DATE DUE

JY 30 '98			

DEMCO 38-296

Italy
Volume II

The International Library of Politics and Comparative Government

General Editor: David Arter
Associate Editor: Gordon Smith

Titles in the Series:

France
David S. Bell

Italy, Volumes I and II
Mark Donovan

Australia and New Zealand
Hugh V. Emy

Germany , Volumes I and II
Klaus H. Goetz

Revolution and Political Change
Alexander J. Groth

Comparative Public Administration
Jan-Erik Lane and Moshe Maor

Gender Politics
Joni Lovenduski

Religion and Politics
John Madeley

Israel
Gregory S. Mahler

New Politics
*Ferdinand Müller-Rommel
and Thomas Poguntke*

Elections and Voting Behaviour
Pippa Norris

Legislatures and Legislators
Philip Norton

**The European Union
Volumes I and II**
Neill Nugent

Nationalism
Brendan O'Leary

Transitions to Democracy
Geoffrey Pridham

United Kingdom
R.A.W. Rhodes

European Security Organisations
Trevor Salmon

The Media
*Margaret Scammell and
Holli Semetko*

National and International Security
Michael Sheehan

**The United Nations
Volumes I and II**
Paul Taylor and Sam Daws

Scandinavia
Derek Urwin

**The United States
Volumes I, II and III**
Alan Ware

**The Politics of the Post Communist
World**
Stephen White and Daniel N. Nelson

Party Systems
Steven B. Wolinetz

Political Parties
Steven B. Wolinetz

Italy
Volume II

Edited by

Mark Donovan

Lecturer, European Politics, School of European Studies
University of Wales, Cardiff

Ashgate
DARTMOUTH
Aldershot • Brookfield USA • Singapore • Sydney

Aldershot
Hants GU11 3HR
England

Ashgate Publishing Company
Old Post Road
Brookfield
Vermont 05036
USA

British Library Cataloguing in Publication Data
Italy. – (The international library of politics and
   comparative government)
   1. Italy – Politics and government – 1976–
   I. Donovan, Mark
   945'.0929

Library of Congress Cataloging-in-Publication Data
Italy / (edited by) Mark Donovan.
        p. cm.– (International library of politics and comparative
   government)
   ISBN 1-85521-637-X (v. 1 and 2)
   1. Italy–Politics and government–20th century. I. Donovan,
 Mark, 1955– II. Series.
   JN5451.I848 1997
   320.945—dc21
                                                                97-25137
                                                                CIP

ISBN 1 85521 637 X

Printed in Great Britain by Galliard (Printers) Ltd, Great Yarmouth

Contents

PART VI   OBSTACLES TO REFORM AND ACHIEVEMENTS TO DATE

Acknowledgements

The editor and publishers wish to thank the following for permission to use copyright material.

Luciano Bardi (1996), 'Party System Change in Italy', *Italian Politics and Society*, Conference Group on Italian Politics and Society (Congrips), Newsletter No. 46, pp. 9–22. Copyright © 1996 L. Bardi.

Frank Cass & Co Ltd for the essays: Donald Sassoon (1985), 'Political and Market Forces in Italian Broadcasting', *West European Politics*, **8**, pp. 67–83; Luca Ricolfi (1997), 'Politics and the Mass Media in Italy', *West European Politics*, **20**, pp. 135–56; Giacinto della Cananea (1997), 'The Reform of Finance and Administration in Italy: Contrasting Achievements', *West European Politics*, **20**, pp. 194–209; Pino Arlacchi (1996), 'Mafia: The Sicilian Cosa Nostra', *South European Society and Politics*, **1**, pp. 74–94; Carlo Guarnieri (1997), 'The Judiciary in the Italian Political Crisis', *West European Politics*, **20**, pp. 1–15.

Comparative Politics for the essay: Yasmine Ergas (1982), '1968–79 – Feminism and the Italian Party System: Women's Politics in a Decade of Turmoil', *Comparative Politics*, **14**, pp. 253–79.

Judith Adler Hellman (1996), 'Italian Women's Struggle Against Violence: 1976–1996', *American Political Science Association*, San Francisco, 28 August – 1 September 1996, pp. 1–14. Copyright © 1996 Judith Adler Hellman.

Oxford University Press for the essay: Tim Mason (1988), 'Italy and Modernization: A Montage', *History Workshop Journal*, **25**, pp. 127–47, by permission of Oxford University Press.

Il Politico for the essay: Sandro Fontana (1984), 'Per una storia del trasformismo (1883–1983)', Il Politico, **XLIX**, pp. 303–20. Translated by Mark Donovan (1997), 'Towards a History of Transformism (1883–1983)'. Funding was supplied for the translation by University of Wales.

Rivista Italiana di Scienza Politica for the essay: Adriano Pappalardo (1980), 'La politica consociativa nella democrazia italiana', *Rivista Italiana di Scienza Politica*, **X**, pp. 73–123. Translated by Jane Brillante and Mark Donovan (1997), 'Consociational Politics and Italian Democracy'. Funding was supplied for the translation by University of Wales.

Routledge for the essays: Donald Sassoon (1995), '*Tangentopoli* or the Democratization of Corruption: Considerations on the End of Italy's First Republic', *Journal of Modern Italian Studies*, **1**, pp. 124–43. Copyright © 1995 Routledge; Raimondo Catanzaro (1985), 'Enforcers, Entrepreneurs, and Survivors: How the *mafia* Has Adapted to Change', *British Journal of Sociology*, **XXXVI**, pp. 34–57.

Series Preface

The International Library of Politics and Comparative Government brings together in one series the most significant journal articles to appear in the field of comparative politics in the last twenty-five years or so. The aim is to render readily accessible to teachers, researchers and students an extensive range of essays which, together, provide an indispensable basis for understanding both the established conceptual terrain and the new ground being broken in the fast changing field of comparative political analysis.

The series is divided into three major sections: *Institutional Studies, Thematic Studies* and *Country Studies.* The *Institutional* volumes focus on the comparative investigation of the basic processes and components of the modern pluralist polity, including electoral behaviour, parties and party systems, interest groups, constitutions, legislatures and executives. There are also collections dealing with such major international actors as the European Union and United Nations.

The *Thematic* volumes address those contemporary problems, processes and issues which have assumed a particular salience for politics and policy-making in the late twentieth century. Such themes include: democratization, revolution and political change, 'New Politics', nationalism, terrorism, the military, the media, human rights, consociationalism and the challenges to mainstream party political ideologies.

The *Country* volumes are particularly innovative in applying a comparative perspective to a consideration of the political science tradition in individual states, both large and small. The distinctive features of the national literature are highlighted and the wider significance of developments is evaluated.

A number of acknowledged experts have been invited to act as editors for the series; they preface each volume with an introductory essay in which they review the basis for the selection of articles, and suggest future directions of research and investigation in the subject area.

The series is an invaluable resource for all those working in the field of comparative government and politics.

DAVID ARTER
Professor of Nordic Politics
University of Aberdeen

GORDON SMITH
Emeritus Professor of Government
London School of Economics and Political Science

Introduction to Volume II

This is the second volume of the reader on Italy published in the *Politics and Comparative Government* series by Dartmouth. The first volume contains the principal introduction to the two-volume set, detailing its overall structure and commenting on the state of studies of Italian government and politics. Both volumes comprise three parts. The first volume is thus devoted to articles dealing with, first: the political and governing institutions of the Republic, often with an evolutionary, or at least historical perspective; second: some of today's most salient, but generally poorly covered policy areas (southern policy, immigration, the environment); and third: the onset of the 1990's crisis. This second volume emphasizes the need for a multi-focused historical perspective on what is a largely unprecedented 'transition within democracy'. The term transition signifies the fundamental nature of change in the absence of the immediate drafting and ratification of a new constitution. It also indicates that the old party system was not immediately replaced with a stably consolidated new system. Rather, whilst a bipolarizing, left-right tendency exerted a weak predominance, multi-polar drives continued to exist. In other words, in 1994 and 1996, competition for government focused on left- and right-wing coalitions yet, simultaneously, a relatively strong centrifugal force existed on the far left of the party spectrum, as did a perhaps weaker, yet potentially more significant, neo-centrist impulse. So long as the interaction of these two subordinate drives could overwhelm the bipolar one, the creation of a tripolar, or three bloc (left-centre-right) party system, as first theorized by Sartori (see Hanning, Chapter 7 in Volume 1), remained possible (Broughton and Donovan forthcoming). However uncertain the final outcome with regard to both constitutional-institutional structures and the array of political forces, the degree of change was clearly so great, in particular in replacing and/or marginalizing the formerly highly stable governing class, that many were tempted to see the events in terms of regime change. Nevertheless, as the phrase 'transition within democracy' also indicates, the process is one of change within a democratic framework, a possible comparison being, then, with the transition from the Fourth to the Fifth French Republic in and after 1958 and not the nevertheless contemporaneous processes taking place in the former Soviet empire.

As stated, Volume II comprises three parts. Part IV is devoted to analyses of Italy's historical trajectory in the 19th and 20th centuries. In the first and perhaps most seminal paper in the collection, John Davis reviews the most important recent attempts to map Italy's path to the 20th century, uncovering possible continuities between the pre-Fascist and the contemporary, or at least post-Fascist, periods. Davis makes clear that any vision of Italy as an economic 'late-comer' suffering from the 'immobilism' of a 'backward' society is profoundly misleading, Italy, including 'the south', having been participant in a changing international political economy for over a century. The interaction of global and local, then, is anything but new – reason enough to beware the ghastly neologism 'glocal'. Timothy Mason's review in Chapter 28 focuses on the concept of 'modernization', first exploring the strange absence of controversy in its use in, and application to, the study of Italian politics, and second arguing that use of the term must necessarily be normative. In invoking values

Mason also refers to the controversies surrounding Italy's political culture and specifically the alleged weakness of its civic culture. This is an issue which has come to the fore once more in the aftermath of the collapse of the First Republic in a welter of revelations of systemic corruption (as outlined in Donald Sassoon's portrayal of the 'democratization' of corruption in Chapter 40). It is to the critical analysis of one particular aspect of the political culture debate, the insistence on the lack of civic culture in the south specifically, which Filippo Sabetti's study is devoted (Chapter 31). Sabetti thus furthers the challenge to the stereotypical misrepresentation of the south condemned by Davis. Sabetti also provides grounds for a positive appraisal of Church influence on Italian society and politics, in contrast to the negative impact of Vatican Catholicism emphasized by Gino Bedani's speculation, in Part III (Chapter 22), on the origins of Italy's ambient corruption and Percy Allum's examination, in Part I (Chapter 3), of the degeneration of the Christian Democratic Party. The challenge to another myth signalled by Davis, that of the 'backward' and inadequate Italian bourgeoisie, is the focus of Raffaele Romanelli's critical essay (Chapter 29). Romanelli delineates the contours of the international debate about the bourgeoisie and 'its' revolution before surveying the Italian case, considering different applications of the term, the urban nature of even Italy's countryside, and hence the inappropriateness of analyses stressing late feudalism; he also notes the relevance of paternalistic industrial enterprise, not least Catholic, thus signalling some of the specificities of Italy's economic development and her institutional and political forms more generally. The fourth essay in this section, that by Leonardo Morlino, emphasizes the decisive role of political parties in the relatively late consolidation of democracy in Italy and southern Europe – late by contrast to north-western Europe, that is. In sum, these essays provide an essential minimal historical and analytical context for understanding the nature of Italy's post-war constitution and supposed *partitocrazia*, or party dominated polity, these being the subjects of the first two chapters reproduced in Volume I by Hine and Calise and which provide a more immediate background to the remainder of that volume.

Part V gathers together a group of articles on major post-war social and politico-cultural developments. Thus in Chapter 32, Yasmine Ergas examines the emergence of the Italian feminist movement in the 1970s in a highly traditional society subject to a male-dominated party system which, nevertheless, introduced divorce and abortion legislation broadly comparable, chronologically and in content, with that of north-western Europe's more liberal polities, and certainly in advance of Ireland. (An up-to-date account of feminist inspired legislation which, finally unimpeded by the constraints of the post-war party system, sets a marker for other European parliaments to follow is provided by Judith Hellman in Chapter 44.) Next, in Chapter 33, Raimondo Catanzaro depicts the survival by adaptation of the mafia, signalling the failure of the simplistic modernization paradigm according to which this phenomenon should have faded away. Then, capturing the rise of Silvio Berlusconi's media empire in the 1980s, Donald Sassoon analyses the disintegration of the state monopoly of the media. This theme of the importance of the media in modern politics is further treated by Luca Ricolfi in Chapter 35 which presents both an overview of developments in this field and a controversial analysis of the impact on voting in the 1994 and 1996 elections of the 'quasi-duopoly' existing between the three public (RAI) and Berlusconi's three private networks. Finally, Part V includes an unusually comprehensive study of Italian terrorism by Marco Rimanelli. Italy's terrorism, concentrated in, but not confined to, the period 1969–82, was several times more intense than that experienced in Germany, the only European country with which it bears comparison given its non-ethno-nationalist bases. The pervasiveness of the terrorist phenomenon rendered it a major national trauma which in the end discredited political violence of left and right whilst making the liberal democratic state (both in principle and in its concrete manifestations), the subject of sustained debate. A learning experience for Italian political culture generally, it had a specific direct impact on the judiciary (see Guarnieri, Chapter 46) and the police (see introduction to Volume I).

The final part of the second volume presents some of the major papers analysing the impact of the changes of the 1990s up to 1996. To begin with, it provides translations of two articles dealing with transformism and consociationalism, phenomena which might, as suggested in the introduction to Volume I, be regarded as touchstones of the extent of change undergone by the putative Second Republic. In Chapter 38, Sandro Fontana provides a century-and-more long overview of transformism, cataloguing the series of positive and negative judgments made of it. In addition Fontana, a life-long Christian Democrat, outlines the social structural causes allegedly underlying this political phenomenon, notably economic dualism which led both to the impossibility of identifying a programme able to reconcile conflicting interests and to the fragmentation of parliamentary representation. Both these characteristics of Italian politics are much remarked upon features of the transition to the Second Republic. Adriano Pappalardo's analysis in Chapter 37 of consociational democracy and its (in)applicability to Italy addresses a related theme which reformers hope the Second Republic will bring about: clear-cut yet cooperative government-opposition relations. Consociational democracy is classically understood as a means of preventing political disorder in an inherently unstable society by institutionalizing cooperation between the elites of the antagonistic social forces. In fact, this theory has been criticized as being inapplicable in practice precisely in those circumstances where it seems to be needed, and as being redundant where elite cooperation in grand coalitions does actually take place. Nevertheless, despite these two ideal-type extremes of irrelevance, one can still usefully look in the messy reality of history for cases where elite cooperation has helped political stabilization and where deeply-rooted societal antagonisms have threatened civil war or political instability. In fact, the literature on democratic consolidation (see Chapter 30 by Morlino) intersects with the consociational perspective. In the Italian case, elite cooperation in the 1944–48 period was crucial in laying the bases of the Republic, yet it was electoral confrontation, rather than continuing cooperation, which helped stabilize the polity. Equally, elite cooperation in the late 1970s was rejected by both Communist and Christian Democratic voters and rank-and-file party members, but was nevertheless of great importance for all that. In the current crisis, and in the aftermath of the revelations of elite collusion in systematic corruption, 'consociationalism' has become a term of abuse and an accusation that elites seek to avoid. At the same time, however, elite cooperation, albeit competitive rather than collusive, is not only essential in any democracy, but is particularly important in contemporary Italy where the fundamentals of politics, the constitution and the country's political economy are being rewritten and restructured.

Luciano Bardi's article on the restructuring of the party system (Chapter 39) reflects concerns about elite and mass interactions. Thus, whilst a two-bloc tendency usually associated with political moderation – i.e. centripetal (or centre-wards) competition – seemed fairly strong in the elections of 1994–96, neither left nor right was able to furnish a government after the downfall of Berlusconi's government in December 1994, and political debate in 1995 was so intense as to be seen by many as a centrifugal process of destabilizing polarization. This led to talk of the re-emergence of 'polarized pluralism' and calls for a return to centre-based government – which would, if anything, tend to consolidate a new edition of polarized pluralism. Donald Sassoon's response to *Tangentopoli* in Chapter 40 focuses on mass attitudes to corruption, especially elite corruption, emphasizing their fundamental ambivalence: on the one hand, everyone does it, no-one is guilty of anything; on the other, politicians are a bunch of scheming and despicable criminals. Sassoon emphasizes the switch from the former attitude to the latter, but the quasi-universal nature of corruption in Italy remains an issue for institutional reformers. Still, Maurizio Ferrera suggests in the next chapter that major barriers to the recreation of the corrupt partitocracy of health care now exist; Vincent della Sala points to the strengthening of the state in its handling of the economy, a strengthening brought about in the context of growing European integration (Chapter 43), and Pino Arlacchi depicts well the new sense of the mafia's vulnerability (Chapter 45). However, none of these authors sees Italy's grave problems in these areas as having been solved. Della Sala, for instance, depicts Italy's political and economic restructuring as a gamble – a gamble that the elites of the First Republic eschewed. Furthermore, in Chapter 42, Giacinto della Cananea contrasts the relative success in reforming the management of the macro-economy in a context framed by European integration, with the failure to reform public administration – an area where the European Union's facilitation of competitive adaptation to global challenges has yet to be brought to bear. Finally, Guarnieri shows in Chapter 46 that that special area of administration, the administration of the law (one hesitates to say justice), is in particularly urgent need of reform, not only given the parlous state of the judicial system, but also because of the urgent need to establish proper relationships between the different branches of government.

In sum, Italy's crisis and her path into the 21st century are a fascinating, challenging and rewarding area of study. Italy's population, economic strength and quality of life equal those of France and the UK, even if her political and diplomatic influence in Europe do not reflect this. Major debates in political science are enormously enriched by examination of the Italian case, as Filippo Sabetti specifically points out in Chapter 31 in his review of the debate on the relationships between political culture, history and institutions. And as the reviews in Part V demonstrate, Italian academic and political debate and research are of considerable importance for how we think about and conceptualize not just Italy's, but Europe's, path to the future. Italy, and southern Europe more generally, have lessons for understanding the transition to, and consolidation of, democracy in central and eastern Europe. More generally, Italy's handling of constitutional and policy issues is of both comparative and direct relevance as European integration proceeds apace. Thus, as discussed in the introduction to Volume I, the policy studies literature has, in recent years, broken out of its Anglo-Saxon constraints. Italy, like the other states of Europe, is in every way a specific case with distinctive idiosyncrasies. But it is not incomparably unique. Italy's contemporary crisis comprises, in concentrated form, a range of challenges common to Europe and beyond.

References

Broughton, D. and M. Donovan (eds) (forthcoming), *Changing Party Systems in Western Europe*, London: Pinter.
Recchi, E. (1996), 'Fishing from the Same Schools: Parliamentary Recruitment and Consociationalism in the First and Second Italian Republics', *West European Politics*, **19** (2), April, pp.340–59.

Part IV
Interpretations and Debates

[27]

Remapping Italy's Path to the Twentieth Century*

John A. Davis
University of Connecticut

For a long time the historical agenda on liberal Italy has been driven by the problems posed by the subsequent collapse of parliamentary government in Italy and the rise of fascism in the early twentieth century. As in the case of Germany, the causes of these failures have been widely linked to Italy's imbalanced and feeble modernization in the nineteenth century or, alternatively, to its failure to achieve a solid or complete bourgeois revolution. Seen from the 1950s and 1960s there was much to justify such a perspective: attributing fascism to economic and social backwardness was inseparable from the expectation that economic progress and social change would regenerate Italian democracy. Seen from the present, such assumptions are more questionable. The titles under review illustrate many of the ways in which Italian historians have been replotting Italy's path to the twentieth century.

---

*The following are the works under review: Aurelio Alaimo, *L'organizzazione della città: Amministrazione urbana a Bologna dopo l'Unita (1859–1889)* (Bologna, 1990); Alberto M. Banti, *Terra e denaro: Una borghesia padana dell'ottocento* (Venice, 1989); A. M. Banti and M. Meriggi, eds., "Elites e associazioni nell'Italia dell'ottocento," special issue, *Quaderni Storici*, vol. 77, no. 2 (August 1991); Giuseppe Civile, *Il comune rustico: Storia sociale di un paese del Mezzogiorno nell'ottocento* (Bologna, 1990); Franco Della Peruta, *Esercito e società nell'Italia napoleonica* (Milan, 1988); *Esercito e città dall'Unità agli anni Trenta*, Pubblicazioni degli Archivi di Stato, 2 vols. (Rome, 1989); Gabriella Gribaudi, *A Eboli: Il mondo meridionale in cent'anni di trasformazioni* (Venice, 1990); Maurizio Gribaudi, *Mondo operaio e mito operaio: Spazi e percorsi sociali a Torino nel primo novecento* (Turin, 1987); David Lo Romer, *Merchants and Reform in Livorno, 1814–1868* (Berkeley and Los Angeles, 1987); Salvatore Lupo, *Il giardino degli aranci: il mondo degli agrumi nella storia del Mezzogiorno* (Venice, 1990); Paolo Macry, *Ottocento, Famiglia, élites e patrimoni a Napoli* (Turin, 1988); Maria Malatesta, *I Signori della terra: L'organizzazione degli interessi agrari padani, 1860–1914* (Milan, 1989); Angelo Massafra, ed., *Il Mezzogiorno pre-Unitario: economia, società e istituzioni* (Bari, 1988); Marco Meriggi, *Il regno Lombardo-Veneto*, Storia d'Italia, vol. 18, pt. 2, ed. G. Galasso (Turin, 1987); C. Pavone and M. Salvati, eds., *Suffragio, rappresentanza, interessi: Istituzioni e società fra '800 e '900*, Annali della Fondazione L. Basso, ISSOCO, vol. 9 (Rome, 1987–88); Marta Petrusewicz, *Latifondo: Economia morale e vita materiale in una periferia dell'ottocento* (Venice, 1989); Paolo Pezzino, *Una certa reciprocità di favori: Mafia e modernizzazione violenta nella Sicilia postunitaria* (Milan, 1990); Raffaele Romanelli, *Il commando impossibile: Stato e società nell'Italia liberale* (Bologna, 1988), and *Sulle carte interminate: Un ceto di impiegati tra privato e pubblico: i segretari comunali in Italia, 1860–1915* (Bologna, 1989); Raffaele Romanelli and A. Annino, eds., "Notabili, elettori, elezioni: Rappresentanza e controllo eletorale nell'Ottocento," *Quaderni Storici*, vol. 69 (December 1988); Simonetta Soldani, ed., *L'educazione delle donne: Scuole e modelli di vita femminile nell'Italia dell'Ottocento* (Milan, 1989). My thanks to J. Morris and L. J. Riall for their helpful comments on an earlier draft of this article.

[*Journal of Modern History* 66 (June 1994): 291–320]
© 1994 by The University of Chicago. 0022-2801/94/6602-0003$01.00

292   *Davis*

In part the reasons for rethinking accepted interpretations of the course of contemporary Italian history have been historiographical, and as in the case of the debates on Germany's *Sonderweg,* the new agenda in Italy began by questioning the teleological assumptions that link the failure of liberal democracy to flawed economic and social modernization.[1] The weakness of the comparative models on which such reasoning depended has been made more apparent by new empirical research that has drawn aside coy ideal-type veils to reveal the markedly heterogeneous social endowments of the most "advanced" nineteenth-century European societies, making the supposed shortcomings and relative "backwardness" of their Italian (or German, or Spanish) counterparts less obvious. All this makes Whiggish assumptions about the fixed and unilinear relationship between modern economic growth and political democracy look increasingly doubtful, and once the relativist character of English political liberalism is acknowledged, for example, the political experiences of liberal Italy, no less than Third Republic France or Wilhelmine Germany (and why not Spain?), clearly need to be reexamined in their own terms.[2] Growing awareness of the complexity of social identities has tended to dissolve even the longest-established nineteenth-century nation-states into "imagined communities," and this also calls for rethinking judgments on the supposed fragility of political or social integration in the newcomers. New emphasis on the variety of different paths along which the European economies have reached the twentieth century has set industrialization in broader, more relative, and more differentiated contexts of economic growth in ways that have also encouraged more pluralistic and relativist approaches to modernization.[3]

The new Italian agenda has a postmodern cast, but its matrix is probably more closely post-1968. Dramatic postwar economic growth has transformed Italian society, making Italy a leading European economy and a showpiece for flamboyantly successful entrepreneurship. Yet this has not been accompanied by commensurate political or institutional change. Formally one of the most flexible democracies in western Europe, Italy's political system has proved remarkably resistant to structural reform and vulnerable to monopolistic domination by political parties; yet continuity of political power and resilience toward the challenge of political terrorism in the 1980s, for example, have gone hand in hand

[1] See R. Romanelli, "Political Debate, Social History, and the Italian Bourgeoisie: Changing Perspectives in Historical Research," *Journal of Modern History* 63, no. 4 (December 1991): 717–39; but also Tim Mason, "Italy and Modernization: A Montage," *History Workshop* 25 (1988): 110–47, on "modernization" as a category for interpreting contemporary Italian and German history; and C. Cassina, ed., *La storiografia sull'Italia contemporanea* (Pisa, 1991), for brief critical surveys of recent historiographical tendencies.

[2] See G. Eley, "Liberalism, Europe and the Bourgeoisie, 1860–1914," in *The German Bourgeoisie,* ed. D. Blackburn and R. J. Evans (London, 1991), pp. 305–7; and, for a more critical view on the revisionist stance, J. Breuilly, *Labour and Liberalism in 19th Century Europe: Essays in Comparative History* (Manchester and New York, 1992), esp. pp. 273–95.

[3] See esp. N. F. R. Crafts, "The New Economic History and the Industrial Revolution," in *The First Industrial Revolutions,* ed. P. Mathias and J. A. Davis (Oxford, 1990), pp. 25–43; S. Pollard, *Peaceful Conquest and the Industrialization of Europe* (London, 1981); and P. O'Brien, "Do We Have a Typology for the Study of European Industrialization in the 19th Century?" *Journal of European Economic History* 15, no. 2 (1986): 291–334.

Remapping Italy's Path to the Twentieth Century 293

with inadequate provision of social facilities, the persistence of processes of government by mediation and "political exchange" that seem to preclude wider structural reforms and initiatives, and impotence in the face of organized crime. None of these things can adequately be explained in terms of the absence of economic change, nor indeed can the persistence, albeit in changed forms, of Italy's "Southern Problem." Profound economic and social change in the Mezzogiorno since the 1950s have not halted social and institutional decay and in many respects may have aggravated situations that grow more threatening to Italy as a whole.

Neither lack of economic progress nor, indeed, lack of modernity now offer plausible explanations, and this, together with the disillusioned expectations of political change that followed 1968, has shaped the new Italian historical agenda. Working from the experience of Italy today, it starts by turning the original "modernization" formula on its head and asking why economic and social change have not been accompanied by broader processes of institutional and political change. That leads to a broader reconsideration of the relationship between state and society in Italy, projected backward over a chronology that begins to break down the conventional periodization of the Risorgimento, liberalism, fascism, and republicanism to explore the elements of continuity in the longer-run formation of relations between state and society. Whereas earlier interpretations identified slow economic development and social change as the principal obstacles to broader institutional change and the deepening of political democracy in Italy, the new agenda tends to locate the peculiarities of Italy's path to the twentieth century in a process that translates somewhat elusively as "modernization without growth" *(modernizzazione senza sviluppo)*.

Although only a random and self-selected sample, the studies under review do illustrate many of the more general features of this revisionist agenda.[4] These include a shift away from political history toward social history and the historical sociology of politics and power, from macro- to microeconomic analysis, from the center to the periphery, from the history of political movements and organized labor to the history of social formation and social relations. Broader aggregate and structural studies give way to local studies, while sectoral analyses are dropped in favor of local studies that look to integrate the economic, social, cultural, and political dimensions of change, drawing on political sociology and anthropology to reconstruct interest groups, networks, and structures of power and influence.

If social history has moved to center stage, the essential jumping-off point for the revisionist agenda lies in a rereading of Italy's economic history. Since the early 1960s, the debates on Italian industrialization have evolved around two

---

[4] A more general discussion would have to take account of major academic publishing ventures like the Einaudi *Storia d'Italia,* its supplementary *Annali* and the more recent *Storia delle Regioni dall'Unità a Oggi;* the volumes in the Unione Tipografico Editoriali Torino (UTET) *Storia d'Italia,* edited by Giuseppe Galasso; and the Laterza urban and regional history monographs. Journals—notably *Quaderni Storici, Società e Storia, Passato e Presente, Studi Storici,* and, more recently and concerned specifically with the south, *Meridiana*—have played a critically important role in organizing research, establishing new questions, and defining new methodologies, as have conferences designed to develop new areas of research. The papers resulting from two of these are included in this selection.

294   *Davis*

images, both of which stressed the partial, patchy, and incomplete nature of economic modernization before 1914. One was Gramsci's "passive revolution," predicated on the economic weakness and immaturity of the Italian bourgeoisie and the sluggish emergence of modern capitalist forms of activity; the second depicted Italy as an industrial latecomer, most notably in Alexander Gerschenkron's formulation, in which industrialization occurred late and was due in large part to mainly external inputs. By emphasizing the relatively feeble force of internal growth throughout much of the nineteenth century, both interpretations conspire to underline how the experience of industrialization constituted in social as well as economic terms an abrupt discontinuity that was accompanied by deep internal dualisms.

Neither interpretation has stood up well to empirical testing, not least because of the absence of data from which to make reliable estimates of the timing and scale of structural change. These issues are far from being resolved and the debate on the Italian economy in the nineteenth century remains bogged down in numerous data gaps, but an influential group of Italian economic historians have for some time been arguing that it is possible to identify longer-term processes of growth. In this new perspective, the role of increased output and productivity in agriculture from the mid-eighteenth century onward has attracted growing attention and is now widely seen as a key motor of growth and the principal source of capital savings.[5]

Such a view is still far from documented, but the work of Franco Bonelli, Luciano Cafagna, and others has begun to redraw Italy's economic landscapes, emphasizing the variety of different regional patterns of growth and in place of sudden leaps and discontinuities drawing attention to the elements of continuity. The image of economic immobilism in turn gives way to a closer awareness of the particular constraints that derived from the subordinate and vulnerable position of Italian producers in changing world markets. By stressing the forces of commercialization and integration into new regional and international markets, the new perspectives on Italy's preindustrial economic growth replace the image of a fragile latecomer that experienced economic change only belatedly and partially for that of a society inescapably caught up from a much earlier moment in what Polanyi termed the "Great Transformation" —the emergence and formation of new market economies that brought Italy and the Italians into a new and recognizably modern world.[6]

---

[5] The best recent general overviews are G. Toniolo, *An Economic History of Liberal Italy* (London, 1990); V. Zamagni, *Dalla periferia al centro: La seconda rinascita economica dell'Italia (1861–1981)* (Bologna, 1990); V. Castronovo, "Storia economica," in *Storia d'Italia*, vol. 4, *Dall'Unità a oggi* (Turin, 1974); G. Mori, ed., *L'industrializzazione in Italia (1861–1900)* (Bologna, 1977); L. De Rosa, *La rivoluzione industriale in Italia* (Bari, 1980); but for an incisive critical overview of recent trends in Italian economic history, see esp. G. Mori, "L'economia italiana dagli anni Ottanta alla prima guerra mondiale," in *Storia dell'industria elettrica in Italia*, ed. G. Mori, vol. 1, *Le origini, 1882–1914* (Bari/Roma, 1992), pp. 1–106.

[6] See F. Bonelli, "Il capitalismo italiano: Linee generali d'interpretazione," in *Storia d'Italia: Annali* (Turin, 1978), 1:1193–1255; L. Cafagna, *Dualismo e sviluppo nella storia d'Italia* (Venice, 1989); G. Federico, "Per un'analisi del ruolo dell'agricoltura nello sviluppo economico

Remapping Italy's Path to the Twentieth Century 295

In this perspective, conventional indicators of Italy's relative "backwardness" are easily turned on their heads. The ruralization of Italian industry (especially textiles) in the second half of the nineteenth century, for example, becomes a sign of entrepreneurial rationality rather than an indication of backwardness. By enabling entrepreneurs to exploit narrow and inelastic comparative advantages offered by cheap labor, low investment costs, and proximity to raw materials, rural production enhanced Italian competitiveness in external markets.[7] Nor did the rural location of manufacturing necessarily inhibit the adoption of rational, modern forms of management and organization of production, nor did hostility toward the social consequences of industrialism make a pioneer of Italian industrial capitalism like Alessandro Rossi—founder of Italy's largest nineteenth-century textile industry, the *Lanificio Rossi* at Schio in the Veneto, and architect of the distinctively Venetian model of entrepreneurship—less dynamic or effective as a capitalist entrepreneur.[8]

The emphasis on longer-term processes of economic change has also refocused attention on the role of agriculture in the broader process of economic growth, and this has been accompanied by a shift from quantitative toward more qualitative forms of analysis. In part this serves to sidestep the data gaps that continue to block the measurement of structural changes in the Italian economies[9] and moves the debate onto the broader terrain of the institutional and social impact of agricultural growth. The preferred targets are those sectors and regions that have been most closely identified with Italy's relative backwardness. At first sight, Lombardy would not seem to fit this category, but in a study almost as wide-ranging as it is long, Maria Malatesta challenges a view widely held by contemporaries that the typical Lombard landowner was a fainéant absentee ("so accustomed to idleness—in the words of the writer Carlo Ravizza—that it no longer even made him feel uncomfortable" [p. 111]) who left the management of his estates to large-scale and aggressively capitalist leaseholders. There were constant struggles between the two because the landowners resisted the leaseholders' demands for compensation for improvements along the lines of the English Agricultural Holdings Act and Settled Land Act (1875; 1882). But the landowners proved to be precociously capitalist in outlook and in economic management. From an early date they employed specialist agricultural advisers to draft contracts giving them close control over their leaseholders, were actively engaged in

---

italiano," *Società e Storia*, no. 5 (1979), and "Mercantilizzazione e sviluppo economico in Italia," *Rivista di Storia Economica*, no. 2 (1986); and K. Polyani, *Origins of Our Time: The Great Transformation* (London, 1946).

[7] There is now an extensive bibliography on rural industrialization: F. Ramella, *Terra e telai: Sistemi di parentella e manufattura nel Biellese dell'Ottocento* (Turin, 1984); A. Dewerpe, *L'Industrie aux Champs* (Rome, 1985); but see also G. Mori, "Industrie senza industrializzazione: La penisola italiana dalla fine della dominazione francese all'unità nazionale," *Studi Storici* 30, no. 3 (1989): 603–35.

[8] See S. Lanaro, "Genealogia di un modello," in *Il Veneto*, ed. S. Lanaro, Storia d'Italia: Le regioni dall'Unità a oggi (Turin, 1984), pp. 60–98; G. Roverato, "La terza regione industriale," in ibid., pp. 170–82; C. Fumian, "Proprietari, imprenditori agronomi," in ibid., pp. 120–51, and *La città del Lavoro: Un utopia agroindustriale nel Veneto contemporaneo* (Venezia, 1990).

[9] See Toniolo, pp. 133–48.

296   *Davis*

establishing networks and associations to promote and protect their interests, and developed close links with urban commercial and financial capital.[10]

Alberto Banti's study of another apparently backward group of northern landowners reveals similarly aggressive patterns of capitalist organization. Land-holdings in Piacenza (Emilia) were smaller than on the Lombard plain, and until the end of the century they were less technologically advanced. But the absence of technological innovation should not be taken as an indication of a lack of capacity to innovate, Banti argues, and it was determined by the unsuitability of available technologies to local conditions. When the agricultural crisis of the 1880s caused prices to fall and wages to rise, the Piacenza landowners were not slow to demonstrate their full-blooded capitalist credentials and their response to the crisis was aggressively modern and organized. Italy's first agrarian purchasing syndicate was created in Piacenza and provided a base from which the landowners rapidly developed concentric networks of credit, insurance, and financial opera-tions that interlocked closely with local administration.[11]

Banti's title—"land and money"—provides a subtext for numerous new local studies that chart the spread of capitalist mentalities, organizations, and institu-tions in different parts of nineteenth-century Italy. From Piacenza to Pisa, from Lucca to Avellino and beyond, land ceased to be a source of status, either to become an object of capitalist investment or else to be discarded in preference for urban property and securities—especially shares in the public debt.[12] Despite the absence of more spectacular examples of economic growth, new and essentially capitalist forms of activity and organization were penetrating the sleepiest corners of provincial Italy, so that well before the onset of industrialization, forms of economic organization, management, and investment in Italy were being trans-formed along recognizably modern and capitalist lines.

It is not surprising that the south—the locus classicus of Italy's economic backwardness—should have been singled out for particular attention. Here too received images of economic backwardness and immobilism are giving way to emphasis on the difficult and unstable conditions within which growth occurred. Despite structural differences, at least until the great crisis of the 1880s economic change in the south was in many cases similar to that in the north. The leading southern commercial port cities—Bari, Catania, Messina, and Palermo—despite a period of crisis after Unification, prospered from expanding agricultural exports and saw the emergence of typically bourgeois urban lifestyles and institutions—clubs, theaters, cafés, and local political organizations.[13]

---

[10] Maria Malatesta, *I Signori della terra: L'organizzazione degli interessi agrari padani, 1860–1914* (Milan, 1988), p. 111. For a general analysis of agrarian politics and political lobbying, see also L. Masella, *Proprietà e politica agraria in Italia, 1861–1914* (Naples, 1984).

[11] Alberto M. Banti, *Terra e denaro: Una borghesia padana dell'ottocento* (Venice, 1989).

[12] A. Banti, "Ricchezza e potere: Le dinamiche patrimoniali nella società lucchese del XIX secolo," and A. Polsi, "Possidenti e nuovi ceti urbani: L'élite politica di Pisa nel ventennio post-unitario," *Quaderni Storici*, vol. 56 (1984).

[13] See E. Iachello and A. Signorelli, "Borghesie urbane dell'ottocento," in *La Sicilia*, ed. M. Aymard and G. Giarrizzo, Storia delle regioni dall'Unità a oggi (Turin, 1987), pp. 110–54. R.

Remapping Italy's Path to the Twentieth Century   297

The crisis of the 1880s severely interrupted their prosperity without reversing the processes of social and institutional modernization, but the crisis (resulting from the collapse of agricultural prices throughout Europe, the abandonment of free trade, and the contraction of export markets) did expose a more permanent and fundamental constraint facing the more advanced sectors in the south—heavy dependence on uncertain and unstable export markets. This, it is argued, offers a key for a more general understanding of the patterns of economic growth in the Mezzogiorno. Uncertain markets encouraged multiple short-term investments and explain the absence of longer-term investment capable of generating structural change; yet these preferences should be seen as rational attempts to spread and minimize the high level of risk inherent in the markets, rather than as signs of entrepreneurial immaturity or organizational incapacity. From the personification of backwardness, Verga's hyperactive Mastro Don Gesualdo becomes a paragon of economic rationality.[14]

Reappraisal of the sectors of southern agriculture that were most directly involved in export trade has also questioned accepted images of that quintessential symbol of southern backwardness: the *latifondo*. The prevalence of an extensive and archaic latifundist sector over the more dynamic but smaller and more fragile pockets of intensive and commercially oriented agriculture has long been seen as the key to understanding the failure of economic growth in the south. But the distinction between what Manlio Rossi Doria called "the flesh and the bones of southern agriculture" is now questioned by growing evidence that the two sectors were often closely integrated.[15]

Drawing on one of the few private estate archives to have been made accessible to researchers, Marta Petrusewicz makes the first documented reconstruction of the internal organization and management of a major latifundist enterprise. Her study of the vast Barraco estates in Calabria in the middle years of the century lends further weight to the revisionist view on the origins and nature of the latifundist "system" and offers further evidence that, far from being a relic of the feudal past, the nineteenth-century *latifondo* grew out of the abolition of feudalism at the beginning of the century, from massive purchases of land during the French period and from later engrossments (including purchases of church lands after Unification—a subject that still awaits systematic study). Petrusewicz also shows how the management of the estates sought to accommodate production to different and varying forms of demand, so that the production of export-oriented cash crops

---

Battaglia, *Mercanti e imprenditori in una città marittima: il caso di Messina (1850–1900)* (Milan, 1992), however, underlines the "limits of growth."

[14] Ibid., p. 131; but see also G. Barone, "Stato, capitale finanziario e Mezzogiorno," in *La modernizzazione difficile: Città e campagne nel Mezzogiorno dall'éta giolittiana al fascismo,* ed. G. Giarrizzo (Bari, 1983), pp. 41–42; L. Masella, "Elites politiche e potere urbano nel Mezzogiorno dall'éta giolittiana al fascismo," in ibid., pp. 99–108; A. Cormio, "Le campagne pugliesi nella fase di transizione, 1880–1914," in ibid., pp. 147–210; S. Lupo and R. Mangiameli, "La modernizzazione difficile: Blocchi corporativi e conflitti di classe in una società arretrata," in ibid., pp. 219–29.

[15] Masella, *Proprietà e politica agraria,* pp. 38–43, 53–60.

was combined with the more traditional extensive sector in ways that enabled the
latifondo to fall back on cereals and grazing and to utilize the "internal" market
provided by the peasant population resident on the estates when export opportunities were poor. The combination was functional, she argues, and enabled the
latifondo to operate as a flexible economic system that could be self-sufficient or
export led depending on prevailing market conditions. But Petrusewicz also draws
attention to the system's limitations, which were fully exposed by the agrarian
crisis of the 1880s. Falling prices, narrower markets, and growing reliance on
casual labor increased production costs, undermined the internal social cohesive-
ness of the system, and caused it to become dysfunctional. Thereafter, she argues,
it took on those features that were widely denounced in the writings of the late
nineteenth-century "Meridionalisti."[16]

Petrusewicz offers additional evidence that the economic problems of the south
had little to do with immobilism, and her study of the management of the Barraco
estates indicates that the latifundists did attempt to respond to changing circumstances in ways that involved innovation. But her argument that this form of
latifondo was transitional, together with the essentially paternalistic picture that is
drawn of social relations on the Barraco estates in this period, is less convincing
because it fails to explain why "rational" exploitation conspicuously failed to
engender broader economic growth. The links between the latifundist system
before and after the agrarian crisis of the 1880s are probably closer than is
admitted here, and the reasons for that need to be explored more fully since they
go close to the heart of the mysteries of modernization without growth. In
particular, closer attention needs to be given to the comparative advantages
utilized by the landowners and their agents—cheap labor, cheap land, tight control
over land, credit, communications, information, and access to markets—to explain
why they continued to depend on inflexible monopolistic controls in ways that
made the rational pursuit of individual profit and commercial expansion cotermi-
nous with the preservation of institutional constraints that directly inhibited wider
processes of economic growth.

These questions are addressed against a broader panorama in Salvatore Lupo's
impressive and deeply researched study of the Sicilian citrus trade in the
nineteenth and twentieth centuries. Before 1914, oranges and lemons were the
south's most valuable export commodities (and later as well: they were what
Mussolini relied on to pay Hitler for German coal and steel). Responding to
growing foreign demand after Unification, it was the latifundists who invested in
citrus production. The investments were substantial, and once again the combination of intensive and extensive production was closely determined by the uncertainties of export markets, resulting in the familiar tendency toward speculative

---

[16] M. Petrusewicz, *Latifondo: Economia morale e vita materiale in una periferia dell'ottocento*
(Venezia, 1989). Earlier studies emphasizing the "modern" features of the *latifondo* include A.
Blok, *The Mafia of a Sicilian Village* (Oxford, 1974); and J. Schneider and P. Schneider, *Culture
and Political Economy in Western Sicily* (New York, 1976). For the older view see E. Sereni, *Il
capitalismo nelle campagne, 1860–1900* (Turin, 1947).

investment and risk spreading. But despite increased output and exports, little progress was made toward closer integration of production, trade, and processing. Nor did market difficulties (growing competition, especially on North American markets from producers in Florida and California) lead to diversification of products or markets: until the twentieth century oranges remained virtually unknown in north Italian cities and the greater part of Sicily's citrus fruit continued to be sold abroad, and mainly in North America.[17]

Lupo's study closely documents why commercial expansion failed to create conditions for broader structural change: in part these derived from markets, but above all from the failure of the Sicilian landowners to adopt new forms of organization and to exploit new opportunities—typified by the defensive reactions to the first incursions of organized capital from the north during the Giolittian era. This leads to the conclusion that the citrus trade represented "the most dynamic face of a still backward society, and not a way of moving beyond that society" (p. 81): a judgment that Maurice Aymard would extend to the more productive and commercially oriented sectors of southern agriculture as a whole. Hence the dramatic impact of the agrarian crisis of the 1880s and the scale of emigration after 1900—a crisis that fully revealed the structural weaknesses of the southern economy and its lack of integration into national markets (the emigrants went overseas, not to northern Italy).

These and other recent studies have begun to revise many aspects of the conventional image of the southern economy, and it is now evident that its problems had more to do with adapting to rapidly and often violently changing economic circumstances than with economic immobilism. It is also clear that the economies that made up the south were neither monolithic nor undifferentiated, yet even the most advanced sectors continued to operate largely outside the confines of national markets until well into the twentieth century.[18] If we have as a result become more aware of the importance of the export-oriented, high value-added sectors of commercial production in the south, this also modifies received images of southern landlordism and hence also of the politics of the southern *agrari*. Petrusewicz and Lupo both offer important additional examples to show that influential groups within the south remained deeply opposed to agricultural protectionism in the 1880s, because they well knew that tariffs would damage their export markets—and indeed southern exports became the principal targets of reprisals against the Italian tariffs. But if southern export interests— unlike the farmers of the Po valley, who were the principal advocates of agricultural protection—remained opposed to tariff protection for commercial reasons, they were willing nonetheless to go along with it for fiscal reasons—and specifically in return for the shelving of a proposal to abolish the tax concessions made to the south at the time of Unification. Nor did their sympathy for free trade

[17] S. Lupo, *Il giardino degli aranci: Il mondo degli agrumi nella storia del Mezzogiorno* (Venice, 1990), with a preface by Maurice Aymard.

[18] See, e.g., Lupo, pp. 180–82; see also L. Cafagna, "Il dualismo economic italiano," now in Cafagna, *Dualismo e sviluppo* (n. 6 above), pp. 183–222.

300   *Davis*

prevent them rallying to Salandra's deeply conservative agrarian platform after
1900.[19]

The political behavior of the southern landowners and their willingness to
sacrifice economic interests for political and fiscal gain might be taken as' a good
example of the consequences (and the causes?) of a process of modernization
without growth; so too might the market constraints that repeatedly inhibited
broader processes of structural and institutional change. But the formula is a
slippery one, and if it serves to restate a problem—Why did economic change not
lead on to more solid processes of institutional and structural change in the
south?—it has not as yet led to any clear new consensus. Some recent contributors
continue to identify natural constraints and external forces—unkind geography
and terrain, ecological devastation, uncertain and unstable markets—as the
barriers to growth.[20] No one—especially the authors of classical writings on the
Mezzogiorno—has ever underestimated the force of these obstacles, but the new
research also offers compelling evidence that the "visible hand" played a direct
and unrelenting role in inhibiting economic growth. Fragmented markets, lack of
vertical and horizontal integration between different sectors, limited access to
credit, and distorted circuits of information were not simply reflections of market
conditions but were also reinforced by the actions and preferences of economic
actors for whom they were instrumental in maintaining power, wealth, and
influence.[21] The reasons why southern entrepreneurs failed to make better use of
admittedly narrow opportunities (although that narrowness should not be over-
stated), their reticence in the face of the incursions of northern capital and, in turn,
the reluctance of northern entrepreneurs to move into the south until government
support became available have also to be understood in terms of the strategies that
guided the visible hand.[22]

Whatever modernization without growth might lack in conceptual or terminological precision, it does reflect the ambivalences and contradictions of the
experience of economic change in the nineteenth-century Mezzogiorno, and these
are examined with exceptional sensitivity in Paolo Macry's study of the changing

---

[19] This has been recognized for some time: see, e.g., Castronovo (n. 5 above), pp. 101–10. For
detailed reconsideration of the political stance of the southern landowners and attitudes toward
protectionism, see esp. F. Barbagallo, *Stato, Parlamento e lotte politico-sociali nel Mezzogiono
(1900–1914)* (Naples, 1980); Giarrizzo, ed.; and Masella, *Proprietà e politica agraria.*

[20] On market and technical constraints, see P. Bevilacqua, "Acque e bonifiche nel Mezzogiorno nella prima metà dell'ottocento," in *Mezzogiorno Pre-Unitario: Economia, società,
istituzioni,* ed. A. Massafra (Bari, 1988), and "Uomini, terre, economie," in *La Calabria,* ed. P.
Bevilacqua and A. Placanica, Storia delle regioni dall'Unità a oggi (Turin, 1985).

[21] Lupo, p. xi; see also F. Barbagallo, "Potere economico e economia assistita nel Mezzogiorno
repubblicano," *Studi Storici* 30, no. 1 (1989): 43–53, and "Il Mezzogiorno come politica
attuale," *Studi Storici* 31 (July–September 1990): 585–96; Pezzino's review of L. D'Antone,
Scienza e Governo del Territorio, Studi Storici 32 (1991): 766; and my discussion of Mafia in this
article.

[22] See, e.g., Lupo, pp. 256–62; cf. also V. Castronovo, "Congiuntura bellico e divario
Nord-Sud," and N. Recuperato, "Analisi sociale e ricerca storica," both in Giarrizzo, ed. Einaudi's
fictitious merchant prince took a brief look at Bari before heading for South America; see
Cafagna, p. 213.

Remapping Italy's Path to the Twentieth Century   301

fortunes of five Neapolitan patrician families.[23] Following a span of three generations, Macry demonstrates how dramatically yet ambivalently the southern patricians made the journey from "land to money." Until the midcentury, land remained both a source of status and above all the means for securing the continuity and integrity of the family. This meant that economic strategy was directed single-mindedly toward the perpetuation of the family by preserving family patrimonies intact in the male line, subjecting individuals to inflexible disciplines that sacrificed younger sons, wives, and daughters to the unbending "logic of the family name."

After Unification all this was to change. Huge increases in taxation (reaching between 25 and 33 percent of net revenues from land) and the fall in agricultural prices in the 1880s decimated revenues and broke up the carefully protected family estates. Macry's families responded to the crisis in different ways, but there were no golden rules for survival: some survived, some did not, but all were drawn willingly or not into a new world of money. Heirs were now more likely to inherit debts than broad hectares, and the patrician family economy gave way to a new and harsher world of economic individualism. Investments shifted from land to urban property, stocks, and shares, bringing the Neapolitan patriciate into closer contact with an array of professionals and specialists—lawyers, accountants, agricultural managers—who were now needed to mediate on their behalf in this new world.

How did their attitudes and behavior change? On this point Macry reserves judgment, illustrating the difficulty of inferring changes in cultural and social values from changes in economic behavior and organization. Although they were drawn into a world of bourgeois affairs, values, taste, and sociability, Macry's Neapolitan patricians never really became part of that world. Modernity in one respect did not necessarily imply modernity in all.

Macry has few rivals in the sensitivity of his analysis of social institutions and cultural values, and of all those under review his book comes closest to adopting an explicitly postmodern agenda.[24] It also builds a bridge from south to north and to a broader discussion of the social dimensions of economic change in Italy as a whole, since it has been widely argued that modernization without growth should be seen as a characteristic not peculiar to the south but to Italy more generally.

It is in this perspective that the middle classes come to hitherto unprecedented prominence. Italy's bourgeoisie has been more widely blamed than studied, and until recently there have been few documented accounts of who the Italian middle classes were and how they thought and behaved, and what was known tended to rely more heavily on the generally hostile observations of contemporary critics and observers than on research.[25] This neglect is now being amply reversed, and

[23] Paolo Macry, *Ottocento: Famiglia, élites e patrimoni a Napoli* (Turin, 1988).

[24] Macry's introduction provides one of the clearest statements of the current agenda of Italian social historians, see also the editors' introduction in *La Campania,* ed. P. Macry and P. Villani, Storia delle regioni dall'Unità a oggi (Turin, 1990).

[25] In addition to Romanelli, "Political Debate" (n. 1 above), see Adrian Lyttelton, "The Middle Classes of Liberal Italy," in *Society and Politics in the Age of the Risorgimento: Essays*

302   *Davis*

bourgeois Italy has been moved back to center stage almost to the exclusion of all
other social groups, its identities being pursued along a variety of intersecting
tracks—some following the broader horizontal and national contours of social and
institutional change, others focusing more closely on localized and regional
processes of social formation.

One result has been to throw into sharper focus the impact of political change
on social formation, emphasizing in particular the formative experience of the
Napoleonic period. The years of Napoleonic rule at the beginning of the
nineteenth century have long been recognized as a critical moment in the
consolidation of agrarian capitalism in Italy, but more recent research now reveals
how this was a key moment in the formation of a new middle class, which was
interrupted but not reversed by the Restoration. The administrative and juridical
restructuring of the Italian states created new opportunities for bureaucratic
employment that offered crucial, albeit inadequate, perches for the formation of
modern professional middle classes but also drew new boundaries between the
spheres of public and private life in ways that established new concepts of
sovereignty, citizenship, and the rule of law.

In many cases the openings were hesitant and without immediate sequel. One
good example was military service, which in the larger dynastic states had already
in the eighteenth century offered opportunities for developing technocratic and
scientific skills.[26] The formation of national armies under the French rulers—as
Franco Della Peruta's massive study of the army of the Kingdom of Italy
illustrates—promised to increase those openings. But military service proved to
have uncomfortably close affinities with political liberalism, with the result that
the Restoration severely limited these opportunities and attempted to reassert the
exclusively dynastic character of the officer corps.[27]

Other opportunities for bureaucratic employment also expanded during the
French period, only to be cut back after the Restoration. Marco Meriggi's new
volume on the Austrian administration develops his earlier thesis that the failure
to meet the growing demand for bureaucratic employment was a principal cause
of middle-class dissatisfaction with Austrian rule in Lombardy-Venetia. Growing
pressure for access to university courses was clear evidence of the new vocational
aspirations of the landed classes, and attempts to choke off demand by constantly
upping the qualifications for entering public service (hence the length of courses
and the costs to the students' families) inevitably increased middle-class resent-
ments against Austrian rule. These middle-class discontents overlapped with the

in Honour of Denis Mack Smith, ed. J. A. Davis and P. Ginsborg (Cambridge, 1991), pp. 217–50;
M. Meriggi, "La borghesia italiana," in *Borghesie europee dell'Ottocento*, ed. J. Kocka (Venice,
1989), pp. 169–83; P. Villani, "Gruppi sociali e classi dirigenti all'indomani dell'Unità," in
Storia d'Italia, Annali (Turin, 1978), 1:863–978.

[26] See the essays in A. M. Rao, ed., *Esercito e società nell'età Rivoluzionaria e Napoleonica*
(Naples, 1990).

[27] F. Della Peruta, *Esercito e società nell'Italia napoleonica* (Milan, 1988); see also W.
Barberis, *Le Armi del Principe: La tradizione militare sabauda* (Turin, 1988), and "Tradizione e
modernità: Il problema dello stato nella storia d'Italia," *Rivista Storica Italiana* 103 (1991):
243–67.

aristocracy's grievances at losing control over local administration, and although the interests and aspirations of the two groups never fully coincided they gave a firm base of self-interest to the opposition to Austrian rule in Lombardy-Venetia.[28]

The contributions to Angelo Massafra's important and wide-ranging volume reveal that similar and in many ways broader developments were occurring in the Mezzogiorno before Unification. Here too public administration offered opportunities, but demand heavily outstripped supply and local administration was of much greater importance. Both geographical size and the dynastic ambitions of its rulers made the Neapolitan Bourbons more heavily reliant on the cooperation of the landed elites than they cared to admit. Bourbon autocracy therefore retained French administrative decentralization, and paradoxically the weakness of the Bourbon state encouraged the development of a relatively autonomous but fragmented provincial bourgeoisie.[29]

Economic change often brought local interests into conflict—and not only in the south. David Lo Romer's study of Livorno in the early nineteenth century examines the development of a mercantile oligarchy and the tensions that developed between Florence and Livorno in these years. The prosperity of Livorno and its merchant community in the eighteenth century was closely linked to the city's privileged status as a free port. But the changing structure of Mediterranean trade in the nineteenth century made these privileges anachronistic and brought the city's mercantile community into conflict with a new and powerful commercial and banking elite in Florence. Lo Romer argues that the Livorno merchants lost the struggle because the revolution of 1848 aroused fears of social revolution that forced them to compromise their reform program. But this well-researched study gains little from the invocation of Gramsci's "failed bourgeois revolution," which introduces the sort of teleology that most of the other studies under review attempt to avoid without offering a convincing interpretation of the situation in Livorno. Comparison with other mercantile communities and the very different economic fortunes of mercantile classes of Florence and Genoa in the same period casts doubt on such fatalistic judgments and suggests that Livorno's fate was sealed less by fear of revolution than by the anachronistic character of its commercial oligarchy and the failure to diversify in the face of changing markets.[30]

[28] M. Meriggi, *Il Regno Lombardo-Veneto*, Storia d'Italia, ed. G. Galasso, vol. 18, pt. 2 (Turin, 1988), develops many of the themes from his earlier *Amministrazione e classi sociali nel Lombardo-Veneto (1814–48)* (Bologna, 1983). Some of Meriggi's arguments are challenged in D. Laven's recent thesis, "Austrian Administration in Venetia, 1814–1830" (Ph.D. diss., Cambridge University, 1991).

[29] The essays in Massafra, ed., now offer the essential starting point for any discussion of economic and social change in the Mezzogiorno in the early nineteenth century. See also P. Pezzino, *Una Certa Reciprocità di Favori: Mafia e modernizzazione violenta nella Sicilia post-unitario* (Milan, 1990), and "Autonomia e accentramento nell'ottocento siciliano: Il caso di Navoro," in *Annali della Fondazione L&L Basso*, vol. 9 (Rome, 1987–88); and G. Fiume, "Bandits, Violence and the Organization of Power in Sicily in the Early 19th Century," in Davis and Ginsborg, eds., pp. 70–91.

[30] David Lo Romer, *Merchants and Reform in Livorno, 1814–1868* (Berkeley and Los Angeles, 1987).

304   *Davis*

But Lo Romer, like Meriggi, does provide further evidence to endorse Greenfield's thesis that Italy's pre-Unification commercial elites never formed a coherent lobby for political change, and in Tuscany as in Lombardy the mercantile interests retained close ties with the land. Yet despite the agrarian character of even the most active elements of the pre-Unification middle classes, it is also increasingly evident from recent studies that commercial expansion, changes in agriculture, and urban growth did create significant new opportunities for professional and technical employment as demand grew not only for lawyers and doctors but also for a range of newer technical skills ranging from civil engineering and estate management to accounting and banking.

One indication of the changing consistency of the middle classes can be found in the rapid expansion of new forms of urban association and sociability. From the 1830s onward, recreational, literary, and philosophical societies multiplied, especially in the northern cities, and their membership offers a valuable guide to the shifting frontiers of "bourgeois" identity as the propertied and wealthy classes of urban Italy opened their doors to commercial wealth and the respectable professional classes. There were exceptions—Turin retained its aristocratic exclusiveness until the end of the century—but, like their counterparts in Europe more generally, these associations played an important part in establishing middle-class identities, redrawing the distinctions between public and private life, integrating different interest and occupational groups (through social contact and marriage), and establishing springboards for wider economic and political initiatives.[31]

During the 1840s and 1850s the Italian middle classes were taking on the tastes and behavioral characteristics of their European counterparts, but Unification dramatically accelerated and strengthened these tendencies. The critical innovation, Raffaele Romanelli has argued, was the introduction of elective local administrations (with a much wider suffrage than the parliamentary electorate), which delegated a range of new obligations and responsibilities to local government. From Bologna to Catania, from Piacenza to Pignataro Maggiore and Eboli, the consequences were dramatically similar. Everywhere local administration now offered the critical interfaces around which bourgeois Italy took shape, partly because local government was an important new source of jobs but above all because it was now a primary focus of economic and political activity.[32] To control local administration was to control access to the wider worlds of provincial and national politics and the resources that flowed from them, thereby conferring the powers of mediation that were prerequisites for promoting and protecting local interests.

---

[31] See the contributions to A. M. Banti and M. Meriggi, eds., "Elites e associazioni nell'Italia dell'ottocento," special issue, *Quaderni Storici*, vol. 77, no. 2 (1991).

[32] R. Romanelli, *Il commando impossibile: Stato e società nell'Italia liberale* (Bologna, 1989); A. Alaimo, *L'Organizzazione della città: Amministrazione urbana a Bologna dopo l'Unità (1859–1889)* (Bologna, 1990); Banti, *Terra e denaro* (n. 11 above); G. Civile, *Il comune rustico: Storia sociale di un paese del Mezzogiorno nell'ottocento* (Bologna, 1990); G. Gribaudi, *A Eboli: Il mondo meridionale in cento anni di trasformazione* (Venice, 1990).

Remapping *Italy's Path to the Twentieth Century* 305

The working of these processes has now been traced through the patient reconstruction of local political and economic networks, which make visible the ways in which local interests were drawn into wider circles, wider contacts, and wider fields of action—each forming a layer with some degree of autonomy, yet each reacting on the other. The worlds of provincial municipal politics studied by Banti, Malatesta, Civile, and Gabriella Gribaudi show how local administration acted as the fulcrum for concentric associations that brought the agrarian elites into contact with other sections of the middle classes and with wider structures of business, finance, and local and national politics.[33]

The attempt to redefine bourgeois sensibilities and collective awareness has also led to new interest in the aristocracies, in an attempt to reconstitute the shifting social contours of the old and the new. But these boundaries are difficult to map, and Italy's aristocracies prove no easier to distinguish as a social group from the wealthier landed gentry than elsewhere in Europe, while aristocratic values and ethos remained as strong as they did in most of the rest of Europe. Paolo Macry shows how the Neapolitan patricians came to terms with a bourgeois world without losing their sense of caste or their aristocratic pretensions, while in an earlier study G. Fiocca showed how the Milanese commercial and industrial classes continued throughout the century to marry into the aristocracy and adopt their lifestyles. The difficulty is to know what significance to attach to this, since the Italian middle classes were hardly behaving differently from their English counterparts and contemporaries, and there is certainly no evidence that the self-consciously aristocratic lifestyles of gentlemen-farmers of the Veneto made their commitment to capitalist farming any less vigorous.[34]

The importance of aristocratic lifestyles and an aristocratic ethic in Italy is complicated by the fact that, in dispossessing six of Italy's seven rulers, Unification had precipitated the political eclipse of the greater part of the Italian nobility. The exceptions were Piedmont and Rome (although the Neapolitans probably also deserve closer attention), and it was the unique status of the House of Savoy that accounted for the conspicuous social exclusiveness of the Piedmontese nobility in Turin that lasted beyond the end of the century.[35]

The Savoy monarchy—which so far has attracted little attention from social historians—was also the reason why Piedmontese noblemen continued to enjoy privileged access to senior military commands, even though they still constituted only a minority in what was, by European standards, a remarkably bourgeois

---

[33] Banti, *Terra e denaro;* Malatesta (n. 10 above); Civile; G. Gribaudi.

[34] Macry, *Ottocento* (n. 23 above); and also on Naples, G. Laurito, "Comportamenti matrimoniali e mobiltà sociale a Napoli," *Quaderni Storici* 56 (August 1984): 434–50; G. Fiocca, ed., *Borghesi ed imprenditori a Milano dall'Unità alla Prima Guerra Mondiale* (Bari, 1983); M. Meriggi, "Lo spirito di associazione nella Milano dell'800," *Quaderni Storici* 77, no. 2 (August 1991): 389–411; Fumian, "Proprietari" (n. 8 above), pp. 129–51. On aristocratic and middle-class families in general, see M. Barbagli, *Sotto lo Stesso Tetto: Mutamenti della famiglia in Italia dal XV al XX Secolo* (Bologna, 1984), and "Marriage and Family in Italy in the 19th Century," in Davis and Ginsborg, eds., pp. 92–127.

[35] A. Cardoza, "Tra caste e classe: Clubs maschili dell'élite torinese, 1840–1914," *Quaderni Storici* 77, no. 2 (August 1991): 365–83.

306   *Davis*

officer corps.[36] Did that make the army a vector for middle-class values in liberal Italy? This question is raised but not fully resolved in the contributions to the volumes on the army and urban society after Unification. In comparison with other professional careers, the army was relatively cheap to enter (much cheaper than law or medicine). Its popularity varied geographically (the Milanese were particularly unenthusiastic), but for the humbler sections of middle-class Italy the army (we know less about the navy) offered accessible opportunities for advancement.[37] Yet despite the absence of an aristocracy, the collective esprit of the officer corps remained aristocratic and exclusive, even if the continuation of rituals like dueling are open to more than one reading. Over time, greater emphasis was placed on merit and skill, reflecting the growing importance of technical training, but the norms of officerly conduct were dictated by codes of chivalry and honor that were neither obviously new nor bourgeois but, like their European counterparts, exclusive and above all martial.[38]

Soldiering also opened doors to social advancement, and Paola Nava describes how the matrons of Modena looked to the cadets from the military academy to fill out an inelastic local marriage market.[39] What awaited them in middle-class domesticity has until recently been of interest primarily to demographic historians, but new windows are now opening on these private spaces of middle-class family life. Macry describes how the Neapolitan patricians adapted the organization and furnishings of their interiors to the more individualistic styles of bourgeois society, while Simonetta Soldani's important volume on women and education contains a wealth of new and original studies that approach the Italian middle-class family through the roles and expectations of women.[40]

Even against the narrow standards set by bourgeois Europe, gender roles in Italy were tightly delimited. Denied the relative emancipation of their aristocratic predecessors—some of whom had been able to participate in the political salons of the Enlightenment and the Risorgimento—the spaces ascribed to the women of liberal Italy were almost exclusively private and deeply influenced by the pietist

[36] Forty-nine percent of German officers were aristocrats in 1872, compared with 7 percent in the Italian army; by 1914 the figures were, respectively, 33 and 4 percent. See A. Cardoza, "An Officer and a Gentleman: The Piedmontese Nobility and the Military in Liberal Italy," in *Esercito e città dall'Unità agli anni trenta*, Pubblicazioni degli Archivi di Stato, Saggi 12, 2 vols. (Rome, 1989), 1:185–200; see the comments by Meriggi and Del Negro in ibid., 1:340–42, and Meriggi, "La borghesia italiana" (n. 25 above), p. 169.

[37] Macry, *Ottocento*, p. 203; Meriggi, "L'ufficiale a Milano in età liberale," in *Esercito e città*, 1:273–96.

[38] P. Mazzonis, "Usi della buona società e questioni d'onore: Etichetta e vertenze cavalleresche nei manuali ufficiali," in *Esercito e città*, 1:229–54; and cf. U. Frevert, "Bourgeois Honour: Middle Class Duellists in Germany," in Blackbourn and Evans, eds. (n. 2 above), pp. 255–92. Historians of the Italian monarchy have paid little attention to its popular image—closely associated with that of the military, but never identical—but it is clear that the Savoy rulers never achieved the popularity of their German or British cousins.

[39] P. Nava, "Ufficiale e gentiluomo: Cadetti e ufficiali dell'Academia militare e nella società modenese tra '800 e '900," in *Esercito e città*, 1:321–36.

[40] S. Soldani, ed., *L'Educazione delle donne: Scuole e modelli femminili nell'Italia dell'ottocento* (Milan, 1981); see also M. Barbagli, "Marriage and the Family," pp. 92–127, and *Sotto lo stesso tetto*.

Remapping Italy's Path to the Twentieth Century 307

tones of the Restoration: "A lady cannot be anything other than wife and mother or virgin: outside these two estates there are no ladies, only females."[41] Apart from the handful of women (mostly foreigners) who graduated before 1914 in medicine (the only professional skill apart from elementary teaching considered suitable to what were deemed to be the special "caring" qualities of womanhood), the world of the professions and of higher education was closed to women. Unlike their counterparts in the French Third Republic, the Italian middle classes showed no enthusiasm for separate secondary schools for girls, nor indeed for secular schooling, preferring to send their daughters (and their sons—the founder of Fiat, Giovanni Agnelli, was the product of a Jesuit college) to religious schools whose numbers increased exuberantly in the late nineteenth century.[42]

A preference for moral and religious instruction rather than learning or training in the education of girls was scarcely unique, but it does illustrate vividly middle-class indifference to the secularizing mission of the liberal state. However, official attitudes were not markedly less ambiguous, as Ilaria Porciani's reconstruction of the controversy that erupted over the selection of representatives for a gallery of "Great Italian Women" well illustrates. Clerical protest ensured that no female *philosophe*, Jacobin martyr, or Anita Garibaldi would enter the pantheon, which without any sense of incongruity did happily accommodate St. Catherine of Siena and Countess Matilda of Tuscany.[43]

The essays in Soldani's volume take important steps toward exploring the still-shadowy world of gender, sexuality, and domesticity in nineteenth-century Italy, as well as opening fascinating windows on the one major form of employment that was open to middle-class women: teaching in primary schools. The conditions of women schoolteachers throw a stark light on life on the lower fringes of bourgeois Italy, where the rapid expansion of primary schools after 1860 offered relatively wide opportunities for women. But this was an area where the issues of gender, religion, and public service converged with often tragic results. To be unmarried was a condition of employment, and in remote provincial towns and village schools the single schoolmistress was exposed to every conceivable harassment and abuse, making the vividly melodramatic portrayals of their plight in novels like *Cuore* seem if anything understated. Targets of unwelcome attentions from administrators on whom they were dependent and of unrelenting denunciations from the clergy for whom they were immoral agents of a godless state, Italy's schoolmistresses were frequently victims of assault, rape, suicide, and death not only from disease (a common enough nineteenth-century occupational hazard) but from hypothermia, malnutrition, and starvation as well.[44] These essays also vividly illustrate how time and again the authorities were unable to ensure that schools were provided or that they were run as the law required—local

---

[41] A. G. Marchetti, "La stampa lombarda per le signorine," in Soldani, ed., p. 459; and the essays in the second part of the volume.

[42] See the contributions by A. Manacorda, M. Raicich, G. Padovani, V. Monastra, M. I. Palazzolo, and A. Buttafuoco in Soldani, ed.

[43] I. Porciani, "Il Plutarco femminile," in Soldani, ed., pp. 297–318.

[44] G. Bini, "La maestra nella letteratura: Uno specchio della realtà"; M. Moretti, "P. Villari e l'istruzione femminile," both in Soldani, ed., pp. 331–62, 497–530.

308   *Davis*

administrators were often the culprits, but the greatest battles were with the clergy and the religious orders, which in many cases simply refused to cooperate in any form with the authorities. Not only were women schoolteachers vulnerable missionaries of the liberal state, but their conditions expose the state's weakness at the periphery as well.

In that sense, the essays in Soldani's volume throw light on two different realms of the private. One concerns domesticity, gender, and sexuality and still remains only very dimly perceived. The other—the realm of private power, authority, and jurisdiction, as opposed to that of public authorities and the state (the two of course meet in the patriarchal family)—is more closely bound up with the particularly Italian experience of institutional change and state formation in the nineteenth century. Indeed, the blurred demarcations between the spheres of public and private authority can be seen as a critical characteristic of the process of modernization without growth, and it is in that sense that the uncertain boundaries between public and private form a central theme in Romanelli's analysis of another group on the lowest rungs of public service and middle-class respectability—local government clerks.

Responsible for ensuring that local administrators observed the law and carried out official instructions, municipal clerks were effectively appointed by and dependent on those they were supposed to oversee. Distinctions between public and private authority as a result remained uncertain, but Romanelli argues that this blurring was far from accidental and should be seen as a direct consequence of the ideological premises and administrative structures of the liberal state. Successive governments after 1860 saw public administration as an instrument of political and social change, while at the same time firmly believing in the need to protect the autonomy of local government. It was for ideological reasons and not just because of meanness that successive ministers rejected the clerks' appeal for recognition as civil servants (which would have entitled them to pensions), for example, since to make them civil servants was thought to be undue interference in local autonomies. But despite their essentially local frame of reference, the clerks did attempt to organize collectively at a national level, and Romanelli argues in *Sulle carte interminate* that their professional manuals and journals reveal forms of political and cultural awareness that went well beyond local confines.[45]

Despite the hardships, clerks and schoolmistresses enjoyed degrees of security and status largely unknown to the mass of working people, and while material conditions were poor they offered ladders for occupational and social mobility. Some time ago Paolo Macry argued that relative security and close dependence on the state and local patrons made the lower middle classes a critical cushion against social unrest in liberal Italy. These studies lend further weight to such a view, as will Jonathan Morris's forthcoming study of Milanese shopkeepers, which takes the discussion into the "private" sector of the petty bourgeoisie. Demonstrating that the shopkeepers of the Milanese working-class suburbs in the late nineteenth century were neither apolitical nor instinctively reactionary, Morris emphasizes

---

[45] R. Romanelli, *Sulle carte interminate: Un ceto di impiegati tra privato e pubblico: I segretari comunali in Italia, 1860–1915* (Bologna, 1989).

Remapping Italy's Path to the Twentieth Century 309

the reciprocal links of dependence that developed between the shopkeepers and their working-class customers, whom they provided with petty credit as well as goods and with whom (at least until the cooperative movement got under way) they shared a common hostility toward the wealthier quarters and commercial interests of the city center.[46]

Viewed from the bottom up, entrenched assumptions about the fragility of middle-class Italy seem to become questionable. Both Banti and Malatesta demonstrate the relatively precocious initiatives taken by northern landowners to establish mutual aid societies, credit banks, and insurance schemes for their laborers—initiatives that initially had clear paternalist overtones but (in the case of Piacenza) began to explore corporatist alternatives to liberal self-help at an early stage. Such institutions reinforced paternalist bonds of deference and dependence, but they were also, as Maria Malatesta puts it, good business, establishing profitable linkages with financial enterprise. Deference and dependence was no less evident in the Veneto, where Carlo Fumian describes the industrial complex at Piazzola (near Padua) created by Paolo Camerini, one of the model Venetian entrepreneurs of the late nineteenth century, as an "autarchic industrial feudal estate and welfare community."[47]

Dependence and deference combined best where the entrepreneurs or landowners worked with rather than against the church, but Italy's industrial, agrarian, and municipal elites were not unprotected. Where conflict did occur, it was more often associated with change and innovation than backwardness, and recent studies on industrial relations before 1914 have stressed how working-class militancy took its lead from the most advanced sectors—especially from the engineering industry—where a highly skilled work force attempted to gain control over the reorganization of production rather than reject technological innovation out of hand.[48] Rural unrest and violence took a greater variety of forms, but the most intractable was the labor militancy that developed where the changes in the organization of the agrarian economy were pushed ahead most vigorously—in the Po valley. In the south, the violent explosions of the Sicilian Fasci in the 1890s or those on the Apulian latifundia in the next decade did not shake the dominant structures of landlordism and could only find an alternative in emigration.[49]

All of this seems to run firmly counter to Gramsci's claim that fear of revolution from below gelded the bourgeois revolution in Italy, and, if middle-class Italy lacked political programs with a popular appeal comparable to Gladstonian

---

[46] P. Macry, "Sulla storia sociale dell'Italia liberale: Per una ricerca sul 'ceto di frontiera,' " *Quaderni Storici* 35 (1977): 522–47, and "Borghesia, città e stato: Appunti e impressioni su Napoli, 1860–80," *Quaderni Storici* 56 (August 1984): 371–72; J. Morris, *The Political Economy of Shop-keeping in Milan (1886–1922)* (Cambridge, 1993).

[47] Fumian, *La città del Lavoro* (n. 8 above); see also M. Zane, "Associazionismo e politica fra '800 e '900 in un paese del Bresciano," *Quaderni Storici* 77, no. 2 (August 1991): 514–37.

[48] See D. Bigazzi, *Il Portello: Operai, tecnici ed imprenditori all'Alfa-Romeo, 1906–1926* (Milan, 1988); S. Ortaggi, *Il prezzo del lavoro: Torino e l'industria nel primo '900* (Turin, 1988); Fumian, *La città del Lavoro;* but cf. D. H. Bell, *Sesto San Giovanni: Workers, Culture and Politics in an Italian Town, 1880–1922* (Los Angeles, 1987).

[49] See esp. R. Vivarelli, "La questione contadina nell'Italia unità," *Rivista Storica Italiana* 102 (1990): 87–165, and "Interpretations of the Origins of Fascism," *Journal of Modern History* 63, no. 1 (1991): 29–43.

310   *Davis*

liberalism,[50] the Italian middle classes were nonetheless relatively well cocooned in vertical organizations strongly impregnated with interclass ideologies. But if local examples provide important correctives to many earlier generalizations, there is still much more that needs to be known about the development of social relations in this period. While at a local level landowners and entrepreneurs did respond to changing economic and social conditions, it is also evident that their attempts to retain deference and dependence were in broader terms far from successful. It is at this point that the relative abandonment of interest in the working classes in recent years becomes particularly noticeable, and this points to the need for a broader reconsideration of the experience of labor in the light of the greater knowledge about the behavior and strategies of the Italian middle classes that is now available. There is room here too for broader comparative discussion, since the Italian case (or cases) would seem to remain much closer to the German rather than the French or British models of social and political integration, following the criteria that John Breuilly, for example, has recently put forward for reconsidering the relationship between liberalism and labor in Europe.[51]

The neglect of labor history is not total, and Maurizio Gribaudi's study of the working-class communities of Turin at the turn of the century offers an interesting but in many ways puzzling attempt to apply the methods of political and social anthropology to class formation. Gribaudi argues that the collectivist values of the working-class communities at that moment were rooted in the social "networks" that evolved among migrant workers as they moved from the neighboring countryside to settle in Turin's rapidly expanding working-class districts at the turn of the century. Reconstructing these networks of migration and settlement from demographic sources, Gribaudi shows how the newly immigrant workers relied on networks of contacts provided by the established communities that enabled them to find jobs, housing, marriage partners, and access to working-class sociability. But, Gribaudi argues, once those factors became less important as the community became more settled, collectivist principles were weakened, and with them the appeal of political socialism. This change in attitudes and values over generations—together with a generational reaction by the young against the values of their parents—provides an explanation, Gribaudi claims, for the attraction exercised by fascism on many young Turin workers in the 1920s.[52]

Gribaudi's approach—which closely mirrors the influence of political anthropology in the other local and community-based studies discussed in this review—reveals both the strengths and the limits of his methodology. On one hand, the emphasis on the relatively autonomous character of working-class communities and self-help institutions provides further evidence of the limited channels of social or political integration or assimilation open to the Italian working classes. On the other hand, the analysis of working-class politics in these terms becomes highly mechanistic and reductionist, while the author's distinctions

---

[50] On the "peculiarities" of Gladstonian liberalism, see Eley (n. 2 above), pp. 307–12.
[51] See Breuilly (n. 2 above), pp. 1–25.
[52] M. Gribaudi, *Mondo operaio e mito operaio: Spazi e percorsi sociali a Torino nel primo novecento* (Turin, 1987).

between class consciousness, political commitment, and "public discourse" remain far from clear.[53]

The discussion of the relationship between liberalism and the working classes in Italy also raises the question of the broader relationship between the Italian bourgeoisie and liberalism. If recent research has illustrated the capacity of the Italian middle classes for organization, innovation, and adaptation to change at a local level, what does this mean in more general terms and how does it change or modify our understanding of the liberal state?

Some critics have detected in the preference for a "view from below" a distorting lens that magnifies the locality at the expense of the whole while shying away from the big questions posed by the liberal state. But this seems unwarranted, since far from simply throwing light on hitherto murky corners of provincial life and politics, local studies have exposed the critical importance of the ties that linked the most distant peripheries to the center. Even in remote communities like Pignataro Maggiore and Eboli, the interdependence between center and locality was close, and we are now much more aware of the ways in which these small rural communities were at every point tied into obligations that ran outward toward regional and national politics. Older political labels and alignments were grafted onto new ones, and external political events were assimilated through filters of local memory, social alliances, and political symbolism, with the result that different layers of identity and allegiance were established. Elements of continuity and change coexisted, so that locality and localism were never synonymous and the dichotomies between local and national identity never absolute.[54]

But if we move back—as at some point we must—to the broader context of state and society, how does the view from below lead to a broader understanding of the nature of the liberal state? Have local studies reaffirmed the essentially localized character of social formation, thereby reinforcing—albeit from new perspectives—an older emphasis on social fragmentation, on municipalism, and hence, to some degree, on the absence or weakness of a "national" bourgeoisie? Despite the outward appearances of agreement there is in reality very little consensus on a broader reinterpretation of politics and society in liberal Italy, and the studies under review serve rather to indicate a range of different and by no means convergent or complementary interpretations.

One sets new emphasis on the agency of the "visible hands" driving economic, social, and institutional change in Italy and locates those forces on the peripheries rather than at the center, within society rather than the state. As a result, an image of the liberal state in which social formation was immature and economic change sluggish gives way to a radically different picture of rampant, or at least unregulated, capitalism, driven and shaped by specific local forces and circumstances and seeking its own solutions. This offers one possible interpretation of the process of modernization without growth, in which free-market capitalism pushed ahead successfully with little regard—or indeed need for—broader institutional or

[53] Ibid., p. xxvii.
[54] Civile (n. 32 above); G. Gribaudi (n. 32 above).

312   *Davis*

structural changes. It is argued most explicitly by Silvio Lanaro, who has ascribed
the success of Venetian entrepreneurship in the late nineteenth century to "the
non-existence of politics, of the institutions of the central State and public
administration as instruments for regulating society."[55] Albeit in more qualified
tones, Banti echoes Lanaro when he argues that authoritarian, nationalist, and
corporatist ideas quickly found support among the landowners of Piacenza
because they related directly to the needs and practices of agrarian capitalism in
ways that liberalism did not. Like Lanaro, Banti also sees authoritarian anti-
liberalism at the end of the nineteenth century as a vehicle of modernization in
Italy, implying that fascism grew out of a modernizing reaction against liberalism
that the particular forms of capitalist development in Italy made anachronistic.

Such conclusions make both liberalism and the liberal state essentially marginal
and effectively unhitch the process of economic growth from the modernization of
the state—indeed, the relationship is inverted in the sense that the specific form
assumed by the liberal state (and in particular the skewing of power from the
center to the locality) is in large part attributed to the centrifugal forces of
localized capitalist development. But such a view poses at least two sets of
problems: one is that it comes very close to simply arriving at the same
conclusions as modernization theory, albeit by a different route; the other is that
it explains away rather than explains the liberal state.

The most systematic attempt to redefine the role of the state and liberalism in
the light of recent research is to be found in the numerous studies on public
administration and political liberalism by Raffaele Romanelli. Some of these
important essays have now been published in a single volume that gives a clear
indication of Romanelli's rethinking of the relationship between liberalism,
politics, and society in Italy.

Romanelli argues that the structural and ideological organization of the liberal
state actively encouraged the development of unregulated capitalism. In part the
reasons were historical, and he emphasizes the contrast between state formation in
Italy and Germany, arguing that because it lacked Prussia's military and economic
resources the Piedmontese monarchy had little option but to preside over what was
in many ways a negotiated settlement that left considerable spaces for regional and
local autonomy.[56] The administrative centralization that followed the annexation
of the south did not reverse those tendencies, Romanelli argues, because liberal
ideology was premised on the autonomy of local government. But far from being
the bureaucratic tyranny denounced by contemporaries, Romanelli insists that the
extensive powers of central government (exercised, for example, by the prefects)
can only be understood in terms of Cavour's conviction that liberalism was the
instrument best suited to bring about the political, social, and moral regeneration
of Italy. The state equipped itself, therefore, with powers to ensure that local

[55] Lanaro, "Genealogia" (n. 8 above), p. 65, and *Nazione e Lavoro* (Venice, 1979), pp. 8–9.
For a more general discussion of the Venetian "model" of entrepreneurship, see D. Bigazzi, *La
storia dell'impresa in Italia: Saggio bibliografico* (Milan, 1990), pp. 46–47.

[56] On the relative unimportance of the region except as an administrative unit, see esp. G. Levi,
"Regioni e cultura delle classi popolari," *Quaderni Storici* 14, no. 2 (1979): 720–31.

administration should adhere to its liberalizing design, which sought to encourage active citizenship, broaden political participation, and foster free enterprise. Cavour's successors were no less convinced that free and participatory local government was the necessary premise for development and the means to extend the liberal revolution from the center, where it had triumphed, to the periphery, where older autocratic and corporatist mentalities lived on.[57]

Romanelli insists, however, that this was an "Impossible Mandate." Unbending respect for the autonomy of local government blunted government's willingness as well as capacity for intervention, while legitimizing free-market capitalism. Hence the blurring of distinctions between public and private at a local level and, in the absence of a stronger response from the localities, a weakening of the impetus for institutional change.

The debates on suffrage reform offer further examples of the ways in which social constraints blocked the wider development of political liberalism. The narrowness of the parliamentary electorate (less than 2 percent of the population at the time of Unification but a greatly increased proportion in 1882 and again in 1911) has frequently been taken as evidence of the weakness of the Italian parliamentary system. Romanelli convincingly argues that, whereas the search for an electorate did illustrate the quantitative narrowness of middle-class Italy, the debate itself revealed again the strength of commitment to liberal democracy. Virtually everyone recognized that the suffrage was dangerously small and that even at its lowest point parliamentary suffrage (the local government electorate was from the start very much broader) already embraced all the propertied and professional classes and many more besides. The obstacles to broadening the suffrage lay not in a lack of will but in finding a way to accomplish that goal without at the same time strengthening the forces hostile to liberalism—in particular, the conservative and clerical Right who would have been the main beneficiaries of universal suffrage (of which they remained the principal advocates until 1911).[58]

The great strength of Romanelli's work is that it seeks to integrate the new perspectives from below and from the periphery into a more rounded and coherent reappraisal of the nature and function of the liberal state. In doing so Romanelli redefines in important ways the nature of the liberal state and the relations between the state and the Italian bourgeoisie (or bourgeoisies). What remains less clear, however, is the significance of this reevaluation in comparative terms. What, for example, was the consequence of the failure—or narrowing, or blunting—of the Cavourian liberal revolution? Did it matter that the liberal revolution became an impossible mandate? The answer to that question is hedged with some ambiguity. Was it the case that the imbalance between public and private power simply reflected a path of political and institutional development that was "peculiar" to Italy—different, but not for that reason either "good" or "bad," a functional response to a peculiarly Italian constellation of circumstances? Liberal adminis-

---

[57] See the essays now collected in Romanelli, *Il commando impossible* (n. 32 above), and also *Sulle carte interminate* (n. 45 above).

[58] "Alla ricerca di un corpo elettorale," in Romanelli, *Il commando impossibile*.

314   *Davis*

trative and political ideology could be said to have stimulated and legitimated free-enterprise capitalism, so that by asserting the absolute freedom of contract and the illegitimacy of anything that intervened in the sphere of private relations between master and servant, landlord and tenant, husband and wife, father and family, liberalism made economic development compatible with the preservation of the principles of *padroni quasi patres*.

Such an interpretation does of course illuminate many features of Italian liberalism and the liberal state (not least cohabitation with a deeply antiliberal church) and comes close to the position adopted by Lanaro and Banti. But it is not the conclusion drawn by Romanelli, both because he is well aware that the state itself was never a constant and because he emphasizes the social and political constraints that blocked the liberalizing influence coming from the center and skewed its impact at the periphery with the consequence that the broader impetus for institutional, political, and cultural change was blunted by the narrow parochialism of Italy's provincial elites.[59] But while there is a clear implication that this was in some way limiting, the consequences of the blunting of liberal revolution "from above" are not spelled out.

If there are uncertainties around the crucial question of whether the liberal state was simply different or whether those differences did contain real blockages to further economic or political change, many of the other studies under consideration stress the ways in which the administrative and political organization of the liberal state were dysfunctional. Mariauccia Salvati, for example, traces the origins of those processes of government through the mediation, "political exchange," and "parallel bureaucracies" that have been identified as characteristics of the contemporary Italian state to the political system of the liberal Italy. She argues that local consultative bodies like the *comizi agrari* and *camere di commercio* were created to establish direct channels of communication between the periphery and central government in ways that deliberately circumvented parliament and the civil service, while the absence of highly professional central bureaucracies comparable to those of the French Third Republic meant that the liberal state's capacity for informed intervention at the periphery was in any case severely limited. This in turn encouraged the formation of central ad hoc consultative committees that increasingly transferred the formulation of policy from the civil service and parliament to organized interest groups and lobbies and undermined the function of parliament and the political process.[60]

There is a risk of anachronism in drawing parallels too directly between past and present, and the growing power of organized political lobbying was certainly not unique to Italy in this period. But Maria Malatesta also draws attention to the

---

[59] See R. Romanelli, "Le regole del gioco: Note sull'impatto del sistema elettorale in Italia, 1848–1895"; A. Signorelli, "Partecipazione politica, diritto al voto, affluenza alle urne: Contribuenti ed ellettori a Catania negli anni '700 dell '800," both in *Quaderni Storici* ("Notabili, elettori, elezioni: Rappresentanza e controllo elettorale nell'ottocento," ed. R. Romanelli and A. Annino), no. 69 (December 1988).

[60] M. Salvati, "Dalla Francia all'Italia: Il modello francese e vie surretizie di modernizzazione amministrativa in uno stato periferico," in *Suffragio, rappresentanza, interessi: Istituzioni e società fra '800 e '900*, ed. C. Pavone and M. Salvati, Annali della Fondazione L. Basso, Issoco (Rome, 1987–88; Milan, 1989), 9:123–66.

ways in which cross-cutting local influences blocked structural reform. She takes two important examples: the moves to introduce compulsory compensation for tenants and compulsory insurance schemes for rural laborers, both of which eventually won the support of the Lombard landowners but were blocked (in defense of "freedom of contract") by the southerners—a good example of the way the political influence of the south goes out by one door only to come back through another. By pointing to the recognized inadequacies of civil law and the difficulty of reform, Malatesta uncovers a critically important dimension of structural modernization in Italy that has as yet attracted too little attention from social historians.[61]

The rule of law is raised in different and more dramatic form by the Mafia. The growing body of research into the origins of the Mafia has exposed the weakness of older cultural interpretations and has emphasized the economic and sociological circumstances that favored the development of the Mafia in nineteenth-century Sicily. But Paolo Pezzino convincingly makes the case that any analysis of the Mafia solely in terms of clientist networks or conditions of economic uncertainty fails to explain why similar conditions did not create Mafia organizations elsewhere. He argues that the critical factors in creating and developing the Mafia in Sicily were political, and working from a set of closely documented case studies he shows how the representatives of the liberal state in the nineteenth century effectively created the Mafia both as a form of political power and as organized criminality. Lacking influence or contacts in Sicilian society, the agents of the liberal state were wary of the established elites and turned systematically to men of violence and crime to enable them to achieve an effective purchase in Sicilian society. Insisting on the criminal origins of the mafiosi and dismissing the self-romanticization of the mafioso as a man of honor, Pezzino demonstrates that the Mafia grew out of Sicilian criminality and social violence. But close and uninterrupted political contacts made it possible for Mafia groups to become more organized, more powerful, and more violent—not least because of the growing attractiveness of the mafioso as a role model in society where alternative career opportunities and channels of upward social mobility were not remarkable.[62]

Pezzino's emphasis on the political dimensions of the Mafia implicitly questions the extent to which the absence of structural change in the south can be attributed solely to constraints imposed by markets and prevailing economic conditions.[63] The visible hand as much as markets determined the process of

[61] Malatesta (n. 10 above), pp. 288, 307–9. Social historians in general have paid little attention to the civil law and modernization, with the notable exception of M. John, *Politics and the Law in Late Nineteenth Century Germany* (Oxford, 1989).

[62] P. Pezzino, *Una certa reciprocità di favori: Mafia e modernizzazione violenta nella Sicilia post-Unitaria* (Milan 1990). See also Blok (n. 16 above); R. Spampinato, "Per una storia della mafia: Interpretazioni e questioni controverse," in Aymard and Giarrizzo, eds. (n. 13 above), pp. 886–900; "Mafia," special issue, *Meridiana: Rivista di Storia e Scienze Sociali*, nos. 7–8 (September 1989–January 1990); N. Tranfaglia, *La Mafia come Metodo nell'Italia Contemporanea* (Bari, 1991); and Lupo (n. 17 above), pp. 121–24.

[63] See n. 62; for an interpretation of Mafia in terms of economic and political insecurity, see D. Gambetta, "Fragments of an Economic Theory of the Mafia," *European Journal of Sociology* 29 (1988): 127–45; and now *The Sicilian Mafia: The Business of Private Protection* (Cambridge, Mass., 1993).

modernization without growth, and set in a broader context this raises a much bigger question: If the Mafia's parentage lay in the absence of structural change in Sicily and the absence of the rule of law, was the Mafia the creature of conditions that were peculiar to Sicily, or was it an extreme form of the essentially autonomous and self-governing systems of power and influence exercised by local elites throughout much of Italy, and hence a reflection of the limits of the rule of law in liberal Italy more generally?

Much more needs to be known about the working of the law in general—and particularly of the civil law—before such questions can really be answered and effective comparisons drawn between realities in Sicily and other Italian regions. This in turn leads to a consideration of the state in much wider terms, and if Sicily provides examples of the negative consequences of state intervention there are numerous examples in these studies of the ways in which the state played a much more proactive role. Not the least of these was taxation, a subject too often neglected by social historians yet one of critical importance. On this the view from below offers compelling new evidence that levels of direct as well as indirect taxation were both relatively heavy and a central political preoccupation in liberal Italy. Macry, for example, eloquently demonstrates the crippling impact of taxation on the southern landowners after Unification, and it was not by chance that the avoidance of additional tax burdens weighed more heavily in the south in the late 1880s than the potentially damaging consequences of tariff protection. Romanelli has also argued that Italy's high personal tax rates imposed a critical brake on the material expansion of the Italian middle classes more generally.[64]

The obvious question that this begs—and it is by no means a new one—is, of course, How was this weak and apparently ineffective state able to impose these burdens and maintain them over time? Any answer to that question must also take account of the closely related issues of the state's strategic role in economic and institutional development through the mobilization of savings and more generally through intervention in the economy, in economic policy, in industrial relations, and in social welfare. While there is wide disagreement on the consequences of state intervention, few historians seriously question the critical importance of the suspension of convertibility (the *corso forzoso*), the sale of church lands, the financial support given to the steel industry (Terni), the shipping industry, the adoption of industrial and agricultural protectionism, and reorganization of the banking system after the crisis of the early 1890s.[65] Indeed, the studies under review offer many additional examples—such as the close dependence of northern capital investment in the south (particularly for

---

[64] Macry, *Ottocento* (n. 23 above); Romanelli, "Political Debate" (n. 1 above).

[65] Bonelli (n. 6 above) argues that the state always stepped in to take the risks and pick up the pieces when things went wrong; but as yet this remains a hypothesis rather than a documented conclusion (pp. 1203–11). But see G. Mori, "Dimensione stato e storiografia economica e sociale: lo stato e la rivoluzione industriale," in *Gli spazi del potere: Aree, regioni, stati: Le coordinate territoriali della storia contemporanea,* ed. F. Andreucci and A. Pescarolo (Florence, 1989), pp. 84–90; R. A. Webster, *Industrial Imperialism in Italy, 1908–1915* (Berkeley, 1975); A. Confalonieri, *Banca e industria in Italia, 1894–1906,* vols. 1–3 (Milan, 1974–76).

Remapping Italy's Path to the Twentieth Century   317

electrification and land-reclamation projects) on Nitti's program of state intervention after the turn of the century.[66]

These interventions also have to be set in the wider context of the institutional and juridical changes that regulated and facilitated the development of joint-stock enterprises, money markets, and banking—the latter, after the spectacular crashes of the early 1890s, being a good example of the move toward more regulated and organized forms of economic activity. But similar changes were evident in the scale of operation of the new banks and the electrical, chemical, iron, and steel conglomerates. In short, both Italian capitalism and the Italian state were changing in ways that are visible but not easily assessed from the periphery. Local elites reacted in different ways—defensively in the south, whereas in the Veneto there was a closer accommodation of old and new. But in either case, the advent of new forms of capitalist organization necessarily changed the framework within which capitalism from below had operated.[67]

The new agenda brings us back to these older but central questions about the nature of the Italian and the liberal state without offering clear new answers. Not that this should be surprising: it is clear that the principal concern has been to test and rethink accepted truths, so it may be unrealistic to expect to find a revisionist consensus. The recharting of the interactions between social change and political organization has served to open up important new perspectives on the liberal state, but it does leave critical uncertainties about the process of change in Italy in this period that cannot be resolved by the formula of modernization without growth. The terms of the oxymoron are insufficiently precise and at times display a disconcerting tendency to become interchangeable, so that the implicit contradistinction between "modernization" (economic and social change) and "growth" (broad, sustained, qualitative, and structural economic growth) is rarely either hard and fast or unambiguous.

The continuing ambiguities that attach to even a revised concept of modernization is not peculiar by any means to the debate on Italy, but there are certain additional complications that are more specific to the Italian debate. One possible source of confusion—especially for those coming to these debates from other historiographical contexts—is that while the terminology of modernization that is used is to a large extent Weberian, the framework of analysis remains essentially (although without explicit acknowledgment) Gramscian. One clear example is the way in which the Weberian distinction between public and private is adapted to Gramsci's distinction between state and civil society and his insistence on the relative importance of the latter as the bastion of bourgeois power in Italy in an otherwise decentralized and amorphous state. The focus has moved from Gramsci's intelligentsia to the local elites, from high culture to the networks through which Italy's provincial elites established themselves in the interstices of

---

[66] Lupo, pp. 209–14; Barone (n. 14 above), pp. 61–79; Mori, "Dimensione stato."

[67] See most recently Mori, ed., *Storia dell'industria* (n. 5 above); L. Cafagna, "L'economia e i suoi problemi: La riforma del settore creditizio," in *Problemi Istituzionali e Riforme nell'Età Crispina*, Atti del LV Congresso di Storia del Risorgimento (Rome, 1992), pp. 396–406; Castronovo (n. 5 above), pp. 137 ff.; Confalonieri.

318   *Davis*

the liberal state. In another characteristic piece of historiographical mutation, Gramsci's failed revolution is transformed into a process of change from below, conditioned and shaped by an unstable and uncertain world of market capitalism that bears the clear imprint of Polanyi's "great transformation" —but the framework remains essentially Gramscian.[68]

Although the terminology of modernization is retained, and indeed the modernizing force of liberalism is recognized, the concept of "modernization" still hovers uneasily between Marxist and Weberian formulations that are never clearly identified and that remain more contradictory than complementary. That necessarily makes comparative judgments uncertain. A good example is that blurring of distinctions between public and private authority that both Romanelli and Meriggi point to as a critical difference in the formation of the Italian and German middle classes: despite comparable dependence on public service, the blurred boundaries between public and private in local administration meant that Italy never developed a state bourgeoisie comparable to its German counterpart and state employees in Italy continued to be as much part of the private as part of the public sector.[69] The distinction is a good one and can lead to a wider descriptive analysis of the differences between social formation in the two states—but are there also political conclusions to be drawn? Here the answer is less clear, and we come back to the same problem: Were things in Italy just different, or did those differences have some bearing on the capacity of the liberal state for political development?

These questions are by no means specific to the new historiography on liberal Italy and are perhaps inseparable from a moment when older criteria of comparison are in doubt and newer criteria are as yet unidentified. But it does mean that if the new agenda has made the "peculiarities" of liberal Italy easier to identify, it has not made those peculiarities any easier to evaluate in a wider comparative European context. Yet if the new agenda leads us back to terrain and questions that are familiar and by no means resolved, it does so along itineraries that are new and revealing. The rediscovery of provincial and municipal Italy and of its professional, mercantile, and landed classes has made major advances in our knowledge of Italian society and the processes of social formation. Windows have also been established on the experience of gender, domesticity, and childhood, and social historians are beginning to widen their horizons to subjects that do not relate only to the historical sociology of local politics, although there is still much that remains to be explored. If for the moment the focus on middle-class Italy has pushed the workers from the limelight, that focus is overdue and should provide the premise for reopening debate on social relations and class identities in ways that will bring working people and their experiences back into the social as well as the political history of liberal Italy.[70]

---

[68] Acknowledgments and reference to Polanyi (n. 6 above) are frequent; but see also G. Sapelli, *Comunità e mercato: Socialisti, cattolici e governo municipale agli inizi del XX secolo* (Bologna, 1986).

[69] Meriggi, "La borghesia italiana" (n. 25 above), p. 175.

[70] See, for example, F. Andreucci and G. Turi, "La classe operaia: Una storia nel ghetto," *Passato e Presente* 10 (gen–aprile 1986): 3–7.

Remapping Italy's Path to the Twentieth Century   319

Beyond those empirical gains, it is also clear that an important achievement of the new agenda has been to rescue contemporary Italian history from the isolation of its categories of historical uniqueness and discontinuity—Risorgimento, liberalism, fascism, Republicanism. By setting these events against a continuum of changing relations between society and state that stretch back to the crisis of the *ancien régime* monarchies, if not earlier, the basis for a new and more comparative approach to Italy's experience in the nineteenth and twentieth centuries is being established. If the first task of the new agenda has to be to free Italy from the weight of misplaced stereotypes and models that derived from earlier criteria of comparison, one of the principal tasks now is to bring Italy back more squarely into the newer comparative debates that are focusing around the processes of state formation in nineteenth-century Europe.[71]

Much of this review has concentrated on the ways in which Italian historians have been concerned to study liberal Italy in its own terms and to free it from those teleologies that make every feature of the liberal state in some sense a prehistory of fascism. If this has led to a new emphasis on the elements of continuity in the longer-run development of state and society in Italy, it is worth asking by way of conclusion whether, looking for a brief moment beyond the confines of the liberal state and forward into the twentieth century, this risks "normalizing" fascism as simply another political form that suited the needs of Italian capitalism at a particular moment, another political blip in the onward march of capital. Lack of consensus in the revisionist camp means that as yet there is no clear reformulation of the question. At least some of the contributors to the debate on liberal Italy would see fascism as the pursuit of capitalist ends under a political system that promised to be more congenial and supportive than liberalism (although realities were clearly to be different from expectations). But far from depicting fascism as a teleologically predetermined outcome of the liberal state, the revisionist interpretation suggests more generally that, while the fascists could draw on clearly defined tendencies in liberal Italy, the central thrust of fascism— strengthening of the power of the central state, elimination of the "private" sphere, the nationalization of culture and ideology—ran directly counter to fundamental traits in Italy's social and political development that had been evident in the nineteenth century. If the new research confirms that liberalism had a weak purchase in liberal Italy, it also provides a wealth of new evidence to explain why fascist attempts to break the decentralized structure of the Italian state were unlikely to succeed. In providing further evidence of the social power and influence of the church,[72] these new studies offer additional examples of the

---

[71] Geoff Eley recently appealed for British and German historians to pay more attention to Italy, and there is clearly plenty of material for them to consider. But the debate needs to be opened out in other directions as well—to Spain (to which there is only one reference in all the studies reviewed here—by G. Ranzato in Pavone and Salvati, eds. [n. 60 above]), where recent research has followed a very similar agenda (see *Passato e Presente* no. 2 [1990] devoted to Spanish industrialization), to the Scandinavian countries, and to Eastern Europe. The emancipation of comparative history from established hierarchies of national importance is still far from complete.

[72] There is a great deal of important new evidence on the behavior of the clergy and the church (esp., but not only, in Simonetta Soldani's volume), yet the social history of the church and popular religion outside the Veneto still remains curiously neglected.

320   *Davis*

weakness of liberalism as a national ideology—yet this was a weakness shared by
fascism and one that Mussolini sought to overcome through the alliance with the
Catholic church. By emphasizing the ways in which fascism ran counter to
tendencies that were powerfully entrenched in liberal Italy, the new research has
begun to sketch out elements of continuity that link liberal Italy not to Mussolini's
fascist state but to the Italian republic that took shape after 1947, setting new
contexts in which to understand the abandonment of fascist attempts at political
and administrative centralization, the return to the politics of exchange, and the
maintenance of a close alliance between church and state, political power and
clerical influence. In that sense, even if it leaves central questions far from
resolved, the new Italian historiography has established new perspectives that will
widen the debate on the course of contemporary Italian history both synchroni-
cally and diachronically, opening the ways to broader comparative exploration and
bringing into new focus the elements of continuity in the longer-term formation of
the state and society in Italy.

[28]

Italy and Modernization: A Montage
by Tim Mason

Debates over modernity (pro-/anti-; pre-/post-) usually resonate far beyond the immediate context in which they arise – in this case, twentieth century Italy. The Italian discussion of modernization, apart from its centrality to political discourse there, takes up many echoes of a big international debate among historians and sociologists, which tended to fizzle out during the 1970s without leaving behind either firm conclusions or conceptual clarity.[1] Its legacy, however, can still be felt in the late 1980s. Within the British Left, 'modernization', 'modernity' are terms which seem destined to become the focus of many arguments in the coming years – already during the 1987 election campaign doubts were expressed about whether the Labour Party ever really had been and could ever become a truly 'modern' political party, whether it does not draw its basic strength from the protection of its constituents. What does it mean for a party of the Left to be 'modern'? Should historians on the Left be enthusiastic or sceptical about the notion of modernization in history? The following notes are intended to raise some questions and perplexities of this kind. I don't write as an expert on Italian history; rather I have been moved to sketch out this essay by a general concern for the precise meaning of key terms in historical writing – in this particular area precision is hard to find. As Gerald Feldman put it recently, the attempt 'to consider any historical period from the perspective of modernization theory is a bit like trying to climb a mountain in a fog'.[2]

* * * *

> The central fact in the history of Italy in this century, a fact which is reflected in full in our historiography, is the country's difficult relationship with that complex of phenomena which we usually call 'modernity', phenomena which constitute the axis of the intellectual and practical experience of the century. This relationship, so difficult and tormented in the historical reality of the country . . . has, on the other side, in the sphere of national culture, taken the form of a pure a simple time-lag, of a radical deafness towards the coming of 'the modern', and a failure to prepare the critical and cognitive tools which are necessary to confront it. . . . this comprehensive time-lag of our culture.[3]

The first striking fact about the Italian discussion is that all the different words which have *modern* as their root form seem to have a much less problematic status in Italian culture than in British, German or American culture. In Italy 'modern', 'modernity', 'modernization' are words which are used freely, easily and positively, as though everyone knows what their import is. In the pens of serious writers the words seem not to carry a big weight of ideological baggage, but rather to be innocent and self-evident in their meaning. (Propagandist uses of the terms do of course carry heavy ideological baggage – see below.) Historians of all schools, including those well to the left, use 'modernity' etc. to denote a value judgement which is also analytical; in most cases the words signify developments which are good and necessary, though not inevitable. Italian historians do often disagree about what the vital substantive components of modernity in history really are. When Renzo De Felice, liberal and anti-marxist, insists upon the specifically modern qualities of Fascism* he is obviously talking about something completely different from the 'slow progress towards the modernization' of industrial relations which is at the centre of the work of Gian Carlo Jocteau.[4] But the fact that the language is shared remains very striking. This fact suggests the existence of a common intellectual property, fundamental commonalities of judgement, disagreements occurring within the framework of a basic common discourse. Outside Italy the whole vocabulary of 'the modern', 'modernization' in the discipline of history is much more often a terrain of dispute and of conflicting interpretations.

In Germany, Britain and the USA historians who work with the concept of modernization normally thereby, in so many words, announce

---

* Fascist in upper-case refers to the Italian party or regime of that name; in lower-case, to fascist movements, politics in Italy, Germany, and elsewhere.

Italy and Modernization   129

their rejection of most of the tenets of Marxism. This antagonism may rest on some bad reciprocal misunderstandings, as Hans-Ulrich Wehler has argued, but it remains an historiographical fact of great importance.[5] Indeed, in the Anglo-Saxon-German discussion the key words are not innocent at all, but rather flags staked out with purposefulness on a theoretical battlefield over which some fierce encounters have been fought: those who have raised the banner-concept of modernization as an all-embracing process of historical change have been accused of expelling class and politics from the subject matter of history;[6] and those who reject the category of modernization are said to be blind to the changing *forms* of class relations and political conflict as well as being indifferent to many other spheres of social development.[7]

I am alive to the fact that conceptual arguments may swiftly become arid. However, it is not only because I am English and therefore infiltrated by logical positivism, that I find it appropriate that the whole vocabulary of 'the modern' should in fact be used by historians *only* in a highly self-conscious manner, for the words are in fact neither innocent nor are their meanings self-evident. Wehler it seems to me is correct in arguing (contrary to most sociologists) that the terms are inevitably and always *normative*.[8] That is, they express value judgements about the past which necessarily have implications for the present and the future.[9] In history (though not in the fine arts or philosophy – one thinks of post-modernism) the value judgements are almost always heavily positive, even when extended from such relatively uncontentious fields as public health, literacy, diet, to basic arguments of political economy such as the alleged origins of the modern mixed economy in the cradle of the Fascist regime of the 1930s. No amount of research and analysis can eliminate disagreements from value judgements of this kind; the best that can be hoped for are clearer boundaries around the areas of disagreement. If different, indeed contradictory things are going to be called 'modern' (good, progressive) then we are left, in the case of this vocabulary of modernity, with what Anglo-Saxon philosophers call an 'essentially contested concept'.[10] That is, a term which is impossible to do without, but about the meaning of which there are irreducible disagreements. To a problem of this kind there are no solutions – try to imagine writing on the history of Italy in the last hundred years without using any of the words modern, backward, modernization! The explicit and consistent use of definitions, however, is conducive to clarity, and robs the terms of that seductive innocence, which makes them even more ideological than they necessarily have to be. Precise definition in this field however will always be conflictual, never consensual. This will be made clear shortly by a consideration of the various different proposals which have been put forward concerning the relationship between Fascism and 'modernisation' – all of them clear and all at odds with each other. A preference for explicit definitions of the modern thus amounts to a preference for open disagreements over suggestive confusion.

To the best of my knowledge, which is still very defective, there do not appear to be many open disagreements among Italian historians about the concept of modernity. It seems to have exclusively positive connotations, and historians appear to differ only over what are, or should be, its precise features and its component parts. If this observation is even only approximately correct, the facts which lie behind it need to be explained. No full explanation can be offered here; the most I can do is to make three suggestions for further discussion:

1) The innocent or enthusiastic use of the terms 'modern', 'modernization' has *not* derived in Italy, as it has in the USA, from a hegemony of the social sciences over the historical method and the historical imagination. The serried ranks of American development experts had no counterpart in Italy in the 1960s and 1970s, and they had less impact on the Italian historical profession than they did on the English and the German.[11] (Italian historians who, like Galli della Loggia, denounce the provincialism of their colleagues should reflect a little on the protection which provincialism offers against waves of transatlantic intellectual fashions![12]) Despite the influential and cosmopolitan work of Gino Germani, the pre-occupation of Italian historians with 'modernity'/'modernization' appears to be national and specific, and to grow out of elements in Italian Marxism and Italian liberalism, combined with points taken over from the *Annales* School. It is indebted to Italian and German philosophy and to French historiography, but it is a truly indigenous growth, not a piece of cultural borrowing from American poiltical science.

2) For many years and with increasing intensity the political parties and the media have placed a truly massive emphasis upon the need to modernize Italy. The vocabulary of modernity is literally omnipresent, and it seems possible that this exercises some influence on the language of even the most sceptical historians. Some random examples. On 11 February 1987 the television news of channel 2 described the institutions of local government as 'businesses' – 'one can say that modern local government is a business'. Shortly before this an expert newspaper commentator (whose name I have mislaid) pronounced the acquittal of Enzo Tortora, a television personality charged with mafia crimes, to mark the beginnings of a 'modern jurisprudence' in Italy. Paolo Virno, ex-militant of the New Left who was wrongly imprisoned on terrorist charges, has written a book described by an approving journalist as 'a hymn to modernity'. Virno criticizes himself and his ex-comrades for having been 'more than reticent towards modernity and innovation'; now it is necessary 'to take possession of the modern' for 'the road to happiness must be sought for . . . in the heart of the modern'.[13] Renato Curzio, founder of the Red Brigades who is still in gaol, is more confident about the modernity of his political work: 'If Italy has changed and modernized itself in so radical a way, this is due to

Italy and Modernization 131

the social conflict of the 1970s of which the Red Brigades were a component'.[14] Modernizing reforms are no longer simply the programme of the Italian Socialist Party, but the mental framework within which such programmes are devised. 'Modernization' has totally replaced Socialism in the vocabulary and ideology of the party's leaders. De Mita, Secretary of the Christian Democratic Party, is a less avid devotee of the same key-words only because some of that party's bosses believe that modernity is a euphemism for their own obsolescence. De Mita's true outlook is really very similar to that of Craxi, which goes a long way towards explaining the bitter rivalry between the two leaders which was so much in evidence in the summer of 1987. Talk of modernity on the poitical Left is less comfortable and brash. Alberto Asor Rosa, professor of literature and heterodox communist, feels unhappy in the company of 'a nostalgic Left . . . which longs for political cataclysms', and he feels the need to affirm in categorical terms: 'Altogether the Left has never had, as a value at the core of its project, control over innovation and modernization'.[15] Whether this is true or not is beside the point. What matters is the explicit fear of being left behind – modernity is a powerful locomotive, nobody should miss the train.

The above random list of examples is not presented as an object for ridicule, nor as a demonstration of the systematic abuse of language by those who determine the rhetoric of public life. It serves the more elementary purpose of showing how clamorously ubiquitous are the words 'modern', 'modernization', how impossible it is to escape from them, even from one day to the next. This cannot fail to have an impact upon the vocabulary of historians, no matter how easy it may be in any particular instance to identify and discount manipulative abuses of the words in question. We have to do here with a whole cultural climate which urgently evokes modernity, and it is difficult for anyone, intellectuctuals included, to remain impervious.

3) One possible reason for this preoccupation with modernity may lie in the (widespread?) belief that Italy is *in fact* a *backward* country, and always has been; that there are still vast areas of 'backwardness' which cry out for modernization. The cult of modernity, that is, may grow out of a concern with its opposite. This reading of the problem is suggested by the recent and very strange book of Carlo Tullio-Altan, *La Nostra Italia*.[16] The author presents the national history as an unbroken story of the remorseless progress of 'socio-cultural backwardness', by which he means clientelism, political transformism, anarchoid rebelliousness, organized crime, lack of civil conciousness . . . This chant of despair is the flip-side of the 'hymn to modernity'. (It remains odd that Tullio-Altan defines only backwardness and does not put forward his own concept of modernity and modernization.) The author's voice is that of passionate maschochist nationalism. He insists endlessly upon the comprehensive backwardness of

Italy, a condition common to all the political forces today, as it was at the time of unification. Italy is thus condemned to repeat in diverse forms, but endlessly, the same basic experience of civic immaturity. Tullio-Altan implies that Italy is a radically less successful modern society/state than the countries with which it compares itself. He attributes this in part to the consequences of the 'dual society', that is to the peculiar influence of the South (meggoziorno) over the whole of Italian society and politics. But he also implies that everything which is distinctively Italian about Italy is backward, and thus leaves an impression that all major positive innovations of the past century have been imported from abroad. From this perspective the struggle for modernity has all the qualities of a defiant (and hopeless) national battle against omniverous, debased forms of public behaviour which are the socio-cultural equivalent of original sin.

But perhaps Tullio-Altan only exaggerates and distorts a very widespread consciousness among historians of the elements of backwardness in modern and recent Italian history. And perhaps this consciousness of backwardness has a long scholarly tradition, a centuries-old sense of peninsular inferiority which rests upon major historical facts – no Italian Reformation, no Italian 1789. Others will be able to judge this better than I can. But it is certainly true that English historians who worked in the 1920s on the 'progress of their nation' (still then a favoured theme) did not have before their eyes, in their own country, realities such as the following: Sardinia around 1920 –

> . . . and the irremediable decay of the fields invested with malaria. It is a spiral. The depopulation of the countryside, the lack of intensive agriculture, irrigation a shambles – all encouraging malaria; for fear of malaria the peasants don't return to the fields; and in the uncultivated countryside malaria advances, scything people down: on average in this period the mosquito killed 9,750 Sardinians in every 100,000 each year. Add on, then, the days of work lost on account of the fevers, an annual total which fluctuates between two and three-and-a-half million.
>
> Tuberculosis advances too, the consequence of exhaustion, hunger and of other illnesses which remained without cure. It killed just less than 2,000 people each year . . .
>
> Public works programmes, already inadequate before the Great War, have now [1919–21] practically ceased altogether. The roads are few and in bad condition. On the mainland for every 1,000 square kilometers of land surface there is a median road network of 603 kilometers. In Sardinia the median is down around 190 kilometers. And the public transport services on these few roads correspond to only a minimal part of the needs. And so it goes on. Only seven of the 364 local government districts in Sardinia have sewage systems. In 250 there is no piped water. In 199 the cemetry is inadequate. In 156 there

Italy and Modernization 133

is no school; and the census of 1921 confirms the disturbing proportions of another phenomenon which is also a cause of backwardness: 366,000 illiterate persons . . . which means that 42 out of every 100 Sardinians don't know how to read and write.[17]

And English historians in the 1960s did not have scenes like the following before their eyes as they struggled to intepret the history of British Puritanism or Methodism:

> The Madonna of the sanctuary of Pollino . . . when they finish the ritual of circling the church the pilgrims cross the threshold and move towards the statue of the Madonna, which is on a pedestal outside the ballustrade; the church is crowded; many women move forward on their knees beating their breasts and some, a few, draw their tongues over the floor. Each group tries to get as near as possible to the statue and begins to interact with it, sometimes silently, sometimes in loud voices which express deep emotion and thus arouse the participation of those present. At 11.30 some women from Albidona enter the church bringing with them three goats, their horns bedecked with coloured ribbons . . .[18]

Have Italian historians felt themselves to be surrounded by contemporary images of their country's backwardness as they studied its past? It is a question. If the answer were positive this could help to explain the general and easy circulation of the pair of concepts, 'modernity/backwardness', as unproblematic components of the professional vocabulary.

*　　*　　*　　*

I want to return later to the question of whether everything that seems backward can in fact be designated in this way; and also to the interdependence of the backward and the modern. But it is first necessary to demonstrate just how problematic the twin concepts really are. This is best done by listing the different ways in which scholars have applied the idea of modernization to Fascism. Most writers on the subject are sure that there exist important causal and phenomenological links between the process of modernization and the rise of Fascism, but there is a bedlam of discord concerning what exactly these links were. The rise of Fascism as part of something called a crisis in the process of modernization? Fascist regimes which either voluntarily or involuntarily push forward certain aspects of the process of modernization? Fascist regimes which modernized simply through the destruction of the old and the traditional? These are in fact very different *types* of positive correlation between Fascism and modernity.

In the case of Italian Fascism the simplest and most frequent approach takes as its point of departure the observation that the Fascist movement and the Fascist regime thought of themselves as and presented themselves as historically novel figures, as agents of modernization. This approach is the immanent approach: it takes (not uncritically) the declared motives, aims and self-image of the historical actors and synthesizes them into an historical interpretation. If the evidence concerning ideas, attitudes and policies suggests a sufficiently serious and sustained Fascist drive towards modernity in at least some sectors of social development and public life, then, it is argued, this is in itself proof of a positive correlation. (The degree of actual success achieved by the regime in transforming and modernizing the country can happily remain a matter for calm discussion, for it is a matter of *secondary* importance in the construction of this kind of immanent interpretation: what mattered were the declared aims of the regime, its general posture towards the 'modern world'.) This kind of argument has been developed with varying degrees of sophistication and missionary zeal by a large number of writers; by Sarti in a manner which is especially precise and cautious, and emphasises the failure of an original modernizing project;[19] by De Felice with an over-strong emphasis upon the Fascist leadership and its plans and daydreams;[20] by Turner and Gregor as part of a heavy and self-confident thesis about the essentially modernizing nature of Fascism;[21] and by most of the contributors to the catalogue of the exhibition 'The Italian Economy between the two Wars' as a rather crude exercise in historiographial revision.[22] The list is far from exhaustive.

  The basic problem of all works which follow this immanent approach is that their concepts of modernity/modernization are almost totally lacking in theoretical rigour; they are at the best elastic and eclectic, at the worst vague and confused. This is necessarily so for they are made up of a mixture of very diverse elements, which do not cohere at a conceptual level. These elements typically fall into three groups:

1) discrete achievements of the regime which Fascists themselves advocated at the time as modern, such as mass communications, the political mobilization of young people, new state interventions in the economy, attacks upon the authority of the Vatican and the Catholic hierarchy, land reclamation, etc., etc.;

2) evidence of continuitites from the Fascist regime to the Italian polity of the 1960s and '70s. Such continuities confer the epithet 'modern' on the regime because they carry the 'same names and maintain their life in the later chronological epoch, up to the present day. The Industrial Reconstruction Corporation (IRI), 'mass society' and the welfare state are the most often cited examples. (But surely their social and political significance, their functions, have in fact changed greatly since the 1930s. And

Italy and Modernization   135

anyway, would we call the witch-hunts of the sixteenth century 'modern' just because they continued in the seventeenth century?);

3) randomly selected elements for the analytical or functionalist treatises of sociological modernization theorists, developments, that is, which were not the goals of deliberate state policies: technological progress, the emergence of new social strata, the increasing differentiation of social roles.

These various elements do not seem to add up to any kind of a clear, coherent and internally consistent concept of modernization. In the writings of the immanent school the term remains elusive and emotive and never develops a critical/analytical potential; it tends to close down discussion and research, rather than open them up. It remains especially difficult within this framework to establish clear criteria for assessing the modernity or otherwise of any particular development of the Fascist decades because the grounds of the argument are always shifting. Fascist propaganda techniques, for example, are widely described as 'modern', although in their pure form they did not survive 1945; IRI is designated as modern because it did survive 1945. Looked at down one end of the telescope the withdrawal of large parts of the Italian population from active engagement in political affairs after 1925 – that is, the apathy which was the main foundation-stone of the so-called Fascist consensus – appears like a big step towards 'modern' political behaviour, but this apathy was to a large (if indefinable) degree coerced, and so one has to ask; was the coercion modern? One also has to ask: was the apathy also perhaps modern? (see conclusion below). It is an easier task to plough the waves of the ocean than to bring any kind of clarity or order into discussions of this kind.

On the other hand, however, the conceptual rigour of certain sociologists offers to us historians little assistance and even less comfort. For A.F.K. Organski, not the least subtle exponent of this functional approach, modernization moves through four stages of economic and social change which can be objectified in terms of indices.[23] For him the category is not immanent, but analytical, scientific, as is appropriate to the study of what is essentially a quantifiable process, and only secondarily a matter of ideologies and policies. Organski argues that at a point of crisis in the second stage of industrial development a paralysis may occur in which the traditional and the modernizing elites block each other while both coming simultaneously under the threat of popular movements from below; the way out is the fascist compromise which is strong only in its repression of the insurgent popular movements, but is characteristically weak in its pursuit of modernising goals and is thus liable to be a transitory regime. This model is not crude/simplistic, but it suffers from the difficulty of not being really appropriate to any one fascist regime (Italian fascism may have been weak in the pursuit of modernizing goals, but it was, regrettably, not especially transitory). A larger defect of the model, however, is one which is common to almost all general models of 'the modernization process' – that is, its functionalist character. The approach gives priority to those aspects of the problem which can be quantified as social and economic formations, between which functional relationships can be established. Modernization has its own trajectory – an uneven trajectory, to be sure – which is more like natural history than human history; specific changes such as new transport systems, agricultural machinery, literacy, administrative efficiency, political mobilization, appear above all in relation to each other as component parts of an overall process. But this process is in fact very narrowly defined, and it is no coincidence that Organski concentrates heavily on the crisis which gives birth to fascist regimes and has little to say about the later history of the regimes. The problem for the historian arises from the fact that so many important themes in the history of fascism simply cannot be analysed within the terms of his model. Such principal realities of fascism as repressive violence, state-organised mendacity, war and mass slaughter cannot be derived from or transformed into sets of indicators which point (even indirectly) towards modernity, or towards its opposite. They burst the frame of the models.[24] The historian who sets out to assess the degree of modernity of fascist Italy or to locate the '20s and '30s in the history of the modernization of Italy cannot avoid speaking at length about dictatorship and the slaughter of war, but it is not possible to do this within the conceptual framework of the sociologists. (That framework permits only vulgar subaltern arguments about whether war and dictatorship were functional or dysfunctional to the modernization of this or that part of the economic system)

Eclecticism on the one hand, restrictive definitions and models on the other. Is there a possible step forward towards a clarity which is also comprehensive?

Gino Germani, whose sociological model of modernization remains the most subtle and sophisticated of all in my view, was acutely aware of these basic difficulties.[25] He sought to make the conceptual dilemma visible, transparent, by attaching special importance to the *political* aspects of modernization, where most historians and sociologists emphasized the technical, social and economic aspects. Unlike Organski, Germani regarded fascism as a phenomenon of a society which was already modern. But he saw clearly that fascist mass society led to an 'inversion of modernization' . . . to 'the very opposite of the individuation process characterizing the rise of modern society, and the denial of its higher values: reason, freedom and individuality'.[26]

This very striking formulation makes it clear that if 'modernisation' is to have any coherent and comprehensive meaning, then it can only be used as a concept which, in the end, has an essentially normative character. There are other reasons for believing that this is so, but in the case of fascism the mere placing of a proper emphasis upon the political dimension of modernity gives this view a compelling power. Empirical descriptions of specific progressive-looking social changes in the 1930s can only be added up into an evocation of modernity which is trivial when set beside the normative and political judgements which are inextricably entailed in the use of this vocabulary. Those who write of modernization in general terms make value judgements about the past and express their commitments with respect to the future; they want their own intellectual work to contribute to a particular form of cultural and political progress. In this ultimate bed-rock sense, fascism for Germani was profoundly hostile to true moderni-zation, for all that many of its trappings and styles, and bits and pieces of its social and economic policies indicated breaches with tradition. But his normative judgement grew out of, and inspired, close study. It was not pronounced with easy moral certainty from on high.

Hans-Ulrich Wehler develops the same argument to a point of theoretical conclusion.[27] And it seems impossible not to agree both with him and with Germani that any valid *comprehensive* concept of modernity or modernization must be informed by value judgements, and thus by a moral and didactic commitment on the part of the writer for the future. (It is very striking that those who participate in the philosophical and aesthetic debates about modernism and post-modernism have absolutely no doubt that their vocabulary is normative, and they are not in the least embarrassed by this fact.[28] Why so many sociologists and historians should strain themselves so much to appear neutral, objective and scientific, remains a little mysterious.) This position does not, of course, give a licence to scholars to define modernity in terms of their own private, idiosyncratic ideals. As Barrington Moore, Jr., has shown in his study *Injustice*, normative judgements of this kind really can be, and have to be, historically realistic as well as logically coherent – they have to refer to the missed opportunities and thwarted potentials in history, to those things which might have turned out different, if . . . , to history's 'suppressed alternatives'.[29] But this mode of conceptual reasoning does confer upon the scholar the right and the duty to designate certain phenomena as on the whole a-modern, destructive of a true, humane modernization. I want to argue in what follows that this is the only meaningful way of specifying the relationship between fascism and modernization; that the eclectic use of the term by De Felice, Turner and others, and the morally abstinent sociological models of modernization are both deeply inadequate. To say 'modernization' is to say something about what 'we' want, what still remains to be achieved. Fascism is in no way part of that.

But it is first necessary to make some further comments on the present day use of this vocabulary by historians and social scientists. Fascist Italy is now very rarely designated as having been comprehensively anti-modern in any of the various senses of the term discussed above. This is in marked contrast to Nazi Germany: the very essence of the Nazi regime is frequently presented as a kind of war against the modernization and rationalization of society. This school of thought took root with the celebrated contemporary essay of Talcott Parsons, and has proceeded through the subtle research of David Schoenbaum and the lofty generalizations of Ralf Dahrendorf to the trench-like positions of Turner and most recently Lipset.[30] The judgement of these writers that Nazism was essentially anti-modern is not explicitly normative, but derives rather from more or less simple sociological models of modernity. To complicate the picture still further the litmus-test of basic attitudes to modernization has been applied to the two regimes by Turner, De Felice and others in such a way as to disqualify the generic concept of fascism! If 'modernization' has been the basic process of the epoch, and if Fascism was modern while Nazism was archaic, how can the two regimes possibly have been of the same genus?![34] The argument is not, I believe, a very strong one and I want to return to it below, but it has the merit of throwing into sharp relief the crucial importance of the definition of such fundamental concepts.

Historians of Italy, on the other hand, who are sceptical about Fascism's role as a modernizing force, do *not* for the most part ground their arguments in attempts to re-define the concept of modernization itself. They allow the concept a degree of innocence and prefer to develop *empirical* arguments concerning the great continuing strength under Fascism of the old/traditional economic, administrative, military and ecclesiastical elites; they emphasise the conservative and restorative functions of the regime, as opposed to its innovations and its self-image of brash novelty.[31] This empirical research and debate is obviously of great intrinsic importance, but even if – which is not possible – agreement could be reached on the regime's relative degrees of reactionariness and modernity, the overall conceptual problem would remain unresolved: what general yardstick is being adopted to define 'modernization', and for what reasons is it chosen? A list of the regime's actual innovations, from mass leisure schemes to the attack on the formal mode of address ('thou') to the persecution of the Jews, does not add up to a concept. And a conclusion to the effect that the regime may have modernized this but not that, so much but not more, is a rather small theoretical outcome for what must be a vast empirical labour. Tullio-Altan is the one recent Italian writer who does indeed deny that there was any positive correlation between early Fascism and modernization. His general concept of socio-cultural backwardness leads him to define the whole framework of Italian politics in the early 1920, together with all the political forces, including Fascism, as backward: Giolitti's system of transformism was backward, and it engendered a backward response in the shape of 'anarchronistically subversive tendencies' on the part of the workers' movement, which in turn provoked 'an anarchic subversiveness of fascist stamp', which was also 'rebellious', and thus backward. In this way the crisis of 1919–1922 can be summarized as

Italy and Modernization   139

'responses to a backward reality which were themselves socially and culturally backward; two sides of the same coin'.[32]

This neat formula satisfies the requirement that key concepts should be both comprehensive and normative. It is however, like much writing which takes modernization/backwardness as its axis, politically undiscriminating – can both the socialist and the fascist movements be described in the same breath as subversive? But the formula is also factually inadequate: however one may want to characterize the fascist movement and the fascist regime, they were certainly *novel*, both in their appearance and in their actions. To concentrate so heavily upon the element of rebelliousness in the movement, and to justify *in this way* the inclusion of Fascism within a so-called syndrome of national socio-cultural backwardness which covers a continuous arc of 130 years, distorts the picture in such a way as to encourage us to forget that these 'rebels' were still in power two decades after 1922.

In order to deny Fascism any title to modernity, it may not be necessary to assert that it was the opposite of modern – i.e. backward. Perhaps it was something quite different, a-modern, beyond the pale of these categories, quite outside any possible normative discourse about modernization: *a novel barbarism*.[34] This involves arguing that lies, irrationality, cruelty, techniques of repression, contempt for human kind, mass slaughter and war were to such a high degree constituitive of the regimes that they permeated all other aspects of Fascist and Nazi achievements, and thus command the centre of the stage for any present-day analysis. As Primo Levi, the most eloquent of all camp survivors, once said, 'I think that from the concentration camp can grow only another concentration camp, that only evil can grow out of that experience.'[35]

That both regimes used novel methods of suasion and coercion is entirely secondary in respect of the cultural, political and moral content which must be central to any meaningful concept of modernization.

There are a number of ways in which such a radical conceptual delimitation can be defended. They all involve confronting the notion of modernization in its richest, most serious and subtle form. First, it is of course a common-place that the overall process of modernization has been, and continues to be, janus-faced: it contains strong forces for disruption and suffering in many sectors of society, and, in the shape of modern applied science, it contains terrible dangers for the future of mankind. Sensible normative concepts of modernization do not entail commitments to utopia, and such concepts can indeed take account of and analyse historic suffering and potential future threats (and there will always be room for disagreement about their specific identity and their severity). But the fear, death and pure destruction wrought by Fascism and Nazism and their wars seem to me to be of a quite different quality from, say, the impoverishment and degradation suffered by many groups of artisans in the course of industrialization, or from, say, the deaths and diseases caused by Chernobyl. The latter can perhaps be understood as the negative aspects of ruthless and dangerous modernizing transformations. But the former, beginning with class war from above and the terrorization and murder of political opponents, and ending with the mass slaughter and genocide of World War Two, were not the negative side of any such project (or even blind process) of modernization. No such link existed. They were not the negative side of anything, rather the central realities of fascism.

A similar but more subtle argument has been advanced in respect of elements in the modernization of the world economy since the sixteenth-century – that is that all forms of progress towards modernity have had their *costs* (and continue to have their costs), and that it is for the social scientists and the historian an obligation to present these costs which, especially insofar as they have been human costs, have often been very high.[36] One can perhaps for example even think of the millions killed in the French Revolution and the Napoleonic wars as a collective price paid for the birth and diffusion of democratic politics.[37] But the suffering and mass murder imposed on the world by Fascism and Nazism were not the cost of anything; they were not a price paid for any identifiable future good, however far distant. Their legacy was horror, a void, death, repression of memory, an incapacity to grieve. The mode of argument about the costs of modernization is enlightening for many questions, but is simply not relevant, not applicable to this case.

Nor, I believe, is another argument often used to connect Fascism and Nazism with modernity – that is the argument that the very destructiveness of these regimes cleared the ground for the development of truly modern societies in Europe after 1945. A good Italian example does not spring to mind, because it was the resistance rather than Fascism which decisively weakened some parts of the Italian *ancien régime*. In the case of Germany, Ralf Dahrendorf has argued that the persecution of many aristocratic families after the 20 July bomb plot of 1944, but above all the liquidation in 1945 of the whole East Elbian aristocracy with its enormous backward agricultural base, and the physical transfer of these lands to Russia, Poland and the DDR, made the construction of a 'modern' social and economic order in the territory of the Federal Republic much easier.[38] This may be a correct observation, but it has nothing much to do with the arguments which are at stake here. The beneficent effects which Dahrendorf identifies were consequences of the *defeat* of Nazism, not consequences of Nazism.[39] But beyond this there is a larger point to be made concerning the destruction of traditions and of traditional forces in the course of modernization. Such destruction has taken many different forms, been more or less violent, been more or less appropriate in its execution to the construction of a better world. The Nazi and late-fascist attacks on traditional forces on the contrary were purely nihilistic, and the removal of the East Elbian aristocracy was an act of simple liquidation. This was a different kind of historical event – violent acts of state – from the overcoming, transformation and absorption of traditional forces in other Western European countries, or from the revolutionary overthrow of the Russian aristocracy in 1917.

*   *   *   *

The main part of this article has been devoted to showing the confusion which surrounds, and is engendered by, the present usages of the vocabulary of modernization in respect of Fascism. I want in conclusion to return to the larger theme broached at the outset of the paper – that of the more general and, as it seems to me, innocent use of these words by Italian writers. Three points need to be made, the first two closely connected with each other.

It is possible to concur with Tullio-Altan in one half of one of his major arguments: that is, that most current notions of modernity and backwardness place far too much emphasis upon the economic and technological components of modernization, and tend to neglect the moral/civic/political dimension. This is perhaps especially true of scholars who in fact understand rather little of economic and technological history, and remain over-impressed by phenomena with which they have little familiarity. Tullio-Altan drastically redresses the emphasis by presenting socio-cultural modernization as a much higher value than, and as totally dissociated from, economic progress; for him, poverty and prosperity seem to have nothing at all to do with virtue. I do not wish to contest this (Aristotelian) judgement here, which seems to me to be a possible one, although I don't share it. But what does seem to me to be quite unacceptable is Tullio-Altan's failure to specify *any* kind of relationship between socio-cultural backwardness and economic backwardness.[40] This failure is the mirror image of the failure of those who give high prominence to economic modernization without paying any attention to the cultural ramifications of such changes. In fact, of course, economic modernization has often gone, and still goes, hand in hand with tyranny and moral barbarism. But it is perhaps less often noted that the civic virtues by which Tullio-Altan sets such high store in his desperate struggle against Italian backwardness have been found precisely in *economically retarded sectors of society*. One example must do for many. Stuart Hood was an English officer, ex-prisoner of war, who fought with the partisans in Emilia and Tuscany in 1943–44. His memoirs are full and precise, not in the least nostalgic. Daily in danger of his life, among the peasants he encountered only decency, generosity and civic commitment. Their practical solidarity with the resistance fighters was absolutely reliable, but it was a part of a most simple life:

In part I was caught by a regression in time. Living with the peasants I saw the last upsurge of peasant life and of an ancient civilisation – *la civiltà contadinesca*. The skills I learned, the crafts I watched, had not changed since Ambrogio Lorenzetti in the fourteenth century painted his great murals in the Town Hall of Sienna. War, blockade, economic autarky had cancelled out such small progress as the last fifty years had seen. Trade had ceased, except for an occasional pedlar with a pack of thread, needles, pins and almanacs. Each family lived to itself and for itself, spinning its own wool, making its own tools, providing its own food. When Dino went out in March to prune his vines with his broadbladed knife or stopped to hone his scythe on the verge of the farm track, he had the exact gestures and rhythms of a peasant from Breughel or some Book of the Hours . . .

Today the brides no longer bring a dowry of chestnut trees. The girls no longer wear the coarse home-spun stockings. The women no longer fan the charcoal stoves. They have methane gas and are the better for it. The young men cavort on their motor-scooters and the girls sit side-saddle, flouncing their nylon petticoats. I am glad – and glad that I saw what went before.[41]

There is thus an evident need to work out with very close empirical precision the relationships between the different strands of what is called either 'modernization' or 'backwardness', if the terms are to have any real meaning. Failing that, the notions remain crude labels or vague banners; they mix up different realms of experience which should be analysed dialectically and distinctly, and then they are better not used at all.

For much the same reasons, enquiries which take modernization/ backwardness as their axis need to look well below the surface of the phenomena which they describe and categorize. Appearances can be very deceiving, especially appearances of backwardness. I have argued elsewhere that much of what appeared to be sentimental, romantic and archaic in the orchestration of public life by the Nazi regime was in fact purely instrumental, and that this 'culture' provided a cover (perhaps not even a popular one) for a fierce drive towards technical and administrative modernization for the purposes of war.[41] It was these latter processes which really mobilized and enthused the cadres of the regime, and gave the regime its awesome power.[42] The endless invocations of community, harmony and the homeland (*Heimat*) were a kind of smoke-screen for the tanks and the concentration camps, not the predominant reality. It still appears to me to be a major distortion to attach supreme importance in interpretations of Nazism to the archaisms, which are surely present, in the text of *Mein Kampf* and in Himmler's letters and speeches, etc. We are not faced with a choice between alternative historical realities – archaic day-dreams *or* technocratic efficiency; everything dominated by forward-looking trends in Italy for De Felice, or by backwardness in Nazi Germany

for Turner. Historical realities can be approached only through detecting
the exact mode of fusion between the modern and the backward in the case
of each specific object of enquiry. That mode of fusion, the exact elements
of the chemical compound, is often hidden and hard to identify. Amalia
Signorelli has made this point very well in a hard and correct criticism of
Tullio-Altan:

> In other words the Italian political class embodies a culture which is
> particularistic and quasi-tribal, and a parallel political practice which is
> clientelistic and transformist. Culture and practice alike have grown up
> within a social system which has adapted itself to them not without
> resistance and friction, sometimes with open and deep conflicts. At the
> level of its shared values the social system is a long way from
> acknowledging the legitimacy either of this culture or of this political
> practice. If we take these facts into consideration we can develop the
> following hypothesis: the culture and practice of the political class are
> not so much, or not only, a heritage from the past, the product of the
> malign growth of the original vice; rather, they are a modern and
> effective system of power designed to integrate into the national
> society masses of people who are dangerously inclined to claim
> democratic participation and their own emancipation. By means of
> clientelist favours and mafia-like intimidation and blackmail, a system
> of power has been constructed which perpetually recreates a condition
> of subalternity for the masses – even if today it is a subalternity
> rendered comfortable, decked out with the trappings of consumerism.
> If this hypothesis is correct, the national vice is thus no longer the age-
> old product of a viscous culture, no longer backwardness, but rather a
> modern political culture: that is, the culture of subsidised dependence,
> or, in the terms of a current witticism, the welfare state, Italian-style.[44]

Referring to the specific instance of the system of power in Italy today, this
critique demonstrates very well how the terms modern/backward can only
generate emotive heat and intellectual confusion if they are applied solely
to the surface contours of historical realities, to the distinctive style of a
public order, instead of to substance and to interconnetions. Of heat and
confusion there is an abundance. I would be grateful to anyone who can
explain what Ernesto Galli della Loggia means by 'modernity' in the
passage quoted toward the beginning of this article.

But we are not confronted here simply with an ivory-tower debate
about the meaning of concepts. This whole discussion has a great political
actuality and strong political implications. 'Modernization' has far too
many contradictory meanings for the term to be invoked lightly, least of all
by anyone on the political Left. In order to underline the provisional and
'montage' character of this essay. I want to raise in conclusion a point
which thus far has only been touched upon. There is still a big argument to

144   *History Workshop Journal*

be conducted with those who, from the Federalists and de Tocqueville on, have seen political *de*-mobilization as an essential feature of civic maturity, and withdrawal from the public arena as a *positive* achievement of modernity. Latter-day anti-jacobinism is especially explicit among conservative political scientists in the USA, among that type of observer, that is, who sees an electoral participation rate of 40% or less as a major source of institutional stability.[45] But very similar trends can be detected in all European countries, especially in Italy, where the modernizers are manifestly attempting to turn political participants into political consumers. Unlike Americans they should vote, yes, but please not do much more . . .

This aspect of the problem seems to be consistently overlooked by democratic and left-wing commentators, who tend to assume, like Tullio-Altan, that the virtues of modernization constitute an indivisible and mutually reinforcing whole; that the diminution of rebelliousness and clientelism will somehow automatically lead to an increase in participatory democracy and civic virtue. Nothing could be more naive. Many varieties of civility go perfectly well hand-in-hand with political apathy, political consumerism and withdrawal into private life, and many influential scholars, politicians and media managers believe that this is how it ought to be. It is not a paradox, but a harsh critique of the text, to point out that for the current modernizers in Italy – for Bettino Craxi, the Socialist Party leadership and the media-managers arrayed behind them – Tullio-Altan's call for *modern* civil virtue and active citizenship must seem like a dangerous archaism. An epidemic of real civic virtue would sweep their corrupt manipulations right off the political table. Is Tullio-Altan the real modernizer, or Craxi? The one answer which seems to be quite inadmissible is that both of them are modernizers, but in different ways.[46]

Notes

1   This is revised version of a paper which first appeared in *Movimento operaio e socialista*, 1987, n.1/2, a special double number devoted to Italian historiography.

2   Gerald Feldman, 'The Weimar Republic: A Problem of Modernization?', *Archiv für Sozialgeschichte*, vol. XXVI, 1986, p. 1. This is an excellent article.

3   Ernesto Galli della Loggia, 'Una storiografia indifferente', *Il Mulino*, 1986, n. 4, pp. 594 f.

4   Gian Carlo Jocteau, 'Corporativismo autoritario e liberalismo conservatore: il nodo di diritto di sciopero', *Movimento operaio e socialista*, 1986, n. 3, p. 475.

5   Hans-Ulrich Wehler, *Modernisierungstheorie und Geschichte*, Vandenhoeck & Ruprecht, Göttingen, 1975. An English edition of this short and incisive book would be extremely useful.

6   See, for example, Tony Judt, 'A Clown in Regal Purple: Social History and the Historians', *History Workshop Journal*, n. 7, 1979.

7   This is the import of much of the recent writing of Lawrence Stone, for example.

8   See Wehler, *op. cit.*, pp. 60 ff.

9   In the English language, 'modernization' first emerged as a distinct new word in the eighteenth and nineteenth centuries with a highly negative charge – see the *Oxford English*

Italy and Modernization   145

Dictionary, 1933 edition; it is a shame that the recent four volume *Supplement* to this work has no entry under this heading.

10   For the origins of this philosophical discussion see W.B. Gallie, *Philosophy and the History of Understanding*, London 1964, ch. 8.

11   One small proof of this is that I have been unable to find in Rome a major American study which applies modernization theory to Italian history: M.F. Neufeld, *Italy: A School for Awakening Countries*, Ithaca, 1961. The book seems to have excited little interest in Italy. It is widely quoted by British and American historians of Italy.

12   'Una storiografia indifferente', *loc. cit.*

13   Gabriella Turnaturi, 'Compagni, viva la modernità', *l'Espresso*, 19 Oct. 1986, pp. 197 ff.

14   Interview in *l'Espresso*, 18 Jan. 1987, p. 28.

15   Statements made in an interview with Elisabetta Rasy, *Panorama*, 8 Dec. 1985, pp. 185 f.

16   The subtitle is *Arretratezza socioculturale, clientelismo, transformismo e ribellismo dall'Unità ad oggi*, (Socio-cultural backwardness, clientelism, transformism and rebelliousness from unification to today), Feltrinelli, Milano, 1986.

17   Giuseppe Fiori, *Il Cavaliere dei Rossimori. Vita di Emilio Lussu*, Einaudi, Torino, 1985, pp. 66 f.

18   Annabella Rossi, *Le feste dei poveri*, Laterza, 1969, reprinted by Sellerio, Palermo 1986, pp. 27 f. The extraordinary photographs have been omitted from the new edition.

19   Roland Sarti, 'Fascist Modernization in Italy: Traditional or Revolutionary?', *American Historical Review*, vol. LXXV, no. 4, 1970.

20   I understand the development and documentation of an immanent version of the modernity thesis to be the red thread which runs right through De Felice's immense work on Mussolini. For some very explicit remarks in this direction, see his *Intervista sul fascimo*, ed. by M.A. Ledeen, Bari, 1975.

21   See Henry Ashby Turner, Jr., 'Fascism and Modernization', *World Politics*, vol. XXIV, no. 4, 1972; and the response in the same journal by A.J. Gregor, vol. XXVI, n. 3., 1974. In his book, *Italian Fascism and Developmental Dictatorship*, Princeton, 1979. Gregor makes the absurd claim that 'The effort to identify Italian Fascism as conservative, reactionary, and anti-modern has produced little more that a tissue of implausibilities' (p. 316).

22   IPSOA, Milano, 1984. I published a critical review of this revisionism in *History Workshop Journal*, n. 21, 1986.

23   Organski presents his schema in an especially clear and succinct way in his contribution to S.J. Woolf, ed., *The Nature of Fascism*, Weidenfeld and Nicolson, London, 1968, pp. 19 ff.

24   For an especially crude example of the effort to turn fascism into a set of indices concerning modernization, see Horst Mazerath and Heinrich Volkmann, 'Modernisierungstheorie und Nationalsozialismus', in J. Kocka, ed., *Theorien in der Praxis des Historikers*, Göttingen 1977 (= Sonderheft n.3 of *Geschichte und Gesellschaft*). The summary of the debate which was aroused by the paper of Mazerath and Volkmann is attached to the text, and is of great interest.

25   Germani worked out his overall argument with a notable subtlety and flexibility in *Sociologia della modernizzazione. L'esperienza dell'America Latina*, Laterza, Bari, 1971. Ch. 2 of this work is essential for any historical discussion of the issues at stake above. See also his *Autoritarismo, fascimo e classi sociali*, Il Mulino, Bologna, 1975.

26   I quote here from the English version of Germani's essay 'Fascism and class', published in S.J. Woolf ed., *op. cit.*, p. 78. For an introduction to Germani's writings on fascism, see the essay by Gianfranco Bettin in Luciano Cavalli, ed., *Il fascismo nell'analisi sociologica*, Il Mulino, Bologna, 1975, pp. 193 ff.

27   Wehler, *Modernisierungstheorie*.

28   Symposium 'Processo alla Modernità', published in *l'Espresso*, 22 Feb. 1987.

29   *Injustice: The Social Bases of Obedience and Revolt*, London, 1978.

30   An extensive bibliography would be out of place here. Schoenbaum remains the least schematic representative of this school of thought: *Hitler's Social Revolution*, London 1966. For Lipset's most recent (and most desperate) contribution on this side of the debate, see 'La rivolta contro la modernità', in *I limiti della democrazia. Autoritarismo e democrazia nella società moderna*, ed. by R. Scartezzini, L. Germani, R. Gritti, Liguori Ed., Napoli 1985,

pp. 117 ff. This essay is followed in the volume by a devastating criticism of Lipset's arguments and use of evidence written by Adrian Lyttelton.

31   All references to Turner are to the essay quoted in n.21, above. De Felice put the same point with great vehemence in his *Intervista*, *cit*. See the excellent critical reply by Enzo Collotti in G. Quazza *et al.*, *Storiografia e Fascismo*, Franco Angeli, Milano, 1985, pp. 25 ff.

32   This, it seems to me, was the main characteristic of the response of left historians to De Felice's *Intervista*: that is, they opposed their facts about fascism to those of De Felice. In the last analysis the critique of De Felice remained empirical, untheoretical, especially with respect to the latter's notion of modernity. Such was the tenor of the volume edited by N. Tranfaglia in the heat of the debate, *Fascismo e captialismo*, Feltrinelli, Milano, 1976. And the essay by Massimo Legnani in *Storiografia e Fascismo* does not advance much on this position. I do not wish for one moment to diminish the importance of empirical arguments, but it seems to me that this response on the part of the 'resistance school' of historians left a part of the ground of the debate untouched.

33   *La nostra Italia*, p. 117. In much the same way, Tullio-Altan uses a species of verbal brute force in order to compel the Italian political developments of the 1970s to fit into his conceptual mould; the effect on the reader is one of incantatory repetition of key phrases, regardless of the facts. See pp. 183 ff., 188–190, 195.

34   This invaluable notion was anticipated by leading socialists of the Second International in their reaction to the horrors of World War I – see the brilliant analysis by Norman Geras, *The Legacy of Rosa Luxemburg*, New Left Books, London 1977, ch. I. Some of the writings of Luxemburg and others were truly prophetic of fascism, and were, I think, conceptually superior to and more sensitive than much of the later Marxist writing on fascism itself in the 1920s and '30s.

35   See the interview with F. De Melis, republished after Levi's suicide, in *Il Manifesto*, 11–12 April 1987. In agreeing with Levi I find myself in my only major disagreement with Wehler, who does believe (but does not demonstrate) that a normative concept of modernization can be helpful in analyzing Fascism.

36   The classic statement of this argument has been made by Barrington Moore, Jr., in *The Social Origins of Democracy and Dictatorship*, London 1966.

37   Some historians and economists would wish to stretch this mode of analysis to cover the costs and benefits of colonialist imperialism. However the calculation may fall out in this case, it is not *a priori* an absurd calculation to make. I believe it is *a priori* absurd in the case of fascism.

38   See *Society and Democracy in Germany*, London 1968.

39   There was, of course, a strong element of populist social envy and resentment in the Nazi movement, but it cannot be argued that this determined the policies of the regime. It was important as one factor among many which the leadership had to take account of in order to maintain the acquiesence of the people.

40   *La nostra Italia* is full of economic statistics and disembodied summaries of economic development. It is not in the least clear why these passages were included.

41   Stuart Hood, *Pebbles from my Skull*, Hutchinson, London, 1963, pp. 149f. An identical picture of the generosity, stoicism and civic virtue of the Tuscan peasantry is drawn in another extraordinary book of memoirs of the years 1943/44: Iris Origo, *War in the Val d'Orcia. An Italian war diary*, now re-printed with a new introduction by Denis Mack Smith, Godine, Boston and Century Hutchinson, London, 1984.

42   'Zur Entstehung des Gesetzes zur Ordnung der nationalen Arbeit vom 20. Januar 1934: Ein Versuch über das Verhältnis "archaischer" und "moderner" Momente in der neuesten deutschen Geschichte', in *Industrielles System und politische Entwicklung in der Weimarer Republik*, ed. by Hans Mommsen, Dietmar Petzina, Bernd Weisbrod, Droste, Düsseldorf, 1974. Annabella Rossi, n.18 above, was very much alive to the strictly modern components in the poor people's pilgrimages which she studied.

43   I have argued this case at greater length in an essay inspired by the terrible figure of Klaus Barbie, *Rinascita*, 1985 n. 18. Feldman makes a similar warning about attaching too much importance to nostalgic rhetoric in his essay on the Weimar Republic, *loc. cit*. He is also very careful to distinguish between different strands of backwardness and modernity in the Germany of the 1920s.

44   *L'Indice*, 1986, n. 8, p. 45. The other reviews of Tullio-Altan's book which I have read are uncritical in the extreme: Nicola Tranfaglia in *La Repubblica*, 5 April 1986; Carlo Fumian in *I viaggi di Erodoto*, vol. 1, n. 1, April 1987, pp. 106 ff. No critic has taken up

Italy and Modernization 147

Tullio-Altan's silence on the contribution of the Catholic Church to the socio-cultural backwardness of Italy.

45 This position was formulated with special clarity by Seymour Martin Lipset in a book which is still regarded in some circles as a classic of its kind, *Political Man*, London 1962.

46 By far the most interesting recent contribution to the general discussion of modernity is a very brief essay by Mark Elvin, an historian of China, in *Past & Present* no. 113, 'A working definition of "Modernity" '. He argues that the essential divide between modern and non-modern societies has to do with *power*. Western societies, he argues, are different because in every sphere of human activity they have increased the sum of power available to individual persons, to groups of people and to institutions. His notion of power is so broad as to be almost a metaphor, for it encompasses power in the economic sense of energy, as well as power over the environment, organisational and political power; in a brilliantly chosen detail he contrasts the 'power' which is embodied in a western symphony orchestra with the lack of such ambition which is typical of most forms of music in Asia. As he develops this idea, his concept of modernity is not normative: power may be used for good or for evil, and in this sense his notion is similar in kind to those sociological models of modernization which see both the dark and the light sides of the process. It is an extremely stimulating intervention, which ought to be widely read, for it could give a new and sharp focus to a discussion which at the moment bears a strong resemblance to a Roman traffic jam: much noise, no rules and little movement.

[29]

Political Debate, Social History, and the Italian
Borghesia: Changing Perspectives in Historical Research*

Raffaele Romanelli
Università di Pisa

In Italy the term *borghesia* has been used rhetorically in political and ideological debate for over a century. Thus its use has had so little connection with scholarly rigor that perhaps it is unwise to use it in a historical context. This is of course equally true in other contexts than Italy: the term, intimately linked with modern European civilization, has a long and complex cultural history. From an origin perhaps in *Burg* or *burgus*, French has derived *bourgeoisie*, German, *Bürgertum*, Spanish, *burguesía*. English, which lacks a related term, speaks of the "middle class" or adopts the French *bourgeoisie* in a more limited sense. Nor is the term habitual in the social sciences, which perhaps should warn us that it is more relational than objective and that its meanings, buffeted by the waves of changing fortune, have shifted through history. The term first arose in the Middle Ages, and it returned in France between the fifteenth and sixteenth centuries. It flourished in the mid-nineteenth century, thanks largely to Marx, who used it in global opposition to the term *proletariat*—retaining, however, the somewhat pejorative tone attached to the word by reference to a mimetic behavior system typical of Old Regime France, a tone that persisted in all the nineteenth-century literature on the subject.[1]

The ambiguity inherent in this term and its rhetorical and ideological use are thus common phenomena on the European scene, but this is particularly true in Italian historiography, where the term is used extensively. There are a number of reasons for this. In particular, clashing ideologies have always been an inherent part of Italy's national identity, given that Italy's national unity is a relatively recent creation and has always been the subject of lively debate. In any event,

---

* Preceding versions of this text were discussed in February 1989 at the Freie Universität, Berlin, Arbeitsbereich Wirtschafts und Sozialgeschichte; in New York at Columbia University, Seminar on Modern Italy; and in Chicago at the University of Chicago, Modern European Studies Workshop, in October 1990.

[1] I have attempted to give an idea of the nineteenth-century career of the term in a study ("Borghesia, Bürgertum, bourgeoisie: Itinerari europei di un concetto") written for Jürgen Kocka, ed., *Borghesie europee dell'Ottocento* (Venice, 1989), a much-reduced Italian edition of Jürgen Kocka, ed., *Bürgertum im 19. Jahrhundert: Deutschland im europäischen Vergleich*, 3 vols. (Munich, 1988). Contributions to this volume will be cited here from the German edition. For an important contribution to thought on the nineteenth-century use of this term, see Philip Nicholas Furbank, *Unholy Pleasure: The Idea of Social Class* (Oxford and New York, 1986).

[*Journal of Modern History* 63 (December 1991): 717–739]

there is a close connection between political and ideological debate in Italy over problems of historical interpretation, which means not only that historiography is extremely politicized (a point stressed by the idealistic tradition) but also that current Italian political ideology makes frequent reference to historical events in the nation's past.

In this framework, the term *borghesia* has a strategic function in the debate concerning modernity and modernization in Italy. All the political groups that were in opposition to the political system of the nineteenth century (and whose opposition dominated subsequent public opinion)—beginning with the radicals and anarchists of the last century and ranging from Catholics and socialists to communists and Christian Democrats in our own day and including the revolutionary fascists—all considered the nineteenth-century liberal regime *borghese*. They meant by this that it was the social and economic regime of the capitalistic middle classes, that it was thus to some extent foreign to local tradition, and that it brought a new harshness and a new spirit of exploitation into social and economic relationships. Although the ideological orientations that shared this opinion varied greatly, it is clear that the term was largely synonymous with *capitalistic* (in the Marxian sense).

If the ruling classes of Italy were accused of being *borghesi*, however, they were also accused of not being *borghesi* enough. Throughout the history of unified Italy, the political opposition has been against "bourgeois civilization" in general, but it has also criticized the governing classes for not being sufficiently modern. Intersecting traditions of both the Right and the Left blamed "un difetto di borghesia"—a bourgeois failing, but also a failure to be bourgeois—for what they held to be the unsatisfactory outcome of the Risorgimento. Much the same occurred later, when liberal Italy was criticized for giving way before fascism, and still later, in the republican era, with criticism of the disequilibrium that accompanied industrial modernization. Something similar happened in Germany when debate concerning the origins of nazism gave a negative cast to the concept of *Sonderweg*. Obviously, judgments of this sort contrast the observable situation in the various "second comer" countries to models constructed by the culture of the time on the basis of the experience of the dominant countries, England and France in particular.[2] Furthermore, in the case of Italy, dependence upon foreign models of modernization is an integral part of the history of public opinion, beginning with the French invasion at the end of the eighteenth century, when the term *passive revolution* was used polemically to signify the "derivative" (thus the incomplete and distorted) nature of the transformations that took place.[3]

In these borrowings and projections, the various facets of the concept of *bourgeoisie* were derived from stereotypes that centered on each particular national experience. Thus, in France, *bourgeois gentilhomme* alluded to a

[2] For a discussion of the "English model" and its uses in the debate on Germany, see David Blackbourn and Geoff Eley, *The Peculiarities of Germany History: Bourgeois Society and Politics in Nineteenth-Century Germany* (Oxford and New York, 1984).
[3] The term *passive revolution*, coined by Vincenzo Cuoco in connection with the Neapolitan republic of 1799, owes its more recent fortune to being picked up again by Gramsci. See John A. Davis, ed., *Gramsci and Italy's Passive Revolution* (London and New York, 1979).

life-style and to habits and values imitated from aristocratic and lordly circles, whereas the connotation of a spirit of innovation and an economic mentality derived from the model of the Calvinist entrepreneur, and so forth. Sociological texts have influenced these cultural premises, starting with the popularizing writings of the Manchester economists and of Samuel Smiles, who was much read and imitated in Italy,[4] and including the Marxist writers as well as German and then American sociologists. Werner Sombart's *Der Bourgeois* (published in English as *The Quintessence of Capitalism*), which sought the roots of a model to compare with modern bourgeoisies in the Middle Ages, was particularly influential in Italy.[5]

Thus a variety of meanings cohabit within the "bourgeois universe," combining notions of exploitation and class conflict with innovation and a spirit of initiative, a conservative image of the gentleman with vague "vestiges of feudalism." Feudalism is in fact another nineteenth-century ideal type that contributes—by opposition and superposition—to the definition of the concept of bourgeoisie. As we shall see, it is especially inappropriate to use feudalism to explain the Italian case, since doing so requires external models—in particular, those constructed by the Marxism of the Second International to fit the German experience, which included nineteenth-century institutional, economic, and cultural phenomena of a "feudal" type or, more accurately, of a type associated with landed lordships.[6] Thus we could say that the Italian *borghesia*—considered in the Marxian sense as the capitalistic class that had the governance of the country— was accused of not being bourgeois enough both because of the role that traditional landownership played in it and because, in a Weberian sense, it lacked a genuine capitalistic spirit. Precisely because of these characteristics, however, it betrayed typically "bourgeois" attitudes in its life-style.

[4] On this phenomenon, see Guido Baglioni, *L'ideologia della borghesia industriale nell'Italia liberale* (Turin, 1974); and Silvio Lanaro, *Nazione e lavoro: Saggio sulla cultura borghese in Italia (1870–1925)* (1979), 2d ed. (Venice, 1990).

[5] Sombart used the French word *bourgeois* in his title to distinguish, within the world of the *Bürger*—the burgher, or city-dweller—the merchants, entrepreneurs, and capitalists from both the old and new middle classes (*Mittelstände*) and the humanistic middle class (*Bildungsbürgertum*). He sought the roots of his model in the class of merchants, entrepreneurs, and bankers that made the cities of medieval Italy famous, which enabled him to state that the capitalistic spirit had first developed in Italy. Obviously, this past grandeur might suggest to Italians that the "failure of the bourgeoisie" was a decline rather than an immaturity, with quite different psychological connotations. Werner Sombart, *Der Bourgeois: Zur Geistesgeschichte des modernem Wirtschaftsmenschen* (München-Leipzig, 1913), first translation in English, *The Quintessence of Capitalism: A Study of the History and Psychology of the Modern Business Man,* trans. and ed. M. Epstein (1915; reprint, New York, 1967).

[6] The most influential representative of this school in Italy was the Marxist historian Emilio Sereni, whose analysis of Italian agrarian and financial capitalism made consistent use of the notion of vestiges of feudalism. Sereni has strongly influenced Marxist economic history, in particular concerning the history of agrarian structures (Sereni's specialty). His school should be distinguished from the branch of Italian Marxism originated by Gramsci, which is more interested in institutional, political, and cultural phenomena. The fact that the works of both men appeared after World War II tends to make us forget that when they were written (in antifascist circles in the 1930s—in Gramsci's case, in prison) there was no contact between the two authors. Sereni noted this parallel and the differences in his inspiration and Gramsci's in the preface to the new edition of his *Il capitalismo nelle campagne (1860–1900)* (1947; reprint, Turin, 1968).

720   *Romanelli*

All this could lead to strange conclusions. Piero Gobetti, a writer and liberal-socialist politician later assassinated by the fascists, reached the conclusion that after World War I the middle classes in Italy were *piccolo borghesi* and that it was instead the communist, revolutionary working class that demonstrated the true bourgeois spirit.[7] Later, the fascist author of a book on the bourgeoisie (a concept he explicitly borrowed from Sombart) wrote that the Italian bourgeoisie, which was predominantly rural in the nineteenth century, was "the negation of the bourgeoisie."[8] Even fascism, then, could be considered either the realization of an "authentic" modern bourgeois revolution or the victory of the reactionary sectors of the bourgeoisie. It is hardly surprising that writers used the term to apply to their own class only in an anticonformist or iconoclastic sense.[9]

It appears, then, that the same word could express economic development and limitations to that development, the growth of a modern nation through the Risorgimento and its inherent fragility. It is hardly surprising that in 1930 Benedetto Croce, after reading the recent works of Groethuysen and Sombart, protested that the concept of bourgeoisie had a "merely metaphorical, imaginative, and expressive function" and was ambiguous, misleading, and loaded with antiliberal attitudes.[10] Croce had no way of knowing that the term, with all its contrasting meanings, would be revived after World War II with the new Marxist and Catholic dominance of historiography. The streets of Italy periodically filled with workers and students joining forces against "il potere borghese," while journalists denounced the "weakness" of the Italian *borghesia*. It was during that period that the antibourgeois leadership—principally the Catholics in the ruling class, but they had the socialists and communists at their side—accomplished Italy's definitive capitalist revolution, giving the country the particular bourgeois style (both entrepreneurial and hedonistic, open to the market but reliant on the state) that characterizes Italy today and gives it a "modernity" that scholars have only recently attempted to describe with appropriate instruments.

REVISIONISM

If our intent is to discern a concrete social group, it is misleading to begin with the concept of *borghesia*, which belongs above all to the history of culture, of literature, and of political ideology. Furthermore, historical research has for some

---

[7] Piero Gobetti, *La rivolutione liberale: Saggio sulla lotta politica in Italia* (1924; reprint, Turin, 1948), p. 137.

[8] Nello Quilici, *La borghesia italiana: Origini, sviluppo, e insufficienza* (Milan, 1932), p. 300.

[9] In general, relational terms denoting lower status on a hierarchical scale (lower middle class, petty bourgeoisie, etc.) are not used for self-definition. In our case, a stigma is attached to the entire concept of *borghesia*, which only exponents of the rightist (at times fascist) opposition embrace. It was in an iconoclastic and anticonformist spirit that in 1950 the journalist Leo Longanesi founded a political weekly entitled *Il borghese*, a review that soon adopted a profascist *piccolo-borghese* orientation and that often criticized the customs of the *grande borghesia*.

[10] Benedetto Croce, "Di un equivoco concetto storico: La borghesia," in his *Etica e politica* (1930), 2d ed. (Bari, 1943), pp. 321–28.

time concentrated on a revision of the concept—if not a decisive repudiation of it, as in French cultural circles.[11]

Repudiations and revisions had a choice between two strongly divergent roads: on one hand lay the deconstruction of texts and a relativization of the various meanings of the term, on the other, refuge in quantitative analysis of social groups, as Labrousse suggested. It is a shame that these roads lead so far apart, because the one cannot easily do without the other. Textual revision without reference to documents only adds a new chapter to the literary history of the term, whereas quantitative analysis without theoretical support is not always clear on what questions it seeks to answer, which leads to unsatisfactory results.

Many studies of this sort are less concerned with responding to a historical question than with proving the need for polemical revision of previous ideological assumptions; hence they are to some extent simply a speculative reversal of those assumptions. This is certainly the case in Labrousse's appeal for concreteness, which sprang from debate on the bourgeois character of the French Revolution and the class nature of social conflict in the Old Regime and was, in the last analysis, a reaction against Marxist constructions. Thus the result of such studies was indirect, a consequence of the fact that more space and more intense reflection were dedicated to the various social subjects under observation than had been the case in the general systems of an ideological matrix. What springs to mind is the fable in which the treasure a father claims is hidden in a field consisted in the result of his sons' assiduous plowing as they looked for it after his death. The "winners" in this exercise were the social subjects and perspectives that had been considered "losers." In the paradigmatic cases of the processes of development—in England, for example, or in France—that this revisionism has tended to investigate and reevaluate, the persistence of values, attitudes, or interests considered typical of the past is often regarded with open sympathy.[12] In Germany, contrary assumptions prevail to some

---

[11] The French historian Ernest Labrousse opened a new phase of social studies in France with his drastic statement at the International Congress of Historical Sciences in 1955: "Define the bourgeois? I disagree. Let us rather recognize—on the spot, in its sites, in its cities—this city species and place it under observation. . . . Inquiry first. Observation first. We will see about a definition later" ("Voies nouvelles vers une histoire de la bourgeoisie occidentale au XVIIIe siècle," in *Comitato Internazionale di Scienze storiche, X Congresso, Relazioni* [Rome, 1955], 4:467).

[12] Although in the case of the social history of popular strata the sympathy for the preindustrial world can be tinged with either conservative or radical attitudes, conservative sentiment seems to prevail in connection with bourgeois elites. This is the spirit in which the American scholar W. David Rubinstein has worked on patrimonial Victorian elites. In his most recent publication, a collection of important essays on the subject, he presents himself as "a foreigner to Britain, a natural-born Tory and conservative" (*Elites and the Wealthy in Modern British History: Essays in Social and Economic History* [New York, 1987], p. 5). Rubinstein further states that his study "reveals a Britain which was much more 'conservative' in its evolution than many historians would credit" (p. 11). The Stones arrive at much the same conclusion in their discussion of the "myth" of the "perennial openness of English landed elite to penetration by large numbers of the newly enriched bourgeoisie." They conclude: "By and large, the power, wealth, and even status of the landed elite survived more or less intact until 1880" (Lawrence Stone and Jeanne C. Fawtier Stone, *An Open Elite? England, 1540–1880* [London and New York, 1984], pp. 284, 282). In France, the quantitative approach and a conservative orientation coincide explicitly in the most recent overview of the question, Adeline Daumard, *Les bourgeois et la bourgeoisie en*

722   *Romanelli*

extent: since, after the experience of National Socialism, *Sonderweg* has been viewed
as a sort of "feudalization" of bourgeois groups, recent social historians have
attempted to verify this thesis, emphasizing the places and manifestations of a
"bourgeois autonomy." Studies have examined the social origins of industrialists, for
example, or the social cohesion of their matrimonial ties, the social choices of their
children, and so forth, concluding that, at least in quantitative terms, "the upper
bourgeoisie and the nobility proceeded on two separate tracks."[13]

No matter who momentarily occupies the central position in this ideological
battlefield, it is littered with the rubble of most of the ideal types that were
constructed concerning modern capitalism and the feudal Old Regime during the
nineteenth century. Only in this rubble can we discern the questions that historians
intended to put to the sources: What was the level of autonomy of the elite strata
that emerged as the nineteenth century progressed, as compared to those of the
Old Regime? What functions did they fulfill in the imperialistic phase of
nineteenth- and twentieth-century history? What were the relationships between
the various strata of the bourgeois world, in particular between the middle and
high bourgeoisie or the old petty bourgeoisie and the new one? Did group identity
depend upon material elements, institutional ones, or ones of a symbolic nature?
And what consistency existed, in the many historical instances, among these
diverse elements? In other words, can one assume necessary connections—as
some theories of modernization would have it—between the development of
economic, civil, cultural, and political institutions?

These are the problems that have emerged from the turbid debate over the
nature of the Italian *borghesia*. Scholarship has proven slow to offer clarification,
however. The aim of the pages that follow is to delineate a few of the paths that
Italian historiography has taken.

ITALIAN NINETEENTH-CENTURY ELITES: LANDED BOURGEOISIE OR PATRICIATE?

One of the chief accusations directed at the Italian *borghesia* is certainly its
numerical exiguity. Calculation was first attempted as soon as national statistics

France depuis 1815 (Paris, 1987). Other authors seem to be moving in the same direction,
however, as Jean-Pierre Chaline, *Les bourgeois de Rouen: Une élite urbaine au XIXe siècle*
(Paris, 1982).

[13] This is the opinion of Hartmut Kaelble, "Französisches und deutsches Bürgertum im
Vergleich," in Kocka, ed., *Bürgertum im 19. Jahrhundert* (n. 1 above), 1:119. For this type of
study, see also Toni Pierenkemper, *Die westfälischen Schwerindustriellen, 1852–1913: Soziale
Struktur und unternehmerischer Erfolg* (Göttingen, 1979); Hansjoachim Henning, "Soziale
Verflechtung der Unternehmer in Westfalen 1860–1914," *Zeitschrift für Unternehmergeschichte*
23 (1978): 1–30; Hartmut Kaelble, "Wie feudal waren die deutschen Unternehmer im
Kaiserreich?" in *Beiträge zur quantitativen vergleichenden Unternehmensgeschichte*, ed.
Richard H. Tilly (Stuttgart, 1985), pp. 148–74; Youssef Cassis, "Wirtschaftselite und Bürger-
tum, England, Frankreich und Deutschland um 1900," in Kocka, ed., *Bürgertum im 19.
Jahrhundert*, 2:9–33; Dolores L. Augustine-Perez, "Very Wealthy Businessmen in Imperial
Germany," *Journal of Social History* 22 (1988): 299–321, in which the author sees "a strong
commitment to capitalism and a strong sense of identity" in the frequency of family relations
among the Germany commercial elite (p. 315).

became available following Italy's political unification in 1861. The overall population of the kingdom was at the time around 25 million inhabitants. Working on the earliest data provided by the new tax on "mobile wealth," one socialist jurist, Pietro Ellero, calculated in 1879 that 250,000 Italians—including women and children—had enough income from capital investment or sufficient real estate holdings to live decorously; one-fifth of these (about 50,000) were the truly wealthy *alta borghesia.* Ellero observed that they were probably "fewer in number than gentlemen—that is, than the citizens whose families were listed, at the end of the last century, as nobles in the councils of our thousand communes."[14]

Although today it has been shown that these data were strongly underestimated (for reasons of tax evasion), the overall number of wealthy persons could not have been high. If we examine the socioprofessional categories listed under "proprietors" in the 1871 tax census (industrialists, priests, state employees, etc.), we find figures similar to those calculated some years ago by an economist, Sylos Labini, according to whom the *borghesia,* properly speaking, ranged from 300,000 to 350,000 persons between 1881 and 1921. That is, there were about 200,000 property owners, entrepreneurs, and owners of business concerns and about 100–150 thousand in the liberal professions.[15]

In the early twentieth century scholars used probate documents in attempts to compare the extent of private wealth in Italy and other lands. Private fortunes, middling and great, turned out to be few in Italy. One of these economists, Francesco Saverio Nitti, calculated that in Italy there were 1,500 "millionaires," as compared to 15,000 in France, 11,000 in Germany, and 30,000 in England.[16] Nitti wrote that the evidence belied the Marxist prediction of progressive impoverishment, but the general "tendency of median incomes to rise and of minimum incomes to diminish in number" also could not be found in Italy, either in terms of income or in terms of wealth: "The *borghesia,* which is the soul of modern civilization and the true factor of development, forms slowly and is rather a bourgeoisie of landed proprietors and professional people than a bourgeoisie of industrialists."[17]

This bourgeoisie constituted about 1.8 percent of the population immediately after Italian unification, a figure nearly equal to the political electorate, which was only slightly more than one million voters in 1882. I should note that public opinion, later echoed by the historians, long complained of voting restrictions, citing the small electorate as an example of deliberate "closing" of the political elite. Close analysis has shown, however, that the political elite was in favor of enlarging the electorate (obviously in order to enlarge their own consensual base), but it was not easy to do so while maintaining the liberal constitutional framework without extending the vote to the illiterate (who made up more than 70 percent of the population). No matter how low the property requirements for voting were set or how generous substitute criteria were, it was difficult to find an acceptable broader

[14] Pietro Ellero, *La tirannide borghese* (Bologna, 1879), p. 30.
[15] Paolo Sylos Labini, *Saggio sulle classi sociali* (Bari, 1974), p. 155.
[16] Francesco Saverio Nitti, *La richezza dell'Italia* (1905), now in his *Scritti di economia e finanza* (Bari, 1966), vol. 3, pt. 1:155.
[17] Ibid., pp. 247, 284–85.

724   *Romanelli*

electorate. The "civic stratum" of the population—even in its broadest definition including clerical workers, some craftsmen, and the wealthiest peasants—was already
included in that 2 percent of the population.[18]

The categories adopted for the classifications used in the nationwide census that
was launched immediately after unification in 1861, when the country was still
undergoing civil war, tell us something of the social profile of this elite. The upper
levels were asked to indicate whether their chief source of income was a
professione or a *condizione*. The first, which presumed some work activity,
included the notion of *proprietario;* the second was defined as *possidente,* a
notion of independent wealth close to that of a rentier or gentleman. (The forms
stated: "whoever exercises no profession and lives on income will be called
capitalist or retiree or *possidente,* according to the case.")

This was a fairly ambiguous linguistic distinction—then as now—and it was
hard to apply. It mixed class and status (in a Weberian sense) in a way difficult to
adapt to the profession-based categories of later sociology, and it is easy to see
why census data have seldom been used by scholars. This distinction was in fact
rarely used, and the elites tended to define themselves with the generic term of
possidenti. This occurred, for example, on the electoral lists, on which many
could have listed themselves according to either their profession or their
titles—their wealth or their income. The official classifications themselves tended
to subordinate specific professional designations to that of *proprietario,* so that in
1871 we find 361,977 *proprietari* and 18,665 *proprietari esercenti industrie
manifatturiere* (property-owner/industrialists), but also 5,215 "property-
owner/functionaries" (lawyers and notaries), 5,859 "property-owner/priests,"
and so forth. Thus focused around the generic notions of *proprietario/possidente*
(with little or no distinction made between capitalistic or entrepreneurial sources
of income and the independent wealth of a gentlemanly rentier), the elite sought
distinctions on the symbolic plane that followed parameters without legal value.
In the south of Italy, for example, the honorific titles "don" and "signor"
typically alluded to a mix of social prestige, power, and wealth.[19]

These considerations all point to the particular importance of property
ownership in the social panorama of nineteenth-century Italy. They are confirmed

[18] The greatest attempt at reform heretofore enacted (and which was accused of partially
perverting the entire system) brought 7 percent of the population into the political electorate in
1882. On the problems brought on by this move, see Raffaele Romanelli, *Il comando
impossibile: Stato e società nell'Italia liberale* (Bologna, 1988), pp. 151–206.

[19] For a detailed analysis of the significance of these titles in a small Sicilian community during
the first half of the nineteenth century, see Paolo Pezzino, "Autonomia e accentramento
nell'Ottocento siciliano: Il caso di Naro," *Annali della fondazione Lelio e Lisli Basso—ISSOCO*
19 (1987–88): 15–94. Pezzino writes, "The title of 'don' was never acquired in the course of
only one generation. . . . The condition of 'don' thus always connoted either an already acquired
status position (as in the case of the nobles) or a status acquired with studies . . . or a patrimony
accumulated by the family of origin that nonetheless (usually with the investment of one member
of the family [who was] made to study and directed toward a post or a profession) in time
permitted a conversion of wealth into prestige" (p. 71). The titles of "don" and "signore" are
treated in another study of a Sicilian community of the same period, Enrico Iachello, "Potere
locale e mobilità delle élites a Riposto nella prima metà dell'Ottocento," in *Il Mezzogiorno
preunitario: Economia, società, istituzioni,* ed. Angelo Massafra (Bari, 1988), pp. 915–34.

by several ongoing studies on the configuration of wealth using probate records, this time based on the original documents.[20] One of the principal coefficients considered in this sort of study is the proportion of landed property within total wealth in the estate, given that the "normal" trend on the pan-European level was a gradual increase in personal wealth (bank deposits, investment in stocks and state bonds, etc.). Here the figures for Italy show a clear difference with respect to France: whereas in Paris and other French cities real estate declined from about 50 percent of total wealth in the mid-nineteenth century to about 30 percent at the beginning of the twentieth century,[21] in Italy real estate holdings still accounted for 50 percent of total wealth at the latter date and in some cases continued to be as high as 75–80 percent up to World War I. As a sort of counterproof of these data, the study of the diffusion of capital invested in stocks and in banks shows that it remained fairly limited even during and after the first boom of the 1870s.[22]

These data help us to understand better Ellero's remarks on the civil identity of the city *borghesia* and *patriziati* and Nitti's statement that the Italian *borghesia* was made up of landed proprietors. Obviously, however, this is not enough to persuade us of the "lack of modernity" of that property-owning elite. Early studies have concentrated on the period of the French Revolution, when state properties were put up for sale. An intense circulation of lands ensued and the number of noble landowners declined. Italy differed radically from France, however. In France such sales had revolutionary origins and involved expropriation from the nobility; in "Jacobin" regimes in Italy—which were in no way Jacobin—the motivation was predominantly fiscal and the sales regarded only demesnial and ecclesiastical holdings. This means that in many cases it was the old landed nobility who bought such lands, thus extending their own holdings, and they did so just when the revolutionary process gave them ownership in the "bourgeois" sense, thus reinforcing their power. Individual instances show enormous variation, however, and there were great differences between northern and southern Italy in both previous landholding patterns and the importance of the so-called *eversione della feudalità* (overthrow of feudalism). Sicily, for example, was untouched by the revolutionary process.

[20] On the problems of the utilization of these sources in Italy, see Alberto Mario Banti, "Una fonte per lo studio delle élites ottocentesche: Le dichiarazioni di successione dell'Ufficio del registro," *Rassenga degli archivi di stato* 43, no. 1 (1983): 83–118, "Les richesses bourgeoises dans l'Italie du XIXe siècle: Exemples et remarques," *Mélanges de l'Ecole française de Rome, Moyen Age, Temps Modernes* 97, no. 1 (1985): 361–79. For the first applications of these questions to Italian cities, see Alberto Mario Banti, "Richezza e potere: Le dinamiche patrimoniali nella società lucchese del XX secolo," *Quaderni storici* 56 (August 1984): 385–432 (on Lucca), and *Terra e denaro: Una borghesia padana dell'Ottocento* (Venice, 1989) (on Piacenza). Preliminary notice of further ongoing work was presented at the annual meeting of the Social Sciences History Association, Minneapolis, October 1990, and included Anthony L. Cardoza, "The Limits of Fusion: Aristocratic Reaction and Industrial Elites in Late Nineteenth-Century Turin"; and Raffaele Romanelli, "Urban Patricians and the Shaping of a 'Bourgeois' Society: Wealthy Elites in Florence, 1862–1904."

[21] See Adeline Daumard, ed., *Les fortunes françaises au XIXe siècle* (Paris and The Hague, 1973), p. 159, table 9.

[22] A pioneering study in this regard is A. Polsi, *Alle origini del capitalismo italiano: Banche e banchieri dopo l'Unità* (in press).

726   *Romanelli*

What relationship can be established between these changes and capitalistic transformations in agriculture? Many studies of the history of landed property during the first half of the nineteenth century show that in Italy, as in England, the greatest innovators were the aristocrats; conversely, historians have reproached the new "bourgeois" property owners with not having a fully capitalistic mentality. In 1961 the Marxist historian Renato Zangheri, studying the region around Bologna (which was among the more advanced areas), wrote, "The new bourgeois property owners brought to country areas a spirit of enterprise unknown to lordly landownership, but they were attracted by the latter toward a semi-feudal conception of property and profits. . . . The great Bolognese proprietors who sought the means of agricultural progress in the Restoration after 1815 were informed concerning modern technology, debated problems of the market, [and] demanded reforms, whether they were bourgeois or nobles. . . . On the other hand, they firmly rejected any idea of the division of landholdings and all proposals for the capitalistic transformation of the means of production."[23]

It is misleading, however, to state that the presence of nobles made this complex situation in any sense "feudal."[24] In the long term, Italian society in the modern age has been characterized by precisely the lack of powerful feudal orders and the existence of a strong, unified nobility, by the urban and mercantile roots of many urban patriciates, and by the close connection between Italy's many small and midsized cities and towns and their surrounding countryside. It is thus a world that reflects the traditions of the communes and the signorie more than that of the feudal system. Furthermore, although Italy saw phenomena of "feudalization" between the sixteenth and seventeenth centuries, Enlightenment reforms operated to inflect them, in many cases anticipating the innovations of the French period. The fact that in Italy there was no genuine revolution of the French type is an essential part of any explanation of the persistence of many elements from the past, but the fact that the revolutionary period was to some extent "absorbed" into preexistent structures reveals the compatibility between those structures and the new nineteenth-century patterns into which the traditional aristocracy and the emerging bourgeoisie fitted perfectly.[25] Thus in Italy there were no forms of "alliance" among groups of the feudal aristocracy and the emergent bourgeoisie,

---

[23] Renato Zangheri, *La proprietà terriera e le origini del Risorgimento nel Bolognese*, vol. 1, *1789–1804* (Bologna, 1961), p. 150.

[24] Some scholars have even stated that for fifteen centuries and until the late nineteenth century Italian economy had a "feudal character." See Ruggiero Romano, "Una tipologia economica," in *Storia d'Italia*, vol. 1, *I caratteri originali* (Turin, 1972), pp. 255–304, quotation on p. 302. Arno J. Mayer, *The Persistence of the Old Regime: Europe to the Great War* (New York, 1981), makes a substantially similar argument. Mayer's book had a cool reception in Italy (see Raffaele Romanelli, "Arno Mayer e la persistenza dell'antico regime," *Quaderni storici* 51 [December 1982]: 1095–1102; and the remarks of S. J. Woolf, Alberto Caracciolo, Claude Fohlen, and Innocenzo Cervelli, "L'ombra dell'ancien régime," *Passato e presente* 4 [1983]: 11–34).

[25] It is not by chance that in Italy, unlike Germany or England, all *juridical* distinction between the bourgeoisie and the nobility disappeared in the liberal Constitution of 1848 (which was in many ways extremely conservative). On this point, see Giorgio Rumi, "La politica nobiliare del Regno d'Italia, 1861–1946," in *Les noblesses européennes au XIXe siècle* (Milan and Rome, 1988), pp. 577–93.

as there were in Germany but, rather (as in France if anywhere), an amalgamation of bourgeois and noble notables whose catalyst "was naturally found in the ownership of landed property, the new escutcheon that substituted for birth as a sign of social distinction"—thus Carlo Capra wrote in a fundamental survey of scholarship that stated the need to "disassociate the concept of bourgeois society from that of capitalistic society, and to characterize the former on the level of institutions and dominant values."[26] I might note that only in this way did Italian historiography begin to accept into the field of social history the thought of Antonio Gramsci, whose elaboration of the theoretical concept of "hegemony" resulted precisely from his reflection on the central social position of the restricted property-owning elite that had taken over guidance of the Risorgimento.[27]

All of this provides a key to the inherent ambivalence in the notion that in Italy the *borghesia* had many nonbourgeois, gentlemanly characteristics but nevertheless acted, as a general class, like a bourgeoisie. And those nonbourgeois characteristics did not prevent it from guiding the capitalistic innovations—on occasion extremely advanced ones—that were introduced in Italy at the end of the nineteenth century. Studying one of these cases, Alberto Mario Banti has shown that networks of familial relationships and political alliances enabled one group of nobles of mercantile origin to acquire the knowledge and the capital needed to effect a number of radical agricultural innovations in the early 1900s; these networks eventually made the group into one of the most striking expressions of the agrarian capitalistic bourgeoisie.[28] Only an assessment of the Italian situation according to German sociological models of French and English derivation—in many ways inapplicable to Italy—makes it seem systematically "lacking," "imperfect," and "limited." It is only recently that this comparison was seen as unsatisfactory; and upon that realization, an investigation was launched in which the same mixture thought to constitute Italian bourgeois society was demonstrated on the basis of the pertinent documentary evidence.

Another topic under recent investigation is association as a typical form of bourgeois social arrival. The same prevalently "property-owning" configuration of the Italian bourgeoisie can explain the limited vitality of the phenomenon of association in comparison to other European models: the greater part of the relational networks in Italy concentrated around the "gentlemanly" figures of the notables without spreading to larger social circles. During the first half of the nineteenth century, the lack of a representative regime and of political liberties in the constitutional framework in Italy contributed to this situation. Even at the end of the nineteenth century, however, the elite was slow to organize into

[26] Carlo Capra, "Nobili, notabili, élites: Dal 'modello' francese al caso italiano," *Quaderni storici* 37 (January–April 1978): 12–42, quotations on pp. 20, 18.

[27] The widespread popularity of Gramsci in Italian Marxist historiography has in fact produced ample reflections in the field of political history but not in those of economic and social analysis, where the classical Marxist canons best represented by Emilio Sereni prevail (see n. 6 above).

[28] Alberto Mario Banti, "Strategie matrimoniali e stratificazione nobiliare: Il caso di Piacenza (XIX secolo)," *Quaderni storici* 64 (April 1987), pp. 153–73, *Terra e denaro* (n. 20 above), and "I proprietari terrieri nell'Italia centro-settentrionale," in *Storia dell'agricoltura italiana,* ed. Piero Bevilacqua, vol. 2, *Uomini e classi* (Venice, 1990), pp. 45–103.

728   *Romanelli*

parties or stable political groups. One study on land ownership in the Po Valley in the latter nineteenth century insists on this point.[29] Thus it is doubtful, in the current state of scholarship, that one could state (as has one contemporary representative of ideological discourse concerning the Italian *borghesia*), that "the lack of generally shared values and of interpersonal relations made lasting by some form of associative network seems a constant of the Italian scene."[30] In reality, the launching of a series of scholarly investigations in this field suggests the existence of a reality that is much more fully articulated and differentiated, and it confirms the need to shift from a simple imposition of external cultural models onto the Italian situation to specific analyses of particular contexts.[31]

THE CHALLENGE OF UNIFICATION: THE STATE

If the concept of "feudal vestiges" fits the Italian scene poorly, the same might be said of the concept of "feudalization," used in the case of Germany to indicate the process by which some factors that promoted the growth of the industrial bourgeoisie were aided and abetted by the forceful intervention of the state and by a related subordination of bourgeois energies to the values and the power of the aristocracy.

In Italy the two terms *state* and *aristocracy* should be kept clearly separate. It is impossible to speak of the autonomous, well-defined power of a feudal aristocracy in Italy. It is undeniable, however, that state intervention played a primary role in the processes of bourgeois affirmation after unification. The topic has been much discussed, and it has been established that in the short term

---

[29] Maria Malatesta, *I signori della terra: L'organizzazione degli interessi agrari padani (1860–1914)* (Milan, 1989). On the problem of political parties, which lies beyond the scope of the present study, see Paolo Pombeni, ed., *All'origine della 'forma partito' contemporanea: Emilia Romagna, 1876–1892: Un caso di studio* (Bologna, 1984); Paolo Pombeni, *Introduzione alla storia dei partiti politici*, 2d ed. (Bologna, 1990), chap. 6.

[30] Silvio Lanaro, *L'Italia nuova: Identità e sviluppo, 1861–1988* (Turin, 1988), p. 28.

[31] The French derivation of these first studies is evident. Such topics were introduced in Italy with the anthology (containing no studies regarding Italy) edited by Giuliana Gemelli and Maria Malatesta, *Forme di sociabilità nella storiografia francese contemporanea* (Milan, 1982). New contributions have subsequently been published: Maria Malatesta, ed., "Special Issue: Sociabilità nobiliare, sociabilità borghese," *Cheiron*, vols. 9–10 (1988); M. Ridolfi and F. Tarozzi, eds., "Special Issue: Associazionismo e forme di socialità in Emilia-Romagna fra '800 e '900," *Bollettino del Museo del Risorgimento* (Bologna, 1987–88); and Maria Teresa Maiullari, ed., *Storiografia francese ed italiana a confronto sul fenomeno associativo durante XVIII e XIX secolo* (Turin, 1990), which concerns confraternities, corporations, and worker sociability. Robust local traditions of labor history and political history have often been subject to historiographical suggestions from beyond the Alps, as in Maurizio Ridolfi, *Il circolo virtuoso: Sociabilità democratica a rappresentanza politica nell'Ottocento* (Florence, 1990). For a suggested transfer of the phenomenon into its proper milieu of the "history of public opinion" and the history of bourgeois society (with an eye to the German experience), see Marco Meriggi, "Associazionismo borghese tra '700 e '800: Sonderweg tedesco e caso francese," *Quaderni storici* 71 (August 1989): 589–627. Meriggi has more recently edited (with Alberto Mario Banti) a special issue of *Quaderni storici*, vol. 77 (August 1991), entitled "Associazioni di élite nell'Italia del XIX secolo."

political unification in 1861 did not create opportunities for the middle classes, whose limited activities at first continued to operate within traditional local markets or to follow the modest flow of preexisting international trade. However, political unification did lead to vastly increased public spending, in particular on public works (primarily the railroads), which brought a concomitant increase in taxes and in the public debt. In this way the state came to play an essential role in mobilizing resources and in financial exchanges, and that had decisive economic effects.

Caution is called for when this assumption is transferred from macroeconomic history or political history to the history of social groups. It is possible that in many cases both fiscal pressures and the attraction of state protection of financial investments depressed the private sector and on the whole contributed to fortifying the profit mentality of the landed bourgeoisie in Italy.[32] But the now traditional interpretation, that this led to "an extremely rapid growth in the political influence of the classes that held personal wealth," thus eventually discouraging productive investment,[33] has not yet been supported by pertinent studies on the nature or the administration of the wealth of the Italian *borghesia*.[34] Furthermore, the idea that all this derived from the particular protectionist mentality and inclination to trust the state on all occasions that some scholars see as typical of the entrepreneurial class in Italy is even less supported by documentation.

Then there is the problem of the expansion of public administration and the excessive influence of the bureaucratic class. This current image is so undisputed that documentary verification has never been suggested. It is hard to say to what extent this is due to a cultural phenomenon recurrent in European liberal sentiment: the aversion to an expanded role for the state, an aversion that, in the case of Italy, is seen as reinforced by the unpopularity of certain Gallic *dirigiste* characteristics in the Italian administrative system and, ultimately, by the turn to authoritarianism in fascism. Some years ago one scholar of public administration questioned the idea that the Italian bureaucracy was ever bloated and stated that

[32] I have discussed this opinion in "La bourgeoisie italienne entre modernité et tradition: Ses rapports avec l'Etat après l'unification," *Mélanges de l'Ecole française de Rome, Moyen Age, Temps Modernes* 97 (1985): 303–23.

[33] Sereni (n. 6 above), pp. 61–62. Sereni continues, "The state's continuing need to take advantage of the capital market led to an extremely rapid growth in the political influence of the classes that held personal wealth. The political balance of power between landed property and personal property that existed at the time of unification soon changed to the clear advantage of the latter more than proportionally to the increase in its economic efficacy." Vera Zamagni states, furthermore, that "the low capacity of accumulation of the agricultural sector prevented a sizeable increase of non-agricultural activities, which ended up in a preference toward financial investments by existing capital not reemployed within agriculture" ("The Rich in a Late Industrialiser: The Case of Italy, 1800–1945," in *Wealth and the Wealthy in the Modern World*, ed. W. D. Rubinstein [New York, 1980], pp. 122–66). The one Italian contribution to this volume of comparative studies differs from the others in its lack of data.

[34] See, however, the studies cited in nn. 20 and 22 above, in particular Polsi (n. 22 above), which will offer a preliminary description of the stock market in Italy. The traditional history of agrarian enterprises has rarely considered the late nineteenth or the early twentieth century.

730   *Romanelli*

the polemics that periodically raise the question have little to do with the actual
size of the administration.[35] Objective parameters for measurement are lacking,
however: at what point can one say that a bureaucracy is superabundant?

On the other hand, certain cultivated bourgeois circles undeniably exerted
pressure on public administration that was linked to phenomena of intellectual
underemployment and to the economic fragility of urban elites. This certainly
occurred in a number of different periods, even in the economically more
advanced regions,[36] but southern Italy was prototypical for its particular economic, institutional, and cultural conditions, to the point of bringing on a rapid
and nearly total southern infiltration of the administration of the Italian state. The
tendency of people in civic life to utilize the administration as well as, more
generally, the historical role of administrative and juridical mediation in the
kingdom of the two Sicilies give this phenomenon a quite special cultural flavor,
which popular opinion has superimposed on the bureaucratic condition along with
a sort of anthropologically coded and unproductive parasite mentality. Only the
force of this image as "normal" can explain why no study has even been
undertaken of the administrative class in southern Italy or even of the class of
lawyers, notaries, and jurists to whom the stereotype has been applied and who
undeniably occupy a fundamentally important place in the overall configuration of
middle-class strata in southern Italy.[37]

But if to some extent (an extent that is by no means clear) one can say that the
Italian *borghesia* had particular "bureaucratic" connotations, it is nonetheless
certain that the bureaucracy itself never had any specific power as a social
stratum, as it did in France or in Germany, where the bureaucratic class inherited
a spirit of hierarchical and authoritarian service that can be linked to the culture
of the Old Regime and perhaps even to "feudal" culture.[38] Nothing of the sort
took place in Italy, particularly in central and northern Italy, where the functionary
was traditionally not so much the ruler's man as a notable in his own right. In

---

[35] Sabino Cassese, *Questione amministrativa e questione meridionale: Dimensione e recluta-
mento della burocrazia dall 'Unità ad oggi* (Milan, 1977).

[36] Marco Meriggi, *Amministrazione e classi sociali nel Lombardo-Veneto (1814–1848)*
(Bologna, 1983), attributes great importance in the formation of an opinion hostile to Austria to
the demonstrated inability of the administration to satisfy the requests for employment coming
from the cultivated bourgeoisie of the provincial cities. On the phenomenon of intellectual
unemployment in general and regarding a later period Marzio Barbagli, *Disoccupazione
intellettuale e sistema scolastico, 1859–1973* (Bologna, 1974), is still a basic text. It is available
in English as *Educating for Unemployment: Politics, Labor Markets, and the School System—
Italy, 1859–1973*, trans. Robert H. Ross (New York, 1982).

[37] For a study that discusses this topic (but does little except note this lack), see Hannes
Siegrist, "Die Rechtsanwälte und das Bürgertum: Deutschland, die Schweiz und Italien im 19.
Jahrhundert," in Kocka, ed., *Bürgertum im 19. Jahrhundert* (n. 1 above), 2:92–123. See also
Paolo Macry, "Notables, professions libérales, employés: La difficile identité des bourgeoisies
italiennes dans la deuxième moitié du XIX siècle," pp. 341–59, and Paolo Frascani, "Les
professions bourgeoises en Italie à l'époque libérale (1860–1920)," pp. 325–40—both in
Mélanges de l'Ecole française de Rome, Moyen Age, Temps Modernes, vol. 97 (1985).

[38] For a comparison of the Italian and the German bourgeoisie in this connection, see Marco
Meriggi, "Italienisches und deutsches Bürgertum im Vergleich," in Kocka, ed. *Bürgertum im
19. Jahrhundert*, 1:141–59.

those regions throughout the nineteenth century and into the twentieth century the high-level bureaucrats, at least, belonged to the same propertied ruling elite as the political and parliamentary class we have already identified as Italy's "general class."

THE HISTORY OF THE ENTREPRENEURS

When Italy became an industrial country the problem of the bourgeoisie changed radically, and for the first time entrepreneurs entered the historical picture. The historical perspective clearly changed in the 1950s when, among other things, the history of the industrial age was accepted as an academic discipline.

Initially, the problem was to pinpoint the origins of the industrial take-off at the beginning of the century. Studies first focused on "macroimpulses" of a structural nature, among which the Italian *borghesia*'s talent for innovation was conspicuously absent. As early as the 1930s, in the same book that defined the Italian middle class as "the negation of the bourgeoisie," Nello Quilici attributed the current "rebirth" of that class to three combined forces: the money sent back by emigrants; foreign investments; and, within Italy, the activities of Jewish entrepreneurs.[39] This was a somewhat naive picture, but later one of the first academic historians who studied the "formation of an industrial base" in Italy, Luciano Cafagna, spoke of "a complex and well-articulated development . . . made possible by the action of two sources of macroimpulses, the state and large banks, who openly destroyed the previous basic equilibrium, in part galvanizing preexistent energies, in part mobilizing new ones."[40]

Attention then focused on those "preexistent energies." In his portrait of Italy's economic take-off, Cafagna stressed the point that state intervention involved fiscal maneuvers and public works and did not touch the entrepreneurial field. Private entrepreneurs played an essential role in the economic boom, especially the large numbers of small-scale entrepreneurs with small, widely scattered ventures. Cafagna declared, "All this limited the advantages of concentration, but at the same time such diffusion meant that there was a more widespread readiness for economic ventures, which is one of the most difficult factors in industrial development. It could probably not have been overcome but for the fact that in the more advanced regions of the [industrial] 'triangle' there was a long-standing tradition of small concerns, especially in the textile field."[41] This was the start of a reevaluation of many proto-industrial activities in northern Italy, beginning with the silk industry, traditional in the region and fundamental to its economy.

At this point, attention turned to the phenomena of "modernity," which were seen, however, as governed by strong constraints and limited to a restricted

---

[39] Quilici (n. 8 above), pp. 368 ff.

[40] Luciano Cafagna, "La formazione di una 'base industriale' fra 1896 e 1914" (1961), now in his *Dualismo e sviluppo nella storia d'Italia* (Venice, 1989), pp. 323–57, quotation on p. 351.

[41] Luciano Cafagna, "Italy, 1830–1914," in *The Fontana Economic History of Europe*, ed. Carlo M. Cipolla (Glasgow, 1962), 4:319. This article was first published in Italy in 1977 and now is included in Cafagna, *Dualismo e sviluppo nella storia d'Italia.*

geographical area that was almost "a small state": "To a certain extent, the process of industrialisation of the three north-western regions of Italy was conducted like that of an autonomous small country."[42] It was stressed at the time that Italian industrial development was rooted in a strong dualism that not only opposed the industrial triangle Genoa-Turin-Milan to the rest of the country but also kept industrial culture at a distance from the capital and from politics, the symbols of the concrete reality of national unity. Interest in the history of entrepreneurship (along with the more traditional interest in the labor movement) was undoubtedly directly connected with the contemporary economic "boom" in northern Italy. Moreover, it was in the universities of the "triangle" where most of the work on this topic took place and where the leading entrepreneurs were treated to studies ranging from rigid "class" criticism to a more detached, scientific approach and even to biographies of an apologetic nature.[43]

Whatever individual scholars' motivations might have been, the overall result was a reevaluation of the contribution of bourgeois initiative to economic development in Italy. Valerio Castronovo has recently declared, "The state was not the sort of demiurge of Italian industrialization that has often been pictured. In the wearisome efforts that enabled the Italian economy to catch up with the general growth of the capitalistic system, entrepreneurs and technocrats represented something more than simple secondary figures, if for no other reason than for their organizational innovations and their ability to adapt to changing conditions."[44]

Who, then, were these entrepreneurs? Major industrialists were obvious choices for study, but curiosity about them also corresponded to a particular interest in heavy industry. Naturally, one of the first industrialists to merit a biography was the pioneer of the automobile, Giovanni Agnelli, the grandfather of the Giovanni Agnelli who heads the firm today. The elder Agnelli was the son of a wealthy landowner in the silk business in Turin who had acquired a patrician villa in the nearby mountains. In his early days a cavalry officer and mayor of "his" mountain village, young Agnelli frequented the meetings of a small group of fanatics interested in automobile racing as an elite sport—"aristocrats and entrepreneurs, professional men and public administrators"[45]—and in 1898, with their aid, he founded the Fabbrica Italiana Automobili Torino (FIAT).

[42] Cafagna, "Italy, 1830–1914," 4:324.

[43] One of the most prolific of these authors wrote works that differ significantly in tone. See Roberto Romano, *Borghesia industriale in ascesa: Gli imprenditori tessili nell'inchiesta industriale, 1870–1874* (Milan, 1977), *I Caprotti: L'avventura economica e umana di una dinastia industriale della Brianza* (Milan, 1980), *I Crespi: Origini, fortuna e tramonto di una dinastia lombarda* (Milan, 1985), and *La modernizzazione periferica: L'Alto Milanese e la formazione di una società industriale, 1750–1914* (Milan, 1990). For a different treatment of the same textile industry, see Giorgio Roverato, *Una casa industriale: I Marzotto* (Milan, 1986); and Piero Bairati, *Sul filo di lana: Cinque generazioni di imprenditori: I Marzotto* (Bologna, 1986). For an overview of the textile industry, see D. Bigazzi, *La storia dell'impresa in Italia: Saggio biografico* (Milan, 1990).

[44] Valerio Castronovo, *Grandi e piccoli borghesi: La via italiana al capitalismo* (Rome and Bari, 1988), pp. xi–xii.

[45] Ibid., p. 76.

This portrait does not perfectly coincide with the ideal type of the entrepreneur, à la Weber, nor does it recall Samuel Smiles's heroes. More than an Italian William Morris, Agnelli was in fact a typical nineteenth-century *borghese-possidente* who had substituted a passion for automobiles in place of a fondness for horses. Furthermore, according to his biographer, his was a nineteenth-century history prototypical of Italian industrial capitalism for its duality, for "the interweaving of business profits and income from [his] position" with "the greatest opening toward the international market and the most advanced technology and, at the same time, the most sullenly closed protectionism and sectorialism; [for] an alternation of liberating and innovative advances and hierarchic and elitist tendencies; [for] the most daringly cosmopolitan projections and reliance on old neighborhood alliances."[46]

The overall connection between the older propertied bourgeoisie and industrial enterprise in the age of the "end of the notables" and the agrarian crisis still needs to be clarified. In any event, it was in that world that the industrial adventure originated, because many Italian entrepreneurs either had been exposed to it or, if they came from more modest trades backgrounds, soon conformed to its model in an immediate and almost natural "gentrification" that had no need to wait out the canonical three generations.

Aside from Agnelli, there was also a somewhat anomalous figure who soon attracted the attention of historians. He was Alessandro Rossi, a man less well known than Agnelli and who died in 1898, one year before Agnelli founded the FIAT company. The leading Italian industrialist in the wool industry in the nineteenth century and a staunch supporter of industry, Rossi initiated technological and organizational advances, transforming the industry he had inherited from his father into a large-scale corporation as early as 1870. But he did not move the plant from its old location in the Veneto countryside, and, in the interest of combining the work ethic with religion and with the virtues of family and living in the country (each worker's house had a kitchen garden, e.g.), he built a company town that he planned to the last detail.

Rossi's concern with the well-being of "his workers" (and with the minutia of their private lives) was based in a defense of the industrialist's autonomy inspired by laissez-faire economics; hence he rejected social legislation and supported state intervention for the creation of structural conditions favorable to industrial development. As a member of Parliament he defended protectionist policies in both agriculture and industry. A skillful politician, he cultivated clientage relations, first as a deputy and later as a senator of the "Catholic party." His social outlook was Catholic, combining activist ethics with a decided paternalism, and while his speeches supported social inequality he also attempted to further worker solidarity and studied schemes for worker profit sharing.

As historians pursued their study of Rossi they found that, although he was exceptional in many ways, in the last analysis he was relatively close to the norm and provided insight into lingering ambiguities in the relationship between capitalism and tradition.

[46] Valerio Castronovo, *Giovanni Agnelli: La FIAT dal 1899 al 1945* (1971; reprint, Turin, 1977), p. xxiv.

734　*Romanelli*

As the studies on Rossi and his background have shown, Rossi's ideas and his economic and social strategies were deeply rooted in the textile industry of the Veneto, so much so that historians speak of a "Veneto model." Among the components of this model was the fusion of modern strategies with ideology and tradition. Rather than large cities, the Veneto had a number of small, historic cities not far from one another. The social structure was dominated by a countryside for the most part divided into small and midsized units of production that were run not as capitalistic enterprises but as *colonìe*—a kind of sharecropping system. The landowners, known as *agrari,* were very much present, both in person and symbolically in the form of their homes, the famous villas of the Veneto. The church was an important part of this model, and the landowners and the church were in total agreement, not only due to the religious faith everyone shared but even more because the function of social control was entrusted to religion and to the clergy (who always supported the government in office).[47]

Many elements in this picture—a homogeneous agriculture, scattered land holdings, and a decentralized agrarian system—can be found in other regions of central and northern Italy. What made the Veneto both unique and normative for contemporary Italy were other elements that emerged more clearly over the long term—in particular, the convergence of social structure and Catholic ideology. The social ideas of Alessandro Rossi (a member of Parliament) were in essence the ideology elaborated by Catholic thought during the course of the century, which stressed the roles of religion and the church in combating the traumas and fractures and mediating the dialectics of the modern world—an area in which Italy set an example for other nations. Rossi held that Italian entrepreneurs had a particularly strong sense of social responsibility and that Italians were free of capitalistic avidity, sensitive to foreign examples but capable of adapting them to Italian needs without excessive stress.

It is tempting to draw a connection between historians' interest in Rossi and the "Veneto model" during the 1960s and the hegemony of Catholics in the political life of the Italian Republic during those same years, when the Veneto had an overwhelming Christian Democratic majority and contributed disproportionately to the formation of the governing class. There are other points of comparison with more recent historical events as well. During the 1970s and the 1980s vast areas of central and northeastern Italy (the Veneto, Tuscany, and the Marches) entered into a new productive phase, becoming so important, socially and economically, that they were dubbed the "third Italy." (The Milan-Turin-Genoa "triangle" formed the "first" Italy and the south, the Mezzogiorno, the "second.")[48] The new industries in the region, whose products ranged from household appliances to fertilizers, from clothing to luxury wines and personal computers, had, on the

---

[47] Silvio Lanaro, "Genealogia di un modello," in *Il Veneto,* ed. Silvio Lanaro, Storia d'Italia: Le regioni dall'unità a oggi (Turin, 1984), pp. 5–96. Lanaro defines the Veneto as a region of "relative backwardness, guided, but not wished for" (p. 69). The interpenetrating categories of landowner, noble, and capitalistic entrepreneur in the Veneto is well illustrated in the figures portrayed in C. Fumian, "Proprietari, imprenditori, agronomi," in Lanaro, ed., pp. 97–162.

[48] Arnaldo Bagnasco, *Tre Italie: La problematica territoriale dello sviluppo italiano* (Bologna, 1977), and *La costruzione sociale del mercato* (Bologna, 1988).

structural level, "low capital intensity, absence of relevant economies of scale, mature technology and slow economic progress, market competition, scattered and changing demand (for example, tied to fashion), small-scale assembly line production."[49] The "new entrepreneurs" who led this development often had craftsman or peasant origins; like their predecessors they had deep roots in their territory and in local institutions. In spite of their markedly different social origins, they were to some extent the sons of the same environment as the first entrepreneur-owners, the bourgeois and the aristocrats who often had served as tenants, sharecroppers, craftsmen, or workers.

Naturally, the historical frame of reference changed over time as well. In the 1950s historiography sought the origins of a development that was in disequilibrium but retained elements that seemed to reflect classical models (big business, heavy industry, urban development, increasing secularization, and so forth). Later, the normative efficacy of many parts of that model seemed to decline, and new developments seemed governed by elements earlier considered of limited scope: a late separation between agriculture and industry (even with a long-standing crisis in the primary sector) and widely scattered small productive units, often family-run. It is worth noting that this shift in perspective synchronized Italian studies with other revisionist trends in the field of economic history that rejected classical categories to "reevaluate" the family business, the small enterprise, and regional industry.[50]

On the specific topic of the social history of bourgeois groups, the new atmosphere has at least contributed to new thinking on the complex relationship between innovation and tradition. Agrarian and industrial paternalism, for example, is far from vestigial in Italy today. "The idea of the good father" (as a recent biography of an industrialist is entitled) long dominated industrial relations.[51] It is now common in this sort of work to stress the integration of family ties into the larger economic picture, from the hiring of workers through kinship channels to familial ties behind the ownership and management of the company. Even Rossi's construction of worker towns was not exceptional; an emphasis on worker housing as a way to integrate industrial labor into a rural social and cultural context was common among Italian industrialists of the period.[52] Such

[49] Willem Tousijn, "I piccoli imprenditori nella struttura di classe," in *I ceti medi in Italia tra sviluppo e crisi,* ed. Carlo Carboni (Bari, 1981), p. 203.

[50] A classic study concerning the nineteenth century is Charles F. Sabel and Jonathan Zeitlin, "Historical Alternatives to Mass Production: Politics, Markets and Technology in Nineteenth-Century Industrialization," *Past and Present,* no. 108 (August 1985), pp. 133–76. This and other similar studies have been particularly well received in Italy. See also Charles F. Sabel, "La riscoperta delle economie regionali," *Meridiana: Rivista di storia e scienze sociali* 3 (1988): 13–71. On the current state of family direction in large corporations, see Piero Bairati, "Le dinastie imprenditoriali," in *La famiglia italiana dall'Ottocento a oggi,* ed. Piero Melograni (Rome and Bari, 1988).

[51] Fabio Levi, *L'idea del buon padre: Il lento declino di un'industria familiare* (Turin, 1984). Levi credits the recent bankruptcy of a cotton company to having continued paternalistic management too long.

[52] For examples of planned company towns, see *Villaggi operai in Italia: La Val padana e Crespi d'Adda* (Turin, 1981). I might note that two such entrepreneurs were foreigners: Francesco De Larderel, who founded flourishing mines in Tuscany, was French, and Isacco Neumann, who

736   *Romanelli*

men not only constructed factory buildings, worker residences, and charitable
works but also built their own city houses and country estates or acquired patrician
residences, in the city or the country; the symbolic value of the latter is difficult
to separate from the economic investment they represent.[53]

We need still to verify to what extent these situations were unique to Italy, given
that a similar revision of "modernizing" sociological stereotypes has occurred in
vast sectors of historiography throughout Europe, as studies and discussions about
paternalism in industrial relations in England attest.[54] But although revisionist
trends may resemble one another, specific situations vary from country to country.
More typical of the Italian context, for example, are the fragmentation and
dispersion of industries—hence the integration of industry into the rural
community—and the roles played by the family, small-scale agricultural production, and Catholic ideology. One of the many variants of this mixture is the history
of large landholders in Tuscany—a group of aristocrats and agrarian entrepreneurs
who played an important role in Italian politics between the unification of Italy
and fascism and whose large holdings (as in the Veneto) were divided into small
productive units (*poderi*) rented to sharecropper families under the owner's
paternalistic control. The commonly accepted picture of such men presents a
conservative elite of the aristocratic type tied to the social and economic
conventions of the sharecropping system and open to innovation only through the
least risky financial investments. Studies that concentrate on the activities of urban
entrepreneurs, the configuration of wealth, or the management of particular
companies present a much more varied and complex picture. One prime example
of this is Baron Ricasoli, a great landowner and member of the feudal aristocracy,
a politician, and a capitalistic entrepreneur, whose investments in state bonds or
in politically guaranteed stocks could be seen not as an example of the flight of
agrarian capital but as an attempt to support capitalistic investment in agriculture
in a phase of incipient economic crisis.[55] The sharecropping system itself,
traditionally presented as "one of the most unprogressive features of feudal-

---

founded textile factories in Piedmont, was Swiss. On the latter, see Gian Albino Testa, "La
strategia di una famiglia imprenditoriale tra Otto e Novecento," *Bollettino storico bibliografico
subalpino* (1981), pp. 603–36. Another example of a company town in the Veneto has now been
studied by Carlo Fumian, *La citta' del larozo: Un' utopia agroindustriale nel Veneto contemporaneo* (Venice, 1990). Various aspects of Rossi's career are discussed in Giovanni L. Fontana,
ed., *Schio e Alessandro Rossi: Imprenditorialità, politica, cultura e paesaggi sociali del secondo
Ottocento,* 2 vols. (Rome, 1985).

[53] Emphasis on "gentrification" often leads scholars to forget that ownership of lands, farms,
or urban dwellings in many cases served the entrepreneur as a way to obtain bank loans. See
Giorgio Fiocca, ed., *Borghesi e imprenditori a Milano dall'Unità alla prima guerra mondiale*
(Bari, 1984). For an exemplary analysis of the phenomenon, not in a bourgeois milieu but among
peasants and home-based weavers during the first half of the nineteenth century, see Franco
Ramella, *Terra e telai: Sistemi di parentela e manifattura nel Biellese dell'Ottocento* (Turin,
1984), chap. 5.

[54] See, e.g., the debate prompted by Patrick Joyce, *Work, Society, and Politics: The Culture
of the Factory in Later Victorian England* (New Brunswick, N.J., 1980).

[55] Giuliana Biagioli, "Vicende e fortuna di Ricasoli imprenditore," in *Agricoltura e società
nella Maremma grossetana dell'Ottocento* (Florence, 1981).

ism,"[56] can be seen in another light not only because of intrinsically "rational" economic elements (great flexibility in the use of resources) but also because certain goals of social preservation that typified it had positive long-term results—for example, in forming the social structure on which the region's small- and midsized industry, luxury agriculture, and elite tourism are based today.

Thus scholarship is moving ever farther away from the practice of applying ready-made, external sociological models to individual cases. Rather, it is beginning to examine specific historical contexts and, within those contexts, the options available to individuals; it is addressing the interplay of challenge and response in a perspective that privileges the moments and rhythms of innovation.[57] In this larger picture, the history of Italy's south—the Mezzogiorno—is an overwhelming and problematic case in point. As long as it was defined only as a "backward" area oppressed by the weight of the past or by new mechanisms of a "dualistic" development, the south offered little occasion for any study of real social transformation. Where sociological deductivism reigned the consequences of social backwardness were known in advance; its overturning has focused attention on the Mezzogiorno, and it is precisely southern Italian society's deviation from the "normal" paradigm of modernity that has provided an opportunity to experiment with new analytical concepts and different explicative models.

A recent study by Marta Petrusewicz on the administration of one *latifondo* (large landholding) in Calabria during the nineteenth century is quite special in this sense, since it deliberately overturns the usual perspective on a phenomenon generally considered among the most backward in nineteenth-century Italian society. Although the property owners in this case study belonged to an ancient noble family and led a gentlemanly life, the *latifondo* was constituted in the early 1800s as a result of changes during the period of French rule, and it was administered with a quintessentially "bourgeois" rigor and a logic that was in many instances "feudal." Only a small and well-defined portion of the production was destined for the market, and the entire administration resembled a tightly integrated, organic, and socially closed world. It is precisely in these elements, however, that Petrusewicz sees the efficiency and "rationality" of the operation, judging it by criteria that measure productive flexibility and capacities for economic and social adaptation to external conditions more than monetary profit.[58]

---

[56] Zamagni (n. 33 above), p. 128.

[57] Banti, *Terra e denaro* (n. 20 above), is an excellent example of this method. Studying an agrarian bourgeoisie of aristocratic origin that was among the most advanced in a capitalistic sense, Banti shows why, by whom, when, and with what means this group adopted fundamental innovations in production techniques. For a different application of the same general methodology, see Alberto Mario Banti, "Gli imprenditori meridionali: Razionalità e contesto," *Meridiana: Rivista di storia e scienze sociali* 6 (1989): 63–90. For a discussion of the concept of "strategy" in this sort of study, see Giovanni Federico, "Azienda contadina ed autoconsumo fra antropologia ed econometria: Considerazioni metodologiche," *Rivista di storia economica*, n.s., 2 (1984): 224–68, and "Contadini e mercato: Tattiche di sopravvivenza," *Società e storia* 39 (1987): 877–913. My own reference to the problem of the moments and rhythms of innovation is indebted to Karl Polanyi, *The Great Transformation* (New York, 1944).

[58] Marta Petrusewicz, *Latifondo: Economia morale e vita materiale in una periferia dell'Ottocento* (Venice, 1989).

738   *Romanelli*

Petrusewicz takes the feudal model of Witold Kula and Edward P. Thompson's concept of "moral economy" as her point of departure, but other scholars of the Italian Mezzogiorno have found inspiration in anthropological literature outside Italy. What counts more than the results of non-Italian scholars' studies of the Mezzogiorno (which tend to be criticized in Italy) is that those studies have helped stimulate theoretical reflection on the Mezzogiorno, which is sorely needed if we are to understand how Italy's southern regions fit into the Italian and European contexts.[59]

Many and varied aspects of the recent cultural and economic evolution of the Mezzogiorno itself enter into this change in perspective, and southern Italian society today makes a more vital and dramatic impact on the national scene. Nevertheless, new studies have introduced an entire set of modifications to the rural and feudal picture, stressing, for example (in relation to the topic at hand), the numbers and the functions of the urban elites, the bureaucratic and professional elites,[60] and the technological[61] or more strictly entrepreneurial elites. Even where the city's *borghese* character is undisputed, as in the case of Naples—not an industrial city but the biggest city of the peninsula and an exceptional case—the urban context has attracted scholarly attention as an example of a "compromise between inheritance and innovation that gives form to the special identity of the nineteenth century."[62]

When historians study the entrepreneurial *borghesia* in the Mezzogiorno, they stress the region's remoteness from international markets, hence the uncertain conditions under which innovative entrepreneurs had to operate. During the latter half of the nineteenth century, when southern agriculture specialized in the production of oil, wine, and citrus fruits, ensuing transformations "derived no

---

[59] It seems to me significant that only recently and after some time have some of these works been translated into Italian. Among such studies are Jane Schneider and Peter Schneider, *Culture and Political Economy in Western Sicily* (New York, 1976), trans. Soveria Mannelli in 1989; Anton Blok, *The Mafia of a Sicilian Village, 1860–1960: A Study of Violent Peasant Entrepreneurs* (Oxford, 1974), Italian translation, Turin, 1986. Space limitations preclude tracing the chronology and the lines of importation of all the texts of historical anthropology that have influenced current Italian thought. Particularly applicable to the present discussion are Polanyi, *The Great Transformation*, translated into Italian in 1974; and Edward P. Thompson, "The Moral Economy of the English Crowd in the Eighteenth Century," *Past and Present* (1977), available in Italian together with other essays in *Società patrizia, cultura plebea: Otto saggi di antropologia storica sull'Inghilterra del Settecento*, ed. Edoardo Grendi (Turin, 1981).

[60] Enrico Iachello and Alfio Signorelli, "Borghesie urbane dell'Ottocento," in *La Sicilia*, ed. Maurice Aymard and Giuseppe Giarzzino, Storia d'Italia: Le regioni dall'unità a oggi (Turin, 1987); "Special Issue: Città," *Meridiana: Rivista di storia e scienze sociali*, vol. 5 (1989), a special issue on cities in the context of southern Italy.

[61] Leandra D'Antone, *Scienze e governo del territorio: Medici, ingegneri, agronomi e urbanisti nel Tavoliere di Puglia (1865–1965)* (Milan, 1990).

[62] Paolo Macry, *Ottocento: Famiglia, élites e patrimoni a Napoli* (Turin, 1988), pp. 261–62. See also Paolo Macry, "Borghesie, città e Stato: Appunti e impressioni su Napoli, 1860–1880," *Quaderni storici* 56 (1984): 339–83, "Tra rendita e 'negozio': A proposito di borghesie urbane meridionali," *Meridiana: Rivista di storia e scienze sociali* 5 (1989): 61–76, and "La città e la società urbana," in *La Campania*, ed. Paolo Macry and Pasquale Villari, Storia d'Italia, le regioni dall'unità a oggi (Turin, 1990), pp. 93–182.

impulse from agronomic and technological innovations, from the efficient use of available resources for productive ends, [or] from the ability to conquer the market by the high road of cost reduction and increased competition"—as a strong paradigm might suggest—"but represented adaptations of varying degrees of competence and efficacy to conjunctural shifts in the market."[63] For the southern entrepreneur (according to the same author), this meant "avoiding the immobilization of sizeable amounts of scarce capital . . . spreading the risk over a broad range of agricultural, commercial, manufacturing, [and] financial initiatives, always [making] small and relatively liquid investments, pulling them out at the first negative market signs; using market variations and the limits of the infrastructure for speculative ends; . . . tightening up production relations founded on peasant self-exploitation rather than on direct exploitation."[64]

Even in southern Italy, then, the portrait of the *borghese* is not clearly defined and it combines the same diverse social elements that we have found in all the elites of Italy: the property owner, the industrialist, the merchant, the rentier, the administrator, and the functionary. The greater structural fragility of Italy's southern provinces accentuates the dramatic nature of this amalgam, however, and carries its theoretical indeterminacy to the extreme. The study of a peripheral area of extreme instability thus suggests the need to concentrate on the relationships between the various components of modernization (economic, cultural, and institutional), measurement of their internal hierarchies, and theoretical evaluation.[65]

Once the term *borghesia* is purged of the rhetorical functions it has taken on, the very ambivalence of the concept may turn out to be extremely rich and prolific. It would not be the first time that the "Italian case" provided a serviceable laboratory for the comparative analysis of processes of modernization.

[63] Biagio Salvemini, "Note sul concetto di Ottocento meridionale," *Società e Storia* 26 (October–December 1984): 917–45, quotation on p. 923.

[64] Biagio Salvemini, "Per un profilo della borghesia imprenditoriale dell'Ottocento meridionale: Una griglia interpretativa generale," in *Le borghesie dell'Ottocento*, ed. Alfio Signorelli (Messina, 1988), p. 73. One of the most noteworthy case studies (on the Florio family, the most prominent entrepreneurs in Sicily in the nineteenth century) confirms the picture of a varied production. For the essential sector of citrus fruit production, see Salvatore Lupo, *Il giardino degli aranci: Il mondo degli agrumi nella storia del Mezzogiorno* (Venice, 1990).

[65] Hence it is often accurate to speak of "modernization" in connection with the Mezzogiorno, as it is accurate to suggest that the modernization that does indeed occur and that often is characterized by culture and custom more than by structural economics is derived and subalternate. In this sense Schneider and Schneider (n. 59 above) spoke of "modernization without development" and Luciano Cafagna of "passive modernization" ("Modernizzazione attiva e modernizzazione passiva," *Meridiana: Rivista di storia e scienze sociali* 2 [1988]: 229–40). Others have spoken of a "submerged modernization." See Giuseppe Giarrizzo's introduction to Lucio Avagliano et al., *La modernizzazione difficile: Città e campagna nel Mezzogiorno dall'età giolittiana al fascismo* (Bari, 1983). See also Paolo Pezzino, "Quale modernizzazione per il Mezzogiorno?" *Società e storia* 37 (1987): 649–74. In this context, it appears significant that the first expressly interdisciplinary review, *Meridiana*, has appeared in southern Italy.

[30]

International Political Science Review (1995), Vol. 16, No. 2, 145–167

Consolidation and Party Government in Southern Europe

Leonardo Morlino

ABSTRACT. Among the essential conditions for a recently installed democracy to survive are that it reduce to a minimum or absorb the inconsistencies of the first moments of transition and that it affirm its solidity vis-à-vis possible threats, whatever their origin. At the center of this process a stable system of political intermediation, able to guarantee the governability of the country in question, must be generated. With these premises, the present article analyzes the topic of democratic consolidation in reference to the crucial role played by political parties. Although the analysis focuses on Spain, Portugal, Italy and Greece, the conclusions may be extrapolated to other European countries.

In the democratic consolidations of Southern European countries, such as Italy, Spain, Portugal and Greece, parties (and party elites) played a key role. Although the Italian experience encompasses the late 1940s and 1950s, whereas the other three took place in the 1970s and 1980s, they all may be defined as *consolidation through parties*. As a result in each of these countries party government, in weaker or stronger form, was established. In all cases a predominant party system was also instituted, though we should make some qualifications regarding Greece. Certain mechanisms of an organizational or institutional kind account for the different processes and outcomes. They include a developed party organization, a stronger role played by parties vis-à-vis pressure groups (related to a large public sector), a cohesive dominant party with a strong leadership, and institutional rules that favor the incumbent party (parties). In the four cases under study, however, those factors are combined differently, as we shall see.

This article is divided into four parts. After some initial theoretical definitions, the first part analyzes the sub-process of legitimation, while the second and the third try to explore the organization of parties and their relationship with interest groups. Finally, the main hypotheses, suggested by the research, and the emerging patterns of consolidation, are presented.

0192-5121 95/02 145–23 © 1995 International Political Science Association

The "point of departure" we have chosen is the moment when once the approval of a constitutional charter has been achieved. This was 1947 for Italy, 1974 for Greece, 1976 for Portugal, and 1978 for Spain. The final moment to be considered is more approximate, but on the whole the focus is on the first years after the installation as the core period of consolidation.[1] The following analysis will clarify why the "point of arrival" for Italy is the end of the 1950s; and for Portugal, Spain and Greece, basically the end of the 1980s.

What is Democratic Consolidation?

In this article, consolidation is defined as the process by which the structures and norms of democracy have been firmly established and supported by the general public so that the regime gains persistence and the capability to overcome possible challenges. In other words, this process implies the strengthening of the democratic regime to avert possible future crises. If adaptation and firm establishment are the main modes by which consolidation is achieved, a preliminary review of our cases suggests that the two main characteristics of the process are the legitimation of the institutions and the self-strengthening of the actors supporting the regime.[2]

The second feature, the self-strenthening of intermediary structures and the other institutions of the regime, creates a self-perpetuating internal system. The institutions thus develop their own vested interests in maintaining themselves, once installed. More precisely, if the rules and procedures of the regime are considered, this means basically the institutionalization of those rules and procedures; if the main actors at the core of the process are analyzed, then some form of predominance or prevalence of those actors should be expected, mainly as a side effect of the competition among actors to achieve more stable ties and the allegiance of various sectors of society.

The first dimension, legitimation, involves the largest possible acceptance or even support for the democratic structures. This is a key part of the whole process. An anti-regime group or party, created during the installation and then firmly established during the following years, may remain unchanged for decades in its opposition toward the regime, or it may change very slowly and gradually, if the regime does not stumble into a crisis.

The two dimensions are strictly related. To some extent, stability of the party system, as a manifestation of the party's strengthening, may be the result of bipolarization. But if it is undermined by widespread anti-democratic attitudes, then consolidation is unlikely. The party system may be organizationally well-structured, but if one or more of the relevant parties is against the democratic order this can only lead to a continuous "trench war" with probable disruptive consequences. A large public sector may control a barely autonomous or dependent society. But if in this society radicalization, violence or non-democratic political alternatives are common, that form of control is irrelevant to consolidation. In this case, the only other possibility would be repression—but this would be a first step toward transforming the regime into a non-democratic order.

Thus, to understand democratic consolidation in the different countries, the *top–down* relationships between parties and party system vis-à-vis the general society must be explored, since these relationships determine how parties *control* society. At the same time, the *bottom–up* relationships between people and parties (as well as other governmental institutions) have to be considered, since they represent the *consensual* component of the consolidating process.

Thus, our main starting point is that consolidation emerges from the interweaving of consensus and control, which bring about the characteristic "mixture" of consolidation in each country; the same factors are always present, but to different degrees, as a side effect of institutional control, and of flexibility, which is an effect of consensus.

Legitimation

All four cases present a process of legitimation, though at different speeds and with different features. In Italy, from the end of the 1940s through the 1950s, the process was very slow. Even in the early 1960s, legitimacy was limited, with anti-regime forces on both the Right, the neofascist Movimento Sociale Italiano (MSI), and the Left, the Partito Communista Italiano (PCI), which together took about 30 percent of the vote. By the early 1960s, the forces that only partially supported the regime, such as the Socialists, with 13–14 percent of the vote, had been integrated. This meant that during the first fifteen years after 1948 these forces basically overlapped with those participating in the governmental coalition formed by Christian Democrats (DC) Liberals (PLI), Republicans (PRI) and Social Democrats (PSDI).[3] In other words, there was an internal party system that excluded fringe parties, Socialists included, and a broader party system with its more radical patterns of competition.[4]

If placed on a sort of continuum, the Spanish case is very distant from the Italian one, much closer to the opposite pole. After the first election, in 1977, the extreme Right disappeared. A formation of the Right (Alianza Popular) found it very difficult to become established and achieved a resounding success only in 1982, thanks to the crisis of the Union de Centro Democrático (Center Democratic Union, or UCD) and its parallel transformation from a semi-proregime force to a more integrated party. The Communist Left showed a great deal of moderation at an elite level and, in spite of deep internal political conflict and a crisis in the leadership, it was fully integrated into the regime from the beginning. The legitimation of regionalist forces was much slower.

Greece and Portugal, which also differ from one another in important respects, are closer to the experience of Spain. In Greece, the Right was very supportive of the newly installed regime, which was created by Karamanlis and Nea Democratia (ND). After the first years, in Portugal as well, the Right also supported the regime. As for the Left, the Greek and Portuguese processes differed. The integration of Greek Communists originated from the weaknesses of the two Communist parties that were caught in an ancillary position vis-à-vis the Socialists after the electoral success of the Panhellenic Socialist Movement, PASOK in 1981. The process of legitimation ended in 1989–90 when the government formed an alliance with Nea Democratia. In spite of the transformations of all Communist parties in Western and Eastern Europe, in Portugal the Communist leadership was able to maintain its position, all the while keeping the party midly in support of the regime and condemning it to a declining electoral trend. Thus, on the whole, the experience of Greece is closer to that of Spain, and in the early 1990s there has been no serious challenge to the legitimacy of either democracy.[5]

To the issue of legitimacy, other important elements should be added. First, in three of the four countries the process has not been linear. In Italy, it basically remained frozen during the most oppressive years of the Cold War (1948–56), until the Hungarian revolt. In Spain, after the installation of democracy, there was a difficult period between 1979 and 1981 with public disenchantment and a crisis in and breakdown of the Union de Centro Democratico (UCD) the main actor in the democratic installation;[6] these were also the years of Basque terrorism, with support coming from different separatist groups that had gained votes in national and regional elections. In Portugal, until the first important constitutional revision in 1982, there was a long phase during which it was not even clear what kind of democracy should be installed and considered legitimate: a radical socialist regime or a pluralist democracy, closer to European models. Only in Greece was the process basically linear: in fact, the legitimation concerned Communists only and there were no important moments of backsliding.[7]

How to explain the differences among the countries? If the key point is that people gradually begin to think that there are no acceptable alternatives to democracy, what are the explanations for the different paths followed by the four countries—especially as between Italy and the other three cases? The answer lies in the nature of the regime prior to democracy—a mobilizational one in Italy, an authoritarian one in the other countries—as well as some determining events during the transition. In Italy, the establishment of the Repubblica Sociale Italiana (RSI) and the civil war account for the presence of an extreme non-democratic Right. Also in Italy, a negative memory of the earlier fascist experience and of the war, the democratic Catholic choice, and the alliance of Christian Democracy with other smaller center parties (Republicans, Liberals, and Social Democrats) are the factors that together with certain policies introduced by De Gasperi, explain the trend towards legitimation.[8]

In Spain, legitimation was the result of the people's collective memory of civil war,[9] the political and economic appeal of other European countries, widespread attitudes favorable to democracy, in the Left[10] as well as the Right and amongst the elite.[11] Crucial to the process of legitimation in Spain were various agreements between the government, unions and private associations, as well as the pacts between center and local elites.[12] In fact, a general effect on these agreements was unavoidably to confer legitimacy on the existing regime and to integrate the social actors and their representatives in that democracy.

In Portugal, as well, the appeal of the European model of a pluralist democracy and the refusal to consider the radical Left alternative were at the heart of support for the kind of regime that eventually was consolidated by Socialists, Social Democrats, and the Social Democratic Center (CDS).[13]

In Greece, the dislike of the previous military regime, widespread democratic attitudes, the shift of the Socialists toward more moderate positions, and the democratic initiative of Karamanlis and his Nea Democratia Party, explain the beginning of the development of legitimation. When, in the second general election of 1977, a right wing party (EP) won nearly 7 percent of the vote, before disappearing in the following elections, this party was clearly not anti-regime.

In trying to give a more general answer to the question of legitimation, two elements stand out clearly. At the beginning of the legitimation period, a decision is made by the founding elites, which is later supported and electorally strengthened by the people. There is, therefore, a double decision: the first at an elite, the second at a mass level, which is manifested in the electoral success of democratic parties.[14] In this vein, the electoral success of the party (or parties) that made the installation is often very important. Thus, in Spain, for example, the breakdown of the UCD created the most difficult moment of the whole process, and the ability with which the Socialists replaced that party and created a democratic alternation was crucial, showing again how widespread democratic attitudes were within Spanish society. The second related aspect is that, in the beginning, a pro-democratic system may be created by a few actors or even by only one party. Later on, during the ensuing process of legitimation, this system may encompass other actors, as well, if only to a limited extent. If so, a virtual circle of legitimation is set in motion. Italy and Portugal are the clearest examples of this.[15]

Thus, on the whole, the reasons for the installation and successful maintenance of a democratic regime depend on a specific constellation of factors related to the memory of the past, a few current aspirations and problems, and the international context of each country in a given historical period. How is consolidation still possible if after a few years there is only a limited legitimacy, as in the Italian case?

Party Organization and Society

The analysis of stabilization in electoral behavior, in patterns of competition and in party elites, gives a preliminary picture of the party systems in the four countries under study.[16] In all cases there is stabilization, but this is highest in Italy and Greece, more recent in Portugal, and, on the whole, lower in Spain. The Spanish situation is mainly characterized by party splits or breakdowns and elite changes in the Right, the center, the extreme Left, and even in the regional parties. But such low stabilization is counteracted by a relatively higher electoral stabilization.

Nevertheless, a key question needs to be addressed, namely, how to explain the differences in form and extent of stabilization among the four party systems? The most obvious explanation is internal to party politics. That is, after the democratic installation, stable equilibrium is achieved in the competition among parties. Possible electoral gains and losses are mutually compensated for among the parties and, at least in appearance, no change occurs. The patterns of party competition remain unchanged. This is more so if a bipolarization emerges in such patterns.

In fact, the two cases with the highest stabilization (Italy and Greece) are also those with the strongest bipolarization. In other words, the hypothesis would seem to be: the higher the bipolarization, the higher the stability, provided that bipolarization does not also entail a move away from democracy. If in Greece a highly non-proportional electoral law may partially account for bipolarization, what are the other possible explanations of that stabilization suggested by our cases?

The development of party organization and of the relationships that are established between interest groups and parties seem to be a plausible answer. These two factors may be considered the two main means for controlling society from a party's perspective. In this and the next section, these phenomena are illustrated and the causal connections are examined.

With regard to the *organizational networks*, and at the same time the resulting relationship of "closeness" with society, the main purpose of organizational structuring is to maintain and enlarge a stable electorate that shares the ideology, values and programs of parties. It is well known, however, that a better, more articulated organization is achieved in special conditions where the ideological dimension is an important feature of the political conflict in the country.[17] At the same time, its main thrust also comes from the logic of party competition: the electoral dynamics, above all, induce parties to create organizational resources to win more votes and maintain their electorate.

First, the organizational aspects may be illustrated by *membership* and *affiliation rates*, as well as by the degree to which activists or militants are present, if such

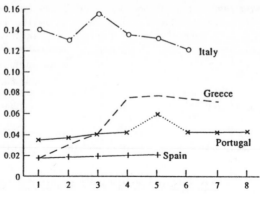

FIGURE 1. *Party Membership Rate.*

data are available. Despite their low reliability, they may still provide the best available measures, if trends rather than yearly figures are considered. Thus, if an estimate of people who are also party members is attempted, to find out the extent of party penetration into society or, from the opposite perspective, the extent of "partisan associability" of society, some interesting results immediately emerge.[18] First, Italy and Greece are the two countries with the highest party membership rate, but the stabilization is higher in Greece than in Italy. In addition, between them the difference in the development of party organization is strong (see Figure 1). Portugal has a lower degree of organization, but not of stabilization (although this is a recent development), and, in comparison, Spain has both a lower degree of development, and of stabilization. In other words, Figure 1 seems to suggest contradictory results. Furthermore, this figure may even suggest a lack of connection between the two phenomena. In fact, in Italy we find stabilization of electoral behavior, party systems and leadership, but at the same time a decline in party membership, and membership rate (Figure 1). In the other countries, even with lower stabilization (as in Spain), the membership rate remains stable.

Assuming that the estimates given in this figure are correct, a developed party organization, as measured by membership rate, is weakly related to stabilization. In addition, the Italian decline of membership rate may give a wrong idea of organization development. In fact, in this country the Left went through a phase of demobilization after the Resistance and civil war (this is explained in detail below), while Christian Democracy had a strong organizational development.

Regarding the trends in membership, both Figure 2 for Italy and Figure 3 for Spain show meaningful results. In Italy the growth concerns only the Christian Democrats; in Spain it refers to the Socialists. This seems to suggest a connection between incumbency (success at the polls) and the growth of membership. That is, the growth of membership paves the way to, and also follows the achievement of, government office. From this perspective, one may suggest that incumbency brings about the organizational growth of the ruling party. As for the other parties in both Spain and Italy, membership is either declining or holding steady.

However, other important differences between the Italian and Spanish democratic installations contradict the apparent connection between incumbency and the growth of membership. The two installations differ mostly in the degree of

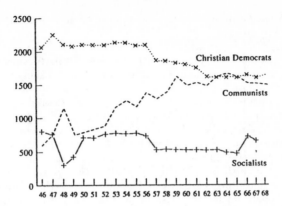

Figure 2. *Trends in Party Membership—Italy.*

mass mobilization that characterized the two processes. On a continuum from a maximum to a minimum of political mobilization, Italy stands at the first extreme and Spain at the second, with very limited popular participation that is also mirrored by a high percentage of abstention.[19] Thus, with regard to membership, the different degree of ideological mobilization (and bipolarization) means that in Italy the number of affiliated people is immediately very high, and much higher than that in Spanish parties (see also Figure 1).

In Italy, with the subsequent, inevitable, decline of mobilization, the high Communist membership was also bound to decline; in Spain this is immediately clear for the Communists (PCE), whose decline began after the first political election, in 1977 (see Figure 3).

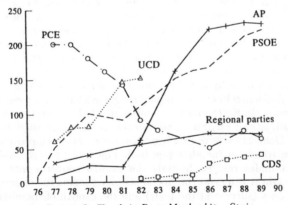

Figure 3. *Trends in Party Membership—Spain.*

In Italy, Christian Democracy has been the party in office from the beginning, that is, since the phase of transition, 1944–46. For this party the problem of building its own organizational network was already evident after the successful electoral results of 1948. In fact, these results came about thanks to the support of Catholic organizations. Later on, at the end of the 1940s and in the early 1950s, efforts were made mainly to build autonomous structures in order to counteract the Communist organization. Within these limits, incumbency is an additional element that accounts for a part of the growth. But it is not the only explanation: as I have just said, Christian Democracy has been the incumbent party since 1944, but the problem of organization emerged during the phase of consolidation and competition with the Communists. Curiously, after some attempt at organization, the Socialists failed to gain more members: they basically accepted an ancillary position vis-à-vis the Communists until the Hungarian uprising of 1956.

For Spain, too, the hypothesis of a relationship between incumbency and growth of membership is put in a better context if one looks at the beginning of the growth of the Socialist Party (PSOE) that took place after the transitional phase in 1976, and continued at a fairly steady pace also after the victorious election of 1982; basically there is no difference between the rate of growth before and after 1982. But electoral competition and the crisis of the UCD also pushed Alianza Popular (AP) toward higher electoral figures and in this case, again, the growth of 1982 was made possible by an increase in membership during the previous year.

What evidence is suggested by the Portuguese parties with regard to incumbency and the growth of membership? Do organizational developments in terms of membership precede electoral victory? May we affirm that such a development paved the way to the resounding success of the Social Democratic Party (PSD) in 1987, which brought about the change in the party system? First, growth of memberhip and electoral victory do not seem associated in the case of the Communists. During the second part of the 1970s and the early 1980s the growth of the Communist Party (PC) was substantial in terms of membership, but after 1983 an equally substantial electoral decline became evident, and even continued: from 18.9 percent in 1983 to 16.0 in 1985, 12.5 in 1987, and 9.0 in 1991. Second, for the PSD and the Socialist Party (PS) the connection between growth in membership and incumbency is not demonstrated. PSD has a steady increase in membership, but stronger growth is evident only when this party achieves a predominant position. From this perspective, the key aspect does not concern incumbency, but the fact of being the only governmental party. Regarding the PS, the decline in membership in the mid-1980s suggests the salience of factors such as the leadership crisis and the reaction of militants to the austerity policies of 1983–85.[20]

In the Greek case, membership figures for PASOK suggest a story that strengthens the conclusions reached for Portugal: the growth of PASOK's membership both preceded and followed the electoral victory of 1981. Even more specifically, after becoming the only governmental party, between 1981 and 1983, the membership nearly doubled, from 110 000 to 200 000. But later, scandals, a too-highly personalized management of public affairs and a poor economic performance by the Socialists caused an internal crisis that made it difficult to maintain the level of membership, which declined sharply to 100 000 in 1990.[21]

An additional question is: how did Italy become the country with the most highly developed party organization? The best answer is supported by research in Italy.[22] This suggests that the Fascist legacy, Catholic structures, ideology, the size of the public sector (see below) and, last but not least, polarization, were very relevant in maintaining those highly articulated structures. On the whole, a complex system was created with different kinds of parties and a number of related, ancillary organizations,[23] which taken together make a strong, continuous appeal to the public and are successful in creating those very stable links with it. This is also evident from the stabilization of electoral behavior. The development of the party organizational framework is, ultimately, one of the main features of Italian consolidation.

Party organizations in the other countries may be seen in contrast to the Italian case. In Spain, a complex, multifaceted modern society, which featured a waning ideology and where anti-party propaganda under Franco was maintained for many years, accounted for a low development in party organization.[24] But as is also suggested by the growth of party membership (see Figure 3), there was a trend toward some institutionalization of parties. There were not, however, the traditional "integration parties" or mass parties recalled by the Italian case of the 1950s, but catch-all organizations with a strong role played by the leaders and only secondary roles for members and the organization.

The dominant force in the party system, PSOE, is the best example of this. On paper the organizational model is the common one to be found in European Socialist parties. In actual fact, mainly between 1977 and 1981, but also later on, PSOE gradually changed through continuous adaptation from a radical divided leftist party to a unified, cohesive, integrated, centrist party of electors with a strong leadership.

After 1981–82 the organizational stabilization of PSOE was not complemented by a corresponding stabilization in the rightist Alianza Popular or in the centrist CDS or even in the Communists. If these organizational features are connected with the stabilization of a predominant party system, then the reason it was brought about may be better understood: such a stabilization, which concerns both the party system and its main actor, the PSOE, was made possible by the weakness and the internal instability of the other parties. Fragmentation and crisis in both organization and leadership are the most distinctive features of the PCE, which recently attempted rebirth through an electoral coalition with a few other leftist organizations, such as the Izquierda Unida (United Left). The picture would be incomplete without mentioning the regional parties. But there is no clear process of stabilization or development of organization for them, while at the same time different organizational models coexisted even in the same subsystem.[25]

On the whole, Spanish parties were altered by the development of the mass media and by the increasing role played by party leaders. There was not only a personalization of political life, but also centralization of the party and success only when unitarian, stable, strong leadership was established, as has been the case with PSOE. In addition, there were clear organizational differences among the national parties, such as the PSOE, AP, CDS, and PCE, and among the regional parties—some of them with more solid grass roots support than the national parties. At a national level, the low ideologization of political conflict and the correspondingly low polarization seem to provide the best explanation for the differences vis-à-vis Italy. No truly developed organizational network can be seen. The fairly stable party system was only based on the relative dominance and cohesion of PSOE, a party with a strong leadership, and at the same time on the weakness, division and instability of other parties. In other words, the stabilization of the party system is ironically confirmed by comparing the "light" structuring of the Socialists and the instability of the others. The change of only one of these aspects is also likely to change the party system.

In Portugal, the Communist Party has the most classical organization of all similar leftist forces, and this has been so from the beginning. That is, there was no trend toward organizational articulation because the party had a highly developed organization from the beginning. PCP was the only political organization with a strong leader, its own tradition of underground opposition, a tight control over membership, and a precise hierarchy of militants.[26] However, after the first period, the electoral decline also carried with it some organizational decline.

From an organizational perspective, the most distant party is the conservative CDS, a loosely structured coalition of independent politicians and local notables, founded in mid-1974 by officials of the previous authoritarian regime (see Bruneau and MacLeod, 1986; Stock, 1986). It may resemble, in many ways, the small Italian opinion parties, provided that a basic difference is stressed: CDS was not continuously in government, as were those parties. For this party, as well, it is very difficult to detect an evident trend toward a higher organizational articulation.

Given the following electoral developments and the established centripetal pattern of competition, for this analysis the two most important parties are the Socialists and the Social Democrats. Both are mass parties with highly organized structures on paper; but they are de facto, catch-all parties with internal factions, which also remained in serious conflict for years.

A profound transformation has also taken place in Greece, since the democratic inauguration, during the subsequent decade or more of consolidation. The key aspect concerns the evolution of the party system from a predominant party arrangement to a polarized, two-party system, with the marginalization and decline of the Communists. Thus, from the beginning (1974) Nea Democratia was a conservative party of notables, relying on "MPs and their clientelistic networks for communication with the electorate and rallying mass support" (Lirintzis, 1984: 106), as well as on a charismatic leader. But basically it had a weak organization.

On the other hand, PASOK resulted from the establishment of a well-structured mass organization in the subsequent years. It was grounded on a populist program, had a charismatic leader, and authoritarian management of internal affairs.[27] In 1977, and even more in 1980, the party had a high and growing membership. The role of Papandreu was very dominant and the middle-level party elite was weak and dependent on the upper echelons.[28] The internal organization itself was, above all, a link between leader and masses; and party activists and cadres drew their legitimation from the relationship with the leader rather than with party members and sympathizers.[29] Also, the transformation into a catch-all party before 1981 and the building of the first non-communist mass party in Greece was a decision made by its dynamic leader.

The elections of 1981 brought about a change in the party in office (from ND to PASOK) and a bipolarization occurred with the disappearance of other center and rightist formations. These two elements had a strong impact on the organization of both parties. Thus, PASOK became much weaker in terms of grass-roots organization. At the same time, Nea Democratia gradually changed its organization, partly because a third factor came into play. That is, ND lost not only its leader, with the election of Karamanlis as president of the Republic, but it also lost office after 1981. Both successors to Karamanlis, Averoff and Mitsotakes, made great efforts to reorganize the party at a local level. And their success was made possible by the high level of established bipolar competition with PASOK, favored by the highly disproportionate electoral law.

To conclude this organizational analysis, two further points should be made. First, if a more quantitative examination casts a few doubts on the connection between the stability of party system (and parties) and party organization (see Figure 2), the addition of qualitative features stresses that in Italy there is a higher stability and also the most developed party organization, whereas in Spain both of these are very low. But organization is not the only explanation. In fact, in Greece there is high stability, as in Italy, but there is less developed party organization. In the former, during the 1980s, in spite of ND's efforts and even its successes, the most characteristic mark of the phase of consolidation does not seem to have been the development of party organizational networks, but rather the "occupation" of the state by the incumbent party, which was PASOK for most of the decade. Thus, an analysis of the relationship between parties and interest groups becomes necessary.

Second, this analysis suggests that a well-developed party organization is not a recurring, necessary feature of democratic consolidation. In fact, Spain contradicts such an hypothesis. However, when the consolidation of a specific kind of democratic regime is considered, party organizational aspects may be more or less important in characterizing the specific pattern of consolidation.

Parties, Interests and the State

A stable, developed organizational structure of one or more parties in a party system may be a condition for democratic consolidation. In a nutshell, the *control* of society by political elites in order to consolidate their power may also be achieved through party organization, including ancillary organizations. Our cases, however, suggest that this is not the only way of gaining this sort of control. A second possibility lies in the establishment of relationships between the parties and more or less organized interest groups or sectors of society through the processes of decision making, the distribution of state resources, or in other ways. In this case the links with the public stem not from ideology and organization, but from economic interest. This is the party control over organized and non-organized interest groups, individuals and micro-interests, directly or through the public sector.

A way of looking at relationships and links between parties and interest groups, or individuals, is to see whether parties and the party system as a whole are able to perform a "gatekeeping" role in controlling access to the decisional arena. If so, for interest groups, party intermediation is the best way to protect their interests.[30] Gatekeeping may become one of the main aspects in the process of consolidation since it causes the most relevant sectors of the public to accept the role of parties and their control over them.

It is possible to sketch at least three scenarios for the party/group relationship, with or without a direct role for the public sector. The first, *dominance* or in a stronger form, *occupation*, envisages the situation where the party system largely dominates society in general, and interest groups in particular. From the beginning, or shortly thereafter, interest groups become mainly ancillary organizations for the parties, which have very solid sources of power in terms of ideology, internal organization and full control of a large public sector. With regard to the public economic sector, not only is it very large, but all positions in that sector have to be filled by party appointment. The second scenario, *neutrality*, foresees no definite links between groups and parties. Parties have their power bases and control of the decision-making process, which reside mainly in the rules of the democratic regime. Basically, they perform a gatekeeping role. More or less organized groups and people are compelled to appeal to parties and party leaders to promote and protect their interests. But no special strong relationship is established between a group and a particular party. This means that the groups are in a more independent position vis-à-vis parties. In the third possibility, *direct access*, interest groups bypass parties (and party elites) because of personal relationships with parliamentary members, ministries and the bureaucracy, or in other ways. Parties have weak autonomous bases and sources of power and they are not able to achieve stronger ones. They perform no gatekeeping role.[31]

To understand how the relationship between parties and interest groups may be defined, three main domains can be taken into consideration. The first directly concerns the relationship between parties and entrepreneurs or propertied organizations; the second relates to parties and unions; and the third is associated with policies toward people or organized and non-organized interests, through the resources of the state-owned economic sector.

In Italy, the 1950s were a period of *party dominance* vis-à-vis society.[32] With regard to interest groups in the agricultural sector, the most meaningful relationhip involved the DC, on the one hand, and Confagricoltura and Coldiretti, on the other. At first, after 1945, the association of landowners, the Confagricoltura, was obliged to defend the interests of its members in the new democratic context and to seek the support of the parties and their leaders, to opt for neutrality and a multi-party appeal. Later on, in the 1950s, this association finally approached the governmental party, DC, and at the same time sought to develop a privileged relationship with other rightist parties, above all the PLI,[33] in order to carry out a dual strategy of internal and external influence of Christian Democracy. This did not apply to the association of small landowners, the Coldiretti, whose political relationship with the DC was that between the party and its trade union. The relationship between the party and the organization of small farmers is better defined in terms of the *dominance* by the party over the latter.

In the industrial sector, as well, the DC was dominant, through a penetration of state-owned enterprises, and the marginalization and isolation of the organized groups of the Left. Basically, party control over access to the decision-making arena was challenged neither by the industrial entrepreneurs' association, the Confindustria, nor by the trade unions. DC dominance vis-à-vis the industrialists was characterized by different phases. Until the exit of the Left from the governing majority (May 1947), the influence of the Confindustria and, more generally, of the entrepreneurs, was very limited and mainly channeled via the PLI. The second major phase started after May 1947: the DC was strong at both a political and a parliamentary level, but it needed an industrial sector committed to reconstruction. It was thus forced to concede decision-making space and influence in the management of economic policy in the solution of the most pressing industrial problems, to the Confindustria, which had maintained its privileged relationship with the bureaucracy from the outset.[34] The third phase of party dominance came when the Confindustria suffered a decline in both membership and political initiative (1953). At this point the DC was weaker in terms of parliamentary seats, but considerably stronger on other levels as a result of party organization, the expansion of the public sector, and credit facilities managed by the public banks. In addition, the fragmentation of entrepreneurs as an interest group had occurred when public entrepreneurs left the Confindustria, and formed a new association of public entrepreneurs, the Intersind.

Also the relationship between parties and trade unions changed with time. In the first period of transition and installation, party dominance was clear-cut and strong: ideological divisions absorbed all aspects of activity and the electoral mobilization of the trade unions was strong and embedded in the overall political mobilization of these years. With the split in the trade unions (1949–50), a second phase began. The parties became even more dominant, partly because of fragmentation and the decline in union membership and participation. A further confirmation of party dominance of the trade unions is the fact that during this period the latter never adopted a clearly autonomous position in the area of industrial relations.[35]

In the picture of party and interest group relationships, the importance of the expansion of the public sector has to be stressed. In the agricultural sector, the Federconsorzi, agrarian reform agencies, public pension agencies, and the agency for the development of Southern Italy (Cassa per il Mezzorgiorno) conditioned all relations between the main party in power, the DC, and the interest group associations. The same applied in the industrial sector. The role played by the Institute for Industrial Reconstruction (IRI) in economic reconstruction, the creation of ENI, the public oil company, (1953) and the Ministry for State Investments (1956), the laws on petroleum products (1957), the activity of the Cassa per il Mezzorgiorno in the industrial sector, the presence of the public banks and the creation of a series of public agencies, all controlled by parties in government, defined and characterized the bases of relationships between governmental parties with entrepreneurs and trade unions.[36] Thus, a clientelistic system, which is at the base of particularistic ties between parties, such as DC, PLI, PSDI, and the public in some southern areas of the country, was basically set up in the 1950s, with the establishment and enlargement of the state-owned economic sector.[37]

The Spanish picture is the very opposite of the Italian one. A different authoritarian tradition, a society and economy developed along different lines at the moment of change, an international situation no longer violently polarized, are the main factors explaining the great distance between the two cases. First, the diversities within the agricultural sector are also mirrored by the several associations set up in these years. In addition, none of them achieved either high political salience or a definite, precise connection with a specific party.[38] The problem of legitimation even as an interest group, which existed in Italy during the 1940s, was not present here during the 1970s and later. Thus, there was no sense in a rightist, perhaps ambiguously democratic, political force becoming the monopolistic representative of such an interest group or of some agricultural association. The political *neutrality* of these associations and the differentiation in the voting behavior of the people belonging to this sector were obvious.[39]

The situation in the industrial sector was organizationally different, but similar in its relationships with parties. In fact, the association of industrial entrepreneurs, the CEOE, also assumed a position of *neutrality* vis-à-vis the parties and the party system as a whole, with a clear distinction between the period before and after 1982. But a well-defined distance always remained between the CEOE and the political class (Pérez Diaz, 1987: 164). From the beginning, the entrepreneurs had no bonds with the centrist UCD. On the contrary, there was a period of tension and conflict during 1977–78 when entrepreneurs protested against the Moncloa Pacts (1977)— that is, mainly the economic agreements reached among the social partners and the government—and governmental economic policy. Later on (1981), an attempt was made to create a party very close to the industrial entrepreneurs, formed by parts of UCD, already in the process of breaking up, and Alianza Popular.[40] This attempt was also justified by the centrist political attitudes of the CEOE and the sympathy for Alianza.[41] Finally, since 1982, given the moderate, pragmatic policies of Socialist cabinets and at the same time the greater strength of the employers associations, a sympathetic neutrality vis-à-vis the Socialist governments was clearly established. An entire decade of economic agreements also contributed to this result, which further strengthened the autonomy, identity and position of employers.[42]

Italy II

During the democratic installation, the main trade unions were the Comisiones Obreras (CCOO), very close to the Communists and already well-organized and rooted in different sectors; the General Union of Workers (UGT) close to the Socialists, and minor independent unions or regionalist associations in the Basque country. In the following years the elections allow us to see the increasing success of UGT, the decline of CCOO and of nationalist unions. From our point of view, what is more important to stress is that since 1980, or even earlier,[43] unions have been considered to be moderate associations, open to bargaining and coordinated action, while any connection between parties and unions has been turned down.[44] In the following years, both the orthodox Socialist economic policies and the moderate stance of the unions led to a greater and greater distance between the Socialist Party and UGT, culminating in the anti-governmental and, consequently, anti-socialist strike of UGT in December 1990.

When the public sector is analyzed, the difference with Italy again emerges. In Spain in a very different economic context, the public sector had shrunk when an industrial plan involving several sectors was almost fully implemented during the 1980s.[45] Despite this, however, in both countries patronage is widespread. Several authors[46] and the press have repeatedly stressed the prevalence of the *spoils system*, or *sottogoverno*, by which thousands of appointments to administrative posts are made both at the national and at the local level, as well as in the existing public sector.[47]

Thus, when we address the question of how the party system was able to achieve its gatekeeping position, the reply seems evident. Not only is the control of the agenda in decision making made possible thanks to the dominant governmental party, but also, the relationship between people and the state is mediated by thousands of professionals in the administration and the public sector. To this, two other considerations should be added. First, because of the mechanisms just described, a large social stratum acquired a strong vested interest both in the maintenance of the existing democracy and in the control of society. Second, the predominant party system at a national level and in many regions, a few strict rules of government, contained above all in parliamentary regulations, in favor of the incumbent party and, at the same time, a strong and unified Socialist leadership, all account for this outcome. There was no real need to build a large party organization: during recent years, ideology and the Cold War, again so "useful" in the Italian case, have moved offstage. Thus, the party system as a whole, and the specific parties, maintain the kind of relationship defined as *neutral*, vis-à-vis the fairly organized interest groups. At the same time, however, a partisan penetration of the state gives the predominant party the possibility of controlling large sectors of society.

Portugal and Greece are closer to the Italian experience than to the Spanish one. For Portugal, the point of departure is the attempt to install a radical, socialist regime. More precisely, both the Constitution of 1976 and a law in 1977 created a very large public sector. Thus, a state monopoly was established in banking and insurance, as well as in all the basic industries and infrastructure industries. Also, the mass media were mainly placed in public ownership. Only with the constitutional revision of August 1989, following a bill in 1983 that had already softened that situation of monopoly was this situation fully reversed. In the agricultural sector, as a result of the agrarian reforms, several cooperatives were created.[48]

All this led to a very different arrangement from that in Spain. Industrial entrepreneurs, for instance, and their two associations, until very recently, had been largely delegitimated by their previous support for the Salazar regime and remained very weak. No autonomous or neutral role of any kind was possible for them.[49] On the other hand, the unions were and are closely linked to the parties. First, the powerful Intersindical Nacional was very close to the Communists. By adopting an old orthodox wording, one could define the unions as having been almost a "transmission belt" for the Communist Party for many years. Only recently (1989–90), following the breakdown of the Communist regimes in Eastern Europe, did the close relationship begin to change.[50] The second most important union, UGT, is linked to the Socialists, but also to the Social Democrats. These links were so strong as to induce the unions always to adopt strategies determined by partisan goals. In addition, the problems that concerned labor in a strict sense were also politicized.[51]

As a result, the party system has achieved its gatekeeping role through a non-linear process, with several moments of crisis and pronounced governmental instability. But in the second half of the 1980s, even the quadripartite Council formed by representatives of the unions, entrepreneurs, landowners, and the government, was entirely dominated by the government. The key point is that this position was achieved because of the resources provided by such a large public sector. Thus, there is a party dominance, which resembles the Italian case, but in comparative terms there are two differences: on the one hand, party organization is less developed and, on the other hand, the *state resources* are relatively larger and consequently the private sector is smaller than in Italy. As in Italy and Spain, in Portugal administrative appointments are common, and there has even been an increase in the size of the bureaucracy.[52] It is likely that all this paved the way to the further key development in the party system: its transformation from a four-party pluralism to a predominant-party system (see above).

At this point it is possible to stress a basic difference between Portugal and the other two countries. In Spain the predominant position in the party system was achieved because of electoral success and the breakdown of the UCD; the gatekeeping role came afterwards. Likewise, in Italy the predominant position—although not as strong as in Spain—is also the result of electoral success, thanks to Catholic support and anticommunist feelings; the gatekeeping role became clear after the elections of 1948 and later. As for Portugal, the gatekeeping role was gradually achieved thanks to the resources of the public sector, which paved the way to the victory of the PSD in 1987 and the consequent transformation of the party system. It should be recalled that between 1983 and 1985 the "central block" was also formed by Socialists. The discontent against them, which coalesced and was expressed by the new party created by President Eanes, and then the loss of their leader (Soares) when he was elected to the presidency, left a vacuum for the Social Democrats, who were able to use it to their advantage. With some caution, due to the partial unreliability of the data, this interpretation is also supported by a sharp decline in Socialist membership after 1983–84.

In the case of Greece, the industrial groups were also weak, as were their associations. As in Portugal, immediately after the democratic inauguration, the Greek industrial interest groups were largely delegitimated because of their ties with the former military regime. During these years, they were not close to Nea Democratia and were openly hostile to the radical PASOK. Later on, after 1983–84 and above all since 1985, their previously conflictual relationship with the Socialists changed, but the Socialist economic policies also became much less radical and more orthodox. By contrast, unions were closely linked to political parties, the Communists more than the Socialists, but at the same time they were fully dependent on funds from the Ministry of Labor. The strong party dominance or, in this case, their occupation of the unions, is further demonstrated by Mavrogordatos (1988) when he discusses party penetration into cooperative, as well as a number of other different associations, even in the agricultural sector.

In Greece, as in Portugal, the position of weak entrepreneurs, dependent unions and other penetrated associations was compounded by a large public sector. During the first PASOK government, this sector was further expanded. For example, not only numerous industrial enterprises, but also banks and insurance companies were included in the public sector. That is, on the whole, nearly 90 percent of financial agencies became state-owned. Moreover, while in power, PASOK governments passed an impressive amount of administrative legislation so that the party totally subordinated state bureaucracy.[53] Thus, party occupation during the PASOK decade seemed to be increasingly penetrating and widespread, so much so that some Socialist supporters expressed concern about the weakening of the Socialist organization.[54] In fact, after they took over the government in 1981, party appointments to the public sector became so numerous that the party organization was largely deprived of people. Although the Greek case is the only one where alternation is a real possibility, and where it actually took place twice (1981 and 1990), the dominance of the Socialists is again the key to understanding the gatekeeping role they performed during their decade in office. On the whole, in Greece the process paralleled that which took place in Portugal, though the different processes of transition and installation of democracy and also the resulting different party systems (a bipartisan system in Greece, and a predominant-party system in Portugal) mainly account for their differences during the years of consolidation.

Empirical Patterns of Democratic Consolidation

With regard to the bottom–up consensual relationship toward institutions, legitimation plays a crucial role in different domains, not only at the level of parties (and the party system). The two poles consist of an incomplete, limited legitimation (*exclusive legitimation*) and a full legitimation (*inclusive legitimation*) of institutions through parties (and the party system).

Thus, in Italy, about fifteen years after the democratic inauguration, the legitimacy achieved was partial and limited. If the positions of the Right and of most of the Left are considered, this may be labeled an *exclusive legitimacy*. Greece represents the opposite case, above all from the moment when the Communists participated in a government with Nea Democratia (1989–90). Largely *inclusive legitimacy* may also be defined as that achieved by Spain, in which some local anti-regime forces may be ignored by the end of the 1980s. Because of the position of the Communists, Portugal still presents some limitation of legitimacy. Thus, the Portuguese case is a *quasi-inclusive legitimacy*.

When the second dimension of the process, *control*, is considered, there are two main possibilities:

(i)   institutions attain a firm control over society up to the point of dominating it through parties (and their organization), state institutions or both (*dominance*); or

(ii) a more active, autonomous, society and/or a situation of low development in party organization gives society more autonomy vis-à-vis state institutions and parties (*neutrality*).

Thus, with regard to internal party organization, Italy stands out as a case in which ideology, initial mass mobilization and bipolarization brought about a more developed party organization, thanks also to Catholic groups, authentic ancillary associations for Christian Democracy. In Spain the opposite is true. The combination of a long, traditional anti-party propaganda under Franco, the waning of ideology, and the modernization of a complex society were strong obstacles to party organization. The development of mass media and other techniques in a modern society led party leaders to appreciate other party models and to transform the old organization based on cells and sections. As shown by my analysis (see above), Greece and Portugal are in the middle, but closer to the Italian case than the Spanish one. After all, strong bipolarization and some ideological tenets contributed to the organizational development of PASOK and, later on, to the transformation and organizational development of Nea Democratia. The same applies to the Portuguese Social Democrats in their competition with the Socialists. Although to a different degree, in all four countries there was a partisan occupation of the state: the phenomenon was relatively smaller in the case of Spain, but greater in the other three countries. Thus, *neutrality* characterizes the relationships between parties and interest groups in Spain; party *dominance* is typical of Italy; in Greece a more accentuated *occupation* during the PASOK decade was the rule; and Portugal again lay between Italy and Greece.

Therefore, in the end the inferences to be drawn from our cases seem to be the following:

(i)   When legitimacy is restricted, if some forms of elite stabilization, party organization and/or control of organized and non-organized groups is not clearly achieved, then even a weak consolidation is not possible, and sooner or later a crisis will occur.[55]

(ii) If, on the contrary, there is widespread democratic legitimacy from the beginning, or shortly thereafter, less party control of society is necessary to achieve consolidation.

(iii) If, in addition to widespread legitimacy, there is a partisan control of society, the second phenomenon is not decisive for the consolidation (see above), but it is still important in characterizing both the process of consolidation and the pattern of consolidated democracy. To fail to analyze this aspect would hinder a deeper understanding of the whole topic.

At this point the main patterns of consolidation may be sketched. If the legitimation of institutions is only partially achieved, then the role of parties and even of other institutions, which penetrate and dominate society, is a necessity for consolidation. Thus, party structures essentially organize and at the same time maintain internal divisions by encapsulating them. When this is the case, party-based consolidation or *party consolidation* is achieved.

In the case of wide legitimation, party structuring is unnecessary; if there is widespread support for democratic values, the role played by elites may be central and quite sufficient for achieving a flexible pattern of consolidation, where adaptation and change is always possible without a serious crisis. This is the elite-based consolidation, or *elite consolidation.*

There are two other possibilities. One involves wide legitimation and the control of society through a large public sector, as well as parties rooted in society which bring about a process of consolidation that is defined here as state-based consolidation or *state consolidation.* When, however, the traditions of the country, historical timing and other features do not allow either a strong control of society or a wide legitimation of democratic institutions, there is only *maintenance*. No consolidation is possible, and a crisis is always likely. Exclusive and weak legitimacy, no party dominance, a fairly developed party system, but one that lacks strong links with various sectors of society would be the main characteristics of this model. In this pattern, only an international context favorable to democracy will allow the existence of such a regime. That is, in this fourth case, the international aspects, which have deliberately been excluded from the picture, may become crucial to the resulting pattern (and the continuation of the regime).

If limited legitimacy, party stabilization, and partisan dominance are stressed, the Italian experience may be labeled a *party consolidation*. In Spain, the process has developed in a very different way. Here, there is no strong stabilization of the party system which is characterized only by a relative continuity, of the political class, no structuring of parties, and a neutral gatekeeping role, however, the Socialist Party and its leader, Felipe González, occupy a key position in the party system and, at the same time, a widespread legitimacy has been achieved in a limited number of years. Therefore, from the point of view of the main actors in the process, Spain features an *elite consolidation*.

In Greece and Portugal some aspects are more similar to the first model and others are closer to the second one. Particularly in Greece there is a strong stabilization of the party system, characterized by continuity in voting behavior, stabilization of the political class, a fairly strong internal party organization and, at the same time, the control of civil society by the incumbent party and a great role played by the public sector, which additionally strengthens that control. The extent of legitimacy grows to the point where it is very close to the Spanish case. Thus, the best definition seems to be *state consolidation*.

Finally, in Portugal, there are various concurrent elements: the recent stabilization of the party system, some stabilization of the political class, a relatively developed internal party organization, party dominance and a strong role played by the public sector until the end of the 1980s, when a reform of the Constitution (1989) permitted some development of private enterprise, quasi-legitimacy, but without the complete integration of the Communist Party. Thus, we again have *state consolidation* with an important role played by the old corporatist authoritarian tradition.

The whole picture is roughly sketched in Figure 4. This figure shows that the strong role of parties may be complemented by limited legitimacy. And also, that widespread legitimacy may be complemented by a weaker intervention of parties in

| | | Legitimation | |
		Exclusive	Inclusive
	Dominance	party consolidation *Italy*	state consolidation *Portugal Greece*
Control			
	Neutrality	maintenance	*Spain* elite consolidation

FIGURE 4: *Models and Cases of Democratic Consolidation.*

society. But it also stresses that at the same time parties, state resources, and legitimacy may contribute to consolidation.

To conclude, this analysis provides support to the hypothesis that there are at least two different patterns of consolidation: one achieved through legitimation and a limited control of society and another through a stronger control that compensates for the limited legitimation. It also suggests that the stabilization of the party system is partially related to consolidation. That is, consolidation may be achieved with low stability and broad legitimation.

Additional confirmation that the process discussed here has definitely been concluded in Portugal, Greece and Spain and that the main aspects of Italian consolidation are changing, is provided by the following facts. In Greece the new government of Nea Democratia seems to have inaugurated a new phase of politics in 1990, so that the main elements that characterized PASOK governments have changed. In addition, PASOK again won the 1993 elections and was returned to power. In Portugal, after 1989, the Social Democratic government made a number of decisions aimed at opening and enlarging the private sector and, thus, in this country also some of the most important features of the past few years will disappear. In Spain, the Socialists lost their majority in the 1993 election, but they remained in power, supported by other forces. In this way, one of the most characterizing elements of Spanish consolidation disappeared. Finally, in Italy, after so many years and recurring crises, the most important features of consolidation have recently been disappearing or changing: party organization is fading away; the planned privatization of a number of agencies, banks and industries will shrink the public sector; parties are no longer able to dominate interest groups; a new party system is emerging. Actually, since the end of the 1980s Italy has entered a new phase of deconsolidation and crisis, which will culminate in the transformation of the present democracy. The approval of two new electoral (quasi-majority) laws for the Senate and Chamber of Deputies in early August 1993 is only the first step in this direction.

Notes

1. More precisely, within the time span under consideration, I refer to the years that follow the installation, during which the core of the process takes place. That is, I expect that the most important features of consolidation will take place within ten to twelve years after the installation. However, the process may go on until signs of crisis and profound change emerge. Basically, the reason for this is the positive role that the passage of time may play. To be more specific, consolidation may partially come to an end in some aspects, while it continues in others, which may also keep changing. All this makes the precise indication of a final point of democratic consolidation more difficult, as a whole, and makes necessary this rather arbitrary assumption (which, however, should be submitted to subsequent empirical evidence).
2. See Morlino (1986).
3. They had broken away from the Socialists in January 1947.
4. See Sartori (1976).
5. A good way of complementing this analysis with other empirical measures at a mass level is to look at the party polarization index. It shows that in 1981, in Greece, the distance between the extreme parties, Nea Democratia and the Communists, on a left–right continuum was .73 (Seferiades, 1986: 426); at the end of the 1970s in Spain it was much lower: .47; in Italy, in the middle of the same decade, it was .64, that is, between Greece and Spain (Sani and Sartori, 1983). However, there is no systematic work on these measures for other years, nor for Portugal. On Spain, see also Sani and Shabad (1986).

164   *Consolidation and Party Government in Southern Europe*

6. To this, the disaffection and alienation from the regime at a mass level should be added. See Morlino and Montero (1994).
7. Only a problem of space prevents me from closely examining these stops and reversals in the legitimation.
8. For details, see Morlino (1991a).
9. See Maravall (1981) and Pérez Díaz (1991).
10. Here, the Spanish Socialist "Bad Godesberg" should be recalled (see above).
11. See Gunther (1992).
12. See Pérez Díaz (1987).
13. Without this basic support—at least since 1981—it is impossible to understand the constitutional revision, approved in 1982, and the law on the army passed in the same year, which changed the regime. In fact, this was a turning point in the neutralization of the army and in the removal of army "protection" for the regime, which had made that democracy an odd case until then.
14. Of course, this second decision is greatly "helped" by the electoral law and by the ability of a democratic party (or parties) to "control" civil society.
15. This point warrants a much closer analysis than is possible here.
16. For the empirical details concerning these aspects, see Morlino (1994).
17. The relationships between ideology and organization are well-illustrated by Barnes (1966).
18. This measure is similar to that adopted by Bartolini (1983: 189), with reference only to membership of social democratic parties.
19. See Montero (1992).
20. However, some of the Portuguese data seem unreliable. Particularly, those of the Communist Party, which after 1988 no longer provided figures on membership, and those of the PSD and PS in 1983.
21. It is not possible to say much about membership in other parties, except to give some low figures of KKE (12 000 in 1983 and 14 000 in 1984) and an exceptional growth of ND after 1985: from 200 000 in 1986 to 400 000 in 1991. Membership stood at 20 000 in 1977 and 97 000 in 1979, that is in the initial but predominant phase of the party. Figures on the ND were given to the author by Takis Pappas.
22. See Barnes (1967), Tarrow (1967), Alberoni (1968).
23. Firstly, the Catholic organizations. On the main interest associations linked to parties, see the next section.
24. For other important considerations on this topic, see Linz (1986: 657ff.).
25. For details on these parties, see Morlino (1993).
26. See, among others, Alves da Costa e Sousa (1983), Bruneau and MacLeod (1986), Pacheco Pereira (1988), Gaspar (1990).
27. See Diamandouros (1991).
28. See also Spourdalakis (1988).
29. See, especially, Sotiropoulos (1991: ch. 3).
30. This analysis is developed in my own research on interest groups in Italy during the period 1945–58.
31. This is a very simplified presentation of a set of relationships between parties and groups, developed in Morlino (1991b) and applied to the Italian case.
32. See also Farneti (1973: 31–40).
33. But, in fact, in some areas of southern Italy, the two small monarchical parties and the MSI need to be included.
34. The research carried out by La Palombara (1964) focuses, primarily, on this aspect.
35. As proof of this, we can also mention the renewed debate on the incompatibility between political office and trade unions after 1958, when there were clear signs of the strengthening of the trade unions in the labor negotiations.
36. For a reconstruction of this aspect, see Maraffi (1991: esp. chaps. 7 and 8), who stresses the role of Fanfani in the construction of the public sector.
37. See Pasquino (1980: 95), and Graziano (1980). A much more detailed analysis of relation-

ships between interest groups and parties in Italy during the 1940s and 1950s can be found in Morlino (1991a).

38. See Pérez Díaz (1987: ch. 13).
39. For a fairly complete picture of agricultural organizations, see De la Fluente Blanco (1991).
40. See also López Nieto (1988).
41. See Pérez Díaz (1987: 163).
42. See also Pérez Díaz (1987: 82). There are only a few studies on entrepreneurs. In addition to Pérez Díaz (1987), see Martínez and Pardo Avellaneda (1985), on business attitudes, as well as Rijnen (1985), and Jerez Mir (1982).
43. See Pérez Díaz (1987: ch. 8).
44. The complex relationships of influence, not control, during the first years of democracy are explored in detail by Fishman (1990: esp. 163ff.).
45. According to the OCDE, one of the outcomes of this plan has been the dismissal of nearly 30 percent of public sector workers.
46. See, e.g., once again, Pérez Díaz (1987: 71), Gillespie (1990: 132); Cotarelo (1992: 307).
47. Based on press accounts, Gillespie (1990: 132) mentions the 25 000 appointments between 1984 and 1987.
48. See Avila de Lima (1991), De Lucena and Gaspar (1992).
49. See De Lucena and Gaspar (1991).
50. See Taborda Barreto (1991: 459ff.).
51. See Stoleroff (1988), Taborda Barreto (1991), and De Lucena and Gaspar (1991). A new situation began to emerge only in recent years (Stoleroff, 1990).
52. See De Vasconcelos (1990: Table 5).
53. A thorough, excellent analysis of this phenomenon has been carried out by Sotiropoulos (1991).
54. See also Spourdalakis (1988: 242ff.), who correctly analyzes the problems and consequences of incumbency for PASOK's internal organization.
55. See Linz (1978) and Morlino (1981).

References

Alberoni, F. (ed.) (1968). *L'attivista di partito.* Bologna: Il Mulino.
Alves da Costa e Sousa, V. (1983). "O Partido Comunista Portugues (subsidio para um estudo sobre os seus adeptos)." *Estudos Politicos e Sociais,* 11: 497–543.
Avila de Lima, J. (1991). "As organizaçoes agricolas socioprofissionaais em Portugal e a integraçao europeia (1974–85)." *Analise Social,* 26: 209–239.
Barnes, S. (1966). "Ideology and the Organization of Conflict: On the Relationship between Political Thought and Behavior." *Journal of Politics,* 28: 513–530.
Barnes, S. (1967). *Party Democracy: Politics in an Italian Socialist Federation.* New Haven: Yale University Press.
Bartolini, S. (1983). "The Membership of Mass Parties: The Social Democratic Experience, 1889–1978." In *Western European Party Systems: Continuity and Change,* (H. Daalder and P. Mair, eds.). London and Beverly Hills: Sage Publications.
Bruneau, T.C. and A. Macleod (1986). *Politics in Contemporary Portugal: Parties and the Consolidation of Democracy.* Boulder: Lynne Rienner Publishers.
Cotarelo, R. (ed.) (1992). *Transición politica y consolidación democrática: España (1975–1986).* Madrid: Centro de Investigaciones Sociológicas.
De la Fuente Blanco, G. (1991). *Las organizaciones agrarias españolas: El asociacionismo sindical de los agricultores y ganaderos españoles en la perspectiva de la Unidad Europea.* Madrid: Instituto de Estudios Económicos.
De Lucena, M. and C. Gaspar (1991). "Metamorfoses corporativas?—Associaçoes de interesses económicos e institucionalizaçao da democracia em Portugal." *Analise Social,* 27: 847–903.

De Lucena, M. and C. Gaspar (1992). "Metamorfoses corporativas?—Associaçoes de inter-esses económicos e institucionalizaçao da democracia em Portugal (II)." *Analise Social*, 28: 135–187.

De Vasconcelos, A. (1990). "Sociedade, partidos e estado em Portugal." Unpublished paper.

Diamandouros, N. (1991). "PASOK and State–Society: Relations in Post-Authoritarian Greece (1974–1986)." In *Greece on the Road to Democracy: From the Junta to PASOK 1974–1986*, (S. Vryonis, ed.). New Rochelle, N.Y.: Caratzas Publishers.

Farneti, P. (1973). "Introduzione." In *Il sistema politico italianso*, (P. Farneti, ed.). Bologna: Il Mulino.

Fishman, R. (1990). *Working-Class Organization and the Return to Democracy in Spain*. Ithaca, N.Y.: Cornell University Press.

Gaspar, C. (1990). "Portuguese Communism since 1976: Limited Decline." *Problems of Communism*, 3: 45–63.

Ghini, C. (1982). "Gli iscritti al partito e alla FGCI 1943/1979." In *Il Partito Comunista Italiano: struttura e storia dell'organizzazione*, (M. Ilardi and A. Accornero, eds.). Milano: Feltrinelli.

Gillespie, R. (1990). "Regime Consolidation in Spain: Party, State and Society." In *Securing Democracy*, (G. Pridham, ed.). London and New York: Routledge.

Graziano, L. (1980). *Clientelismo e sistema politico: Il caso dell'Italia*. Milano: Angeli.

Gunther, R. (1992). "Spain: the Very Model of Modern Elite Settlement." In *Elite and Democratic Consolidation in Latin America and Southern Europe*, (J. Higley and R. Gunther, eds.). Cambridge: Cambridge University Press.

Jerez Mir, M. (1982). *Business and Politics in Spain: From Francoism to Democracy*. Barcelona: Institut de Ciències Politique i Socials.

La Palombara, J. (1964). *Interest Groups in Italian Politics*. Princeton: Princeton University Press.

Linz, J. (1978). "Crisis, Breakdown, and Reequilibration." In *The Breakdown of Democratic Regimes*, (J.J. Linz and A. Stepan, eds.). Baltimore: Johns Hopkins University Press.

Linz, J. (1986). "Consideraciones Finales." In *Crisis y Cambio: electores y partidos en la Espana de los anos ochenta*, (J. Linz and J.R. Montero, eds.). Madrid: Centro de Estudios Constitucionales.

López Nieto, L. (1988). *Alianza Popular: estructura y evolución electoral de un partido conservador (1976–1982)*. Madrid: Centro de Investigaciones Sociológicas.

Lyrintzis, C. (1984). "Political Parties in Post–Junta Greece: A Case of 'Bureaucratic Clientelism'." In *The New Mediterranen Democracies: Regime Transition in Spain, Greece and Portugal*, (G. Pridham, ed.), pp. 99–118. London: Frank Cass.

Maraffi, M. (1991). *Politica ed economia in Italia: La vicenda dell'impresa pubblica dagli anni trenta agli anni cinquanta*. Bologna: Il Mulino.

Maravall, J.M. (1981). *La política de la transición 1975–80*. Madrid: Taurus.

Martínez, R. and R. Pardo Avellaneda (1985). "El asociacionismo empresarial español en la transición." *Papeles de economía española*, 22: 84–114.

Montero, J.R. (1992). "Las elecciones legislativas." In *Transición política y consolidación democrática*, (R. Cotarelo, ed.). Madrid: Centro de Investigaciones Sociológicas.

Morlino, L. (1981). *Dalla democrazia all'autoritarismo: Il caso spagnolo in prospettiva comparata*. Bologna: Il Mulino.

Morlino, L. (1986). "Consolidamento democratico: definizione e modelli." *Rivista italiana di scienza politica*, 16: 197–238.

Morlino, L. (1991a). "Democratic Consolidations in Southern Europe: Theoretical Guidelines for Empirical Analysis." Unpublished paper.

Morlino, L. (1991b). *Costruire la democrazia: Gruppi e partiti in Italia*. Bologna: Il Mulino.

Morlino, L. (1995). "Political Parties and Democratic Consolidation in Southern Europe." In *The Politics of Democratic Consolidation in Southern Europe*, (N. Diamandouros, R. Gunther, H. Jurgen Puhle, eds.). Baltimore: Johns Hopkins University Press.

Morlino, L. and J.R. Montero (1995). "Legitimacy and Democracy in Southern Europe." In *The Politics of Democratic Consolidation in Southern Europe*, (N. Diamandouros, R. Gunther and H.J. Puhle, eds.). Baltimore: Johns Hopkins University Press.

Pacheco Pereira, J. (1988). A Case of Orthodoxy: The Communist Party of Portugal." In *Communist Parties in Western Europe: Decline or Adaptation*, (M. Waller and M. Fennema, eds.). Oxford: Basil Blackwell.

Pasquino, G. (1980). *Crisi dei partiti e governabilità*. Bologna: Il Mulino.

Pérez Díaz, V. (1987). *El retorno de la sociedad civil: Respuestas sociales a la transición política, la crisis económica y los cambios culturales de España 1975–1985*. Madrid: Instituto de Estudios Económicos.

Pérez Díaz, V. (1991). "The Emergence of Democratic Spain and the Invention of the Democratic Tradition." Estudios Working Papers no. 1. Madrid: Instituto Juan March.

Rijnen, H. (1985). "La CEOE como organización." *Papeles de economía española*, 22: 115–121.

Rossi, M. 1979. "Un partito di anime morte? Il tesseramento democristiano tra mito e realtà." In *Democristiani*, (A. Parisi, ed.). Bologna: Il Mulino.

Sani, G. and G. Sartori (1983). "Polarization, Fragmentation and Competition in Western Democracies." In *Western European Party Systems: Continuity and Change*, (H. Daalder and P. Mair, eds.). London and Beverly Hills: Sage Publications.

Sani, G. and G. Shabad (1986). "¿Adversarios o competidores? La polarización del electorado." In *Crisis y cambio*, (J. Linz and J.R. Montero eds.). Madrid: Centro de Estudios Constitucionales.

Sartori, G. (1976). *Party and Party Systems: A Framework for Analysis*. Cambridge: Cambridge University Press.

Seferiades, S. (1986). "Polarizzazione partitica e non proporzionalità elettorale in Grecia." *Rivista italiana di scienza politica*, 16: 401–437.

Sotiropoulos, D.A. (1991). "State and Party: The Greek State Bureaucracy and Panhellenic Social Socialist Movement (PASOK), 1981–1989." Doctoral diss., Yale University.

Spini, F. and S. Mattana (1981). *I quadri del PSI*. Firenze: Nuova Guaraldi.

Spourdalakis, M. (1988). *The Rise of the Greek Socialist Party*. London and New York: Routledge.

Stock, M.J. (1986). "Os partidos do poder dez anos depois do '25 abril." Universidade de Evora.

Stoleroff, A. (1988). "Sindicalismo e relaçoes industriais em Portugal." *Sociologia*, 4: 147–164.

Stoleroff, A. (1990). "Reflexoes sobre a evoluccao do sindicalismo e do movimento operario na era dos governos Cavaco Silva." *Vertice*, 31: 45–55.

Taborda Barreto, J.M. (1991). "A formaçao das centrais sindicais e do sindicalismo contemporaneo em Portugal." Doctoral diss., University of Lisbon.

Tarrow, S. (1967). *Peasant Communism in Southern Italy*. New Haven: Yale University Press.

Biographical Note

LEONARDO MORLINO is a professor of Political Science at the Università degli Studi di Firenze, where he is Dean of the Faculty of Political Sciences. Among his many books, the following are of particular importance: *Como cambian los regimenes políticos; La scienza politica in Italia; Dalla democrazia all'autoritarismo;* and *Costruire la democrazia.* ADDRESS: Facoltà di Scienze Politiche, Università degli Studi di Firenze, Via Laura 48, 50121 Firenze, Italy.

[31]

Path Dependency and Civic Culture: Some Lessons From Italy About Interpreting Social Experiments

FILIPPO SABETTI

Robert D. Putnam's *Making Democracy Work: Civic Traditions in Modern Italy*[1] seeks to account for differential performance of regional governments in terms of culture and for systemic variance between north and south in terms of the medieval legacy of civic norms and networks. At a time when the study of comparative politics seems increasingly to privilege crossnational analysis, *Making Democracy Work* stands out as an important reminder and attestation that "comparative political research of the broadest philosophical and theoretical implications can be executed within a single country."[2] Putnam's work makes other contributions to comparative inquiry. It brings the study of Italian politics "back in" and broadens it, precisely at a time when favorite Italian research topics among comparativists—such as Left parties and national trade unions—no longer have the old currency. It further suggests that, contrary to the view often expressed, Italy's past need not always be viewed as a burden. Indeed, it is the use of the past to explain differential effectiveness in contemporary regional governments that makes Putnam's study an important work. It is, in turn, path dependency analysis

An earlier draft of this article was presented at "The Workshop on the Workshop," Workshop in Political Theory and Policy Analysis, Indiana University, Bloomington, Indiana, June 1994. I benefited from discussions with Workshop on the Workshop participants and, later on, with Arturo Parisi and Thomas Row in Bologna. I much appreciate the written comments made by Tommaso Astarita, Frank J. Coppa, Alfred Diamant, Miriam Golden, John A. Marino, Anthony C. Masi, Hudson Meadwell, Elinor Ostrom, Vincent Ostrom, Anthony N. Schratz, and the members of the editorial board of *Politics & Society*, especially Margaret Levi, on subsequent drafts. Financial support from the Social Science Committee of the Graduate Faculty of McGill University is gratefully acknowledged.

POLITICS & SOCIETY, Vol. 24 No. 1, March 1996 19-44
© 1996 Sage Publications, Inc.

that sharply distinguishes *Making Democracy Work* from its earlier (1985) Italian-language version,[3] adds more lustre to the former, and endows Putnam's argument with a strong sense of intellectual closure and a seemingly flawless protective belt.

Putnam states some unsurprising findings when he reports that the medieval monarchical and republican regimes worked differently, that modern public institutions work better in some parts of Italy than in others, and that the south has fewer expressions of voluntary joint or collective efforts than does the north. But for Putnam's explanation of these findings to hold, three things must be true. The first is that the Italian regional experiment was a "natural" experiment to be approached in the same way that "a botanist might study plant development by measuring the growth of *genetically identical seeds* sown in different plots."[4] The second is that patterns of civic culture best, or decisively, explain differential effectiveness in regions. The third is that these modern social patterns are plainly traceable to the monarchical and republican regimes of medieval times.

One objective of this paper is to show that neither logic nor evidence bears out such an interpretation. The regional experiment was hardly a "natural" experiment. Patterns of civic culture do not explain all of the story about regional government performance. Institutions more modern than the medieval ones Putnam considers have shaped the civic society and constitute a south different from what Putnam and many of the authors he cites take for granted. Differential behaviors in different regions cannot be explained unless one introduces the rich historical diversity that characterizes each region—and this Putnam is prevented from doing by the very method of analysis he uses. The other, and more general, objective of the paper, then, is to show that the substantive claim about how development proceeds is responsible for making some findings of Putnam unsurprising and the great majority of his other findings either misleading or wrong.

To be sure, not all the problems in *Making Democracy Work* are attributable to the assumptions of path dependency. For example, Putnam begins his inquiry with sketches of Bari and Bologna, the regional capitals of Apulia and Emilia Romagna respectively. The stark contrast is an effective literary device. The problem is that the "facts on the ground," in so far as they can be independently verified, do not quite fit; they mislead readers who have to rely on the author for a description of those cities and for civic practices throughout Italy.[5] It seems petty to point out inaccurate and exaggerated small details—minutiae in a rich story—but such details assume importance only because Putnam has effectively employed them to paint a picture that is not quite true.

It is the contention of the paper that a path dependency *forma mentis*, or mind set, goes a long way in accounting for the flaws that disable *Making Democracy Work*. The strength and allure of path dependency as a substantive claim about how development proceeds consist in combining fortuitous contingencies of an initial phase with a deterministic logic concerning the subsequent process—both people and their behaviors are locked in as a consequence of their past history.[6] In the first section of the paper, I shall point to the problems that path dependency analysis creates for Putnam's understanding of the medieval legacy; in the second, I shall advance the argument that institutions more modern than the medieval ones Putnam considers have shaped the civic society and constitute a south different from what Putnam and others take for granted. From this vantage point, it should be easier to see that the creation of regional government and differences in regional government performance have been deeply misunderstood. Above all, I shall argue that Putnam has drawn the wrong lessons from history and from the creation and performance of regional government. This is not to suggest that there are no north-south differences, but rather to point out that differentials in development remain still poorly understood.

THE MEDIEVAL LEGACY

Putnam's inquiry into the historic roots of contemporary problems is very much part of the tradition of Italian scholarship and public discourse. Perhaps one of the best known practitioners in this tradition is Carlo Cattaneo (1801-1869), a Milanese publicist with a reputation as an uncompromising Risorgimento radical democrat, who shares Putnam's interest in civic community and social capital. In a set of essays entitled "The City as an Organizational Principle for Understanding the Course of Italian History," written in 1858, Cattaneo used the legacy of medieval Italy to place in sharp relief the Italian civic tradition, to argue against the creation of a unitary, monarchical regime, and to press for a federal, republican solution to the making of modern Italy in the 1860s.[7] Moreover, the title of Putnam's 1985 Italian-language book on the Italian regions, *La pianta e le radici*, is taken from Carlo Cattaneo's characterization of liberty as a plant of many roots; several passages from Cattaneo's work also grace the frontispiece of the book, fittingly published under the aegis of the Cattaneo Research Institute of Bologna, a prestigious independent social science research center. How Cattaneo approaches the past clarifies what is new and what is old in Putnam's thesis and why they differ. Writing in 1839, in an essay setting out what became a life-long research program, Cattaneo noted the challenge awaiting those interested in issues of political development: how to navigate between the doctrines of extreme rationalism of the past two centuries and the deterministic doctrines of his own time so as to understand how particular institutions emerge, how they change over time and how institutional arrangements affect individual and institutional behaviors as well as development potentials more generally. The pressing task, he stressed, was to construct a "public science or economy" incorporating history, institutions and culture, and, pari passu, individuals *not* as blind instruments of a particular time and culture but as beings capable through their actions of destroying, derailing or refashioning the heredity of the past.[8] In the end, and after more than twenty volumes, Cattaneo did not quite succeed in fashioning this new "public science." He seldom had the time, or the inclination, to return to his ideas and develop them fully, so that, for example, he did not pursue the implication of his (and his mentor's, Gian Domenico Romagnosi) insights about transaction analysis. But his dynamic view of the world and his appreciation that "the state" may be nothing but rules manipulated for public and private ends sharply differentiates his logic of inquiry from Putnam's. Cattaneo also shares little of Putnam's benign view of government.

In the 1858 city essays, as throughout the entire corpus of his work, Cattaneo argues that the most productive way to make sense of the vicissitudes of the more than two thousand years of recorded history of Italy is to examine the question of self-government as an empirical and theoretical question. The essays can be read at different levels: the city as a conceptual variable about human association (*consorzio umano*), as a historical community, and as a manifestation of the struggle for self-governance over time.

Cattaneo goes back to ancient times—to the civic culture of *Magna Graecia* in the south, and of the Etruscan communities in the center and the north. He identifies several periods in the history of Italian cities; draws no sharp differences between city and countryside, a feature of Italian life that sharply differentiates its rural population from northern European counterparts; and ends his account with the city republics in the fourteenth century. Unlike Putnam, Cattaneo identifies characteristics of civic traditions *throughout* Italy: the local community in the historic memory and consciousness of people; the importance of municipal institutions; and the cities as self-governing, and law-making, entities.

Cattaneo credits the municipal institutions in the south for keeping alive remnants of civic life in Italy after the fall of the Roman Empire, when municipal institutions had become nearly extinct in the north. Though the portrayal is generally considered accurate as far as it goes, it stops precisely when northern communes were declining as free cities.

Cattaneo draws attention to two dissimilar sources of ruptures, but with roughly similar results: the creation of a medieval kingdom in the south and the insufficiency of city republics in the north. The position of southern cities in the new political economy changed for the worse. Local communities, including the free cities of Amalfi and Naples (one of the oldest Greek cities), were now subordinated to the extraneous and adverse principle of domination. Soon they became powerless, servile, and dull, while their inhabitants became estranged and indifferent to the place in which they lived:

And so it was that the Byzantine era lasted until modern times for a large part of Italy. . . . [southern Italy], whose people had inflicted the greatest loss of life on the Romans as they tried to conquer them, now became the golden dream of every adventurer hoping to gain a piece of land. What a difference between the vast and sick Kingdom of Two Sicilies . . . and the humble set of lagoons from which the people of Venice resisted Charlemagne, Sulemein and the League of Chambray![9]

Cattaneo equally suggests the insufficiency of the northern civic tradition for the constitution of a self-governing society. He attributes this insufficiency to three factors, better documented since Cattaneo's time: (1) the opportunities provided by governmental institutions for the rise of self-perpetuating local oligarchies; (2) the practical absence of overlapping arrangements among city republics (i.e., a federal or polycentric system of governance); and, more important, (3) the intellectual failure to conceptualize the possibility of federal arrangements. These factors led to the breakdown of fiduciary relationships among the people of communes, the transformation of differences into factional struggles, despotic governments (the *signorie*), and, eventually, foreign domination and conquest. By the fourteenth century, deep ruptures in civic culture took place in varying degrees and, for different reasons, throughout Italy.

Cattaneo and Putnam share a particular, retrospective, view of "feudalism" and both tend to use a very wide brush to paint their canvas. But Putnam's method of analysis leads him to exaggerate more than Cattaneo and to lock people and their behaviors in predetermined games of life for centuries. This absolves Putnam of the responsibility of looking at how and which history matters over time. Thus, Putnam presents us with sharply different political consequences over a long period: in the north, the people were citizens, in the south subjects; authority was dispersed in the north, monopolized by the king in the south; horizontal relations in one, vertical social hierarchy in the other; collaboration, mutual assistance, civic obligations, and trust in one, hierarchy, domination, mistrust, and *incivisme* in the other. Whereas collective life in north Italy is viewed as almost always healthy and strong, in the south collective life is viewed as blighted for a thousand years and more.[10] The characterization not only overstates the case but also does several other things wrong.

First, it endows pre-1860 southern kings (or their respective viceroys) with monopoly powers they seldom had, in theory or practice. The Neapolitan parliament, tamed to servility and silence, fell into desuetude only by 1642, without, however, undermining the hold that the aristocracy had in running the Naples city government (the *Seggi*). Indeed, between 1642 and 1734, when Naples acquired its own Bourbon king, viceregal authority was compelled to come to terms with the *Seggi* functioning as a kind of new Neapolitan parliament. The Sicilian parliament, though weakened in its organization and powers, stubbornly clung to its last vestiges of authority in matters of taxation and its claim of representing the Sicilian nation (i.e., the baronial class) before the monarch as late as 1812.

Hence, whereas the Neapolitan aristocracy became—if at all[11]—a court nobility only after 1734, the Sicilian aristocracy that controlled parliament retained some of the functions inherent in the prerogatives of rule as late as 1812. The parliamentary barons' boast that they were "associates of the sovereign" in governing Sicily was no empty boast. Many different Sicilian parliamentary barons managed, over time, to be successful agrarian capitalists. Thus, just as the

24   POLITICS & SOCIETY

king's monopoly powers were checked by parliamentary barons, so the monopoly
powers of parliamentary barons were checked by dynastic, community, and
market-economy requirements that applied to the fiefs as political, social, and
economic ventures. Both monarchs and parliamentary lords faced common constraints: the entrepreneurial skills required to manage each "family firm" and the
residual earnings could not always be continued by inheritance. The history of
Sicilian fiefs as capitalist enterprises engaged in the production and sale of grain
in Sicily and Europe as late as the seventeenth century—"the golden age of
baronial jurisdiction"—has not yet been written, but one thing seems clear: the
history of baronial jurisdiction is not just the history of exploitative relationships
of rulers to ruled, ruinous lordships, and antiquated agrarian economies.[12]
A concern with how people create and maintain efficiency-enhancing and
inefficiency-prone institutions led Cattaneo—in a set of notes on Britain, written
in English around 1834 and published only in 1959[13]—to suggest the need to
compare the evolution of Norman institutions in England and Sicily. This is an
insight that Putnam's explanatory scheme does not allow him to pursue: the route
to modern representative institutions in south Italy had the potential of passing
through feudal institutions.

Second, and not surprising, the characterization tends to fuse long periods of
time and to obscure the norms of generalized reciprocity and the network of civic
engagement that could be found in the rich variety of self-governing collective
efforts at the neighborhood level and among guilds and mutual-aid societies in
the different southern cities, towns, and villages under varying political-economic
regimes. Third, the characterization of perennial exploitation glosses over successive, and sometimes successful, efforts at overthrowing exploitation and dependence in the larger context in which ordinary people lived and worked. John A.
Marino's *Pastoral Economics in the Kingdom of Naples*[14] brings to life additional
problems for Putnam's characterization.

Marino studies the "Dogana di Foggia" (1447-1806), the Neapolitan equivalent to the better known Castilian Mesta located in Capitanata, the most fertile
region of Apulia. It was through the Apulian Mesta, covering some 4,300 square
kilometres of winter pasture in one of the largest plains in the Italian peninsula,
that the Kingdom of Naples became a major supplier of raw wool to Europe. Wool
production was critical to the internal revenue of the Kingdom and, until the early
nineteenth century, the sheep customshouse of Foggia served as one of the most
important financial institutions of the state. Many worlds converged at Foggia and
their extraordinary permutations are ably traced by Marino in his 350-year
analysis of continuity and change. I draw on his work only to emphasize facets
of southern history generally missed.

The Foggia Customshouse received its definitive charter around 1447, but
pastoralism and its accompanying council of graziers or mesta charged with the
task of regulating matters of common concern in southern Italy as in the former

Papal States (where they were part of the Customshouse of the Pastures) can be traced back to ancient times. Grazier associations in Capitanata, in particular, antedate the feudal state. As Marino puts it:

The sheepowners' organization . . . was an indigenous invention to establish and enforce a set of norms to allow for continued economic cooperation among the pastoral population. From the southern European transhumant cousins—Mesta and dogana—the centralized medieval state incorporated those already existent sheepowners' institutions as partners in the royal plan to pacify and profit from the marginal zone.[15]

Class conflict among rich and poor sheepowners did exist; but what emerges from the historical record of the parliament of graziers is the rich associational life that allowed the graziers to put aside or resolve their differences and to confront their common enemies together, be they doganal officers or merchants. "Thus, the sheep customshouse of Foggia developed a model for participatory democracy from below—even within the hierarchical world of an Old Regime monarchy."[16] Marino makes evident that horizontal, as well as vertical, bonds of solidarity and relationships, together with a fairly high degree of self-government, did exist in one of the most important sectors of the political economy of the Kingdom of Naples for several centuries. Bonds of fellowship also extended to others: "Ongoing works of mercy were part of the [graziers' organization's] pious duties and associational responsibilities."[17]

There is at least one important difference between the common people of Apulia and the common people living in central and northern signorie. Whereas commoners in the north did not have the right to bear arms for fear of causing disorder or rebellion, the graziers on the Apulian plain had such a right, one of the oldest and dearest rights of citizenship. What in the south was the right of the lowest of social classes, in the north was the prerogative of the highest of social classes and their retainers.[18]

Marino's history does not fit the prevalent strands of the reigning orthodoxies about the south.[19] This highlights a serious historiographical problem in Putnam's analysis. He uses an approach that leads him to be insensitive to the antifeudal (and anti-Spanish) bias that has marked much of the literature on south Italy since the eighteenth century. But if one is prepared to go beyond the vista interposed by this literature, it is possible to find an extraordinary quantity and variety of documents on civic traditions and the pursuit of collective or joint economic and political opportunities. This documentation suggests that, below the power of alternating monarchies, successive viceroys, and self-perpetuating oligarchies, there were, in the cities, towns, and villages of southern Italy, certain vestiges of communal self-governance that, although half destroyed, were still distinguishable over the entire life of the Kingdom of Naples or the Two Sicilies. These vestiges represented small-scale *civitates*—dense patterns of social civic assets involving collaboration, mutual assistance, civic obligation, and trust.

Problems of commanding the services of impartial government officials or of sustaining existing agreements against new demands and unilateral cancellations of contracts were serious; but what is striking in reading archival documents of the period, in Sicily as in the mainland south, is the trust that ordinary people had in written agreements even when they could only barely sign their names with a cross, in negotiation, and in the law as conflict transformed into a contest of ideas. These norms are as much a feature of the history of southern communes as they are of the history of city republics or tyrants—and even of the history of Montegrano and Pietrapertosa if their notarial archives mean anything. Paolo Grossi offers a rich documentary data base in his important 1977 work on collective property.[20]

In an unintended way, Putnam presents evidence that undermines his own claim about how development proceeds. Putnam finds, in chapter 55 of Book One of Machiavelli's *Discourses*, what he says he might term the "iron law of civic community." Machiavelli, Putnam notes, has "a passage of remarkable relevance to [his] own task of understanding institutional success and failure."[21] Putnam has Machiavelli say that in provinces like Naples "there has never arisen any republic or any political life, for men born in such conditions are entirely inimical to any form of civic government. In provinces thus organized no attempt to set up a republic could possibly succeed."[22] But what are the provinces that Putnam says Machiavelli regards "like Naples"? This question goes to the heart of Putnam's argument. Putnam fails to indicate that these provinces are the Papal States, Romagna, and Lombardy—that is, provinces identified by Putnam with an almost unbreakable civic tradition are identified by Machiavelli as having such an uncivic tradition that no attempt to set up a republic or "good government" could possibly succeed there! Typical of Machiavelli, he thought that good or virtuous citizens could be found only in Tuscany (and, possibly, Venice). But the main problem is that what Putnam is inclined to call Machiavelli's "iron law of civic community" is not supported by Machiavelli's own empirical evidence. If Machiavelli is correct in his empirical observation, then he is mistaken in his "iron law"—and Putnam is mistaken in giving Machiavelli's observation the standing he does. Machiavelli contradicts the claim he was mustered to support.

To sum up, Putnam is correct in drawing attention to two distinctive types of political regimes in early medieval Italy and to the negative consequences of monarchical government. Cattaneo's work shows that this thesis is an old one. What is new in Putnam is, unfortunately, the fruit of some profound misunderstandings. A path dependency perspective leads Putnam not to consider (1) that the roots of civic cultures throughout Italy are much older than medieval times; (2) that civic traditions were not entirely extinguished in the south by the creation of the medieval kingdom, just as they were not entirely extinguished in the north by the dissolution of city republics; and (3) that the civic practices and civicness of any area are more fluctuating than the logic of path dependency would lead us to believe. Cattaneo's work shows more of an awareness of the interplay of complex factors over time that cannot be accommodated by particular "iron laws," be they simplistic renderings of history or deterministic conceptions of development.

The work of Cattaneo and Marino can be brought together to advance an alternative argument about north-south differentials: graziers on the Apulian plain and water appropriators on the Lombard and Po river plain operated *terra terra* with roughly similar norms and networks of civic engagement, but the critical difference in their exigencies of life and work had to do with the megaconstraints imposed by geography, location (earthquake areas in the south), economics, and politics. These larger constraints, more than civic norms and networks, are the key for understanding differentials in development. Some of these constraints, such as geography, are constants; others are variables, and to these I specifically turn next to pinpoint their historical legacy for contemporary Italy.

A DIFFERENT KIND OF HISTORICAL LEGACY

Since the medieval legacy portrayed in *Making Democracy Work* cannot provide the appropriate historical context for understanding regional government performance, which history matters then? I suggest that what matters are the theoretical and practical growth of governmental institutions since the eighteenth century and the enduring presence of ecclesial infrastructures in civil society. Whereas the basic logic of governmental arrangements generally sought or worked to dissolve local civic assets in the south, the basic logic of ecclesial arrangements sought or worked to build them up. While church-affiliated organizations have a long history, they ceased to be the only major network in civil society by the 1890s. The growth of autonomous workers' solidarity leagues, not long after national governments stopped putting them down, suggests that horizontal norms and networks of solidarity can emerge under conditions that many analysts have steadfastly, and mistakenly, described as *culturally* infertile terrain for such norms and networks to grow. I thus advance another argument: that institutions more modern than the medieval ones Putnam considers have shaped the civic society and constitute a south different from the north and from what Putnam and others take for granted.

The Role of Governmental Institutions

The growth of governmental institutions in Italy involved two transition periods; each transition period shaped in turn the subsequent structure of political and economic life. The cumulative impact or historical legacy of these transitions went into making a new south.

The first transition period was brought about by the Enlightenment, which Sicilian, Neapolitan, Lombard, and Tuscan intellectuals and statesmen, who often were one and the same, shared with their counterparts elsewhere in Europe. Italy gave the general clash between "reform and utopia"[23] its own color.

When allowance is made for the constraining presence or liberating absence of foreign rule, the differential impact of the intellectual, political, and economic forces of the Enlightenment among the Italian states, including the Papal States, can be summarized as follows: the more abstract the ideas, the more tabula rasa the attempts to liquidate the heredity of the past, as in the case of the south, the least likely their prospect of success; the more practical the ideas, the more "marginal" the changes, as in the case of the Papal States, Tuscany, and Lombardy, the higher their prospect of success. Sicily stood in relation to Naples almost exactly as Lombardy stood in relation to Austria. What explains the policy variance then, given the fact that these regimes were all autocratic in nature and that "elite public opinion" in both Lombardy and Sicily favored reforms? Two critical variations explain the different attempts at reform. One is the relative bargaining power, transaction costs, and discount rates[24] of Lombard and Sicilian "rulers" vis-a-vis their respective viceroys: the Sicilian parliamentary barons were stronger and more united than were their Lombard counterparts who represented different and conflicting interests. The other had to do with alternative Enlightenment conceptions on how best to repair failings in government and agriculture: whereas Austrians and Lombards shared, for different reasons, the same "ideology" for remedial action, Sicilian barons looked to Britain, "Sicily's sister island," while Neapolitan viceroys looked to France. This is why the tabula rasa liquidation of the heredity of the past failed in Sicily, and why the more modest reforms in Lombardy and elsewhere succeeded. Two important consequences are worth noting for pinpointing sources of modern regional diversity.

First, the moderate reforms in land, as in the community-based enclosure movement in Tuscany; in taxation, as in the tax reform in Lombardy which drew praise from Adam Smith;[25] and in local administration, as in the Papal States—all were evolutionary in nature and contained, in varying degrees, mechanisms for correcting problems as they emerged. Second, by contrast, neither constitutional nor secondary changes were possible, especially in Sicily. Its parliamentary barons had also, by the 1790s, acquired a new awareness of their constitutional rights. For these reasons, the second transition period brought more profound changes in the south than in the north.

In northern Italy, the greatest impact of the French revolution and the Napoleonic period was more in fostering and promoting the growth of Italian nationalism than in fundamentally recasting existing institutional arrangements. By contrast, in the two politically separate parts of the Kingdom of the Two Sicilies, the impact went much deeper precisely because earlier successes in preventing a tabula rasa of the past now made ancient institutions stand in sharper relief. Three profound ruptures took place in the political economy of the south between 1805 and 1865.

First, there was a basic restructuring of property rights in rural land, albeit for different reasons and by different actors. On the mainland south, French-inspired Neapolitan liberals abolished in 1806 remnants of feudal privileges of the nobility, transformed complex forms of property in land into private property largely for themselves, and initiated what eventually took place in Liberal Italy in 1865, the disbandment of the Apulian Mesta. In Sicily, parliamentary barons went further. In 1812, they gave up all the former privileges of their rank, transformed fiefs into private property for themselves, and prevailed on the Bourbon king to promulgate a new Sicilian constitution endowing Sicily with a system of parliamentary monarchy and taxation far more representative than that of Britain.

A complex matrix of choices involving internal and external events brought a second rupture by 1816. A reformulated, absolutist, Kingdom of the Two Sicilies was established with a system of government and administration borrowed from the French and supported by Austrian arms. All the kingdom was divided into provinces; Sicily lost almost all the vestiges of its nationhood and independence, including flag and parliament. The enforcement of regulations issued from Naples became subject to serious institutional weakness and failure; at the same time, control over agricultural resources now gave new southern landowners, Sicilian barons, and their agents a political power they had never had before.

The earlier economic and political ruptures weighted the constitutional out-come of the Risorgimento in the direction of a centralized system of government and administration. The making of Liberal Italy fits Hobbes's Leviathan better than the making of the medieval monarchy: ordinary people had the constitutional right to say "yes" or "no" to the creation of a united Italy, but lost that right and became mere subjects as soon as the new commonwealth was proclaimed. The third rupture for the people in the south lay elsewhere, however, in the whole remodelling of secondary laws and other institutional arrangements that directly impinged on everyday life as well as on the intergenerational cycle of life—from state monopolies on tobacco, matches, fire arms, stamp paper, and salt (on whose economy cities like Trapani depended) to military conscription, from a radically new system of excise duties to pay for the new national debt to numerous mutations in currency, weight and land measures, and in new linguistic meanings of common and juridical terms. It was these "mundane" changes, more than the constitutional regime change itself, that would make Sicily—as the Sicilian political economist Francesco Ferrara (1801-1900) was bold enough to tell Cavour in July 1860—"the Ireland of Italy."[26]

Let me now bring the two transition periods and the ruptures in the second transition period together and sketch, in a brief and stylized fashion, their impact on civic society in the south. I shall then compare this sketch with Putnam's presentation.

One legacy is the creation of great estates under single proprietorship. Unlike Sicily and Calabria, Capitanata became the heart of latifundism in Apulia only by the late 1860s, but the transformation was just as profound. The abolishment of the Dogana di Foggia did away with all the infrastructures, including social capital, connected with wool production. It was the "scramble for land" affecting about 4,000 square kilometres of the plain that led Capitanata to be known as "the California of the south" and the "Texas of Apulia." Two classes of people could be found there by the end of the nineteenth century: large landowners and a proletarian work force. The entire plain was now owned by no more than 500 landlords; up to 85 percent of those who cultivated the land were landless daily laborers.[27]

The phenomenon of southern latifundism, far from being a relic of medieval times, is of more recent origin—the intended and unintended consequences of the political changes in the nineteenth century. As Sidney Sonnino (1847-1924), a London-born Tuscan nobleman and future prime minister of Italy, observed in the now classic study of Sicilian rural conditions he wrote with Leopoldo Franchetti, his travelling companion and fellow Tuscan nobleman:

The situation we found in 1860 persists today [1876] . . . We have legalized the existing oppression and are assuring the impunity of the oppressors. In modern societies, tyranny of the law is restrained by fears of remedies outside the law. In Sicily, with our institutions patterned on liberal formalism rather than informed by a true spirit of liberty, we have furnished the oppressing classes the legal means to defend their oppression and to take over all public positions by the use and abuse of power that was and continues to be in their hands.[28]

And, in a sharp disagreement with the parliamentary commission on Sicilian conditions (R. Bonfadini, Rapporteur) which had just reported that "In Sicily there exists neither a political question nor a social [i.e., agricultural] question,"[29] Sonnino continued:

We are now strengthening the oppressors' hands by reassuring them that, no matter how far they push their oppression, we will not tolerate any kind of illegal remedy, while there can be no legal remedy, for they have legality on their side.[28]

Most ordinary people thus found themselves locked in what Sonnino called an "iron circle." On one hand, they suffered labor contracts imposed by the monopoly of large landowners or their agents and supported by the arms of the state; on the other, they bore the cost of government—including more than three years of conscription for young males—without voice and with little benefit. A logic of mutually destructive relationships came to dominate work and community life, and only in this period does Gramsci's characterization of the south as a great social disaggregation apply somewhat.

Whether local mafias were *ab origine* part of the oppressing classes, or whether such expressions of collective action developed as attempts by some ordinary people, after 1860, to alter a game of life rigged against them, to become in the end only new forms of predatory rule on other ordinary people, landowners, and the state, is still an open historical question. Whether, or the extent to which, antimafia forces, including political parties and social movements, managed *not* to become the mirror image of what they sought to destroy also remains an open historical question.[30] But, in the popular and scholarly literature, the latifundia legacy of southern Italy continued to exist even after a series of nested and stacked events—the growth of agricultural cooperatives by the 1890s, the "land invasions" between 1919 and 1921, market demands of grain with declining labor population due to exit, new labor and sharecropping laws in 1944-1945 placing considerable limits on the property rights of big landowners—had by 1947 largely relegated the latifundia legacy to the past. A reliable survey of the National Institute of Agricultural Economics (INEA) conducted between 1946 and 1947 revealed the extraordinary number of private holdings, the very small size of most properties, and the relatively small extent of genuinely large holdings in the south. Moreover, the rapid industrialization then taking place in north Italy and the demand for labor abroad stood to provide powerful incentives for people to leave the rural areas and thus to undermine the prospect of land reforms premised on the assumption that a large number of southern people should "remain on the farm" as small landowners and cultivators. But, under pressures from the Left parties, land reform came to be accepted by most Italian politicians as a major remedy for the ills affecting south Italy and the year 1950 was the year for land reform legislation. The reform did, in time, do away with the few remaining large landholdings in Sicily and Calabria without, however, achieving the anticipated improvements in agricultural productivity and in the working and living conditions of the rural population. The reform also did little to improve the electoral success of the Left, as it revealed that the "Italian Way to Socialism" itself was based more on myths than facts about the south.[31]

A second legacy is one that Italy shares with other countries with representative systems of government: the presupposition of parliamentary sovereignty. Government policy making since the post-unification period confirms the view prevalent among both Italian radical democrats and public finance specialists after the 1860s: "the monopolistic process of legislation is a spontaneous product of parliamentary regimes."[32] It has produced, in fact, two parallel, if contradictory, tendencies in problem solving by legislation: nationalization and privatization. The effects have often been the same. The disastrous effects in south Italy of nationalizing the rich horizontal and vertical mosaic of local and interlocal religious and nonreligious ventures at self-help and public beneficence that existed from feudal times, and of privatizing what previously had been a vast bundle of alternatives to private property are well documented by successive generations of Italian scholars. There is no intention here to idealize the status quo ante; most long-enduring local ventures as social civic assets had developed serious failings by the 1860s and were in need of reform. What I want to stress are two overlapping points: (1) by retaining the greatest number of social civic assets from its feudal past, the south was especially vulnerable to problem-solving by national legislation, and (2) by attempting to reform, direct, and supervise almost all those local undertakings, national legislators effectively (a) excluded the possibility that communities of citizens —groups of principals— could take part in repairing institutional failings and (b) exposed those long-enduring civic ventures, often still endowed with considerable financial assets, to predatory rule by members of the national governing class itself. Beginning in the 1880s, the Italian parliament attempted to rectify some of the problems that previous legislative measures had created, often through special laws for the south.[33] But the earlier nationalization or privatization of social civic assets could not be undone, while special or "exceptional" national laws for the south became increasingly standard practice, to reach dramatic proportions in scope after World War II. Special laws and funds for the south have over time had the effect of bringing, within the reach of most people, amenities of modern life and standard of living unexampled in the history of the area. Pari passu, however, they also served to enhance the prerogatives of state and party officials and allowed them to dominate local and regional development.[34]

A third legacy is that members of the governing class—shown in the political career of Sidney Sonnino between 1880 and 1919, for example, as well as in many of the parliamentary debates until Fascist times—were themselves critically aware of the shortcomings in the structure of basic social institutions. The problem was that changes in the instrumentalities of government would have given support to localized groups intent on asserting an inherent right of self-government in the whole area of political economy, and thus, it was feared, demolished the work of the fathers of unification. This problem persisted after World War II and the creation of a regionalist state—widely debated at least since Ferrara's memorandum to Cavour of July 1860[35]—was one solution. But before World War II, another solution was put in place by 1896, lasting almost until Fascist rule: keep the machinery of government as it is, but apply leniently or leave unenforced many unjust, harsh, and arbitrary laws. This, in the end, gave Giovanni Giolitti's "New Liberalism" a bad reputation, especially among intellectuals; however, in the process, many new forms of voluntary collective efforts emerged in the south as in the north, unimpeded by governmental action.

Norms of generalized reciprocity and networks of horizontal associations ranged from knitting circles or "schools" among women to local musical bands and olive- and wine-producing consortia among men and women, and these have continued to present times. New and unprecedented forms of associations were established with the purpose of interesting the greatest possible number of people in matters of the commonweal. By 1922, Sicily had acquired the highest number of locally constituted and operated farmer cooperatives and the second highest number of locally established (Catholic and non-Catholic) rural credit institutions in Italy; the three regions comprising what is now Calabria had as many rural credit institutions started and operated locally as did Tuscany.[36] But it was in the Capitanata region of Apulia that there emerged a labor movement, we now know, stronger and more powerful than its counterpart in Emilia Romagna. This story is worth elaborating in some details.

The land workers of Capitanata had been locked in Sonnino's iron circle with the disbandment of the Dogana di Foggia in 1865. A great social disaggregation had followed the "scramble for land." But the data gathered by Frank M. Snowden[37] show that by the turn of the century the landless workers on the Apulian plain had successfully learned to do three things: (1) extricate themselves from the logic of mutually destructive relationships; (2) organize themselves into a powerful peasant movement placing serious limits on the rights of large land-owners; and (3) maintain a high degree of internal democracy in their local and provincial associations by insisting, among other things, that their leaders should come only from their ranks and that no political movement should possess a doctrine beyond the comprehension of its members. It took at least a generation of landless workers to extricate themselves from "the iron circle," but by 1911 they had created a strong and powerful labor movement. The Capitanata town of Cerignola became the center and model of union activism throughout Apulia. In part for this, it became known as "the Bologna of Apulia."[38]

The workers' movement in Apulia shared with that of Emilia-Romagna several common features, including a strong sense of workers' solidarity. But the Apulian movement differed in one important respect. As it spread throughout and beyond the towns of Capitanata to other regions of Apulia, it maintained internal democracy, with a high degree of leaders' accountability. In contrast, by 1920 the workers' leagues in the Po valley had become so centralized and hierarchical in nature as to be quite unresponsive to local members.[39] The differences between Apulian and northern workers' organizations were real and became critical as Fascists —Mussolini was Romagna's native son— sought to come to power. In Apulia the workers' movement contested the advance of Fascism town by town and showed considerable resilience in the face of Fascist (squadrist) assaults on local headquarters of workers leagues. By contrast, in the Po valley, including Emilia Romagna, it was enough to strike only a few individuals to bring chaos to the workers' leagues, as happened in 1921-1922. This is what made Apulia stand apart during the advent of Fascism.[40] Norms of generalized reciprocity and networks of associations did not become entirely extinct under Fascist rule; this way Giuseppe Di Vittorio emerged as the most respected national workers' union leader after 1944. It seems evident that the Apulian land workers had built more solid foundations for generalized norms of reciprocity and networks of associations than had their counterparts in Emilia Romagna.

Compare now this sketch of southern conditions with Putnam's claim of the continuity of a great social disaggregation and individual *scioltezza*, or atomism, from medieval times to Gramsci's time and to modern times. Putnam's claim can be advanced and perpetuated only at great cost.

First, Putnam's method of analysis does not allow him either to observe or to explain what happened, in the course of the nineteenth century, to the rich and dense panoply of social civic assets that had been features of southern civil society since medieval times. Putnam misses almost altogether the role that governmental action played in dissolving those small-scale *civitates*.

Second, the view of atomized southern individuals, or *scioltezza*, that Putnam and others he cites in support of that view—from Turiello and Franchetti in the nineteenth century to Gramsci, Tarrow, and Graziano for this century and until the middle of the 1960s—has currency only if we (1) accept Putnam's benign view of government or (2) assume, as do the other analysts, that southern peasants and artisans should entrust their aspirations and needs to an enlightened and benevolent "Modern Prince"—be it a national parliament for Turiello and Franchetti, or a Marxist-Leninist party for Gramsci and others. Both positions are questionable. They call for an examination of other key texts Putnam uses to weave his story.

The statement in the 1863 Pasquale report to the effect that society in Calabria Ulteriore is not held together by economic bonds, but only by natural, civil, and religious bonds can be reinterpreted as an indirect confirmation both of the upheaval created by the "abolition of feudalism" and of the still strong presence of civil and religious structures of village life characteristic of the ancien regime. In fact, Pasquale's last sentence in the paragraph that Putnam quotes from noted that "The propensity for mutual aid can be found everywhere [in Calabria], especially in villages."[41] Putnam uncomplicates his narrative by omitting this important sentence. Mack Smith's discussion, in his modern history of Italy, of the absence of community sense in Liberal Italy does not refer, as Putnam seems to suggest, to the absence of community spirit among southern villagers and the like; rather, it refers to the widespread lack of support for the post-1860 central government and policies throughout the entire country—which is an entirely different matter than what Putnam wishes to convey.[42]

Even Franchetti's often cited views about Sicilian *scioltezza* take on a different meaning when they are ranged alongside the analysis advanced by his travelling companion, Sonnino. Franchetti's description is "institutions free"; it tells us how individuals behave when they are locked in a many-person analogue to the prisoner's dilemma. Sonnino provides the missing links in Franchetti's account by telling us about the rules or constraints of the game. Gramsci's great social disaggregation, then, does not mean a lack of community concern, or an inability to act, or a proclivity for vertical, clientelistic politics, but, rather, the presence of governmental institutions that create serious impediments to both voluntary and public initiatives. The "iron circle" sketched by Sonnino explains great social disaggregation better than the "ethos laws" advanced by Putnam and Banfield.[43]

Third, Putnam's explanatory schema does not allow him to confront contradictions in his own argument. He cannot explain the network of secondary associations and community organizations that developed especially after the 1890s: if *scioltezza* is as universal as it is alleged, how have successive generations of ordinary people in the south, as presumed rational egoists or amoral familists, managed to overcome the logic of collective *inaction* and the oligarchical tendencies inherent in organizational life? North-south differences in group action and other joint voluntary undertakings are not really comparable unless we take into account the differential impact of governmental action. By contrast, Sonnino's method of analysis gives him greater predictive capacity because he did not view ordinary people just as "prisoners" and because he understood better than Franchetti and Putnam the rig of the game and how to change its rules.[44]

Fourth, Putnam's method of analysis allows him to overlook similarities in social civic practices throughout the country. He can observe horizontal bonds of reciprocity, trust, and the continuous ad hoc mutual aid and exchange of services among neighbors (*aiutarella*) in north Italian communities, can call up similar practices among residents of Mexico City, Java, other parts of the world, and even among prisoners of some Latin American jails, but cannot come to terms with the fact that the same social practices can be found among neighbors of south Italian cities, towns, and villages. The tenacity of his presumptive knowledge did not prepare him well for his voyage of inquiry to Pietrapertosa; it led him to ignore visible facts on the ground.

Finally, just as Putnam's explanatory schema allows him to take only a benign view of governmental action in promoting social capital, so it allows him to ignore completely the role that a big institution of civil society has had in creating social capital in the south. I reserve a longer discussion below.

Organized Religion and Civic Society

The view is put forward in chapter 4 of *Making Democracy Work* that organized religion is an alternative to, or works against, the civic community in Italy. This view is advanced on the strength of historical and modern events that, however, suggest the opposite.

From medieval times to unification, the church in the north is portrayed as only one civil institution among many, itself a local affair with horizontal religious allegiances and alignments. For the same period, by contrast, the church in the south is portrayed as a single entity, as a powerful and wealthy proprietor in the feudal order,[45] with presumably negative consequences for the civic community. It is not clear whether what is meant by "church" is the same in the two contexts; what is less unambiguous is that a unitary-actor model can produce gross distortions of the historical record.

The church was and is a single entity in spiritual and doctrinal matters, but it was not organizationally a single entity or proprietor in the south. Sicilian exceptionalism applies to the church as well. Sicilian churchmen and lay organizations enjoyed considerable autonomy from Rome under the Apostolic Legateship as late as the nineteenth century. On the mainland south, it was only in 1867 that the system of local churches run entirely by lay people, with appointed priests to administer the sacraments and say Mass, and where the local bishop had no right of jurisdiction except in matters *quoad spiritualia*, was abolished. Strong indications exist in the available literature that local parishes, known as *chiese ricettizie*, were more the norm than the exception throughout the mainland south for many centuries; quite a few of them were run synagogue-like. As a corrective to any tendency to idealize this particular tradition in retrospect, it would do well to emphasize that, over time, the *chiese ricettizie* developed critical failings and abuses that could not be easily repaired. The chief point remains, however: the church in the south was a complex and overlapping system of individual and local churches, lay confraternities, and congregations of men and women,[46] mutual-aid societies, and public-spirited societies (*opere pie*) running hospitals, linked in different ways to all sorts of diocesan institutions and to several kinds of monastic orders—each with its own bundle of property rights and with considerable entrepreneurial initiative in providing material and spiritual benefits to distinct, and often overlapping, political communities. For centuries, and as late as the 1880s—when State regulations effectively destroyed their capacity to act as essential coproducers of many collective services—all those entities remained very visible neighborhood institutions, passing on an ethic of community involvement, social responsibility, and mutual assistance among different classes and social equals.[47] It was in this sense that the church on the mainland south, in the words of a British analyst, "represented, in a curious form, the embryo of democratic institutions."[48] Sonnino observed, paradoxically, that the key factor which made local parishes in Sicily stand out in community life was precisely that "civil society appears to the Sicilian peasant only in the form of rapacious landlords, tax collectors, conscription officers and police officials. . . . Outside of [the church], he finds nothing but toil, sweat and misery."[49]

The papal *non expedit* ban to Catholics from participating in Italian national life for some time after unification is also used to argue that Catholicism and civic involvement are antagonistic. Three aspects of the injunction, seldom noted, give a more nuanced, and less negative, interpretation of the ban. Keeping in mind the tense church-state relations of the post-1859 period, including the fall of papal Rome in 1870, the *non expedit* does not appear to be a strong Vatican response to the nationalization of church properties in 1865 and the serious threats to the liberty of the church itself. Moreover, given the very limited franchise for the first thirty years of the new kingdom, the *non expedit* applied in practical terms to a relatively small portion of the population: for example, up until 1882 only 2 percent of the population was eligible to vote (about 620,000 male voters). At the same time, the ban did not apply to local elections and, in fact, did not negatively affect Catholic community efforts and civic involvement. On the contrary, beginning in 1874 there took place a considerable renewal in Catholic social action that emerged with particular strength in Sicily and Calabria after the 1890s. Church-sponsored associations allowed villagers to realize mutual benefits and to participate in self-governing efforts to a degree not possible in public, governmental, affairs; membership in these associations also served to provide the primary political leadership and social capital for other types of concerted action. Far from negating or opposing civic involvement, the *non expedit* ban actually encouraged committed Catholics to renew their grassroot efforts just at the time when the central government was bent on dissolving social civic assets from the ancien regime. It was these grassroot efforts, undertaken as part of his apostolic work, that by 1919 propelled a Sicilian priest and nobleman, Luigi Sturzo, to national prominence as leader of the newly formed Catholic Popular Party. Sturzo's commitment to self-governance was as strong as Di Vittorio's.

A third line of contention that organized religion in Italy is an alternative to the civic community, and not a part of it, derives from the period especially following the Vatican II Council in the 1960s. Data drawn from aggregate Eurobarometer surveys in 1976, 1985, 1988, and 1989 and some qualitative accounts are used to suggest that "churchgoers seem more concerned about the city of God than the city of man."[50] The conclusion follows: the civic community in today's Italy is a secular community.[51]

First, the Eurobarometer surveys for Italy, on which Putnam relies, are well known to be methodologically flawed and notoriously unreliable. In the absence of more reliable surveys, it can be argued that they are the best we have and thus can be used. There is, however, little or no evidence of caution in the way Putnam has constructed his index of clericalism on the basis of Eurobarometer studies.[52] The Putnam index conflates religiosity with clericalism and civic community with secularism, and erects a false dichotomy between civic community and religious faith. Second, even if the sources cited correctly portray what they observe, it does not mean that they can be taken as accurate representations of Catholic theology, teaching, and practice. In fact, the play on words about the title of Saint Augustine's book, *The City of God*, reveals mistaken notions about Catholicism. The Roman Catholic church teaches the inseparability of one's love of neighbor from the love of God, and not a substitution of one for the other. The journey onward toward salvation for the Christian begins—in Saint Augustine's work as in the more recent Vatican Council II document *Lumen gentium* no. 31—not so much with the flight from the world as with self-examination and self-control, and with a commitment to sanctify the world from within through one's ordinary circumstances of life and work. Third, the call to human dignity and solidarity, and the inseparability of one's love of neighbor from the love of God, have served to build new infrastructures of collective efforts and community development in Apulian, Basilicata, Calabrian, and Sicilian towns. A large part of the voluntary-action sector throughout Italy is connected with social movements inspired by the teachings of the Catholic church. Christian roots may not always be visible enough to account for social civic assets and community efforts in contemporary Emilia Romagna but it is a mistake to overlook those roots and civic assets in other parts of the country.[53]

REGIONAL GOVERNMENT

I have shown that two of the three pillars on which Putnam's analytical and empirical scaffold rests cannot withstand close inspection: the historical legacy portrayed by path dependency analysis is profoundly mistaken and cannot be used to explain differential effectiveness in regions; cultural patterns and associational networks dissimilar from, and richer than, Putnam would lead us to believe have shaped, and have been at work in, the south. Moreover, taking the basic analytical perspective of representative government with a presupposition of parliamentary sovereignty places any inquiry about "making democracy work" at risk of drawing the wrong conclusions about legislative output. Whether the legislative output of regional governments is interpretable as Putnam suggests remains open. But can Putnam's other pillar withstand close inspection? Was the creation of regional government a "natural" experiment?

Putnam says that "the border of the new governments largely corresponded to the territories of historical regions of the peninsula, including such celebrated principalities as Tuscany and Lombardy."[54] Though it is not clear from the text what he means by "largely," he may be somewhat correct in matching the present regional boundaries with the territories of Tuscany, Lombardy, and Emilia Romagna as representing political entities with historic identities. The situation in the south, beginning with what used to be called Abruzzi e Molise, is more complicated than Putnam allows. The more south one goes, the harder it is to find regional states, or the present regions, in history. Several facts stand out.

The regional governments created in 1970 do not match the regions that have existed in southern history, at least not in the same way that they match the historic regions in the north. For centuries, there were at least three Apulias, two Abruzzos, generally three Calabrias, and perhaps the same number for what is now known as Campania—each with its own territorial boundaries, capital, distinct political economy, historical consciousness, and cultural identity. This helps to explain why almost all these areas have been known in Italian in the plural—the Abruzzi, the Puglie, the Calabrie. The creation of regional government made them singular. To be sure, the areas politically brought together shared the same name, but this did not give the regional experiment there a more spontaneous and less contrived nature.

There were two exceptions: Basilicata, with its relatively small size and historically distinct boundaries, was left as it was; Molise was allowed to break away from Abruzzi and form its own regional government, even though the people of Abruzzi (or the Aquila and southern part of it) and Molise have been historically linked and share close identities. Putnam does not tell us why Molise was allowed to secede from Abruzzi and have its own regional government, even though the historic reasons for such a move are not strong.[55] The fact that some Molisan intellectuals and politicians who favored the creation of the Molise region were, or had close ties with, powerful leaders in the national center-left governing coalition may explain the Molise exception. This exception reinforces the view that the regional experiment was not a natural experiment: the borders of the new governments were, as much historical legacies as political contrivances of national legislators. This point can be illustrated in another way.

National legislators also had authority over which cities should be regional capitals. This decision may have constituted a mere formality, in the cases of, say, Turin for Piedmont, Milan for Lombardy, and Bologna for Emilia Romagna, but not so for the southern regions. There was even some opposition in Basilicata and Campania, where it was difficult to question the historic importance and claims of Potenza and Naples, respectively. The choice of regional capitals elsewhere proved more contentious. Mass protests were organized in cities with equal claims to be capitals—like Pescara in Abruzzi and Reggio Calabria in Calabria. The protests in Reggio Calabria were strong, cutting across right-left party and trade-union barriers; so intense did they become that some citizens lost their lives as police tried to contain demonstrators during the so-called revolt of Reggio Calabria in 1970-1971. The riots against Catanzaro as the regional capital caught national legislators, including those from the region, by surprise. The mass revolt explains why Calabria is the only region to have its central machinery of government in two different cities: the de jure regional capital, where the regional government and its central administration are located, remained Catanzaro; but the regional assembly was moved to and now meets in Reggio Calabria.

The fact that Apulia and Calabria seem, in Putnam's analysis, to be the worst-governed regions may, in part, be due to the way national legislators disregarded historic borders and regional identities and imposed what, from the perspective of ordinary people in Capitanata and Crotone, appeared to be one more consolidated—and distant—layer of government between localities, the provincial field services of the national system of public administration, and Rome itself.[56] Putnam's evaluation of the institutional performance in Apulia and Calabria may coincide with the constituency evaluation there,[57] but the *criteria* for the constituency evaluation may be grounded in an interpretative scheme that Putnam and his collaborators failed to explore seriously. By paying little or no attention to the riots of Reggio Calabria and to the resultant regional government arrangements, Putnam misidentifies Reggio Calabria as the regional capital,[58] and—more important—he misses an opportunity to explore the suggestion advanced earlier by some Italian analysts that the way the Calabrian regional experiment took effect had a negative impact on, or slowed down, its legislative performance.[59]

The present regions are, then, in part, historic entities and, in part, arbitrary administrative contrivances. This is to say that the design principles of regional government did not embody similar meanings and thus the creation of regional government cannot be reasonably construed as constituting a single, uniform political experiment across Italy.

This conclusion leaves no pillars in Putnam's analysis standing. But it would not have surprised many nineteenth-century publicists—from Cattaneo in the north to Napoleone Colajanni and Edoardo Pantano in the south—who took part in or followed the regionalist debate between 1860 and 1945.[60] These analysts did not assume that the extension of representative institutions built on a logic of parliamentary sovereignty could be equated with self-government; they, in fact, anticipated that central government decentralization, far from being a neutral policy instrument, would be a political contrivance more sensitive to the demands of the governing classes than to the regional diversities of Italy. This point was made by Cattaneo in the 1860s. About thirty years later, Colajanni and Pantano amplified it: they likened proposals to decentralize central government authority as attempts to shorten the handle of the hammer when the hammer of centralized government and administration itself was the problem. The southern analysts may have been too radical in their predictions. But Putnam imperiled his own experiment as his method of analysis did not allow him to profit from the rich regionalist debate in Italy since 1860.

CONCLUSIONS

Putnam's explanation of Italian regional government performance is questionable and does not withstand close inspection. His analysis advances a strong argument for path dependency but, as I have shown, also accentuates its fatal shortcomings. My conclusions are threefold. First, Putnam's model reminds us that history matters and then proceeds to mess it up. A path dependency *forma mentis*, or mind set, can lead, and has led, to a caricature of the north and the south and to the neglect of fluctuations in both. Second, Putnam's explanatory scheme leads him to draw the wrong lessons from history and the regional experiment. I have shown that north-south differences are not really comparable unless we take into account the differential impact of governmental action, something which Putnam is prevented from doing by the explanatory scheme he uses. Third, the transitions and ruptures I have sketched in the growth of governmental institutions since the eighteenth century point to the constraints on development that have other than a path dependent structure; they support the argument that the continuing interplay of economic and political factors at the local, regional, and national level has far more profound implications for development or inertia than any particular path dependent structure. Thus fatal flaws disable *Making Democracy Work* both from making sense of the Italian regional experiment and from being a classic in comparative politics research. As we unlearn the lessons taught by *Making Democracy Work*, we are challenged to provide less flawed accounts of how history, culture, institutions, and individuals come together to matter. Cattaneo's life-long intellectual struggle and Putnam's own twenty-year poking around the regions of Italy suggest that the task is not an easy one. This essay suggests that the struggle is still worthwhile.

FILIPPO SABETTI 41

NOTES

1. With Robert Leonardi and Raffaella Y. Nanetti (Princeton, NJ: Princeton University Press, 1993).

2. Joseph LaPalombara, review of *Making Democracy Work*, by Robert Putnam, *Political Science Quarterly* 108, no. 3 (fall 1993): 550.

3. Robert Putnam, Robert Leonardi, and Raffaella Y. Nanetti, *La pianta e le radici* (Bologna: Il Mulino, 1985).

4. Putnam, *Making Democracy Work*, 7, emphasis added.

5. Putnam, *Making Democracy Work*, 5-6. Putnam says of Bari: "Like visiting researchers, ordinary Pugliesi must first locate the nondescript regional headquarters beyond the railroad yards" (5). The regional headquarters may have been nondescript and hard to locate in 1970, but not so at least since the second half of the 1970s. Street signs in the area point to it; the building is clearly marked. Moreover, the regional headquarters is not located beyond the railroad yards but on the backside of the Bari main railway station in downtown (*centro*) Bari. The railroad yards are more than four kilometres away. Putnam does not stop long enough in Bari to tell us why the building which houses the regional government is still rented from private sources. As for Bologna, Putnam refers to its central piazza, "famous for its nightly debates among constantly shifting groups of citizens and political activists, and those impassioned discussions about issues of the day are echoed in the chambers of the regional council" (6). What he describes here is not unique to Bologna's central piazza and applies equally well to the central piazzas of the other regional capitals and of almost all the towns and villages in the south, Pietrapertosa included. It is also very likely that, among the constantly shifting groups of citizens and political activists that can be observed pacing up and down the Bologna piazza, can be found transplanted southerners continuing there a civic tradition of their natal villages and towns.

6. E.g., Geoffrey M. Hodgson, "Economic Evolution: Intervention Contra Pangloss," *Journal of Economic Issues* 25 (June 1991): 519-34.

7. Carlo Cattaneo, "La città considerata come principio ideale delle istorie italiane," in *Scritti storici e geografici*, ed. G. Salvemini and Ernesto Sestan (Florence: Le Monnier, 1957), 2:383-437.

8. Carlo Cattaneo, "Su la 'Scienza Nuova' di Vico," in *Scritti Filosofici*, ed. Norberto Bobbio (Florence: Le Monnier, 1960), 1:95-142.

9. Cattaneo, "La città," 431.

10. E.g., Putnam, *Making Democracy Work*, 162, 163.

11. I owe this point especially to Tommaso Astarita's insightful study *The Continuity of Feudal Power. The Caracciolo di Brienza in Spanish Naples* (New York: Cambridge University Press, 1992); see also, Giuseppe Galasso, *Napoli spagnola dopo Masaniello*, 2 vols. (Florence: Sansoni, 1982).

12. For the mainland south, see Astarita, *The Continuity of Feudal Power*, 108-58.

13. Robert G. Murray, "Un inedito di Cattaneo sull'Inghilterra," *Rivista storica italiana* 71 (1959): 611-52.

14. (Baltimore: Johns Hopkins University Press, 1988).

15. Ibid., 114.

16. Ibid., 10.

17. Ibid., 111.

18. The right of selected common people in the south to bear arms was, especially after Unification, the source of much misunderstanding as national leaders sought to suppress or strictly regulate it.

19. In fact, one would never know it from reading almost all the English-language text on the "Southern Question." In fairness, one would know of it even by reading Benedetto

Croce's classic Italian text, *The History of the Kingdom of Naples,* ed. H. Stuart (University of Chicago Press, 1970).

20. Paolo Grossi, *An Alternative to Private Property: Collective Property in the Juridical Consciousness of the Nineteenth Century* (Chicago: University of Chicago Press, 1981), originally published in Italian in 1977. Equally worth reading is Grossi's more recent collection of essays entitled *Il Dominio e le cose. Percezioni medievali e moderne dei diritti reali* (Milan: Giuffre, 1992).

21. Putnam, *Making Democracy Work,* 132.

22. Nicoló Machiavelli, *Discourses,* ed. Bernard Crick, trans. Leslie J. Walker (London: Penguin, 1970), 246.

23. Franco Venturi, *Utopia and Reform in the Enlightenment* (Cambridge, UK: Cambridge University Press, 1971).

24. I am drawing here on the conceptual elaboration and empirical application in Margaret Levi, *Of Rule and Revenue* (Berkeley: University of California Press, 1988).

25. Adam Smith, *The Wealth of Nations* (New York: Random House Modern Library Edition, 1965), 886.

26. Francesco Ferrara, "Brevi note sulla Sicilia," reprinted in *Camillo Cavour. La Liberazione del Mezzogiorno e la formazione del Regno d'Italia* (Bologna: Zanichelli, 1949), 1/2:300.

27. On the strength of the 1901 census figures supported by other sources of the time: see, e.g., Frank Snowden, *Violence and Great Estates in the South of Italy. Apulia 1900-1922* (Cambridge, UK: Cambridge University Press, 1986), 10, 20-2.

28. Sidney Sonnino, *I contadini in Sicilia,* vol. 2 (1877), quoted in Filippo Sabetti, *Political Authority in a Sicilian Village* (New Brunswick, NJ: Rutgers University Press, 1984), 48.

29. Giunta per l'inchiesta sulle condizioni della Sicilia (R. Bonfadini, Rapporteur), *Relazione* 1876. Reprinted in *L'inchiesta sulle condizioni sociali ed economiche della Sicilia 1875-1876,* ed. Salvatore Carbone and Renato Grispo (Bologna: Cappelli, 1969), 2:1077.

30. See, Sabetti, *Political Authority in a Sicilian Village,* 111-217; and F. Sabetti, "The Mafia and the Antimafia: Moments in the Struggle for Justice and Self-Governance in Sicily," in *Italian Politics: A Review,* ed. Raffaella Y. Nanetti and Raimondo Catanzaro (London: Pinter, 1990), 4:174-95.

31. This paragraph draws heavily on Sabetti, *Political Authority in a Sicilian Village,* 174.

32. Antonio De Viti De Marco, "La politica commerciale e l'interesse dei lavoratori," in *Nuova antologia della questione meridionale,* ed. Bruno Caizzi (Milan: Comunità, 1962), 249. The essay by De Viti De Marco was originally published in 1903.

33. Grossi, *An Alternative to Private Property.*

34. For a more developed argument than I can present here, see Carlo Trigilia, *Sviluppo senza autonomia. Effetti perversi delle politiche nel Mezzogiorno* (Bologna: Il Mulino, 1994), and his "Economia e società nel Mezzogiorno contemporaneo" (paper presented at the "Convegno Strutture e metodi del consenso nell'Italia repubblicana," Pisa, 29 March - 1 April 1995).

35. See note 26 above.

36. See Sabetti, *Political Authority in a Sicilian Village,* 6, for supporting sources, and, among others, Anna Caroleo, *Le banche cattoliche dalla prima guerra mondiale al fascismo* (Milan: Feltrinelli, 1976), 45-78 passim, 175. A useful source of other evidentiary material is the *Bollettino dell'Archivio per la storia del movimento sociale cattolico in Italia,* edited and published at the Catholic University in Milan.

37. Snowden, *Violence and Great Estates in the South of Italy*. There is also a rich Italian-language literature on the subject, some of it cited by Snowden.

38. Ibid., 100.

39. Ibid., 190-1. See also, Anthony L. Cardoza, *Agrarian Elites and Italian Fascism: The Province of Bologna 1901-1926* (Princeton, NJ: Princeton University Press, 1982), 364-408, for how and why the very organizational success of the Bolognese *Federterra* among the agricultural proletariat "depended on the unhampered authority of the league leaders and their ability to enforce strictly all rules and regulations" (365).

40. Snowden, *Violence and the Great Estates in the South of Italy*, 190; and Cardoza, *Agrarian Elites and Italian Fascism*, especially chaps. 7 and 8.

41. Pasquale quoted in Piero Bevilacqua, "Uomini, terre, economie," in *Calabria*, ed. Piero Bevilacqua and Augusto Placanica (Turin: Einaudi, 1985), 296. Putnam cites from this source.

42. Denis Mack Smith, *Italy: A Modern History* (Ann Arbor: University of Michigan Press, 1959), 34-35, quoted in Putnam, *Making Democracy Work*, 143.

43. Some "Montegranesi" now suggest that Banfield seriously misunderstood what he observed, and that what he observed among villagers did not even get at the basic structures of village life in 1954-1955. (Interviews by author with three leading villagers, including the Left-wing mayor of Chiaromonte—"Montegrano,"—August 8, 1994.) The villagers' view about the unreliability of Banfield's fieldwork in 1954-1955 is impossible to verify. A cursory look at the historical record of Chiaromonte—before and after the period Banfield spent in the village—suggests that Banfield's description and explanation of village life may not be empirically grounded, as Putnam and others have imagined. Chiaromonte seems to have had the panoply of community organizations—ranging from mutual aid societies, lay congregations of men and women, and wheat banks before Fascism, to more recent forms such as farm workers' organizations and cooperatives, as well as the many ad hoc joint efforts among friends and neighbors—that characterizes local life in much of the south. For a more extended discussion, see report of work in progress in replicating Banfield's study: Filippo Sabetti, "A Different Way of Knowing: A Research Note on the Real 'Montegrano,' " *Italian Politics & Society*, no. 44 (Fall 1995): 18-25.

44. He noted a capacity among ordinary Sicilians for changing the constraints, and breaking out, of their iron circle. He reported on cases he observed of tenant farmers seeking to impose limits on the rights of large landowners in some Western Sicilian towns and villages in the 1875-1876 sowing season, even though the tenant associations and the strikes they proclaimed were illegal and were put down by the arms of the state. I have examined in some detail how one such agrarian association developed, the role that the social capital accruing from participation in church confraternities played in overcoming the logic of collective inaction among peasants—a point that Sonnino also seemed to be aware of—and how the association was forcibly put down. See Sabetti, *Political Authority in a Sicilian Village*, 86-8, 90-1.

45. Putnam, *Making Democracy Work*, 130.

46. It is generally not well known that Catholic lay congregations of women were the first self-organized and self-governed collective women's groups throughout Italian society and the only ones until the second half of the nineteenth century. For an initial elaboration of this point in a comparative context, see Maurizio Ridolfi, *Il circolo virtuoso. Sociabilità democratica, associazionismo e rappresentanza politica nell'Ottocento* (Florence: Centro Editoriale Toscano, 1990).

47. There is a huge and growing literature on the topic. Most of the research is being done by historians and include the following: Enrica Delle Donne, *Chiesa e potere nel Mezzogiorno. Istituzioni ed economia 1741-1815* (Salerno: Edisud, 1990); Giuseppe

Galasso and Carla Russo, eds., *Per la storia sociale e religiosa del Mezzogiorno d'Italia* (Naples: Guida, 1980); and Francesco Volpe, ed., *Studi di storia del Mezzogiorno offerti ad Antonio Cestaro da colleghi ed allievi* (Venosa: Edizioni Osanna, 1993). Most of these works have been deeply influenced by the historical research of Gabriele De Rosa, cited therein. By nonhistorians, see the extracts from John Chetwode Eustace, *A Tour through Italy* (1815) in *Naples: A Travellers' Companion*, ed. Desmond Seward (New York: Atheneum, 1986).

48. R. M. Johnston, *The Napoleonic Empire in Southern Italy and the Rise of Secret Societies* (London: Macmillan, 1904), 1:13.

49. Sonnino, *I contadini di Sicilia*, 145, quoted in Sabetti, *Political Authority in A Sicilian Village*, 90.

50. Putnam, *Making Democracy Work*, 107.

51. Ibid., 109.

52. Ibid., 214, n. 52, where one would have equally liked to see some caution in accepting at face value what seem to be the results of a 1982 survey showing that fully half of the citizens of Sicily and Sardinia claimed to have heard nothing at all about their own regional governments, by then more than thirty-five years old.

53. E.g., CENSIS, *Il raccolto della solidarietà. Chiesa impegno nella società e sostegno economico* (Milan: Franco Angeli, 1994); Pierpaolo Donati, "Carità e solidarietà nella società post-moderna," *Acta philosophica* 2 (1993): 233-60; and Franco De Leo, "Volontariato e cooperative di solidarietà sociale in Basilicata," *Sociologia* 25 (1991): 237-59.

54. Putnam, *Making Democracy Work*, 5.

55. The "contado" of Molise emerged in modern times as a jurisdisdictional and administrative unit only around 1806. It was created by the French-inspired Neapolitan government as a kind of buffer zone or "Switzerland" where Campania, the Abruzzi, and the Apulian Capitanata meet. Molise ceased to be such a unit after 1860; the Italian government, rather than returning the Molise territory to the different areas from which it had been taken, simply incorporated Molise into the larger Abruzzi administrative system. See, e.g., Luigi Picardi, "Il Molise centrifugo," *Nord e Sud* 14, no. 94 (October 1967): 84-95.

56. Historically, the people of Apulian Capitanata have had, by almost all measures, more ties with the inhabitants of Molise than with the other two Apulian parts to which now Capitanata is administratively and politically joined. Since the consolidation of the Calabrias into one regional government, the Crotonose area has succeeded in gaining recognition as a new political and administrative entity, the province of Crotone, within Calabria, as have people of Isernia in Molise.

57. Putnam, *Making Democracy Work*, 76-81.

58. Ibid., 54, where Putnam says: "For many southerners . . . being ruled from Bari or Reggio Calabria is not much better than being ruled from Rome."

59. See, e.g., Giuliano Amato, Sabino Cassese, Enzo Cheli, Stefano Rodotà, and Donatello Serrani, "Materiali per una discussione sullo stato dell'attuazione delle regioni," in AA. VV., *Dalla parte delle regioni. Bilancio di una legislatura* (Milan: Edizioni di Comunità, 1975), 41.

60. See, e.g., Massimo Ganci, *Da Crispi a Rudinì: la polemica regionalista, 1894-1896* (Palermo: Flaccovio, 1973); Roberto Ruffilli, *La questione regionale dall'unificazione alla dittatura, 1862-1942* (Milan: Giuffrè, 1971).

Part V
Social and Politico-Cultural Developments

[32]

1968-79—Feminism and the Italian Party System

Women's Politics in a Decade of Turmoil

Yasmine Ergas

Historically, protest, understood as an autonomous mobilization that confronts the principal actors of political systems, has been an infrequent avenue for women. Yet in the late 1960s and early 1970s a new wave of feminism swept over the Western world, often assuming the characteristics of autonomous political movements and gathering strength especially in countries like Italy, where other forceful opposition movements had developed.

This paper will attempt to examine the factors that affected the emergence and evolution of the Italian feminist movement, exploring the movement's "internal" development as well as its interaction with, and dependence on, external forces. The feminist movement gained impetus, coming to form a political body, from the widespread mobilization that the students' (1968) and workers' (1969) rebellions gave rise to in Italy. Throughout the principal phases of its growth, until 1976, the mainstream[1] of this movement combined its focus on the transformation of female identity and of male-female relations with a highly "political" character, not only turning a great deal of its attention to the nexus between the liberation of women and the transformation of society, but also engaging in direct confrontation with some of the main actors of the political system.

Following the changes registered in the political system, the feminist movement's "politicization" has become increasingly problematic, and, since the general elections held on June 20, 1976, it appears to have accentuated its orientation toward cultural and microsocial objectives with only sporadic forays in the broader political realm.[2] Thus, though significant crises have affected its primary organizational structures (consciousness-raising groups, collectives, coordinating committees)—whereas more informal patterns of aggregation have been strengthened—feminism's political difficulties have been exemplified by its silence in the political arena. Explaining this silence, as well as the collapse of many of the centers of women's autonomous

0010-4159/82/0415-0001$05.00/1

253

Comparative Politics   April 1982

grass-roots organization that sprang up early in the 1970s, is the major task of this paper. I shall argue that the Italian women's movement suffered the fate of many other such movements that appear on the scene as part of general movements of social protest: to be pushed to the sidelines ultimately as the "parenting" movement changes and as the political system moves into a new phase. It is beyond the scope of the paper to compare Italian feminism over the past decade to other social movements, specifically either to other women's movements or to other movements in Italy. The paper draws on the literature relating to these fields, first to outline a general framework for the analysis of women's movements in conflictual political contexts, subsequently to examine the specific case of Italian feminism with reference to the development of women's movements in the post–World War II period, and finally to look at the social factors underlying the rebirth of feminism and to follow its itinerary from its origins in the New Left of the later 1960s up to the repercussions of the 1976 general elections.

Women's Movements, Mass Mobilization, and Political Institutionalization

The Italian feminist movement's important, albeit seemingly chimeric, breakthrough into the arena of "conventional" politics echoes recurrent patterns in women's history and ought, therefore, to be situated in an interpretative framework that examines some of the general features of women's mobilizations. Autonomous women's movements have often emerged in the wake of sweeping mass mobilizations and at moments of general social crisis; yet their "political" lifespan has usually been brief. Like the movements of women demanding their rights that arose in the wake of the French Revolution, of the American Abolitionists' campaign, of the Bolshevik Revolution, and of the Italian antifascist struggle, the renaissance of feminism in Italy raises the general problem of the relationship between women's movements and wide-ranging mobilizations of new political actors. The general hypothesis of this paper is that the factors enabling women to penetrate—however fleetingly—into the realm of "conventional" politics are directly tied to the dynamics of political systems and, specifically, to the importance within them of new social actors.

    Women's entry into politics is facilitated when politics itself is in a state of disarray, when the rules of the game and the roles of traditional actors are already being challenged by emerging forces. As the "newcomers" mobilize, not simply to further their immediate interests but, more fundamentally, to modify a system's functioning, they open a general debate over access to the system's rewards. In the ensuing struggle, women have sometimes attempted to revolutionize their own standing. New states of equilibrium, however, usu-

254

Yasmine Ergas

ally restrict the negotiating area once again. Frequently excluded from the conventional political arena, women's movements have often grown nonetheless, tackling problems on the plane of the social organization of everyday life.

Furthermore, the link between the development of women's autonomous political movements and "revolutionary" social movements seems to be the outcome of three distinct but interrelated processes. First, "revolutionary" movements may provide particular incentives that bring women into active roles, thus leading to significant increases in their normally low participatory rates. Second, recruitment into "revolutionary" movements stimulates processes of political socialization and furnishes access to political resources (theory, organizational and communications networks, leadership skills). Finally, the "revolutionary" movements provide a "wedge" into conventional politics to actors who are otherwise normally excluded from its arena.

How do these processes operate? Underlying the capacity of these general movements to catalyze new levels of female participation are at least two sets of motivating factors. In the first place, the expectation of change and the enthusiasm such movements register at their peak[3] may also promote the expectation of a radical transformation of individual identity definition. In this sense, political demands represent the projection of desires for change experienced on an existential plane. In the second place, moments of collective enthusiasm may foster an experimentation in social relationships that, while rarely attaining equality between the sexes, can increase women's dignity. The equalizing aspect of mobilization thus constitutes a real incentive for political involvement.[4]

The focus of women's commitment, may, however, shift from the original social movement to autonomous mobilization as the former recedes from the heights of collective enthusiasm to face the problems created by its role in the political system. Processes of "institutionalization" of protest movements are often accompanied by a reduction of militancy; however, although activism decreases, access to hitherto unavailable political resources has already been gained. Women can consequently use the skills and resources acquired within such movements to address the issue of their own position in society.

Recruitment and subsequent political socialization are, however, insufficient to explain access to the sphere of conventional politics. Studies of modern party systems have repeatedly stressed their particular responsiveness to sectors of society that can either affect key economic processes by organizing around their specific interests in the economy or influence the electorate. Recent analyses have, moreover, shown that political systems must continually confront their own need for legitimacy,[5] which allows less powerful groups access to resources. Along which of these axes do autonomous women's movements enter into a direct relationship with political systems?

The primacy of women's roles in the family with respect to their other eco-

255

nomic functions, the very structure of household organization and of domestic labor, the nature of the identification processes linked to work in and for the family—these are some of the elements that have militated against women per se constituting effective, broadly based interest groups. Although in the context of their familial functions (as consumers, as utilizers of public services, as homemakers) women have been organized around their specific interests, the focus of such participation has been, by definition, their role in the family rather than the relations between the sexes. Undeniably, women have also been part of the labor force's struggles. Again, however, these movements have revolved around occupational goals without necessarily questioning sex and gender roles. In recent years, changes in women's roles and the resurgence of women's movements have somewhat reinforced the latter's lobbying activities.[6] Nonetheless, at least in Western Europe, women have not generally constituted a category organized in such a way as to question the economic priorities of political markets or to engage in confrontation on this plane over the sexual division of society.

However, women's relationship to conventional politics seems to be no more linked to their electoral behavior than to their economic role. Viewed in a historical perspective, women have been excluded until relatively recently from suffrage. Even after the extension of suffrage, as has been insistently noted, they have failed to change politics significantly. In fact, the interaction of women's movements with political systems preceded suffrage extension and does not appear to be bound by their performance at the polls.

Legitimation does not merely hinge on formal political expression. Habermas's observation that "legitimacy means a political order's worthiness to be recognized" makes it clear that strong protest movements represent a threat to an order's claims "to be recognized as right and just."[7] The bearers of such a threat must thus be dealt with; through exclusion, negotiation or co-optation, the political system must establish a relationship with them. Thus, as broad opposition social movements denote and deepen a legitimacy crisis, women's movements that may be linked to them find a point of entry into the political arena. They then, however, labor under specific liabilities, since their dependency on others for access to politics easily exposes them to being made marginal. Moreover, because whenever legitimacy is in question matters of principle become central, women's political movements tend to focus on women's status. This emphasis has often constrained the development of negotiable goals, thus hindering the evolution of "normal" institutional integration and of "routine" political activity.

The recent history of the Italian feminist movement exemplifies these processes. Born when the appearance of strong general protest movements seriously menaced the party system's role in the relationship between society and state,[8] genetically linked to the New Left, the movement has seen its political

Yasmine Ergas

fortunes vary, as we shall see, with the acuteness of the country's political crisis.

The New Left and the Women's Movement

The background The Resistance during World War II and the fall of the Fascist regime catalyzed the appearance of strong women's movements in Italy. The two major women's associations of the postwar period were both founded in 1945: CIF (Centro di Iniziativa Femminile) by the Christian Democratic party and UDI (Unione Donne Italiane) by the left-wing parties, the Communist party (PCI) and the Socialist party (PSI). In the same year, important speeches were dedicated to women's political role by both Pope Pius XII and Palmiro Togliatti, head of the Communist party. The following year women were granted the vote. These events all testify that by the end of the year women had acquired noticeable political visibility. Their visibility as a specific political force was, however, to decline over the following two decades.

The Cold War forced the left-wing parties—and especially the Communists—to an entrenchment in defensive positions. In the context of the repression that characterized the first half of the 1950s and the isolation that marked the second half, the family came to represent a "cell of resistance" for the Left against a hostile world. Gradually dropping organizational methods aiming at involving women separately in the party, the PCI increasingly channeled its relations with women through the family. The Cold War also accentuated the Communist tendency to view the party as the prefiguration of socialist theory and, therefore, to underestimate the inequalities in its ranks. Moreover, it was not until the Twentieth Congress of the Soviet Communist party in 1956 that the policy followed by most communist parties—in Italy as elsewhere—of treating social movements as devices for the direct transmission of their own policies was questioned. The PCI, especially throughout the first half of the 1950s, used the UDI to convey its policy, largely suppressing the specific point of view represented by the theoretically autonomous women's association.[9]

The vicissitudes of women in the Christian Democratic party followed a different rhythm. The breakdown of rural modes of social organization resulting from the transformation of the Italian economy and from the country's massive urbanization provoked a crisis in Catholic associationism. By the early 1960s, membership in Italian Catholic Action had dropped dramatically, signaling the difficulties in which one of the Christian Democratic party's primary channels of recruitment floundered. With the decline of female membership in Azione Cattolica (from 1963 to 1969 women's enrollment fell by

257

Comparative Politics   April 1982

66.8 percent—from a total of 1,895,000 to 630,000), female registration in the Christian Democratic party suffered proportionately.[10]

Throughout the 1950s and the first half of the 1960s, complex economic, social, and political factors widened the gap separating women from politics, even as women were being affected by changes in the labor market and in the distorted development of Italy's highly politically penetrated bureaucratic state. The complex system of alliances constructed by the Christian Democrats effectively worked against the realization of equality for women.[11] In particular, the social services essential to women's activities outside the home were not developed publicly. Women were forced, on the one hand, to intensify their domestic labor in order to make up for the lack of public services and, on the other, to assume the burden for managing the multiplication of bureaucratic duties—ranging from relations with schools to dealings with the health care system—assigned to the family by the state in the latter's expansion.[12]

Furthermore, the essential character of the limitations placed on women was not clearly perceived until the middle and late 1960s. While women were being expelled from both the agricultural and the industrial labor force,[13] public awareness was dimmed by the emergence of strong ideological currents exalting women's role as homemakers. Public sensitivity to the issue of sexual discrimination was further diminished by the generalized belief, generated in the climate of the "economic miracle" of the late 1950s, that the evolution of modern society would progressively eliminate the "residues" of preceding forms of social organization.

Why, and how, was this trend toward the increasing alienation of female participation in politics reversed by the generation of women (and their immediate successors) who would, first, become involved in the movements of 1968 and 1969 and, then, go on to constitute the core of the new feminist movement? In examining the context in which the new feminism developed, in order to answer this question adequately, one must take both social and political factors into account. Turning first to the social roots of the feminist movement one realizes that an adequate analysis ought to provide a double explanation: on the one hand, of the "strain" underlying the emergent movement; on the other, of the available role option concretely expressed in the behavioral patterns associated with militance within it.[14] In other terms, both the "motive for" and the "possibility of" protest are elements that need to be explained. The main readings thus far set forth of the social causes underlying the rebirth of feminism deal only with the first aspect of the problem.

The "motive" for feminist protest has often been attributed to the relative deprivation experienced by young women at the end of the 1960s. Thus, for example, Jo Freeman has noted that whereas young women's expectations have changed with their mothers' employment, their own college experience, the (at least partial) legitimation of women's function as providers, and the

Yasmine Ergas

growing approach of their educational preparation to that of men, nonetheless "women's share of both quantitative and qualitative occupational rewards decreases each year."[15] And, according to Maren Carden, "Denied access to the more rewarding forms of paid employment, and denied socially applauded alternative activities inside and outside the home, American women have initiated, out of their sense of frustration, the twentieth century revival of feminism."[16] However, relative deprivation is insufficient even as an explanation of the basic strain manifested in the feminist movement, for it cannot explain why women did not simply mobilize in a new emancipatory movement demanding equal rights but, instead, paid great attention to the complex significance of *liberation*, therefore accentuating personal change and attributing a basic function to consciousness raising.

A second reading of the social roots of feminism attempts to account for precisely this particular characteristic of contemporary feminism. According to Bortolotti, "Liberation can turn to the psychological sphere" in industrialized nations where youth has gained economic independence, while the family, Bortolotti argues, has become increasingly useless as an economic unit.[17] The reason seems to be that where the family is obsolete as an economic unit the forms of sexual oppression associated with the family become obsolete as well. However, far from becoming economically obsolete, the family has modified its tasks, retaining its rule as one of society's foremost functional structures.[18] The emergence of a "psychological" orientation in feminism cannot, therefore, be explained by referring to the "archaic" nature of sexual oppression.

Neither relative deprivation nor the changes in the family's economic functions appear to explain satisfactorily even the strain underlying the resurgence of feminism in the 1960s and 1970s. Alternatively, I would argue—at least in reference to the Italian case—that by the second half of the 1960s, a substantial role conflict characterized the condition of young women, in such a way that their expectations and behavior were polarized between "emancipation" (understood as access to social parity) and family-centered feminine models. By the mid-1960s, young Italian women's lives and prospects differed greatly from those of preceding generations. The first female generation for which enfranchisement was a "natural" right reached maturity having attained high levels of education. These young women had, moreover, gained access (albeit in a state of semi-illegality) to new contraceptive methods . They could take many, relatively recent, political and social rights for granted. Finally, they faced the prospect of bearing smaller families than those in which they had been brought up and could look forward to the likelihood of finding employment in the tertiary sector.[19] At the same time, however, everyday family life and profoundly internalized values revolved around differentiated sexual roles.

For the first time it seemed that for large numbers of young women—par-

259

Comparative Politics   April 1982

ticularly those in the higher social classes—the two sets of messages that had underlain much of their socialization could become concrete reality: the strain toward equality, and the desire to remain attached to a clearly recognizable feminine identity. These two vectors, however, also carried somewhat contrasting identification codes and differing relational models, easily generating conflicting behavioral expectations.[20]

It was in the university context that such role conflict reached a peak. On the one hand, by furnishing the highest degree of preparation for effective integration into society, it represented the maximum level of emancipation. On the other hand, for the young women who attended it, the university also represented the new arena of the marriage market and, in any case, the setting in which they could (were expected to and themselves expected to) establish relations of a matrimonial type.[21] The tension generated by role-conflict in female identification processes was eventually reflected in feminism's emphasis on the models and patterns of women's socialization. At the same time, and as a by-product, legitimation had been broadly attributed to egalitarian attitudes and to corresponding behavioral models that provided the role option for the type of behavior required by political activism.

The Italian "1968" By the end of the 1960s the environment of the universities provided the opportunity for the political development of the tensions inherent in the previous generation. The universities were profoundly shaken by the students' movement, to which many young women were attracted. Activism itself did not always represent a break with previous life patterns, for it also constituted a form of continuity with preceding experiences of participation in Catholic and other youth associations. The New Left commonly emphasized the need to bypass the normal routes of institutional politics by substituting for them direct action and strong mobilizing tactics. It developed a set of basic convictions—differently interpreted by each group—concerning the tangibility of radical change and the extensive delegitimation of the ruling Christian Democracy. Finally, by and large, the New Left shared some fundamental tenets: anticapitalism, antiauthoritarianism, anti-imperialism.[22]

The "new politics" openly questioned the validity of the existing party system and of the political culture that had developed since the war. In the tracks of this critique, feminism could attempt to redefine politics further. A process of mobilization with such far-reaching goals as those proclaimed by the 1968 movements could satisfy an intricate series of needs: by placing its militants "in the mainstream of history," it seemed to meet the young women's demands for equality; by postulating a radical-utopian transformation of society and favoring an expectation of catharsis, it could allow them to defer their problems of defining a precise social identity while allaying some of their existential tensions; finally, by constituting itself as a "total experi-

Yasmine Ergas

ence,'' it could become the new locus of everyday life, in which ''normal'' social relations would be established in new, experimental ways. In the words of a woman recounting her experiences in the students' movement of Turin:

> The positive element which I managed to grasp was that these people wanted to change the world, that one was among many, that the revolution was near . . . within a year we would have all been on the barricades. . . . Everything was motivated by this atmosphere of great precariousness, by our anticipation of the moment in which we would have overturned the state, in which we would have changed the world. Neither studying nor working mattered any longer.[23]

This striking participatory tension, in which individuality appears to have been literally molded into a collective identity, suffered as militancy in the New Left began quite quickly to weigh heavily upon women. Alternative lifestyles experimented with by many couples maintained important aspects of the traditional division of labor and of the customary sexual hierarchy,[24] often generating strong feelings of frustration. Politics itself became increasingly unsatisfactory. The diffusion of the feminist debate initiated abroad—taken up first by groups of Italian women outside the New Left, then by groups within it—heightened the activists' tendency to compare their political groups' theories and practices with the new proposals. Finally, in the general elections held in June 1972, in which the New Left Manifesto group was defeated, the Communist party augmented its votes slightly and the Right increased its vote, intensifying both the divisions within the New Left and the institutionalizing tendencies of its groups. Consolidating their organizational structures, the latter tended to accentuate the sexual division of labor and power within themselves.

In the meantime, however, women had gained access to political resources hitherto unavailable: they had been able to acquire some basic political skills and to generate leadership capacities; they had become part of associational networks and had had some access to the organizational resources of the New Left; they had acquired an ideology, which could motivate and justify their rebellion in the context of the New Left; and, finally, they were integrated into an international cultural circuit. For the women involved, the organizations of the New Left could constitute an optimal reference point for evaluating women's position. Comparisons—and their interpretation in political terms—were in fact favored by the proximity of the New Left and by the distinctive character the New Left's segmentation and institutionalization lent its various organizations, as well as by the salience of politics itself, both in the conventional sense of the term and as lifestyle politics.[25]

Furthermore, the basic tenets of the New Left's ideology (especially its egalitarian antiauthoritarianism and anti-institutionalism) played an impor-

Comparative Politics   April 1982

tant role in undermining the legitimacy of the rules of the game by which women had apparently been placed in a subordinate position within these organizations. Ideology thus became the terrain on which women's groups could construct their identity by continually redefining their position vis-à-vis their reference groups. Much "early" writing by feminists in the New Left reads like an open letter to the militants' political organization, harking back, more or less explicitly, to their basic beliefs.

The "consumeristic" exploitation of women both as housewives and as sexual objects; the "imperialism" and the "chauvinism" of male values; the "authoritarianism" of male-female relations in the family, in politics, and in all other places of social interaction were forcefully denounced. Similarly, feminists expounding on women's estate insistently emphasized the "anticapitalistic" nature of their movement and its economically, socially, and politically revolutionary potential.[26] The extension of the debate on male-female relations to the various organizations of the New Left signaled the expansion of feminism. The segmentation of the movement favored bloc-recruitment and the development of internal female leaders. The outcome of these processes led to the formation of collectives prevalently constituted by the militants (or ex-militants) of specific New Left organizations.[27]

Of the many processes that favored the consolidation of the feminist movement, the creation of areas of solidarity and the processes of interaction with the political system proved especially important. The formation of collectives and the adoption of consciousness-raising techniques generated closely knit female networks. Participants' attitudes toward their daily lives were often affected as women came to represent more substantial referents for each other than they had done before. Furthermore, by attributing a political valence to sexual oppression (thereby redefining the parameters of justice), these feminist groups tried to promote changes in values. The new ideology, upheld by the social organization of the collectives, became part of systems of interaction in which militants could reciprocally reinforce their commitment.

Starting in 1974, with the development of direct action for abortion, the feminist movement also began tackling other problems of female existence. Initially, a few feminist collectives and the Movimento di Liberazione della Donna—the women's group linked to the Radical party[28]—organized trips of women needing abortions to legal clinics in Britain and to an illegal center in Florence. Within less than a year, the abortion issue had emerged as the potential locus for common action by feminist collectives. By early 1975, discussions were under way in Rome—and soon thereafter in other cities such as Bari, Turin, and Venice—to establish coordinating committees for initiatives concerning abortion.[29] These discussions involved feminists' collectives and the three major organizations of the New Left: Lotta Continua, Avanguardia Operaia, and the Partito di Unità Proletaria per il Comunismo. At the same

Yasmine Ergas

time, the Radical party, joined by large segments of the feminist movement and of the New Left, opened a campaign calling for a referendum to abrogate the surviving fascist law regulating abortion.

By mid-1975, the combination of tactics devised (weekly chartered trips abroad and the direct practice of abortion) enabled the feminist movement to aid several hundred women each month. The movement thus managed to extend its influence well beyond the boundaries of the collectives fostered by the New Left. By engaging directly in service delivery, feminism both established new centers of recruitment and developed new sources of legitimation.

The Women's Movement and the Party System

During the first five years of its development, the Italian feminist movement was normally treated by the principal political forces (parties and trade unions) as a substantially marginal, elitist, and fairly insignificant phenomenon. This approach to feminism essentially reiterated the stance generally taken by the political parties toward the New Left in general. The consistent underestimation of the mobilization that had emerged in part reflected social factors. Overall, the recruitment patterns (and, hence, internal composition) of the major political parties had not kept up with the transformations of Italian society.[30] As far as women are concerned, perhaps the most striking case of a skewed distribution of party membership is that of the PCI: in 1975, over 50 percent of its female membership was concentrated in two regions (Emilia-Romagna and Tuscany), which together accounted for 23 percent of the total female population.[31]

The political strategies of the major parties also led them—each for specific reasons—to downplay the significance of the emerging movements and the legitimacy of their demands. The parliamentary elections of 1972 reinforced the tendency in the Christian Democratic party to seek new sources of consensus in the conservative electorate.[32] In particular, under the leadership of Senator Amintore Fanfani, the DC attempted to characterize itself as the only viable, stabilizing, and moderate force in Italian politics. Through what came to be known as the "strategy" of opposite extremisms," the Christian Democratic party highlighted and stigmatized the disruptive and radical connotations of the extraparliamentary movements of both Left and Right, attempting to attribute responsibility for their behavior not only to the movements themselves but also to their alleged "parent" organizations: the PCI for the left, the MSI (Movimento Sociale Italiano) for the right. In contrast to these "fomenters of disorder," the DC purported to reinstate "law and order" and to reaffirm traditional values. Thus, in preparing for the referendum to be held in May 1974, the party's leadership campaigned heavily in favor of repealing the law legalizing divorce. The referendum dealt a severe blow to the Christ-

Comparative Politics   April 1982

ian Democratic party, for 59 percent of the electorate voted in favor of maintaining divorce. Notwithstanding this result—and the increasing intraparty
conflict to which it contributed—the party leadership pursued the same
strategy up to the regional elections held in June 1975.[33] Consequently,
throughout the first half of the 1970s, a consistently hostile stance was maintained toward feminism and the issues that it raised. By stressing the movement's "destructiveness" of traditional values, the Christian Democracy attempted to reinforce and increase women's loyalty.

"Neo-feminism: the wrong way to treat an important problem," proclaimed the PCI's women's commission in a 1973 issue of *Donna e politica*,
its official publication. Throughout the first half of the 1970s, the party's
strategy of alliances favored the tendency to maintain a diffident—and sometimes overtly hostile—attitude toward the feminist movement. The first years
of the decade witnessed a shift to the right in the politics of the Christian Democracy and in important sectors of public opinion. Attempting both to stave
off the "backlash" against the mobilizations of 1968-69 and to promote reformist governmental policies, the PCI worked to build an alliance with the
Christian Democratic party, to direct the emerging social movements toward
demands requiring the mediation of political parties, and to avoid exacerbating societal cleavages.[34]

In this perspective, the feminist movement appeared disruptive. It focused
on themes, ranging from women's control over their sexuality and reproductive functions to the distribution of power in the family, which could easily be
perceived as accentuating societal cleavages and therefore jeopardizing the
party's policy of social recomposition. Moreover, since religious divisions cut
across the PCI, much of whose membership and leadership did not subscribe
to anticlerical values, the feminist movement's positions could be seen as
damaging to internal party unity. Furthermore, feminism raised policy issues,
such as abortion, around which mediation with the Christian Democratic party
was likely to prove extremely difficult. Consequently, by legitimizing
feminist concerns and translating them into policy demands, the PCI risked
provoking a confrontation with the DC that might strengthen its right-wing
tendencies.

Since the late 1950s, the Socialist party has often proved particularly receptive to the modernizing sectors of Italian society. The forcefulness with
which it has defended progressive legislation has, however, been conditioned
by the party's general policies and its relationship to the other major political
parties. At the end of the 1960s, the PSI faced a dilemma.[35] Electorally weak
and internally divided, the party encountered great difficulty in developing an
autonomous strategy. At the same time, the construction of an alliance with
either the DC or the PCI seemed fraught with danger. The preceding decade's
experience in coalition governments appeared to show that close cooperation

Yasmine Ergas

with the Christian Democracy spelled a loss of identity and of electoral support. However, the increasing influence of the PCI seemed to condemn the Socialists to being the weaker partner in any left-wing alliance that, moreover, was rejected by the Communists themselves. Caught in this quandary, the Socialists oscillated between "frontist" stances and participation in governments with the Christian Democracy, at times appearing receptive to the issues raised by the left-wing protest movements and, at others, downplaying the same issues.

For the feminist movement, interaction with the PSI was further complicated by the Socialists' relationship to the Radical party. Although formally a party, the PR actually functioned, especially in the first half of the 1970s, as a conglomerate of single-issue movements whose basic, unifying trait lay in their focus on civil liberties. This peculiarity of the Radical party enabled it to adopt a policy of "dual membership." Members of other parties were encouraged to join the PR without having to renounce their previous allegiances. Through this policy, the Radicals extended and consolidated their influence within the Socialist party. The alliance with the Radicals—although informal and frequently unstable—allowed the Socialists to maintain a link with parts of Italian society that had been influenced by the mobilizations spawned in 1968 and 1969, but it excluded the mainstream of the New Left, which tended to follow "workerist" and Marxist-Leninist orientations. The Socialists thus developed a working relationship with the Movimento di Liberazione della Donna (MLD), the women's group affiliated with the Radical party, but not with the principal part of the feminist movement, which had developed within the New Left.

The abortion controversy Abortion functioned as a "breakthrough" issue for the feminist movement, enabling it to extend its influence, even within the constituencies of the main political parties, and to acquire visibility as a political actor. In February 1975 the Constitutional Court declared unconstitutional several articles of the legal code introduced under Fascism governing abortion. The ensuing legislative confusion made it imperative for Parliament to establish a new law. When the parties' bills were presented in the spring of that year, they seemed largely unaware of the free abortion movement, for none of them accepted the requests for the liberalization and protection of abortion that had been put forth. The Socialist party promised to amend (but never actually did) the proposal it had presented in 1973 permitting abortion, subject to the approval of three medical specialists, when a woman's health was endangered. The Communist proposal also attributed decision-making power to a committee of specialists, who had to certify that serious harm to the woman's life would ensue from pregnancy and childbirth. Under full steam, the abortion campaign faced a negative response from the established

Comparative Politics   April 1982

Table 1

	Decision (adult women)	Decision (women under legal age)	Payment
Socialist Party	3 MDs	+ parents or tribunal for minors	Free
Communist Party	2 MDs + 1 social worker	+ parent legally responsible	Free
Christian Democratic Party	ABORTION	ILLEGAL	
Social-Democratic Party	Woman	+ 1 parent	Woman, if income greater than minimum wage level
Republican Party	Woman, if less than 12 weeks pregnant, 2 MDs if life or health endangered	+ 1 person legally responsible	Woman, if health not endangered by pregnancy
Liberal Party	Woman	+ both parents or tribunal for minors	Free

political spectrum. A situation thus appeared in which the male political system appeared to be denying a women's demand that had already aroused widespread support. The PCI's tepid reform proposal, for example, aroused both a reaction from UDI—which proclaimed its independence on this issue and put forth a different proposal—and a revolt of some of the party's own militants.[36]

Table 1 summarizes the parties' first legislative proposals with reference to two of the main requests advanced by the feminist movement in the campaign for the liberalization of abortion: i.e., that the decision be solely up to the woman and that abortion be state-subsidized so as to be free of charge.[37]

Corresponding to the pattern Touraine has described in analyzing the dynamics of social movements,[38] the ensuing confrontation increased both the internal cohesion of the movement and the processes of female identification around it that favored recruitment. As the only component of the abortion campaign that was ideologically equipped to underscore the sexual antagonism revealed by the official party system's proposals, and as the strongest center of women's organizational capacity, the feminist movement came to represent one of the main points of reference for women, whether or not they had other political affiliations. Spurred by the party system's appa-

Yasmine Ergas

rent inability to recognize and successfully mediate women's emerging demands, the feminist movement's force of attraction reflected the general crisis in the parties' capacity to organize and represent the policy needs of the new collective actors whose development the profound transformations of Italian society had fostered.[39] Thus, while the tie established during the abortion campaign between feminists and activists of conventional political organizations elicited new attention for issues regarding women (and occasionally led to changes in policy), the feminist movement came to be recognized as the foremost political force expressing female concerns.

The confrontation over abortion in 1974-75 favored a strengthening of the women's movement, which was to be consolidated further in the first half of the following year. During this period, collectives mushroomed in all areas of social life—from neighborhood communities to work places and schools. By the summer of 1975, neighborhood collectives had set about establishing women's health centers in several cities.[40] At a national meeting called in October 1975 in Bologna by Turin's coordinating committee, a series of initiatives was decided on, culminating in a national demonstration to be held in Rome on December 6 of that year. It was agreed that the demonstration would be "separatist" and that identifying banners and posters would carry only the names of women's organizations. UDI and the PCI women's commission refused to participate, while the Socialist party adhered and sent delegations from various major cities.

What of New Left groups and parties? Although none of its organizations had enthusiastically accepted the separatist nature of the demonstration, only Lotta Continua actually infringed the rule: members of its Roman federation arrived in force, repeatedly charging the women's march. These events precipitated a crisis in Lotta Continua. New dissent was also sparked within the PCI. *"Sono del PCI eppure sono qui"* (I am a Communist, but I'm here) read the placard a Communist militant bore as she joined the feminist march, which counted over 50,000 participants.[41]

A point of no return had been reached: feminism could no longer be ignored either by the mass media or by the main political parties. Thus, for example, *L'Unità*—the Communist party's newspaper—broke its customary silence and ran a series of articles on the movement.[42]

Changes were provoked even within the feminist movement, since Lotta Continua's behavior gave rise to a clarification in its relations with the New Left. The committees coordinating initiatives concerning abortion generally decided that the political organizations should withdraw their formal representation. Significantly, in many cases the women who had acted as representatives of these organizations stayed on, for in the months that had elapsed between the founding of the committees and the Rome demonstration, they themselves had often become involved in autonomous feminist collectives.

267

Comparative Politics   April 1982

On April 3, 1976, after the abortion bill proposed by the Parliamentary Committee had been defeated by the joint views of the Christian Democratic party and the Neo-Fascists, a new nationwide demonstration was staged, this time with the participation of UDI and of the women's commissions of the Republican, Socialist, and Communist parties. This extensive mobilization—again called for and organized by the coordinating committees of the feminist movement—made it clear that it was time to pass from a purely oppositional to a propositional phase.

Feminism had developed a variety of organization forms: the decentralized, segmentary, and capillary network[43] of the collectives and consciousness-raising groups had given rise to coordinating committees whose somewhat more formal and stable system of representation could, at least in theory, have helped to engage in bargaining within political institutions. But what institutional strategy had actually been developed that could support the required change in attitude? The evolution of the abortion campaign indicates that, as far as strategies vis-à-vis institutional politics were concerned, the feminist movement's link to the New Left had remained intact, notwithstanding the fact that the latter's conditioning had been transcended as far as both the interpretation of women's condition and the critique of politics were concerned.[44]

The campaign for abortion had centered primarily around direct action and had been characterized by the feminist movement's prevailing tendency to presume its own autonomy (real or potential) rather than dedicate attention to the construction of a system of alliances, even with other segments of the women's movement. For example, at the April 3 demonstration, all the participating organizations had to adhere to the initiative's separatist nature even though only the feminist collectives accepted the principle of separatism. These lines of action were clearly dependent on a firm belief in the possibility of transforming the existing order by bypassing the normal routes of political negotiation.

However, when the task of designing the guidelines for a new law on abortion had to be faced, the difficulties inherent in the New Left's strategy came to the fore. At the same time, the weakness of the internal cohesion that had taken place in the oppositional stages of the campaign led the way to lacerating divisions—centering around the movement's attitude toward institutional politics—that rendered general agreement impossible.

The 1976 elections and the problems of the women's movement The stage for the most significative encounter between the feminist movement and the political system was set by the parliamentary elections of June 20, 1976, whose results were to deal a heavy blow to the entire spectrum of the New Left, while carrying the official Left into the majority. Following its success

Yasmine Ergas

in the regional elections held the previous year, the PCI faced the new round of elections aiming, on the one hand, at mediating between the opposition movements that had developed since 1968 and the institutional framework; on the other hand, the PCI purported to use its oppositional strength in order to ensure a transition—without reactionary counterattacks—toward new modes of government and new relations between the dominant sectors and the emergent "positive forces" of Italian society. In order to reinforce its legitimacy by strengthening its position as mediator, the party would have to represent the new forces while defeating their more radical "fringes." Thus, in the general renewal of its candidate lists—which included attributing an unprecedented number of safe seats to non-Communists drawn from among leading Catholics and intellectuals—the presence of female candidates was greatly increased. However, although the number of women elected on the Communist ticket doubled,[45] those actually elected were rarely representatives of the women's movement. In particular, no leading feminists were elected. The electoral defeat of the New Left highlighted the insufficiencies of many of its assumptions. At the same time, the PCI obtained the investiture it had sought, thus reducing the margins for autonomous political negotiations conducted directly by the movements themselves.

The New Left movements also had to face difficulties of a different sort in their dealings with the political system—difficulties stemming from the complex process of "institution-building" undergone by the Italian governmental structure.[46] Forms of representation and of self-government involving non-party "social forces" were established at this time in many sectors of society in which the development of strong movements had underscored the acuteness of the political order's legitimacy crisis. The new institutions—whose inauguration gained momentum between 1975 and 1977—ranged from the governance of the school system to that of neighborhood communities. Despite their enlarging the scope for participation, they were actually accorded little decision-making power. Moreover, the social forces' original nonpartisan character quickly receded, accentuating instead the emergence of a new type of party politics.[47] This tendency was enhanced both by the political professionalism stimulated by the institutions themselves and by the fact that participation proved easier for forces—such as the major political parties—with an organized system of activism and with reserves of party militants.

The new institutions presaged significant changes in the context of the New Left's mobilization and growth. The high degree of centralization that was characteristic of the Italian system of government until the early 1970s had made the central decision-making bodies the primary focus of mass pressure. The new multiplication of institutions—and of negotiating partners—dispersed tensions and, to a certain extent, routinized political confrontation into procedurally regulated bargaining. This weakened the New Left's opposi-

Comparative Politics   April 1982

tional thrust and thereby altered the climate surrounding the feminist movement.

Women, moreover, also obtained their share of new institutions: regional
and municipal governments set up *"consulte femminili,"* through which
women's associations were to be consulted on matters directly concerning
women. The establishment of these organisms congealed the pattern of more
informal contacts that had previously been developed by many branches of
local government and, at the same time, proved unsuccessful in stimulating
participation that was not based on the old system of designation by the political parties. For the feminist movement, lacking the organizational structures
necessary to enable it to develop stable forms of representation, the obstacles
hampering its participation in these bodies generally proved to be insurmountable.[48]

While such changes in the context and in the institutional framework curtailed the feminist movement's effectiveness in the political sphere, its difficulties were accentuated by a basic slant in its approach to politics. Since the
referendum on divorce in 1974 the feminist movement had embodied wom-
en's tendency to establish themselves—in a redefined identity—as a new collective actor.[49] Both the intensity of the ideological debate carried out within
the New Left and the attention dedicated to the creation of specific symbols of
identity (the adoption of pink—as opposed to red—as the distinctive feminist
color, the replacement of the clenched fist by the touching of index fingers
and thumbs held over head as a hand signal in demonstrations, even the evolution of particular modes of dress) indicated the crucial nature of this issue to
the groups involved.

Viewed in this light, the threat that a large part of the movement perceived
as coming from negotiating with the "official" parties over abortion becomes
intelligible, for it symbolized the latent fear that the movement's nonnegoti-
able goal (the full-fledged acceptance of feminism) might be overshadowed or
basically compromised in the course of processes of bargaining over specific
goals. Working out long-term strategies and implementing tactics does not
easily meld with a demand largely skewed toward the affirmation of a new
identity.

The weaknesses manifested in the expression of specific demands were
compounded by the kinds of responses produced through the legislature by the
party system, especially in relation to the question of abortion. The Christian
Democracy did not actively participate in the last phases of the parliamentary
debate concerning abortion. After the 1975 regional elections, the new leadership that emerged aimed at relegitimating the party as a popular, progressive
force. Zaccagnini, the new secretary, therefore steered the party away from
stances that could provoke widespread opposition. Thus, to avoid a repeat
performance of the reaction that had been aroused by the joint vote with the

Yasmine Ergas

Fascists in the spring of 1976, the Christian Democrats decided to abstain from the final vote in Parliament on abortion, thereby enabling new legislation to be approved in 1978.

The Communist party, however, did not abandon the attempt to consolidate the relationship with the Christian Democracy even on the substantive content of the abortion bill. The Communists therefore insisted on restricting women's "right to choose" in accordance with principles they deemed to be generally acceptable to the Catholic masses, constituents of both the DC and the PCI.

The new law had important consequences for the feminist movement that greatly complicated its dealings with the party system. Although feminists had not reached a unified stance on the ideal contents of a law on abortion, certain priorities had been expressed from the outset. The slogan, *"aborto libero, gratuito e assistito,"* for example, enunciated some basic points: that the woman be the only decision maker, and that the state recognize abortion as a form of necessary health care, therefore subsidizing it and making adequate provision in medical facilities. Furthermore, distinguishing between the right of women over and under a certain age to an abortion was expressly rejected, and it was insisted that "conscientious objection," that is, medical personnel's right to be exempted, on moral grounds, from performing abortions, be severely controlled.

These demands carried a double valence. They evidently sought to obtain the best conditions for women needing abortions. They also, however, attempted to redefine the symbolic significance implicit in the legislative order so as to free women's status through this law from the hallmarks of patriarchal authority. The fundamental thrust of the mobilization around abortion was the right of women (all women) to self-determination. In this context, the insistence on controlling conscientious objectors and on the provision of adequate facilities must be seen as expressing not only the demand for particular conditions but also the aim of ensuring the effectiveness of women's decisional power. Not by chance, a tune was set to the words "How come / How come / We never decide? / From now on / From now on / We will be the only ones to decide."[50]

In the phases preceding the final parliamentary debate, the left-wing parties had recognized that, were the "justifiable causes" for abortion to be restricted to those incurring serious risks for women's health, in many cases authorization would be impossible to obtain. "Social circumstances" were therefore introduced as a sufficient motivation for abortion. With this catchall phrase, a loophole was opened through which it could be expected that abortion would actually be made free (in the sense that women would find a suitable cause for their request) without compelling the authorities to accept the principle of female self-determination. Furthermore, the principle of paternity was also

271

Comparative Politics   April 1982

incorporated into the new legislation. A clause was introduced indicating that the physician authorizing the abortion ought to consult the "presumed father of the conceived" unless the mother specifically objected.

Notwithstanding these two clauses, the final decision was still to be left to the individual adult woman, who consequently would now find herself in the peculiar position of needing an authorization that she could—theoretically—insist on being granted! Though the law's formulation made abortion a difficult procedure, its significance did not stem simply from the obstacles it placed in the path of those wanting to interrupt pregnancy.[51] On the contrary, the complicated twist in reasoning that adamantly established authorities that might then be disregarded indicates clearly that the real meaning must be sought elsewhere. It is to be found in the symbolic reaffirmation of the partial character of women's rights to self-determination. The process of seeking approval was a yoke to be passed under; it was, especially, a symbolic tribute to patriarchy.

The law on abortion not only had symbolic significance for feminism. It also contributed to the demobilization of the movement as an organized political actor. In particular, the service institutions around which the movement had grown were severely undermined. Most of the feminist movement's activities concerning social services were affected by the traditional emphasis of left-wing cultures on the state as the primary body responsible for social welfare. Direct action around abortion had therefore usually been envisaged as having a temporary character. By delivering and organizing abortions—and by organizing women's health centers—the feminists' aim was to highlight what the state was not, but ought to have been, doing and, in the process, to establish new standards for health services. Consequently, when the new law attributed responsibility for abortion to public health institutions and to specifically authorized private clinics, the previously engaged-in forms of direct action lost legitimacy amongst feminists themselves as well as in public opinion. The motivation toward civil disobedience then declined while the new regulations concerning abortion confirmed the illegality of the practices developed by the feminist movement.[52] As the initiatives based on direct action collapsed, the feminist movement lost both its center of recruitment and organization and its legitimating functions.

Conclusion

With the elections of 1976, the Italian "1968" ended.[53] They effectively marked the closure of the period of widespread mobilization that had been inaugurated by the students' revolt. As the PCI's vote jumped from 27 to 34 percent, the question of its role in government became unavoidable. At the

Yasmine Ergas

same time, the resilience demonstrated by the Christian Democratic party in holding on to its 38 percent of the electorate indicated widespread resistance to change. Discussion and negotiation centered around the participation of the various parties in government and, specifically, around that of the hitherto leading force of the opposition. The PCI, aided by its expansion into the "peripheral" areas of the New Left[54] as well as by the latter's electoral weakness, tended to concentrate political representation of New Left forces in its own hands.

Furthermore, in 1976, following the elections, the PCI, by abstaining in the vote of confidence, permitted the newly formed government headed by Christian Democrat Giulio Andreotti to survive. (Two years later, on the same day that Aldo Moro was kidnapped, the PCI voted in favor of the DC minority cabinet, thus entering into the parliamentary majority supporting the government, for the first time since 1947.) Again in 1976, a Communist became speaker of the Chamber of Deputies, and Communists received seven committee chairmanships in Parliament, four in the Chamber of Deputies, and three in the Senate. These events are emblematic of the changes evoked by the PCI's entry into the "area of government," which directly affected or menaced the position of organized sectors of society, thus making the relevant interest groups the primary forces articulated in the party system.[55] As processes of new institution building modified the form of government of segments of society in which dissent had been especially acute, favoring party representation and dispersing tensions, the focus of political discussion shifted back to the relations between the traditional actors of the political system. In fact, the processes synthesized by the 1976 elections significantly altered the characteristics of the "crisis of representation" epitomized by the insurgence of the New Left.

The PCI's entry into the governmental sphere seemed to seal the working class's effective attainment of new levels of citizenship. That its integration into the dominant political framework was in fact only partial and actually left unresolved large portions of the demands of many of the preceding decade's emerging collective actors has become increasingly apparent as the Communist party both encountered insurmountable limits blocking its direct involvement in government and lost ground within the sectors of society expressing critical stances toward the country's principal institutions. But, though a series of events—ranging from a youth revolt (March 1977) to the referendum on the attribution of public funds to political parties (May 1978) to the most recent legislative (June 1979) and regional (July 1980) elections—indicates that the party system's crisis is not "over," the movements arising out of the 1968-69 mobilizations have proved unequipped to deal with the changes that had intervened in the political system. The wall separating them from the seats of traditional political activity has thus thickened. Negotiations over the po-

Comparative Politics   April 1982

litical system's statute and, in particular, over the PCI's role have culminated—albeit after the introduction of significant changes—in a restriction of
the forces involved, which left the women's movement, among others, on the
sidelines.

In this changed context, these movements have increasingly turned to the
development of new lifestyles.[56] Thus, in the feminist camp, while the coordinating committees established during the abortion campaign dwindled out of
existence—after the elections but well before the approval of the new law—
collectives centering around cultural issues ("women and the visual arts,"
"women and writing," "women and culture," and so on) gathered momentum. Collectives without a specific thematic orientation, however, often stopped meeting and, after a while, even some of those built around precise topics
drifted apart. Feminism seemed to continue its expansion both in more imperceptible ways—through the multiplication of informal contacts—and in
specific organized sectors of society (professional associations, trade unions,
even the major political parties) while losing the structures that had characterized its existence in its more dynamic phase of growth.

Those structures had, in fact, been genetically linked to the New Left,
which had constituted a terrain of mediation and socialization facilitating the
expansion of feminism.[57] The conduciveness of these settings had stemmed
from the frustration generated by the perpetuation of a situation of strain
linked to the role conflict experienced by young female students, the women's
subordinate standing in their organizations, and the lack of recognition of their
importance in a "revolutionary" process. This combined with the generation
of new political resources necessary to allow women's frustration to be transformed into mobilization: resources like leadership skills, organizational
structures, communication networks, and ideology.

The main core of the feminist movement had therefore emerged in relation
to a highly politicized reference group. Consequently, the comparison on
which it could base its differentiation and demand its own recognition was
largely skewed toward the political system. This politicization was, however,
rooted in a particular historical context, largely dominated by an upsurge of
working-class mobilization in which the PCI could renegotiate its role in the
political system. In the situation created by the elections of 1976, the loss of a
"New Left" reference and sources of political socialization, the failure of the
institutional strategies implicitly adopted, and the changes in the political-
institutional framework combined to foster the decline of autonomous
feminist interaction with the political system. The global, separatist subculture protecting the movement from effective demise has, moreover, followed
a basic orientation toward social and cultural change. Shifting its attention
from (improbable) macrotransformations of the political order to the problems
of everyday life, feminism can, presumably, continue to "talk to" and "talk

Yasmine Ergas

of'' those changes in women's attitudes that the national referendum on abortion, held on May 17-18, 1981, so eloquently reflected. In the referendum that pitted a proposal to severely restrict abortion rights, presented by a Catholic-dominated ''right-to-life'' movement, against a proposal to liberalize it totally, supported by the Radical party, Italian voters upheld the 1978 legislation by an overwhelming majority. The ''right-to-life'' proposal won consent from only 32 percent of the electorate. Public opinion has thus shifted toward a far more positive attitude toward women's rights than could have been expected at the end of the 1960s. Whether feminism can, however, on its own, generate the resources necessary to redevelop a general negotiation of women's status with the political system or whether this will have to wait for a new, more general mobilization of oppositional forces in Italy remains to be seen.

NOTES

As always, the merits of this article are due to many; the responsibilities are mine. Thanks go to Judy Adler, Laura Balbo, Bianca Beccalli, Victoria De Grazia, Peter Lange, and Simonetta Piccone Stella for their careful comments. Both Sidney Tarrow and Marcello Fedele read, discussed, and helped to revise the article with greater interest and patience than could decently be asked for. I also wish to thank one of the anonymous readers of *Comparative Politics*, whose detailed comments helped to improve greatly an earlier version.

1. Throughout this paper an abstract term—*the feminist movement*—will be used to refer synthetically to the multiform aggregation of women that emerged after 1968. In fact, this movement has always been composed of many strands with differing orientations. It is my intention to attempt to trace only the principal phases of the development of the *mainstream* of the feminist movement and to focus on its interaction with the political system.

2. Alberto Melucci has pointed out that movements differ in fundamental ways according to the planes of the sociopolitical systems they act upon. Alberto Melucci, ''L'azione ribelle. Formazione e struttura dei movimenti sociali'' in *Movimenti di Rivolta*, ed. Alberto Melucci (Milan: Etas Libri, 1976), pp. 3-66.

The feminist movement's increasing difficulty in dealing with political problems has been widely debated within the movement. See, for example: ''Movimento e istituzione,'' *Donna Woman Femme* 4 (1977): 5-45; and the monographic issue on politics, *Differenze: speciale politica* (1979).

3. Francesco Alberoni has given a penetrating description of this stage—for which he has coined the term *stato nascente*—in the genesis of social movements. Francesco Alberoni, *Movimento e istituzione* (Bologna: Il Mulino, 1977).

4. Luisa Muraro, discussing the biographies of women involved in the Resistance, has noted that ''women have shown . . . that they want to obtain equality as a *lateral effect* of the struggle for other objectives. . . . It's logical enough. . . . How can someone say that she wants to reach equality when she thinks she is equal and she has just proven that she is better than so many others?'' Luisa Muraro, ''Simili a donne,'' *Quaderni Piacentini* 60-61 (October 1976): 208.

5. For recent contributions, see Claus Offe, *Lo stato nel capitalismo maturo* (Milan: Etas Libri, 1977); Alan Wolfe, *The Limits of Legitimacy* (New York: The Free Press, 1977); and Jurgen Habermas, *Communication and the Evolution of Society* (Boston: Beacon Press, 1979).

6. Joyce Gelb and Marian L. Palley, ''Women and Interest Group Politics,'' *American Politics Quarterly* 5 (July 1977): 331-352.

7. Jurgen Habermas, op. cit., p. 178.

Comparative Politics   April 1982

8. Sidney Tarrow, "Aspetti della crisi italiana: note introduttive," in *La crisi italiana*, ed. Luigi Graziano and Sidney Tarrow (Turin: Einaudi, 1979), p. 3-40.

9. The evolution of the Communist party's recruitment policies is documented in *La presenza sociale della DC e del PCI*, ed. Agopik Manoukian (Bologna: Il Mulino, 1968). Further data are in Maria Weber, *Il voto delle donne*, Quaderni di Biblioteca della Liberta 8 (Turin: Editrice Bdl di A. Guerrini & Co., 1977). UDI's history has been recently reconstructed by Giulietta Ascoli, "L'UDI tra emancipazione e liberazione," *Problemi del Socialismo* 17, no. 4 (October-December 1976): 109-159. For an analysis of the Communist party in the 1950s, see Pietro Ingrao, "L'indimenticabile 1956" and "Ancora sulla svolta del 1956" in his *Masse e potere* (Rome: Editori Riuniti, 1977), pp. 101-176.

10. The 66.8 percent membership drop refers to the total female enrollment in Azione Cattolica, i.e., Unione donne and Gioventù femminile. In 1963, the sum total of AC's membership (men and women, all age groups) was 2,778,000; in 1969, it had fallen to 929,000. For data on women in Azione Cattolica and in the DC, see Agopik Manoukian, ed., op. cit. and Maria Weber, op. cit.

11. See Paolo Farneti, "I partiti politici e il sistema di potere" in *L'Italia Contemporanea*, ed. V. Castronuovo (Turin: Einaudi, 1976), pp. 61-104, especially p. 68.

12. Laura Balbo, *Stato di famiglia* (Milan: Etas Libri, 1976); Fortunata Piselli, *La donna che lavora* (Bari: De Donato, 1976); and Chiara Saraceno, *Anatomia della famiglia* (Bari: De Donato, 1976).

13. See Massimo Paci, *Mercato del lavoro e classi sociali in Italia* (Bologna: Il Mulino, 1973); Luigi Frey, *Lavoro a domicilio e decentramento nell'attivita produttiva* (Milan: Franco Angeli, 1975); Luigi Frey. Renata Livraghi, Giovanni Mottura, and Michele Salvati, *Occupazione e sottoccupazione femminile in Italia* (Milan: Franco Angeli, 1976); Mea Furnari, Giovanni Mottura, and Enrico Pugliese, "Occupazione femminile e mercato del lavoro," *Inchiesta* 18 (1975): 3-29.

14. On the importance of including the analysis of role options as well as of stress in explaining protest and deviant behavior, see Richard Cloward and Frances F. Piven, "Hidden Protest: The Channeling of Female Innovation and Resistance," *Signs* 4, no. 4 (1979): 651-669.

15. Jo Freeman, *The Politics of Women's Liberation* (New York: Longman, 1975), p. 31.

16. Maren Carden, *The New Feminist Movement* (New York: Russell Sage Foundation, 1975), p. 158.

17. Franca Pieroni Bortolotti, "Movimento femminista e movimento operaio. Appunti di storia," *Critica Marxista* 16, no. 5 (1978): 106.

18. See Laura Balbo, op. cit.

19. For example, the percentage of women amongst university students rose from 26.5 in 1952-53 to 28.9 in 1962-63 to 36.1, in 1967-68.

Changes in family size may be gathered from data concerning the order of childbirths in families. From 1953 to 1968, for every 1,000 legitimate births, firstborn children increased by 18.2 and secondborn children by 48.9, whereas fourthborn children decreased by 5.5, fifthborn by 16.5, and sixthborn by 13.7. While officially registered female employment decreased between 1959 and 1969 by 1,050,000 units in agriculture and by 196,000 units in industry, it increased by 82,000 units in the service sector.

The evolution of women's sociopolitical status is exemplified in the legislation. Some of the most significant passages may be recalled: 1946—suffrage, 1947—recognition of equality of the sexes in the constitution, 1950—protection of working mothers, 1956—ratification by the president of the Republic of the International Labor Office's Convention establishing the principle of equal pay, 1962—banning of work layoffs because of marriage, 1963—both equal access to careers and pension rights for housewives, 1964—establishment of the principal of "just causes" in employment layoffs.

20. The psychological and psychoanalytic literature concerning women's difficulties in identifying with extrafamilial roles is too vast to recall. An excellent analysis of the contradictions linked to female emancipation is U. Prokop, *Realtà e desiderio: l'ambivalenza femminile* (Milan: Feltrinelli, 1978).

21. Simonetta Piccone Stella analyzes in depth the attitudes of a sample of women students at the University of Salerno in her *Ragazze del Sud* (Rome: Editori Riuniti, 1978). Reports of similar

Yasmine Ergas

research carried out in other Italian universities are in "Speciale Donna," *Inchiesta* 18 (1975).

22. Carlo Donolo,"La politica ridefinita," *Quaderni Piacentini* 35 (July 1968).

23. Daniela Del Boca and Elena Dorigotti, "Storie di compagne," *Ombre rosse* 15/16 (July 1976): 97, 99-100. Other biographies of women active in the New Left are in Giulietta Ascoli et al., *La parola elettorale* (Rome: Edizioni delle donne, 1976). I am also basing these considerations on a set of unpublished interviews gathered in 1978.

24. See the biographical materials cited above: Laura Grasso, *Compagno padrone* (Florence: Guaraldi, 1975); and L. Merenda, "Le donne nelle copie della nuova sinistra," *Inchiesta* 27 (1977): 70-80.

25. John Urry, *Reference Groups and the Theory of Revolution* (London: Routledge and Kegan Paul, 1973) indicates proximity, saliency of a particular dimension, and distinctiveness of the object as the key factors favoring structural comparisons.

26. Collections of documents produced by the italian feminist movement are to be found in: Rosalba Spagnoletti, *I movimenti femministi in Italia* (Rome: Savelli, 1973); Bianca Maria Frabotta and Giuseppina Ciuffreda, eds., *Femminismo e lotta di classe in Italia* (Rome: Savelli, 1974); and Bianca Maria Frabotta, ed., *La politica del feminismo* (Rome: Savelli, 1976). A detailed analysis of the development of feminist theory is in *Lessico politico delle donne* vol. 3, *Teorie del femminismo*, ed. Manuela Fraire (Milan: Gulliver, 1978).

27. Oberschall stresses the importance of segmentation in the recruitment patterns of social movements in his *Social conflict and social movements* (Englewood Cliffs: Prentice-Hall, 1973). The effects of the New Left's segmentation on the recruitment of the feminist movement is clearly exemplified in the formation of "feminist-communist" collectives, largely made up by militants of the *Manifesto* and, with the latter's founding, of the Partito di Unita Proletaria per il comunismo.

28. Since the late 1960s, the Radical party has essentially functioned by promoting a series of single-issue movements focusing on civil liberties. Although in the early 1970s it occasionally established "working arrangements" with specific groups of the New Left, profound differences with the New Left itself remained. Whereas the Radicals espoused a libertarian, rather spontaneous and fundamentally nonmaterialistic ideology that granted little attention to "class conflict," the New Left's politics was steadfastly couched in the language of the "class struggle." On the Radical party, see Massimo Teodori, Piero Ignazi, Angelo Panebianco, *I nuovi radicali* (Milan: Mondadori, 1977); Piero Ignazi and Angelo Panebianco, "Inchiesta sui militanti radicali—mutamenti tra il congresso 1976 e il congresso 1977," *Argomenti Radicali* 7 (1978): 42-57; and Angelo Panebianco, "Fratture sociali e conflitti politici: la crisi del partito di massa e la politica radicale," *Argomenti Radicali* 11 (1979): 34-51.

29. Separately, the Radical party–based CISA (Centro Italiano Sterilizzazione e Aborto) also established illegal abortion centers. Clandestine abortion groups functioned in Turin, Milan, and Bologna, as well as in Rome.

30. Marcello Fedele, *Classi e partiti negli anni settanta* (Rome: Editori Riuniti, 1979).

31. Marcello Fedele, op. cit.: p. 229.

32. See Paolo Farneti, op. cit.: p. 93.

33. When the regional elections held in June 1975 both delivered to left-wing forces the government of regions in which the DC had previously had a central role and showed an especially marked increase in support for the PCI, the Christian Democrats changed strategy. The party then chose new leadership, nominating Benigno Zaccagnini secretary and Aldo Moro president, and aimed at reviving its popular image and reconstructing its channels of communications with society. Furthermore, until his death, Aldo Moro sought to steer the DC away from hostile confrontation with the PCI, favoring, instead, a more collaborative stance.

34. See Peter Lange,"Crisis and Consent, Change and Compromise: Dilemmas of Italian Communism in the Seventies," *West European Politics* 2, no. 3 (1979): 110-132.

35. See Paolo Farneti, op. cit., p. 96; and David Hine, "Social Democracy in Italy," in *Social Democratic Parties in Western Europe*, ed. W.E. Paterson and A.H. Thomas (London: Croom and Helm, 1977), p. 67-85.

36. In the concluding document of a seminar on maternity, UDI had refused to accept the principle of a system of "cases" within which abortion could be consented (February 1 and 2, 1975).

37. These proposals were subsequently modified during the same legislature by both the PCI

277

Comparative Politics   April 1982

and the DC. The PCI shifted decision-making power from a committee of three specialists to one MD; and the DC accepted abortion in cases of incest or of violent assault.

38. Alain Touraine, *Production de la société* (Paris: Editions du Seuil, 1973), p. 391-392.

39. See Marcello Fedele, op.cit., pp. 245-254.

40. Women's health centers were opened by militants of the feminist movement in at least the following cities: Rome Turin, Milan, Aosta, Palermo, and Bologna. They were planned, however, in many more cities ranging from Venice to Bari.

41. *Espresso*, 6 December 1975.

42. Luisa Melograni, "Il caleidoscopio del femminismo," *L'Unità*, 24 March 1976; "Femministe nei quartieri," 26 March 1976; "Libri fatti da donne," 30 March 1976.

43. Luther Gerlach and Virginia Hine, *People, Power Change: Movements of Social Transformation* (Indianapolis: Bobbs-Merrill, 1970) discuss movements based on decentralized, segmentary, and reticular structures.

44. Mariella Gramaglia, "1968: il venir dopo e l'andar oltre del movimento femminista," *Problemi del Socialismo* 17, no. 4 (1976): 197-201.

45. Karen Beckwith, *Female Communist Deputies to the Italian Parliament: A Thirty-Year Retrospective* (Paper presented at the Conference of Europeanists, Washington, D.C. March 39-31, 1979).

46. This process of "institutional incrementalism" is discussed by Bruno Dente and Gloria Regonini, "Urban Policy and Political Legitimation: The Case of Italian Neighborhood Councils," *International Political Science Review* 1, no. 2 (1980): 187-202.

47. The functioning of the new institutions has been discussed by Alberto Testa, *Intervista alla citta* (Bari: De Donato, 1979). Antonio Milanaccio, *La partecipazione subalterna* (Torino: Einaudi, 1979) examines the functioning of the "consigli di fabbrica" (factory councils).

48. In fact, the "consulte femminili" introduced a new filter between the institutional level of politics and the feminist movement. Examination of the relevant regional legislation demonstrates two points: (1) the presence of the autonomous women's movement is clearly outweighed by that of other forces; (2) the insistence of the national organization of the women's associations to be represented, as that on their democratic structure and on their statutory aims, impedes the participation of the feminist movement, whose organization, structure and aims are entirely informal.

49. The concept of *collective identity* as a motivating factor in political actions is set forth by Alessandro Pizzorno in "Le due logiche dell'azione di classe" in *La politica nell'Italia che cambia*, ed. Alberto Martinelli and Gianfranco Pasquino (Milan: Feltrinelli, 1978), pp. 230-253.

50. "Come mai/come mai/noi non decidiamo mai?/D'ora in poi/d'ora in poi/decidiamo solo noi!"

51. As the law now stands, within the first ninety days of pregnancy, if its continuation or childbirth or maternity constitutes a serious danger, physically or psychologically, in relation to the woman's state of health, to her economic, social, or familial conditions or to the circumstances in which conception occurred, she may turn to a family health center (*consultorio*), to a medical structure expressly recognized for this purpose by the regional government, or to a physician in her confidence (article 4). The physician or structure called upon must ascertain her medical condition and examine with the woman and with the "father of the conceived," if the woman agrees, possible solutions for avoiding abortion. If the physician considers the case urgent, he immediately gives the woman a certificate enabling her to request abortion in a publicly recognized hospital. If the physician does not consider the case urgent, he gives the woman a document, which she also signs, on the basis of which she must wait seven days before requesting the abortion from an appropriate structure (article 5). After ninety days' pregnancy, abortion is consented to only when (1) pregnancy or childbirth represents a serious threat to the woman's health or (2) the presence of pathological processes is ascertained.

52. The law explicitly states that abortions may be performed only by specified institutions and in specific circumstances.

53. Carlo Donolo, *Mutamento o transizione?* (Bologna: Il Mulino, 1977).

54. Marzio Barbagli and Piergiorgio Corbetta, "Base sociale del P.C.I. e movimenti collettivi" in Alberto Martinelli and Gianfranco Pasquino, eds. op. cit., pp. 144-170.

55. The Radical party obtained 1.1 percent of the popular vote and four seats in the Chamber of Deputies. Proletarian Democracy won 1.5 percent of the vote and five seats in the Chamber.

Yasmine Ergas

Together they consequently totaled nine deputies out of 630. For a few of the significant contributions concerning the effects of the 1976 elections, see Carlo Donolo, *Mutamento o transizione?*, op. cit.; Federico Stame, *Societa civile e critica delle instituzioni* (Milan: Feltrinelli, 1977); and Marcello Fedele, op. cit.

56. The change in focus of the New Left's movements is emblematically expressed in Luigi Manconi, Gad Lerner, and Marino Sinibaldi, "Le altre stagioni del movimento di primavera," *Ombre rosse* 22/23 (October 1977): 3-39.

57. Jo Freeman, op. cit., also attributes an important role to the organizations of the New Left, as a system of intermediate groupings, in the formation of the feminist movement.

[33]

Raimondo Catanzaro

Enforcers, entrepreneurs, and survivors: how the *mafia* has adapted to change*

ABSTRACT

This article seeks to explain the reasons for the persistence and transformation of the *mafia*, a problem not addressed directly in the literature. The cultural codes of honour and of instrumental friendship are analysed. These codes served to train groups and individuals to competitiveness and to a particular relationship with the state. This led to the emergence of *mafia* when, with the Unification of Italy, the Sicilian periphery encountered the Italian national state. The promotion of economic development over the last thirty years has had the effect of helping the *mafia* to spread rather than that of eliminating it.

The thesis of the article is that the continuity of the *mafia* derives from its capacity to adapt continually to change. This happens because the *mafia* groups are not relics of the past, but were formed as a result of a specific combination of ancient and modern, a mixture of private violence and the legitimate violence of the state, of competition for economic resources in the market and the absence of regulatory standards for economic activities other than violence. In this sense, the *mafia* is a phenomenon typical of what can be defined as a process of social hybridization.

INTRODUCTION

The recrudescence of the *mafia* in the last few years raises disturbing questions. One no longer thinks of *mafia* simply as an expression of Sicilian backwardness; today one wants to ask why the *mafia* and its modes of behaviour have lasted, what its social roots are, and how it has been able to adapt to new economic and social contexts.

The literature on *mafia* has not yet confronted this problem. While interesting analyses of traditional *mafia* exist — of its codes of behaviour and its recent move towards entrepreneurship[1] — the continuity/transformation of the cultural codes and behaviour which

The British Journal of Sociology Volume XXXVI Number 1

permit the perpetuation of the *mafia* are mentioned only rarely. The limited goal of this article is to make a contribution to the understanding of the ways in which, throughout the *mafia*'s history, its typical codes of behaviour and values have always adapted to changes in socio-economic and political conditions.

The article is organized around four basic points. I will first analyse two traditional codes of Sicilian culture, and particularly of *mafia* culture: the code of honour and the code of instrumental friendship. My argument is that these codes, and their accompanying behaviour patterns, are not traditional, in the sense that they are not feudal or pre-capitalistic vestiges; rather they derive from economic activities and networks of political and social relationships which are modern, even if not industrial or capitalistic.

The second point is that these cultural codes and modes of behaviour have trained individuals and groups both to competitiveness — albeit in a market with such idiosyncratic characteristics as regulation by violence — and to a relationship with the public administration that was particularly useful at the moment of the impact of the Italian nation-state upon the Sicilian periphery.

The third point is that the *mafia* emerged right after the building of the Italian state as a consequence of three aspects of that process. These are: the communication gap between centre and periphery and the consequent delegation to the local ruling class of social control over the peasants; the diffuse nature of the Italian public administration system of the periphery; and patronage system of local government.

The fourth and last point is based on the observation that in the last thirty years the economic development efforts taken by the state in Sicily have not eliminated the *mafia* but, rather, have accentuated its visibility and relevance. The *mafia*'s values and modes of behaviour have adapted to the new situation of the welfare state, changing meaning and aims, but continuing to function as cultural tools for the enlargement of the *mafia* and its expansion to the national and international level.

The main thesis of the article is that the continuity of the *mafia*, if only in its capacity for profound transformation, derives from the fact that the *mafia*'s behaviour has always been a specific combination of ancient and modern, a mixture of private violence and the legitimate violence of the state, of competition for economic resources in the market and the absence of regulatory standards for economic activities other than violence. Exactly because they are not relics of the past the values and modes of behaviour of the *mafia* have been able to adapt to every form of social change that has taken place in Sicily. Indeed, the *mafia* has sometimes played a leading role in such processes precisely because of its historical ability to hybridize traditional and modern values.

36   *Raimondo Catanzaro*

I. THE CODE OF HONOUR

Mafia behaviour is, by definition, determined by honour. The *mafioso* is
a man who can earn respect unaided by the law or even by successful
violation of it. The code of honour pervades much of Mediterranean
culture[2] and, in order to understand honour as the basis of *mafia*
behaviour, it is necessary to understand its social connotation. This
connotation is double and contradictory. Along with a 'static' notion
of honour, which is related to conditions of inequality, there coexists a
second, 'dynamic', notion deriving from the subjective pretence of
equality. This manifests itself in the competition between individuals
and groups.[3]

   In its static aspect honour is the socially recognized ability of the
head of a family to guarantee his family a standard of living at their
level of resources. This is thus related to the ability to care effectively
for the family's property and its unity against attacks from outside,
with particular regard to the protection of the chastity of the wife and
the virginity of the daughters. Honour is thus a socially recognized
means of evaluating the distribution of statuses with reference to three
aspects of individual behaviour: (1) living at the level of the economic
resources possessed; (2) assuring the protection of those resources;
and (3) effectively guarding the sexual integrity of the women of the
family. A number of anthropological studies[4] show that, in the culture
of Mediterranean peoples, these three elements are related. For
example, a woman who is a spendthrift or wears clothes or colours not
suited to her rank is probably an adulteress as well. If a man cannot
guarantee the chastity of his women it is probably because he is a
good-for-nothing. And so forth.

   Two aspects of this notion of honour should be emphasized: first,
treating women and property as equal in terms of honour and loss of
honour; second, the social duty of living according to one's means and
station. In a society which holds to the principle of living within one's
means, property is given, transmitted by inheritance, not acquired
through processes of social mobility. This notion of honour is applied
to women. As can be inferred from the expressions 'honoured' or
'honest' women, the woman is merely a passive subject of the
attribution of honour: honour is a quality that she has at birth and
which is lost only by inappropriate behaviour. By this definition, the
only one which applies to women — but applies not only to them —
honour is a code of behaviour which reflects the fixed distribution of
ascribed statuses. A person is honoured because he was born in an
honoured family. In this way honour has a purely static connotation;
it is a reflection of an ascribed status.

   But in Sicilian culture one can be not only an honoured person but
also 'a man of honour'. The difference is that one is not born a man of
honour but becomes one. In this second sense, honour is a particular

ability consisting in strength and cunning or in some other individual gift which inspires admiration and respect and helps one make one's way in life. For example, the man of honour, even if his origins are humble, has become wealthy and respected by bullying. Or he has killed and been acquitted for lack of evidence; in which case he can count on *omertà*, the silence of others obtained by threat of violence. In this case, honour is conceived of as an extraordinary individual ability reinforced by the accumulation of a capital of successful violence.[5] The more effectively a man is able to use violence the higher he rises on the scale of honour. The struggle for honour is therefore a competition for social mobility in a society that is still a stranger to the capitalistic market. One fights to acquire honour and so to alter the pre-existing fixed distribution of honour. This second is a dynamic conception of honour as an achieved status.

Honour is, therefore, on the one hand an ascribed status deriving from the family condition, and so a typical product of social inequality arising from social stratification. On the other hand, it can also result from an extraordinary individual ability, that is, a status achieved by means of the struggle for honour. In this second aspect honour is related to conditions of social equality.

It should thus be emphasized that the competition for honour is not open to everyone but operates among subjects who either are equal or who can claim equality.[6] If a baron seduced the wife or daughter of a peasant, or appropriated his property, it was not usually an occasion for conflicts in terms of honour. The social inferior accepted these events as part of his earthly lot. But when the offences came from his peers conflicts over honour would break out. These conflicts are particularly violent for two reasons. First, because honour is perceived as a fixed amount; the conflicts are zero-sum games. When someone acquires honour someone else loses it in the same measure.

But there is a second and more pertinent reason why the struggle for honour has crucial importance. In a society in which resources are scarce people who compete successfully for honour win a symbolic resource that permits greater access to material resources. Honour is, in fact, a system of stratification that

> describes the distribution of wealth in a social idiom, and prescribes appropriate behaviour for people at the various points in the hierarchy; it entails acceptance of superordination and subordination . . . Honour stratification invites equals to quarrel, and asserts the cooperative dependence of those who have less honour on those who have more.[7]

Honour is an idiom in the language of competition for access to resources, a competition in the form of physical violence that takes place between individuals and groups. These groups are defined according to networks of kinship, quasi-kinship (*comparaggio*, that is,

Raimondo Catanzaro

co-parenthood, relationships between godparents and godchildren
and between parents and godparents of the same children) and
instrumental friendship.

2. INSTRUMENTAL FRIENDSHIP

Every friendship has two components. The emotional component
consists in the pleasure of the company of friends. When this
component is emphasized the friendship is an end in itself. The other
is an access-to-resources component which manifests itself in the
voluntary exchange of favours. When this aspect is emphasized,
friendship becomes an instrument for attaining goals outside the
friendship itself. This is nearly the ideal type of instrumental
friendship. The essence of instrumental friendship, therefore, lies in
the possibility of reciprocity in the exchange of resources, either one's
own or acquired; in the potential continuity of such exchange; and ,
finally, in the largely open nature of the relationship. In fact, each of
the friends acts as a potential link with others.[8] But in instrumental
friendship there is always an emotional component, even if it is mainly
symbolic-ritual.[9] Instrumental friendship is essentially, however, a
sort of credit card which takes the form of such expressions as 'Say
that I sent you', or 'Mention my name'. This creates bonds structured
according to typical networks, which common parlance calls 'friends
of friends'.[10]
    What functions does instrumental friendship perform? It serves
essentially to create non-corporate groups, networks of informal
relationships that compete with one another for economic and
political resources. In the networks of instrumental friendship,
solidarity is based on trust in the fulfillment of obligations on the
principle of balanced reciprocity.[11] It is trust, then, which characterizes
these non-corporate groups and not the stable network of relationships
and impersonal obligations typical of modern corporate groups.
Networks of instrumental friendships based on informal relationships
of trust played a crucial economic role in pre-unification Sicily. In
fact, they made the principal economic and commercial transactions
possible. The basic instrument for this was made from *ad hoc* — that
is, temporary and task-oriented — coalitions. Such coalitions were
destined to dissolve as soon as the task was completed. Naturally this
meant that they were largely unstable, and so they continually
redefined and re-formed themselves. Moreover, the informal trust on
which they were based required constant reconfirmation by actions.[12]
Without this the coalition dissolved even before the goal was attained.
    Such an informal structure of interpersonal relationships was
typical of a society into which the principles of the capitalistic market
had not yet penetrated but which, nevertheless, had economic
relations with those centres in which the world system of the

European capitalist economy was being formed.[13] In other words, it belonged to the periphery of the European capitalistic system in formation. Let us see how instrumental friendship began.

3. THE GENESIS OF INSTRUMENTAL FRIENDSHIP AND THE CODE OF HONOUR

Before we examine the origins of instrumental friendship and the code of honour it will be helpful to outline some economic and political characteristics of Sicily under the Spanish empire (sixteenth and seventeenth centuries). Two very important developments occurred during this period: the reinforcement of the latifundistic structure of landownership; and absenteeism on the part of the barons. These developments, which had a marked effect on western Sicily, gave rise to a particularly active rural entrepreneurship which profited from the increasing demand of Spain and, later, north-central Europe for a foodstuff, durum wheat, whose cultivation was the specialty of the western Sicilian latifundia. Earlier, between the thirteenth and fifteenth centuries, a structure of human settlements based on agrotowns had progressively taken shape; the rural villages (*casali*) disappeared as the Catalan barons promoted sheep farming as well as the cultivation of grain. The small settlements of agricultural population in the countryside disappeared, as did inter-city markets, roads, and centres of artisanal production. There resulted, particularly in the area of the latifundia, a structure of less differentiated and complex settlements. Sicily, especially in the west, saw the disappearance of a structure in which villages, rural centres, and cities were integrated by means of bureaucratic and commercial hierarchies. Each agrotown became differentiated internally, but all resembled one another; there was neither division of labour nor any hierarchic order among them. Each settlement was connected to the outside world mainly by the export of grain.[14] The agrotowns were isolated and travel in the surrounding countryside was made dangerous by bandits and highwaymen. The administration was not able to guarantee public order. This lack of order spurred the rural entrepreneurs to create a system of self-defence based on the indiscriminate use of violence. The organization of armed bands of guards (*campieri*) and caretakers of latifundia later constituted the operative structure of *mafia* violence.

The absence of links between the agrotowns, the lack of commercial and market hierarchies and the need to get export goods to European markets all necessitated the creation of networks of connections which would be farther-reaching than merely local ones of kinship and quasi-kinship. Without a network of impersonal relationships, as would have been typical of the capitalistic market, the only, or at least the principal basis for trust was instrumental friendship and its main operative tool the temporary coalition of friends. Both served to define networks of exchange of economic resources. The code of instrumental friendship should, therefore, be interpreted as an organizational response of the rural entrepreneurs to the opportunities for commerce and export which opened up to them under Spanish rule.[15] The necessity of responding in these terms was accentuated by the nature of the Sicilian administrative system under Spain. The system of distribution of offices was prebendary and the behaviour of the bureaucracy certainly did not correspond to the Weberian ideal type. To obtain authorization, licences, concessions, and administrative passes, one needed to have entry to the right offices. One needed to be able to count on the favours of persons whom one would one day repay in kind. In other words, one needed one's own network of acquaintances in order to lubricate the slow mechanisms of bureaucracy.[16] Instrumental friendship was served for this too. In the absence of a capitalistic market and modern state, it functioned as an informal parallel structure which interacted with the administration. In a sense, instrumental friendship was to temporary coalitions as the state was to entrepreneurial associations in early capitalism: 'It lent credibility to contracts and a modicum of predictability to affairs.'[17]

The absence of a capitalistic market and modern state also helps to explain the reinforcement and institutionalization of the code of honour: by allowing the family to defend its property (including the women, for their productive and reproductive functions) against attacks from outside, it was an ideology of defence of the family and kinship groups.

From where does this ideology of defence derive and how has it established itself? One explanation which appears convincing is that of J. Schneider,[18] who adopts a thesis of Wallerstein on the different ways in which the capitalistic and the empire systems control peripheral areas. Unlike capitalistic economies, which use market mechanisms to control society, empires control their peripheries essentially by means of administrative instruments that tend to impede or slow up the private accumulation of capital. In Sicily, various elements threatened the unity and strength of the family with respect to property. In addition to laws dictating the division of property among the heirs at the death of the head of the family, and the dowry for the daughters who married, there were the principles of the Catholic Church. The Church's ban on marriage between cousins impeded the consolidation of property and 'subordinated the community of blood to the community of faith'.[19] Both the Church and political power exerted strong pressures that tended to limit the power of kinship groups in society. Thus the code of honour emerged and grew in strength as a response to the attack of the Church and of political power against the integrity of the family and its property.

The situation of Sicily before the unification of Italy cannot, therefore, be interpreted either in terms of feudalism or in terms of isolation. On the contrary, conditions developed which trained individuals and groups to both competitiveness and solidarity beyond the confines of the family. Competitiveness appeared in that particular arena in which honour was understood as a social idiom in the language of stratification by wealth. It is important to note that, unlike the market, where the opportunities for gain are formally peaceful and the actors are pledged not to use predatory and violent methods,[20] this is an arena in which the basic means of acquiring resources is violence. This gives business undertakings a temporary life in that possibility of violence precludes long-lasting trust and thus long-term investments. For this reason, *ad hoc* temporary coalitions based on networks of instrumental friendship constitute the ideal corporate tool. They have a flexibility which allows the alliances to orient themselves quickly to the sudden and unforeseeable changes that occur in a market whose main regulative instrument is violence. Furthermore, they provide a modicum of predictability insofar as they permit manipulation of state agencies for private ends. This economic and political system has been called 'broker capitalism',[21] being different from both feudalism and capitalism. In this system the functions of brokerage assume a crucial role.

4. THE IMPACT OF THE NATION-STATE AND THE RISE OF THE *MAFIA*

Throughout roughly five centuries of Spanish rule and the Kingdom of the Two Sicilies, Sicily was the periphery of either the Spanish Empire or the nascent European capitalist economy. After 1860 it became a periphery of the Italian state. This was a change of no small significance. Communication with the centre became crucial, and three aspects of the process of system-building assumed especial importance: 'penetration (state-building)', 'standardization (nation-building)', and 'equalization of the rights of participation (establishment of political citizenship)'.[22] And it is exactly while these were under way that conditions were created for the *mafia* to emerge as the institutionalization of the two codes we have discussed. The *mafia* emerges as the institutionalization both of private violence as means of social control for those who hold the monopoly of honour and of instrumental friendship as means of penetrating the public administration for private purposes (patronage). To understand the rise of the *mafia* it is necessary, therefore, to outline the social structure existing on the periphery and the manner in which the administrative and political system was constructed in the course of the formation of the Italian national state.

The *mafia* is not a relic of the past but a modern product of the process of formation of the Italian national state. To the extent that

42   *Raimondo Catanzaro*

violence was used as a private instrument of social control the *mafia*
was a means of easing tensions or a form of connection between formal
requirements of the national political society and the demands of the
periphery. Whoever performs such a function can be called a power
broker and, in fact, this is what the original *mafiosi* were. Their role was
to control the channels linking the local population with the national
society as a whole.[23] The structural conditions for the emergence of
the *mafia* can be traced back to the nature of the economic and social
structure of west-central Sicily during the crisis of the latifundia and
to the state's inability to use its monopoly of physical violence.[24]

The structure of the latifundia of west-central Sicily was atypical,
inasmuch as it was based on three social classes: absentee landed
aristocracy, agrarian bourgeoisie (represented by the *gabelloti*[25])
and peasants. There was no class of landless rural wage earners
(*braccianti*). The liberalization of commerce in land and the sale of
Church properties which followed unification did not produce a class
of peasant owners; they reinforced the power of the *gabelloti*, who
resembled the landed aristocracy in the scale of their landownership
and in that they did not exploit their holdings capitalistically.
Further, they imitated the aristocracy in their social behaviour. Thus,
despite the marketability of land the market remained extremely
small. Land was rarely sold and, when it was, it was sold in parcels so
large that most peasants were *de facto* kept out of the market. On the
other hand, rental contracts passed all the risks on to the peasants [26]
Therefore, the liberalization of the land market did not eliminate —
indeed, with the abolition of the rights to use common fields, it
accentuated — the hunger for land and competition for its possession.
Because the landowners were absent and a class of rural wage earners
did not exist conflicts were not between social classes ranked vertically
but were largely competition for the possession of land between
parallel groups. Land then remained essentially a source of power;
and, for this reason, possession of it or control over its use remained
conditions for the attributions of honour to individuals.

Under the conditions just described social tensions were aggravated.
The years 1812–60 saw the birth of a new class of bourgeois
landowners (the *gabelloti*), and increase in the numbers of landless
peasants and a growing interdependence of city and country and of
social classes.[27] This growing interdependence collided with the need
for centralized control typical of a newly formed national state. There
were two reasons for this: first, continuing interests of the absentee
landowners as the principal force of Sicilian society; second, the
strongly segmentary nature of rural Sicilian society which was related
to the self-sufficiency of the agrotowns and to the lack of efficient
communication networks between them and the society as a whole.
One of the most important aspects of this segmentation was caused by
the exclusion of the peasants from the labour market, because they

were not yet a labour force, and from the political market, because they did not have the right to vote. As a result, a state superimposed from outside, as the Italian one was, was unable to guarantee effective control and manipulation of social tensions. Recourse to violence certainly was not a novelty; but now, unlike in the past, it occurred in the context of weak authority of a state which formally claimed to hold a legitimate monopoly of physical violence.[28] This, in turn, forced the state, in the context of general choices of alliances among the industrial bourgeoisie of the north and landowners of the south,[29] to come to terms with whoever exercised *de facto* power at the local level, and to hand over to them the monopoly of legitimate violence. When it became understood that the sovereignty of the state did not actually exist violence became generalized. Thus the *mafia* represented a response to the strains among peasants, landlords and *gabelloti*, and between them and the central government. It was a way to manage these strains by means of a particular behaviour in which *mafiosi* specialized as power brokers.[30] Once characterized as holders of the honour monopoly, the *mafiosi* were able to exercise social control legally, playing a role of political and economic intermediaries. Their functions of mediation and liaison were not limited to control of the electorate and prevention of peasants' rebellions (or their repression by violence), but were based on their position of supervision and management on the absentee landlords' estates. In this sense it is possible to say that the economic base of *mafiosi* as power brokers finds an equivalent in the existence of broker capitalism. Thus as broker capitalism rises to fill the gap between agricultural production and marketing, similarly, at the level of social control, the *mafioso* as power broker appears to fill the gap between peasants and state, assuming from the state the management of physical violence. 'In terms of actual control and authority, *mafia* constituted a pragmatic dimension of the State.'[31]

This characterization of the *mafia* was facilitated by the nature of the central Italian administration at the periphery level, as well as by the organization of local administration.

The unified Italian state was characterized, right from the start, by the need to control the periphery with very strong instruments in order to prevent social disorders. This forced the central government to prefer the French administrative system, based on the figure of the prefect, to the English.[32] Nevertheless, the prefect was not an instrument for effecting the inter-ministerial unity of the administration in the French manner. In France, the prefecture controlled the activities of all the ministries at the territorial level, whereas in Italy, the prefecture as extension of the Ministry of Internal Affairs controlled only justice and local government. This led to a lack of administrative integration between centre and periphery and gave a diffuse quality to the Italian administrative system; this meant that

44   *Raimondo Catanzaro*

the administration penetrated to the periphery insufficiently and that
its control was weak. As a result the liberal élite slowed down the
introduction of universal suffrage thus depriving the local opposition
of the instrument of electoral representation.[33]

On the other hand, the local government did not manage to
mediate between society and the state. The introduction of local
autonomy where there had been no political participation and where
suffrage was very limited concentrated the resources in the hands of a
few local powerful men or their trusted collaborators. This caused
competition for the conquest of power at the local level to intensify.
Such competition nevertheless could only take the form of particularism
and patronage, given that the groups possessed of local political
power were the same ones which held the material bases of power at
the social level. In general, there occurred a form of patronage-based
competition for power. In fact, joining a patronage group was the only
means available to protect oneself from the consequences of an illegal
and discriminatory use of power.[34] Patronage, which began as an
instrument of social control in the absence of political participation,
was not the best tool for promoting it. The great masses of the
population remained shut out from any relations with the state and
their integration was entrusted not to political-administrative tools
but to the manipulation of local politics through patronage. In the
areas in which *mafia* was developing this meant, essentially, a powerful
interweaving of *mafia* and political power both at the level of the local
political-administrative system and of the peripheral branches of the
central administration. And, besides, the *mafia* groups, trained by the
networks of instrumental friendship to move skilfully through the
labyrinths of the administration, were certainly not shy about
entering the vital nerve-centres of the state. When the Left came to
power (1876) suffrage was partially extended (1882) and *trasformismo*[35]
became government practice; by then the institutionalization of *mafia*
as an expression of the interweaving between state and local
potentates could be said to have been completed.

5. THE *MAFIA* AS CAUSE AND EFFECT OF SOCIAL HYBRIDIZATION

The *mafia* was born as a response of the periphery to the impact with
the centre; but it could not assert itself without the centre's support.
The state authorities' use of *mafia* power indicates that the *mafia*
phenomenon should be looked at in the context of systems of alliances
among social classes and political interest groups that occurred at the
local level but which had to cross the boundaries of the local political
system to negotiate at the national level. The regional alliance
between the agrarian bourgeoisie (the former *gabelloti*), the intellectual
petty bourgeoisie, and the latifundist aristocracy was able to sustain

itself only because of the *mafia's* repression of the peasants. In order that this power might be exercised with impunity, a national alliance was necessary between southern latifundists and the northern industrial bourgeoisie which delegated to the latifundists, through the governing class, the repression of the peasants.[36]

The *mafia* was born of the incapacity of the state to use its monopoly of legitimate violence; but the reasons it was able to take root socially were more numerous. The reasons it was able to persist are different from those of its genesis. The *mafia* has acquired an autonomy which guarantees, automatically as it were, its reproduction and makes it difficult to uproot.

Police repression of the *mafia* under Fascism can supply an example of this.[37] The state's assumption of the monopoly of violence, and the suppression of elections, took away the social bases of *mafiosi* as power brokers. The *mafia*, which had supported the liberal anti-Fascist party at the beginning of the regime, apparently collapsed; small *mafiosi* who did not join the black shirts were eliminated. The large landowners, once the repression of the peasants was guaranteed by the apparatuses of the state, were happy to shake off the economic weight of *mafia* mediation[38] and joined the regime. As a result, when prefect Mori, in charge of the police effort, began to take aim at the landowners, he was promptly dismissed. The *mafia* re-emerged in 1943 with the same apparent characteristics that it had had at the beginning of the century. But some years afterwards a profound process of crisis, transformation, and restructuring would overwhelm it, causing it to re-emerge in new and perennially changing forms from the beginning of the 1960s.

What are the reasons for the *mafia's* ability to persist, to adapt to change, altering forms but succeeding often in becoming even more pervasive?

It has been stressed that one of the fundamental models of behaviour for the *mafia* consists in resistance to social changes but, when these appear inevitable, to exploit them for its own ends.[39] One of the many possible examples would be the resistance to the introduction of co-operativism among the peasants and the subsequent organization of co-operatives by *mafiosi* themselves. *Don* Calò Vizzini, one of the principal *mafia* chiefs of the first half of this century, began to organize agricultural co-operatives among soldiers returning from the First World War. He continued this activity after the Second World War and succeeded, with the use of a typical instrument of peasant unionism, to throw the peasant movement into disorder.[40]

One of the consequences of this model of behaviour is that new institutions come to be utilized for the fulfilment of traditional values. A double process thus occurs: on one side, the modern institutions are modified and employed for ends other than those for which they were originally intended. On the other, the traditional values do not

46 *Raimondo Catanzaro*

disappear; they are not replaced by new values, but are adapted to make traditional use of new institutions. This process of social hybridization of which the *mafia* is, perhaps emblematically, at once cause and effect, constituted the basis of the *mafia's* power and of its extraordinary capacity to survive and reproduce. To understand this process better we can examine the example of the co-operativistic organization promoted by the *mafia* chief. He manages to have the regional authorities block a co-operative founded by the peasant movement; then he forms his own. The peasants, who have seen their proposal fail, depend on him for their very survival. Whoever is admitted to the co-operative feels lucky and regards admission not in terms of a normal economic transaction but as a form of unconditional concessions of benefits. Whoever feels thus benefitted 'becomes his protector's man in the feudal sense of the word; he has, in a certain sense, received his life from him in fief, and, from then on, is ready to serve him'.[41]

What are the consequences of the persistence of this pre-contractual[42] conception of the economic transaction and of its combination with relationships which belong to a market economy? The nature of the unconditional concession of benefits is that the party that receives the benefits is not asked for anything specific in return. But, in a social atmosphere like that described in these pages, the vagueness of the repayment is translated into the perpetual debt of proofs of moral obligation — that is, of symbols and pledges of loyalty. The receiver of benefits can thus be asked for a percentage of his economic activities or for a vote for a candidate in elections. He can be asked to become a killer. Thus economic functions and functions of social control and political power combine tightly in the *mafia*-style obligation. In general terms, one can say that economic resources are converted into political resources: that is, into control over people with an increase in resources. In fact, obligations based on loyalty constituted a credit, a potential always and repeatedly due.

This explains why the *mafiosi* were able, ever since first making their presence felt in west-central Sicily, to adapt to processes of economic transformation of a society which, although it was unable to develop industrially, was far from static. Indeed, it showed notable dynamism in economic enterprises.[43] The constant adaptation of this model of behaviour to the changing of the historical conditions has been the *mafia's* strength. It was this capacity that has made possible the remarkable recovery which the *mafia* has enjoyed since the Second World War.

6. THE PUBLIC POLICY OF ECONOMIC DEVELOPMENT AND THE SPREAD OF THE *MAFIA*

Repression by the Fascist regime did not cut off the *mafia* economic and social roots but struck at its most visible manifestations.

Moreover, at the time of the repression, bonds between the Sicilian *mafia* and American organized crime had existed for some time as a result of transoceanic migration. Today these bonds constitute one of the main organizational tools of the international drug traffic.

The re-emergence of the *mafia* at the end of the Second World War cannot, however, be understood except with reference to the new functions assumed by the Italian state in the context of a more general policy for the development of the *Mezzogiorno*. The basic problem has been that of institutionalization of the rights of social citizenship.[44] In other words, in the post-war period, a policy of redistribution of resources began which was typical of the welfare state. Alongside it existed a policy of economic development. The state then has had two faces in the Mezzogiorno and Sicily. It has promoted development, and thus has allowed the capitalistic market to be introduced into the Mezzogiorno, thereby opening the region to trade and exchanges and to European markets. At the same time it has assumed the welfare-related duties of redistributing resources and of assisting the people of the south with pensions, subsidies, and various other social benefits. The state thus becomes both agent of social change and defender of the traditional balance of power.[45]

In this context, economic and political activities become more and more tightly interwoven, a situation which favours yet again those groups and individuals who were already trained to move through political labyrinths and to penetrate the public administration. But other groups emerge together with these: in particular, new groups of economic operators, typically entrepreneurs whose private economic activities and social rise are guaranteed by a privileged relationship to the sources of public support of such economic activities.[46] From the beginning of the 1950s, in fact, private entrepreneurial groups emerge as a result not of selective functioning of the free market but of state support to firms. The state has promoted an economic policy oriented towards the creation of infrastructures and development of building activities; moreover it has promoted entrepreneurship, granting financing at low interest rates and free subsidies to enterprises. In this way, a relationship of exchange is created between entrepreneurs, the party system (especially the Christian Democrats), and the political-administrative system. The *mafiosi* understand that the essential virtue of modern man is that of acquiring capital through economic activity. They understand the possibility of increasing their volume of business and their economic power by exploiting privileged relationships with the party in power and so with the development apparatus of the state.

But other processes, too, characterize the more recent developments of the *mafia*: namely expanding markets for local entrepreneurs and the opening up of new opportunities in illegal economic activities.

In the course of the 1970s, the assisted entrepreneurs of eastern Sicily, traditionally considered safe from the *mafia*, began to do

48   *Raimondo Catanzaro*

business in the markets of western Sicily. They were obliged to come to terms with the relationships between economy and polity existing there. The differences are not many: it is a question of adapting the practice of clientelism in a *mafia*-patronage dimension. In this way an enterprise that appeared 'clean', in that it was immune from *mafia* methods, was 'polluted' by these methods after conquering new markets. For those who had always been *mafia* entrepreneurs the inverse occurred. Their expansion on markets originally not penetrated by the *mafia* set off a process of transformation of local political systems in the *mafia*-patronage sense. These phenomena are important because it is not only a question of changes of quantity or intensity of *mafia* activities. We are witnessing a process of potential depersonalization of the *mafia's* power.

Traditionally *mafia* power had a personal quality. That was because of, first, the role of *mafiosi* as brokers. Moreover, the *mafioso* often assumed public duties including those which represented the community to the outside. This community aspect was related to a third characteristic of *mafia* power; a power with geographical limitations. The decline of its intermediary functions and the *mafia* organization of modern economic and entrepreneurial activities potentially spelled the end of the personal nature of its power. The formation of *mafia* enterprises not only caused the community aspect to disappear but, after the expansion of the scale of activities of the assisted entrepreneurs, the geographical limitation explodes too.[47] *Mafia* power thus tends to become an impersonal market power.

This tendency is limited by the persistence of, and sometimes by the emphasis on, violence as a tool for regulating economic competition among *mafia* groups. The end of geographical limitation of *mafia* power exacerbated the violent struggle between rival *mafia* groups for the conquest of markets or, at least, for economic opportunities.[48] Certain facts which reinforce the process of depersonalization of *mafia* power should not, in any case, be forgotten. These are the pure economic links, thus links of interests, between *mafia* enterprises and others: the other enterprises to which jobs are subcontracted or with which agreements are stipulated or cartels formed; the banks into whose vaults flows money of *mafia* origin in the form of deposits; the many individuals who earn incomes from the circulation of this money. All of these form a constellation of interests on which the impersonal market power of *mafia* groups is based.[49] Even if this process is not unilinear, because of strong counter-tendencies, the anonymity of market forces informs the process of depersonalization of *mafia* power. But, as a consequence of the processes just outlined as well as of the proliferation of the illicit economic activities of the *mafia*, it assumes more of the features of a hidden power.

7. HIDDEN POWER AND ILLICIT ECONOMY

The *mafia's* power was not always hidden; in fact it operated openly. And this was true for both of the aspects of the traditional *mafiosi's* career: the violent destructive one and the institutionalized one legitimized by acceptance by the population as a result of success in the use of violence.[50] In both cases, the open display of power by *mafiosi* derived from the combination of their brokerage functions and the state's delegation of the use of violence. To be a broker, the *mafioso* must enjoy a reputation in society and must be considered as a man of honour; and this derives from his having previously proved himself highly skilled in the use of violence. Having been thus recognized, he no longer needs to use open violence because he can earn an income from normal economic activities which are based on a fortune acquired illegally.

Both of these processes — from violence to legitimization and from illegal to legal economic activities — have slowed down from the 1950s on. The requirements of social control by traditional methods were sharply reduced and both the state's delegation of its monopoly of violence and the brokerage functions of the men of honour have come to a halt. The *mafia* is no longer the pragmatic dimension of the state and, as a result, its power is less visible. Alongside these processes, the growth in importance of the illegal sector of the *mafia's* economic activities has brought with it a tendency to assume the lineaments of a hidden power. Ever since the 1950s, *mafiosi* have constantly been immersed in illegal practices; and not only, as in the past, in the early stages of their career. The organization of increasingly economic activities by the *mafia* is associated with the beginning of the drug traffic in the 1950s.[51]

The expansion of the drug market and the Sicilian *mafia's* rise to pre-eminence in it[52] have a series of consequences the first of which can be seen in the banking system. The direct and indirect conditioning of the banking system by *mafia* groups is evident. On the one hand, private banks grow as a consequence of profits deriving from assisted entrepreneurial activities and *mafia* entrepreneurship. On the other hand, the conditioning power grows as a result of the enormous quantity of cash in *mafia* hands.[53] An idea of the dimensions of this power can be had by considering that by the 1960s the Anti-Mafia Commission set up by the Italian Parliament was finding irregular cases of credit granted to known *mafiosi* not only by small private local banks but also by commercial national banks.[54]

The expansion and scale of *mafia* activities today have upset the traditional relationships between *mafia* and political power. How did this occur? What role do the traditional tools of instrumental

50   *Raimondo Catanzaro*

friendship and patronage play in the present structure of the
relationships between the *mafia* world and politics? To answer these
questions it is necessary to look at the ways in which traditional values
have adapted to changes in *mafia* behaviour and to the needs that have
grown out of these changes.

8. THE ADAPTATION OF TRADITIONAL CULTURAL CODES

The passage of the *mafiosi* from power brokers to entrepreneurs is a
change of great importance. The use of market mechanisms and
privileged relationships with the state bureaucracy to construct
economic empires combining legal and illegal activities constitutes a
further example of the capacity of *mafia* groups to blend old and new,
traditional and modern.[55] An old pattern repeats itself in this new
combination: traditional values do not disappear but change function
and meaning. This holds true for both honour and instrumental
friendship.

Once they have joined the game of market competition the *mafiosi*
must adapt to its rules. The functions of instrumental friendship, of
allowing trust and predictability in economic transactions, are largely
reduced and are replaced by legal and commercial guarantees; but
not altogether. In fact, in a dependent economy it is difficult for local
entrepreneurs to foresee trends in demand, given the unbalanced
nature of the commodities market and the marked fluctuations caused
by external investments. The problem of predictability is resolved by
state policy which, systematically favouring certain sectors of economic
activities with its financing, allows the entrepreneurs to identify low-
risk opportunities for investment.[56] To ensure predictability instrumental friendship is increasingly changed into both a patronage-
exchange relationship between entrepreneurs and politicians and into
the formation of groups and alliances between business groups,
political factions and parts of the apparatus of the state. The
relationship loses all vestiges of its symbolic-emotional nature and
becomes purely instrumental.

As for the problem of trust, if the need for recourse to instrumental
friendship is reduced in the legal sector of the economy it remains
urgent in the illicit sector. Here, however, given the scale of the
interests in play, instrumental friendship is no longer able to furnish
sufficient guarantees. The functioning of the illicit sector cannot, by
its very nature, rest on transactions which are exposed to the light of
day and which are based on the normal relationships of trust proper
to the market. As long as business must be hidden, the only system for
making the illicit machine function is an intense network of fiduciary
relationships. For these reasons, *mafia* groups organize themselves by
reviving traditional values and basing themselves on relationships of

kinship and quasi-kinship.[57] But, however much these bonds can be
extended by means of matrimonial strategies, *comparaggio*, and so on,
it always remains necessary to have recourse outside the networks of
kinship and quasi-kinship. In these cases, which are very numerous,
especially when alliances between different *cosche* are concerned,[58] the
traditional code of honour has fundamental importance. Respect for
the obligations undertaken and conformity to what has been decided
within the *cosca* both demand behaviour which conforms to the code of
honour. This code then becomes the main instrument on which
relationships of organizational trust in illegal activities are based.
Honour loses its cultural significance for regulating standard of
competition for social mobility. Now that even the *mafia* is oriented
more towards accumulating capital than gaining respect, honour
serves to promote internal cohesion within *mafia* groups.

Nevertheless, this cohesion is not easy to maintain because of the
many temptations offered by the illegal market. One successful
operation is enough to make a fortune: for example holding back the
proceeds of the sale of drugs instead of delivering the shipment to the
owners. It was exactly an episode of this sort which touched off the
violent conflict between *cosche* which characterized one of the many
fasi calde ('hot phases') which Palermo went through at the beginning
of the 1960s.[59] The suspicion that two couriers had withheld part of a
drug shipment destined for the USA caused one *cosca* to break its
alliance with the others and to kill one of the presumed traitors (the
other had gone to ground) and many of their relatives and friends,
causing a chain reaction of vast proportions.

One could say about this episode that a sort of 'in-house conflict'
was resolved by recourse to violence. Thus violence has become the
basic instrument of economic competition among *mafiosi*. It is not that
it was not such before; it is that now it assumes a new, more open
meaning, without ideological overlays and justifications. Up until the
1950s, *mafia* violence found a legitimacy in three factors: the state's
delegation of the use of violence; the community nature of *mafia* power
as public management of order; the ownership of its monopoly
justified in terms of social attribution of honour. Now that these
conditions have been exhausted the use of violence appears for what it
is even in the substitution of the machine gun and TNT for the
traditional sawn-off shotgun: pure, brutal, often indiscriminate
demonstration of the rule of physical force.

The great transformation of *mafia* during the last thirty years has
brought with it an upset and a re-adaptation of the traditional
cultural codes. Instrumental friendship is no longer a delicate balance
between instrumentality and symbolic solidarity. The first is subsumed
under relationships of interests and exchange between individuals and
groups and specialized brokerage agencies. The second, as far as *mafia*
groups are concerned, tends to be replaced by honour. Honour loses

52   *Raimondo Catanzaro*

the connotation of an idiom in the language of material wealth and of a regulatory instrument of the competition for social mobility. The ambivalence of the concept of honour is thus reduced. Replaced by wealth as a standard of social status and symbol of power, honour contributes to the institutionalization of trust in the organization of the illicit economy. Its former competitive function is assumed by violence. Violence, in its actual exercise and in the threat of recourse to it, not only regulates competition between *mafia* groups but is asserted as a normative system in relationships between *mafioso* and non-*mafioso* sectors of the economic system. The *mafia* use of violence to discourage competition, in all its forms, from non-*mafia* enterprises is an apt example of the attempt to impose brute force as a general regulatory norm of the market.

9. *MAFIA* AND POLITICAL POWER: FROM THE PERIPHERY TO THE CENTRE

Mafia violence, stripped by now of its symbolic cloak of honour, does not present itself only as a regulatory tool of economic competition. It is increasingly becoming a political force entering into open conflict with the powers of the state. For more than ten years representatives of the powers of the state, judges, officials of police and officers of the *carabinieri*, even a president of the Sicilian regional government and a prefect of the Republic, have systematically become *mafia* targets and victims. The phenomenon is completely new; except for rare cases, concerning the rural *mafia* or shootings between *mafia*-gangsters and forces of police and *carabinieri*, the *mafia* had never before attacked the powers of the state.

The causes of this change are rooted in the destabilized conditions of *mafia* existence which we have discussed. In brief, the expansion of the illegal economy, the volume of business sparked off by *mafia* dealings, and the national and international dimensions of the interests involved have led to a double phenomenon: on the one hand the need of the *mafia* groups to take direct possession of the crucial parts of the state machinery; on the other hand, that of openly combatting those parts of the state apparatus which resist such domination and oppose the spread of *mafia*.

A thesis has recently been advanced that the growth of *mafia* power is characterized, as compared with the traditional model of the relationships between *mafia* and politics, by the novel element of the political autonomy of *mafia* power. Such autonomy expresses itself, according to this thesis, in two forms: the 'internalization of political representation of *mafia* groups'; and the formation of *mafioso*-political lobbies based on 'relationships of common economic interest among *mafia* leaders, political leaders, and sectors of the local and national economic and financial world'.[60] This thesis may appear convincing

in the light of the growth of *mafia* power; it does not adequately define
the autonomy of *mafia* power and the new forms in which it appears.

In the first place, it is difficult to define what is meant by the
political autonomy of *mafia* power. If it means the capacity to affect
policies fundamental to the political system, the *mafia* is not
autonomous. If, however, it means the capacity to influence policies
with reference to a given geographical area or economic sector then,
paradoxically, it was so once, but is not now. Traditionally, in fact,
the *mafia*, after being delegated the use of violence, became a power
with a broad sphere of autonomy both at the territorial level and at
the level of management of economic policies for agriculture. As we
have seen, this autonomy was realized in the context of a relationship
of exchange in which state non-interference with the power of the
southern landowners was bartered for support for the government
policy of protection of the development of industrial interests in the
north. In this sense, the autonomy of *mafia* power existed as a
delegated power and was limited to the periphery. That, however,
does not mean that interest groups combining political and *mafia*
components were not created which combined important economic-
financial and political interests at the local and national level. On the
contrary, the existence of these groups seems to demonstrate that the
phenomenon of the internalization of political representation was
present even then.[61]

The autonomy of *mafia* power, intended in this meaning of
delegation of dominion over the periphery, runs through its entire
evolution up to the 1950s, when the delegation of violence to the *mafia*
came to a halt. And it is exactly during this period that a crisis in the
autonomy of *mafia* power occurred. The end of the monopoly of *mafia*
brokerage and the assumption of the roles of mediation, social control
and protection of the traditional sectors of Sicilian society by the
Christian Democratic party and by politicians, constituted a formidable
challenge to traditional *mafia* power. Its reorganization, in the forms
we have discussed in the preceding pages, has been accompanied by
the organization of illegal trade and, as a consequence, the end of the
mafia's being restricted to the periphery, both of which are relevant to
an analysis of new forms of *mafia* power.

From this it follows that, perhaps, the newest aspect of *mafia* power
is that it is no longer delegated by the state. This begins in the 1950s
and it is from the same date that a process of conquest of new parts of
the state apparatus begins. Even this is not new: it first occurred with
the consensus of the state for managing social control on the periphery
in the interests of the local ruling classes. Now, however, the state
keeps its monopoly of violence; but illegal economic activity is on such
a scale as to surpass interests which are solely or largely those of the
periphery — and which have national and supra-national dimensions.
Consequently the profound difference between the new *mafia* power

54 *Raimondo Catanzaro*

and the earlier form lies in the fact that it has become a phenomenon that involves the entire Italian political system. From the periphery, where *mafia* power arose, it has moved toward the centre seeking to win power there. The killings of judges, politicians, and high state and police officials show that the fight between the *mafia* and those sectors of the state apparatus which oppose this march is far from being won. These crimes can only be read in the light of a violent struggle between power groups which operate from within the state institutions and fight for their control.

The *mafia* has become pervasively part of the economic, financial, and political systems. Its presence is no longer restricted to a limited geographical area within the state, even if its political and economic brain remains in Sicily. The *mafia* can no longer be seen as a special group, but asks to be interpreted as a social sub-system which articulates its own presence in most of the vital nerve-centres of society. And it is exactly this which today constitutes its strength and its danger.

Raimondo Catanzaro
Dipartimento di Scienze Sociologiche
Università di Catania

NOTES

* An earlier version of this article was presented at the conference on 'Islands of Europe' held at the University of Edinburgh in April 1983. I am grateful to Nino Recupero for some insightful conversations on the subject, to Francesco Cossentino for the term 'social hybridization' and to Donatella della Porta, Umberto Di Giorgi, and Maureen Fant, all of whom read the manuscript and made valuable suggestions.

1. See respectively A. Blok, *The Mafia of a Sicilian Village: 1860–1960*, New York, Harper & Row, 1974; H. Hess, *Mafia and Mafiosi: The Structure of Power*, Westmead, Farnborough, Hants, Saxon House, 1973; P. Arlacchi, *La mafia imprenditrice*, Bologna, Il Mulino, 1983. See Hess, op. cit., for proof of the inexistence of the *mafia* as a secret society or as a single, rigidly hierarchical organization. Rather, there exist *mafiosi* individuals and groups. This idea is by now accepted in the scholarly literature and is the sense in which the term *mafia* is used in this article; hence the use of the lower case 'm'.

2. For a review of the theme of honour in Mediterranean societies, see J. Davis, *People of the Mediterranean*, London, Routledge & Kegan Paul, 1977.

3. Some references on the duality of the concept of honour can be found in Davis, op. cit., from whom I have taken the materialistic interpretation of honour as social idiom related to the allocation of resources.

4. See Davis, op. cit., p. 92.

5. The accumulation of such capital is a consequence of an economy regulated not by the peaceful means of the market but by violence.

6. See Davis, op. cit., p. 93; J. Schneider and P. Schneider, *Culture and Political Economy in Western Sicily*, New York, Academic Press, 1976, pp. 100–1.

7. Davis, op. cit., p. 98.

8. On the concepts of emotional and instrumental friendship, see Eric R. Wolf, 'Kinship, Friendship, and Patron-Clients Relations in Complex Societies', in Banton,

Enforcers, entrepreneurs, and survivors 55

The Social Anthropology of Complex Societies, ASA Monograph 4, London, Tavistock, 1966, pp. 10–13.

9. An interesting description of symbolic rituals of exaltation of friendship is given in Schneider and Schneider, op. cit., pp. 104–7.

10. Blok, op. cit., p. 146.

11. On the concept of balanced reciprocity, see Marshall D. Sahlins, 'On the Sociology of Primitive Exchange', in Banton, *The Relevance of Models for Social Anthropology*, A.S.A. Monographs 1, London, Tavistock, 1965, pp. 139–236.

12. On *ad hoc* coalitions in Sicily, see P. Schneider, 'Coalition Formation and Colonialism in Western Sicily', *European Journal of Sociology*, vol. 13, 1972, pp. 255–67.

13. This is the thesis held by Schneider and Schneider, op. cit., taking the centre-periphery model proposed by I. Wallerstein, *The Modern World System. Capitalistic Agriculture and the Origins of the European World-Economy in the Sixteenth Century*, New York, Academic Press, 1974.

14. Taking this analysis from Schneider and Schneider, op. cit., pp. 32–55.

15. Ibid., p. 109.

16. On the characteristics of the Spanish administration in Sicily, see D. Mack Smith, *A History of Sicily: Medieval Sicily, 800–1713*, London, Chatto & Windus, 1968, pp. 115–68.

17. Schneider and Schneider, op. cit., pp. 108–9.

18. J. Schneider, 'Of Vigilance and Virgins: Honor, Shame and Access to Resources in Mediterranean Societies', *Ethnology*, vol. 10, 1971, pp. 1–24.

19. Quoted by S. W. Mintz and E. R. Wolf, 'An Analysis of Ritual Co-parenthood', in Potter, Diaz, and Foster, *Peasant Society: A Reader*, Boston, Little, Brown, 1967, p. 179.

20. M. Weber, *The Protestant Ethic and the Spirit of Capitalism*, New York, Charles Scribner's Sons, 1930, pp. 16 ff.

21. Schneider and Schneider, op. cit., pp. 10–14, 54–5, *et passim*.

22. This interpretative model of the formation of the national state was proposed by Stein Rokkan, 'Dimensions of State-Formation and Nation-Building: A Possible Paradigm for Research on Variations Within Europe', in Tilly, *The Formation of National States in Western Europe*, Princeton, N.J., Princeton University Press, 1975, pp. 562–600.

23. Blok, op. cit., p. 7.

24. Ibid, pp. 89 ff.

25. The *gabelloti* were large tenants of the landed aristocracy to whom they paid a sum in rent called *gabella*. They in turn sublet land in small parcels to the peasants for higher rent and pocketed the profit. Literary descriptions of the *gabelloti* can be found in G. Verga's *La roba* and *Mastro Don Gesualdo* and G. Tomasi di Lampedusa's *The Leopard*.

26. On the characteristics of the production relationships in Sicilian agriculture of the second half of the nineteenth century, see E. Sereni, *Il capitalismo nelle campagne*, Turin, Einaudi, 1948, pp. 184 ff.

27. Taking this analysis from Blok, op. cit., pp. 92 ff.

28. Ibid., pp. 92–3.

29. G. Salvemini, *Scritti sulla questione meridionale (1896–1955)*, Turin, Einaudi, 1955, pp. 46, 62, *et passim*.

30. Blok, op. cit., pp. 95 ff.

31. Ibid., p. 96.

32. S. Tarrow, *Between Center and Periphery. Grassroots Politicians in Italy and France*, New Haven and London, Yale University Press, 1977.

33. Ibid., ch. 2.

34. L. Graziano, *Clientelismo e sistema politico: il caso dell'Italia*, Milan, F. Angeli, 1980, pp. 113–28.

35. The Left which came to power after the so-called Parliamentary Revolution of 1876 was composed largely of republicans (former supporters of Mazzini and Garibaldi), opponents of Cavour's liberal Right. Under the government of the Left, a system of forming parliamentary majorities became established which ignored party or political-group loyalties: this was *trasformismo*. The Left could count on the vote of deputies of the Right who would support the government in exchange for favours (usually using the state's administrative structure to intimidate deputies' constituents to ensure the deputies' re-

56   *Raimondo Catanzaro*

election). *Trasformismo* is thus a deputy's being elected with a mandate of
one sort and then voting another. It was
especially prevalent among southern
and Sicilian deputies, many of whom
became known as 'ministerial' or 'government' deputies for their tendency always
to vote in favour of the government,
whatever its composition and policy.
On this degeneration of the Italian
parliamentary system, which had important effects on the origins of patronage in the Mezzogiorno, see G. Mosca,
*Partiti e sindacati nella crisi del regime
parlamentare*, Bari, Laterza, 1949.
   36. Salvemini, op cit., pp. 41–9.
   37. See F. Renda, 'Funzioni e basi
sociali della mafia', in *Il movimento contadino
nella società siciliana*, Palermo, Edizioni
'Sicilia al lavoro', 1956; Hess, op. cit.,
pp. 172–6; Blok, op. cit., pp. 182–9.
   38. See C. Mori, *Con la mafia ai ferri
corti*, Verona, Mondadori, 1932, pp. 351,
354, *et passim*.
   39. Schneider and Schneider, op. cit.,
p. 183; E. J. Hobsbawm, *Primitive Rebels.
Studies in Archaic Forms of Social Movements
in the 19th and 20th Centuries*, Manchester,
Manchester University Press, 1959, ch.
3.
   40. See M. Pantaleone, *Mafia e politica*,
Turin, Einaudi, 1962, pp. 100, 118.
   41. L. Franchetti, *Le condizioni politiche e
amministrative della Sicilia*, Florence, Vallecchi, 1974 (first published 1875), pp.
109–10.
   42. L. Graziano has called attention to
the characteristics of the Mezzogiorno as
pre-contractual society: 'Clientelismo e
sviluppo politico: il caso del Mezzogiorno',
in *Clientelismo e mutamento politico*, Milan,
F. Angeli, 1974, p. 339.
   43. For an analysis of the dynamic
tendencies and of the attempts at development of modern economic initiatives
in Sicily, see Giuseppe Barone, 'Stato,
capitale finanziario e Mezzogiorno' and
Salvatore Lupo, Rosario Mangiameli,
'La modernizzazione difficile: blocchi
corporativi e conflitto di classe in una
società arretrata', both in Avagliano,
Barbagallo, Barone *et al.*, *La modernizzazione difficile*, Bari, De Donato, 1983.
   44. On the institutionalization of the
rights of social citizenship as process of

formation of the state and nation, see
Rokkan, op. cit.
   45. G. Gribaudi, *Mediatori*, Turin, Ro-
senberg & Sellier, 1980, pp. 23–8 *et
passim*.
   46. See R. Catanzaro, *L'imprenditore assistito*, Bologna, Il Mulino, 1979.
   47. P. Arlacchi, 'Mafia e tipi di società',
Rassegna italiana de sociologia, vol. XXI,
no. 1, 1980, pp. 3–49.
   48. Arlacchi, *La mafia imprenditrice*, pp.
180–5.
   49. On the concept of domination by
virtue of a constellation of interests, see
M. Weber, *Economy and Society*, New York,
Bedminster Press, 1968, vol. 3, p. 943.
   50. On these two moments in the
mafioso's career, see Hess, op. cit., pp. 45
ff.
   51. See the biographies of 11 *mafiosi*
made by the *Commissione antimafia* of the
Italian parliament and published in Li
Causi, *I boss della mafia*, Rome, Editori
riuniti, 1971, pp. 69 ff.
   52. With the present state of documentation we are not able to state whether
the pre-eminent position of the Sicilian
mafia in the world drug traffic was such
from the beginning of the 1970s, as
Arlacchi maintains (*La mafia imprenditrice*),
or was already in the 1950s, as is
maintained in the McClellan report,
taken by the *Commissione parlamentare
d'inchiesta sul fenomeno della mafia in Sicilia*,
vol. 4, tomo 13, parte prima, p. 202. It is
however, certain that the availability in
mafia hands of huge sums of illegal origin
should have been noticeable already at
the end of the 1950s, if the Commission
itself documents payments of 1300 thousand million lire (at current price) by the
Americans to a Sicilian mafia group for
the supply of 361 kilos of heroin in the
period 1958–61.
   53. On the multiplication of banking
initiatives in Sicily, see S. Ruvolo, 'Mafia
e speculazione edilizia', in *Accumulazione e
cultura mafiosa*, bulletin of the *Comitato di
controinformazione 'Peppino Impastato'*, Palermo, Editrice Centofiori, 1979, p. 5;
Arlacchi, *La mafia imprenditrice*, pp. 234–5.
In-depth research has not yet been done
on the subject, however.
   54. See Li Causi, *I boss della mafia*, pp.
346–60.

55. For a review of the recent literature on the Mezzogiorno relating to the themes mentioned above, see R. Catanzaro, 'Struttura sociale, sistema politico e azione collettiva nel Mezzogiorno', *Stato e mercato*, vol. 3, n. 8 (1983), pp. 105–49.

56. Catanzaro, *L'imprenditore assistito*, pp. 41–51.

57. Arlacchi, *La mafia imprenditrice*, pp. 222–8.

58. The world *cosca* (pl. *cosche*) in Sicilian dialect means the leaf of an artichoke and symbolizes the tightness of relationships between members of the *mafia* groups.

59. See Li Causi, *I boss della mafia*, pp. 241, 272–94.

60. Arlacchi, *La mafia imprenditrice*, pp. 193–4 ff.

61. It should be sufficient to cite only the famous scandal of the murder of Notarbartolo, ex-director general of the Bank of Sicily, in 1893. A deputy to Parliament was convicted of having instigated the crime, but was acquitted on appeal. The case brought to light a series of collusions between economic, financial, and political interests which went beyond the boundaries of Sicily. For an analysis of the relationship between the mafia, the representative system, and economic and political interests which takes off the case in questions, see Mosca, op. cit., pp. 249–56.

[34]

Political and Market Forces in Italian Broadcasting

Donald Sassoon

Italy is the only European country with a multi-channel radio and television system much of which is not subjected to any form of state regulation. Any private person or company can set up a transmitting station, produce their own programmes or purchase them and broadcast them. The only restriction is that the broadcast must be local. The law, however, does not specify the dimensions of local broadcasting. Furthermore, a network of local companies can decide to broadcast locally at the same time the same programme with the use of previously distributed videotapes.

According to figures made available in September 1983 there are in Italy between 700 and 800 private television stations with over 5,000 transmitters and between 6,000 and 8,000 radio stations.[1] Many of these simply occupy an air wave and broadcast a signal while they try to develop proper programming, while others can only broadcast programmes around a few square miles. Only 50 per cent of television stations are able to broadcast regular programmes.

In the last few years something approaching an embryonic network system has emerged. Four 'national' companies linking together 125 stations are poised to become the keystone of Italy's private broadcasting system. They are: *Retequattro* (24 stations), *Italia Uno* (31), *Euro TV* (32) and the most successful of them all, *Canale Cinque* (38). By 1984 70 per cent of the population were able to receive these four networks. If we add to these the other local television stations and the three state channels run by the Radio-televisione Italiana (RAI) we obtain the following result: something approaching 32 million Italians are able to tune into between seven and 11 television channels for something approaching 13 hours a day. In many large cities the choice increases to 18 to 20 channels. In some it is possible, thanks to special equipment, to receive foreign broadcasts from Switzerland, France, Monaco, Austria and Yugoslavia. This has enabled Italy to have the highest density of radio and television stations in the world: there is one radio station for every 16,000 inhabitants against one in 25,000 in the USA, and one television station for every 93,000 inhabitants against one in 274,000 in the USA.[2]

An unregulated system of broadcasting means that the only rules which are applicable are those established by existing *general* legislation such as those regulating pornography. There are no *special* restrictions concerning the broadcasting of sexually explicit material, no rules concerning unfair treatment of minorities or individuals, no obligation to report facts in a fair and unbiased manner, no restriction on the kind of programmes to be shown during the day when children may be watching and no requirements to broadcast a certain amount of cultural or educational material. A private television company can broadcast, if it so wishes, non-stop adult movies or cartoons or both.

State television is, of course, subjected to all these restrictions and is therefore competing from a position of inferiority. Italy's private system of broadcasting thus provides an example of what might happen to a West European country which decided to develop a system of unregulated cable television. If this system was financed by advertising, as private radio and television companies are in Italy, there would probably be very similar effects in terms of what happens to advertising revenue, the content of television output and the ethos and organisation of established 'public service' broadcasting.

In this article we shall examine all of these but before doing so it will be necessary to explain the origins of the present system.

STATE TELEVISION: ORIGINS AND DEVELOPMENTS

The RAI is a public company which is entirely owned by the Istituto per la Ricostruzione Industriale (IRI), a stateholding company which had been created in the 1930s by the fascist regime. Television broadcasting began in 1954 and was available to nearly half the population. Two years later it covered virtually the whole territory. A licensing fee provided television with its sole source of revenue until 1957 when the RAI was allowed to accept advertising. This was strictly regulated: it had to be 'bloc' advertising at the beginning or at the end of a programme.[3] This is still the case.

Soon after 1945 the RAI came under the political control of the Christian Democrat Party (DC), which had emerged from the war as the leading Italian political party. Between 1945 and 1954 the DC relied heavily on the political machine of the Roman Catholic Church in order to maintain its electoral base. In the early 1950s it began to use its control over the public sector to develop its own network of clienteles so that it would not have to be so dependent on the Church. In this period, under Amintore Fanfani, the Christian Democratic Party began to appoint its own supporters to positions of power and influence. This was also a device used to develop its own network of experts and specialists.

The RAI was obviously an important terrain for this kind of political 'colonisation'. Television was seen as a powerful instrument of propaganda which could be far more easily controlled than Italy's highly diversified press. It was also a potential cultural industry which would give jobs to technicians and intellectuals. The DC did not intend to control the content of the entire output: what really mattered was the news and current affairs section. Fiction programmes were allowed freedom from overt political control. In fact they were dependent on prevailing conceptions of decency which, until the mid-1960s, tended to be those of traditional Catholicism. These could not compete with Italy's thriving cinema industry.

In the late 1950s a private group, *Il Tempo-TV*, began to exercise pressures for the development of commercial television. The DC tried to prevent it and the Constitutional Court was asked to arbitrate. This decided that the state monopoly of broadcasting was legal and justified on a purely

POLITICAL AND MARKET FORCES IN ITALIAN BROADCASTING 69

technical reason: the shortage of frequency bands available. The Court, however, also declared that some sort of competition was necessary and this led the RAI to begin broadcasting on a second channel (RAI-2) in 1961. By 1967, RAI-2 could be received by 86 per cent of the population.[4] RAI-2 was politically controlled just like RAI-1 but its programming policies were of a more cultural nature and the bulk of the audience continued to turn to RAI-1.

Political opponents of the DC, much of the press and the intellectuals continued to criticise the RAI: news programmes showed government ministers performing edifying tasks such as inaugurating schools, kissing children, receiving flowers, being greeted and acclaimed. Opposition leaders (in Italy's case, Communist Party leaders) were never to be seen, their policies never mentioned. Only in 1963, during the electoral campaign, did the Communist leader Palmiro Togliatti appear for the first time on the screen in a political broadcast in which he was interviewed by the press.

It is difficult to assess the political consequences of DC political control over the RAI in terms of votes. Television certainly did not enable the DC to increase its electoral base. After its victory in the 1948 elections the Christian Democratic Party tumbled to 40 per cent in 1953, moved up to 42 per cent in 1958 and then settled around the 38–39 per cent mark until 1983 when it lost heavily and went down to 33 per cent. The Italian Communist Party, on the contrary, moved from 22 per cent in 1953 to around 25–27 per cent in the 1960s. In 1976 it reached its peak (34.4 per cent) although it lost a few points in 1979 and 1983 (down to 30 per cent). At the European elections of 1984 it obtained 33.3 per cent of the votes overtaking for the first time the DC, if only by 0.3 per cent. The total of the Communist and Socialist vote in Italy has been around 40–45 per cent, which corresponds to the percentage of votes that left-wing parties obtain in most other West European countries, including those where television is not under the direct control of political parties.

In spite of widespread criticisms and the lack of any evidence of electoral gains, the DC never relented in its pursuit of control over the RAI. In 1961 it named as director general Ettore Bernabei who would remain in charge until 1974. Bernabei was a personal friend of Fanfani and had been the editor of the DC daily, *Il Popolo*. Bernabei's rule saw a further expansion of the patronage system of the DC, but the general approach had to change radically to take account of the presence of the Socialists in a new coalition system.[5]

Between 1948 and 1963 the DC had governed Italy in alliance with three minor parties of the centre: the Social Democrats, the Republicans and the Liberals. During this period, and particularly between 1958 and 1963, Italian economic development reached a very high rate of growth: the so-called 'economic miracle'. This expansion had been largely left to the private sector. When this period of growth came to an end in 1963 many of Italy's traditional problems had remained unsolved, such as the gap between the developed north and the agricultural south, and new ones had been created by the uncontrolled internal migration which had deprived the southern countryside of its labour force and overcrowded the industrial cities of the north. The DC, under the leadership of Aldo Moro and Amintore Fanfani, decided that it was necessary to ditch the anti-interventionist Liberal Party, include the Socialist Party in the coalition and initiate a programme of reforms. This was all the more necessary so as to stop the Italian Communist Party from extending its influence. The entry of the Socialist Party in the coalition government brought to the DC a partner which intended to obtain some share of control over the public sector (which, under the aegis of the new centre–left government, expanded very rapidly). The DC could no longer hope to have the exclusive monopoly over appointments in the public sector; now it had to negotiate with the Socialist Party (PSI). This was done through a quantitative increase in jobs. Thus the entry of the Socialists into the RAI in the 1960s under Bernabei was simply part of a process which was going on elsewhere in the public sector.

Bernabei increased the personnel of the RAI in an uninhibited manner, not only to accommodate the Socialists but also to make friends and extend his own power and that of his party. To counter the constant criticisms of intellectuals he developed a system of consultancies and freelance contributors well in excess of what was needed. Writers and journalists, academics and other personalities would be paid a retainer, on a yearly basis, plus a special contribution for occasional services.[6] When the student movement erupted in 1968, soon to be followed by the wave of workers' unrest in 1969 (the so-called 'hot autumn'), dissent threatened to engulf large sections of educated public opinion. The Bernabei system could no longer hope to diffuse criticisms by the simple policy of co-option.

The structural reforms promised by the centre-left government never materialised. After the social unrest of 1968–69 the DC faced a deep crisis. In 1974 it tried to re-establish control over the Catholic electorate by initiating a referendum to reverse the 1970 Divorce Act. It failed. In 1975 the Communist Party made sweeping gains in the local elections and took control, with the Socialist Party, of most major cities: Milan, Florence, Venice, Turin and, eventually, Rome and Naples. In 1976 the Communist Party further increased its electoral strength at the general elections. It was now the party of 34.4 per cent of Italians, a few percentage points behind the DC.

The DC felt it could no longer monopolise the public sector (and hence the RAI). Consequently, it offered the PSI a wider share of political power. The subsequent battle for control allowed other political forces to enter the fray and in particular the PCI. This led to the most important reform of the RAI to date.

THE REFORM OF THE RAI AND THE END OF DC MONOPOLY

The PCI was ill-equipped to enter the battle for the reform of broadcasting. Its main guiding principles were all connected to the conception of broadcasting as a 'public service' and the necessity to democratise it. Democratisation entailed the transfer of control over the RAI from the government to Parliament. This was also the only way in which the PCI could obtain some

POLITICAL AND MARKET FORCES IN ITALIAN BROADCASTING 71

influence over the RAI because, although excluded from government, it had obviously a very strong presence in Parliament. The PCI was also committed to improve relations with the PSI, but if it had decided to fight unrelentingly against the carving-up of the RAI (the so-called *lottizzazione*) it would have had to oppose the PSI. Of course, the PCI could have also attempted to bypass the PSI and deal directly with the DC in the hope of obtaining a share more or less commensurate with its strength. But this strategy would have damaged the prestige of the PCI as the one party unsullied by corruption and would have divided it from those RAI journalists and technical staff and the broadcasting unions who saw the PCI as their main representative. Virtually paralysed in its attempts to initiate a more thoroughgoing reform, the PCI ended up by insisting on two principles: democratisation (that is, parliamentary control) and decentralisation.

The principle of democratisation was enshrined in Law 103 (1975).[7] This established that the RAI was now under parliamentary control. A parliamentary committee on broadcasting was set up. This consisted of 40 members appointed by Parliament in proportion to the strength of the parties. The task of this committee was to ensure that the state television system was managed according to the principles of political pluralism and that it fulfilled the obligations set out in its charter and those established by the law (for example, that there should be open access, educational programmes, etc.). The parliamentary committee was also required to appoint ten out of the 16 members of the *Consiglio d'Amministrazione* (the Board of Governors), the remaining six being appointed by the 'shareholders' of the RAI, that is, the IRI.

The principles behind the reform were good. The application of the principles less so. Within the parliamentary committee a majority was constituted which reflected the government. In other words the same parties which were in coalition in government joined together to appoint governors who could be relied on to support them. Furthermore the president of IRI, whose job it was to appoint six governors, was himself a government appointee and was instructed to follow the advice of the government department in charge of IRI. The PCI was given less than its fair share of the governors, but that was immaterial in view of the fact that *all* governors were political appointees and that the majority of the Board would in any case have been made up of loyal supporters of the governing majority. Thus control by the executive branch was reasserted via the devious route of establishing parliamentary control. The governors always behaved as 'politicians' and sought to defend the interests of their masters. This was, once more, seen essentially in terms of ensuring a 'correct' news coverage. The political importance of television fiction bypassed them nearly completely.

Law 103 established the 'official' reform of the RAI. Alongside it there was a parallel hidden 'reform': the formal carve-up of the two channels between the DC and the PSI. A 'secret' agreement (which leaked immediately) was reached in a locality near Rome between the representatives of the coalition parties.[8] The most significant point of this agreement was that RAI's two main television channels were given two distinct structures. RAI-TV 1 would be under DC control, whilst RAI-TV 2 was placed under Socialist control.

This has been the situation ever since. In 1984 the state of play was the following: the President and Vice-President of the RAI are members of the PSI, while the director-general is a Christian Democrat. The DC also 'has' the directors of RAI-TV 1 as well as the director of the news programmes on the first channel, whilst the Socialists control the entire second channel. Radio has suffered a similar political carve-up: Radio 1 has a Social Democrat for director, but its news are jointly run by a Socialist and a Communist. Radio 2 (including the news) is the exclusive property of the DC. Radio 3 (which is similar to its British equivalent) is mainly devoted to cultural programmes and is run by an independent close to the PCI while its news bulletins are run by a Social Democrat.[9]

The extent of politicisation in Italy is such that virtually all journalists and many RAI employees are members of political parties. In the shake-up that followed the DC–PSI agreement journalists were allowed to opt for one or the other channel. Most Socialists opted for the second channel, whilst the Christian Democrats opted for the first.[10]

The carve-up was not 'fair', not even by the rules of the *lottizzazione*: by choosing the first channel the DC obtained the channel with a mass following and thus retained the lion's share of the RAI audience.

As a sop to the decentralising demands of the PCI, a third television channel was also established. This was expected to devote a large amount of programming to broadcasts of a local and regional nature. It never stood a chance because the first and second channels were beginning to face the challenge of private television and more and more economic resources were poured into them in order to make more popular programmes and to purchase films from the USA. As a result, the audience share of the third channel has always been insignificant.

In retrospect the attempt by politicians to monopolise television can be seen to have had little effect. Mass behaviour is not affected by news programmes alone but by the entire communication system. Television too depends on a cultural industry of great diversity: press, publishing, theatre, cinema, the educational system and all other disseminators of information including those of other parts of the world. The colonisation of the RAI by the governing parties could not prevent the growing autonomy of the broadcasting media from the political elites because these (that is, the media) were becoming increasingly subordinated to the (largely American) world communication and cultural industries. Furthermore, the crucial event which would transform the contours of Italian broadcasting and enable the development of a sizeable private sector was about to empty the political carve-up of the RAI of much of its significance. This event was the decision, in 1976, of the Italian Constitutional Court that the state monopoly over broadcasting was not legal.

DEVELOPMENT OF PRIVATE BROADCASTING AND ITS CONSEQUENCES

A year after the 1975 Reform Law was passed, the Constitutional Court

POLITICAL AND MARKET FORCES IN ITALIAN BROADCASTING 73

assembled once again to consider the question of the state monopoly over broadcasting. It decided that this was now valid only at the national level. Local private broadcasting was to be allowed. In so doing the Court probably destroyed also the emerging hopes of the cable industry because over-the-air broadcasting is much cheaper: it does not require an expensive network of cables and any additional expenditure on the part of viewers over and above the licence fee.

The way was now open for the unrestricted expansion of private radio and television stations. Of course the government could have stepped in and established some sort of regulatory framework, but the DC, having seen its power at the RAI somewhat diminished, hoped that it could reassert it, at least partially, in the developing private sector. There were no great pressures for regulation from the PCI whose position was still that television should be a 'public service'. It took a few years before the Communists accepted the idea of private broadcasting. It should also be said that the diffusion of private broadcasting companies was greeted by near-universal approval. The prestige of the RAI, never very high, had been tarnished by the spectacle of political parties fighting over the spoils. It was also assumed that competition would improve programmes all round. The press could have been expected to resist private broadcasting which would be an obvious competitor for advertising. It did not do so because most of it is under the control of large publishing conglomerates such as Mondadori and Rizzoli who were quick to enter the field of private broadcasting. The far-left groups as well as radicals and libertarians felt that this was a golden opportunity for the diffusion of community programmes with a high political content. As the initial capital required for this kind of operation was quite low, they hoped to initiate a whole network of 'alternative' broadcasting. Eventually even the PCI established its own network of radio stations (and some television stations) in the major cities, although with little success. Italian intellectuals, who have always had a snobbish attitude towards television, hoped that the new private sector would open up the possibility for more and better cultural programmes.

The hopes of all these were soon dashed. Those who benefited were some of the entrepreneurs who threw their energies into this new enterprise (but many had their fingers burnt and withdrew) and, of course, the audience whose demand for more popular television could no longer be satisfied by the RAI. As could be expected the cultural content of the private programmes was quite low. Most private radios offered an undiluted diet of pop music and some amateurish news reporting. Private television stations soon found out that they could never afford anything more than games shows, old films and a constant run (and re-run) of American products.

There is no doubt that the bulk of the audience wants to watch films. The ratings for the main types of programmes give a 75 per cent for films, but there is also a strong demand for news (74 per cent).[11] This is probably due to the low level of press readership and the habit of eating dinner during the news (that is, between eight and nine in the evening). At 8.30 p.m. the news programme is over and virtually all television channels schedule the beginning of their main programme. The search for a film starts. This is when the private television audience reaches its peak: 13 million viewers between 9.00 p.m. and 10.00 p.m.

Taking a day at random in the Rome area it is possible to classify thus the supply of television: 16 channels, including the three RAI channels, offer 196 hours of television, 23 per cent of which is produced by the companies themselves, and the rest purchased; 4.6 per cent of the total output is devoted to sports; 6.4 per cent to news; 11.4 to games and pop music; 15.4 per cent to cartoons; and 61.7 per cent to purchased films. Thirteen out of the 16 channels show films after 8.30 p.m., most of which (and of the cartoons) have been purchased abroad and dubbed in Italian. Nearly all imported films are made in the USA.[12]

Thus the Italian television system has become a huge network of terminals transmitting programmes produced in and around Los Angeles. In 1981 Italian television companies (both private and the RAI) imported 2,369 films plus 2,043 made-for-TV films and episodes of television serials. This makes a total of 4,412 units of which only 18 per cent were bought by the RAI. The total sum spent for all TV imports *and* for films to be shown in cinemas was 102 billion lire in 1981. In the same year Italy exported television material and films worth 29 billion. The deficit is therefore one of 73 billion lire (roughly £12.6 million), which indicates that the financial resources available for television and film are not invested internally but are directed towards the USA. In practice the Italian broadcasting system acts as the distribution network for products manufactured by a few multinational companies: centralisation of production and decentralisation of distribution go hand in hand.

This is, of course, not only an economic problem but also a cultural one: there is an increased Americanisation of Italian society. It will be remarked that this is not imposed on the Italian viewer by some evil outside force. Nobody compels anyone to watch *Starsky and Hutch*, *Dallas* and *Happy Days*. This is true, but it is not the whole story. Television viewing is now the principal, though not exclusive, focus of people's leisuretime throughout the advanced industrial world. There is no other activity to which masses of people can turn so frequently and so easily. Italians may well want to see films, but there is no evidence that they get the films they really want or might want if they had a wider choice. On the contrary, there is some evidence that the audience is getting bored. They do not switch off but they use frenetically the now widespread remote control instrument in a desperate search for 'something better on another channel'.

The dominance of American-made products is not only due to a cultural hegemony which has been established by the Hollywood film industry between the wars, but also to the fact that it is much cheaper to buy their products than to make new and original ones. Private television stations do not have the resources to invest heavily in their own production, although soon, the larger ones will. As for the RAI the fear of being left with a small share of the audience has driven it to compete with the private companies on their own ground, diverting resources towards the purchase of foreign products.

The spread of private television companies has also had a massive impact

POLITICAL AND MARKET FORCES IN ITALIAN BROADCASTING   75

on advertising. In the first place the widespread diffusion of local television has enabled local advertising to find a space. Until then national advertisers could use the press, the RAI, the cinema, etc., to the benefit of products with a national market. Local advertising had no outlet until private local radio and television stations emerged. This in turn caused the development of new advertising agencies specialising in local advertising. To sell a 'spot', however, it is necessary to have a programme of fairly good quality. The early programmes were mainly chat-shows and badly dubbed poor quality foreign films, and so the agencies themselves began to purchase a better product which they passed on to the companies together with the advertising spot. The local companies became mere relay stations whilst the agencies continued their 'vertical growth' by purchasing equipment from electronic companies.[13]

Soon there emerged something akin to a network situation. The advertising companies became *de facto* distributors. They convinced a number of local television stations to carry the same programmes at the same time with the same advertising (which by now is both local and national). They thus provided the stations with the advertising revenues which would be returned to them to pay for the programmes, thereby establishing their control over most of the financial aspects of private broadcasting. The advertising companies/distributors then organise the production and distribution of comic books, novels, T-shirts, toys and other goods which relate to the programmes shown.[14] Thus the local television companies, far from being examples of a new dynamic entrepreneurship are but the agents of a few oligopolies which dominate the market. They are mere terminals for distribution.

Some local broadcasting stations are financed by capital already connected to advertising. Backed by powerful interests they soon emerged as the market leaders. The top three private television companies have cornered most of the advertising revenue going to the private TV sector.[15] Of these the most powerful is *Canale Cinque* whose owner, Silvio Berlusconi, has become the virtual master of the entire private system since he bought both *Italia Uno* and *Retequattro*. Berlusconi's own financial empire includes housing estates, shopping centres, and electronic companies, the right-wing Milan newspaper *Il Giornale* and Italy's leading television weekly magazine. His complex network of couriers distributes videotapes to hundreds of relay stations around the country thus creating the effect of a national network. The system he has created includes a financial company, Cofint-Finanziaria, a company for the purchasing and distribution of videotaped programmes, a production centre, a technical centre with a high and low frequency band, a television broadcasting station *Telemilano* (the original element in the network), and an advertising company. Technically speaking *Canale Cinque* is a network which broadcasts daily the entire programme schedule of *Telemilano*.[16]

In 1982 *Canale Cinque* bought the Italian option for the entire output of the major American TV company, CBS. Another company, *Retequattro*, made a similar deal with ABC. The RAI was forced to follow suit with NBC, but by June 1984 it still had not received from the Ministry of Trade the authorisation to purchase the necessary foreign currency. In 1984 the RAI was able to obtain the exclusive Italian rights for the Los Angeles Olympic coverage, but this meant that the Eurovision network (of which the RAI is a member) had to pay over the odds to defeat Berlusconi's challenge. The RAI had to agree to participate in this operation to the tune of six million dollars. Without Berlusconi, it would not have had to pay more than two-and-a-half million dollars.[17]

In 1983 Berlusconi bought *Italia Uno* thereby establishing a commanding strength. In 1984 he bought from Mondadori, Italy's largest publishers, *Retequattro*. Thus Berlusconi has acquired control over all three leading private TV stations, and consequently over 80 per cent of advertising revenue. He is likely to expand this further by also obtaining control over the remaining two minor networks, *EURO-TV* and *Rete A*. It was quite clear that Mondadori had tried to find another buyer. Its president, Mario Formentor, declared, when he accounced the sale in September 1984, that at first he had been trying to sell to another firm (the building company of Vincenzo Romagnoli) until he realised that Romagnoli was acting on behalf of Berlusconi. While the negotiations were going on, Mondadori's shares began to show a constant fall in value because of heavy sales. It has been widely suggested in the Italian press that this was a concerted action inspired by Berlusconi.

Having achieved the conquest of virtually all major national private networks, Berlusconi's next move could well be to weaken further the RAI. He has already begun to exercise considerable pressure on the government to abolish the RAI's licensing fee or to forbid it to carry advertising. He is also asking that he should be allowed to broadcast news every half-hour and has declared that 'any new law on broadcasting must not re-examine problems which have already been overtaken by the workings of the market'.[18] Clearly from now on the struggle will be directed entirely against the public sector. It is quite possible that the Berlusconi empire is not constitutional because the Supreme Court had already made its opinion known that even an oligopoly would not be legal. But this is not likely to deter Berlusconi. As a member of the secret masonic lodge P2 (his name was on a list deemed to be authentic by the parliamentary commission investigating the allegation), he has obviously enjoyed the help of influential political friends and has always acted in the knowledge that there would not be any regulation which could be an obstacle to his plans.

The entire operation which led to the establishment of a number of private networks occurred under the aegis of a *laissez-faire* ideology which had a major libertarian component. It was not only a question of establishing a free market in the broadcasting sphere, but also a demand for a pluralistic system of broadcasting which would not be confined to the state sector. Given the RAI's traditional subservience to the governing political parties, the development of private broadcasting had considerable public support. Yet no-one should be under any illusion that the development of the private sector was occurring despite the political establishment. There is little doubt that active encouragement had come, at crucial stages, from the governing parties. Only this can explain the extreme reluctance to initiate any legislation throughout the period of expansion of the new private system and the extreme ease with

POLITICAL AND MARKET FORCES IN ITALIAN BROADCASTING 77

which thousands of television and radio transmitters have been installed throughout the national territory. Italy has a maze of regulations and a large and well-entrenched bureaucracy notorious for its delaying tactics. It is not unusual to have to wait months and even years in order to obtain permission to enlarge one's house or open a newsstand. Yet the widespread diffusion of transmitters occurred without any reaction on the part of the authorities. Clearly the dream, or perhaps the utopia, of a hundred stations broadcasting against the monopoly of state television has faded away. Power and control were at first diffused, then concentrated in a few hands and an oligopolistic situation was created. By the end of 1984 even this situation came to an end. There is now a duopoly: RAI and Berlusconi's TV empire.

ADVERTISING AND AUDIENCE SHARES

Available figures show that the remarkable growth in advertising which occurred between 1977 and 1981 benefited the private sector more than the RAI. Between 1978 and 1980 the RAI's share of advertising revenue decreased. In 1981 it increased again.[19] This is probably due to the fact that the amount of advertising broadcast in the private sector is reaching saturation point. The private companies may well have reached what is considered to be the natural limit of advertising per hour, namely, 14 per cent (eight-and-a-half minutes) whilst the RAI, which broadcast more hours, has still some way to go. But there is another explanation for the RAI's increase in revenue after 1980 and it is political.

During the battle for control between the DC and the PSI the RAI had succeeded in acquiring some form of independence. In the years 1976–79 the Italian Communist Party had supported the Christian Democrat government as part of its strategy of 'historic compromise'. This encouraged many producers and journalists to behave more independently. It was assumed that the difficult situation in which the DC was finding itself (electoral losses, necessity to co-operate with the PCI, etc.) meant that political control over the RAI could not be so tightly exercised as in the past. This was not the case. The DC and the PSI re-established control through the financial side: the real value of the licensing fee was allowed to decrease, while at the same time the amount of advertising revenue the RAI was allowed to obtain was not increased.[20] This amount, according to the RAI Reform Law (Law no. 103), must be established by the appropriate parliamentary committee, in other words, by its governing majority. Thus the RAI lost revenue on both the advertising and the licensing fronts. In 1980 many independent-minded functionaries and broadcasters were sacked and 'political protection' returned; advertising revenue and the licensing fee went up.

Clearly, the control exercised by political parties has had no tangible benefits for the RAI. The necessity to be on good terms with the governing political parties has meant that no-one can be particularly original, daring or critical; routine is much safer. There is also a growing inefficiency. In spite of its large personnel (14,000 employees, 800 executives, 1,100 journalists) there is a massive use of outside facilities and personnel on contract. For example, the RAI has paid an outside company ('Video Italia') to edit its

78   BROADCASTING AND POLITICS IN WESTERN EUROPE

own presentation spots: about 100 a year (length of spot: 40–50 seconds).
The contract amounts to 3,500 million lire a year (roughly one-and-a-half
million pounds). The RAI's director-general is not allowed to negotiate
contracts for sums greater than 100,000,000 lire (£43,000), so these kinds of
deal must be authorised by the majority of the 16 members of the Board of
Governors (whose expertise on matters of television financing is not particularly great).[21] Clearly the chances of kickbacks are very high.

The leading private television companies have made major inroads into
the RAI audience. The ratings for December 1983 made available by the
ISTEL research organisation (considered fairly reliable by both the private
and the public broadcasting sectors) show that *Canale Cinque* has now
got the second largest share of the peak-time audience (8.30 p.m. to
11.30 p.m.):

	Percentage
RAI-1	28.9
Canale Cinque	25
Italia Uno	14
Retequattro	12
RAI-2	9.9
RAI-3	1.4
Others	8.8

This means that the three leading private networks have three million
peak-time viewers more than all three RAI channels put together (the total
audience is 27.380 million). This is not a 'freak' result; it is confirmed
by the average ratings for the whole autumn of 1983. It also shows a trend
unfavourable to the RAI, because the ratings for the spring of 1983 had seen
the three RAI channels 'beating' the top three private networks by three
million peak-time viewers.[22]

THE FUTURE OF ITALIAN BROADCASTING

The development of the private broadcasting system could not have taken
place without the deliberate help of the governing political parties. Its
appearance can be justified on many counts: the RAI monopoly was
increasingly untenable; there was a widespread demand for television
products that the RAI alone could never hope to satisfy; competition could
have improved the public service; there was a need for more local broadcasting and so on. What is not so obvious is why the ruling coalition has never
regulated this system, why it has allowed this untrammelled growth and
why, nine years after the decision of the Constitutional Court, there is no
evidence that the government is about to produce even the draft of a
comprehensive regulatory bill.

1. The Position of the DC

The Christian Democratic Party never fought very hard to defend the
monopoly of the RAI. In the first place it was clearly beginning to lose the
total control it once enjoyed. The fact that it had to share power with the PSI

POLITICAL AND MARKET FORCES IN ITALIAN BROADCASTING   79

had already been a sign that it could not assume that it could control in perpetuity a monopolistic public system. In the second place it hoped that it would be able, sooner or later, to deal directly with the emerging networks. The DC may have had to give up important sectors of its empire, but it has retained absolute control over the banking system. This has given it access to the private sector of industry which depends on the banks for much of its finances. Through the banks the DC can always negotiate with the private television companies.

The best card the DC can play with respect to the private sector is the regulatory system. It can tailor it so that it will benefit those companies which will accept to collaborate, but there is no point in playing this card before the private system has gone through an initial phase during which a few companies will have acquired a dominant role. This phase has now been reached, but various things have happened to the DC in the meantime: it has suffered a serious defeat in the 1983 general elections (a defeat which was confirmed in the European elections of 1984); it has had to give up the Prime Ministership to the Republican leader Spadolini in 1982 and to the Socialist leader Bettino Craxi in 1983, the first time since 1945 that non-DC politicians have obtained this post; it is at the mercy of a Socialist Party which has always had the option of joining the PCI in opposition, thus depriving the DC of the necessary parliamentary support. A weakened DC may not be able to impose on restless coalition partners the regulatory system it wants, but it is still strong enough to prevent any regulation whatsoever.

Finally, the DC is in reality concerned mainly with the television coverage of news and current affairs. Here the RAI still reigns supreme and, within the RAI, the DC-controlled RAI-1 has the overwhelming share of the audience for news programmes. Thus the leadership of the DC can obtain the 'right' sort of messages where it really matters. DC backbenchers have a different attitude; they need private radio and television because they can obtain from them what they cannot obtain from the RAI: publicity for their own activities at the local level. The opportunity to establish a local television image can be crucial to DC politicians during an election campaign. Italian voters must vote for a party, but can then write in the names of their favoured three or four candidates from within that party's list (the so-called preference vote). Before the development of the mass media, local candidates could keep in touch with their electorate through public meetings. Now they can no longer obtain a large audience; everyone stays at home watching television. Local notables can only enter private homes through small television stations which beam their message for a distance of 10–20 miles.[23] They will, of course, pay for it, but they can also do so by blocking in Parliament any reforms because, as far as local television stations are concerned, the best way in which they can be helped is by leaving untouched the present *laissez-faire* system.

2. *The Position of the Socialist Party*

Some of the arguments used to explain the position of the DC can be applied to the PSI as well. However, the support that the PSI has given to the private

80   BROADCASTING AND POLITICS IN WESTERN EUROPE

companies is also due to its general strategic perspective. Since Craxi became the Socialist leader, the party has attempted to create for itself a new image. It has proceeded to shed many of its traditional working-class connotations and to espouse a view of modernisation characteristic of many new and old centrist parties in Europe (such as the British SDP). According to this analysis it is necessary to link up with the emerging middle classes of technicians and professional people who are in the forefront of technological progress and whose aspirations have been repressed by the existence in Italy of a Christian Democratic Party which has always protected backwardness and inefficiency in order to maintain its electoral strength. Nor can the PCI be the vehicle for these new groups because – the PSI claims – it is still a traditional working-class party which will protect these entrenched interests against any rationalisation of the economy. Given this outlook, the PSI has cultivated from the very beginning the new private television sector. It welcomed the end of the RAI monopoly, declaring that a mixed market system would open up opportunities for all.

The PSI has also tried to develop the image of a party which seeks to defend and extend civil liberties and the right of the individual against the populist spirit of DC clericalism and the collectivist spirit of the PCI. The diversification of the broadcasting system was seen as a golden opportunity for expanding access and was made to fit the new libertarian image of the PSI. The fact that the reality of oligopolistic control contradicted the dream of 'let a hundred television channels bloom' never seemed to matter.

3. The Position of the Italian Communist Party

Until the 1970s the PCI had conceived of the television system purely in terms of a 'public service' which had to remain under the control of the state. It had not appreciated that television had also become an industry which would soon have to face competition from the private sector and be subjected to the requirements of the market as well as to political and professional control.

In the 1970s and 1980s the party began to understand the great importance of the mass media as a crucial sector which linked industry, culture and the new technologies. It established a special section of the Executive Committee which dealt exclusively with the media and was the only political party to present a comprehensive proposal for reform during the life of the 1979–83 Parliament. The main points of this proposed law were:[24]

(a) The Constitutional Court's principle that companies must operate only at the local level must be upheld. However, the local dimension cannot be too restricted and so it is suggested that the 20 Italian regions be the framework for roughly as many private companies.

(b) Networking would be allowed provided that effective anti-trust legislation ensures that ownership is not concentrated in a few hands.

(c) Private companies would be required to produce and transmit their own programmes for at least 30 per cent of their total weekly broadcast time.

(d) A national broadcasting authority would be created with specific tasks: to allocate frequency bands, specify when and how much of the internally produced programmes would have to be shown and supervise the application of codes of conduct. The governing body of this authority would be appointed in part by the government and in part by the parliamentary committee on broadcasting (although clearly this might launch a new *lottizzazione* struggle).

(e) A single national news programme should be broadcast by the private sector which would be in charge of its production. 'Live' news broadcasts would be provided by a publicly owned company.

Virtually every political party has agreed with at least some of these proposals. For instance, the DC accepts the principle of a single national news programme and of a statutory limit to advertising. Along with the small Republican Party it also accepts the need for anti-trust legislation which is, however, opposed by the Socialists (who seem to have become the main upholders of unrestricted capitalism).

The Communist proposals, in spite of the positive comments with which they have been received, are unlikely to become law. The chances are that there will not be any regulation of the private sector for some time to come. The present government coalition is too weak and divided and faces powerful interests. Furthermore, all existing proposals for reform do not get to the heart of the matter, which concerns both the relationship between the private and the public sector and the connection between television broadcasting and the entire information industry.

CONCLUSION

A modern mixed system can no longer assume a rigid demarcation between the public and private sectors of broadcasting; both are subjected to market forces and both must be liable to some form of state regulation. There is no reason why the two should be kept separate. The state could, through the RAI, establish some sort of framework within which a system of mass production of television products can be established and in which the private sector can play a part. So far the private sector has been an importer. A way should be found to transform it into a producer. The RAI has been successful in forging links with the film industry by acting as a producing company as well as a distributor of films both on television and in the cinemas. Well-known directors such as Olmi, Bertolucci and the Taviani brothers have produced important films through this system. It could be expanded on a more commercial basis and the private sector could be involved in it. This would allow Italian broadcasting to compete with American products, particularly if it were to take advantage of the fact that a number of European and Third World countries are increasingly concerned at American 'cultural imperialism'.

The advent of satellite broadcasting will go a long way towards destroying the national basis of television systems. In these circumstances reforms can no longer be conceived purely at the national level. The tasks facing the Italian political elite are thus considerable; it must achieve the modernisation of Italian telecommunications and promote – with other European countries – a concerted entry into the technological software market as well

82   BROADCASTING AND POLITICS IN WESTERN EUROPE

as into the international TV market. It must try to eliminate at least the worst aspects of *lottizzazione* (which has not given it the advantages expected) through the professional training of competent cadres and the establishment of some form of demarcation between technical and professional competence on the one hand, and political control on the other.

The main danger facing Italy at this stage is in the field of information technology. The development of unrestricted private television has dealt a blow to the possibility of the expansion of cable systems. Viewers who can receive up to 20 channels for free are unlikely to pay to get 30 more channels transmitting *Dallas*-type programmes all over again. The long-term purpose of rewiring an entire nation is not to provide programmes (these are only the means to convince consumers to pay for the installation of cables), but to provide the whole country with an interactive (two-way) system of information; consumers will no longer be the passive recipients of messages manufactured and transmitted by a few senders, but will actively intervene in a network of data which will permit shopping, learning, working and communicating by cable. The unrestricted over-the-air broadcast explosion may have cut Italy off from these crucial developments. The consequences may be that Italy will be left out of the advanced sectors of the 'information revolution'. For a country which is still paying the price for having been a 'late comer' in the industrial revolution, this is a daunting prospect.

NOTES

1. Figures made available by the RAI-Documentazione e Studi.
2. Figures in Carlo Gagliardi, 'La televisione in Italia: tendenze del sistema misto', *Sociologia e ricerca sociale*, no. 9 (1982).
3. Franco Chiarenza, *Il cavallo morente* (Milan: Bompiani, 1978), p. 91.
4. Giovanni Cesareo, *Anatomia del potere televisivo* (Milan: Franco Angeli, 1970), p. 80.
5. For an analysis of Bernabei's management see F. Pinto, *Il modello televisivo* (Milan: Feltrinelli, 1980).
6. Cesareo, op. cit., pp. 45–6.
7. A fuller description of the law can be found in Fabio Luca Cavazza, 'Italy: From Party Occupation to Party Partition', in Anthony Smith (ed.), *Television and Political Life* (London: Macmillan, 1979), pp. 105–8.
8. See Chiarenza, op. cit., p. 22 and Massimo Pini's autobiographical 'confessions', *Memorie di un lottizzatore* (Milan: Feltrinelli, 1978), especially pp. 63–72.
9. *Il Gazzettino*, 5 Feb. 1984.
10. C. Fracassi, 'Poltrona per poltrona tutto il potere lottizzato alla RAI-TV', *Paese Sera*, 6 March 1982.
11. Data in Giuseppe Vacca, *L'Informazione negli anni ottanta* (Rome: Riuniti, 1984), p. 155.
12. My calculations on the basis of data in S. Balassone and A. Guglielmi, *RAI-TV L'autarchia impossibile* (Rome: Riuniti, 1983), pp. 64–8.
13. Renato Venturini, 'Verso un sistema misto', *Studi sociali*, no. 1–2 (1983), p. 106.
14. Ibid., pp. 111–2.
15. Data in Vacca, op. cit., p. 167.
16. See Venturini, op. cit., pp. 111–2, and the *Financial Times*, 14 March 1984 for information on Berlusconi.
17. Chiara Sottocorona, 'Effetto biscione', *Panorama*, 19 March 1984.
18. Quoted in Mimmo Scarano, 'Il predatore del network', *Rinascita*, no. 35 (1984), p. 7.
19. Data in Balassone and Guglielmi, op. cit., pp. 81–5.
20. The Italian licensing fee is one of the lowest in Europe: approximately £32 for colour

POLITICAL AND MARKET FORCES IN ITALIAN BROADCASTING   83

television (only one-third of receivers are colour). The real value of the fee dropped 16 per cent between 1974 and 1979, but by 1981 it had returned to its 1974 level.
21. See reports in *La Repubblica*, 22 Feb. 1984.
22. See ISTEL reports in *Il Giornale*, 24 Jan. 1984.
23. Venturini, op. cit., pp. 98–9.
24. See Luca Pavolini, 'TV, la legge bloccata', *Rinascita*, no. 1 (Jan. 1983); Antonio Bernardi, 'Regolare così RAI e private', *Rinascita*, no. 5 (Feb. 1984) and reports in *La Repubblica*, 30 Nov. 1983.

[35]

Politics and the Mass Media in Italy

LUCA RICOLFI

This examination reviews the changes which have occurred in the links between politics and the mass media in recent years in Italy. It should be stressed that such an analysis must be largely conjectural. Although empirical studies analysing media content are fairly numerous, there are very few touching upon the two areas which are essential for adequately reconstructing the events of the last decade, namely a vertical study, through panel data or comparable measures, of the evolution of public opinion,[1] or a study of the effects of the media on electoral behaviour. This analysis is divided into three sections. The first describes some of the changes which have occurred over the last few years in the links between mass media, the Italian public and the political system. The second presents the available empirical evidence on the effects of television on electoral behaviour. Finally, the third discusses various problems relating to the regulation of political communication in the mass media (the so-called par condicio – equal access regulation).

LINKS BETWEEN THE POLITICAL SYSTEM AND THE MEDIA

Reconstructions of the links between politics and the mass media in Italy have been frequent in the post-war period. The majority of commentators seem to agree on distinguishing between at least five periods. The first of these, extending from the immediate post-war period until the introduction of television into Italy around 1954, is characterised by the political system's domination of the media. The formation of public opinion stemmed mainly from the mass political parties – the Christian Democrats (DC), the Communists (PCI) and the Socialists (PSI) – and in the case of the intellectual élite, via the classic mechanisms of mediation by leaders of opinion. In the following 15-year period, from the birth of television to the outbreak of the student and workers' revolts, television caught up with the classic media of radio, newspapers and periodicals, and soon became the main information source for the bulk of the population. During the regional elections of 1960, the TV programme, *Tribuna Elettorale*, first appeared. This provides a good illustration of the relationship between television and politics in the 1960s: television, far from developing an autonomous role in political innovation and content, instead restricted itself to offering existing political parties a channel for communicating their respective manifestos.

136   CRISIS AND TRANSITION IN ITALIAN POLITICS

The subordination of television to the political parties began to break down towards the end of the 1960s, with the concomitant onset of a difficult period of political upheaval – the student and workers' revolts, 'Red' (left-wing) and 'Black' (right-wing) terrorism, feminism, the first referendum conflicts and the crisis of the DC. Whilst remaining heavily dependent upon the party system, television used the volatility of civil society to gain some measure of independence from the political system. Giving society its own voice permitted television to contribute to the political renovation and cultural modernisation of the country.[2] This slow (and incomplete) development of independence of television from politics proceeded along two main lines: structural innovation and the diversification of supply. In the period from 1968 until the mid-1970s,[3] various experiments in political broadcasting were tried: open-house debates, popular tribunes, self-compiled propaganda, etc. At the same time, the process of pluralising televisual broadcasting, which a few years later led to the law reforming the RAI (State broadcasting corporation),[4] began with the creation of the third RAI channel, mainly contracted to the PCI, and to the birth of commercial television.

In the decade and a half which spanned the middle of the 1970s to the end of the 1980s, the situation changed once more. The end of the collective movements coincided with the emergence of an apparently renovated PSI, led by Bettino Craxi, and built on the ruins of left-wing unity, the marginalisation of the PCI, and an organic alliance of most of the small parties (except the fascist MSI) with the DC in the so-called *pentapartito* (five-party) alliance. The history of the *pentapartito* is also that of the gradual but inexorable takeover of the RAI. Having lost their vitality and their links with civil society, the Italian parties found the carving up of the broadcasting network – and of other sectors[5] – the best means of survival and self-perpetuation. Simultaneously, commercial television grew in size and power, especially in its ability to guide Italy's cultural modernisation. After an initial period of excessive proliferation, small private channels (of which there were almost one thousand at the beginning of the 1980s) yielded to the stronger entrepreneurs, and were virtually all absorbed by the beginning of the next decade. At the end of the 1980s, with the purchase of almost the entire commercial network by Silvio Berlusconi and his company Fininvest (now Mediaset, after the floating of the shares on the securities market), radio and television had developed into a duopoly, based on a division of the audience between private and public, the latter forming a kind of 'petrified pluralism' through the distribution of offices and sectors within this 'public' service. The so-called Mammì law,[6] which regulated radio and television broadcasting in Italy, served only to duplicate this situation in the legal domain.

However, even if the control of the media, both public and private, by the political system remained as solid as ever, the 1980s saw a major transformation of the relationship between the two. Through the influence of commercial television, this decade saw political parties first using advertising slots, and then politicians experimenting with new channels of communication, such as appearing on talk shows and entertainment programmes. The relationship between television and politics switched in many respects to one of mutual exchange. Whilst it is certainly true that the parties controlled television through job appointments (for the RAI) and concessions (for private channels), it is also true that the means of communication was always firmly in the hands of the operators, who consequently used politicians to glamourise their shows.

With the 1990s, this arrangement again began to change. The first evolution, very gradual and almost imperceptible, was the increasing amount of air-time given over to new political themes. The *Lega Nord* (LN – Northern League) of Umberto Bossi and the referendum movement of Mario Segni, while not actually created by the media, benefited from a boost in publicity that would have been unthinkable before television. Then, very gradually, the political system began to spiral out of control following the *'Mani Pulitie'* ('clean hands') affair, resulting in the electoral trouncing of the *pentapartito* in the elections of 6 April 1992, and the victory of the supporters of a referendum, finally held on 18 April 1993, which instigated a change in the electoral law towards a majoritarian system.

The battle between the old and fading nomenclature and the new political élites (those who were pro-referendum, members of the Lega, and ex-fascists who had previously always been excluded from the sharing-out of broadcasting) considerably broadened the role of the media which, within the space of a couple of years, found itself not only fulfilling its traditional function of agenda-setting, but also acting as the cog in the transition from old to new, from the first to the second Republic. This process culminated with the entry of Silvio Berlusconi into the fray, after the creation of *Forza Italia* (FI).

Although accepting that the role of the television channels which Berlusconi controlled directly was anything but marginal in FI's victory in the 1994 elections (as shown in sections three and four below), the key to Berlusconi's success is less his ability as a communicator (an aspect which has been over-emphasised) than his faultless timing, and the means which he used act. During a period when change was the most pressing objective, in the context of a media which was striving ever harder to create new 'spectacles', a brand new party like FI was by definition already ahead of the field. Television relies upon events, and Berlusconi's chief success was turning this political novelty into exactly that. Leaving aside the *nature* of the reaction to it by the various national channels, the birth of FI was the

138   CRISIS AND TRANSITION IN ITALIAN POLITICS

central event in politics for many weeks, becoming the yardstick by which other actors were measured. More fundamental even than media control was the electoral affinity with the product, and the consequent victory for Berlusconi.

After the victory of the right in the elections, and despite the growing interference of politics in television, which culminated in the appointment of the new Council for the Administration of the RAI,[7] the power of journalists over politics otherwise grew. Politics in the 1990s has an ever increasing reliance upon television, and this is not lost upon those who are working in it. As individuals they can be in the vanguard of political and economic power; but together they are propelled by a logic which is often in contradiction with their political counterparts. The realm of televisual information is acting more and more like a lobby, pursuing its own interests and ignoring the political affiliations of its members.

These changes can be illustrated by the reactions to the drawing up of the 'Gambino' law on *par condicio* – (equal access) – which aims to introduce some rules into the management of political broadcasting during elections.[8] Despite many of these regulations being inspired by the left, the editorial staff of RAI 3 – the channel closest to the *'Progressisti'* (Progressives' alliance) of the left – has been the fiercest critic of the bill, not because of its effectiveness in combating the abuse of television, but because of its negative effects on journalistic 'freedom'. Similar reasoning can be ascribed to other journalistic initiatives, such as the *'Abbonato alza la voce'* ('Subscribers, Raise your voices') campaign, the *'Telesogno'* project led by two presenters, Costanzo and Santoro,[9] and more generally the attitude of the media as a whole during the referendum on televisual information (April 1995). In all of these cases, televisual information has become a leading political issue, covering personal interests which are often opposed to the powers on which they depend.

Despite the resistance and hostility of those in broadcasting, the rules on equal access have had some sort of impact on the form of political communication. In the 1996 electoral campaign, the format of politics on television underwent a fundamental restructuring[10] and the context of competition seemed less inclined to presenting politics as a show. Further-more, faced with the new regulations, the producers tried to synthesise them, adapting the style of political propaganda to the new equal access regime. This contributed to the cooling of competition, and to the main-tenance of the broadcasting élites at the centre of political communication.

The result of these changes has been a new type of relationship between the media and politics. Midway through the 1990s, politics and journalists find themselves linked in a perverse kind of Laocoontian embrace.[11] The heat of the political and economic battles has certainly increased the reliance of journalists and their careers upon the strategies of opinion leaders. However, the centrality of television in information supply has also changed the face of politics, making it more dependent upon access to mass communication.

In this game of mirrors and exchanges between the media and the political system, the main losers are the audience. Especially during the years straddling the 11th and 12th legislatures (the three-year term from 1993 to 1995) the 'spectacularisation' of political competition opened the doors to talentless personalities with so-called 'gifts' of aggression, verbal pugnacity and domineering manners. Furthermore, the appearance of many new political groups allowed these same politicians to use the mass media ever more unscrupulously. Desperately searching to remind the voters of their existence, leaders on the left and on the right took on board a new method of survival: the continuous production and reproduction of artificial events. Slogans guaranteeing an interview; blazing declarations triggering polemic; broken alliances which were immediately patched up again; insults against adversaries which had to be countered, and which were already claimed to be responses to previous slander; and statements whose seriousness was inversely proportional to the electoral strength supporting them – these were the means by which politicians fought on television and in the newspapers, and the journalists were left to cover a political agenda which had very few *real* events to offer.

Similarly – and this should be seen as probably the most important effect of the changes since 1989 – the complex relationship between information and political alliances changed. At the point when the main interest of the media was in increasing its own freedom, the regulation policy traditionally promoted by the left finally met the interests of the broadcasting élite head on. A broadcasting network which aims to maximise its own freedom does not need to be controlled by the political right to be in tune with it. It is only natural that today, the right being the foremost supporter of market forces and deregulation in television, the latter sector should lean towards that particular political camp. The left, which for half a century has been accustomed to providing patronage for cultural movements, or at least major branches of them, does not seem to be fully aware of this major change. Winning the 1996 elections, and the probable future alignment of state television with them as a result, only makes it more difficult for the left to adapt to this change in the relationship between the political system and the media.

THE EFFECTS OF TELEVISION ON VOTING: THE 1994 ELECTIONS

The electoral campaign of 1994 was exceptional for many reasons. The 1994 elections were the first to take place under the new (partially) majoritarian

140   CRISIS AND TRANSITION IN ITALIAN POLITICS

electoral law, as well as being the first since *Tangentopoli* (February 1992).
These two aspects are tightly interwoven in the mentality of the Italian
electorate. The extraordinary success of the two referenda on electoral laws
(1991 and 1993) would be inexplicable without the growing antipathy
towards the political class which had dominated the scene for the past 15
years, under the guise of the *pentapartito*. The apparent concerns of the
1991 referendum on the preference vote and its 1993 successor on the
majoritarian system were the electoral system, but the underlying and
motivating force was to change the political class.

This context, characterised by loud demands for innovation, was stronger
than ever in the spring of 1994, notably when the entrepreneur Silvio
Berlusconi entered the arena at the head of FI. Newspapers, opinion polls
and maps of the electoral space all attest to this. For example, some studies
on perceptions of electoral space carried out a few months before the birth
of FI do not arrange the parties in a uni-dimensional space (such as left-
right or progressive-conservative axes) but in a bi-dimensional space.

Cross-cutting the traditional left-right axis, a second axis appeared,
probably at the beginning of the 1990s, based on the juxtaposition of

FIGURE 1

DIMENSIONS OF ELECTORAL SPACE

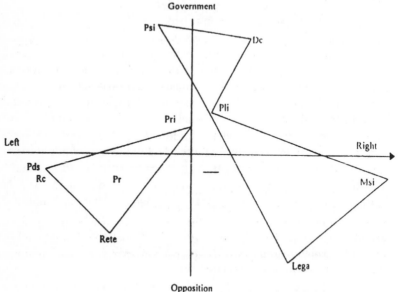

Key: Psi (Socialists), Dc (Christian Democrats), Pli (Liberals), Pri (Republicans), Psd
(Democratic Party of the Left), Rc (Communist Refoundation), Pr (Radical Party), Msi
(Neo-Fascists)

POLITICS AND THE MASS MEDIA 141

government and opposition parties, or, if one prefers, of new and old parties. Moreover, this new dichotomy became more important (or more precisely, a better description) than the old left-right axis (see Figure 1)[12].

In this situation, characterised by intense demands for change, the appearance of a new actor (Silvio Berlusconi) at the head of a new party (FI), with the technological support for the type of communication that had just become important in political competition (opinion polls, focus groups, advertising slots, political broadcasts) created a truly exceptional combination of conditions – which needs to be emphasised if we are to understand the subsequent dramatic electoral results.

In an econometric-style study of the evolution of Italian political preferences in the 1994 electoral campaign I have attempted to estimate the effects of exposure to the RAI channels (public television) and to the Fininvest channels (commercial television, controlled by Berlusconi) on voting behaviour.[13]

FIGURE 2

THE EFFECT OF TELEVISION ON THE VOTE

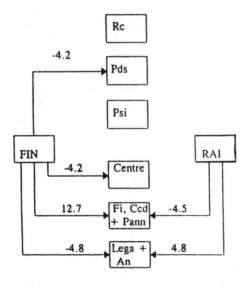

Key: FIN (Fininvest), Fi (Forza Italia), Ccd (Christian Democratic Centre), Lega (Northern League), Pann (Pannella), Rc (Communist Refoundation), Psi (Socialists), An (National Alliance), Pds (Democratic Party of the Left).

The results are impressive. The impact of the three RAI channels together is on at least five per cent of the electorate, whereas that of the three Fininvest channels is on at least 13 per cent. The total of all the movements

142   CRISIS AND TRANSITION IN ITALIAN POLITICS

induced by the RAI channels roughly equals zero, whilst for the Fininvest channels there is an increase of about four percentage points in favour of the centre-right, and especially at the expense of the PDS (the former communists) and of the two Catholic centre parties (the successors to the DC). To this we should add that a simulation of electoral constituencies has shown that, without the effects of television, the composition of Parliament would be very different indeed. Under the most conservative estimate, the centre parties *Partito popolare* (PPI) and the *Patto Segni* would have held the balance, and under the most likely scenario, the *Progressisti* would have won an absolute majority of seats.

These results, in agreement with both common sense and also with the most recent methodological and political science studies,[14] have caused strong reactions in Italy, especially in the broadcasting sector (worried as they are by possible negative repercussions on the level of freedom accorded to them) and amongst some mass media experts (still often adhering to the theory of limited effect). Apart from the robustness of the results, the *extent* of the effects predicted by the model is surprisingly large. Before estimating the parameters of the main behavioural equations, I expected a movement of about 3–4 per cent, whilst *a posteriori* the actual results were triple that figure. What tends to confirm the results was the emergence of two further pieces of empirical evidence congruent with the other findings, but obtained through different methods and different data.

The first piece of evidence congruent with the econometric model came from the Osservatorio di Pavia on the content of television transmissions. From these data, it is possible to see for each political party the bias in time accorded to each by the Fininvest channels and RAI channels.[15] This data can be compared with difference in vote volatility caused by the Fininvest channels and the RAI channels. Surprisingly the two series correspond almost exactly:

FIGURE 3

TIME BIAS AND VOTER MOVEMENT

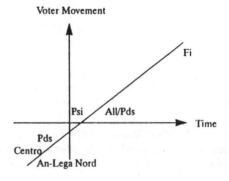

POLITICS AND THE MASS MEDIA 143

It is difficult to interpret this result in any way other than a confirmation of coverage on television – measured simply by direct coverage time – having an effect on electoral choice.

The second element of proof comes from an independent study by a young sociologist at the University of Naples.[16] The author, Angelo De Lucia, lives in the small village of San Felice a Cancello, in the province of Caserta. This locality has special characteristics because, due to the geography of the area, not all of its districts receive all television channels. RAI 3 (on the political left) and the three Fininvest channels (on the centre right) are received by different districts. San Felice a Cancello is therefore an ideal place to perform an experiment (of sorts) – and consequently a sociological rarity. Subdividing the districts according to which particular channels they receive, one can try and measure the differing effects in each. This is in substance what De Lucia did, using variance analysis to try to isolate the effects of the Fininvest channels and of RAI 3. Table 1 presents his statistically significant results.

TABLE 1

EFFECTS OF TELEVISION IN SAN FELICE A CANCELLO

	Fininvest	RAI 3
Forza Italia	8.9	–
Alleanza Nazionale	–5.2	–
PDS	–	4.5
Patto Segni	3.0	–
Others	–4.1	–3.6

Source: A. De Lucia, 'L'influenza della televisione sul voto. Un caso esemplare: S. Felice a Cancello', *Sociologia e Ricerca Sociale* 49 (1996).

The comparability of these results with those of my study is limited by at least three factors: the different structure of political supply (in the south of Italy, the Lega does not field candidates); the weakness of the left in San Felice; and the different operationalisation of the RAI in the two studies (grouped in my study, RAI 3 is isolated from the other two channels in his). The weakness of the left, visible even in the 1992 results, particularly narrows the possible volatility of votes moving to the centre-right. This aside, De Lucia's study also demonstrates a large influence of the Fininvest channels in favour of FI (+8.9 per cent), partly at the expense of *Alleanza Nazionale* (AN) and local political groupings. Perhaps the most interesting result is the current favourable effect RAI 3 is producing *vis-à-vis* the PDS (+4.5 per cent). This reinforces one conjecture which arose from my study: it is likely that the neutrality of the three RAI channels, rather than being a by-

144   CRISIS AND TRANSITION IN ITALIAN POLITICS

product of the quality of their broadcasting, is a result of a talented distribution of patronage by the parties.

Even if De Lucia's results do not allow us to draw general conclusions about television influence on the vote, due to the limited sample size, they at least reinforce the results of my own study: in the 1994 elections, the extent of television's effects on the vote was of a size equal to – if not greater than – that needed to determine the outcome of the ballot (5–10 percentage points).

A 'BRAIN-WASHED' ELECTORATE?

Should we conclude from this that the electoral result of 27 March 1994, and the victory of the forces led by Silvio Berlusconi, was due to radio-televisual 'brain-washing'? Definitely not. In reality, the depth of our study only confirmed that television almost certainly influenced the result, and that such influence was of a size sufficient to determine the outcome. But this is as much as can be claimed. It is one thing to say how much television had an effect, but quite another to say how this worked. The former describes the behavioural effects, the latter would have to explain the communicative, emotional and cognitive mechanisms through which such effects were produced.

Whilst the existence of effects from radio and television broadcasting on electoral behaviour is incontrovertible, and there is undoubtedly a serious problem of regulating the access to such a system, the analysis of such effects is open to interpretation. The influence of media on behaviour can always be read in two different ways: on one extreme, there is the theory which sees political communication as a manipulation of public opinion, while on the other, there is the opposite theory, which views communication merely as information. Evidently this does not mean that the way in which public opinion can be influenced by communication cannot be subject to empirical testing. Rather, it means that to understand what happened in the 1994 campaign we must go beyond the results of the model, and try to get inside the black box of voting behaviour.

The theory of manipulation, often promoted by the left in retrospect as a convincing (and soothing) explanation for their failure, clashes with two principal empirical problems. The first is that the two main groups on the left – the PDS and its allies – are the only ones to experience negative effects from both the Fininvest and RAI channels. Such negative effects do not appear in Figure 2 because of the lower percentage levels and significant statistical uncertainty. Table 2 presents the complete effects.

This seems to absolve the RAI from the accusation of having played to the left. But it also suggests a possible alternative perspective on voting, and one which is distinctly more worrying for left-wing leaders. The fact

POLITICS AND THE MASS MEDIA 145

TABLE 2

THE EFFECTS OF TELEVISION ON THE VOTE

Parties	RAI	Fininvest
RC, Rete, Verdi, AD	(–0.6)	(–0.4)
PDS	(–0.7)	(–4.2)
PSI	(–0.4)	1.0
PPI, Patto, PRI	(1.4)	–4.2
FI, CCD, Pannella	–4.5	12.7
Lega Nord, AN	4.8	–4.8

(The figures in parentheses indicate the effects which drop below the 5% threshold of statistical significance.)

that the left on television never produces positive results in voting terms would suggest that the defeat of the left was also due to their inability to use television,[17] that is their failure to strike the correct chords in a medium largely divorced from traditional means of mobilisation (rallies, leaflet distribution, debates, etc.).

The manichean theory of a direct linkage between television and voters is also weakened by the fact that those sections of the population that turn out to be most sensitive to influence appear also to be those who 'think more', that is, who possess the greatest cognitive resources.[18] It seems that the theory of manipulation should at least provide a minimally convincing interpretation of these results. Nevertheless, the opposite approach – which absolves the media of all responsibility for the 1994 results – also encounters problems. Who would truly believe that the voters are individuals with totally free choice, blessed with complete rationality or an ability to assess relative value, which immunises them to any form of conditioning? This view not only contradicts half a century of studies on the process of decision-making, but also the surprising results presented above (Figure 3): the difference in effect of Fininvest and RAI on public opinion mirrors exactly the bias in time allocated by the two broadcasting agencies to the respective political parties.

The significant level of correspondence between the two measurements seems on the one hand to be a confirmation of the reliability of our results (otherwise, is it a near-miraculous coincidence?); while on the other it suggests that the reading of the impact coefficient should be far lighter (that is, less extreme) than those discussed until now. It may seem banal, or too close to common wisdom about politics, but our diagram (Figure 3) suggests that in general, *time is equal to approval*. Certainly, the reliability of the information, the non-sectarianism of presenters, and the balance between the different groups can also play a role, and these should surely be introduced as fundamental ethical imperatives for those working in the broadcasting sector. But, above all, visibility, time and focus – whether through

146   CRISIS AND TRANSITION IN ITALIAN POLITICS

advertising or report coverage – that the parties obtain for themselves are what count the most. This is the greatest lesson of advertising in the consumer sector ('As long as you get people talking about you ...'); and is one of the main discoveries in international research. Television does not change opinions directly, rather it changes individual orderings by determining the salience of issues. In short, it plays a critical role in setting the agenda.[19]

If viewed from this perspective, problems such as partisan broadcasts or the freedom of voters appear in a different light. It may be that when bias or a partisan element is found in a RAI or a Fininvest broadcast, it may be due more to the planning itself than to the nature of broadcasting management. RAI and Fininvest allocated time to the different political groupings in a markedly unbalanced manner, and these differences have a significant effect on the volatility of the voters aligned with each broadcaster. The extent of the volatility caused by Fininvest is greater than that of RAI, above all because the bias in time allocated to *Forza Italia*, as opposed to the other political parties, is correspondingly larger.

This perspective considerably transforms the question of the voters' freedom of choice. The voter/viewer is not a passive subject who absorbs everything that is placed before him, but rather an information processor who reformulates the information he/she receives.[20] The crucial point is that the result of this process depends upon the quantity and content of the mix of information received. We can restate this point by saying that the voter is free by definition and that, whatever the connection between the stimuli which he receives and his behaviour, his choices are to be considered a manifestation of his true beliefs. More realistically, we might surmise that the fact that the 'menu' presented by television strongly affects our choices poses certain problems for democracy, if not to our freedom. However, before turning to this more speculative point, it is worth re-examining the effect of the media on elections under the less exceptional circumstances of 1996.

THE EFFECTS OF TELEVISION ON VOTING: THE 1996 ELECTIONS

The lower exceptionality, or greater normality, of the 1996 elections is due to two factors. The first is a certain 'cooling' of political passions since 1994, partly due to the spontaneous reduction of tensions over the previous two years (*Tangentopoli*, rebellion against *partitocrazia*, etc.), but also because of the attempt by the Dini government (the successor to the Berlusconi government, supported by the Lega, the PPI and the PDS) to introduce elements of control and to civilise the broadcasting network. At the beginning of 1995, with the approval of the President of the Republic, the Minister for Postal and Telecommunications, Antonio Gambini, presented a bill (subsequently made into a decree) limiting the amount of advertising

POLITICS AND THE MASS MEDIA   147

and opinion polls in electoral campaigns, and imposing certain regulations guaranteeing equal access to the broadcasting network and mass communication by all political groups.

The second reason for this cooling of the political climate is the absence both of a media event on the scale of Silvio Berlusconi's arrival on the political scene, and of the birth of a new party, such as FI. The entry into the political fray by prime minister Lamberto Dini with *Rinnovamento Italiano* was in no way comparable to that of its predecessor: Berlusconi created a new coalition, whereas Dini only allied himself with one of the existing alliances (Polo, Ulivo, Lega). Furthermore, Dini's entry was immediately neutralised by accusations by his adversaries of incorrect behaviour, partisan bias, lies, betrayal, all of which were immediately seized upon by the mass media and forced the Prime Minister to be constantly on the defensive.[21]

The lack of spectacle in the 1996 campaign does not mean that the public was less interested in the televisual treatment of the campaign and elections than in 1994; rather, the nature of their interest had changed. In 1994, the public's interest was suffused with emotion, caused by antipathy towards the political class, and the demonising tactics of the two adversaries. In 1996, as has been demonstrated by the Mediamonitor group in the University of Rome,[22] interest in political broadcasts took on an intensely cognitive character. The public turned to television for information-gathering and the reduction of uncertainty, rather than for the show. In spite of a reduction in the total amount of broadcasting by both RAI and Fininvest, the interest in political information remarkably increased, as revealed by the higher parity of sharing-out compared with 1994.[23]

In other words, the 1996 campaign represented a return to the old style of politics or, more exactly, an improvement in content which contrasted with the 'game of mirrors' played two years before. The use of advertising and opinion polls was drastically reduced, while the key themes of political debate returned: tax, employment, education, welfare, law and order. Moreover, in contrast to the past, the different political parties did not oppose each other by championing a single issue, but rather by promoting different programmes dealing with the same issues.[24] In the end, it was thanks to its ability to meet the public's demands that the centre-left coalition, a group with a clear disadvantage against the centre-right, managed to make up this deficit at the eleventh hour of the campaign.

The different dynamics of the two campaigns has been reconstructed using a very similar methodology to monitor television supply and public demand. Thanks to the data on political broadcasting collected by the Mediamonitor group in the University of Rome, and also to the weekly public opinion data collected by Cra-Nielson,[25] a detailed picture can be presented of the imbalance between supply and demand of political issues (Tables 3a to 3c).

148   CRISIS AND TRANSITION IN ITALIAN POLITICS

TABLE 3a

THE STRUCTURE OF PUBLIC DEMAND

Themes	10/3	17/3	24/3	7/4	14/4	21/4
Work and training	46.6	49.0	50.0	52.1	53.9	54.9
Tax and deficit	24.8	22.0	20.8	19.2	17.4	15.5
Welfare	11.8	12.3	12.6	12.4	13.3	14.3
Law & order/immigration	2.9	3.6	3.7	3.8	3.7	3.5
Justice/'*Tangentopoli*'	2.7	3.3	3.8	4.0	3.5	3.3
Other laws	7.4	6.2	5.7	5.7	5.5	5.5
Future government	1.1	0.8	0.9	0.8	0.9	0.9
Europe and miscellaneous	3.0	2.8	2.5	2.0	1.8	2.1

Source: Cra-Nielsen.

TABLE 3b

THE STRUCTURE OF POLITICAL BROADCASTING SUPPLY FROM THE CENTRE-LEFT

Themes	1	2	3	4	5	6
Work and training	14.3	25.4	16.7	15.5	12.0	17.6
Tax and deficit	20.8	13.6	18.2	15.1	15.7	16.5
Welfare	11.0	20.3	15.3	11.3	11.6	12.8
Law & order/immigration	1.9	1.1	5.9	2.1	2.3	1.1
Justice/'*Tangentopoli*'	22.1	10.7	12.8	15.8	21.8	14.4
Other laws	16.2	19.2	16.7	20.6	25.5	20.2
Future government	13.0	9.6	12.8	16.8	9.3	13.3
Europe and miscellaneous	0.6	0.0	1.5	2.7	1.9	4.3

Source: Mediamonitor

TABLE 3c

THE STRUCTURE OF POLITICAL BROADCASTING SUPPLY FROM THE CENTRE-RIGHT

Themes	1	2	3	4	5	6
Work and training	8.1	18.8	17.3	22.9	26.6	19.3
Tax and deficit	19.4	18.8	20.4	12.6	12.2	12.7
Welfare	10.6	16.8	19.0	13.7	15.4	12.7
Law & order/immigration	3.1	7.4	0.9	2.3	3.1	2.0
Justice/'*Tangentopoli*'	16.3	6.9	5.8	17.1	11.9	10.2
Other laws	22.5	17.8	20.4	18.9	14.0	13.9
Future government	20.0	11.9	15.5	10.3	16.1	24.2
Europe and miscellaneous	0.0	1.5	0.9	2.3	0.7	4.9

Source: Mediamonitor

POLITICS AND THE MASS MEDIA   149

As can be seen, out of eight thematic areas studied, three dominate public interest over time: employment and its development, welfare, and tax and the public deficit. Contrary to what many observers believe, themes such as justice, moral questions (such as *Tangentopoli*), law and order, immigration, and broadcasting and political control are of interest mainly to the parties, whilst most voters are virtually indifferent to them. Indeed, it was due to the differing capacities of the two wings to synthesise public interests, amending their own programmes along the way, which made the difference between the centre-left and the centre-right. To measure the correlation between the content of political communication and public interest, we have constructed on a weekly basis an index of the shift between public expectations and the composition of the two camps' communications to the voters.[26] The difference between the shift on the centre-right and that of the centre-left was compared with the change in strength of the two camps (a simulation of the single vote for the Lower Chamber) collected in an electronic panel-study by Cra-Nielsen.

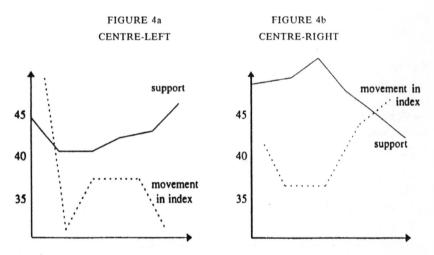

FIGURE 4a
CENTRE-LEFT

FIGURE 4b
CENTRE-RIGHT

The link between the shift in the composition of the parties' messages and the evolution of electoral support is quite evident. During the first three weeks, allowing for fluctuations, the movement in the index on the centre-left (Figure 4a) is greater than that of the centre-right (Figure 4b), with the centre-left suffering an electoral deficit of between about four and eight percentage points. At the beginning of the fourth week, the centre-left index begins to fall, as opposed to the centre-right's which rises. Correspondingly, the electoral handicap for the centre-left drops, eventually becoming a lead of three points. Significantly, such a change is due more to the fall of the centre-right than to the growth of the centre-left: the defecting part of the

150   CRISIS AND TRANSITION IN ITALIAN POLITICS

centre-right heads in the main towards the Lega and smaller parties – local
movements and the *Movimento sociale–fiamma tricolore* (neo-Fascists)
rather than to the centre-left.

If this analysis of the 1996 elections has a firm basis, it would be
reasonable to expect that, given the greater 'nomality' of the 1996 campaign
compared with that of 1994, the effects of exposure to either RAI or
Fininvest channels would be smaller. At the time of writing this article,
definitive and detailed estimates of the effect of television on the vote are
not yet available: but some evaluations are already possible.[27] In particular,
there has been an attempt to estimate the effects that exposure to RAI and
Fininvest would have had just on the choice between centre-left and centre-
right.[28] If we analyse these first estimates, we see the following (Table 4):

TABLE 4

EFFECTS OF TELEVISION ON 1996 ELECTIONS (INITIAL ESTIMATE)

	Centre-left	Centre-right
RAI	2.8	–2.8
Fininvest	–3.9	3.9

Similarities with the 1994 results are quite minimal: they have in common
simply that exposure to television broadcasting has some effect on voting
behaviour; and the effect of Fininvest seems slightly greater than that of
the RAI. The differences are far more interesting. At the moment, we can
make three conjectures:

• the difference in effect between Fininvest and the RAI is much smaller
  than in 1994;
• the net effect of exposure to television is negligible (the effects of
  Fininvest and the RAI counter each other almost completely);
• and RAI broadcasting, which in 1994 only had redistributive effects
  within the centre-right, has ceased to be neutral.

This third conjecture is perhaps the most worrying result to emerge from
the initial analyses. In spite of the RAI's position being heavily influenced
after 1994 by the interests of the victors, the RAI's broadcasting during the
1996 campaign was more in harmony with the centre-left than the centre-
right. This paradoxical situation can be explained by the desire of those
appointed by the centre-right not to appear too supine towards their
masters;[29] or, more simply, as a result of the change in majority after 1995
(the Dini government supported by the centre-left) and the traditional
acquiescence of RAI journalists to the government.

The behaviour of the RAI is worrying because, in view of the history of

POLITICS AND THE MASS MEDIA 151

its journalism, it is more than likely that over the next few years we will witness a pro-government stance, rather than a critical attitude towards the executive. We have become accustomed to thinking that the problem with television in Italy is the dominance of Berlusconi; and this is true to a certain extent. However, it is possible that over the next few years, the nature of this problem will change drastically. Fininvest's power is set to change after the judgement of the Constitutional Court which fixed a limit of two national channels per private owner;[30] on the other hand, there does not seem to be any move to reduce the acquiescence of the public service towards the government.

EQUAL ACCESS, BUT FOR WHOM?

In Italy, the term *par condicio* means the right of all political actors to equal access to mass communications. Until now, the regulations on equal access, contained in a series of decrees, have been applied in the 1995 regional elections, and to the 1996 legislative elections. The most severe criticisms of equal access stem from two main actors: the centre-right coalition and the broadcasting world as a whole, including many RAI 3 journalists. The regulations which govern opinion polls, advertising and, above all, the time allocated to each party are seen as an intolerable imposition on the freedom of expression, a bureaucratic and authoritarian means of regulating broadcasting.

There are many other facets to this argument, not least the idea that regulating, controlling and sanctioning on the basis of *content* is impossible, even from a technical point of view, due to the sheer size of the sector. In the west, the strength and the appeal of *laissez-faire* arguments regarding information are based on systemic considerations linked to the size and complexity of the structures which are being controlled. But, amongst the critiques of par *condicio,* there is also an underestimation of the unique position of Italy as regards broadcasting. Not only is almost the entire commercial network controlled by one individual, who also happens to lead of one of the two major political camps, but there are also two socio-historical facts of primary importance: the meagre professionalism and independence of a large number of journalists; and the long tradition of dependence of television journalists on political forces.

A more general anomaly should be added to these, one on which all discussion of links between politics, culture and means of mass communication can be based. Among western countries, Italy has the lowest average level of education and the largest cultural gap between young and old. But most importantly, it is the country in which linguistic unity has occurred most recently, and almost entirely because of television. In Italy,

152   CRISIS AND TRANSITION IN ITALIAN POLITICS

as opposed to other countries, high culture – learned in school, through reading and through written media – does not form a solid traditional foundation onto which television has been added, but rather something which, for about half the population, has been something of mysterious taboo area, which they would not know how, or indeed wish to, deal with. More than any other Westerners, Italians have been homogenised by television. Many have learnt to speak, to think, and even to read and write through television. Television is not simply *one* means of communication, but – for the majority of the population – the *only* means of communication, almost to the point of being an element of collective identity. This is also probably the reason why the referenda on television were won by the pro-Fininvest camp which promised to protect the integrity of radio and television broadcasting. But, above all, this is the reason why in Italy, with all its peculiarities, the problem of regulating radio and television has become an extremely delicate business. This is why it is difficult to give a balanced assessment of the equal access regulations.

The claim that journalists have the right to produce information without interference or external influence is sacrosanct. However, this claim would be more credible if its subjects could claim a long tradition of professionalism and independence, rather than their sad heritage of servitude to economic and political power. Evaluation of the equal access regulations is also difficult on purely technical grounds, and merely at the level of their effectiveness in comparison with their scope. It is true that many of them are complicated, muddled and consequently difficult to implement securely and on time. Furthermore, it is also true that the so-called *'autorità garante'* (regulating authority) has the means neither to survey the implementation process, nor to bring sanctions into force quickly enough to be effective. Nevertheless, what can be said is that, in the last two campaigns – the 1995 regional elections and the 1996 national elections – the conflict between the two camps has been decidedly more civilised than in 1994, and attention to content has been much higher. The role of a regulation is not only to prevent or punish certain behaviour, but also to discourage it, or at least to make it less likely. From this point of view, we cannot rule out the possibility that the improved electoral climate is in part a result of the equal access regulation. However debatable, intricate and difficult it may be to enforce generally, it is possible that its mere existence, backed up by observers, monitors and claims to legitimacy, may have produced in both groups and individuals a more cautious, intelligent and generally well-balanced style of communication, or simply more willingness to observe and limit oneself, if not actually to censure.

Beyond the judgements that can be made of the effectiveness of equal access regulation, there remains the fact that all debate on radio and

POLITICS AND THE MASS MEDIA   153

television broadcasting in Italy revolves around the problem of competitive equality in politics. The close integration of political and media systems, and the frequent exchange of roles and functions between broadcasters and politicians, has reduced this question to little more than an internal problem of the politico-journalistic establishment. The logic of equal access regulation follows the logic of regulations which prevent unfair competition in the economic and advertising sectors. This perspective would seem to be reasonable but narrow. In the economic sphere, it is not simply reciprocal rights to market competition which are protected, but also the rights of consumers. It is not clear why the same principle does not apply to television broadcasting in general, and to the politico-electoral sphere in particular. For next to the rights of the politicians are those of the voters. There are times when there is no reason to find in favour of Party A over Party B, but rather to respect the clear right of the viewer/citizen/voter.

What is this right? Simply, it is the right to truth, the right to information that does not excessively distort the facts. This may seem like a simple nicety, or maybe even a truism, but it is not. Every day, there are thousands of violations, some of which are serious, to the right to truth which are invisible and go unpunished because the injured party (i.e. the public) is too diffuse or the organisation is not strong enough to begin legal action. Newspapers, radio and television know this all too well, and play on the fact that the right to clarification and to refutation has too high a price.

It is worth emphasising that this is first and foremost a cost–benefit mechanism, rather than an ethical shortcoming. Providing a documented, balanced service costs more time and effort than producing a montage of voices and agency clips. Producing a scandal sheet for spectacle or for effect pays better than performing a rigorous enquiry. The risk of economic or legal sanctions is almost always minimal in comparison to the rewards. Above all, it is the structure of prizes and punishments which makes for bad journalism. If the professional level of journalists in Italy is low, it is because there are no disincentives on producing shabby work. Neither laws, standard procedures nor moral sensibilities protect readers, listeners and viewers from bad broadcasting.

Amongst this lack of solid institutions answerable to the public, we can discern the weakness in the associational fabric of civic culture which has been the eternal thorn in the side of the Italian version of western democracy.[31] But on closer inspection, in this imbalance between the power of the apparatus and the rights of the individual, there is an issue of relevance to all post-industrial societies. The concentration of media ownership occurring throughout the world, together with a growing dependence of citizens on information sources, means it will become progressively more difficult to guarantee both the freedom of expression and the right

154   CRISIS AND TRANSITION IN ITALIAN POLITICS

to truth – or more prosaically, the pluralism of information and its accuracy. *Par condicio* (equal access) amongst political groups is only one side of the problem. The other side is the *impar condicio* (unequal access) between the establishment which controls information (the political class, state bodies, private editors, software manufacturers, telecommunications companies, etc.) and the individual users who are always much weaker and more dependent on a system they cannot easily influence.

To resolve this problem, there have been as many *laissez-faire* and neo-conservative suggestions as there have been interventionist ones.[32] The former, whilst right to emphasise the impossibility of governing the enormous flow of information channelled by the media, seem to ignore the problems of the degradation of communication that this logic brings. The latter, whilst right to point out such dangers, do not seem to have taken on board the kernel of truth to be found in laissez-faire theory, that is, the *technical* impracticality of governing a media system via its content. The problem of integrating freedom of expression, pluralism of radio and television broadcasting, and the rights of the users to a minimum of accuracy in information does not seem to be uniquely Italian. The media landscape of the next few years will very much depend on the way in which this particular problem is confronted.

NOTES

1. The unique exceptions being the studies on 'The reading habits of Italians' carried out by Istat every six to seven years, and opinion surveys by the RAI agency. These could potentially be valuable sources, but are underused and are almost completely unknown in sociological research.
2. This partial increase in the autonomy of information from political influence is relevant not only to television but also to the printed word. Notably in not directly political areas, such as divorce, newspapers assumed a very important role in sensitizing and educating, removing a noticeable amount of influence from the traditional party links. See C. Marletti, 'Il 'potere dei media': sulla crescente interazione fra comunicazione e politica', *Il Mulino* 4 (1983).
3. The mid-1970s is considered by most authors writing on the evolution of the media as a watershed, even if the year held to be the turning point is not always the same. In his *Dalla Tv di partito al partito della Tv* (Florence: La Nuova Italia 1995), Edoardo Novelli, for example, isolates the 1976 elections as the pivot, whereas Peppino Ortoleva, in his very original reconstruction of 'ventennio a colori' ('20 years in colour'), takes the referendum on divorce as his point of departure. See P. Ortoleva, *Un ventennio a colori. Televisione privata e società in Italia (1975–1995)* (Florence: Giunti 1995).
4. At the institutional level, the first clear indication of the new tendency was supplied by the Constitutional Court judgement no. 226, July 1974, which concerned the incompatibility between monopoly ownership of the means of mass communication and pluralised society. See *Novelli, Dalla Tv di partito al partito* (note 2) p.132.
5. As became clear after 1992, with the advent of inquiries into all aspects of society, 'sharing out' is a phenomenon occurring everywhere, and not just in information: 'At the moment when the great wave of political participation began to recede, the first manifestations

POLITICS AND THE MASS MEDIA 155

of society being highly dominated by the parties began to emerge. Still supported by mass membership, the parties set out to occupy all available spaces, a process which culminated in the 1980s' (Novelli, note 2, p.147).

6. The 'Mammì law' (from the name of its proposer, the Republican party deputy Oscar Mammì) refers to law no.223 of 1990, which for the first time regulated radio and television broadcasting, which had grown enormously during the 1980s.

7. As of the summer of 1994, the state management of television was regulated by a long series of decrees ('Urgent dispositions for the restructuring and reorganisation of the RAI'). The first of these in particular gave the Presidents of the two Chambers the power to select members of the governing council. In 1994, the two presidents (Irene Pivetti and Carlo Scogna-miglio) were both members of the centre-right (Irene Pivetti was a member of the LN until summer 1996 when she was expelled for her refusal to adopt Bossi's separatist line in place of federalism, Carlo Scognamiglio of FI).

8. The bill by Minister Gambino was never passed into law, but rather into a series of decrees, each issued at a different electoral expiry date (regional elections, single constituency by-elections, referenda, legislative elections).

9. Maurizio Costanzo and Michele Santoro are two of the most well-known presenters of current affairs programmes – the first on *Canale 5* (*Fininvest*), the second on RAI 3 (the public channel close to the PDS). In the course of 1994 and 1995, the two presenters discussed on many occasions the possibility of creating a third television group in Italy, which would be autonomous from the RAI and Fininvest. The project was named '*Telesogno*' ('Dream TV') by the mass media.

10. M. Morcellini, forthcoming in *Problemi dell'informazione*.

11. Laocoontes, a Trojan priest, was crushed to death with his two sons by two enormous serpents.

12. L. Ricolfi, 'Politica a quante dimensioni', *Il Mulino* 1 (1994) and Left, voice and God. 'Riflessioni sulla geometria del mercato Macao elettorale', *Micro & Macro Marketing* 1 (1994).

13. L. Ricolfi, 'Quanti voti ha spostato la tv', *Il Mulino* 6 (1994).

14. L. M. Bartels, 'Messages Received: The Political Impact of Media Exposure', *American Political Science Review* 2 (1993) pp.267–85.

15. F. Rositi, 'Sette televisioni nazionali quasi ventimila casi', *Problemi dell'informazione* 3 (1994).

16. A. De Lucia, 'L'influenza della televisione sul voto. Un caso esemplare: S. Felice a Cancello', *Sociologia e Ricerca Sociale* 49, 1996.

17. This incapacity can either be attributed to the limitations of the *Progressisti*'s leadership (Achille Occhetto in the 1994 elections) or, more generally, to the culture and mentality which is typical of the left in Italy. Alberto Abruzzese, *Elogio del tempo nuovo. Perché Berlusconi ha vinto* (Genova: Costa & Nolan, 1994) supports the latter explanantion.

18. Ricolfi, 'Quanti voti ha spostato al tv' (note 13).

19. On the theory of agenda-setting, see, e.g. M.E. McCoombs and D.L Shaw, 'The Agenda Setting Function of the Mass Media', *Public Opinion Quarterly* 2 (1972) and M.E. McCoombs, and L. Mastel-Walters, 'Agenda-Setting: A New Perspective on Mass Communication', *Mass Communication Research* 2 (1976). For a critical account, see G. Mazzoleni, *Televisione elettorale e televisione politica. Materiali per un bilancio della ricerca sugli effetti* (Milan: Unicopli 1984).

20. The idea that certain aspects of the mind's functioning can be seen in terms of information elaboration is not simply metaphorical, but forms the basis of much cognitive psychology. See the monumental text by P.H. Lindsay and D.A. Norman, *Human Information Processing: An Introduction to Psychology* (NY: Academic Press 1977). The Italian translation is *L'uomo elaboratore di informazioni. Introduzione cognitivista alla psicologia* (Florence: Giunti Barbera 1983).

21. Prime Minister Dini presented the logo of his party (*Rinnovamento Italiano*) on 28 Feb. 1996. Both in polls prior to this date and in those immediately afterwards, support for the Dini list was estimated at 6–8 per cent (Abacus, Cra-Nielsen, Unicab polls) with a potential electorate of over 10 per cent. In the following weeks, support dropped

156   CRISIS AND TRANSITION IN ITALIAN POLITICS

noticeably to 4 per cent. It cannot be ruled out that this decline was in part due to the huge number of negative statements Dini had been subject to on the right (Trojan horse, traitor, Pinocchio) and on the left (toad, lizard, villain), and the notable relish with which these labels were used in the television news. According to a study by the Studio Frasi, five times the amount of time was devoted to negative statements about Dini than to negative views of leaders such as Berlusconi and D'Alema. Only Romano Prodi bettered Dini's score (*La Repubblica*, 19 April 1996).

22. The Mediamonitor group in Rome is directed by Professors Mario Morcellini and Sara Bentivegna, to whom credit is due for some of the material in this text on the differences between the 1994 and 1996 campaigns.

23. Morcellini, (note 10).

24. I owe this observation to Professor Carlo Marletti, who formulated it during a CATTID (Centre for Communications) conference of opinion poll and mass media experts in Rome on 8 June 1996.

25. The electronic panel survey by Cra-Nielsen is a panel of families whose members are interviewed every week by modem, via a computerised interview system. On the differences between modem and telephone interviews, and on the advantages of the former, see L. Ricolfi, 'Fra incertezza e verità', in F. Di Spirito, P. Ortoleva and C. Ottaviano (eds.) *Lo strabismo telematico* (Turin: Utet 1996).

26. The index has not been calculated for the last week before the election, when references to the 'future government' could have provided misleading results. Even if the explicit occurrence of this phrase is low, it seems reasonable that with the immediacy of the vote, political parties' references to the future government might increase. In Figs. 4a and 4b, the two groups of electoral support and of the weekly shifts in the index are out of phase by one week (support at time t, as against the shift in the index in the week falling between time t-1 and t-2).

27. Among the experiments that I carried out is an analysis of those who watched and those who did not watch the debate between Prodi and Berlusconi transmitted on *Canale 5* (the largest Fininvest channel). A comparison of the two groups shows that the main effect from watching the programme was one of reinforcement: changes in electoral orientation in the last week before the election were small for those who watched, and broader for those who did not. The direction of change was the same (favourable to the centre-left) in the two groups.

28. The effects were analysed using a regression model similar to that used for 1994. The dependent variable was taken from the choice of centre-right or centre-left (with the exclusion of LN voters and those who abstained). The independent variables were estimates of exposure time to RAI and Fininvest channels. Included in the control variables were socio-demographic characteristics (treated as dummies); electoral orientation at the beginning of the campaign, measured on a 10-step proximity scales, submitted for each of the 13 parties; and exposure to other mass communications media (radio, daily press, periodicals). The R^2 of the regression was equal to 69 per cent.

29. I owe this conjecture to a conversation with S. Bentivegna.

30. This concerns judgement no.420, 7/12/94. See *Giurisprudenza Italiana* (1995), I, C.129 ff., and in particular the note by S. Ambrosini, 'Anti-trust e informazione radiotelevisiva: incostituzionalità della norma sulla concentrazioni'.

31. See e.g. G. Almond and S. Verba, *The Civic Culture. Political Attitudes and Democracy in Five Nations* (Princeton UP 1963), R. Putnam, *Making Democracy Work: Civic Traditions in Modern Italy* (ibid. 1993) – translated into Italian as *La tradizione civica nelle regioni italiane* (Milan: Mondadori 1993) – and R. Cartocci, *Fra Lega e Chiesa* (Bologna: Il Mulino 1994).

32. On this issue, see M. Ricolfi, 'La convergenza tra telecommunicazioni, informatica e mass media e sistema giuridico', *Mediario* 62 (1995).

[36]

Terrorism, Volume 12, pp. 249-296
Printed in the UK. All rights reserved.

0149-0389 89 $3.00 + .00

Italian Terrorism and Society, 1940s–1980s: Roots, Ideologies, Evolution, and International Connections

MARCO RIMANELLI

U.S.-European Relations and International Law
Public Affairs Department
George Mason University
Fairfax. VA 22030-4444

Terrorism, History, and Society in Italy

Definitions, Statistics, and Historical Roots

Terrorism is commonly defined as a violent form of political struggle employed by revolutionary groups to maximize their meager forces and topple domestic regimes through a strategy of terror. This systematic and indiscriminate strategy of violence against governmental structures and innocents alike is targeted to foster generalized political instability and domestic tension, as well as to psychologically sever the traditional ties of trust and protection between state and people once the government is perceived to be unable to defeat terrorism without resorting to equally indiscriminate repression. *Terrorism* as a political term still covers all too wide an array of definitions (over 109 in the 1936–1981 period) and criminal activities (murders, bombings, kidnappings, robberies, hijacking, etc.), committed either by revolutionary groups or by governments (state-sponsored terrorism). Yet regardless of its origins, perpetuators, and instigators, its intended victims are both the actual symbolic targets and, even more, the general population (target audience), whose behavior and political beliefs are to be altered through the fear of terror into new patterns politically dictated by the terrorists themselves. Thus terrorism is always a form of psychological propaganda by deeds (as the Russian anarchist Piotr Kropotkin expressed it in the late 1800s). Therefore, it has become especially effective in the "television age," when the spectacular aspect of political violence and/or state repression is reinforced by the media's unwitting complicity in conveying the impression that behind the terrorist onslaught exists a vast, well-organized revolutionary group bent on mobilizing the population against the regime by exploiting political chaos and state weaknesses.

Along its violent course, both terrorists and authorities end up locked into rigid politico-moral postures which stress self-righteousness and firmness against the threat.

This study is a thorough reelaboration of a lecture given at the Center for Conflict Resolution, George Mason University. Fairfax, VA, January 27, 1989.

Address correspondence to Dr. Marco Rimanelli, U.S.-European Relations and International Law, Dept. of Public Affairs, George Mason University, Fairfax, VA 22030-4444.

On one hand the terrorists incrementally develop a centralized organization and complex ideological justifications to rationalize their initial spontaneous grass-roots violence, while escalating the terror campaign through actions and propaganda (spectacular blood-baths and name-calling further dehumanize selected opponents and innocent victims alike into symbolic abstract targets). Democratic states, on the other hand, struggle between respect for constitutional individual rights (which uphold personal liberty and due criminal process strictly through incrimination evidence) and the need to use sweeping emergency powers to accomplish their institutional task of protecting the country from internal destabilizing threats. For the terrorists, the state is the Moloch oppressing the people, and they are the "victims" willing to sacrifice themselves to rescue society through blood. For the state, the hidden terrorists are mere political criminals, oppressing society and authorities ("victims") through a reign of terror meant to destroy the very fabric of democratic life in the name of totalitarian ideologies.[1]

Hardly a novelty in Italian history, political violence and terrorism were analyzed by Machiavelli and played a subtle role during the 1815–1870 struggle for national unification (the 1815–1870 Carbonari and Mazzinian secret nationalist-revolutionary groups; the 1874 anti-Italian Accoltellatori Sect; the 1861–1870 pro-Bourbon banditry in Southern Italy). Spontaneous and collective bouts of political violence as byproducts of socio-economic tensions increased dramatically between 1860 and 1920 and from the 1940s to the 1960s (peasants' and workers' strikes, antitax and bread riots, antiwar disorders, land seizures, factory occupations), with only a brief respite during the Fascist dictatorship. Yet organized terrorism developed seriously only with the erratic, but spectacular, attacks of the Italian Anarchist Federation (organized in the 1870s by the Russian Mikhail Bakunin), which stressed the revolutionary overthrow of the system and retaliations to the authorities' repression of popular protest and trade unions. Thus from the 1870s through the 1920s, the Italian Anarchists unleashed sporadic waves of terrorism as symbolic political propaganda through deeds: semi-insurrectional attempts (Bologna, 1874); bomb-throwing at patriotic processions (Florence, Pisa, Naples); bombing crowded places (Milan's Kursaal Diana Theater in 1921, 21 dead, 104 wounded); assassination campaigns against symbols of "state repression" (such as royal and high governmental figures, including several attempts to kill King Vittorio-Emanuele II and the murders of the French president in 1894, of Spain's premier, of Austria's empress, and of Italy's King Umberto I in 1900). Inevitably the authorities reacted to Anarchist terrorism with further repressive bouts, while "criminalizing" the opposition (anarcho-syndicalists, republicans, and socialists) in an effort "to prove a single master conspiracy."[2]

Yet while pervasive and persistent, the anarchists were hardly a well-organized revolutionary force (their own ideology opposed well-established hierarchic structures), nor could they seriously destabilize society and state. Fascist extremism, instead, provided a highly organized use of political violence to subvert the system in the name of totalitarianism and a systematic quest for absolute power. Thus political violence and terrorism resurfaced during the Fascist rise to power in 1919–1926, when paramilitary bands of Fascist thugs (*squadristi*) used systematic assaults, cruel theatrical ridicule, kidnappings, and murders, to intimidate, humiliate, eliminate political opponents (Catholic priests, communist militants, unionists, or even such national party leaders as the socialist Giacomo Matteotti). Mussolini even went as far as to promote "state terrorism" against antiFascist expatriates (i.e., the 1937 murder in France of the Rosselli brothers, leaders of the "Giustizia e Libertà" movement), and to destabilize neighboring countries Albania and Yugoslavia by providing safe havens, covert training, arms, and support for Croatian terrorists (*ustashas*) bent on creating a separate pro-Italian homeland (in 1934 Croatian terrorists also assassinated King Alexander of Yugoslavia and French Foreign Minister Louis Barthou in Marseilles).[3] Mussolini himself escaped several assassinations, while sporadic bombings and sabotage occurred in 1928 (the Fiera bombings in Milan, 18 dead and 40 wounded), in 1932 (bombings in Bologna, Genova, Turin, and Milan), and 1933 (St. Peter's Square bombing in Rome, four injured). Mussolini's collapse in the wake of the Allied invasion of Southern Italy during World War II led to military stalemate and partisan warfare in Northern Italy (1943–1945), with Resistance hit-and-run guerrilla attacks in the countryside against Nazi-Fascist communications, forces, and strongholds, while the Allies were slowly inching their way northward. However, smaller procommunist urban partisans (GAPs: Partisan Action Groups in Roma, Milan, Turin, Genova, Padova, Florence, Bologna, etc.) widely resorted to terrorist bombings, kidnappings, and assassinations of Fascist leaders, party members, and troops to promote a vicious cycle of Black repression and popular insurrection (i.e., the executions of Fascist philosopher Giovanni Gentile and Fascist commander Ricardo Muti, or the Via Rasella bombing of a German company in Rome which led to the Nazi execution of 1100 political prisoners in reply, or the widespread postwar execution in 1945 of 2000 ex-Fascist officials.[4]

Notwithstanding these historical records, never has terrorism festered so uncontrolled and widespread in Italy as in 1969–1982, arming and motivating both neo-Nazis and ultraleftists in the common effort to destroy the despised democratic regime. Terrorism's 14-year-long onslaught has been unanimously considered by foreign and domestic observers to be the single most important political threat to Italy's fragile stability. Moreover, its modern dramatic impact stemmed not only from its deadly efficiency, vast organizational network, and antidemocratic goals, but especially from the uniqueness of the Italian case. Italy is a traditionally fragile country, without a strong sense of state or national identity, beset by structural domestic socioeconomic problems of development, labor strikes, and political crises. It is a geostrategically vital NATO country in the turbulent Mediterranean basin, at the center of East-West and North-South tensions, as well as home to both the Catholic Church and the largest communist party (PCI) in the West. This unique combination of weaknesses and international relevance, as well as Italy's traditionally strong politicization, provided fertile ground for different kinds of terrorist movements, both domestic (separatist, anarchist, neo-Fascist, ultraleftist) and international (Arab-Palestinian, Armenian, Libyan), with extensive financial backing, training, and arms from the Middle East and the Soviet bloc.[5]

Yet regardless of the importance of foreign connections in exacerbating domestic violence, Italy's terrorism remained essentially an internal phenomenon with its own original politico-ideological and socioeconomic roots, and vast domestic complicities. In 1978 the Minister of the Interior (law and order), Francesco Cossiga, identified to the Italian Parliament 147 terrorist and extremist groups, 12 of which were neo-Fascist and 135 ultraleftist. A 1978 PCI report, moreover, estimated there were 700–800 full-time terrorists with 10,000 supporters, while recent studies count 5000 active terrorists operating between 1969 and 1982. Acts of terrorist violence totaled between 12,000 and 15,000 from 1968 to 1989, steadily escalating from 173 actions in 1968 to 439 in 1969; 554 in 1970; 832 in 1971; 776 in 1972; 648 in 1973; 816 (or 573) in 1974; 467 (or 702) in 1975; 685 (or 1353) in 1976; 1805 (or 2128) in 1977; and peaking to 2723 (or 2238) in 1978 and 2139 (or 2514) in 1979. (Differences in data reflect contrasting statistics on terrorist acts and political violence between the Ministry of the Interior's 1977–1982 estimates, shown in parenthesis, and the more recent ones in 1984 by Francesco Bruno and Francesco Ferracuti, Professors of Criminal Medicine and Forensic Psychiatry at the State University of Rome.)

Paradoxically, however, the Anni di Piombo (or Leaden Years, as the period of terrorism is commonly remembered), far from bringing the ailing country to its knees, strengthened its internal fabric while underlining once again Italy's successful art of survival. The unexpected emergence of national consensus and renewed sense of state, spurred by the political maneuvering during the Red Brigades' kidnapping and murder of the Christian-Democrat President and ex-Premier Aldo Moro, made organized and relentless counterterrorism finally effective and decisive in the equally spectacular demise of terrorist violence. Terrorist acts declined from 833 (or 1184) in 1980 to 908 (or 791) in 1981, 346 in 1982, and only 30 from 1983 to 1989. Casualties of terrorism from 1969 to 1989 totaled over 1184 people, of which 770 were injured and 414 dead (363 killed by terrorists and 51 terrorists killed "in action"). Over 1100 terrorists were arrested throughout 1968–1981, and 1045 in 1982 alone, with over 3000 extremists in prison in any given year (considering average prison-term turnovers) from 1978 to the early 1980s.[6]

Terrorism and Political Change: Theories and Sociopolitical Interpretations

What were the sociopolitical and ideological roots of Italy's terrorism? Several hypotheses have been put forward to explain the terrorist phenomenon, but even when failing to unravel its complex roots, they have often sought to shield governmental and national responsibilities while "demonizing" terrorism as an external plague. Thus psychological and conspiracy theories denied the domestic roots of Italian terrorism by insisting that the brutality and cruel efficiency of modern terrorism reflected foreign influences, clearly alien to Italy's traditionally chaotic but good-natured way of life. Terrorism, in this view, could only derive from foreign enemies plotting to destabilize the nation (from Bakunin in 1870 to modern-day Arab and KGB *agents provocateurs*). Yet these conspiracy theories ignore the multifaceted domestic roots and history of terrorism, which found in Italy a centuries-old humus of violent politico-ideological confrontation, revolts, and philosophico-cultural exaltation of "forceful action," or violence, to overcome the confines of a static society and attain power. In Italy, therefore, the appeal of violence as a means of domestic social change and springboard for terrorist-revolutionary acts emerged from the conflicting cultural odd-mix of Machiavelli's political "realism," anarchist nihilism, Georges Sorel's brand of revolutionary-syndicalism, futurism's artistic destructiveness, Marxist-Leninist revolutionary theories, Gabriele D'Annunzio's wild political romanticism, Mussolini's Fascist doctrine of "movement," Nazism's totalitarian extermination of any opposition or symbol of impurity, third world revolutionary myths, and the 1968–1969 labor-student unrest.[7]

Sociological theories, on the other hand, stress the relevance of domestic socioeconomic factors in fostering terrorist outbursts: recurrent economic crises; widespread unemployment; the transformation of the poor southern Italian peasantry into an exploited urbanized proletariat in the industrial North (Lewis effect); the breakdown of the education system; the cultural-economic crisis of the petite bourgeoisie; wild labor strikes and deteriorating urban and financial standards of living. This view seemed to explain why terrorism was common in the industrialized North, but rare in the economically backward South. But it could not explain why terrorism had failed to emerge as a permanent destabilizing force in the aftermath of World War II, when Italy faced military defeat, domestic reconstruction (1945–1955), generalized misery, 2 million unemployed, mass migration, economic crisis, and a permanent political gridlock between the pro-Western centrist governments and the pro-Soviet leftist opposition. Instead, except for widespread uncoordinated political violence, and a brief emotional, semi-insurrectional outburst in 1948 after the Left's electoral defeat and the attempted murder of the PCI leader Palmiro Togliatti, leftist terrorism disappeared as a significant social phenomenon from 1949 to 1967.[8]

A parallel politico-moral theory further expands on the theme of internal crisis, social collapse, and revolt. Thus, given the overwhelming popular dissatisfaction with the system, terrorism becomes the only possible mass reaction to an inefficient, corrupt political regime based on economic exploitation and sociopolitical stagnation. Yet this view of terrorism as a means of social reform flatly ignores its true antidemocratic objectives, or its emergence in such politically efficient systems as Germany. It is true that the cold war and the domestic confrontation between the ruling parties and the PCI-Left opposition overheated the internal political scene in the 1947–1976 period, reinforcing the Left's condemnation of the system. Yet earlier sporadic outbursts of leftist violence disappeared by the 1960s with the spectacular political rise of the PCI to a close second place (27% of the electorate from 1968 to 1975, 34.4% in 1976, and 30.4% in 1979), right behind the leading Christian Democrats (DC), as well as its integration in the mainstream of Italian society and culture. It seemed just a matter of time before the PCI would enter the government through a "historical compromise," trading communist full support of the system for the DC's influence as a domestic and international guarantor. Still the PCI's much-heralded internal democratization and "Euro-Communist" independence from Moscow's influence (essential preconditions to joining the government) were stifled by the internal opposition of the pro-Soviet Stalinist wing and persistent skepticism by both the ruling parties and the United States.

Thus, given the PCI's pervasive fears of a showdown with Moscow (which would split it and create a neo-Stalinist party with full Soviet support), as well as of alleged U.S. support for anticommunist military coups as in Chile (the K factor), the party neither fully pursued an independent Euro-Communist path, nor forced a final confrontation with the ruling DC for government power-sharing after the Left's dramatic electoral victories in 1975 and 1976. Consequently, the difficult task of controlling various internal pressure groups left the PCI in the 1980s still excluded from power, divided, and losing its popular volatile electoral support (falling from 34.4% of the vote in 1976 to 30.4% in 1979 and 27% during the 1980s).[9]

Equally influential has been the DC's absolute political preeminence in Italian life since 1945. If on one hand the DC's stable leadership fostered Italy's pro-Western alignment, postwar recovery, and the 1958–1963 "economic miracle" that made her the seventh most industrialized Western country, on the other hand it has been unable to manage the country's rapid socioeconomic transformations. Accelerated industrial and cultural development combined with massive internal migrations from the rural, backward South to the industrialized urban North to overstrain sociocultural traditions and local administrative structures, whose inefficiency was aggravated by the DC's scandal-prone, nefarious system of local patronage and corruption (*clientelismo*). Domestic political tensions, already rising under the postwar ideological confrontation and traditional popular distrust of the state, were not eased even with the 1963 integration of the Socialist Party into the government. Instead, this opening to the left neither reformed the system nor overcame the government's recurrent political crises and immobility.

By the early 1970s it seemed that only the uncorrupted PCI could reform the system. Yet its hopes of presenting itself as a new democratic alternative to the weak DC-led government met sizable hostility from both the DC and the Right. Still greater opposition came from the growing ultra-Left, whose radical revolutionary beliefs had been traumatized both by earlier ideological shocks (Khrushchev's 1956 de-Stalinization campaign; the 1963 Sino-Soviet split of the international communist camp) and the PCI's new reformist line. The ultra-Left now realized that it would be impossible to pursue their mythical dream of an Italian communist revolution under the PCI's leadership (symbolically reenacting the 1943–1945 Resistance struggle). Instead, the PCI itself was now becoming "bourgeois"![10]

After the great student/labor demonstrations of 1968 and 1969, several dissatisfied uncoordinated splinter Marxist-Leninist groups emerged in the late 1960s and early 1970s, attracting many old PCI cadres: the Maoist Communist Party of Italy (Marxist-Leninist), Manifesto, Partito di Democrazia Unitaria Proletaria, and Democrazia Proletaria. Instead, Lotta Continua, Potere Operaio and Autonomia Operaia had a predominantly youth-oriented, eclectic base. In an uncoordinated, emotional way they sharpened through their own publications their politico-ideological opposition to both the Italian system and the PCI's reformism, while expanding their appeal by exploiting a national cultural base strongly pervaded by Marxist intellectual concepts. This new extra-Parliamentarian Left rejected bourgeois democracy and heralded instead Maoism's "long-term revolutionary change" as a necessary strategy to counteract the absorption of the working class and reformist Left (PSDI, PSI, PCI, the unions) into the capitalist system, as well as to preserve the ultra-Left's ideological purity from the threat of Soviet-style state bureaucratization.

Thus, third world revolutions (like Castro's Cuba, or Vietnam) galvanized the ultra-Left's criticism against international capitalism and U.S.-Western multinationals, as well as the renegade PCI and reformist Left. The highly charged 1968–1969 labor/student unrest (Hot Autumn) further pushed domestic politics towards ultraleftist nihilist violence. In fact both the unions and the ultra-Left conducted excessive wage-hike campaigns with a confrontational attitude under the influence of old anarcho-syndicalism, which glorified labor unrest as a victorious political tool to wrestle huge economic gains from management, regardless of the price that the whole national economy would then pay in the 1970s in declining international competitiveness, inflation, massive youth unemployment, and national deficits (further aggravated by the 1973–1974 and 1979–1980 oil crises). In summary it was only logical then for the more extreme militants to resort to political violence, vicious street protests, urban guerrilla tactics, or even full terrorist participation, to accelerate the "inevitable change" in the ailing capitalist system.[11]

Thus the most important influences which pushed leftist and neo-Fascist extremists toward terrorism were

(1) Popular dissatisfaction with Italy's "blocked" political system, utterly unable to overcome its inefficiency, stagnation, and corruption, notwithstanding the country's rapid socioeconomic transformations.

(2) The end of the "economic miracle's" unprecedented growth, and the sharp politico-syndicalist cleavages of 1968–1969 which further weakened the state and exacerbated the economy's growing marginalization of large unemployed social sectors (mostly young university graduates and poorly integrated Southern blue-collar workers in the North).

(3) The recurrent urban tug-of-war and brawls between the Left and the young neo-Fascist extremists (paradoxically considers as lackeys of the system by the ultra-Left).

(4) The deep disillusionment of young communist cadres after the PCI's turn toward democratic-reformist respectability, and the failure of the 1968–1969 unrest to bring about the collapse of the ailing bourgeois system.

(5) The collapse of traditional social and religious values, which in the past used to reinforce the society's unwritten sociopsychological bonds of conformism, obedience, discipline, and respect for all forms of authority.

(6) The growing radicalization of leftist youth, influenced by American student unrests and the 1968 French May, worldwide anti-Vietnam War demonstrations, Mao's Cultural Revolution, anti-Americanism, Latin American terrorism and third world revolutionism, all of which favored the ultraleftist unrealistic romantic expectation of an impending revolutionary situation in Italy.

Thus the Red extremists believed it necessary to accelerate the inner disintegration of the Italian system by undertaking a vast terrorist campaign capable of tilting Italy's "prerevolutionary situation" toward a classic Marxist-Leninist proletarian insurrection. But the most immediate factor that push most ultraleftist revolutionaries underground was the neo-Fascist "strategy of tension" from 1969 to 1973. Developed to counteract the perceived collapse of governmental authority under the domestic onslaught of the labor/student/leftist front, the Fascist "strategy of tension" launched an indiscriminate terrorist bombing campaign nationwide to foment mass hysteria in the country, and to strengthen the Movimento Sociale Italiano (MSI, the official legalitarian neo-Fascist party) calls for a pro-Fascist military coup to "restore law and order" and eliminate all leftist threats. Consequently a widespread fear of a Latin American type of military coup deeply influenced Italian politics and opinion in the 1970s, further exasperating domestic tension while encouraging the Red terrorists to intervene too, in the hope of channeling the country's political chaos toward a Marxist-Leninist revolution.[12]

Structural and Organizational Traits of Italian Terrorism

In structure and organization Italy's Red terrorism shared many traits with its German and Latin American counterparts. With the German RAF (Rote Armee Faktion) it shared the cultural narrowness of an intellectual anti-Parliamentarian environment, devoted to political violence under the influence of Marxist-Leninist theories and foreign revolutionary myths. Yet the Italian terrorists counted on a much vaster social and intellectual base of support than the Germans, because while the RAF mainly attracted middle-class anarcho-revolutionary intellectuals, the Italian cadres were always evenly divided between middle-class and proletarian elements. Like its Latin American model, Italy's Red terrorism had a strong societal emphasis, a sophisticated organizational structure, and a vast recruitment base, which attracted also marginalized *lumpenproletariat* ("underproletariat") and "politicized" (converted) common criminals. Latin America's urban guerrilla and third world national liberation wars exerted a major ideologico-mythical influence on Italy's Red terrorists, who saw the third world as a "global Vietnam": an international battlefield upon which they fought the global predatory network of American imperialism, Western bourgeois values, and neocolonialist multinationals. Only revolutions and terrorist "pedagogical violence" could save the society, keep the class struggle alive, and protect the proletariat from absorption into the corrupting capitalist system.[13]

On an operational level, Italian and Latin American terrorism (more than Germany's) were domestically oriented and originated. There was only limited contact or cooperation with international terrorism (Palestinian Liberation Organization [PLO], Libya, Syria) and other national terrorists groups (RAF, France's Action Directe, etc.) except for occasional financing, weapon exchanges, and training. "Targeting" techniques were derived from Latin America, with a preference for continuous intimidating attacks on business, police, and the judiciary (hated symbols of the "repressive bourgeois system"). Unfortunately, Italy's traditionally inefficient judiciary and police were ill-served by the demotion in the 1970s of the domestic Secret Services (heavily compromised by both golpist right-wing ties and recurrent sharp competitive rivalry among the services), which left the democratic state divided and without effective tools to rapidly seize the initiative against the mounting twin Black-Red terrorist onslaught. Overall casualties from 1969 to 1989 totaled 1176 people, of which 363 were murdered by the terrorist (102 police officers and guards, 11 magistrates, 13 managers, 8 party-governmental officials) and 51 were terrorists killed. The bloodiest years were 1969, 1974, and 1980, owing mainly to wanton neo-Nazi massacres of bystanders (123 victims), while overall terrorist violence peaked from 1977 to 1980 under the leftist lead. As far as totals, however, the smaller and less effective neo-Nazi threat produced the highest body count with 763 casualties (dead and injured, or 68% of 1132 victims), of which 192 were deaths (53%). The Red terrorists, although commanding the field, left 368 casualties (32%), of which 170 were deaths (47%).

Both Italy's Red Brigade (BR) and the German RAF believed in being the new Marxist-Leninist revolutionary vanguard, sharing a dogmatic misunderstanding of the proletariat's needs, the rejection of capitalist materialism, and the praise of a mythical anticolonial third world. Common also was the attempt to "unmask the state's true Fascist nature" by using terrorism to provoke the state's indiscriminate repression. Thus in the beginning the Italian Red terrorists directed their offensive against selected symbols of the business and industrial community, to provoke the revolutionary involvement of the proletariat. Later, however, having failed to raise the proletariat's revolutionary consciousness, they concentrated instead on attacking the heart of the state and the symbols of its oppression: the institutional-legal establishment (police, judiciary, media, political and intellectual circles). Black terrorists, instead, first concentrated their bloody bombings on crowds of innocent bystanders (123 deaths), aiming solely at maximizing shock, terror, and horror nationwide to politically provoke a right-wing military coup and restore order against the portrayed leftist violence. Later, however, the last neo-Nazi groups closely emulated the BR in their attack against the system itself. Yet in the end, neither Italian nor German leftist terrorist groups (or the neo-Nazis) succeeded in developing coherent strategic goals for their revolution; instead they merely focused on the total supremacy of terror over political ends.[14]

Finally, the psychological weakening of national identity, religion, and major traditional social values (heroism, patriotism, loyalty) as a long-term reaction to national defeat in World War II helps explain the widespread domestic rejection of state and system by both the Italian and German youth cultures (enhanced in Italy by the constant wave of political scandals, instability, and lack of national self-esteem). The complex influence of domestic and foreign historico-cultural models, modern socio-politico-economic problems of industrialization, political intolerance, and immobility, coalesced then in an explosive, powerful exaltation of terrorist violence for the most economically marginalized and culturally/psychologically alienated extremist minorities. Finally the powerful lure of terrorism's dark romanticism and action-packed lifestyle, the belief in immunity from an inefficient judicial system, and the instant notoriety that spectacular terrorist actions elicit from the media allowed both Black and Red extremists to keep expanding their recruiting base far beyond their natural political environment.

In the end. however. the terrorists' dream of destroying the democratic system to forge in blood their nearly mystical vision of a totalitarian state (be it neo-Stalinist or neo-Nazi) was impossible to attain. It was impossible not only given the state's clear long-term organizational superiority (notwithstanding common and well-proven stereotypes of Italy's efficiency), but also because of the terrorist's antihistorical ideological blindness to domestic and international societal trends. If most neo-Nazis were hopelessly lost in their recycled neo-pagan mystique and violent warrior-cult supremacism, the Red terrorists' "pure revolutionary isolation" also totally blinded them to the changing socioeconomic realities of technological postindustrial societies and the slow erosion of traditional proletariat-syndicalist power. Equally deadly was the terrorists' naive mistake of believing the workers' and public opinion's hostility, or indifference to state and politics, concealed widespread prorevolutionary support. Instead, when the state finally marshalled a full-scale efficient repression, the terrorists found themselves alone under the squeeze.[15]

Terrorism's hopes were doomed also by the international realities of power and Italy's vital geostrategic position within the U.S.-dominated Euro-Atlantic security system. On the one hand, maybe the most lucid among the neo-Fascist leaders could still logically confide that antidemocratic military coups would elicit some form of support, or indifferent acceptance from an American superpower still too concerned with the global communist threat to challenge any pro-Western reactionary status quo in the Mediterranean or Latin American (where Greece, Spain, Portugal, Argentina, Chile, Paraguay, and Brazil were the most clamorous success symbols). But on the other hand, only ideologically blind Marxist-Leninist extremists could have seriously believed in creating a neo-Stalinist Italian popular democracy, disrupting in this way the cold war's fragile nuclear bipolar balance without even a flicker from either Washington or Moscow. Both superpowers, in fact, were traditionally known for their interference in other countries due to their obsessive fear since the mid-1940s that revolutions, external interventions, and even minor challenges to their bipolar geostrategic balance could spill over into World War III and global nuclear holocaust.[16]

In the end the democratic regime prevailed by (1) successfully frustrating the terrorists' destabilizing strategy (the state kept control of the society without resorting to indiscriminate antidemocratic repression, while widening arrest campaigns and nationwide vigilance); (2) shrewdly exploiting dogmatic infighting within the terrorist organizations (which tore apart, during 1978–1980, the very soul of the BR) and using lenient prison terms to foster the terrorists' cooperative "repentance." In fact the internal differences over terrorist tactics, ideology, and political influence sharply split the BR leadership since the Moro kidnapping, just as the state sharpened its antiterrorist offensive and new laws. The ideological-moral dissatisfaction of several terrorists, short-circuited by the hard-liners' dogmatic reliance on total violence, helped start the phenomenon of "repentance," as more and more militants were captured by the authorities and the hope of a victorious terrorist revolution became more desperate. The terrorist grip finally shattered when personal psychological crises (paradoxically reminiscent of the Stockholm syndrome's psycho-identification between terrorists and victims) led to the dramatic confessions of leaders like Patrizio Peci, Fabio Fioroni, Valerio Morucci, and

Adriana Faranda. The phenomenon became a real political flood, once the state exploited the carrot of sharply reduced prison terms to encourage even apprehended multiple-killer terrorists to betray their colleagues and ideological past.

Of course, to repent meant not a pseudo-Christian rejection and reparation of past wrongdoings (although similar moral crises were the reason for the first dramatic breaches in the terrorist wall of silence by Peci, Fioroni, Morucci, and Faranda). Instead it meant officially abandoning the armed struggle and fully cooperating with the enemy (the democratic state) to uncover and destroy the secretive, elusive terrorist network. Regardless of threats, in-prison attacks and ideological condemnation as traitors, the repentance phenomenon became a real flood involving 45% of the imprisoned terrorists, and finally doomed the terrorists' network and cadres. Not even the atrocious murders by the BR of "repented" terrorists' relatives could stop the pressure to bail out of life sentences through betrayal (even Massimo Svasta himself, the last of the hard-line BR leaders, immediately cooperated with the police after his capture during the Dozier case). Thus through better antiterrorist coordination, shrewd exploitation of the "repented" phenomenon, national support, and luck, Italy survived the Leaden Years. Fifteen years of terror (1968–1983) had not crushed her, but fully reasserted instead at home and abroad the surprising vitality of her democratic values.[17]

Neo-Fascist Terrorism in Italy

Separatist and Anarchist Terrorism: First Rumbles of the Storm

Terrorism first reemerged in postwar Italy under the cloak of ethnic extremist separatism. The first case started in Sicily immediately after World War II as a parallel separatist-banditry movement (the Bandito Giuliano saga and the political struggle of the Sicilian Separatist Movement). Sicilian separatism sought alternatively either independence or annexation to Great Britain or the USA, but quickly tapered off by 1948 through a combination of police raids and the concession of regional autonomy. More serious instead remained the separatist tensions in the ethnically divided border region of Alto Adige-Süd Tirol, annexed from Austria after World War I and predominantly German-speaking.

Brutal Fascist attempts to "Italianize" the region from 1923 to 1943 (suppression of German language and culture, immigration of Italians), or ease out the German population through emigration (1939 Italo-German Accords) only exacerbated local hostility. After being briefly annexed to Nazi Germany after Italy's military collapse (1943–1945), the region was claimed by Austria (1945–1946) but returned to Italy by the Allies. Although the 1946 Italo-Austrain De Gasperi-Gruber Accord provided for local regional autonomy, its incomplete implementation promoted renewed Austrian and UN political pressures on Italy to broaden it, while annexionist calls mounted in Austria and locally (by the conservative nationalist Südtiroler Volks Partei [SVP] and the neo-Nazi Befreiungsausschuss Süd Tirol). Although Italy resisted all Austro-UN pressures, the local terrorists expanded their separatist campaign in Northern Italy from 1956 to 1967 (financed by Austrian and Bavarian nationalist groups), with over 300 bombings of power lines, hydroelectrical installations, houses, patriotic monuments, and military posts, 30 shootings involving Italian forces, and 22 deaths.[18]

Tension abated after 1969 when a new Italo-Austrian treaty broadened local autonomy, while the terrorists, now lacking popular and Austrian support, were expelled from the SVP and crushed by the Italian forces. Separatism resurfaced only in 1978 with sporadic bombings of monuments and power-lines by the Tiroler and Tiroler Schutzbund groups (financed by Bavarian ultranationalists), but the dramatic regional economic and touristic growth in the 1970s under a moderate SVP leadership undercut all popular support for terrorism. However, the growing isolation of the minority Italian ethnic group led to a brief revival of interethnic clashes, electoral support for the MSI (the Movimento Sociale Italiano, Italy's neo-Fascist party) and sporadic attacks on ethnic German business by local right-wing Italian terrorist groups (Associazione Protezione Italiani and the ambiguous Movimento Italiano Adige, believed to be a German *provocateur* group). Yet by the mid 1980s organized local ethnic terrorism was basically over.

On the Island of Sardinia, occasional separatist terrorism briefly emerged after World War II, but in the early 1970s, with the financial and ideological support of the leftist publisher and millionaire Gian-Giacomo Feltrinelli, the more stable leftist-separatist terrorist group Barbagia Rossa emerged. Its strong ambiguous ties with both local criminality and ultra-Left extremists fostered intermittent raids on governmental archives and military installations, as well as providing some logistical support to the Red Brigades. But Barbagia Rossa never adopted Feltrinelli's delirious dogmatic vision of Sardinia as a new campground for a Cuban-style communist insurgency to spread nationwide. Finally popular indifference and successful antiterrorist police raids in 1979 eliminated separatist extremism too.[19]

Equally important has been anarchist terrorism's intermittent influence on Italian politics (from its 1870s start, to the 1900 murder of King Umberto I, and the 1921 bombing of the Kurssal Diana Theatre in Milan). Although anarchism's ideological legacy and use of spectacular terroristic deeds strongly influenced Italy's ultra-Left, anarchism itself had waned since the 1920s. A mere shadow of itself in the 1960s, it mostly provided some ambiguous minority influence on both Black and Red terrorisms, although it is still hard to separate effective cooperation from instrumental *provocateur* infiltration of anarchist groups by neo-Nazis (aiming to blame the Left for Black terror). An enigmatic symbol of this was the joint indictment and 10-year-long trials of Piero Valpreda's anarchist group together with the neo-Nazis Franco Freda and Giacomo Ventura for the December 1969 bombing of the crowed National Bank of Agriculture (BNA) in Milan and Rome (16 dead, 104 wounded). Freda, Ventura, and Delle Chiaie repeatedly escaped to Latin America when in trouble, but were all extradited back at different times. However, the Piazza Fontana case was never really solved, and amid ferocious controversies all detained anarchists and most neo-Nazis were released from prison by the late 1970s and mid 1980s.

On May 17, 1973, in Milano, four died and 20 were wounded when the anarchist Giuseppe Bertoli threw a hand grenade into a crowd gathered at the provincial police headquarters to commemorate the late deputy commissioner, Luciano Calabresi, former chief of the Milan Politial Bureau. Calabresi himself had been killed in 1972 by other anarchists for his alleged responsibility in the 1969 death of the arrested anarchist Gianni Pinelli, who "fell" from the fifth floor of the Milan police headquarters while being questioned for the BNA bombings. Anarchist activities briefly resurfaced in 1976 and 1977, with selected terrorist attacks against the prison system by the anarcho-communist Azione Rivoluzionaria group of Gianfranco Faina (comprising anarchists, leftist terorists, and common criminals recuited in jail). Yet with their demise all anarchist activities have ceased too.[20]

Ideological Origins and Evolution of Neo-Fascist Terrorism

Black terrorism emerged from a confused ideologial background, with its roots in Nazi-Fascism, postwar authoritarian creeds, and hero-worship myths. Equally interesting was the dual nature of Italy's right-wing front. On the one hand the neo-Fascist MSI party commanded some 2 million votes (6% of the electorate), and repeatedly sought to return to power by stressing its support of law and order and authoritarian values against leftist, materialist, and democratic influences corrupting modern societies. On the other hand, a coterie of fanatic Nazi-Fascist extremist groups, nurtured in the MSI's shadow, rejected its legalistic approach and favored instead an autonomous terrorist drive against the despised democratic regime.

Unchanged for both was the traditional rejection of the bourgeoisie's "corrupt" mercantilistic and materialistic values, as well as the nostalgic reactionary heralding of a hierarchical, heroic, rural past. A mythical past based on individual and nationalistic values of loyalty, generosity, and obedience to the laws of a natural authoritarian order (exposed by Edmond Burke, Joseph de Maistre, Louis de Bonald, Maurice Barrès, Charles Maurras). Thus capitalism, scientific progress, the democratic values of the American and French Revolutions, as well as the irresistible mass-populizing process of industrialized Western societies, were thoroughly rejected by the reactionary Right ever since the French Revolution. This antibourgeois trend was further strengthened from 1910 through the 1920s by the intellectual-artistic futurist movement of Carlo Marinetti and Gabriele D'Annunzio, who promoted an exasperated alternative modernist rupture with the old atrophied bourgeois system. It was a rupture which called for the preeminence of a younger romantic and heroic generation, capable of all sacrifices and even death under the banners of patriotism and charismatic leadership. Then from 1920 through the 1940s Benito Mussolini and Adolf Hitler succeeded in unifying these reactionary-nationalistic influences with the elitarian quest for a superhuman model-leader, while ruthlessly building hierarchical totalitarian regimes based on total individual subservience to the state.[21]

After the Nazi-Fascist collapse in World War II, all these ideologico-cultural roots were intellectually revived by the new Italian Right, spiritually closer now to the most radical Nazi experiences, rather than to Mussolini's original social-populist creed. While the neo-Fascist MSI reasserted itself in national politics, all neo-Fascist terrorist groups were deeply influenced by Baron Julius Evola and his philosophical disciples Adriano Romualdi and Giorgio Freda (all MSI members in the 1950s before adopting more independent and neo-Nazi violent policies). Evola and his colleagues dogmatically rejected the modern world, Western progressive values, democracy, the bourgeoisie, and industrial societies. The ideals of the American and French Revolutions, science, industry, finance, Zionism, capitalist individualism, liberalism, socialism, and communist collectivism were all condemned for their "perverted" materialistic roots, which diluted and dehumanized individual values, while destroying the natural hierarchic, authoritarian, and heroic order of the past.

Evola's new virile and spiritual society instead would be dominated by a revived aristocratic-elitist Nazi-Fascism, a new leading warrior caste spiritually and racially superior to the decadent capitalist West and communist East, and capable of leading the masses toward a glorious future. The crisis of modern societies and materialism's global grip could be overcome only by faithfully worshipping the heroic-militaristic values of the past, through a spiritual lifetime commitment to the sacred bonds of obedience, honor, and fidelity, and the abandonment of all corrupting material comforts. Sparta,

Roma, and Prussia were the traditional militaristic-spiritual societies to venerate and re-create (as in Japan's *Bushido* code, or Islam's *jihad* [holy war] concept), while the bourgeois Judeo-capitalist plutodemocracies, deeply corrupted by trade and wealth, had to be destroyed. True militants therefore would engage in endless heroic struggles against the capitalist socioeconomic system at home and abroad, while transforming the Black international fraternity of Fascist regimes and movements into an integrated federal-imperial Fascist "Third-Force Europe," independent of both Soviet communism and American capitalism.[22]

Evola's revival of militant heroic life and charismatic leadership also promoted the ultra-Right's revival of the Spanish Falange, the Waffen-SS combative heroic self-sacrifice, and Corneliu Codreanu's role-model ideology (the 1930s Romanian leader of the Fascist "Iron Guards"). Codreanu's semireligious, stern vision was of legionary-warrior elites who fought and sacrificed themselves for the nation and even for lost causes, in much the same way as Hitler's Waffen-SS in World War II (combat SS Panzer divisions). This in turn revamped D'Annunzio's earlier vision of life as a constant challenge against death, to succeed in dominating personal destinies and escape the corrupt modern enfeebling tyranny of wealth. Ezra Pound and Drieu La Rochelle, too, provided further cultural-literary backing to the neo-Fascist rejection of wealth, Zionism, and modern techno-materialism, as well as of the egalitarian principles derived from democracy and communism, both mortal enemies of elitist societies. Thus La Rochelle's vision of a resurgent gilded Middle Ages, capable of resurrecting man from the corruption of modern bourgeois mediocrity, met halfway Pound's neo-romantic rejection of warmongering capitalism, industrial monopolies, "financial usury," and communism, all instrumental in corrupting society and human personality.[23]

Concerning national politics, Evola and most young neo-Nazi extremists rejected the MSI's recurrent attempts to pursue a "legalistic and moderate" domestic political line, casting itself as a law and order party to attract anticommunists and dissatisfied conservatives without wrecking the despised democratic system. For Evola, instead, all attempts to change the system from inside were doomed to failure, as proved by the MSI's failure to gain a governmental role from 1955 to 1960: All Western democratic states in fact were seen as inherently weak, overtly concerned with society's wavering moods. The true new totalitarian state, instead, would be militaristic, vigorous, and would sternly prevent the weaker society's natural slide toward chaos and disintegration. Thus the MSI remained hostage to its traditional cleavage between the nostalgic conservative majority and the hard-core activist ultras. Common to both was the nostalgic revival of Fascism's epic and especially Mussolini's desperate last stand with the 1943–1945 Social Republic of Salo' (or RSI, a tightly controlled satellite of Nazi Germany). All neo-Fascists ended romanticizing the RSI as the purest Fascist state (rather than Mussolini's historic Fascism), self-deluding themselves with the odd dogmatic opinion that its demise came only by the betrayal of its bourgeois friends who courted the Allies' military might, rather than from the reality of local antiFascist partisan warfare and the Allies' conquest of Italy in 1943–1945. Yet while the MSI envisaged Fascism as the only healthy part of the nation, its ideology is permeated also by a deep cultural pessimism and sense of doom for the irresistible decadence of modern society and traditional values. Neo-Fascism therefore rejected all social progress (sexual freedom, racial and sexual equality, mass democratic participation), seen as mortal enemies of sacred family values and mythic authoritarian-hierarchic societies, of which only the neo-Fascist "warriors" were the true spiritual harbingers.[24]

Yet neo-Fascism would remain hopelessly divided over strategies. The dogmatic pessimism and blindness of Evola's disciples to the realities of modern industrialized democratic societies and international relations clashed sharply both with Mussolini's past positive ideological undertones (to create a vital society open to the future), as well as with the MSI's own choice of legal respectability and political integration from the right into the despised democracy born from the ashes of Fascism. Both MSI leaders, Arturo Michelini (1950–1969) and Giorgio Almirante (1969–1988), when in command, stressed political integration with the DC as the only strategy to regain power. Yet success was always marginal and elusive. The nationwide antiFascist opposition (the only postwar unifying political factor) always kept the MSI locked in total isolation, while permanent internal criticism by Almirante's and Pino Rauti's minority hard-core extremists (who accused Michelini of betraying Fascism's ideological purity) left the party in disarray by the period of 1956–1968. Rauti himself seceded from the MSI to found the terrorist Ordine Nuovo group in 1956.[25]

Almirante instead, once renominated secretary in 1969 (he had been ousted in 1950 by Michelini's moderates), gradually traded his extremism for the strategy of respectability, in a bid to win over to the MSI both the anticommunist bourgeoisie and the underprivileged violent youth of the slums. This newly adopted strategy ("double-breasted business suits covering Black Shirts"), in combination with both the 1969 student/labor unrest and the dramatic rise of the PCI in the early 1970s, doubled the MSI's electoral base from 4.5% in 1968 to 8.7% in 1972 (three million voters). But if Almirante had secretly unleashed from 1969 to 1972 his violent FDG youths (Fronte della Gioventù, the MSI party's youth league), winning back such extremists as Rauti, the MSI's 1972 electoral success could not overcome either the party's total isolation or the growing rivalry of Rauti's neo-Nazi ultras during the 1970s and 1980s. Instead, while Almirante inched towards legalitarian conservatorism, the terrorist "strategy of tension" waged by the rebellious neo-Nazis and FDG members weakened the party's authority over the extreme right and forced Almirante to alternate vitriolic attacks against Red terrorism (the "only" source of all violence) with defiant praise of the neo-Fascists' "right to self-defense."

Yet Almirante's desperate bid to maintain an image of respectability, minimize his militants' violence, and bridge the gap between national-conservative forces and Rauti's neo-Nazi ultras couldn't prevent the loss of the MSI's moderate elements in 1976 (the brief "Democrazia Nazionale" split) and an electoral decline to 6.1%. Moreover, the 1973 expulsion of the rebellious neo-Nazis from the MSI had not quashed their independence and upon their reentry into the party (late 1970s) they steadily undermined Almirante's charismatic influence and almost ousted him at the November 1987 MSI Congress of Sorrento. Almirante's line prevailed, but even his last political success, establishing from 1975 to 1988 the MSI's leadership of the Euro-Right in the European Parliament over Jean-Marie Le Pen's French Front National, the Spanish Frente Nacional, the Irish Unionist Party, the Greek Enosis, and other groups, could not stop the party's domestic decline (6.1% of the vote in 1976; 5.3% in 1979; 6.8% in 1983; 5.9% in 1987 and a virtual collapse in the 1988 administrative elections after his death).[26]

Black Terrorism: Groups, Tactics, and the Italian Society

Apart from sporadic minor bombings and traditional open political intimidation and street violence against the Left, neo-Fascist terrorism emerged seriously only in the late 1960s. Although at the time it was perceived as the most dangerous and bloody form of terrorism, it would never parallel the later Red terrorist sophistication. The main differences between Red and Black terrorism were ideological, structural, and operational. The lack of a systematic ideological base left the neo-Fascists under the confused and contrasting influence of the 1920s Fascist squadrism, authoritarian nationalism, anticommunism, racial supremacism, hero-worship, and neo-pagan mythology. Yet the transition from street clashes with the Left to underground terrorism was the logical development of their philosophical extremism of means and irrational hate against the all-pervasive capitalistic society.

Early extremist groups emerged in the 1950s under Evola's ideological influence (Figli del Sole, Legione Nera, Fasci d'Azione Rivoluzionaria [FAR]). At the same time, Romualdi attempted to rationalize Evola's doctrinary visions by stressing the need to win over to the extreme Right those few vital sectors of the society, or "separate corps" (military, police) which came closer to Evola's warrior caste and could provide a revolution from above through a coup d'état and military dictatorship. Yet the original neo-Fascist groups remained mostly inactive and incapable of providing the political leadership for Romualdi's "separate corps." Their 1956 merger into Rauti's Ordine Nuovo (ON), which with Avanguardia Nazionale (AN) and Fronte Nazionale represented the most active new Black factions, provided renewed stimuli for terrorism and the implementation of Romualdi's plans. ON promoted both militant terrorism and ideological proselytism to hand down to new generations the purest revolutionary Fascist and Evolian concepts, while fostering the ideologico-cultural politicization of high schools and universities. After Rauti's reentry in the MSI, ON was reorganized in 1969 by Clemente Graziani and Elio Massagrande, and although it never really attempted to become a mass party, it still ambiguously rivaled the MSI. Instead, ON modeled its structure on Evola's vision of elitarian cadres becoming the fanaticized vanguards of a Black revolution, as well as the leaders of the masses in the final struggle against Western societies. Even its political horizons were enlarged beyond the old Fascist nationalism: The destruction of both the bourgeois system and leftist culture would usher in a new transnational, integrated Black Europe, capable of resuming her old superior civilizing role.[27]

The rigidly indoctrinated neo-Fascist terrorists underwent extensive secret paramilitary training to prepare for their "Black revolution" against the Left and the democapitalistic system. Rapidly spreading in the North and throughout Italy with thousands of members, ON developed strong ties with the Black international and right-wing dictatorships in Europe and South America, as well as with conservative Italian sectors disenchanted with parliamentarian politics. Equally so Stefano Delle Chiaie's 2000-strong AN (a 1960 ON offshot), praised Evola's "heroic" ideology and pursued countless acts of neo-squadrist violence against the Left, hoping to entice a military coup to "save the nation." Also, influential conservative civilian-military groups and sectors of the Secret Services adopted Romualdi's military coup ideas and sought to exploit the neo-Fascists as a counterrevolutionary force against the perceived collapse of governmental authority under leftist encroachment, during the "opening to the Left" (the PSI entry in the government) of the early 1960s, and the 1969 politico-syndicalist Hot Autumn crisis. The pervasiveness in the West, and Italy too, of the fear of communist-inspired guerrillas, or insurgency (dramatized by the 1954–1962 Algerian War and by Vietnam), stimulated active planning for rightist military countermeasures and attempted coups.

In the late 1950s General Giovanni De Lorenzo, head of the military intelligence (SIFAR), proposed the plan "Solo" for an emergency military intervention to ward off potential leftist threats, or guerrilla insurgenices. Again in 1964 during a major governmental crisis following the PSI's withdrawal from the Center-Left government, President Antonio Segni and De Lorenzo (by then head of the prestigious Carabinieri police) were protrayed as discussing behind closed doors the need to garrison Rome against any threat. Although Segni denied preparing with De Lorenzo an eventual military intervention, this fear had already promoted the PSI's precipitous reentry into the governmental coalition, while subsequent parliamentary hearings uncovered De Lorenzo's "Solo" plan and his misuse of the SIFAR to fund patriotic and right-wing groups (ON and AN), as well as investigating and creating secret dossiers on many political leaders of the Left and the Center too. The scandal led to the disbanding and reorganization of the Secret Serices in 1967 and again in 1974 and 1975, but recurrent instances of their continuous occult support of right-wing forces during the strategy of tension undermined their effectiveness, impartiality, and credibility throughout the 1970s.[28]

Another symbol of these occult civilian-military and neo-Fascist complicities was the infamous clandestine Pollio Convention for Historic and Military Studies (Rome, spring 1965), which aligned leading right-wing military, intelligence, and civilian groups with ON and AN to implement a comprehensive counterrevolutionary military plan and turn Italian society against the "mounting leftist subversion." Although all these connections have not been fully clarified, soon afterward the MSI and neo-Fascist ultras were heavily involved in urban-guerrilla warfare during the 1970–1971 popular uprisings in Reggio-Calabria, as well as with the 1969–1973 destabilizing terrorist strategy of tension. This terrorist plan involved indiscriminate bombings against heavily crowded public places and facilities, city squares, banks, trains, and train lines, like the infamous 1969 Piazza Fontana bombings of the BNA banks in Rome and Milan (16 dead, 104 wounded); or the 1970 bombing and derailing of the *Freccia del Sud* train at Gioia Tauro (6 dead, 129 wounded). Its apparent aberrant purpose was to create widespread random terror and chaos at all levels of society through spectacular indiscriminate mass slaughter of innocent victims. The bloody brutality of the attacks, the generalized hysteria and insecurity they provoked, and the neo-Fascist charges that leftists and anarchists were responsible (whose groups, like Valpreda's anarchists, had been infiltrated by Black *provocateurs*), would have then provoked a massive popular reaction against the "criminal Left" and the "incompetent" democratic regime, as well as fostering a right-wing military coup to "restore law and order."[29]

Throughout the 1970s Black terrorist leaders heavily recruited among the MSI's most extremist cadres and its youth organization (FDG), among semi-independent neo-Nazi groups with no apparent ties to the MSI, and from right-wing nostalgic and military groups whose aim was to promote a Fascist military coup. Thus on the one hand ON succeeded in coordinating all independent Black terrorist activities through both its military arm, Avanguardia Nazionale (AN) and other groups (Squadre Azione Mussolini [SAM], Lotta di Popolo, La Fenice, Fronte Delta, Movimento Azione Rivoluzionaria [MAR], Europa Civiltà), all secretly trained in paramilitary camps in mountainous areas. On the other, the moderate-conservative forces promoted the parallel reemergence of Prince Valerio Borghese (an old glory of the Fascist era) and his Fronte Nazionale, a vast catch-all front critical of the MSI's ineffectiveness and uniting the heterogeneous extra-parliamentarian Right (nostalgic Fascists, old RSI soldiers, active and retired military officers and parachutists, military clubs, bourgeois and aristocratic notables, as well as militants from ON, AN, Fronte Delta, and Europa Civiltà). Borghese planned to restore public authority and the collapsing state through a secret anticommunist military coup, organized by his armed underground units, while ostensibly preaching the maintenance of law and order. This plan was temporarily supported also by Black terrorists, given their common goal of destroying the PCI/Left and parliamentarian system by any means.

Borghese's indecisiveness led to the utter failure of this golpe (December 7 and 8, 1970) and the consequent dissolution of this fragile front (through internecine conflicts, exile, or incarceration). Another golpist plot in 1973 by the Rosa dei Venti military group (financed by small industrialists and including dissatisfied high military cadres, retired officers, ex-ON and RSI militants, and common criminals) was preempted by massive police raids. Yet if the strategy of tension had finally been unmasked as a Fascist-led plot to foment a military golpe, throughout the 1970s Black golpists still received obscure forms of support from vast sectors of the armed forces, judiciary, police, and Secret Services, which enhanced Italy's inner fragility and hampered her repression of terrorism. These occult complicities were unmasked anew during the 1975 indictment of General Vio Miceli, ex-head of the "reconstituted" SID secret service, and the 1983 secret Masonic Lodge P.2 scandal. Licio Gelli's powerful and secret P.2 Masonic Lodge, especially, was charged with infiltrating leading state structures (P.2 members included 300 top-ranking military, police, politicians, intelligence, etc.). Moreover, Gelli (another RSI Fascist veteran) had originally sought to undermine Italy's democracy and block the PCI's electoral surge, by financing and supporting right-wing military coup plans from 1960 to 1975 (the strategy of tension, Borghese, and the Rosa dei Venti). After 1975, instead, the P.2 "reconciled" itself to democracy, but only to indirectly and more effectively wield power through greed and politico-financial manipulation of the major Center and Right parties.[30]

After its peak in 1971, Black terrorism fell into disarray because of its failure to topple the government through terror, and also because of the concomitant 1973–1974 massive police crackdowns on both ON and AN after the Piazza della Loggia and *Italicus* train massacres (Graziani, Massagrande, and other leaders fled to Franco's Spain). The most fanaticized surviving members of AN, SAM, La Fenice and Lotta di Popolo, then formed a new terrorist organization, Ordine Nero. Under Gianni Esposti's leadership it created a loose cellular structure covering several urban areas, while training in secret mountainous camps together with the MAR group. But once Esposti died in a 1974 shoot-out during one of the numerous police antiterrorist raids in the mountains, Ordine Nero too retrenched, reeling from internal frustration and criticism of their past ruinous destabilization strategy. Finally, under pressure from the parallel Red terrorist onslaught against the state, the neo-Nazis devised a new strategy and social model at 1975 meetings at Albano-Laziale, Corsica, and Nizza. All underground leaders (Graziani, Massagrande, Delle Chiaie, Signorelli) decided to amalgamate their surviving forces to continue terrorism through a leaner, more efficient group. Evola's doctrines and military coup plans were canned, while communist theories instead and the Red Brigades' efficient terrorist organization and self-financing robberies were analyzed and thoroughly imitated.[31]

Ordine Nero's most clamorous actions were the 1974 bombings of Brescia's crowded Piazza della Loggia during an antiFascist gathering (8 dead, 94 wounded); the bombing of the train *Italicus* near Bologna (12 dead, 48 wounded); and the 1976 killing of Assistant State Attorney Vittorio Occorsio in Rome (who had crushed ON and prosecuted other Black terrorist groups too). The state's repression and the crude reality of clandestine life eroded all ideological pretensions, forcing Black terrorists toward petty crime, bank robberies, and kidnapping for financing. Total secrecy dominated the neo-Nazi groups, while their terrorist attacks, murders, and elimination of "traitors" in and out of prisons were often only initialed and seldom explained to the larger public. Thus the neo-Nazis never capitalized on one of terrorism's most effective tools: propaganda and media coverage, whose use they despised.

Instead, under Freda's influence (imprisoned for life following the 10-year-long trial for the 1969 Piazza Fontana massacres that ushered in the strategy of tension), neo-Nazism and Ordine Nero degenerated into the most extreme anarchism and naked terrorist bloodbaths (trains, governmental offices, and individuals killed as symbols), in the futile attempt to destroy an unredeemable state through a chain reaction of hysteric popular unrest, random state repression, and spontaneous revolution. Freda's sharp condemnation of the MSI's legalistic tricks, and his paradoxical praise of the PLO and international leftist guerrilla movements (in Vietnam and Latin America) as true living incarnations of Evola's heroic mission against the bourgeoisie, showed also the controversial extent of ideological rapprochement between neo-Nazism and the ultra-Left in their shared hatred of democracy. Thus Freda's aberrant Nazi-Maoists, totally independent from the MSI and divested of all past neo-Fascist ideologies (and anticommunism too), focused on destroying bourgeoisie, colonialism, capitalism, and democracy, as well as the European Community, to create instead a totalitarian hierarchical popular state. Private property would be abolished and its ownership centralized together with political power in the hands of an executive regent, state commissaries (ministers), and politcial presidium.[32]

Neo-Fascist terrorism could maximize its impact thanks to a vast network of sympathizers and financiers, domestic and international political ties, and a connection with secret services and international terrorism which facilitated arms trafficking and military training in Labanese camps (both Christian and Palestinian, as the 1982 Israeli invasion proved). Often strong proterrorist sympathies in the MSI led to spontaneous terrorist acts by young MSI members, such as the murder of police officer Antonio Marino, or the incrimination of Sandro Saccucci for killing a young communist during a Fascist raid at Sezze-Romano. In the end, however, Black terrorism suffered the most from its own structural weakness: its small, disorganized, and individualistic groups (six- to eightman units), unsophisticated strategy, confused ideology and operative goals, as well as extensive reliance on drugs to maximize individual courage. All these defaults therefore made it relatively more easy for the Italian authorities to discredit Black terror by the mid-1970s.

Neo-Nazi terrorism reemerged, however, from 1977 to 1982 with a new ruthless generation, mainly Roman high school and university graduates, through Costruiamo l'Azione (1977–1979), FUAN-NAP (Revolutionary Armed Nucleus, 1979–1982), MPR (Popular Revolutionary Movement), and Terza Posizione (founded by Signorelli and ideologically directed by Freda through his prison correspondence). While copying the Red Brigades' organization and strategy, these groups were strongly influenced by Freda's nihilism and the Tolkien Mania (from fantasy writer J. R. R. Tolkien's *Hobbit* saga of adventure and heroism), the last cry in the neo-Nazi ideological desert. On one hand, through Camp Hobbit 1977 and the rejection of rigid Left-Right ideological rivalry, they vainly sought to recreate Freda's Nazi-Maoist fusion of Black and Red terrorism against the common enemy: the capitalist, bourgeois state. On the other hand, they expanded the use of firearms rather than bombs in terroristic attacks, following the BR example also in selectively targeting their victims with individualized murders and woundings, or raids on PCI sections, newspapers, and state symbols of authority. Yet all lacked serious political goals or strategy, focusing instead on violence per se.

Terza Posizione was the better organized and nationally widespread terrorist group (territorial nuclei), yet its 1979–1980 actions quickly tapered off owing to major internal conflicts (spontaneous terrorism as an expression of Evola's legionnaire spirit vs. hierarchically planned revolutionary goals and actions). Costruiamo l'Azione instead was the more effective in 1978–1979: the daylight raids in Rome of the *Messaggero, Tempo,* and *Paese Sera* newspapers; the daylight raid on the PCI's Via Cairoli section (23 wounded); the bombings of the city hall, the Foreign Affairs Ministry, and the Regina Coeli prison. Destroyed by police raids, its role was taken by the reckless NAR (Revolutionary Armed Nucleus) group of Fioravanti and Mambro with new waves of bombings, killings, and raids. Relentlessly hunted down by the police, the young NAR terrorists suffered serious setbacks but kept attacking, killing also in June 1980 Prosecuting Magistrate Mario Amato in Rome, and bombing Bologna's railway station at noontime in August 1980 (the bloodiest terrorist attack ever in Italy: 85 dead, 200 wounded). Finally, with all its members captured or killed in bloody shootouts with the police, NAR and Terza Posizione were destroyed during the period of 1981–1984, and the NAR links with the French neo-Fascist FANE were uncovered. Yet national frustrations did not abate due to the extreme length of the trials and the even more disturbing exposure of Black terrorism's secret high-placed supporters in the army, judiciary, Secret Services, parties, and police (the 1983 P.2 Masonic Lodge scandal), which forced the fall of the government and a new reorganization of the Secret Services.[33]

Red Terrorism and International Connections

Red Terrorism: Ideological Roots and Italian Politics

The ideological roots of leftist terrorism derived from both the general mainstream of Marxist-Leninist philosophy (spanning from Sorel's anarchic-revolutionary syndicalism to Marxist-Leninist theories on the proletarian revolution), and from the new radical Left and student movement's pseudorevolutionary struggles of the 1960s and 1970s. Other major trends which influenced Italy's extra-parliamentarian Left and Red terrorism were

(1) The vision of a new revolutionary communist party, as a modern vanguard of the proletariat against the corrupt materialist democracies and closely patterned after third world Marxist-Leninist revolutionary movements.

(2) The old Hobsonian-Leninist visions of Western imperialism as the extreme phase of the "dying international capitalist" structure.

(3) The inherent flaws of the capitalist system, whose uneven economic develoment and systematic exploitation of the society nurtures in its midst the future proletarian revolution.

(4) Anarcho-communist traditions of terrorism and insurgency, as well as Lev Trotzkij's concept of a "permanent world revolution" which would strengthen anti-Western solidarity between the international proletarian and anticolonialist movements (a vision later modernized by the Marxist guerrilla doctrine of Mao Tse-Tung, Che Guevara, Castro, Régis Debray, Lin-Piao, and Vo Nguyen Giap, as well as by the imagery of the Latin American urban guerrilla: Carlos Marighela, the Tupamaros, and the Montoneros.

(5) The major cultural fortune of Marxism in postwar Italy, both as criticism of the bourgeois system and as a historical analytical discipline.

(6) The complete rejection of the traditional Reformist Left (PCI, PSI, PSDI) "grown too soft and bourgeois," in favor instead of third world role-models (Mao's Long March and the Cultural Revolution; Che Guevara's and Castro's Cuban revolutionary mystique; anti-Americanism; the Vietnam War; anticapitalism in Latin America and Africa; anti-Zionism; the PLO's *fedayeen* terrorists).[34]

More immediately, Red terrorism emerged also as an extremist ideological outgrowth of the political split between the "historical reformist" Left (PSI/PSDI/trade unions, which had attracted the "renegade" PCI too) on one side, and the dogmatic extra-parliamentarian new "revolutionary" Left on the other (Partito Comunista d'Italia–Marxista-Leninista, Il Manifesto, Lotta Continua, Avanguardia Operaia, Democrazia Proletaria). This radical ultra-Left was strongly influenced also by the student movement (the unorganized leftist front of high school and university students), but after the benchmark 1968–1969 years when student/labor protest failed to destroy the severely weakened capitalist state, the most extremist elements switched from violent street protests to terrorism by adopting domestically the same tactics of their cherished third world Marxist-Leninist terrorist-guerrilla groups (Vietcong in Asia, Tupamaros in Latin America, the PLO in the Middle East). Thus in their hardened ideological beliefs, they hoped that an armed insurrection would foster an internal proletarian revolution and the rapid disintegration of Western capitalism in its weakest link: Italy.[35]

Italy in fact seemed ripe for collapse under the multiplicity of internal stains: rampant socioeconomic crises, massive labor and student unrest (1968 and the 1969 Hot Autumn), chronic governmental instability and political immobility, inefficiency, scandals, stalled internal reforms, and the ideological clash between the largest political parties (DC and PCI), each struggling to monopolize the political and sociocultural system. All this fed upon the country's tumultuous transformation from rural to industrialized with massive internal migration flows and the collapse of traditional values; the sharp syndicalist struggles much idealized by the extreme Left as symbolic tools in undermining the capitalism; the identity crisis of the petite bourgeoisie threatened by social changes and the opposition of dissatisfied youths attracted to political extremism in reaction to a mediocre lifestyle. Finally, to most leftist extremists, Italy represented the Western ideological counterpart of Vietnam: an ideal battlefield against Western values, international interventionism, and the monopoly-dominated capitalistic system.[36]

Red Terror: Groups, Organizations, Goals, and Tactics

In contrast to the deep ideological confusion of Black terrorism, Red terror had clearer political goals, ideology, and target selectivity, aimed at "striking the state's authority at its heart" and promoting the old Marxist-Leninist revolutionary dreams. Operationally both neo-Nazi and Red terrorists shared paradoxically the same goals: the violent overthrow of the democratic system through generalized violence and bloody terrorist acts. The consequent breakdown of governmental authority would promote a pro-Fascist military coup to restore law and order, thus making of the leftist terrorists the only viable guerrilla organization capable of leading a new general popular resistance war against the military dictatorship, and transforming Italy into a new popular democracy.

These original visionary plans were abandoned only in the late 1970s, when the state's unforeseen resistance to the terrorist onslaught, and the aborted string of neo-Fascist coups (Borghese, Rosa dei Venti), forced the Red terrorists to accept the inevitability of a long painful struggle, as well as the self-destructive nihilism common to the neo-Nazis. Also, political targeting reflected terrorism's total war on the system: university professors, officers in the police, judiciary, mass media, business, political figures, and activists were all considered as lackeys of the regime, and either killed or ritualistically humiliated and wounded ("knee-capped") in attacks meant to demonstrate the system's weakness. The main political enemy remained the DC, while the PCI and trade unions were also strongly criticized but seldom attacked (the Castellano and Rossa killings).[37]

The structure and dynamics of the different Red terrorist groups were clearly modeled on five major operative patterns derived from Latin American urban guerrillas:

(1) Rigid clandestine activities and systematic violence.
(2) Close interrelation between terrorist armed struggle and political indoctrination of the masses.
(3) Spontaneous sporadic terrorist activities.
(4) Coordinated actions by different terrorist groups against common targets.
(5) Operative reliance on and recruitment of popular sympathizers for auxiliary and part-time terrorist activities.

The first pattern was generally implemented by the Red Brigades (BR) and the NAP (Armed Proletarian Nucleus), who preferred total armed struggle over politics, directing their attacks against any symbol of the "repressive capitalist regime." The second pattern strengthened instead the correlation between force and political action; it was promoted by Prima Linea (Front Line) who opposed total clandestinity because it would have prevented the necessary indoctrination of the masses. The third policy reflected both the uncoordinated activities of small, inexperienced, and short-lived terrorist groups (privileging sporadic arson and bombing, as well as training of new recruits for larger organizations). The fourth policy, common by the late 1970s, promoted joint planning and actions againt important targets by two or more terrorist groups, with joint liaison officers. The last model concentrated on operational-logistic support of terrorism, namely the reliance on auxiliaries and political sympathizers drawn from the extra-parliamentarian Left to provide intelligence, recruits, logistic cover, medical and legal assistance, as well as parallel support through street demonstrations and urban guerrilla violence.[38]

By the late 1970s these operative models were simplified: the first, second, and fourth models were combined, while the third and fifth disappeared after the massive waves of police arrests, which led to the seizure of operational logistic bases, and to mass confessions which fully exposed the terrorists' clandestine organization and tactics. Moreover, the forced camaraderie, the common fight, and the joint operational planning against the system allowed the BR to prevail over and absorb smaller, declining terrorist groups (NAP, GAP [Partisan Action Group], Circolo XXII Ottobre), while adopting their rival operational tactics (like Prima Linea's "double-life" pattern of clandestine terrorist activities and parallel open-air political propaganda).

By the early 1970s, therefore, the BR emerged as the strongest terrorist group, and a living inspiration to scores of radical extremists. Born as a radical offshoot of the 1960s labor/student unrest, the BR's historical leadership (currently imprisoned) comprised ex-Catholic students of the State University of Trento's sociology department (Renato Curcio, "Mara" Cagol); dissatisfied ex-activists from the PCI and its youth organization (Federazione Giovanile Comunista Italiana, or FGCI) from the heavily communist Emilia-Romagna region (Alberto Franceschini, Prospero Gallinari, Luciano

Azzolini); and ultraleftist militants (Mario Moretti, Corrado Alunni), often with worker-syndicalist backgrounds in the northern industrial concerns.[39]

The leading influence of ex-Catholic elements in founding the BR seems paradoxical only if we focus on traditional cliches. Instead, the common psychologial traits of dogmatism, unchallengeable self-righteousness, and fanatic revolutionary solidarity easily mixed with Marxist-Leninism's dogmatic proletarian struggle. Yet the BR's fascination with Marxist-Leninist revolutionarism and third world liberation theories proved also to be their major hindrance in truly understanding the socioeconomic dynamics of the working class in Italy's postindustrial society. Instead, unshakeably convinced that Italy's sociopolitical situation mirrored the crises-ridden Latin American and Asian models, the BR regularly condemned social change as another tool of exploitation by the capitalist system, while fostering guerrilla-terrorist warfare to promote a violent communist revolution and the overthrow of the system. Thus from 1969 to 1981 the BR expanded their national operational presence while constantly altering their terrorist strategy.[40]

Initially they pressed for radical social changes, and heralded the incoming "armed struggle" for communism. But when the PCI officially condemned terrorism, the terrorists totally rejected the "corrupt capitalist system." In this first "revolutionary phase" in Milan (1969–1972), the BR concentrated on clandestine distribution of subversive Marxist-Leninist leaflets in factories (to politically prepare the workers for the revolution) and sporadic bombings and sabotage against private and industrial property. Their lack of resources forced them to rely on bank robberies for financing (justified as "proletarian expropriations"), and on demonstrative kidnappings to intimidate the society. All violent activities, although unorganized and confused, attempted to unmask the state's inner weaknesses and reactionary onslaught, which the BR would have then exploited to promote a popular civil war against the "neo-Fascist state."

This dual strategy of terrorist attacks for propaganda and underground political proselytism in the factories was expanded throughout northern Italy's industrial triangle (the Milan-Turin-Genova area) during the second phase (late 1972 to mid-1974). The systematic rise of terrorist violence, political abductions and dramatic "political trials" of governmental officers (like the 1974 abduction of Assistant State Attorney Mario Sossi in Genova, released in exchange for imprisoned terrorists) gained full media coverage and sympathetic support from radical politico-cultural sectors. As a result, the BR further expanded their recruiting base among fanatic extremists and disillusioned youth attracted to terrorism by a misperceived sense of heroic adverturism and existentialist rejection of modern life's anonymity.[41]

Since its inception, terrorism could have been easily repressed had the government and the police intervened decisively. Yet their apparent downplaying of the events, their inefficient organization, and their refusal to tackle the real roots of terrorism (simplistically dubbed the "opposite extremism strategy"), allowed it to grow uncontrollably until the moment when the BR attacked the judiciary too (the Sossi abduction). The police thereafter captured Curcio, Cagol (later killed), and most of the founding BR leadership by 1974. But the emergence during the third period (mid-1974 to early 1976) of a new, efficient, and ruthless second generation (ex-members of the dissolved extra-parliamentarian group Potere Operaio, and disillusioned PCI militants) rapidly escalated terrorist violence, with widespread assassinations, armed robberies, abductions and knee-cappings of journalists, businessmen, governmental, and DC midlevel officers. Yet the terrorist dream of a generalized armed struggle was gradually abandoned, given also the apparent hostile indifference of the working class and open condemnation by the unions and the PCI.

Clandestinity instead became an extremely rigid way of life, or mission, centered on combat planning, ideological debates, and political subversion in the factories. The BR's tightly knit organization was capped by an executive committee supervising terrorist strategy, with subcommittees for logistics, information, and propaganda. Yet this total ideological commitment to clandestine struggle and complete separation from social daily life completely distorted the terrorists' psychology, while enlarging the gulf between their stated goals and the hostile reaction of the society at large. During the fourth phase (1976 to early 1979), only Moretti of the historical founders remained active (until his 1980 capture), yet the BR quickly reached their mature phase, rapidly expanding nationwide by creating autonomous "firing columns" in major cities, and unleashing a breathtaking onslaught of murders, ambushes, bombings, and knee-cappings which drove the authorities and society almost to hysteria (5700 actions during the peak 1976–1979 years, with attacks almost every other day).[42]

Organizationally the BR formed a pyramidal structure (Figure 1) based on noncommunicating "cells" (three to five members per cell), organized in "brigades" (two autonomous cells per brigade), with every two to four brigades organized in "firing columns" for each major city (Milan, Genova, Turin, Rome, Naples) and few selected regions (the less organized Venetian, central Italian, and Emilian columns). Each operative level was sealed so that the arrest of any terrorist would expose only his cell and cell commander, but not the members of other cells, known only by the brigade chief. The system, very efficient in the North but almost nonexistent in the South, reflected various underground structural models derived from World War II partisan wars in Europe, from Latin American terrorism, and from the theories of Brazilian revolutionary Marighela. The BR's innovative creation of semiautonomous brigades based on noncommunicating twin cells (as in Figure 1:C-Bx2-Ax8) allowed the column to operate constantly and safely whenever the police captured any one cell, while favoring also the rapid self-regeneration of the lost limb by the rest of the brigade structure. All activities (short- and long-term policy planning and terrorist operations) were supervised by an executive committee operating within a larger strategic command uniting political and military leaderships.[44]

Life in the underground had very strict rules dealing with both internal secrecy and security, while an external false image of bourgeois respectability (clean, shaved, well-dressed, reserved, and polite professionals) fooled neighbors and police alike. The rigid habits of internal secrecy and discipline were enforced by conforming all personal lifestyles (from meals to love) to the column standards and the supervision of the respective chiefs. Everybody was subjected to the same rules and risks (men and women alike), while clandestine activities required minimal visibility, concealed heavy firepower, and involved frequent juggling between bases. Unsuspected terorists and/or auxiliaries bought and rented scores of apartments, which were transformed into makeshift bases and "political prisons," forcing the state to impose national mandatory preregistration of all new rents and sales to the local police precincts, as well as nightly monitoring of all hotel reservations.

While the other columns were mostly based on the proletarian-factory realities of the North, the 1975 creation of the "anomalous" Roman column by Moretti introduced new heterogeneous elements from the bureaucratic-retail area of the Center-South (where the industrial base was minimal): urban underproletarians, young unemployed,

Italy II

M. Rimanelli

ORGANIZATIONAL CHART OF TWO OF THE FOUR EXISTING COLUMNS
OF THE RED BRIGADES (ROME, MILAN, TURIN, GENOA)

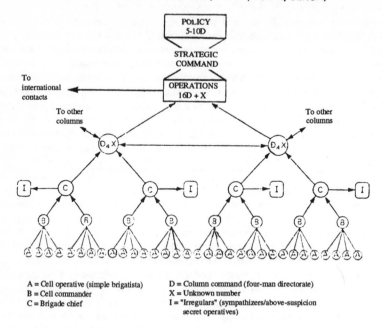

A = Cell operative (simple brigatista)   D = Column command (four-man directorate)
B = Cell commander   X = Unknown number
C = Brigade chief   I = "Irregulars" (sympathizers/above-suspicion
            secret operatives)

Figure 1. The *Brigate Rosse* organizational chart.[43]

and tough extra-parliamentarian militants from the urban ghettos (Barbara Balzerani of the Potere Operaio section in the Borgata Tiburtina; Valerio Morucci and Adriana Faranda of the Comitati Comunisti Rivoluzionari, and members of Viva il Comunismo group). Both the Roman column and its similar Neapolitan cousin were ideologically despised and feared by the more orthodox Northern proletarian columns. Yet the Roman one, especially, was essential for striking the Italian state at its core, as during the 1978 Moro affair.[45]

Traditional self-financing (robberies and kidnappings) was expanded now with foreign funds and weapons, while attacks and targeting techniques were patterned on a highly selective and ideologically symbolic hit list. All terrorist attacks were carefully planned by commando units (one or more terrorist cells) exploiting the target's daily habits. Murder, maiming, and well-planned destructive raids on governmental and business offices to steal personal files and create new hit lists were routinely implemented and publicized. Major attacks were often carefully timed to capture the media's coverage and produce major politico-psychological ripple effects (such as the blocking or postponing of highly visible antiterrorist trials). Minor arson and bombings against property and institutions instead of people had specific symbolic meanings and training purposes for recruits, but often went unclaimed. Invariably all BR terrorist acts, regardless of their cruelty, were immediately underwritten and praised by imprisoned leaders and terrorists, who used their trials as a media show to propagandize the armed struggle and keep some fleeting ties with their underground comrades-in-arms.

Of all terrorist groups (Black and Red), only the BR had the organizational skills, manpower, and firepower to conduct large-scale and extremely complex attacks, such as the 1978 Moro abduction, or the 1979 Piazza Nicosia raid. In the first case a 12-terrorist commando unit carefully planned and successfully abducted Moro (the influential DC president and ex-premier), kiling his five-man escort; changed getaway cars while escaping in daytime rush-hour traffic; repeatedly contacted authorities, the DC, the PSI, the media, and Moro's relatives to dictate their conditions; disseminated dozens of Moro letters in the attempt to split state and country; frequently transferred his secret prison hideout during a two-month-long, ineffective, nationwide police hunt; and then executed him and symbolically delivered his corpse in broad daylight, halfway between the heavily guarded DC and PCI national party headquarters in downtown Rome. In 1979, 50 BR terrorists raided in broad daylight the DC party offices of Piazza Nicosia in downtown Rome, overpowering guards and clerks, killing a police patrol, bombing the buildings, and stealing files before disappearing unmolested.[46]

In the mid-1970s new recruits came from the ranks of common criminals (in-prison "politicization"), and the powerful ideological base of the Movimento Studentesco (the leftist student front) dominated by Autonomia Operaia (the ultraleftist league of unaffiliated students, underproletarians, and unemployed and disqualified workers). The students' numeric expansion and pent-up grievances on curricula and job prospects fueled the growth of Autonomia's blind violence, especially in the radical university hotbeds of Rome, Bologna, Milan, and Padova. Rejecting society and politics alike, Autonomia instigated "spontaneous" street unrest against the system, while sourly criticizing also the PCI's reformist and Euro-Communist line. To them any cooperation with the despised bourgeois system smacked of ideological betrayal. Thus from 1976 to 1979, parallel to the terrorist wave, Autonomia too gave its disorganized contribution to political chaos through street violence, vandalizing the inner cities, openly praising the terrorist armed struggle, participating in sporadic shootouts, and adopting urban-guerrilla tactics against the PCI, the trade unions, and the police during its cordoning of public demonstrations.

The police reaction led to several deaths in crossfire, arrests, tons of tear-gas sprayed throughout the inner cities, use of armored personnel carriers often fitted with water-cannons, closing of the universities, and finally a two-month-long curfew on all public demonstrations. The PCI too intervened vigorously in support of the government. Deeply involved in the difficult transitional period of the "historic compromise," it stressed now both internal party democratization and integration in the government under the DC's suspicious cooperation. Yet the PCI's reformist line had to ocvercome its old militant myths, like the armed revolutionary tradition of Pietro Secchia, of the Spanish Civil War (1936–1939) and of the Partisan War (1943–1945), which strongly influenced the soul of the party and the neo-Stalinists. Yet the PCI always condemned terrorism and fully supported the state's repression (even when the BR killed Castellano and Rossa, two PCI unionists favoring labor-management cooperation). To Enrico Berlinguer, the PCI leader, any hesitation would have doomed the party's democratic and governmental aspirations, while allowing both superpowers to exploit any ideologial cleavage to influence the PCI. The party equally dreaded a U.S.-sponsored right-wing military coup as in Chile (the "K factor," symbolizing America's steadfast opposition to any communist or Euro-Communist governmental role in Western/NATO countries), as well as Moscow's opposition to Euro-Communist independence (with the risk of "excommunicating" the PCI by supporting its internal split and the emergence of a rival neo-Stalinist party).[47]

Meanwhile Autonomia steadily increased its violence under the influence of its more radical elements (from the disbanded Potere Operaio and Lotta Continua) and the intellectual leadership of Professor Toni Negri (Padova), Orazio Scalzone (Milan), Franco Piperno (Rome), Lanfranco Pace, and their newspaper *Rosso*. Autonomia's new goals were to seek operational coordination with the BR and to destabilize the state, while opposing the PCI/unions influence on the working class and Left (symbolically, Autonomia's goliardic "Metropolitan Red Indians" ignited in Rome the 1977 student riots by trashing in a mega-melee the PCI-supported trade unions rally at the University of Rome). The BR instead, manipulated Autonomia as a recruiting ground and rudimentary "fighting communist party" to expand their appeal and reach whenever they would be able to seize power. Yet the BR-Autonomia relationship (known only at its leading levels and involving only its most extreme fringes) was also fraught with deep internal political clashes, as well as routine cooperation (Negri published in the *Rosso* newspaper many BR documents, while his concept of the "Imperialist State controlled by the international multinational corporations" was loudly adopted by the BR too). Yet internal conflicts became extreme when Autonomia's leadership tried to exert political control over the BR before and during the Moro affair (by supporting Morucci and Faranda, leaders of the Movimentist wing in their fight for political control against Moretti's hardliners), as well as through the later Project Metropolis, a pseudocultural organization created by Piperno and Pace to secretly expand terrorism's popular support and establish unitarian coordination of all terrorist groups.[48]

Undoubtedly the killing of State Attorney Francesco Coco and his two-man escort in 1976 (he had opposed in 1974 any exchange of imprisoned BRs for the abducted Sossi), as well as of DC President Moro and escort in 1978, represented the most clamourous and best-organized surprise terrorist strikes at the democratic system (and an Italian "copycat version" of the German RAF's 1977 Schleyer Affair). Moro's abduction, "political trail," and execution, in particular, were part of a well-orchestrated strategy to destroy Moro's delicate political balancing of a government coalition including the PCI ("historical compromise") as the only solution to the country's crises and weakness. In fact the PCI's inclusion in a reform-minded, authoritative, "national emergency" government would have strengthened the state and favored the demise of the terrorist epidemic. Instead the dramatic symbolism of Moro's abduction just hours before the Parliament approved the new government rocked the crisis-ridden Italian system, destroying the "historical compromise" by politically wounding both DC and PCI, while rallying to the terrorists' cause vast proletarian support. The BR skillfully transformed Moro's "popular trial" (the real "godfather" of Italian politics) into a national and international showcase, publicized through BR communiqués and dozens of Moro's own prison letters to the DC leaders (with which he hoped to buy time and negotiate his way out by expounding the terrorists' requests and exhorting his shocked governing colleagues to work out a compromise). While Moro hoped for a negotiated breakthrough or an even more improbable police rescue raid, the BR hoped "to reveal to the people enormously damaging DC secrets" and wreck the government into capitulating to the terrorist demands (recognizing them as an official political antagoinst, and not merely bandits, and possibly even exchanging prisoners). Finally, Moro's "execution" would have forced the state to engage in unpopular repressive counteractions, further "exposing the true Fascist nature of the Imperialist Police-State."[49]

Instead the "Moro trial" also became the BR's political graveyard: Moro did not "confess" any devastating political secret or international subservience to the U.S. as hoped; the deeply divided political system suddenly rallied to the banner of the "sense of state" responsibility (yet a call traditionally unthought of by any Italian politician except in the most tense of crises) and rejected outright all BR conditions (Moro's release in exchange for all imprisoned terrorists, and recognition of the BR as a national political force); and moreover, the political credibility of Moro's embarrassing pleas and prison letters was doggedly and callously negated by the DC, the media, and the whole political establishment (excluding Craxi's pronegotiation socialists). Instead the DC power establishment (il Palazzo) shielded itself behind the preposterous assertion that Moro was either coerced and totally drugged (but how could he write otherwise in such a lucid way?), or had cracked down under the fear of death into cooperating wholeheartedly with the terrorists. Thus the devastating "Moro effect" was wholly eliminated from national policymaking by officially pronouncing him as "politically and civicly dead" well before his physical demise (thus discrediting both his importance as a captive hostage and leader, and as an embarrassing mediator between "his establishment friends" and the terrorists), all the while eulogizing the "good Moro" of past memories, whose role as a statesman, as a martyr of democracy and Christianity, made him the necessary and most vaunted symbolic "sacrificial lamb" of the state's innocence against brute terror. (Unfortunately, the still-living "bad Moro" kept "refusing to cooperate" from prison, vehemently protesting, unheard, his desire to survive the competing political death choreographies forged by both his captors and his "friends"!)

Finally the political clash inside the BR over Moro's fate split the terrorit front to the core. On one hand Morucci, Faranda, the BR Movimentist wing, and Autonomia's leadership pressed for Moro's release, fearing that his death would make him a martyr and unite a revengeful state behind a massive antiterrorist military onslaught and destroy both Red terrorism and Autonomia. Piperono and Pace, moreover, sought to exploit the BR's internal power struggle to impose their political leadership on the terrorist movement. On the other, Moretti and the BR hard-liners dominating the Roman column killed Moro to consolidate their own faltering authority over the BR and reimpose their uncompromising ideological vision, as well as to reap futher propaganda windfalls and expand recruitment from the radical Left.[50]

Both the Moro and Piazza Nicosia affairs totally exposed the state's ineptitude and inefficiency against terrorism. In fact, after ten years of terror no antiterrorist strategy yet existed, and even Questor Santillo's antiterrorist inspectorate had been disbanded. The Secret Services too were virtually nonexistent after being disbanded and prosecuted three times in 20 years for their complicity with Black extremism. The police did not fare better: Notwithstanding their large manpower and search warrants, Moro's secret prison could not be found until months later, while police and Secret Services kept separate, incomplete files and spent most of their efforts trying to out-maneuver each other rather than the terrorists. Under these humiliating circumstances, Minister of Interior Cossiga resigned, while the "historical compromise" slowly whittled away: Prime Minister Giulio Andreotti, although closely collaborating with the PCI (not officially included in the government in 1978 and 1979, but treated as a leading member nevertheless), extracted Berlinguer's political support for deep controversial national economic and judicial reforms regardless of the political costs for the PCI, while still refusing to repay the PCI's loyalty with official full governmental leadership.

By 1980 the PCI returned to the opposition again, but not before the DC-controlled political system had partially recovered from the politico-economic crisis and started a highly successful antiterrorist drive. In fact, by 1979 the reorganized antiterrorist apparatus and controversial new laws expanded police powers and favored the repentance of imprisoned terrorists by trading drastically shortened life sentences in exchange for complete confessions and the betrayal of their peers (1979 Cossiga Act; 1982 Act on the

Repentants). Both the slowly increasing surge of mass confessions and the new police powers allowed the state to mount relentless nationwide waves of arrests, shootouts, and imprisonment of hundreds of terrorists and extremists, including the entire BR and Autonomia leaderships.[51]

Yet the decimation of the BR "second generation" in 1979 and 1980, and of all smaller Red terrorist groups, did not extinguish terrorism as hoped: a new BR third generation suddenly surfaced in 1981 with unexpected vitality, kidnapping five officers, killing another four, and perpetuating daytime bank robberies and armed propaganda in factories and city squares (Rome, Milan, Turin, Naples). These new blows were remarkable both for their organizational efficiency (for the first time four targets were contemporaneously abducted in different cities by a perfectly coordinated action between local BR columns), as well as for the symbolic choice of targeting the country's politico-economic-military structure. Two abducted were leading northern industrial managers (reflecting the BR's traditional anticapitalist tactics against the "Imperialist Multinational State"). In Naples the victim was a prominent DC leader in charge of state reconstruction after the 1979 earthquake (underlining the BR's new interest in exasperating existing socioeconomic cleavages between the unemployed and the state). The last victim was the innocent brother of Peci, the most famous "repented" terrorist: For the first time, the BR's deadly revenge turned on the innocent families of repented terrorists, whose confessions had decimated the secret "firing columns." By killing innocent relatives, the BR severed the only social value they had always respected in a desperate effort to stop the wave of confessions and arrests (Peci's brother and one industrialist were killed, the other two were released under ransom), but in the end this only hastened the inevitable.[52]

Finally, the abduction in late 1981 of the American NATO General John L. Dozier in Vicenza by the Savasta group symbolized the BR's first attack on foreign military personnel in Italy and on Italy's role in NATO. By "internationalizing" their fight and imitating similar anti-NATO terrorist acts perpetrated by the German RAF, the BR attempted to mask their weaknesses by ideologically revamping their third worldist and "anti-imperialist" myths against U.S. "neocolonialism" and U.S. military presence abroad. Even more worrisome was the discovery that in the whirlpool of foreign secret services' involvement in Italian affairs, the Bulgarians (well known for their local espionage on behalf of the KGB) had unsuccessfully tried to obtain NATO secrets from the BR holding Dozier. The Savasta group refused, for fear of being entrapped in a deadly spy game which, after exploiting the surviving BR for anti-NATO purposes, would then sacrifice them to the Italian police (similarly, all BR groups in the past had doggedly resisted strong foreign interferences, manipulation, or controls, for fear of losing their own ideological purity and independence). Italy's intelligence instead, while resisting strong U.S. pressures, finally succeeded in penetrating the terrorists' weakest new echelons (the BR's desperate effort to re-create lost cadres had dangerously lowered security by recruiting vulnerable drug-addicted youths). With carefully planned raids in early 1982 by special combat swat teams ("Teste di Cuoio"), General Dozier was freed and all remaining terrorist groups (Red and Black) wiped out. Logistic bases, arms caches, and apartment bases were seized around-the-clock, while 1045 terrorists were arrested in 1982 along (867 Red and 178 Black), adding to the 1837 already imprisoned extremists (1357 Red and 480 Black).[53]

Terrorism's final collapse was the result of several causes:

(1) The police's newly efficient antiterrorist efforts.
(2) The terrorists' endemic internal factionalism and politico-moral crisis after the

Moro affair, which led many of them to betray the group once captured (also the RAF leaders, once defeated, lost their inner politico-moral drive and committed suicide).

(3) New legislative acts favoring repented terrorists' collaboration.

(4) Popular hostility and shrinking recruitment.

The state had won, yet Red terrorism had not totally disappeared. Although the economy boomed in 1980, all the national social roots of dissatisfaction had not been solved by the state. Instead the country's mood had changed and the fad of political extremism withered, most of the repented ex-terrorists had been released from prison (and often expatriated to protect their security), and other condemned terrorists and Autonomia leaders (Negri, Scalzone) abandoned the struggle and exiled themselves abroad (France). Yet a few among the BR terrorists still at large always refused to surrender, and two to three times a year from 1982 to 1989, they regrouped to commit a few scattered, dramatic murders (in 1983 the U.S. Ambassador William Hunt, head of the Multilateral Force Organization in Rome patroling the Sinai after the U.S.-Israeli-Egyptian Camp David Accords; in 1985 the PCI economics professor Enrico Taliercio at the State University of Rome; in 1986 the Italian army general Luigi Galvaligi; in 1988 a personal top aide to a DC minister; and some others). But however deadly, and linked to international terrorism, this fading BR threat against the system is now virtually nonexistent, given the frequent police raids and the impossibility of the surviving BR to rebuild their original terror network.[54]

With regard to the other Red terrorist groups of the 1970s, the majority remained rather limited in their geographico-ideological influence and in the sophistication of their attacks. Moreover, their own organizational weakness and the state's counterattacks led to their rapid dissolution and/or absorption by the BR. The most important ones were the Circolo XXII Ottobre (formed by disillusioned ex-PCI Stalinists), and the Partisan Action Groups (GAP) (by extra-parlamentarian leftist radicals, old communist partisans, migrant workers, as well as politicized Sardinian bandits and common criminals). Contemporaries of the BR, the Circolo XXII Ottobre briefly operated in Genova, but was soon decimated by the police, and its surviving members were subsequently absorbed by the GAP, financed by the publisher Feltrinelli. Operating in Milan, Genova, and the neighboring countryside, the GAP attacked shipyards, oil refineries, warehouses, and industries. But early attempts to merge with the BR failed for tactical reasons: The BR insisted on a rigidly urban-guerrilla warfare, while the GAP stressed rural attacks. Thus a practical division of operational responsibilities ensued between them until Feltrinelli's death in 1972 (he accidentally blew himself up while mining a power line near Milan), which forced the GAP to merge with the BR.

The Neapolitan Armed Proletarian Nucleus (NAP) was formed in 1974 by radical Lotta Continua extremists and "politicized" converted common criminals (with extensive contacts in the prison system). Their goal was to generalize the armed struggle into the streets and especially the prisons to liberate the "wretched of the earth." Quickly expanding to Rome and the North, they financed themselves through armed robberies, kidnappings, and bombings, while adopting the BR's more sophisticated techniques of ambushes, murders, political abductions, and knee-capping. Although operating jointly with the BR in attacking police barracks and facilities nationwide, the NAP's suicidal carelessness with explosives, rudimental security, and inability to replace lost cadres (dead or imprisoned) forced them to merge in 1978 with the BR, who inherited the NAP's strategy of recruiting common criminals and targeting the prison system.[55]

Prima Linea (a 1976 offshoot of Turin's Lotta Continua security service) was the most successful rival of the BR, raiding and bombing industrial facilities. Having overcome initial costly mistakes with explosives and security, it rapidly expanded to Milan, Florence, Naples, and Cosenza, paralleling the BR's operational sophistication and sharing their ideologico-military goals. While cooperating with the BR since 1978, their major difference remained the policy of semiclandestinity, alternating covert activities with sudden open-air political activities for propaganda indoctrination. Their most important action was the carefully planned, spectacular 1979 broad-daylight seizure of the Turin School of Industrial Management, overpowering 130 professors, students, and staff, and wounding 10 professors in a symbolic mass leg-shooting before disappearing. But after the police's 1980 "great spring offensive," and mass confessions by repented members, Prima Linea also collapsed, its remaining militants joining the surviving BR units.

Other minor Red terrorist groups were more difficult to analyze after 1976, given their complete emulation of the BR and Prima Linea operational techniques, and often close connections as training appendices of the larger groups. While the rural pro-BR Barbagia Rossa remained mainly committed to a confused idea of Sardinian separatism, only the Unita' Comuniste Combattenti emerged with an individual personality and social-populist strategy, capturing the media's attention (as when they kidnapped a wealthly Roman meat-dealer and released him in exchange for the free distribution of underpriced meats). However, all minor terrorist groups were also wiped out by the 1980 police raids.[56]

International Connections: Transnational Terrorism and Foreign Financers

Italy's terrorism was the direct ultimate result of domestic politico-cultural cleavages and frustrations affecting the society at large, caught in a pluridecennial struggle between self-disillusionment (the impossiblity of becoming a respected international politico-economic power) and survival (from a host of recurrent domestic crises). Still we should not discount the yet unclear role of foreign influences. Indeed, since 1970 the possible interrelations between domestic terror, foreign terrorists, and subversive states has been hotly but unconclusively debated in the media and Parliament.

Both Paris and London had been traditional hideouts for international and Italian terrorists, political refugees, and spies (with neo-Fascists preferring London and Latin America, while Reds relocated to the culturally stimulating Paris). France's permissive asylum policy for foreign political refugees benefited scores of Italian extremists on the run and the top leadership of Autonomia in the 1980s (Negri, Scalzone, Piperno). Yet the infamous Black international network, which had helped the postwar Black extremists seek safe havens abroad and keep political-military ties, has now almost waned away, although until the late 1970s it still helped many Italian neo-Fascists relocate in Latin American dictatorships (Argentina, Paraguay, Uruguay, Chile, Brazil). Time and the 1974–1975 collapse of neighboring safe-havens in the Mediterranean (Franco's Spain, the Greek military regime, Portugal, the Lebanese Civil War), as well as the general prodemocratic trend influencing most of Latin America, has made it increasingly dangerous ever since for Black extremists to find stable refuge abroad except in Paraguay or Chile (as Delle Chiaie and Gelli discovered when extradited from Argentina and Uruguay).[57]

Regular contacts between Italian terrorists (especially the BR) and the German RAF went on since the early 1970s, and with the French Action Directe since the late 1970s.

Italian Terrorism, 1940s–1980s   279

The BR-RAF relationship was especially strong, with frequent Italian journeys by German terrorists. Both shared the Marxist-Leninist vision of being a revolutionary vanguard, the common deep dogmatic misunderstanding of the proletariat's real needs, the rejection of capitalism's wealth-oriented society and international multinational system, and the praise of a mythical anticolonial third world. Although both sought through terror to unmask the state's "true Fascist nature" by provoking its repression, neither seemed capable of following up and theorizing coherent strategic goals for their revolution, favoring instead only naked terror over political plans. However, BR and RAF frequently exchanged weapons and ideological debates on their common struggle, with the BR paradoxically pressing their German colleagues to open up to their own societal needs and be less pro-Soviet.

Italian terrorists developed strong ties also with the French Action Directe, with whom they exchanged weapons and explosives. But more importantly they benefited from the political support and sanctuary offered by Paris's cultural milieu; both the linguistic institute Hyperion (created by Simioni and Mulinaris, cofounders of the BR in 1969 with Curcio and Cagol) and the Centre International de Culture Populaire, were cultural covers for the terrorists' international contacts. Other similar centers who sheltered Negri and other leaders of Autonomia abroad were under strong Soviet influence: the Centre International Nouvelles Espaces de Liberté, the Conseil Mondial de la Paix and the Centre Henry Curiel. The Hyperion institute, especially, favored BR contacts with French and German terrorists, as well as the PLO, the Irish Republican Army (IRA), and the Basque ETA (but the strong nationalistic component of the Irish and Basque terrorism prevented serious political ties). German and French terrorists were arrested in Italy in the late 1970s for supplying weapons to their Italian counterparts, while some form of joint but unproven Italo-German terrorist coordination was strongly suspected in both the Moro and Dozier cases (the former was closely modeled on the 1977 Schleyer abduction by the RAF, while the latter was the BR's first contribution to the international-German terrorist campaign against U.S. and NATO installations). Also, several Italian terrorists were tracked down and arrested in France by joint Franco-Italian police raids in the early 1980s, most notably eight Prima Linea militants in Paris and three BR in Toulon in 1980.[58]

While traditional Latin American contacts remained minor (notwithstanding Feltrinelli's personal ties to Fidel Castro), early PLO-BR relations, also organized by Feltrinelli in the late 1960s, expanded by the mid-1970s through the Institute Hyperion. The BR's deadly efficiency, in fact, had won the Palestinians' admiration, who sought unsuccessfully to trade their support in exchange for BR attacks on Israeli and NATO targets in Italy. Instead, Palestinian terrorists and Libya provided to Italian and other transnational terrorists military training in Libya and Lebanon (until Israel's 1982 intervention destroyed the local PLO terrorist bases), while selling and shipping large quantities of modern weapons and even Soviet-made bazookas (smuggled by PLO terrorists apprehended in Italy during one of these arms transfers). Much ambiguity still surrounds all claims of international conspiracies, especially alleged U.S. involvement in the Moro affair (in revenge for his opening to the PCI, as his simple-minded widow doggedly insists, although the menacing and abusive Kissinger of her recollections was long out of power), or Israel's secret service (Mossad) in the attempt to use the BR in 1975 to destabilize an increasingly pro-Arab Italy and force the U.S. to increase instead its politico-economic and military relationship with a more loyalist Israel.[59]

However, the most important influence on Italian terrorism has come from the Soviet and Eastern European secret services (especially Czechoslovakia). Throughout the 1970s, Italian authorities ambiguously dismissed any rumors of Soviet-Eastern Bloc influence on domestic Red terrorism (correctly assessing the Reds as internally originated and financed). Yet parallel to this, Rome regularly and quietly expelled large numbers of Czech and Eastern Bloc diplomats as secret agents: 29 were expelled in 1968 after the student unrests; 21 more expulsions were planned in 1972 after Feltrinelli's death, but then the DC premier Andreotti let the matter drop; 19 others were expelled from 1975 to 1978 during the Red terrorist peak, with scores of later unconfirmable reports of Czech diplomatic cover for BR getaways during the Moro abduction. Once out of office, Andreotti publicly admitted in a 1974 parliamentary hearing his full knowlege of Czechoslovakian involvement in training during the late 1960s, and first generation of Italian Red terrorists; yet by 1980 he retracted his previous statements regardless of all evidence to the contrary.

It now seems certain, however, that both the flamboyant publisher Feltrinelli and the BR's "historical leadership," as well as a few other terrorists, frequently visited Prague, where they undertook secret guerrilla training from 1968 to the early 1970s. Also, General Jan Sejna of the Czech intelligence, after defecting to the West before the 1968 Soviet invasion of Czechoslovakia, repeatedly confirmed the fundamental role played by the Soviet KGB and GRU (military intelligence) in using Czechoslovakia since 1964 as a major training ground for international and Italian terrorists. These facts, and the intensification of terrorist movements in and out of that country, were subsequently confirmed in 1970 by the Milan prefect Luigi Mazza and in 1980 by repented terrorist leader Peci, regardless of the continuous public dismissals by the Italian establishment (until the early 1980s when President of the Republic Sandro Pertini strongly and dramatically condemned all "Eastern European and Soviet complicities" in fomenting Italian terrorism). Yet Peci's confessions, while pinpointing foreign logistic support, always stressed also that no foreign interferences directed or influenced the BR's strategy and ideology. Therefore, notwithstanding the Italian terrorist ties and frequent contacts (mostly arms and finances) with international terrorists, the PLO, and foreign powers, neither of them ever succeeded in masterminding or influencing Italy's terrorism, which remained essentially a domestically generated, internally oriented and controlled movement.[60]

However, dark conspiracy theories and the disturbing contradictory Western policy of half-confirmations and open rebuttals were cunningly rationalized by Claire Sterling's controversial claims of a secret Soviet proxy strategy in supporting international terrorism. By using satellites (Czechoslovakia, Bulgaria, Cuba), client states (Syria, PLO) and friends (Libya, North Korea), the Kremlin would never risk being exposed while coordinating the flow of arms, training, and financing and providing sanctuaries and international connections for international terrorism. Training camps and safe havens, moreover, are scattered globally, according to regional state-supported terrorist strategies (North Korea, Cuba, Syria, Libya, Lebanon, Algeria, South Yemen, Eastern Europe, and in Russia's countryside too).[61] Moreover, ideologically and practically,

> Cuba and the Palestinian resistance . . . had better revolutionary credentials
> than Soviet Russia for the 1968 generation, and a more magnetic appeal for
> the Third World.[62]

If violence breeds violence, the logic of leftist terrorist tactics is disturbing both in its goals and its methods, which paradoxically emulate right-wing ones: Terrorism is used to radicalize and destroy Western democracies through internal reactionary coups, while attacking unions, media, election officers, judiciary, moderate leftist personalities, and independent left-leading governments. Since 1968, international terrorism has seemed to flourish mainly in industrialized Western democracies and the crisis-ridden third world, while leaving almost unscathed the Communist Bloc countries and most right-wing dictatorships. If we cast aside ethnic-religious terrorism, rampant throughout the third world, political international terrorism according to Sterling is aimed mainly at subverting the West and NATO, while it cannot thrive in the rigidly repressive communist and Fascist societies. Yet according to this highly sophisticated conspiracy theory, Moscow's role in enhancing domestic cleavages and terrorist outbursts, had no immediate revolutionary aspiration. Well aware of the terrorist's limited insurgency capability, Moscow instead would easily have used terrorism as a stealth weapon to weaken and demoralize the West, so that overriding domestic concerns would prevent their effective cooperation against the Soviet empire.[63]

Western reluctance to cooperate against terrorism, or expose Moscow's occult support of international terror, depended instead on a combination of factors: the "unconfirmed and uncontrollable nature" of foreign mastermind allegations; the domestic presence of large leftist politico-economic forces; the difficulty of retaliating against the East (where terrorism is claimed to be the result of the Western "rotten democratic societies"); the fear of rocking an unstable East-West détente, with unpleasant political and commercial consequences; the paralyzing role of nationalisms in stalling international antiterrorist coordination and extradition among the West; the relatively low degree of transnational terrorist coordination of strategies and objectives; the mainly domestic nature of most terrorist phenomena compared to the politically charged, obscure foreign or Soviet arms and financial support to existing local extremists (yet even a Mussolini, well known in the 1930s for his state-sponsored terrorism in Europe, could underline the strong political responsibilities binding semi-independent terrorists and their proxy financers).[64]

Although in the late 1970s and early 1980s Libya and Islamic Iran emerged as major financers and "godfathers" for international terrorism, their role has abated in the 1980s. Palestinian terrorism was severely wounded by Israel's 1982 Lebanese campaign, which destroyed the PLO bases, scattering the fedayeen in new unfortified camps throughout the Arab world (under heavy local control, to prevent armed PLO "states within a state" as in Jordan in 1970 and Lebanon 1975–1982). Syria then masterminded an inner split of the PLO against Arafat during a major power struggle for political control beginning in 1983. Equally important had been also the mounting Libyan domestic economic difficulties stemming from the oil glut; the Western economic sanctions/boycotts; the depletion of finances for expensive arsenal building (yet the unused weapons stocked in the desert suffer weather erosion too); the lavish support of all terrorist causes worldwide; and the Chadian military intervention. Libya's declining support for international terrorism was briefly revived from 1983 to 1986 during her political clash with the United States, Britain, and France, and her defeats in Chad. But the unprecedented 1986 U.S. air raids on Libyan military targets (in retaliation for her sponsorship of anti-American terrorism), and the 1986–1987 Libyan defeat in Chad, compelled Qaddafi to minimize his open support of terror. Also, Iran and the Lebanese terrorists have reduced their activities.[65]

Finally, even more controversies seemed to erupt out of the dramatic 1981 attempt to kill Pope John Paul II, which trapped in a complex web of deceit the Italian government, the Bulgarian diplomatic and secret services, the Turkish "Mafia," and political extremists. The clamor of the case, the transnational arrests and trials of Turkish extremists, criminals, and Bulgarian agents (other diplomats involved were hastily repatriated), also ignited endless politico-diplomatic quarrels between Rome, Sofia, Ankara, and Moscow, especially when the convict felon Ali Agca reversed himself and openly accused the Bulgarian secret services (and the KGB) of masterminding the failed assassination attempt. Moscow's interest in "liquidating" the pope through Bulgarian and Turkish proxies steemed from the Vatican's political support and secret financing of the Polish Solidarnosc trade union, whose defiant fight in 1981 had almost destroyed the Polish communist regime.

Although in the end Agca's unsubstantiated confessions and notorious unreliability discredited even his most interesting allegations, the bitterness of the Italian authorities in tracking Bulgarian complicities stemmed also from Sofia's past espionage record in Italy on behalf of the KGB and her 1982 bumbled attempt to obtain NATO secrets from the BR when it was holding U.S. General Dozier. Interestingly enough, the United States (normally the leading anti-Soviet critic) repeatedly warned Italy in private of the impossibility of proving Moscow's involvement in international terrorism or in the pope's case. In the end the Agca case popped empty, with all accused released but Agca. Although suspicions are hard to quell, the repeated allegations of Soviet terrorist complicity have waned, especially now that the Kremlin has been totally absorbed by its own economic and leadership problems.[66]

Conclusion: What Defense Against Terrorism?

Are there any effective defenses against terrorism in an increasingly integrated, interdependent, high-tech, but vulnerable world? Almost 15 years of terror in Italy might suggest the opposite, or at least might underline the difficulty of wiping out domestic terrorism without losing in the process those very democratic values that terrorism seeks to destroy. Kupperman and Trent put much hope in an antiterrorist strategy based on (1) intelligence, (2) target hardening of installations and individuals, (3) damage limitation through cost-benefit analyses, (4) integrated crisis management covering all possible occurrences, (5) a balance of actions (to preserve civil liberties while fighting terror) and media self-restraint (to prevent the terrorists from engaging in bloody propagandistic attacks to win media coverage), and (6) international cooperation.[67]

All of this was finally applied by Italy during the late 1970s to counteract terrorism, but the final success came ony as a result of combined massive police raids and dramatic confessions by repentant terrorists, enticed to betray their peers by the promise of easy prison terms. Thus, using such questionable methods, Italy succeeded in overcoming her past intelligence and counterterrorism weaknesses. Yet repression alone is not a solution and can backfire if the domestic socioeconomic and political roots of terrorism are not addressed too. No society can live indefinitely with widespread terror in its midst; yet it must avoid the opposite psychological trap of indiscriminate bloody counterterrorism and torture. Otherwise the price of destroying terrorism would be the disintegration of national social values. Fragile and weak democracies would find it the most difficult to justify indiscriminate counterterrorism by appealing to positive social symbolisms (courage, patriotism, idealism, equity, etc.). The society's moral fiber instead would fall prey either to the terrorist onslaught and mass hysteria or to government-led repression, thus besieging the whole society with death, fear, and violence (as happened in Argentina and Uruguay in reaction to Tupamaros and Montoneros terrorism, and as almost happened in France during the Algerian War and in Britain during the Northern Irish terrorism).

Thus only when the socioeconomic roots of terrorism are fully eliminated will the dark politico-cultural symbols of violence be rejected by the society, and only when the state has subordinated counterterror to higher moral values (avoiding indiscriminate torture or counterviolence) will the dark romantic vitality of domestic terrorism wane and its perpetuators die. Parallel to effective counterterrorism, the state must never forget that only appropriate socioeconomic and political reforms will really overcome the domestic causes of terrorism. Thus, regardless of existing international connections and financiers, terrorism should never simply be labeled a political demon or a foreign plot devoid of internal causes. In most cases, instead, it is a terrible domestic socio-politico-cultural cancer, corrupting from the inside any "stagnant" society, incapable of overcoming its inner contradictions and fragility. Prevention often can really be the best counteraction to the terrorist threat, rather than blind and idle waiting for the "barbarians among us."[68]

Notes

1. Franco Ferracuti, "A Socio-Psychiatric Interpretation of Terrorism", in *Annals of the American Academy of Psychiatric Social Sciences* 463 (September 1982):129–40; Leonard Weinberg and William L. Eubank, *The Rise and Fall of Italian Terrorism* (Boulder, CO: Westview Press, 1987), pp. 1–2; Francesco Bruno, "Il Terrorismo, Aspetti Generali e Definitori," in *Note sul Terrorismo: Appunti per una Ricerca Criminologica*, ed. Francesco Bruno (Roma: U.G.R.I.S.-Universitas, 1984), pp. 7–10; Massimo Carducci, *Componenti Storico-Sociali del Terrorismo in Italia ed in alcuni Paesi Europei*, Laurea dissertation, (Roma: Universita' La Sapienza, 1985), pp. i–ii, 82, 95–96; Bruno, "Problematiche relative al Fenomeno del cosiddetto Pentitismo," in *Note sul Terrorismo*, ed. F. Bruno, p. 79; Robert H. Kupperman and David M. Trent, *Terrorism* (Stanford, CA: Stanford University Press, 1979), pp. 1–6; Richard E. Rubenstein, *Alchemists of Revolution* (New York: Basic Books, 1987), pp. xiii–xxi, 3–85, 195–236; Walter Laqueur, *Terrorism* (Boston: Little, Brown, 1977), pp. 2–16; Benjamin Netanyahu, "Defining Terrorism," in *Terrorism: How the West can Win*, ed. B. Netanyahu (New York: Farrar, Straus & Giroux, 1986), pp. 3–9; Geoffrey M. Levitt, ed., *Democracies Against Terror*, CSIS, (New York: Praeger, 1988), pp. 1–24; Brian M. Jenkins, *Talking to Terrorists* (Santa Monica, CA: Rand Corporation, 1982), pp. 5–15; Alex Schmidt, *Political Terrorism* (New Brunswick, NJ: Transaction Books, 1983); Leonardo Sciascia, *L'Affaire Moro* (Palermo: Sellerio Ed., 1978), pp. 18–21, 77–78; Robin E. Wagner-Pacifici, *The Moro Morality Play* (Chicago: University of Chicago Press, 1986), pp. 58–61, 234–35; David C. Rapoport, *Assassination and Terrorism* (Toronto: CBC Merchandising, 1971), pp. 5–42; and in *Inside Terrorist Organizations* ed. D. C. Rapoport (New York: Columbia University Press, 1988), see: D. C. Rapoport, "Introduction," pp. 1–10; Martha Crenshaw, "Theories of Terrorism: Instrumental and Organizational Approaches," pp. 13–31; Bonnie Cordes, "When Terrorists do the Talking: Reflections on Terrorist Literature," pp. 150–71; and Grant Wardlaw, "Terror as an Instrument of Foreign Policy," pp. 237–59.

2. Niccolo' Machiavelli, *The Prince and other Political Discourses* (New York: Penguin Classics, 1985); Marcel Prélot and Georges Lescuyer, *Histoire des Idees Politiques* (Paris: Dalloz, 1984), pp. 206–17, 595–632; Carducci, *Componenti Storico-Sociali*, pp. i–ii, 82, 95–96; Weinberg and Eubank, *Rise and Fall of Italian Terrorism*, pp. 19–21; Alessandro Coletti, *Anarchici e Questori* (Padova: Marsilio, 1971), pp. 7–8; Charles Tilly, Louise Tilly, and Richard Tilly, *The Rebellious Century* (Cambridge, MA: Harvard University Press, 1975), pp. 304–309; Pier-Carlo Masini, *Storia degli Anarchici Italiani nell'Epoca degli Attentati* (Milano: Rizzoli, 1981); Romano Canosa and Amadeo Santuosso, *Magistrati, Anarchici e Socialisti* (Milano: Feltrinelli, 1981); Wagner-Pacifici, *Moro Morality Play*, pp. 47–49, 284–85; Rubenstein, *Alchemists of Revolution*, pp. 56, 59, 141–57; Lev Trotzkiy, *Against Individual Terrorism* (New York: Pathfinder, 1974).

284   M. Rimanelli

3. Weinberg and Eubank, *Rise and Fall of Italian Terrorism*, pp. 21–24; Renzo De Felice, *Mussolini il Fascista: la Conquista del Potere, 1921–1925* (Turin: Einaudi, 1966); Carducci, *Componenti Storico-Sociali*, pp. i–ii, 82, 95–96; Federico Chabod, *L'Italia Contemporanea* (Turin: Einaudi, 1961), pp. 41–89; Adrian Lyttelton, *The Seizure of Power: Fascism in Italy, 1919–29* (London: Weidenfeld and Nicolson, 1973); Wagner-Pacifici, *Moro Morality Play*, pp. 16, 25, 29, 33–35, 48, 82, 109, 293; Mario Cancogni, *Gli Squadristi* (Milano: Longanesi, 1980); Denis Mack-Smith, *Mussolini* (New York: Vintage Press, 1982), pp. 3–86; Carlo Maletti, "Immagine, Pubblicita' e Ideologia del Terrorismo," in *Dimensioni del Terrorismo Politico*, ed. Luigi Bonante (Milano: Angeli Ed., 1979); Charles Delzell, *Mussolini's Enemies* (Princeton: Princeton University Press, 1961), pp. 5–160; Jean-Baptiste Duroselle, *Histoire Diplomatique de 1919 à nos Jours* (Paris: Dalloz, 1970), pp. 22–25, 71–72, 91–93, 157–60, 214, 270–71.

4. Chabod, *L'Italia Contemporanea*, pp. 74–143; Delzell, *Mussolini's Enemies*, pp. 5–243; Mack-Smith, *Mussolini*, pp. 143–45; Weinberg and Eubank, *Rise and Fall of Italian Terrorism*, pp. 23–24; Duroselle, *Histoire Diplomatique*, pp. 169–385; Norman Kogan, *Italy and the Allies* (Cambridge, MA: Harvard University Press, 1956); Giorgio Bocca, *Storia dell'Italia Partigiana* (Bari: Laterza, 1977), pp. 5–130, 135–41, 207–15; Soccorso Rosso, eds., *Brigate Rosse* (Milano: Feltrinelli, 1976), pp. 13–14.

5. Antonio Minucci, *Terrorismo e Crisi Italiana, Intervista di Jochen Kreimer* (Roma: Editori Riuniti, 1978); Luigi Garruccio, *Italia senza Eroi* (Milano: Rusconi, 1980), pp. 242–45; Weinberg and Eubank, *Rise and Fall of Italian Terrorism*, pp. 1–6, 25–26; Bruno, "Il Terrorismo," in *Note sul Terrorismo*, ed. F. Bruno, pp. 7–10; Bruno, "Il Terrorismo Politico Italiano," ibid., pp. 27–49; Stefano Silvestri and Marizio Cremasco, *Il Fianco Sud della NATO*, I.A.I. (Milano: Feltrinelli, 1982); Wagner-Pacifici, *Moro Morality Play*, pp. 22–33, 36–37; 40–43, 46–47, 55–58, 63–64. 71–80, 102, 123–25, 145–66, 174–80, 193–94, 202–203, 207–209, 215–16, 233–40, 275–276; Luigi Graziano and Sidney Tarrow eds., *La Crisi Italiana*, 2 vols. (Torino: Einaudi, 1979), pp. 3–558, 609–763; N. Kogan, *A Political History of Italy* (New York: Praeger, 1983), pp. 1–291; L. Sciascia, *L'Affaire Moro*, pp. 38–44, 46–65, 87–93.

6. VittorFranco Pisano, *Structure and Dynamics of Italian Terrorism* (Gaithersburg, MD: International Association of Chiefs of Police, 1980), pp. 1–2; Sergio Provvisionato, "Bilancio del Terrorismo '81: Diminuiti gli Attentati ma cambia la Strategia," *Il Progresso* (Jersey City, NJ), January 3, 1982, p. 10; Mauro Galleni, ed., *Rapporto sul Terrorismo* (Milano: Rizzoli, 1981); pp. 3–49; Bruno, "Il Terrorismo Politico Italiano," in *Note sul Terrorismo* ed. F. Bruno. pp. 27–49; L. Sciascia, *L'Affaire Moro*, pp. 38–44, 46–65, 77–93, 104–108, 117–22, 130–37; Weinberg and Eubank, *Rise and Fall of Italian Terrorism*, pp. 77–118.

7. Ferracuti, "A Socio-Psychiatric Interpretation." pp. 129–40; Garruccio, *Italia senza Eroi*, pp. 246–47; Franco Ferrarotti, *L'Ipnosi della Violenza* (Milano: Rizzoli, 1980), pp. 36–51; Weinberg and Eubank, *Rise and Fall of Italian Terrorism*, pp. 6–13, 19–21, 31, 41, 53–54; Pisano, *Structure and Dynamics*, pp. 1–2; Claire Sterling, *The Terror Network* (New York: Holt, Rinehart and Winston, 1981), and *The Time of the Assassins* (New York: Holt, Rinehart and Winston, 1983); Bruno, ed., *Note sul Terrorismo*, especially Bruno, "Il Terrorismo Politico Italiano" (pp. 27–49), Bruno and Ferracuti, "Aspetti Psicopatologici ed Aspetti Socio-Politici nel Terrorismo Politico Italiano" (pp. 50–67), and Bruno, "Il Fenomeno del Terrorismo in Italia: Aspetti Metodologici di Studio e di Prevedibilita'" (pp. 11–26); Giovanna Guidorossi, *Gli Italiani e la Politica* (Milano: Angeli, 1984), pp. 59–65; Mino Monicelli, *L'Ultrasinistra in Italia, 1968–78* (Bari: Laterza, 1978), pp. 33–41; Luigi Bonante, ed., *Dimensioni del Terrorismo Politico*; Marino Regni, "Labor Unions, Industrial Action and Politics," in *Italy in Transition*, ed. Peter Lange and Sidney Tarrow (London: Frank Cass, 1980), pp. 49–66; Sergio Turone, *Storia del Sindacato in Italia* (Bari: Laterza, 1975), pp. 488–99; Prélot and Lescuyer, *Histoire del Idees Politiques*, pp. 206–217, 566–78, 595–646, 650–92; Giordano B. Guerri, ed., *Patrizio Peci: Io l'Infame* (Milano: Mondadori, 1983), pp. 171–72; Sabino Acquaviva, *Il Seme Religioso della Rivolta* (Milano: Rusconi, 1979), pp. 16–42; S. Acquaviva, *Guerriglia e Guerra Rivoluzionaria in Italia* (Milano: Rizzoli, 1979), pp. 17–28; Rubenstein, *Alchemists of Revolution*, pp. 49–64. 89–191.

8. Giuseppe Mammarella, *Italy After Fascism* (Montreal: Casalini, 1969), pp. 75–358; L. Garruccio, *Italia senza Eroi*, pp. 242–45; Alessandro Silj, *Mai piu' senza Fucile!* (Firenze: Vallecchi, 1977), p. XIII; Bruno, "Il Fenomeno del Terrorismo in Italia: Aspetti Metodologici di Studio e di Prevedibilita'," *Note sul Terrorismo*, pp. 19–22; F. Ferracuti, "A Socio-Psychiatric Interpretation," pp. 138–40; Pisano, *Structure and Dynamics*, pp. 2–3; F. Chabod, *L'Italia Contemporanea*, pp. 137–84; Kogan, *Political History of Italy*, pp. 1–42, 45–59; Giampiero Carocci, *Storia d'Italia dall'Unita' ad Oggi* (Milano: Feltrinelli, 1975), pp. 322–50; Donald L. M. Blackmer, "Continuity and Change in Post-war Italian Communism," in *Communism in Italy and France*, ed. Donald L. M. Blackmer and Sidney Tarrow (Princeton, NJ: Princeton University Press, 1977), pp. 32–58; Le Monde, *L'Economie Italienne sans Miracle* (Paris: Economica, 1980), pp. 13–23, 73–77, 155–62; Graziano and Tarrow, eds., *La Crisi Italiana*, pp. 3–763; Acquaviva, *Seme Religioso della Rivolta*, pp. 16–42; Acquaviva, *Guerriglia e Guerra*, pp. 17–28; Donatella della Porta, "Le Cause del Terrorismo nelle Societa' Contemporanee," in *Terrorismo e Violenza Politica*, ed. Gianfrano Pasquino and D. della Porta (Bologna: Mulino, 1983), pp. 19–38; Weinberg and Eubank, *Rise and Fall of Italian Terrorism*, pp. 13–21, 24–26; Miriam Mafai, *L'Uomo che sognava la Lotta Armata* (Milano: Rizzoli, 1984), pp. 4–71; Wagner-Pacifici, *Moro Morality Play*, pp. 25–26, 105–106, 171.

9. Graziano and Tarrow, eds., *La Crisi Italiana*, pp. 3–422, 609–756; della Porta, "Le Cause del Terrorismo," pp 19–38; Weinberg and Eubank, *Rise and Fall of Italian Terrorism*, pp. 13–19, 32, 135–39; Howard Penniman, ed., *Italy at the Polls 1976 & 1979* (Washington, DC: American Enterprise Institute, 1977 and 1981); Garruccio, *Italia senza Eroi*, pp. 242, 246–47; Ferracuti, "A Socio-Psychiatric Interpretation," pp. 138–40; Peter Lange and Sidney Tarrow, eds., *Italy in Transition*; Kogan, *A Political History of Italy*, pp. 224–40, 277–91, 293–324, 329–42; L. J. Wollemborg, *Stelle, Strisce e Tricolore* (Milano: Mondadori, 1983), pp. 226–582; Carocci, *Storia d'Italia*, pp. 322–64; Guidorossi, *Gli Italiani e la Politica*, pp. 5–65; Robinson Rojas, *The Murder of Allende and the End of the Chilean Way to Socialism* (New York: Harper & Row, 1976); Blackmer, "Continuity and Change," pp. 3–15, 22–23, 55–68; Robert D. Putnam, "The Italian Communist Politician," in Blackmer and Tarrow, eds., *Communism in Italy and France*, pp. 177–217; Stephen Hellman, "The P.C.I.'s Alliance Strategy," ibid., pp. 377–419; Giacomo Sani, "Mass-Level Response to Party Strategy: The Italian Electorate and the Communist Party," ibid, pp. 456–503; Peter Lange, "Dilemmas of Change: Eurocommunism and National Parties in Postwar Perspective," in *Communist Parties of Italy, France and Spain: Postwar Change and Continuity*, eds. Peter Lange and Maurizio Vannicelli (Harvard University's Center for European Studies. London: Allen & Unwin, 1981), pp. 1–21; Ugo Finetti, *Il Dissenso nel PCI* (Milano: Sugar, 1978), pp. 164–292; Congressional Research Service, *Report on Western European Communist Parties* (Committee on Appropriations, U.S. Senate, Washington, DC: Government Printing Office, June 1977), pp. 29–73; Marco Cesarini-Sforza and Enrico Nassi, *L'Eurocomunismo* (Milano: Rizzoli, 1977), pp. 5–15, 17–141; Neil McInnes, *Euro-Communism*, C.S.I.S., Washington Papers No. 37 (Beverly Hills-London: Sage Publications, 1976), pp. 5–28, 35–64, 68–78; Don Sassoon, *The Strategy of the Italian Communist Party: from the Resistance to the Historic Compromise* (New York: St. Martin's, 1981); R. Grant Amyot, *The Italian Communist Party: the Crisis of the Popular Front Strategy* (New York: St. Martin's, 1981); Wagner-Pacifici, *Moro Morality Play*, pp. 22–31, 36–37, 40–43, 63–64, 79–80, 102, 123–25, 145–80, 202–203, 209, 215–16, 275–76.

10. Kogan, *A Political History of Italy*, pp. 2–61, 66–68, 81–94, 98–102, 123–47, 151–57, 161–97, 213–40, 252–64, 277–91, 293–324, 329–36; Weinberg and Eubank, *Rise and Fall of Italian Terrorism*, pp. 13–19, 53–54; Carocci, *Storia d' Italia*, pp. 323–64; Giorgio Galli, *Il Bipartitismo Imperfetto* (Bologna: Il Mulino, 1966), *Storia della Democrazia Cristiana* (Bari: Laterza, 1978), *L'Italia Sotterranea: Storia, Politica e Scandali* (Roma: Laterza, 1983); Carducci, *Componenti Storico-Sociali*, pp. 82–83; Sassoon, *Strategy*; Amyot, *Italian Communist Party*; Corrado Strajano, *L'Italia Nichilista* (Milano: Mondadori, 1982); Giovanni Bechelloni, *Cultura e Ideologia della Nuova Sinistra* (Milano: Comunita', 1973); Giuseppe Vettori, ed., *La Sinistra Extra-Parlamentare in Italia* (Roma: Newton Compton, 1973); Soccorso Rosso, eds., *Brigate*

Rossa, pp. 5-34; Monicelli, *L'Ultrasinistra in Italia*, pp. 5-41; Pisano, *Structure and Dynamics*, pp. 2-4; Finetti, *Il Dissenso nel PCI*, pp. 164-292; Pasquino, "Differenze e Somiglianze per una Ricerca sul Terrorismo Italiano," in *Terrorismo e Violenza Politica*, eds. Pasquino and della Porta, pp. 237-63; Guidorossi, *Gli Italiani e la Politica*, pp. 59-65; Lange, "Dilemmas of Change," pp. 1-21; Congressional Research Service, *Report on Western European Communist Parties*, pp. 29-73; Mammarella, *Italy After Fascism*, pp. 87-353; Blackmer, "Continuity and Change," pp. 32-58; Le Monde, *L'Economie Italienne*, pp. 13-23, 73-77, 155-62; Paolo Sylos-Labini, *Saggio sulle Classi Sociali* (Roma: Laterza, 1976); Wollemborg, *Stelle, Strisce e Tricolore*, pp. 62-537; Hellman, "The P.C.I.'s Alliance Strategy," pp. 377-419; Sani, "Mass-Level Response," pp. 456-503; Wagner-Pacifici, *Moro Morality Play*, pp. 22-33, 36-37, 40-43, 55-58, 63-64, 71-80, 102, 123-25, 145-66, 174-80, 193-94, 202-203, 207-209, 215-16, 233-40, 275-76.

11. Weinberg and Eubank, *Rise and Fall of Italian Terrorism*, pp. 13-19, 31-32, 41, 53-59; Silj, *Mai piu' senza Fucile!*, p. 191; Federico Orlando, *P. 38* (Milano: Garzanti, 1978); Alberto Ronchey, *Accadde in Italia, 1968-1977* (Milano: Rizzoli, 1977); Regni, "Labor Unions," pp. 49-66; Turone, *Storia del Sindacato*, pp. 488-99; Paolo Stoppa, "Revolutionary Culture Italian-Style," *Washington Quarterly* (Spring 1981):100-113; Carducci, *Componenti Storica-Sociali*, pp. 83-84, 95-97; Pisano, *Structure and Dynamics*, pp. 1-2; Pisano, *Contemporary Italian Terrorism*, pp. 3-7; Le Monde, *L'Economie Italienne*, pp. 13-23, 73-77, 155-62; Minucci, *Terrorismo e Crisi Italiana*, pp. 12-32; Kogan, *A Political History of Italy*, pp. 232-342; Garruccio, *Italia senza Eroi*, pp. 246-47; C. Strajano, *L'Italia Nichilista*; Bechelloni, *Cultura e Ideologia*; Vettori, ed., *La Sinistra Extra-Parlamentare*; Soccorso Rosso, eds., *Brigate Rosse*, pp. 5-34; Monicelli, *L'Ultrasinistra in Italia*, pp. 5-47; Finetti, *Il Dissenso nel PCI*, pp. 164-292; Pasquino, "Differenze e Somiglianza," pp. 237-63; Guidorossi, *Gli Italiani e la Politica*, pp. 59-65; Giorgia Manzini, *Indagine su un Brigadista Rosso* (Torino: Einaudi, 1978); Giampaolo Pansa, *Storie Italiane di Violenza e Terrorismo* (Roma: Laterza, 1980); Luigi Bobbio, *Lotta Continua* (Roma: Savelli, 1979), pp. 5-21; Prélot and Lescuyer, *Histoire des Idees Politiques*, pp. 595-646, 650-92; Rubenstein, *Alchemists of Revolution*, pp. 17-34, 49-125, 141-91; Wagner-Pacifici, *Moro Morality Play*, pp. 17, 24-25, 40-47, 57, 72, 79-80, 85, 88, 131, 145-66, 202-203, 209, 275-76; "'68: Una Storia Aperta," *L'Espresso*, special supplement, January 25, 1988, pp. 3-130.

12. Carducci, *Componenti Storico-Sociali*, pp. 88-89, 95-97; Rubenstein, *Alchemists of Revolution*, pp. 17-34, 49-191, 206-227; A. Silj, *Mai piu' senza Fucile!*, pp. xi-xiii; Weinberg and Eubank, *Rise and Fall of Italian Terrorism*, pp. 8-11, 13-19, 31-32, 39-44, 53-56; Pisano, *Structure and Dynamics*, pp. 7-21; Pisano, *Contemporary Italian Terrorism*, pp. 5-12; Minucci, *Terrorismo e Crisi Italiana*, pp. 13-35; Garruccio, *Italia senza Eroi*, pp. 10-247; Sassoon, *Strategy*; Amyot, *Italian Communist Party*; Stoppa, "Revolutionary Culture," pp. 100-113; Carocci, *Storia d' Italia*, pp. 324-64; Kogan, *A Political History of Italy*, p. 232-342; Galli, *Bipartitismo Imperfetto*; Galli, *L'Italia Sotterranea*; Wollemborg, *Stelle, Strisce e Tricolore*, pp. 226-333; Graziano and Tarrow, *La Crisi Italiana*, pp. 3-558, 609-718; Daniel Singer, *Prelude to Revolution: France in May 1968* (New York: Hill & Wang, 1970); Allan Priaulx and Sanford J. Ungar, *The Almost Revolution: France 1968* (New York: Dell, 1969); Sergio Romano, "The Roots of Italian Terrorism," *Policy Review* 25 (1983):25-27; Vincent E. McHale, "Economic Development, Political Extremism and Crime in Italy," *Western Political Quarterly* (March 1978):59-79; J. Bowyer Bell, *A Time of Terror* (New York: Basic Books, 1978), pp. 5-208; Camera dei Deputati, *Relazione della Commissione Parlamentare d'Inchiesta sulla Strage di Via Fani e sul Sequestro e l'Assassinio di A. Moro, e sul Terrorismo in Italia* (Majority Report on the Moro Case) (Roma: Tipografia della Camera), 1983; Regni, "Labor Unions," pp. 49-66; Turone, *Storia del Sindacato*, pp. 488-99; "'68: Una Storia Aperta," pp. 3-130; Martin Oppenheimer, *The Urban Guerrilla* (Chicago: Quandrangle Books, 1969), pp. 15-101, 169-73; Crenshaw, "Theories of Terrorism," pp. 13-31; Zeev Ivianski, "The Terrorist Revolution: Roots of Modern Terrorism," in *Inside Terrorist Organizations*, ed. Rapoport, pp. 129-49; Rapoport, "The International World as some Terrorists have seen It: A Look to a Century of Memoirs," ibid., pp. 32-58; Acquaviva, *Seme Religioso della Rivolta*, pp. 16-42; Acquaviva, *Guerriglia e Guerra*, pp. 17-28; della Porta, "Le Cause del Terrorismo," pp. 19-38; Stragano, *L'Italia Nichilista*; Bechelloni,

Cultura e Ideologia; Pansa, *Borghese mi ha detto* (Milano: Palazzi, 1971), pp. 42–43; "Radiografia del Fascismo Romano," *Rinascita*, November 29, 1972, pp. 18–20; Giuseppe Gaddi, *NeoFascismo in Europa* (Milano: La Pietra, 1974), pp. 4–34; Interior Minister Franco Restiveo report, in Senato, *Atti Parlamentari* (Roma: Tipografia del Senato), 22 (25 February 1971):21-325-21-333; James E. Dougherty and Robert L. Pfatzgraff, *Contending Theories of International Relations* (New York: Harper & Row, 1981), pp. 213–50; Prélot and Lescuyer, *Histoire des Idees Politiques*, pp. 670–92; Vettori, ed., *La Sinistra Extra-Parlamentare*; Soccorso Rosso, ed., *Brigate Rosse*, pp. 5–34; M. Monicelli, *L'Ultrasinistra in Italia*, pp. 5–47; G. Bocca, *Il Terrorismo Italiano* (Milano: Rizzoli, 1978), pp. 5–22; Finetti, *Il Dissenso nel PCI*, pp. 164–292; Pasquino, "Differenze e Somiglianze," pp. 237–63; Guidorossi, *Gli Italiani e la Politica*, pp. 59–65; Manzini, *Indagine*; Pansa, *Storie Italiane*; Bobbio, *Lotta Continua*, pp. 5–21; Daniele Barbieri, *Agenda Nera: Trent'Anni di Neo-Fascismo in Italia* (Roma: Coines, 1976), pp. 145–84; Ronchey, *Accade in Italia*, pp. 4–100; Marco Fini and Andrea Barberi, *Valpreda: Processo al Processo* (Milano: Feltrinelli, 1974), pp. 4–105.

13. Carducci, *Componenti Storico-Sociali*, pp. 84–86, 95-97, 103-112, 114–19; Rubenstein, *Alchemists of Revolution*, pp. 17–34, 49–191, 206–227; Silj, *Brigate Rosse e Stato* (Firenza: Vallecchi, 1978); Weinberg and Eubank, *Rise and Fall of Italian Terrorism*, pp. 2-8, 119–25; Pisano, *Structure and Dynamics*, pp. 24–21; Pisano, *Contemporary Italian Terrorism* pp. 25–35; Minucci, *Terrorismo e Crisi Italiana*, pp. 37–54; Garruccio, *Italia senza Eroi*, pp. 249–50; Stoppa, "Revolutionary Culture," pp. 100–113; Peter Allum, "Political Terrorism in Italy," *Contemporary Review* 1951 (August 1978); Camera dei Deputati, *Relazione della Commissione Parlamentare . . . Moro*; Crenshaw, "Theories of Terrorism," pp. 13–31; Ivianski, "The Terrorist Revolution," pp. 129–49; Rapoport, "The International World," pp. 32–58; Rote Armee Faktion, *La Guerriglia nella Metropoli* (Verona: Bertani Editore, 1979); Lillian Becker, *Hitler's Children* (New York: Lippincott Co., 1977); Konrad Kellen, *On Terrorists and Terrorism* (Santa Monica, CA: Rand Corp., 1982); U.S. Senate, *Terrorism and Security: the Italian Experience*, Report of the Subcommittee on Security and Terrorism, U.S. Senate Judiciary Committee (Washington, DC: Government Printing Office, 1984).

14. Weinberg and Eubank, *Rise and Fall of Italian Terrorism*, pp. 2-8, 77–125; Carducci, *Componenti Storico-Sociali*, pp. 84–86, 95-97, 103-112, 114–19; Rubenstein, *Alchemists of Revolution*, pp. 65–85, 158–91; Silj, *Brigate Rosse e Stato*; Pisano, *Structure and Dynamics*, pp. 24–21; Pisano, *Contemporary Italian Terrorism*, pp. 25–35; Minucci, *Terrorismo e Crisi Italiana*, pp. 37–54; Garruccio, *Italia senza Eroi*, pp. 249–50; Stoppa, "Revolutionary Culture," pp. 100–113; P. Allum, "Political Terrorism in Italy,"; Camera dei Deputati, *Relazione della Commissione Parlamentare . . . Moro*; Rote Armee Faktion, *La Guerriglia nella Metropoli*; Becker, *Hitler's Children*; K. Kellen, *On Terrorists and Terrorism*; Renzo Vanni, *Trent'Anni di Regime Bianco* (Pisa: Giardini Ed., 1976), pp. 149–58; Stefano Rodota', "La Risposta dello Stato al Terrorismo," in *La Prova delle Armi*, ed. G. Pasquino (Bologna: Mulino, 1984), pp. 86–87; Vittor Franco Pisano, *A Study of the Restructured Italian Intelligence and Security Services* (Washington, DC: Library of Congress, 1978), pp. 5–69; U.S. Senate, *Terrorism and Security: Italian Experience*, pp. 53–54.

15. Rubenstein, *Alchemists of Revolution*, pp. 49–138, 158–69, 206–227; Galli, *L'Italia Sotterranea*; Carducci, *Componenti Storico-Sociali*, pp. 89–93, 95–101; Silj, *Brigate Rosse e Stato*, pp. 3–146; Weinberg and Eubank, *Rise and Fall of Italian Terrorism*, pp. 2-3, 9–10, 13–19; Minucci, *Terrorismo e Crisi Italiana*, pp. 36–50; Garruccio, *Italia senza Eroi*, pp. 251–53, 261; F. Ferrarotti, *L'Ipnosi della Violenza*, pp. 7–14, 36–51; Camera dei Deputati, *Relazione della Commissione Parlamentare . . . Moro*; Bocca, *Terrorismo Italiano*, pp. 5–159; Bocca, *Noi Terroristi* (Milano: Garzanti, 1985); Acquaviva, *Seme Religioso della Rivolta*, pp. 16–42; Acquaviva, *Guerriglia e Guerra Rivoluzionaria*, pp. 17–28; della Porta, "Le Cause del Terrorismo," pp. 19–38; Strajano, *L'Italia Nichilista*; Bechelloni, *Cultura e Ideologia*; Vettori, ed., *La Sinistra Extra-Parlamentare*; Soccorso Rosse, eds., *Brigate Rosse*, pp. 5–34; Monicelli, *L'Ultrasinistra in Italia*, pp. 5–47; Bocca, *Terrorismo Italiano*, pp. 5–22; Finetti, *Il Dissenso nel PCI*, pp. 164–292; Pasquino, "Differenze e Somiglianze," pp. 237–63; Manzini, *Indagine*; Pansa, *Storie Italiane*;

Barbieri, *Agenda Nera*, pp. 145-84; Ronchey, *Accadde in Italia*, pp. 4-100; Fini and Barberi, *Valpreda*, pp. 4-105; Petra Rosenbaum, *Neofaschismus in Italien* (Frankfurt: Europaeische Verlagsanstalt, 1975), pp. 1-117; Pietro Secchia, *I Comunisti e l'Insurrezione (1943-45)* (roma: Edizioni di Cultura Sociale, 1954), pp. 10-513, all; Giulio Salierno, *Autobiografia d'un Picchiatore Fascista* (Torino: Einaudi, 1976); L. Bonante, "Teorema del Terrorismo," *Il Mulino* 258 (July-August 1978):574-89.

16. Weinberg and Eubank, *Rise and Fall of Italian Terrorism*, pp. 6-7, 122-32; Guerri, ed., *Patrizio Peci*, pp. 171-72; Wollemborg, *Stelle, Strisce, e Tricolore*, pp. 19-582; Peter Calvocoressi, *World Politics Since 1945* (London: Longman, 1982), pp. 2-45, 54-60, 114-85, 217-56; John Spanier, *Games Nations Play* (Washington, DC: Congressional Quarterly Press, 1987), pp. 142-47, 206-254, 338-45, 367-79, 385-430, 556-64; Charles W. Kegley Jr. and Eugene R. Wittkopf, *American Foreign Policy: Pattern and Process* (New York: St. Martin's Press, 1987), pp. 35-186, 549-96; Stephen Ambrose, *Rise to Globalism: U.S. Foreign Policy since 1938* (New York: Penguin, 1986); Alfred Grosser, *The Western Alliance* (New York: Vintage, 1978).

17. Bruno, *Note sul Terrorismo*; Carducci, *Componenti Storico-Sociali*, pp. 101-126; Weinberg and Eubank, *Rise and Fall of Italian Terrorism*, pp. 6-7, 49, 74, 119-40; Cordes, "When Terrorists Do the Talking," pp. 150-71; Crenshaw, "Theories of Terrorism," pp. 13-31; Guerri, ed., *Patrizio Peci*, pp. 171-77; Vittorio Grevi, "Sistema Penale d'Emergenza: la Risposta Legislativa al Terrorismo," in Pasquino and della Porta, eds., *Terrorismo e Violenza Politica*, pp. 17-24; Pisano, *Restructured Italian Intelligence*; S. Rodotà, "La Risposta dello Stato," pp. 86-87; U.S. Senate, *Terrorism and Security: Italian Experience*; Pier-Luigi Vigna, *La Finalita' del Terrorismo d dell' Eversione* (Varese: Giuffre', 1981), pp. 21-83; "Prima Linea: des Deserteurs du Terrorisme temoignent," *Liberation* (Paris) 2072 (13 October 1980); Luciana Stortoni, *Analisi d'una Organizzazione Terroristica: Prima Linea*, Laurea dissertation (Florence: Universita' degli Studi di Firenze Scienze Politiche, 1983), pp. 3-330; Gabriele Chelazzi, *La Dissociazione dal Terrorismo* (Varese: Giuffre', 1981), pp. 5-53; Luigi De Ruggiero, "I Problemi dei Processi di Terrorismo," in Magistratura Democratica, eds., (Milan: Angeli Ed., 1982), pp. 29-36; Maurizio Laudi, *I Casi di Non-Punibilita' dei Terroristi Pentiti* (Verese: Giuffre', 1983), pp. 11-148, Sue E. Moran, ed., "Court Depositions of Three Red Brigadists," Rand Co., N-2391-RC, February 1986; Wagner-Pacifici, *Moro Morality Play*, pp. 72-73, 125, 143-44, 244, 249.

18. Duroselle, *Histoire Diplomatique*, pp. 18, 155, 223-24, 327, 360, 412; Alfonso Sterpellone, "Vent' Anni di Politica Estera," in *La Politica Estera della Repubblica Italiana*, ed. Massimo Bonanno (IAI, Milano: Ed. Comunita', 1967); Mammarella, *Italy After Fascism*, p. 59; Pisano, *Structure and Dynamics*, pp. 3-4; Bell, *A Time of Terror*, pp. 3-209; Kogan, *A Political History of Italy*, pp. 7-9, 21, 75, 148-50, 209-210.

19. Mammarella, *Italy After Fascism*, pp. 31-32, 59, 166-69, 186; Pisano, *Structure and Dynamics*, pp. 3-4; Bell, *A Time of Terror*, pp. 56-179; Kogan, *A Political History of Italy*, pp. 21, 209-210, 239, 321.

20. Prèlot and Lescuyer, *Histoire des Idees Politiques*, pp. 614-32; Weinberg and Eubank, *Rise and Fall of Italian Terrorism*, pp. 9-17, 20-21, 40-42, 45-46, 57-58; Fini and Barberi, *Valpreda*; Guido Lorenzon, *Teste a Carico* (Milano: Mondadori, 1976); pp. 33-76; Coletti, *Anarchici e Questori*; George Woodcock, *Anarchism* (New York: Penguin Books, 1975); Masini, *Storia degla Anarchici Italiani*; Canosa and Santuosso, *Magistrati, Anarchia, e Socialisti*; Tilly et al., *Rebellious Germany*, pp. 304-309; Bell, *A Time of Terror*, pp. 241-45; Pisano, *Structure and Dynamics* pp. 4-5; Wagner-Pacifici, *Moro Morality Play*, pp. 41, 48-49, 53, 83, 141, 152, 244, 284-85; Vittorio Berraccetti, "Aspetti e Problemi del Terrorismo di Destra," *Questione Giustizia*, April 2, 1983, pp. 870-71.

21. Prèlot and Lescuyer, *Historie des Idees Politiques*, pp. 529-42, 556-78; Jean-Jacques Chevallier, *Grandes Oeuvres Politiques* (Paris: A. Colin, 1949), chapters 9, 14, 15; A Lyttelton, ed., *Italian Fascism: From Pareto to Gentile* (London: Jonathan Cape, 1973); Geoffrey Barraclough, *Introduction to Contemporary History* (New York: Penguin, 1977), pp. 124-52; M. Rimanelli, "The Super-Human Myth in Literature, Political Philosophy, Science and Science-Fiction," paper (pp. 1-25) and lecture at the State University of New York at Albany, Albany, NY

September 1988; Carducci, *Componenti Storico-Sociali*, pp. 1–3; Michele De Micheli, *Matrici Ideologico-Letterarie dell'Eversione Neo-Fascista* (Milano: CLUP, 1975), pp. 3–234; Rosenbaum, pp. 217–25; Franco Ferraresi, ed., *La Destra Radicale* (Milano: Feltrinelli, 1984); Weinberg and Eubank, *Rise and Fall of Italian Terrorism*, pp. 33–34; Mario Stanganelli, "Un Doppiopetto con Camicia Nera," *Messaggero* (Roma) (May 23, 1988):3; Gaddi,*NeoFascismo in Europa*, pp. 13–43; Julius Evola, *Il Mito del Sangue* (Milano: Hoepli, 1942), pp. 1–6; Giorgio Freda, *La Disintegrazione del Sistema* (Padova: Edizioni AR, 1969); Wagner-Pacifici, *Moro Morality Play*, pp. 16, 25, 29, 33–35, 48, 82, 109, 293.

22. Ann Jellamo, "J. Evola, il Pensatore della Tradizione," in *La Destra Radicale*, ed. Ferraresi, pp. 215–47; Franco Ferraresi, "Da Evola a Freda: le Dottrine della Destra Radicale fino al 1977," ibid., pp. 13–41; Ferraresi, "La Destra Eversiva," ibid., pp. 65–73; Patrizia Guerra and Marco Revelli, eds., "Bibliografia Essenziale per la Conoscenza della Nuova Destra Italiana," in *Fascismo Oggi: Nuova Destra e Cultura Reazionaria negli Anni Ottanta*, ed. Guido Quazza (Cuneo: Instituto Storico della Resistenza, 1983), pp. 423–26; Carducci, *Componenti Storico-Sociali*, pp. 3–6; F. Ferraresi, "I Riferimenti Teorico-Dottrinali della Destra Radicale," *Questione Giustizia*, April 11, 1983, pp. 881–92; Pino Romualdi, ed., *L'Italiano: Adriano Romualdi a Dieci Anni della sua Scomparsa*, 24 February 1976; De Micheli, *Matrici Ideologico-Letterarie*, pp. 3–204; Stanganelli, "Doppiopetto con Camicia Nera," p. 3; Rosenbaum, *Neofaschismos in Italien*, pp. 2–85, 95–203; J. Evola, *Mito del Sangre*; Freda, *Disintegrazione del Sistema*; Giuseppe Bessarione, *Lambro Hobbit: La Cultura Giovanile di Destra in Italia e in Europa* (Roma: Arcana, 1979), pp. 3–174.

23. Carducci, *Componenti Storico-Sociali*, pp. 6–10, 39–41; Ferraresi, "I Riferimenti Teorico-Dottrinali" pp. 881–92; De Micheli, *Matrici Ideologico-Letterarie*, pp. 30–201; Rosenbaum, *Neofaschismus in Italien*, p. 2–240; Weinberg and Eubank, *Rise and Fall of Italian Terrorism*, pp. 34–35; Gaddi, *NeoFascismo in Europa*; Bessarione, *Lambro Hobbit*, p. 3–150; Jellamo, "J. Evola," pp. 215–47; Ferraresi, "Da Evola a Freda," pp. 13–41; Ezra Pound, *Cantos* (Leuven: Acco, 1980).

24. Stanganelli, "Doppiopetto con Camicia Nera," p. 3; Carducci, *Componenti Storico-Sociali*, pp. 6–7, 13–16; Rosenbaum, *Neofaschismus in Italien*, p. 217–225; Bessarione, *Lambro Hobbit*, p. 3–150; Ettore Chiarini and Paolo Corsini, *Da Salo' a Piazza della Loggia* (Milano: Franco Angeli, 1984); De Micheli, *Matrici Ideologico-Letterarie*, p. 95; Jellamo, "J. Evola," pp. 215–47; Ferraresi, "Da Evola a Freda," pp. 13–41; Ferraresi, "La Destra Eversiva," pp. 65–73; Guerra and Revelli, eds., "Bibliografia Essenziale"; Ferraresi, "I Riferimenti Teorico-Dottrinali," pp. 881–92; Romualdi, ed., *L'Italiano*; Weinberg and Eubank, *Rise and Fall of Italian Terrorism*, pp. 33–36; Gaddi, *Neofascismo in Europa.*

25. Stanganelli, "Doppiopetto con Camicia Nera," p. 3; Giuseppe De Dio, "Aveva detto: Lasciatemi morire in piedi!," *Il Messaggero* (Roma) (May 24, 1988):3; Ferraresi, "I Riferimenti Teorico-Dottrinali," pp. 881–92; Weinberg and Eubank, *Rise and Fall of Italian Terrorism*, pp. 34–36, 41–44; Salierno, *Autobiografia d'un Picciatore Fascista*; Carducci, *Componenti Storico-Sociali*, pp. 13–16, 39–40; Rosenbaum, *Neofaschismus in Italien*, p. 45–96; Ferraresi, "Da Evola a Freda," pp. 13–41; Ferraresi, "La Destra Eversiva," pp. 65–73; Guerra and Revelli, eds., "Bibliografia Essenziale"; Pisano, *Contemporary Italian Terrorism*, pp. 104–105; Chiarini and Corsini, *Da Salo' a Piazza della Loggia*, pp. 3–207; De Micheli, *Matrici Ideologico-Letterarie*, p. 95; Mario Tedeschi, *Destra Nazionale* (Rome: Ed. Borghese, 1972); Giorgio Almirante, *La Strategia del Terrorismo* (Roma: SAIPEM, 1974); Armando Plebe, *Il Libretto della Destra* (Milano: Ed. Borghese, 1972).

26. Stanganelli "Doppiopetto con Camicia Nera," p. 3; De Dio, "Aveva detto," p. 3; Ferraresi, "Riferimenti Teorico-Dottrinali," pp. 881–92; Weinberg and Eubank, *Rise and Fall of Italian Terrorism*, pp. 34–36, 41–44, 135–39; Salierno, *Autobiografia d'un Picchiatore Fascista*; Carducci, *Componenti Storico-Sociali*, pp. 13–16, 39–40; Rosenbaum, *Neofaschismus in Italien*, pp. 45–96; Ferraresi, "Da Evola a Freda," pp. 13–41; Ferraresi, "Destra Eversiva," pp. 65–73; Guerra and Revelli, eds., "Bibliografia Essenziale"; Pisano, *Contemporary Italian Terrorism*, pp. 104–105; Chiarini and Corsini, *Da Salo' a Piazza della Loggia*, pp. 3–207; De Micheli, *Matrici*

Ideologico-Letterarie, p. 95; Penniman, ed., *Italy at the Polls*; Wagner-Pacifici, *Moro Morality Play*, pp. 25-29, 44-49, 56, 82-84.

27. Ronchey, *Accadde in Italia*, pp. 109-205; A.A.V.V., *Indagine Conoscitiva sulle Attivita' Neo-Fasciste nel Lazio* (Roma: Azienda Tipografica Editoriale, 1975), pp. 3-207; Carducci, *Componenti Storico-Sociali*, pp. 20-25, 27-28; Weinberg and Eubank *Rise and Fall of Italian Terrorism*, pp. 25-26, 34-38; Geurra and Revelli, eds., "Bibliografia Essenziale"; Rosenbaum, *Neofaschismus in Italien*, pp. 100-238; Pisano, *Contemporary Italian Terrorism*, pp. 104-105; Secchia, *I Comunisti e l'Insurrezione*, pp. 80-103; Salierno, *Autobiografia d'un Picchiatore Fascista*; Wagner-Pacifici, *Moro Morality Play*, pp. 244-45.

28. Pisano, *Restructured Italian Intelligence*; Ruggero Zangrandi, *Inchiesta sul SIFAR*, (Roma: Ed. Riuniti, 1970); Barberi, *Agenda Nera*, pp. 94-99; Vanni, *Trent' Anni di Regime Bianco*, pp. 149-58; Weinberg and Eubank, *Rise and Fall of Italian Terrorism*, pp. 7-10, 38, 43-45, 122-26; Senato e Camera, *Relazione della Commissione Parlamentare . . . Via Fani*, p. 56; Senato e Camera, *Relazioni di Minoranza*, Commissione Parlamentare sulla Strage di Via Fani (Roma: Tipografia del Senato, 1983), p. 21; Wagner-Pacifici, *Moro Morality Play*, pp. 244-45; Tina Anselmi, "Il Complotto di Licio Gelli: Relazione di Tina Anselmi, Presidente della Commissione Parlamentare sulla P2," *L'Espresso*, special supplement (May 20, 1984); Wagner-Pacifici, *Moro Morality Play*, pp. 25-29, 44-49, 56, 82-84.

29. Weinberg and Eubank, *Rise and Fall of Italian Terrorism*, pp. 9-10, 31, 38-44; Pansa, *Borghese mi ha detto*, pp. 42-43; "Radiografia del Fascismo Romano," *Rinascita* (November 29, 1972):18-20; Gaddi, *NeoFascismo in Europa* pp. 4-34; Interior Minister Franco Restiveo report, in Senato, *Atti Parlamentari*, n. 22 (Roma: Tipografia del Senato), February 25, 1971, pp. 21-325-21-333; D. Barbieri, *Agenda Nera*, pp. 94-99, 145-184, 193-98; Ronchey, *Accadde in Italia* pp. 99-205; A.A.V.V., *Indagine Conoscitiva*, pp. 3-157; Silj, *Mai piu' senza Fucile!*; Carducci, *Componenti Storico-Sociale*, pp. 22-25; Regni, "Labor Unions," pp. 49-66; Turone, *Storia del Sindacato*, pp. 488-99; Rosenbaum, *Neofaschismus in Italien*, pp. 100-117; Ferraresi, ed., *La Destra Radicale*, pp. 150-240; Pisano, *Structure and Dynamics*, pp. 5-7; Pisano, *Contemporary Italian Terrorism*, pp. 101-116; Fini and Barberi, *Valpreda*, pp. 90-105; Lorenzon, *Teste a Carico*, pp. 33-76; Berraccetti, "Aspetti e Problemi," pp. 870-71; Vanni, *Trent' Anni di Regime Bianco*, pp. 149-58; Salierno, *Autobiografia d'un Picchiatore Fascista*; Fabrizio D'Agostini, *Reggio-Calabria* (Milano: Feltrinelli, 1972); Anselmi, "Il Complotto di Licio Gelli"; Wagner-Pacific, *Moro Morality Play*, pp. 25-29, 41, 44-49, 53, 56, 82-84, 141, 152, 244, 284-85.

30. Ferraresi, ed., *La Destra Radicale*, pp. 98-200; Carducci, *Componenti Storico-Sociale*, pp. 23-27, 29; Rosenbaum, *Neofaschismus in Italien*, pp. 30-117; Ronchey, *Accadde in Italia*, pp. 4-289; Pisano, *Contemporary Italian Terrorism*, pp. 104-105; Weinberg and Eubank, *Rise and Fall of Italian Terrorism*, pp. 9-10, 39-45, 49; Ricciotti Lazzero, *La Decima MAS* (Milano: Rizzoli, 1984), pp. 9-42; Pansa, *Borghese mi ha detto*, pp. 42-43; "Radiografia del Fascismo Romano," pp. 18-20; Gaddi, *NeoFascismo in Europa*, pp. 4-34; Interior Minister Franco Restiveo report, pp. 21-325-21-333; Camera dei Deputati, *Relazione della Commissione Parlamentare d'Inchiesta sulla Loggia Massonica P.2* (Roma: Tipografia della Camera, 1984); Barbieri, *Agenda Nera*, pp. 193-98; Anselmi, *Il Complotto di Licio Gelli*; Giancarlo Scarpari, "Il Processo per la Strage dell'Italicus," in *Questione Giustizia*, idem, pp. 893-911; Wagner-Pacifici, *Moro Morality Play*, pp. 25-29, 44-49, 56, 82-84.

31. Ferraresi, ed., *La Destra Radicale*, pp. 139-203; Ferraresi, "La Destra Eversiva," pp. 72-74; Carducci *Componenti Storico-Sociali*, pp. 29-35; Weinberg and Eubank, *Rise and Fall of Italian Terrorism*, pp. 41, 43-46; Rosenbaum, *Neofaschismus in Italien*, pp. 37-117; Ronchey, *Accadde in Italia*, pp. 95-189; Chiarini and Corsini, *Da Salo' a Piazza della Loggia*, pp. 311-44; Berraccetti, "Aspetti e Problemi," p. 871; Guerra and Revelli, eds., "Bibliografia Essenziale"; Pisano, *Contemporary Italian Terrorism*, pp. 104-105; Restiveo, in Senato, *Atti Parlamentari 22*, pp. 21-325-21-333; G. Scarpari, "Il Processo per la Strage dell' Italicus," pp. 893-911; Corte d'Assise d'Appello di Firenze, *Sentenza*, November 11, 1977 and April 9, 1976; Wagner-Pacifici, *Moro Morality Play*, pp. 25-29, 44-49, 56, 82-84, 244-45.

32. Weinberg and Eubank, *Rise and Fall of Italian Terrorism*, pp. 32-33, 35, 40-42, 44, 46-

47; Ferraresi, ed., *La Destra Radicale*, pp. 45-146; Chiarini and Corsini, *Da Salo' a Piazza della Loggia*, pp. 102-104, 311-44; Berraccetti, "Aspetti e Problemi," pp. 870-71; Carducci, *Componenti Storico-Sociale*, pp. 10-13, 31-35; Lorenzon, *Teste a Corico*, pp. 33-72; P. Rosenbaum, idem, pp. 37-117; Pisano, *Structure and Dynamics*, pp. 5-7; Pisano, *Contemporary Italian Terrorism*, pp. 101-116; Freda, *Disintegrazione del Sistema*; Guerra and Revelli, eds., "Bibliografia Essenziale"; Marco Sassano, *La Politica della Strage* (Padova: Marsilio, 1972), pp. 39-47; Corte d'Assise d'Appello di Firenze, *Sentenza*, April 9, 1976, November 11, 1977, and December 12, 1978; Pier-Luigi Vigna, "L'Omicidio del Magistrato Vittorio Occorsio: i Processi ed alcune Riflessioni," in *Questione Guistizia*, pp. 913-33; Wagner-Pacifici, *Moro Morality Play*, pp. 83, 244-45.

33. Weinberg and Eubank, *Rise and Fall of Italian Terrorism*, pp. 10, 43-44, 46-50; Bell, *A Time of Terror*, pp. 242-43, 245-48; Pisano, *Structure and Dynamics*, pp. 5-7; Pisano, *Contemporary Italian Terrorism*, pp. 101-116; Ronchey, *Accadde in Italia*, pp. 45-203; Carducci, *Componenti Storico-Sociali*, pp. 33-35; Rosenbaum, *Neofaschismus in Italien*, pp. 97-117; Gaddi, *NeoFascismo in Europa*, pp. 13-43; Stanganelli, "Doppiopetto con Camicia Nera," p. 3; Ferraresi, ed., *La Destra Radicale*, pp. 43-168; Camera dei Deputati, *Relazione della Commissione Parlamentare . . . P.2*; Anselmi, *Il Complotto di Licio Gelli*; Giancarlo Capaldo et al., "L'Eversione di Destra a Roma dal '77 ad Oggi: Spunti per una Ricostruzione del Fenomeno," in *Questione Giustizia* April 2, 1983, pp. 939-48; Thomas Sheehan, "Italy: Terror on the Right," *New York Times Review of Books* (27:21) (1981):23-26; Marco Revelli, "La Nuova Destra," in *La Destra Radicale*, ed. Ferraresi, pp. 119-214; Marco Nozza, "Quex': Spontaneismo o Progetto Nazional-Rivoluzionario?" in *Fascismo Oggi*, ed. Quazza, pp. 267-77; G. Galli, "La Componente Magica della Cultura de Destra," ibid., pp. 279-86; Franco Coppola, "Bologna, 4 Ergastoli per l'Omicidio Amato," *Repubblica* (April 6, 1984):12; Wagner-Pacifici, *Moro Morality Play*, pp. 83, 162, 243-45; Claudio Gerino, "Ora stiamo braccando i Latitanti dei NAR," *Repubblica* (October 7, 1982):10; "Avvocato di Parte Civile si dimette dal Processo per la Strage di Bologna," *Repubblica* (July 23-24, 1989):6.

34. Weinberg and Eubank, *Rise and Fall of Italian Terrorism*, pp. 53-59; Carducci, *Componenti Storico-Sociali*, pp. 45-48; Sylos-Labini, *Saggio Sulle Classi Sociali*, pp. 34-165; Bechelloni, *Cultura e Ideologia*; Vettori, ed., *La Sinistra Extra-Parlamentare*; Soccorso Rosso, eds., *Brigate Rosse*; Bobbio, *Lotta Continua*; Pansa, *Storie Italiane*; M. Monicelli, *L'Ultrasinistra in Italia*; Regis Debray, *Revolution in the Revolution? Armed Struggle and Political Struggle in Latin America* (New York: Grove, 1967); Finetti, *Il Dissenso nel PCI*; Strajano, *L'Italia Nichilista*; Carlos Marighella, "Appendix: Minimanual of the Urban Guerrilla," in *Urban Guerrilla Warfare*, ed. Robert Moss (London: Institute for Strategic Studies, 1971); Ernst Halperin, *Terrorism in Latin-America* (Beverly Hills, CA: Sage, 1976); Alain Labrousse, *The Tupamaros: Urban Guerrilla in Uruguay* (Harmondsworth, UK: Penguin, 1973); Anthony M. Burton, *Urban Terrorism: Theory, Practice and Response* (New York: Free Press, 1975); Maria-Esther Grillo, *The Tupamaros Guerrillas* (New York: Saturday Review Press, 1970); G. Manzini, *Indagine*; G. Woodcock, *Anarchism* all; Oppenheimer, *The Urban Guerrilla*, pp. 15-101, 169-73; Stortoni, *Analisi d'una Organizzazione*, pp. 4-45; Prèlot and Lescuyer, *Histoire des Idees Politiques*, pp. 633-42, 650-700; Theodore A. Couloumbis and James H. Wolfe, *Introduction to International Relations, Power and Justice* (Englewood Cliffs, NJ: Prentice-Hall, 1986), Chapters 11, 18; Z. Ivianski, "The Terrorist Revolution," pp. 129-49; Rapoport, "The International World," pp. 32-58; Barraclough, *Introduction to Contemporary History*, pp. 153-233; Dougherty and Pfatzgraff, *Contending Theories*, pp. 213-50; Wagner-Pacifici, *Moro Morality Play*, pp. 10, 17, 23-24, 40-42, 47-54, 59-60, 82-83, 151-52; Rubenstein, *Alchemists of Revolution*, pp. 65-85.

35. Rubenstein, *Alchemists of Revolution*, pp. 89-125, 141-91; Carducci, *Componenti Storico-Sociali*, pp. 48-50; Weinberg and Eubank, *Rise and Fall of Italian Terrorism*, pp. 53-59; Sylos-Labini, *Saggio sulle Classi Sociali*, pp. 34-156; G. Bechelloni, *Cultura e Ideologia*; Vettori, ed., *La Sinistra Extra-Parlamentare*; Soccorso Rosso, eds., *Brigate Rosse*; Bobbio, *Lotta Continua*; Pansa, *Storie Italiane*; Monicelli, *L'Ultrasinistra in Italia*; Finetti, *Il Dissenso nel PCI*; C. Strajano, *L'Italia Nichilista*; Manzini, *Indagine*; Oppenheimer, *The Urban Guerrilla*, pp. 15-

101, 169–73; Stortoni, *Analisi d'una Organizzazione*, pp. 4–41; Wagner-Pacifici, *Moro Morality Play*, pp. 10, 17, 23–24, 40–42, 46–54, 58–61, 82–83, 151–52, 234–35.

36. Weinberg and Eubank, *Rise and Fall of Italian Terrorism*, pp. 31, 41, 53–59; Carducci, *Componenti Storico-Sociali*, pp. 50–55, 57; Sylos-Labini, *Saggio sulle Classi Sociali*, pp. 109–198; Bocca, *Terrorismo Italiano* pp. 3–245; Rubenstein, *Alchemists of Revolution*, pp. 89–125, 141–91; A.A.V.V., *Terrorismo in Fabbrica* (Roma: Ed. Riuniti, 1978); Bechelloni, *Cultura e Ideologia*; Vettori, ed., *La Sinistra Extra-Parlamentare*; Soccorso Rosso, eds., *Brigate Rosse*; Bobbio, *Lotta Continua*; Regni, "Labor Unions," pp. 49–66; Turone, *Storia del Sindacato*, pp. 488–99; Pansa, *Storie Italiane*; Monicelli *L'Ultrasinistra in Italia*; Finetti, *Il Dissenso nel PCI*; Strajano, *L'Italia Nichilista*; Manzini, *Indagine*; Stortoni, *Analisi d'una Organizzazione*, pp. 4–45; Wagner-Pacifici, *Moro Morality Play*, pp. 24–25, 40–43, 47–49, 79–83, 145–66, 202–203, 209, 275–76; "'68: Una Storia Aperta," pp. 3–130.

37. Carducci, *Componenti Storico-Sociali*, pp. 57–68; Sylos-Labini, *Saggio sulle Classi Sociali*, pp. 109–200; Bocca, *Terrorismo Italiano*, pp. 3–245; A.A.V.V., *Terrorismo in Fabbrica*, pp. 3–239; Weinberg and Eubank, *Rise and Fall of Italian Terrorism*, pp. 53–59; Bechelloni, *Cultura e Ideologia*; Vettori, ed., *La Sinistra Extra-Parlamentare*; Soccorso Rosso, eds., *Brigate Rosse*; Bobbio, *Lotta Continua*; Pansa, *Storie Italiane*; Monicelli, *L'Ultrasinistra in Italia*; Finetti, *Il Dissenso nel PCI*; Strajano, *L'Italiano Nichilista*; Manzini, *Indagine*; Stortoni, *Analisi d'una Organizzazione*, pp. 4–45; Pansa, *Borghese mi ha detto* pp. 155–85.

38. Pisano, *Structure and Dynamics*, pp. 7–8; Pisano, *Contemporary Italian Terrorism*, pp. 29–85; Orlando, *P.38*, idem, pp. 3–267.

39. Weinberg and Eubank, *Rise and Fall of Italian Terrorism*, pp. 55, 59–64; Pisano, *Structure and Dynamics*, pp. 7–8; Pisano, *Contemporary Italian Terrorism*, pp. 29–85; Soccorso Rosso, eds., *Brigate Rosse*, pp. 26–85; "'68: Una Storia Aperta," pp. 66–67; Corte d'Assise d'Appello di Milano, *Sentenza N. 7/80*, 1/9 Aprile 1981, pp. 2–29, 51–52; Giudice Istruttore Francesco Amato, *Ordinanza/Sentenza N. 10607/69*, Tribunale Penale di Roma, pp. 771–76; Corte d'Assise di Rome, *Sentenza 31/81RG*, 24 Gennaio 1983, pp. 5–703; Vincenzo Tessandori, *BR: Imputazione Banda Armata* (Milano: Garzanti, 1977), pp. 28–58; Silj, *Mai piu' senza Fucile!*, pp. 3–117; Wagner-Pacific, *Moro Morality Play*, pp. 38, 50–52, 71, 91.

40. Carducci, *Componenti Storico-Sociale*, pp. 57–60; Edgar O'Ballance, *Language of Violence* (San Raphael, CA: Presidio, 1979), pp. 3–250; Pisano, *Structure and Dynamics*, pp. 7–8; Pisano, *Contemporary Italian Terrorism*, pp. 29–85; Bocca, *Noi Terroristi*, pp. 123–245; Bocca, *Terrorismo Italiano*, pp. 3–23; Sylos-Labini, *Saggio Sulle Classi Sociali*, pp. 23–79; Soccorso Rosso, eds., *Brigate Rosse*, pp. 26–85; Corte d'Assise d'Appello di Milano, *Sentenza N. 7/80*, pp. 2–29, 51–52; Giudice Istruttore F. Amato, *Ordinanza/Sentenza N. 10607/69*, pp. 771–76; Corte d'Assise di Roma, *Sentenza 31/81RG*, pp. 5–703; Tessandori, *BR: Imputazione Banda Armata*, pp. 28–58; Silj, *Mai piu' senza Fucile!*, pp. 3–117; Weinberg and Eubank, *Rise and Fall of Italian Terrorism*, pp. 18–19, 55, 59–64; Monicelli, *L'Ultrasinistra in Italia*, pp. 4–41; Wagner-Pacifici, *Moro Morality Play*, pp. 38, 50–52, 71, 91, 145, 160, 187, 247–48, 272; D. A. Strickland and Peter P. Krauss, "Political Disintegration & Latent Terror," in *The Politics of Terrorism*, ed. Michael Stohl (New York: Marcell Dekker, 1983), pp. 77–177; Acquaviva, *Seme Religioso della Rivolta*, pp. 16–42; Acquaviva, *Guerriglia e Guerra*, pp. 17–28; Ferrarotti, *L'Ipnosi della Violenza*, pp. 5–51.

41. Carducci, *Componenti Storico-Sociali*, pp. 59–61; Soccorso Rosso, eds., *Brigate Rosse*, pp. 26–85; Corte d'Assise d'Appello di Milano, *Sentenza N. 7/80*, pp. 2–29, 51–52; Giudice Istruttore F. Amato, *Ordinanza/Sentenza N. 10607/69*, pp. 771–76; Corte d'Assise di Roma, *Sentenza 31/81RG*, pp. 5–703; Tessandori, *BR: Imputazione Banda Armata*, pp. 28–58; Silj, *Mai piu' senza Fucile!* pp. 3–117; Giudice Mario Sossi, *Nella Prigione delle Brigate Rosse* (Milano: Editoriale Nuova, 1979), pp. 7–81; Weinberg and Eubank, *Rise and Fall of Italian Terrorism*, pp. 59–65; Pisano, *Structure and Dynamics*, pp. 7–81; Silj, *Brigate Rosse e Stato*, pp. 34–156; Pisano, *Contemporary Italian Terrorism*, pp. 29–85; Bocca, *Noi Terroristi*, pp. 123–250; Bocca, *Terrorismo Italiano*, pp. 34–209; Wagner-Pacifici, *Moro Morality Play*, pp. 52–54, 142–44, 240, 260–61.

Italian Terrorism, 1940s–1980s 293

42. Carducci, *Componenti Storico-Sociale*, pp. 61–62; Pisano, *Structure and Dynamics*, pp. 7–86; Silj, *Brigate Rosse e Stato*, pp. 43–189; Pisano, *Contemporary Italian Terrorism*, pp. 29–85; Bocca, *Noi Terroristi*, pp. 109–200; Bocca, *Il Terrorismo Italiano*, pp. 33–223; "Terrorism in Italy," special issue of *Terrorism* 2 (3/4) (1979); Soccorso Rosso, eds., *Brigate Rosse*, pp. 26–85; Corte d'Assise d'Appello di Milano, *Sentenza N. 7/80*, pp. 2–29, 51–52; Giudice Istruttore F. Amato, *Ordinanza/Sentenza N. 10607/69*, pp. 771–76; Corte d'Assise di Roma, *Sentenza 31/81RG*, pp. 5–703; Tessandori, *BR: Imputazione Banda Armata*, pp. 28–58; Silj, *Mai piu' senza Fucile!* pp. 3–117; Sossi, *Nella Prigione*, pp. 7–81; Crenshaw, "Theories of Terrorism," pp. 13–31; Cordes, "When Terrorists Do the Talking," pp. 150–71; Weinberg and Eubank, *Rise and Fall of Italian Terrorism*, pp. 59–65; Emilio Papa, *Il Processo alle Brigate Rosse* (Torino: Giappichelli, 1979), pp. 20–52; Wagner-Pacifici, *Moro Morality Play*, pp. 52–54, 142–44, 240, 260–61, 272.

43. The BR Organizational Chart is printed in Katz, *Days of Wrath*, p. xv. Reprinted by permission of Sterling Lord Literistics Inc., 1980 copyright by Katz.

44. Carducci, *Componenti Storico-Sociali*, pp. 61–62; Pisano, *Structure and Dynamics*, p. 9; Robert Katz, *Days of Wrath: the Ordeal of Aldo Moro* (Garden City, NY: Doubleday, 1980), pp. 3–326; Pisano, Comtemporary Italian Ter'sm, pp. 9–85; Bocca, *Noi Terroristi*, pp. 134–89; Bocca, *Il Terrorismo Italiano* pp. 129–57; "Terrorism in Italy," *Terrorism* 2 (3/4); Crenshaw, "Theories of Terrorism," pp. 13–31; Cordes, "When Terrorists Do the Talking," pp. 150–71; Marighella, "Appendix: Minimanual of the Urban Guerrilla"; Camera dei Deputati, *Relazione . . . sulla Strage di Via Fani e . . . sull'As sinio di A. Moro*; Leonardo Sciascia, *L'Affaire Moro*. pp. 14–146; Wagner-Pacifici, *Moro Morality Play*, pp. 52–54, 60–294.

45. L. Sciascia, *L'Affaire Moro*, pp. 14–146; Wagner-Pacifici, *Moro Morality Play*, pp. 22–294; Carducci, *Componenti Storico-Sociali*, pp. 63–64; Pisano, *Structure and Dynamics*, p. 9; Katz, *Days of Wrath*, pp. 4–239; Pisano, *Contemporary Italian Terrorism*, pp. 29–85; Bocca, *Noi Terroristi* pp. 123–245; Bocca, *Terrorismo Italiano* pp. 198–234; Camera dei Deputati, Relazione della Commissione Parlamentare . . . Moro.

46. Pisano, *Structure and Dynamics*, pp. 10–12; Katz, *Days of Wrath*, pp. 14–230; Bocca, *Il Terrorismo Italiano*, pp. 200–235; Bell, *Assassin!* (New York: Basic Books, 1979), pp. 277–81; Kupperman and Trent, *Terrorism*, p. 24; Camera dei Deputati, *Relazione della Commissione Parlamentare . . . Moro*; Wagner-Pacifici, *Moro Morality Play*, pp. 1, 24, 58–63, 68–71, 97, 125, 131, 138, 192, 205–213, 224–38, 240–43, 246–70, 296–302; Sciascia, *L'Affaire Moro*; Weinberg and Eubank, *Rise and Fall of Italian Terrorism*, pp. 65–74, 90–102, 105–125.

47. Carducci, *Componenti Storico-Sociali*, pp. 53–54, 64–65, 67–71; Katz, *Days of Wrath*, pp. 7–154; Silj, *Brigate Rosse e Stato*, pp. 167–289; Orlando, *P. 38*, pp. 67–242; Stoppa, "Revolutionary Culture," pp. 100–113; Bocca, *Noi Terroristi*, pp. 234–57; Bocca, *Il Terrorismo Italiano*, pp. 123–66; Rojas, *The Murder of Allende*; Sassoon, *Strategy*; Amyot, *The Italian Communist Party*; Giorgio Statera, *Violenza Sociale e Violenza Politica nell'Italia dell'Anno '78* (Milano: Franco Angeli, 1983); Camera dei Deputati, *Relazione della Commissione Parlamentare . . . Moro*; Cesarini-Sforza and Nassi, *L'Eurocomunismo*, pp. 5–141; McInnes, *Euro-Communism*, pp. 5–78; Pietro Secchia, *Lotta Anti-Fascista e Giovani Generazioni* (Milan: La Pietra, 1973), pp. 5–180, all; Wagner-Pacifici, *Moro Morality Play*, pp. 22–33, 36–37, 44–47, 57, 63–71, 78, 108–110, 123–25, 174–80, 202–203, 215–16, 240, 291.

48. Carducci, *Componenti Storico-Sociali*, pp. 65, 67–71; Katz, *Days of Wrath*, pp. 19–198; Pisano, *Contemporary Italian Terrorism*, pp. 29–85; Orlando, *P. 38*, pp. 5–234; Wagner-Pacifici, *Moro Morality Play*, pp. 44–45, 47, 72–73, 87–88, 121–22; Stoppa, "Revolutionary Culture," pp. 100–113; Bocca, *Noi Terroristi*. pp. 123–245; Bocca, *Il Terrorismo Italiano*, pp. 150–98; Statera, *Violenza Sociale*, pp. 4–283; Camera dei Deputati, *Relazione della Commissione Parlamentare . . . Moro*; Toni Negri, *Crisi e Organizzazione Operaia* (Milano: Feltrinelli, 1974); T. Negri, *Proletari e Stato* (Milano: Feltrinelli, 1976); Judge Francesco Amato, Giudice Istruttore, *Ordinanza/Sentenza N. 10067/79* (Roma: Tribunale di Roma-Ufficio Istruzione, 1979), pp. 61–209 (the indictment of Autonomia and T. Negri); Daniele Mastrogiacomo, "Autonomia: 7 Secoli di Carcere," *Repubblica* (April 16, 1984):5; Giancarlo Scarpari, "La Vicenda del '7 Aprile'," pp. 37–63, in *La Magistratura di fronte al Terrorismo e all'Eversione di Sinistra*, ed. Magistratura

294   *M. Rimanelli*

Democratica (Milano: Angeli Ed., 1982); Wagner-Pacifici, *Moro Morality Play*, pp. 24, 44, 67–71, 78, 108–110.

49. Sassoon, *Strategy*; Amyot, *The Italian Communist Party*; L. Sciascia, *L'Affaire Moro*; Katz, *Days of Wrath*, pp. 19–198; Wagner-Pacifici, *Moro Morality Play*, pp. 1, 22–33, 33–38, 53–59, 62–64, 68–81, 93–97, 123–25, 127–80, 192–94, 202–203, 210–211, 215–17, 233–43, 246–49, 251–53, 264–69, 289–91; Carducci, *Componenti Storico-Sociali*, pp. 73–79; "Terrorist Grip on Italy," *Boston Globe Magazine*, May 31, 1981, p. 7; Pisano, *Contemporary Italian Terrorism*, pp. 48–56; Bocca, *Terrorismo Italiano*, pp. 132–234; Camera dei Deputati, *Relazione della Commissione Parlamentare . . . Moro*; Weinberg and Eubank, *Rise and Fall of Italian Terrorism*, pp. 7, 11, 69–71, 124–38; Bonante, "Teorema del Terrorismo," pp. 574–89.

50. Weinberg and Eubank, *Rise and Fall of Italian Terrorism*, pp. 7, 11, 69–71, 124–38; Sciascia, *L'Affaire Moro*; Katz, *Days of Wrath*, pp. 19–198; Wagner-Pacifici, *Moro Morality Play*, pp. 20–24, 47, 62–63, 68–71, 88–92, 120–25, 127–63, 192, 205–215, 217–20, 224–38, 240–43, 246–70, 273–78, 283–85, 288–89, 291–92, 296–302; Carducci *Componenti Storico-Sociali*, pp. 73–79; "Terrorist Grip on Italy," p. 7; Pisano, *Contemporary Italian Terrorism*, pp. 48–56; Bocca, *Terrorismo Italiano*, pp. 132–234; Camera dei Deputati, *Relazione della Commissione Parlamentare . . . Moro*; Judge Francesco Amato, Giudice Istruttore, *Ordinanza/Sentenza N.10067/79* (Roma: Tribunale di Roma-Ufficio Istruzione, 1979), pp. 61–209 (the indictment of Autonomia and T. Negri); Daniele Mestrogiacomo, "Autonomia: 7 Secoli di Carcere," *Repubblica*, April 16, 1984, p. 5; Giancarlo Scarpari, "La Vicenda del '7 Aprile'," pp. 37–63, in *La Magistratura di fronte al Terrorismo*, pp. 574–89, ed. Magistratura Democratica.

51. Katz, *Days of Wrath*, pp. 19–209; Carducci, *Componenti Storico-Sociali*, pp. 77–80; "Terrorist Grip on Italy," p. 7; Pisano, *Contemporary Italian Terrorism*, pp. 2–54; Bocca, *Terrorismo Italiano*, pp. 150–209; Bocca, *Noi Terroristi*, pp. 123–230; Camera dei Deputati, *Relazione della Commissione Parlamentare . . . Moro*; "Terrorism in Italy"; Crenshaw, "Theories of Terrorism," pp. 13–31; Cordes, "When Terrorists Do the Talking," pp. 150–71; Pisano, *Structure and Dynamics*, pp. 10–12; Bruno, "Problematiche relative," pp. 79–94; Bruno, "Il Terrorismo Politico Italiano," pp. 43–49; Acquaviva, *Seme Religioso della Rivolta*, pp. 16–42; Sassoon, *Strategy*; Amyot, *The Italian Communist Party*; Wagner-Pacifici, *Moro Morality Play*, pp. 72–73, 123–25, 143–44, 174–80, 193–94, 202–203, 215–16, 233–44, 249, 291.

52. "Terrorist Grip on Italy," p. 7; Crenshaw, "Theories of Terrorism," pp. 13–31; Cordes, "When Terrorists Do the Talking," pp. 150–71; Pier Vittorio Buffa and Pier-Luigi Ficoneri, "Problema: chi ci difendera'? E in che modo?" *L'Espresso*, August 16, 1981, pp. 7–10; "Un-'azione preventiva," in *Il Progresso* (New Jersey), January 3, 1982; Carducci, *Componenti Storico-Sociali*, pp. 80, 122–23; Camera dei Deputati, *Relazione della Commissione Parlamentare . . . Moro*; "Terrorism in Italy," p. 151; Weinberg and Eubank, *Rise and Fall of Italian Terrorism*, pp. 7–8.

53. Rubenstein, *Alchemists of Revolution*, pp. 123–25; Crenshaw, "Theories of Terrorism," pp. 13–31; Cordes, "When Terrorists Do the Talking," pp. 150–71; "Terrorist Grip on Italy," p. 7; Luca, idem, pp. 5–7; Wagner-Pacifici, *Moro Morality Play*, pp. 25, 30, 75, 143–44, 209; Buffa and Ficoneri, "Problema: chi ci difendera'?" pp. 7–10; "Un'Azione preventiva"; Carducci, *Componenti Storico-Sociali*, pp. 80, 122–23; Camera dei Deputati, *Relazione della Commissione Parlamentare . . . Moro*; "Terrorism in Italy," p. 151; Weinberg and Eubank, *Rise and Fall of Italian Terrorism*, pp. 7–8.

54. Carducci, *Componenti Storico-Sociali*, pp. 80–81; Bruno, "Problematiche relative," pp. 79–94; Bruno, "Il Terrorismo Politico Italiano," idem, pp. 43–49; Wagner-Pacifici, *Moro Morality Play*, pp. 72–73, 125, 143–44, 244, 249; Weinberg and Eubank, *Rise and Fall of Italian Terrorism*, pp. 49, 74, 119–40.

55. Soccorso Rosso Napoletano, eds., *I NAP: Storia dei Nuclei Armati Proletari* (Milano: Collettivo Editoriale Libri Rossi, 1976), pp. 3–133; Weinberg and Eubank, *Rise and Fall of Italian Terrorism*, pp. 59–61, 63–65; Sossi, *Nella Prigione*, pp. 79–81; Corte d'Assise d'Appello di Milano, *Sentenza N. 7/80*, pp. 2–29, 51–52; Giudice Istruttore F. Amato, *Ordinanza/Sentenza N. 10607/69*, pp. 771–76; Silj, *Mai piu' senza Fucile!* pp. 119–157; Pisano, *Structure*

and Dynamics, p. 9; Pisano, *Contemporary Italian Terrorism,* pp. 29–85; Bell, *A Time of Terror,* pp. 246–50.

56. Weinberg and Eubank, *Rise and Fall of Italian Terrorism,* pp. 59–61, 63–65; Stortoni, *Analisi d'una Organizzazione,* pp. 5–330; Pisano, *Structure and Dynamics,* pp. 4, 8–12; Pisano, *Contemporary Italian Terrorism,* pp. 29–85; Bocca, *Terrorismo Italiano,* pp. 201–254; Corte d'Assise di Torino, *Sentenza N. 17/81,* July 28, 1981, pp. 11–112; Corte di Firenze, *Sentenza,* April 4, 1983, pp. 135–36.

57. Rubenstein, *Alchemists of Revolution,* pp. 35–64, 126–32; Michael Ledeen. *L'Internazionale Nera* (Milano: Sugar, 1970); Pisano, *Contemporary Italian Terrorism,* pp. 2–56; Weinberg and Eubank, *Rise and Fall of Italian Terrorism,* pp. 6–7, 41, 45–46; Bonante ed., *Dimensioni del Terrorismo Politico;* Guerri, ed., *Patrizio Peci,* pp. 171–77; Cesare De Simone, *La Pista Nera* (Roma: Editori Riuniti, 1972), pp. 38–42; T. Anselmi, "Il Complotto di Licio Gelli."

58. Weinberg and Eubank, *Rise and Fall of Italian Terrorism,* pp. 6–7; Bonante, ed., *Dimensioni del Terrorismo Politico;* Guerri, ed., *Patrizio Peci,* pp. 171–77; Vittorio Lojacono, "La Foto-Chiave dei Collegamenti Internazionali delle Brigate Rosse," *Il Progresso* (New Jersey), December 30, 1981; "Un'azione preventiva"; Pisano, *Structure and Dynamics,* pp. 13–14; Carducci, *Componenti Storico-Sociali,* pp. 103–112, 114–23; Jan Schreiber, *The Ultimate Weapon: Terrorism and World Order* (New York: William Morrow, 1978), pp. 3–234; Rote Armee Faktion, *La Guerriglia nella Metropoli,* pp. 4–233; Kellen, *On Terrorists,* pp. 14–67, 87–198; Becker, *Hitler's Children,* pp. 2–57; Paolo Calderoni and Franco Giustolisi, "Il Grande Vecchio abita a Tripoli," *L'Espresso,* Milan, January 31, 1982; Camera dei Deputati, *Relazione della Commissione Parlamentare . . . Moro,* pp. 151–52; Luigi Migliorino, "L'Italia e il Terrorismo Internazionale," in *Dimensioni del Terrorismo Politico,* ed. Bonante, pp. 313–46.

59. Pisano, *Structure and Dynamics,* pp. 13–14; Schreiber. *The Ultimate Weapon,* pp. 3–234; Camera dei Deputati, *Relazione della Commissione Parlamentare . . . Moro;* Carducci, *Componenti Storico-Sociali,* pp. 121–22; Calderoni and Giustolisi, "Grande Vecchio"; Weinberg and Eubank, *Rise and Fall of Italian Terrorism,* pp. 6–9; Bonante, ed., *Dimensioni del Terrorismo Politico;* Migliorino, "L'Italia e il Terrorismo Internazionale," pp. 313–46; David T. Schiller, "A Battlegroup Divided: The Palestinian Fedayeen," in *Inside Terrorist Organizations,* ed. Rapoport, pp. 90–108; C. Wardlaw, "Terror as an Instrument," ibid., pp. 237–59.

60. Ray S. Cline and Yonah Alexander, *Terrorism: The Soviet Connection* (New York: Crane Russak, 1984); Pisano, *Structure and Dynamics,* pp. 13–14; V. Pisano, *Communist-Bloc Covert Action: the Italian Case* (Washington, DC: I.A.C.P.-Library of Congress, 1981), pp. 1–78; Sterling, *Terror Network,* pp. 289–92; Sterling, *Time of the Assassins;* Kupperman and Trent, *Terrorism,* p. 25; Schiller, "A Battlegroup Divided," pp. 90–108; Wardlaw, "Terror as an Instrument," pp. 237–59; Weinberg and Eubank, *Rise and Fall of Italian Terrorism,* pp. 6–12; Guerri, ed., *Patrizio Peci,* pp. 171–77; Bonante, ed., *Dimensioni del Terrorismo Politico;* L. Migliorino, "L'Italia e il Terrorismo Internazionale," pp. 313–46.

61. Sterling. *Terror Network;* Sterling, *Time of the Assassins;* Levitt, ed., *Democracies against Terror,* pp. 1–47, 57–92; Schiller. "A Battlegroup Divided," pp. 90–108; Cline and Alexander, *Terrorism: The Soviet Connection;* Wardlaw, "Terror as an Instrument," pp. 237–59; Rubenstein, *Alchemists of Revolution,* pp. xix, 34–64.

62. Sterling, *Terror Network,* p. 293.

63. Rubenstein, *Alchemists of Revolution,* pp. xix, 34–64, 123–25; Sterling, *Terror Network,* pp. 34, 294–95; Cline and Alexander, *Terrorism: The Soviet Connection;* Levitt, ed., *Democracies Against Terror;* pp. 1–24, 57–92; Weinberg and Eubank, *Rise and Fall of Italian Terrorism,* pp. 6–8; Wardlaw, "Terror as an Instrument," pp. 237–59; Paul Wilkinson, *Terrorism and the Liberal State* (New York: John Wiley, 1977); Wagner-Pacifici, *Moro Morality Play,* pp. 25, 30, 75.

64. Netanyahu, ed., *Terrorism: How the West Can Win;* Rubenstein, *Alchemists of Revolution,* pp. xiv–xx, 34–64, 123–25; Levitt, ed., *Democracies Against Terror,* pp. 1–24, 57–105; Wagner-Pacifici, *Moro Morality Play,* pp. 25, 30, 75; Cline and Alexander, *Terrorism: The Soviet Connection;* Sterling, *Terror Network,* p. 294; Calderoni and Giustolisi, "Grande Vecchio"; I.A.I., *Libya* (Roma: I.A.I., 1983), pp. 1–123; Pisano, *Communist-Bloc Covert Action,* pp. 2–3;

296   *M. Rimanelli*

Kupperman and Trent, *Terrorism*, pp. 9–10; Laqueur, *Terrorism*; Wilkinson, *Terrorism and the Liberal State*; Wardlaw, "Terror as an Instrument," pp. 237–59; Weinberg and Eubank, *Rise and Fall of Italian Terrorism*, pp. 6–12, 22–23; Duroselle, *Histoire Diplomatique*, pp. 71–72, 91–93, 157–60, 214, 270–71.

65. Rubenstein, *Alchemists of Revolution*, pp. xiii–xx, 34–64, 132–38, 201–205; Weinberg and Eubank, *Rise and Fall of Italian Terrorism*, p. 9; Calderoni and Giustolisi, "Grande Vecchio"; I.A.I., *Libya*, pp. 1–123; Migliorino, "L'Italia e il Terrorismo Internazaionale," pp. 313–46; in Levitt, ed., *Democracies Against Terror*, pp. 1–47, 57–92; Schiller, "A Battlegroup Divided," pp. 90–108; Wardlaw, "Terror as an Instrument," pp. 237–59.

66. Rubenstein, *Alchemists of Revolution*, pp. xiv, 51–53, 55–56; Sandro Acciari, Paolo Calderoni and Mario Scialoja, "Una Pistola Marca K.G.B.," *L'Espresso*, Milan, December 12, 1982; Sterling, *Time of the Assassins*; Wagner-Pacifici, *Moro Morality Play* pp. 25, 30, 75, 143–44, 209; Franco Coisson, "E ora Fanfani cosa fa?" in *L'Espresso*, December 19, 1982; Weinberg and Eubank, *Rise and Fall of Italian Terrorism*, p. 9; Paul Henze, *The Plot to kill the Pope* (New York: Scribner, 1985).

67. Kupperman and Trent, *Terrorism*, pp. 9–10; Netanyahu, ed., *Terrorism: How the West Can Win*, Levitt, ed., *Democracies Against Terror*, pp. 1–47, 93–118.

68. Philippe Pons, "La Faillite des Brigades Rouges," *Le Monde Hebdomadaire*, Paris, March 12 and 15, 1982; Enzo Biagi, *Il Buon Paese* (Milano: Mondadori, 1981): Pier-Vittorio Buffa, "Il Rullo Compressore," *L'Espresso*, February 28, 1982; Buffa, "Fu un Fantasma a dare l'Ordine," *L'Espresso*, July 18, 1981; Laqueur, *Terrorism*, pp. 5–198; Kupperman and Trent, *Terrorism*; Garruccio, *Italia senza Eroi*, pp. 254–56; Jan M. Coetzee, *Waiting for the Barbarians* (Johannesburg, South-Africa: Raven Press, 1985).

Part VI
Obstacles to Reform and
Achievements to Date

[37]
Consociational Politics and Italian Democracy*

Adriano Pappalardo

Translated by Jane Brillante and Mark Donovan

According to Arend Lijphart, consociational democracy is characterised essentially by the priority given to co-operation by the elites of divided and mutually hostile subcultures, and this co-operation is established 'with the deliberate aim of counteracting disintegrative tendencies in the system'. One is clearly dealing with a definition which stresses 'the voluntary, rational, purposive, and contractual elements' of the consociational model, in accordance with the conviction that it can be adopted with 'a creative and constructive act of free will'.[1] However, this conviction is not shared by all, or at least not for everyone is it the best methodological starting point. So, for example, Val Lorwin observed that 'building effective elite co-operation into the definition' opens one to the risk of neglecting 'to examine the conditions which induce, and those which inhibit or frustrate such co-operation'.[2] In fact, this is one of the limitations of Lijphart's approach, ample space being dedicated to the historical, structural and cultural conditions of consociational democracy, but without the necessary rigour, without adequately justifying the selection of undoubtedly plausible conditions and putting these together with many others that are, on the contrary, doubtful and counter-productive.[3] However, this difficulty is not insuperable because on closer examination of the relevant literature it is possible to discard what needs discarding and to conclude, unambiguously, that what contributed to the success of consociational initiatives in countries such as Austria, the Netherlands and Belgium were:

- the stability of the subcultures that the elites represented, and
- a high degree of elite power over their followers, assured by the latter's incorporation in pervasive, deeply-rooted and highly centralised, organisational structures, and by a deferential, or politically acquiescent, political culture.[4]

I have argued in a previous work that these are, logically, the only reliable conditions for predicting consociational outcomes, thus obviating another limitation of the 'voluntaristic' approach. This limitation is precisely that, in fact, the elite variable is not a good predictor and, as Lijphart himself writes, serves at most better to explain the consociational 'paradox':

*Translation of 'La Politica Consociativa nella Democrazia Italiana', *Rivista Italiana di Scienza Politica* (1980), 73–123.

that is, the fact that fragmented systems in which one would have expected instability and inefficiency have instead given optimal proof of stability and efficiency. But this does not change the fact, Lijphart continues, that 'Elite behaviour seems to be more elusive and less susceptible to empirical generalisation than mass phenomena'. The '*explanatory* power of this type is therefore quite considerable, but its *predictive* power is for the same reason rather limited'.[5]

Nevertheless, Lijphart did not abide by this careful theoretical premise when he extrapolated the future attitudes of the elites from past ones in order to predict, with great optimism, that the Netherlands of the late sixties would remain consociational. This means that he did not refrain from basing everything on 'the quality of leadership', even at the risk of being mistaken. If one thing is certain, it is that in practice Dutch politics has followed another course entirely. It is equally certain that this course could have been more correctly identified by giving more consideration to the conditions indicated above.[6] But, why, then, does Lijphart not do so?

Well, in my opinion the reason is substantially extra-scientific, and this seems clear if one considers that for this author the consociational model is of use not only for explaining a phase of development in the Netherlands and other small European democracies, that is for a merely historical purpose (since they have, to a greater or lesser extent, left that phase behind). Additionally, there is the fact that 'The consociational experiences of Austria, Belgium and the Netherlands ... provide concrete examples of how democracy can be a stable and effective system of government in ... societies' that are profoundly divided. As such, these examples provide as many 'normative' challenges to the conventional pessimism of the seventies regarding these societies,[7] so long as, be it understood, they are easily exportable. The answer is most certainly positive if what counts for successfully implementing a consociational enterprise is 'a constructive and creative act of free will'. And this is because – explains Lijphart – such an act can well be replicated given the single condition that the apprentices know how to profit from the 'transnational diffusion of knowledge' so as to imitate the Dutch, Belgian and Austrian lessons.[8]

Thus, it has to be admitted that to privilege the role of the elites makes things very easy. And precisely for this reason it is permissible to suspect that Lijphart is so forcefully optimistic regarding the consociational future of the Netherlands, seeking above all to secure in advance the basis for his normative discourse. Otherwise this optimism would not be justified, being founded on a variable like leadership quality which he too finds of scarce predictive power. But, if this is the case, in choosing the 'voluntaristic' approach, it is probable that prescriptive motivations prevail, from which one would only be able to deduce that the consociational model *should* be exported, and not whether it *can* be or not.

Nevertheless, it goes without saying that the second issue is crucial for evaluating the ability of this model to satisfy the demand for democratic stability and efficiency in countries which are currently unstable and inefficient. And here, analysis of the conditions would seem to me to be obligatory, for two reasons. Firstly, because it is much more productive than postulating an act of imitation carried out by creative and well informed elites, as per Lijphart. This, in fact, is an alternative which – independently of its prescriptive flavour – leaves unaltered the predictive limitations of the elites variable. Indeed, it makes them worse, in that we know for certain that even consolidated coalescent behaviour is not sufficient to predict the continuation of a consociational system which is already stable and efficient.[9] As a consequence, relying on the elites variable alone to predict the consociational evolution of systems which are neither stable nor efficient would evidently be even more hazardous,[10] in that such an evolution presumes a deliberate *change* in the behaviour of these elites.

Furthermore, Lijphart himself maintained that the attitudes and behaviour of the elites must conform to four 'prerequisites' for a successful imitation of his model. This, in fact, requires the ability:

- to recognise the dangers inherent in a fragmented system;
- to commit oneself to assuring the survival of the system;
- to transcend subcultural cleavage at the elite level, and
- to forge appropriate solutions to subcultural demands.[11]

The point is, that the possession of such abilities by elites in transition towards a consociational settlement depends to a large extent on (a) there being stability between the subcultures and/or (b) on the strength of the elites over their own followers. Therefore it is all the more necessary to conclude that the dynamics and outcome of that transition can be foreseen with reasonable safety only on the basis of our conditions.[12]

The Prerequisites of the Elites: A Preliminary Discourse

As we will see later on, a series of facts corroborates the previous conclusion, proving the existence of a clear relationship between the [two] conditions [stated above] and the elites' prerequisites. But even before being empirically founded, the stated relationship is logically plausible. To demonstrate this, let us begin by taking the first prerequisite, that is, the elites' 'ability to recognise the dangers inherent in a fragmented system'.[13] As Lijphart specified, this means that 'The leaders must be fully aware of the system's unstable tendencies caused by subcultural cleavages'. And in my opinion, for this it is necessary that further divisions are not added *within* the subcultures because, if they are, the additional divisions would obscure the first ones, reducing or inhibiting the perception of their danger. In fact, if internal divisions exist, the elites will have other things to think about. So, for example, they will probably have to give priority to the struggle against possible splits from their own bloc fed by those divisions. Alternatively, they will have to defend themselves from oppositional factions whose objective is to depose them and take their place, rather than provoke a split. But in both cases, a large part of the ruling elites' time, attention and energies will be dedicated to these problems, that is to reinforcing or protecting their weak and threatened power; whereas, where this power is unquestioned from the outset, conflicts with other forces in the system and the fate of the system as such would more easily stay at the centre of their attention which, as Lijphart suggests, is 'particularly important at the crucial stage of the initial establishment of consociational practices'.[14] Which is like saying that his first prerequisite will be fulfilled if, and to the extent that, the second of the previously recorded conditions is fulfilled.

But to install a lasting consociational democracy, equally indispensable for Lijphart is 'the commitment to system maintenance', that is, the will of the elites 'to make an effort to halt and reverse the disintegrative tendencies'.[15] Stability between the subcultures can tell us a lot about this other prerequisite once the idea is discarded that its existence depends exclusively or predominantly on there being a widespread and genuine consensus (which a profoundly divided system cannot enjoy, by definition). In fact, if consensus does not exist (at all, or at least in part), the pro-system commitment of the elites can be explained (wholly or in part) by the argument that no one expects to gain anything by supporting disaggregative tendencies; on the contrary, indeed, everyone fears losing something.

There may be various reasons for this: for example, because the one side expects to be defeated in a struggle with opponents who are stronger; or because the other side, despite starting out with a relative advantage, does not expect to win, excepting at costs which are too high; or because the relationship of forces between the contenders is such as to create general uncertainty about the outcome as against the certainty of embarking on a tough, long and wearying contest. But whatever is the case, it is clear that the common basis for all these expectations is the other's perceived incoercibility or, very much to the point, the awareness of operating in a substantially stable system. The more widespread this awareness is among the elites, the more likely it is that they will prefer co-operation in defence of the *status quo* to the risk-laden changes that conflictual strategies would provoke.

We come to the third prerequisite, that is to the 'ability to transcend subcultural cleavage ... to break through the barriers to mutual understanding caused by subcultural differences, and to establish effective contacts and communication across these cleavages'.[16] Is it possible for elites lacking adequate power over their own followers to have this ability? It is possible, yes, but not as probable as in the opposite case. The main reason is that breaking the barriers to understanding and compromise brought about by cultural differences is initially difficult for any leadership which, by doing so, departs radically from its usual conflictual behaviour. But it is even more so if that leadership is weak and therefore has to take into account both the difficulty of overcoming its own psychological resistance to change and the risk of losing, as a consequence, one of the few remaining sources of power that it has left. In other words, that is, resistance to change can itself be indispensable for avoiding a serious power crisis which may precipitate the elite's overthrow by powerful internal rivals or an outward flow of followers towards external competitors. And since this is particularly likely in profoundly divided societies where the bulk of followers are hostile to every significant conciliatory move, one can be sure that a weak leadership will not miss the opportunity to provide grounds for continuing support. On the contrary, the greater the weakness, the more the leadership will have to show that it knows how to maintain continuity with the past. And from this position not only will its ability to understand and conduct a dialogue beyond the subcultural cleavages evidently suffer, but so will its perception of those others – to whom more hostility will probably be attributed than they actually harbour, and to whom little credibility will be granted if they in turn become promoters of conciliatory initiatives.

But let us suppose that the leadership is relatively strong – even if not absolutely unquestioned – and let us ask ourselves if Lijphart's prerequisite can be satisfied from this less difficult position. Let us even hypothesise that initially it is satisfied, thanks to the fact that a given leadership doesn't have to deal with an already organised, powerful internal opposition nor to fear rapidly losing support and so giving advantage to external competitors. After which let us ask ourselves what could happen once it has made the first efforts to transcend the subcultural cleavages. The answer will most likely be pessimistic, for two reasons. Firstly, these efforts may in fact be indispensable for initiating a dialogue with the others, but they don't bring immediately useful results (and indeed they may even distance them if the overtures by one side serve merely to show that the other side doesn't want to know). Furthermore, if the conciliatory leadership is not unquestioned, its move will at the least sow discord, confusion or irritation at the grassroots. And even if these reactions can officially be ignored or minimised by the establishment, it is easy to foresee that they will make life more difficult for it, provoking the concern that they will, sooner or later, encourage the formation of a counter-elite capable of challenging its power. This does not automatically mean that from our second example one should return to the conclusions of the first. Indeed, at first sight these problems could well stimulate an attempt to speed up the process of consociational agreement in the hope of quickly showing the rank and file that the dialogue is 'paying off'.

If it were not for the fact that, as I said, the preliminaries must not be confused with the results; all the less in a profoundly divided society where distances between the different groups are presumably wide and cannot, therefore, be closed rapidly. Further, the time taken will also depend on the attitude of the opposing side whose interest in lengthening the process may be all the greater the more it perceives the first side's need for urgency and its growing difficulties caused by its own delaying tactics. And, finally, the results achieved might not themselves be welcomed by the followers, thus increasing the discontent that in the intentions of the leadership was expected to lessen.[17] Therefore, the most probable thing is that, facing so many uncertainties, this leadership will react by displaying a less coherent behaviour, alternating, that is, readiness to transcend the subcultural cleavages with the renewal of their closing in upon themselves. If this is not exactly the same as what an initially weak leadership would do, it is, however, certain that it would provoke a prolonged situation of stalemate mid-way through the process which a very strong leadership would more easily be able to avoid.

All this, finally, applies all the more to the fourth and last prerequisite, which Lijphart regards as the most important and which consists, as one will remember, in the 'ability to forge appropriate solutions for the demands of the subcultures ... to develop both institutional arrangements and rules of the game for the accommodation of their differences'.[18] In fact, in this case too, one is dealing with the breaking of past attitudes and, simultaneously, the elaboration *ex novo* of the above mentioned rules and arrangements (grand coalitions, proportionalism, reciprocal veto, etc.) without any certainty that they will bear the desired fruits, without sufficient experience of bargaining with yesterday's 'enemy', and without the reciprocal trust that only a long habit of collaboration can bring about.

Consequently, it is clear that the elites will face an accumulation of uncertainties sufficiently discouraging in themselves to feed a strong temptation to cling to the *status quo*. And this temptation will probably become irresistible if the will for change is not accompanied by the power necessary to impose it on the mass base, which is particularly important in the phase in which one prepares the instruments and defines the criteria upon which the costs and benefits of consociational co-operation, and their distribution among all those concerned, will be based. On this point, we know enough plausibly to maintain that the perceptions the elites have of each other will usually differ very greatly from those of their respective followers. And if, for example, we admit that the former do think it advantageous to embark on grand coalitions, to institutionalise the proportional system and the right of veto in the decisional process, then one can easily foresee that the mass base will react negatively to these moves, for a variety of reasons. It will realise immediately that a grand coalition may bring with it the sacrifice of some of the values and partisan symbols to which it is most emotionally attached, as well as placing more or less rigid constraints on the expression of hostile sentiment and long-held wishes of revenge towards the adversary. The proportional method will be perceived equally negatively in that, to make space for everyone, it will oblige each and everyone to do without a number of expected or hoped-for material benefits, and it will be accused by some of reducing the power of their own side below what is permissible, and by others of not providing for adequate recognition for the other side.

On the other hand, the elites will certainly do everything to forestall these recriminations by emphasising the benefits of co-operation and by stressing that without it, the system would be destined to certain collapse, with disastrous effects for everyone. But so long as things are not speeded up, the mass base will probably find it difficult to appreciate that it is worth paying a high price in order to avoid an apparently hypothetical loss; and the very benefits that the elites can assure the public in the short term are likely to easily pass unobserved since they are collective benefits allocated fairly (that is proportionally) between members of the two or more contending parts. Furthermore, any benefit will be taken for granted by most and, once acquired, will be seen as demonstrating one's own strength rather than the adversary's reasonableness. Lastly, most of the promised benefits will be of the indirect type (such as the safeguarding of the well-being of the system) or due at some future date, thus appearing less 'real' than the evident costs to be met immediately.

In sum, the problem is this, that the mass base is used to considering and choosing within a narrower temporal horizon than the elites, and it feeds upon far larger expectations than the elites have.[19] Exactly the opposite, that is, of what the 'institutional arrangements' and the consociational 'rules of the game' presuppose. So, it's one or the other: either this acute attitudinal dissonance is kept under control by organisational and cultural resources sufficient to organise one's followers in a disciplined and deferential bloc, or the elites that are not capable of this will not even try to implement these arrangements and rules, or, at most, they will make little progress in this direction, moving between growing uncertainty and a temptation to go back to square one as the malaise among their own ranks grows.

Whatever is the case, it is clear that the last of Lijphart's four prerequisites is also no exception to the rule already confirmed by the other three, being equally susceptible to explanation and prediction by one of our conditions of consociational democracy. Neither is this proven solely by logic, because there are certainly facts supportive of the previous argument. And the remainder of the present essay proposes precisely to show this, examining to that end the case of Italy. In the last few years, in fact, 'predictions' of a consociational future have been made, more or less cautiously, for this country.[20] It is thus worthwhile pursuing the argument according to my perspective which, as we will see, leads to very different conclusions and ones much closer to the real course of events.

The Case of Italy

In my opinion, to anticipate a consociational course for the Italian crisis of the seventies is unproductive and misleading because it implies excessive concessions to voluntarism and optimism *à la* Lijphart.[21] In other words this forecast is only tenable if one is confident that coalescent behaviour by our major parties depends exclusively on the good will and ability of the elites, neglecting even a rudimentary analysis of the relevant conditions.[22] However, when such an analysis is attempted, it is far too easy to show that these conditions scarcely apply to Italy, especially from 1968 onwards. And my argument is precisely that it is in part because of this that the Italian elites have, up to now, lacked most of the necessary prerequisites to consolidate the various attempts at institutional co-operation that have been made since the appearance on the scene of such formulae as the historic compromise or the government of national unity.

On the other hand, these prerequisites (and the pertaining conditions) have not been entirely lacking because the historic compromise and the like do truly have a structural and psychological base. But the essential fact is that this is also the only one, and as such can serve only to explain why one and the other formula for extended co-operation have been taken into consideration by our political forces; while if these same forces find difficulty in putting them into practice it is because of the countervailing effect of the conditions that were acting decidedly against the surviving prerequisites, which we shall see below. For now, it is worth beginning with the favourable point which is, in my opinion, the stability between the subcultures and the consequent evolution of the elites (especially communist) towards the idea of avoiding a break in the system that would have dangerous repercussions for whomever tried it.

This point can initially be illustrated by observing that, like Austria, Belgium and the Netherlands, Italy has been, and for the most remains, a country of highly inclusive 'spiritual families' powerfully determining electoral behaviour, even if neither one nor the other of these characteristics has presented itself with the intensity found in the first three countries at the peak of their consociational experiences.[23] Nevertheless, the fact is that the research that we have available documents a high level of continuity in the party preferences of members of the same subculture, across the passage of the generations.[24] In addition, it is even more notable (and more important for our purposes) that the majority of the flow of votes recorded is seen to pass 'between similar parties, or at least more or less neighbouring ones, at least in the eyes of the voters – on the left-right spectrum. ... Decisions implying a switch ... that is votes that may be called conversion or [re]alignment votes, are, on the other hand, much less frequent.'[25] And if it is true that this alignment logic weakened in the mid-seventies, with the decline of the moderate-catholic subculture in favour of the socialist one, and particularly the PCI one, the rupture that took place does not exclude continuity with the past. In the first place because to decline does not mean to collapse; and indeed, in response to the question as to whether the hold of subcultural traditions is still strong, 'analysis of the data suggests a fundamentally affirmative answer'.[26] In the second place, because the incidence of one of the components of recent changes in the balance of forces (generational renewal) was particularly elevated in 1976, given the exceptional concentration of first-time voters, and will be less in the future.[27] Lastly, because the second component (defection from one subculture to another) was already falling in 1976 compared to the previous year, and it was certainly insignificant in the 1979 elections.[28]

So, even without excluding further long-term changes arising from other factors which have been suggested,[29] it is to be believed that for now Italian stability is not a thing of the past. However, what counts for our purposes is not just the fact, but also the *perception* of it by the elites of the major parties whose strategies reveal the conviction – maybe exaggerated, but not any the less significant in its consequences for that – that little has changed, that today is more similar to yesterday than it is different from it. So, yesterday the strategy of the DC and PCI was an ostentatiously conflictual one, conducted, however, within the limits of an 'uncertain compromise', of an uncomfortable *modus vivendi* accepted by both parts out of fear of the other's strength and of the other's prevarications.[30] The most salient manifestations of this compromise, from which a situation of real and psychological deadlock was inevitable, are, as is well-known, the pre-1948 institutional agreements. But this deadlock endured – after that year's pause and the harshest moments of the cold war – with the more or less obligatory adaptation to the limits placed on action by a system whose [fragile] equilibrium did not allow anyone to play any other game but the democratic one. And the communist elites in particular – for whom this process was less taken for granted and more demanding – took due note of it, launching the 'Italian road to socialism' in which analyses and concerns came together which centred entirely on the risks of a head-on encounter with the other side which would have definitely been lost, and was judged in this light.[31]

It is for this reason that the 'Italian road' banished from the party's strategy the logic of 'the worse the better' and committed the party to professing its loyalty to a system that – *faute de mieux* – came to be recognised as capable of opening to it the door to power, albeit on certain conditions. Such conditions have been described repeatedly by an extensive literature which it is neither necessary nor possible to examine in detail here.[32] But it is well known that it emphasises the fundamental role that the Communists, in the march to power, have for long attached to a policy of alliances (and compromises) with classes or groups different from their traditional supporters and more recently with their traditional political representatives. I say more recently, because it is not clear whether the PCI in the past included or excluded the greater part of the DC among its desired allies or whether it counted on a split in this party between the progressive component (with which to come to an arrangement) and an integralist or conservative part (to isolate).[33] But the question had to be superseded anyway in 1971–72 when the strategy of the historic compromise was born (even if the label came later) with which 'Berlinguer now made an explicit assumption and drew an equally explicit conclusion: the assumption was that the DC had an electoral base that was both popular and quite stable; the conclusion, that the PCI would abandon any attempt to split off the presumably healthy parts of the DC and would hereafter act to make Christian Democracy *as a whole* accept the necessity of governing with the Communist party'.[34]

In other words, that is, at the beginning of the seventies the leadership of this party evidently appeared to be convinced of the solidity of the opposing alignment in a way that it never had been before and, from this, it derived good reason for rejecting every aggressive and destructive initiative in the most direct, explicit and committed way possible (that is by asking to collaborate with the DC in government). And yet precisely this leadership had started out very differently, in that Berlinguer himself, at the outset, was a man on the left of the PCI and, prior to 1971, had sympathised with the great collective movements (student and worker) which then dominated the Italian scene, setting to work to stress the radical nature of the party's policy and political image.[35] And so, everyone suggested that 'Italian life' would get harder rather than easier under his leadership. And if the opposite then happened, it is for reasons well summarised by Hellman and which are perfectly in line with the general premise of my analysis. In fact, this author has rightly emphasised that at first Berlinguer followed the example of the upheavals of 1968–69 in the expectation that the instability resulting from them would be to his advantage; whereas the immediate effect of these upheavals was the right-wing backlash of 1970–72 which showed that 'the PCI was not prepared to launch a head-on attack on the DC and on state power' and, indeed, 'convinced the PCI that an aggressive approach to the DC, based on constant confrontation and polarisation of the kind that had occurred during the hot autumn, might well result in the isolation that has been the PCI's special nightmare since the fascist era'.[36] Hence the change in Berlinguer's behaviour, a Berlinguer 'mark II' dictated by the confirmation of clearly unfavourable electoral equilibria and 'by defensive self-interest or even by outright fear' rekindled by these:[37] an instinct and fear that the PCI showed again in 1973 when faced with the events in Chile, when its analysis emphasised that 'confrontation and frontal collision' with the DC would lead 'to a split, to a real and thorough-going division of the country into two parts that would be disastrous for democracy and would overwhelm the very foundations of the democratic state'. And so, the conclusion was, once again, that in the interest of the system (and more concretely, of the party), an agreement can and must be found, given above all the imminence of 'a stable and organic union between the centre and the right'.[38]

Nevertheless, precisely this union was developing in 1974 with the divorce referendum which the PCI, quite coherently, did everything to avoid, by whatever compromise; it embarked upon it, fearing the worst, only because forced by the intransigence of others; and unexpectedly it came out of it a winner. But it did not, on this account, change its perception of the situation, seeing that not only was Berlinguer concerned immediately to warn his followers not to overvalue the importance of the result obtained, but also that he formulated a series of proposals intended to create difficulties for the promoters of later referendums and declared himself to be convinced that it is precisely when the 'forces of progress' advance that there is more reason to fear a conservative counter-offensive to be in the offing.[39] Which is like saying that even the test that has just been overcome reinforces the urgency of the historic compromise, rather than weakens it. And if it is true that this [strategy] was conceived at a difficult time, the very different events of 1974 (and 1975) did not change its defensive significance, as we know from the argument that 'even if the left-wing parties eventually reached, election after election, 51% of the votes, this majority would not in itself be enough to form a government capable of lasting, of withstanding the frontal attack of the remaining 49% and at the same time carrying out the job of transformation which would be at the heart of its programme'.[40] Which argument is all the more valid in 1976 when the PCI got over 34% of the vote and came close to 47% with the other left-wing parties. Yet confronting a DC fully recovered compared to 1975 it took steps, as per usual, to exorcise the feared risk of polarisation. Thus, it claimed 'not to be surprised' by the recovery of this party, confirming (beyond what was consented by the evidence) that it remained stable, strong and popular, and proceeding to seek to persuade it, for the whole of the successive legislature, to permit a full government alliance.[41]

However, these moves were only partially successful because, right up until the final dissolution of parliament, they come up against the Christian Democrats' resistance to go beyond the programmatic majority of the fourth Andreotti government. But even so it is clear that the [Christian Democrats] have in turn adapted to the idea of an agreement with the opposition, and for reasons that fit my hypotheses perfectly. Indeed, it is the case that the idea in question took shape immediately after the failure of the conflictual strategy that Fanfani pursued up until the mid-seventies. And from my viewpoint, the important thing is that that strategy – which culminated in 1974 – resulted from the conviction that ample profit was to be drawn from the weakness shown by the left after the hot autumn, and from the victories of the extreme right for whom he rightly predicted easy reabsorption. Except that in the year of the referendum on divorce, his principal adversaries [the PCI] took clamorous revenge. And if that wasn't enough to free the latter from fearing the worst, the same fear now seized the DC as well, persuading it to change direction. So, it quickly got the fourth Moro government under way, which treated the Communists as privileged interlocutors. The secretary, Fanfani, meanwhile was left with just one last chance: the 1975 elections. And, when this trial of strength also failed, the hand passed to Zaccagnini and his demiurge Moro – not, it has rightly been observed, that they trusted the Communists any more than Fanfani did; but they were more pessimistic about the fate of a party whose opposition was stronger than ever and whose traditional allies were in revolt.[42] It was precisely for this reason that they launched the strategy of *confronto* [an ambiguous term meaning confrontation but also competition and even comparison] and confirmed the DC's accommodating U-turn, thus repeating the itinerary run by Berlinguer, beginning with the realisation that the structure [*assetto*] of the system – and its stability (real or perceived) – does not promise anything other than isolation to anyone who tries to support 'disintegrative tendencies'.

Neither is all this simply yesterday's history, as subsequent events, such as the PCI's return to opposition and the simultaneous abandonment of the grand coalition, show. As is quite clear, these events did not, in fact, follow a significant change in the global balance of strength *between* the subcultures, both because they preceded the last elections [1979] and because such change was missing [even] in 1979 (even if there was a shift at the expense of the PCI *within* the socialist subculture). And, what is more, both the Communist elites and the Christian Democratic elites in the 'Zaccagnini area' continue to maintain that the other's strength remains such as not to leave any suitable alternative to a policy of co-operation – more or less specific and institutionalised – in the interest of system maintenance.[43] Consequently, on the one hand, one cannot deny that these elites still possess the second prerequisite postulated by Lijphart and that it is supported by conditions of lasting stability. Yet, on the other hand, it is also true that a step backward has taken place in respect of the seventh legislature [1976–79] and it has to be explained, if possible, in terms compatible with my interpretative scheme. Which in my opinion is feasible, bearing in mind that according to this system one prerequisite alone is not sufficient to ensure the success of a consociational initiative. As I have in fact already said, to achieve this the other three are also necessary, together with the relevant condition (that is, that the different elites should have a high level of power over their followers, guaranteed both by a deeply rooted and centralised organisation and a deferential political culture). And this condition, to the contrary, was glaringly absent in 1970's Italy, creating serious obstacles to the emergence and consolidation of an adequate ability in the elites to recognise the dangers inherent in a fragmented system, to transcend the subcultural cleavages and to forge appropriate solutions to the demands of the subcultures via the institutional arrangements of the consociational game and based on its rules.

So, the hypothesis is that it was these obstacles that complicated the move towards *rapprochement* between the DC and the PCI and, in the end, determined an initial failure which, let it be clear, may not be final. It is precisely for this reason that [the failure] should be examined in the light of the interaction between elite-mass relations and the prerequisites of the elites, in the belief that this is crucial both in formulating a retrospective explanation and for proffering reasonable forecasts regarding the fate of any further attempts at coalescence. It is to this interaction that the next few pages will be dedicated, seeking to break it up into its various components, beginning with one of the most important: the attitudes and images by which the two major parties' electorates evaluate each other.

This component is important for ascertaining whether, and by how much, the attitudes and images of the base differ from those of the elites, stated or implicit, in their conciliatory moves: a point about which we know enough to say that there are differences and that they are profound. So much so, that the available literature speaks accordingly of 'hostility, antagonism and reciprocal distrust .... at the mass level' on many crucial questions and at times along unexpected dimensions.[44]

Confirmed by different sources, research techniques and differing analyses, these attitudes emerge with clarity in a synthesis by Sani who reveals, among other things, 'the different attitudes that (the DC and PCI voters) display towards social groups and other political forces'. So, for example, 'the Communist voters give a largely positive evaluation to groups and movements such as the unions, the Socialist Party and the student movement, to which the DC's base is, on the contrary, hostile or neutral; whereas DC voters express a positive orientation towards the clergy, the police and large-scale industry'.[45] This is particularly important to us in that these data, collected at the end of 1975, are similar to others dating to 1972 and therefore suggest that the configuration of the lines of division at the mass level stayed reasonably unchanged precisely during the period in which the elites were moving very quickly.[46] After which it seems obvious that the base was reluctant to follow them, at least in respect of the points indicated by Sani. And this reluctance changes into outright opposition in other areas where the survival of substantially negative reciprocal images is apparent. In other words, in fact, 'there are very few interviewees (in the 1975 survey cited) who give a positive judgement of the other party, many who give a largely negative evaluation'. This same diagnosis also emerges from other data. A high percentage of Communist voters considered the DC to be an old party (80%), inefficient (74%), dishonest (76%), clerical (76%), two-thirds describing it as 'the bosses' party'. On the other hand, half of the DC's voters consider the PCI to be a revolutionary and not at all a democratic party. And if to all this one adds the fact that the self-placement of the interviewees from the two parties on the left-right spectrum remains markedly divergent, then one has a much more complete picture of the diversity of views, positions and orientations that characterise the two electorates, and consequently one can be sure that 'the encounter between the two major Italian political traditions will generate powerful tensions inside the two parties in which they express themselves'.[47]

However, it is less clear how much these tensions affected and will continue to affect the consociational project because they are, in reality, inevitable, foreseeable and expected in any profoundly divided society. Lijphart's model, of course, stipulates that the elites operate in a largely hostile environment, whilst not excluding their success on this account.[48] Consequently, not even the historic compromise can be considered a lost cause, despite its recent failures, simply on the basis of there being resistance or opposition from the grassroots. After all, even if there is resistance or opposition, the elites could pull everyone into line had they the adequate organisational and cultural resources. And if this is true, convincing explanations and predictions should not obscure this other analytical component, especially as from it emerge crucial differences between Italy and the classic consociational democracies. In fact, whilst the creators of the latter could count on the deference and political acquiescence of the masses encapsulated within highly centralised structures,[49] the same cannot be said of Italy, as I mentioned a little while ago. On the contrary, it is clear that here, deference, acquiescence and monolithic internal organisation within the subcultural blocs are today scarce and diminishing following the long erosion to which they have been subjected by over a decade of intense social mobilisation resulting from the interweaving of a crisis of distribution and a crisis of participation.[50] With the effect that the power of the elites is often limited and contested and, for the same reason, to make use of it with the necessary freedom of action is as problematic as it is dangerous.

As everyone knows, this is especially valid for the Catholic bloc which recovered better than was expected from the electoral misfortunes of 1974 and 1975; but it has certainly not recovered a discipline that was never elevated and which the events of the final years of the sixties reduced to a minimum. During those years, in fact, it was rent by the strongest centrifugal forces signalled by the disengagement of traditional flanking organisations such as ACLI and CISL and a context in which the doctrine of the political unity of Catholics was rapidly becoming obsolescent. And the DC, as a structure dependent upon those organisations and on that doctrine, suffered dreadfully the consequences. So much so, that its collapse as an associational instrument of aggregation and mobilisation of the population for collective ends was all but complete. Nor can one say that its subsequent attempts to create a new space for itself and to equip itself with a new image with which to return to organising civil society have succeeded. Indeed, they have been limited, timid and contradictory ever since their first appearance at the 1976 congress.[51]

Already then, in fact, the personal success of Zaccagnini was matched by his political defeat because the minimal margin obtained over Forlani evidently means that party unity isn't possible, least of all around the new party secretary's proposal to 're-found' the party. Hence, from the beginning he has had to adapt to an exhausting series of mediations, a habitual end in themselves for his predecessors, without any hope that they will lead to a 'clear identification of orientation points and a precise identification of political objectives'. And yet it is exactly orientation and precise objectives that are needed for the organisational reconstruction of the DC which,[52] on the contrary, is proceeding slowly because the debate on both points is still entirely open. Indeed, it is a fact that this debate is taking place between political positions whose labels and fortunes may change over time, but whose substance remains 'exclusive and incompatible'.[53] One of them is the Catholic-populist position of the 'Zaccagnini area' whose openings to the PCI aim (according to Massimo De Carolis) at 'an impossible reconciliation between an integral Christian identity and the practice of power'.[54] Another is the integralist position of movements such as Communion and Liberation which is so jealous of the party's confessional identity that it prefers the path of opposition to that of compromise with 'society's radicals'. And both are strongly contested by the vast lay-moderate political alignment, represented simultaneously or successively by the 'Democratic Pole', the 'Hundred', 'Proposal' or by the factions and fragments of traditional factions brought together by a political project of recovering a solid majority without the Communists.

So, the DC's situation is a complex one but it leaves no room for doubt concerning what interests us. From the preceding, in fact, one can conclude that the party has, until recently, been governed by an alignment which is strongly aware of the need to repair its ties with its base in order to avoid losing it amidst the 'power play' with the PCI to which it is hostile.[55]

And yet, the same base was simultaneously the object of penetration by other forces who prized its traditional values in one way or another. It is certain that this has placed limitations on the Zaccagnini leadership which the latter has tried to break precisely by consolidating its control of the party. But since this attempt did not work out, this same leadership settles on a strategy that – for all its concessions – remains well this side of Communist demands; thus, this leadership continually confirms that national solidarity is a temporary and obligatory experience required by the economic-institutional emergency; and thus it is that this leadership goes as far as the programmatic majority, yet puts in charge of it a government representing the cream of the party's right-wing.[56] This means that the tempering of advances by steps backward has been continuous and absolutely does not augur the 'comprehensive and far-reaching' agreements 'forged within a relatively short period of time' that are achieved by consociational elites elsewhere.[57] But the point is that such accords presuppose a politics undertaken by rigorously authoritative plenipotentiaries for whom the parliamentary and party apparatus are but the executive arms, and the party members obedient spectators. In the DC, however, the parliamentary party is in perpetual revolt; the apparatus is too weak to guarantee the consensus of party members and these are virtually free to follow their own anti-consociational inclinations by placing themselves behind those parts of the party willing to represent them.

For these reasons I cannot see how the historic compromise can be tolerated by this side of the equation, even at some future date. But the PCI too, which continues to propose it, has many problems because the solidarity of its bloc soon showed itself to be more apparent than real in at least two respects. One of these concerns the party's relations with the union which in the past was a fundamental instrument used by the party to regiment its considerable worker base. Today, however, it is not very efficient and scarcely ready to perform this function even if its readiness has increased since reaching an extremely low point at the end of the sixties and the beginning of the seventies. At that time, and especially in the three years 1970–72, the union, in fact, experienced a season of the greatest autonomy from the parties and the most complete identification with the collective movements born of the hot autumn.[58] So much so that it wed their contractual objectives, including the most radical and destabilising ones (theorising, for example, the salary as an 'independent variable'). But above all it channelled the movements' strength into action for reforms, thereby challenging the parties' monopoly of political representation of the base. And [the parties], which at first couldn't, or didn't want, to defend that monopoly, consequently found themselves facing a process of horizontal transfer of power (from the political elites to the union elites) which firmly established a party-union dualism in every bloc troublesome for all of them, but especially for the PCI.

As we know, it was, in fact, in 1971–72 that the [PCI] set in motion its moderate turn-around in order to reach an agreement with the DC; and in order to succeed in this – and in the gradualist and top-down politics implied by it – it needed a unity of command equal if not superior to that when the union was little more than a 'conveyer belt'. Exactly the opposite of what was happening as a consequence of the new-born autonomy of the CGIL, of the radical demands being placed on it by the collective movements, of the process of union unification and of the increased strength that the leadership had at its disposal for pursuing those demands. Yet it is clear that all this had to be urgently reorganised, if not even suppressed. And to do this, a PCI 'fearful, on the one hand, of every possible disturbance of the general political balance and, on the other, of the difficulties of political management created by the presence of a large, autonomous union movement, returned to the practice of strict control over the workers' organisations'.[59] Or at least it tried, because in reality it is difficult to maintain that things went back to the way they were before, or that the union demobilised to the extent required by the new consociational course. Rather, from 1974 the union leadership (with Lama to the fore, Macario close behind and Benvenuto trailing) took to launching appeals for moderation clearly dictated by the changed political situation. And this same strategy was put into practice in great style in the dispute with Confindustria [the Italian industrial association] in the winter of 1976–77, which was unusually responsible and, in many respects, even easygoing.[60]

Faced with this, the ultras were quick to express their pessimism about the union's future central role and to judge a *fait accompli* its abdication in favour of the parties.[61] But from a less unilateral perspective the judgment has to be reconsidered because many of the facts seem to indicate otherwise. And one of the first is that among the few or many concessions of 1976–77 there were none at all on the subject of wage-indexing which was an issue which the union showed a readiness to battle for and an ability to force the PCI (initially open to the possible revision of the mechanism) rapidly to resume a tough stance. Furthermore, the PCI also showed signs of unease about the demonstrations announced by the engineering workers in Rome in December 1977. And only faced by a *fait accompli* did it accept the consequences, shifting its position to put the government, dependent on its abstention, into crisis. After which it was the turn of the programmatic majority – which fell, as is known, on two issues which were profoundly unpopular to the unions (the European Monetary System and the three year plan) and, of course, to the PCI itself. But it is a fact that, again, the party intervened only when a general strike was already fixed (for February), limiting itself to anticipating the obvious result of this decision by a few days.

So, it is obvious that the limited readiness to make concessions manifested to date by the union leadership has not been sufficient. And as far as I can see there is no likelihood of it increasing in the foreseeable future except at the expense of its efficiency in organising mass consensus. In fact, as soon as one asks how these masses would react to a coherent policy of moderation, the answer is always pessimistic: everyone speaks, with varying nuances, about the 'significant problems in controlling members' or even reminds us that 'in periods of tension the workers are able to use the union, via battles within its organisation, to express themselves directly'.[62]

This is what happened in 1968–72 when the union was shaken by a profound structural transformation which caused a drastic vertical transfer of power (from the leadership to the base). And if it is true that the organs through which this transformation was expressed (especially assemblies and factory meetings) are weakening today, nobody is under the illusion that things can go back to the conditions of near absolute hierarchical subordination dominant before 1968. Especially if one considers just a few of the problems of the past few years, among which it is sufficient to recall the union's conflictual relationship with the young (above all with students), its difficulties in organising the unemployed and the marginalised, its powerlessness in the face of the extremism of certain categories, its weakening in favour of the autonomous unions in the public sector. In brief, a combination of facts from which emerges the image of a leadership which is weak and aware of its weakness. This was shown, above all, in the space dedicated to these problems by Lama and other leaders.[63] It was also demonstrated by attempts to demobilise some of the most uncontrollable unrest in authoritarian fashion. But it was shown especially in the union's recently renewed will to fight – which might be useful for regaining credibility in the eyes of its members but certainly is not auspicious for the consociational objectives of the PCI.

Come to that, these objectives have for some time been a source of difficulty within the party which is otherwise known as a model of organised strength and cohesion. And quite rightly. Its large membership, its capillary diffusion throughout the entire country, with about 12,000 sections and centres, its communication network provided by a diversified and widely diffused media, and the efficiency of democratic centralisation in preventing breakaways are all indicators of an extremely good state of health, certainly far better than that of any other party.

All the same, this does not remove the fact that at least some of these indicators now show negative, which is all the more relevant in that this comes after a period of rapid evolution in the opposite direction. Thus, the membership of the party increased constantly from the beginning of the seventies after a long decline from 1954 to 1968. And just as this decline took place via a large number of defections only partially compensated for by new intakes, so the new increase is accompanied by a reduction of the former and an increase in the latter.[64] But neither the one nor the other lasted beyond 1976 which is also the year that they reached record percentage numbers of members (both downward and upward). In fact, in 1977 the total number of members stagnated (1,797,075 against 1,797,597 of the previous year); those of the new intake reduced both absolutely (129,351 against 170,966) and in percentage terms (going to 7.2% of members from 9.5%) and – more importantly – the non-renewed membership returns increased (from 88,564 to 129,873, 5.2% of members to 7.2%), bringing the PCI's organised strength close to that of the years of decline.

Furthermore, this decline became even greater in 1978 when the number of members fell (to 1,772,992), as did those of the newly recruited – both in total (100,074) and as a percentage (5.6%) – while non-renewed card-holders exceeded the latter in total (124,157) and in percentage (7%) for the first time since 1969.[65] Clearly one can speak of 'notable difficulties' – which are clear too from an examination of the monthly membership returns. The year begins on 1 November and closes on 31 October following, and the returns have had a very different progression over the period 1974–78. So much so, that while 'from 1974 to '76 the "initial rush" (that is of the first three months) of card-holding members increased progressively, it decreased in 1977, and even more so in 1978. In particular, comparison of the 1976 renewal pattern with that of 1977 gives an idea of the effort made by the central leadership and by the federations to "reach 100%". But it also leads one to think that, as was the case in other difficult periods, a part of these efforts was directed to plugging the gaps by recruiting from the families of loyal comrades who were already members.'[66]

Anyway, the operation was quite successful in 1977 but less so in 1978 when losses could not be avoided altogether. But even this is better than what happened in the Communist Youth Federation [FGCI] which in truth has always been rather weak. All the same, initially it too benefited from the new course of the seventies, even though later than the party itself and thanks to the huge efforts to improve its organisation and to the ebbing of student protest.[67] The combination of these variables in fact allowed the FGCI rapidly to make up ground after the terrible collapse of 1969 and 1970 (68,648 and 66,451 members against the 125,438 of 1968). But it is precisely a recovery, rather than an organisational expansion, if it is true that in the most fortunate year (1976) it settles at about 142,200 members, that is at a strength little higher than the already modest 1968 level. And even this recovery soon revealed itself to be ephemeral because in 1977 and 1978 the losses begin again at a highly sustained and growing pace: of 10.6% in the first year (with 15,057 fewer members) and of 14.5% in the second (16,122 fewer).[68] As a result of which, with 111,021 members, the youth federation returns to the position it was in seven years previously, or to a position that, on the one hand, remained distant from its historic minimum; but on the other was reacquired *after* the huge reorientation in favour of the communists by young people in 1975 and 1976.[69] Thus, the 1978 situation is the worst that has ever existed, at least judging by the relationship between the enormously expanded potential membership of the FGCI in this and the immediately preceding years, and its meagre and diminishing ability to organise them.

But this ability has lessened in the party, too, the proof being in the number of votes per member in 1976 (7.02 against 5.76 in 1972) and in its slight increase in 1978 (which contrasts with the reduction seen from 1972 to 1975).[70] And if we look for an explanation for this and the previous data it is not difficult to show that it lies where I suggested at the beginning of my analysis: that is, in the fact that the communist leadership – as strong as it may be – is not strong enough to lead party members united along the road of the historic compromise. This is confirmed by the authors from whom I quoted most of the previous data and for whom the difficulties encountered by the PCI in the first year and a half of the seventh legislature 'are certainly due to the political line followed after 20 June and especially to the position of "non no-confidence" assumed towards the Andreotti government'. So much so that there are exceptional coincidences between this position and the progression of the final enrolments which were massively delayed right until the very end of November 1977 (196,000 members less compared to two years previously); enrolment then picked up extremely rapidly in the interval between the communist withdrawal of its abstention and the formation of the programmatic majority;[71] it then went on to the disappointing results of October 1978 as an undoubted consequence of the party's entrance into the latter.

However, the resistance of party members is all the more explicit in their disagreement with party leaders on the most important questions of the time: on the attitude to take towards the church, on relations with the Soviet Union and on the historic compromise itself. Regarding the first two questions, recent research has shown that members did not like the party's open and flexible religious policy and even less its timid efforts to distance itself from the USSR.[72] And yet one knows that these are important, if not determining, conditions of the success of the strategy of the historic compromise which, therefore, was born and continues to develop under extremely unfavourable auspices from both points of view. And as if this were not enough, the strategy itself is – as I stated – massively contested, both in the final objectives and in the forms assumed to date. Without pausing on the former, disagreement over which would provoke serious consequences for the unity of the party only in circumstances not yet verified,[73] let us examine these forms and ask ourselves how party members reacted to the PCI's accord to abstain in the vote of confidence on the Andreotti single party government.

Well, the answer comes from two sources, one of which is unfortunately limited, but much richer and more articulated than the second. The first comprises the minutes taken at local branch meetings held by the Emilian federation in February and March 1977, analysis of which reveals a chorus of criticisms and accusations. The main object is, obviously, abstention as such, which provokes 'incomprehension', 'perplexity' and even the fear of leading the party to the same political and electoral disasters experienced by the PSI at the time of the centre-left. Not even the politics of austerity is spared the members' attacks. And on this, Barbagli and Corbetta point out: 'the accusations that are directed at the leadership group are the toughest of those traditionally thrown within the workers' movement: it speaks explicitly of "authoritarianism" [*verticismo*], "retreat" and the "social democratisation" of the party. After which it is not surprising to hear that the decisional method used to govern the party is questioned, that the decision of the party leadership to abstain is openly criticised, and that a tighter relationship between party members and the party elite is declared to be a "necessity".'[74]

Furthermore, all this evidently underlies the results of the Doxa National Survey conducted in autumn 1977, according to which 'three quarters of party members are willing to recognise that Andreotti has been a little better than his predecessors. But a good four out of ten give a negative judgment to the government and six out of ten think that both his government and the DC will do everything possible not to fulfil the programmatic accord.' Thus, it has to be admitted that, 'in the second half of 1976 and the whole of the following year, that is in the most delicate phase of implementation (of the historic compromise), there were strong tensions between the party members and the leaders'. While further data reveal that 'at the beginning of 1978, with the fall of the Andreotti government, these tensions slackened', then to return, presumably growing as from the spring.[75] And so? Well, the conclusion is that the PCI found itself, and will continue to find itself, facing a recurring dilemma: 'whether to toughen its stance vis-à-vis the DC right up to the point of rupture, with the risk of having to abandon a political line elaborated over many years or whether, alternatively, to carry on in its march towards government, with the danger of weakening its links with the masses, exactly when it needs them'.[76]

More than one alarm bell is sounded in this respect, for various reasons, by the tensions among members and the consequent weakening of the organisational strength of the party. For example, these tensions certainly reflect a state of unease in the ordinary voter, although probably less acute and less widespread.[77] But such a probability does not make a substantial difference in my opinion, not even given the fact, often quoted, that the huge majority of those who vote communist look favourably on the formation of a grand coalition government formally including the PCI.[78] This is in fact, first and foremost, an opinion about the future and as such does not necessarily cover current behaviour nor the actual reactions to the different functioning to that supposed of such a coalition. Besides which, it is an opinion which is just as largely shared by members, whose ideas about the length and outcome of a condominium of the DC-PCI and/or others are, however, very much in contrast with those of the party leaders.[79] And finally, it is an opinion which is in decline following the high point reached in 1976.[80]

Therefore, at the moment it is surely more important to know that the members are recalcitrant also because they are 'subjected daily, in the factories, in the offices and in the schools, to never-ending criticism of the party's behaviour';[81] it is more important to know that if the former can be considered the heralds of its ideological purity, the electorate is not far behind, judging from the data previously quoted in Sani's summary; and above all it is more important to know that in 1979 the PCI has fewer members and fewer votes.[82] In fact with all these elements, the prognosis on the elites' freedom of movement cannot be positive, and likewise the forecast of their cohesion, unless the tendencies of the party base heretofore expressed do not change soon. But although this is not to be excluded in principle, it does not seem to me that these changes are either imminent or probable.[83] Even more so given that a PCI in organisational decline certainly does not promise to exercise effective control over the electorate. On the contrary, if it is true 'that the number of members is a cause (even if not the only one) of the electoral success' of the party,[84] worse can be predicted. As has been observed, in fact, the membership campaigns have their part in this success in that 'they serve to consolidate the consensus obtained and, in turn, the human resources thus recruited are used to further expand the strength of the party'.[85] Hence, when the membership falls – and the defections begin – the minimum to be considered is a slackening of this strength. And from here to a real and proper decline the step may be brief, as the results of the last election seem to show.[86]

With these and the other tensions previously mentioned, the PCI felt directly the progressively growing disadvantages of its consociational efforts. And, although not giving up, it had at least to run for cover, beginning by alternating periods of co-operation and opposition, and choosing in the end to stay with the latter for a period which we do not yet know if, or how long, it will last. Nevertheless, what is certain is that its behaviour revealed itself in this way to be scarcely, or not at all, compatible with Lijphart's prerequisites. As the same prerequisites are even less satisfied by the DC, my judgment is easily imaginable in this respect too, which calls into question the third and last component of the present analysis.

Thus, if we take the ability to recognise the dangers inherent in a fragmented system (that is, the first prerequisite), what evidence is there of this in what the elites have done up to now? Evidently little or none, because the proven test of this ability would be a coherent effort in favour of a stable convergence designed to counter-balance these dangers. And, as I mentioned before, the DC leadership was, and continues to be, reluctant to adopt any solution of this kind, and especially that of a coalition government with the PCI. Furthermore, I also said that the less demanding steps made by the party in the seventh legislature were justified only in terms of the pressure of the economic-institutional emergency (which was considered to be transitory) and not in terms of seeking to undo the permanent 'knots' in the system, to neutralise its profound subcultural divisions. Indeed, these knots are explicitly held to be conducive to encouraging dangerous tensions, internal and international, precisely if put to the test of a consociational experiment such that they represent, in the Christian Democratic interpretation, the main obstacle to such an experiment, whereas the Austrian, Belgian and Dutch elites, on the contrary, found in them the principal incentive. But evidently the latter reasoned in very different terms precisely because they were moving in conditions extremely favourable to the most ambitious political manipulation, whereas the DC leadership is continually distracted by its weakness, which requires continuous genuflexions to the 'physiological' distinction between the majority and opposition to keep itself in the saddle. And even if these genuflexions are less than convinced, what they cost in time, energy and attention is all stolen away from a consociational analysis of the causes of the Italian crisis and from the adoption of the concrete measures stipulated by this analysis to overcome them.

Nevertheless, it will be said, the consociational analysis is not absent at least among the communists who go on and on about the seriousness of the problems in question, consider the emergency a long-term if not permanent problem and, anyway, say they are convinced that the policy of national unity 'certainly responds to today's pressing demands but it has much more profound and general causes' destined to remain to the fore in the future.[87] Except that all this has, up to now, been repeatedly contradicted by the facts because, as we have seen, the fall of the third and the fourth Andreotti governments was provoked by the PCI. And even if it claims to want to force the DC into a true and proper grand coalition, things don't change much, if for no other reason than that one cannot forget the judgment that this party passed down on the PSI when it made the fourth Moro government resign. Then, in fact, the former accused the latter of carelessly risking the country's life which the government was seeking to save by secretly bargaining for the opposition's support. And although the PSI said that the crisis should have served precisely to accelerate open co-operation which was tighter, more official and therefore more effective, this was not sufficient to absolve it in the eyes of its elder cousin. Today, therefore, this [party] cannot claim to meet the requirement regarding the ability to recognise the dangers of subcultural divisions, having contested it in others when they were doing exactly the same things with the same intentions. At most, it is more likely that the Communist leadership was only reluctantly 'distracted' from the problems of the system. This may be, but one has to ask oneself if it could have behaved differently when facing a rising tide of union and party member discontent; or one has to ask oneself if it could have done differently with a congress imminent, with the risk of being exposed to a threatening opposition incited by that discontent. And as the answer is negative in both cases, the first prerequisite – in the best of hypotheses – remains lost among the most fainthearted and inconsistent intentions with which the history of the historic compromise is strewn.

Mutatis mutandis, the same is true – for the same reasons – of the capacity to transcend subcultural cleavages, to promote reciprocal understanding despite the differences that arise. And yet again it is the DC that leaves most to be desired, which is obvious if one thinks that both one and the other thing require elites sufficiently strong to be able to risk putting aside values, principles and ideologies that keep cleavages and differences alive. If this is true, it is not surprising that very weak leaders such as Zaccagnini continue strongly to affirm the Christian identity of their party; they praise, maybe with less energy but still very clearly, its traditional anti-Communist position; they claim to be the carriers of a vision of society 'different and alternative' to that of their counterpart and, finally, they deny that they are disposed to dialogue or open to possible compromise if this should involve fundamentals.

So, the dialogue in discussion has been interrupted and will probably continue on issues such as abortion, the European monetary system and the three-year plan which are – each in their own way – rooted in continuity with the DC's past ideals and practice. And so the conciliatory messages cannot find ears willing to take them at face value but are destined to be decapitated at the outset by a cognitive system congruent with that continuity. So much so that the PCI's attempts at doctrinal review are always doubted by the Christian Democrats who certainly have many good reasons for judging them incomplete or insincere. But they could also be left entirely without these and still not change their attitudes if, and so long as, the formidable screen of rancours and suspicions, rooted in traditional ideology and the incompatibilities emphasised by it, remains between them and their interlocutor.

Anyhow, for now this is only a plausible hypothesis because – as I said – a rational analysis may be enough to consider insufficient what the communist elites have in their turn done to transcend the subcultural cleavages. At least up to now, in fact, 'the impression is that this party moves between adaptability and rigidity, manoeuvring between inflexibility and supermarket ideology. It outlines revisions and openings but at the same time digs itself in, defending a hard ideological nucleus.' For this reason, Fisichella observes, it pushes itself to the point of embracing democracy but not its liberal and competitive attributes; it admits the possibility of alternation of society's governing majorities but continues to glorify the merits of democratic centralism which impedes such alternation within the party; and proclaims pluralism without, however, giving up the ideal of a 'homogeneous society' which is, in the words of Bettino Craxi, 'organically totalitarian'.[88]

On other crucial questions the rigidity of the party was confirmed unequivocally right in the middle of the politics of national unity. Thus, in the summer of 1978 we find Berlinguer's interview in *La Repubblica* and his Genova speech in which he proclaimed 'the value of Lenin's works for the whole world', defining it 'a complete inheritance', to take or to leave in its entirety and opting for the first alternative, concluding that 'if others want to forsake it, let them do so. Certainly we, out of deep conviction, will never do so.'[89] Further, the tone adopted in that same summer is equally orthodox in various comments about real socialism and the Soviet Union, alignment with which is not lacking even on the tenth anniversary of the invasion of Czechoslovakia.[90] And when, in September, the party returns for the umpteenth time to the experience of the German Social Democrats, it is to repeat that there will not be a Bad Godesberg of Italian Communism, that it will not let itself be trapped in the logic of capitalism accepted by the German Social Democrats, and that it will not give up the construction of 'socialism with a human face, yes, but socialism'.[91]

So, if the DC leadership stuck firmly to its values, the communist one didn't distance itself much from its own. And maybe this is the price to be paid so long as the fruits of co-operation are not sufficient to compensate for more incisive sacrifices by the party's rank-and-file; either because continuing Christian Democrat resistance to accelerating the Communist march towards power suggests Berlinguer should not deprive himself of too many ideological resources so as not to end up short of both the one and the other; or precisely because the massive employment of these resources is necessary in order to keep in line the many discontented by what the great majority has been able to do. Whatever it may be, the impasse clearly resides in the fact that effective co-operation is impossible unless the subcultural cleavages are transcended first; while a leadership that is no longer so strong can do very little in this second respect unless, first, the co-operation has been successful enough to show party members that the path of compromise and dialogue is the right one. And so? So, things are going badly here as well, and this can do nothing but negatively influence the ability to forge the rules of the game and appropriate institutional solutions to the demands of the subcultures.

It is not by chance that even this last and most important prerequisite has not up to now been satisfied by the elites, even if it is true that the allocation to the communists of the chairmanship of seven parliamentary committees and the presidency of the Chamber in 1976 was in the spirit of consociational engineering, along with the government formulas of the seventh legislature themselves. But meanwhile there was practically nothing left of this in the following legislature.[92] And it has to be said too, that the large majorities have not been very innovative at all under the decisional profile, confirming, rather, the historic inability of the Italian elites to choose between a potentially unanimous proportional system and its majoritarian counterpart. As Di Palma has shown, this inability finds confirmation 'in the constitutional and political events of the last thirty years and in the ways that the political classes conceive of their own decision rules' which reveal that disagreement exists 'on the role of government and of opposition in the process of decision formation, and that this disagreement coexists with a constitutional order which is not clearly either majoritarian or proportional'. As if to say, in sum, that in Italy there are no 'unanimously agreed decision rules and there is no agreement on what is constitutionally prescribed', not even 'inside single parties and factions of the majority or opposition'. It is this state of affairs that 'in parliament, opens conflict on "unnatural" legislative alliances, blocks the most important legislative initiatives, but at the same time allows parliamentary alliances – often open to the opposition – freely to engage in transactions regarding marginal legislative matters'.[93]

In this picture, that sums up the components of a chronic decisional inefficiency, the proportional system has never been able to be carried through in depth; yet because sufficient space has been given to it to block important legislation and to feed the petty trade of trivial exchanges, of patronage and the distribution of spoils, its limited use 'ended up worsening the negative consequences of fragmentation that it should have kept at bay'.[94] In other words, it has in fact increased the difficulties of the decisional process, condemning it to inactivity, dissipating its energies in wasteful extravagances that are, to a certain extent, intrinsic in the system and as such inevitable in classic consociational democracies.

However, in the latter neither inactivity nor spendthrift behaviour has stopped the formulation and execution of wide-ranging policies because the greater difficulty of aggregating a very wide range of interests was compensated by a more generalised disposition towards making reciprocal concessions, by a greater commitment in terms of resources and capabilities, by a higher level of mutual tolerance and, lastly, by a larger concentration of power in the hands of the elites. Whereas in Italy all this is continually put into question by the pressures of a mobilised society, barely controllable and determined to ensure that its own ideological idiosyncrasies and particular interests are acknowledged. So that, whilst it is true that it can happen that, in an emergency, the elites will find the strength to take responsible decisions based on mutually acceptable sacrifices – and the anti-inflationary measures of 1976 and 1977 demonstrate this – nevertheless, when one tries to go further, the consensus once again becomes precarious; the correct balancing of mutual sacrifice becomes controversial. This was apparent in the three-year plan wherein both sides exchanged accusations of iniquity or of irresponsibility to the point of severing relations. And it was seen with the police, university, pensions and agricultural reforms, all of which ended up being shelved as a result of reciprocal vetoes, while elsewhere the impasse could only be overcome by resorting to majority rule (European Monetary System). And when an important joint decision, such as fair rent, reached approval after an agitated passage in parliament, its application provoked such furious reactions among the parties' clienteles that the parties were forced immediately to renegotiate it in order to dilute and heavily distort it.

So, things have not changed that much compared to the past because diluting, distorting, permanently postponing and occasionally legislating via majoritarian imposition means that the institutionalisation of a co-operative decision system continues to be misunderstood. And the elites can well lament it, preaching that without co-operation the country is heading for disaster. But the fact is – I repeat – that 'people want everything and they want it now' regardless, and they are capable of penalising immediately anyone who proves inadequate.[95] The PCI knows this well, having lost votes in the south and the big cities because thus judged.[96] After which it hastened to bolster its image as 'the party of struggle' that is attractive to its mobilised and exacting party members, delaying until better times its vocation as a 'party of government', flexible and accommodating, which is so important to the functioning of the proportional system.

But will these better times really come? Or will the pushing and pulling that impedes the maturation of the prerequisites necessary to ensure the success of the consociational project continue indefinitely? It is difficult to say, because it depends on how much the elites are able to do to re-establish a power which has been shaken for more than a decade by the mobilisation of the masses. What is certain, however, is that communist and union attempts at demobilisation, to which I referred previously, have proven inadequate to this end. And even if they were to have a better fate in the future, it is not guaranteed that the new circumstances would last long. On the contrary, upon taking a good look, the opposite is more likely, because it will be necessary to reward demobilisation with some recompense. For example, to demobilise the working class on an enduring basis, material incentives (financial and/or occupational) would be necessary, the scarcity of which would prolong and exacerbate the distribution crisis; or at least a serious commitment to reform would be necessary, which is also problematic due to the lack of resources and because it would have to begin with the dismantling, certainly unpopular, of many bankrupt 'reforms' of the sixties; but it would be necessary above all to find some credible and acceptable value that would take the place of the ones that mobilisation has rooted in the collective social mind. Of all the requirements this is the most desperate one because, concretely, the exchange should take place between (political) stability and participation, that is between a value that is still shared but undervalued and another (to be given up) largely overvalued and incarnated in institutions by now untouchable.

This is why my predictions regarding the possibility of transplanting consociational democracy in Italy remain negative even in the long term. The divergences from the classic examples are too many and too profound, whilst the latter lasted only until the elites' power was broken by the mobilisation activated by the participatory ethos of the seventies; and they were able to avoid the distribution crisis, in its turn shaking the quiescence of the masses thanks to two circumstances that I have examined elsewhere: the existence of favourable economic conditions – which contrasts with the poverty of resources which renders Italy quite unable to overcome this crisis; and the minimal salience of ideology in various class-based conflicts compared with the abundance of 'non-negotiable ends' (Pizzorno) that impede the consociational treatment of those conflicts in our political system.[97]

The Hegemonic Model

In such a situation, the solution to the Italian crisis – if there is one – must obviously be sought in other directions which take more notice of the constraints and of the objectives declared by the political actors. These objectives certainly do carry weight in orientating the predictions game, although they are always less important than the constraints. So it is not useless briefly to evaluate the model of society that a party such as the PCI says it wants to bring about, a model that is of particular interest above all specifically since it is at the antipodes of the consociational model. Furthermore it has a considerable coherence (at least on paper) and it was the object of a considerable elaborative effort which permitted some authors to indicate fairly precisely its general traits even though it never came into being. Thus, Lange was able to write that the foundation of this model is a 'hegemonic coalition' directed by the PCI and characterised by the intention to build socialism in a democratic context. For this reason, the said coalition 'would tend above all to gradually transform the economy towards having more social control over the most important decisions regarding investment and production', promoting to this end greater state intervention and increasing 'the power of the workers both in the employment market and in terms of political power'. Thereby, these latter would acquire a key role that would offer them a first recompense for the sacrifices 'nevertheless necessary' to overcome the economic crisis. While a second recompense would come from the planning of 'reforms to reduce the divisions within the masses, bettering the professional competence, organisation and political power of the marginalised', thus favouring their integration 'into the country's economic and political life'.[98]

All the same, the key role of the working class and the unions would not prevent the hegemonic coalition from making room for the 'non-organised part of this class and other subordinate classes' and 'the well-populated strata of the middle classes, including small and medium entrepreneurs, as well as for those social sectors in favour of the reforms'. Of course, 'the problem is understanding how such a heterogeneous coalition will be formed and consolidate itself', obtaining at the same time 'the necessary consensus to bring about a policy of economic transformation'. And concerning this 'the key element is the nature of the decisional process' which would favour the gradual imposition of 'an awareness of socialist ends and of the necessary processes for implementing them thanks to the diffusion of new principles of collective solidarity and collective decisional mechanisms in the social and economic fields. Which in turn require more numerous and intense opportunities for participation not just in political office (decentralisation), but also in the workplace and in society (schools etc.)'. By reason of which 'consensus will be born out of the collective mobilisation of the interested forces, mediated by growing awareness of the ends and the means to implement them' which will mature 'in the numerous arenas in which participation is articulated'.[99]

So, it is clear that the almost insurmountable obstacles that arise in the construction of a consociational alliance would, rather, be points of strength in a hegemonic coalition. Indeed, mobilisation and participation should be encouraged and amplified. The unlikely prospect of transcending the subcultural cleavages would be replaced by the resolute affirmation of 'the socialist aims' of the leading coalition party. These aims would be carried out on the strength of the widespread social consensus that would support them, rather than within a framework – hitherto unproductive – of proportional bargaining by the elites. But of course all this is not enough to make this solution possible or likely – even though there are those who believe it.[100] And this is not so much because, as I have said, it lacks historical precedents. There are other reasons, above all there is the fact that the PCI loves, yes, to emphasise its willingness for profound, radical transformation; but it has never withdrawn Berlinguer's statement that 'in the relationship between reforms and alliances, the problem of alliances has always to remain the priority, the starting point' to which reforms will, if necessary, be sacrificed.[101] This could mean many things, all incompatible with the hegemonic design. In the worst hypothesis one could think that we are facing a disposition, smacking of transformism, to barter everything that is barterable in exchange for some modicum of power. But without coming to this, that judgment contains at least the (consociational) awareness that the working class's *social* alliances would not be complete without a *political* alliance with the DC; and if and so long as the DC will be an indispensable interlocutor, it will be necessary to meet it at least half way, with no illusions, as some hold (but clearly not Berlinguer) of being able to hegemonise it.[102]

Yet the difficulties do not end here because 'the most important task' to which a PCI committed to the construction of a hegemonic coalition should attend 'is the spreading of values and attitudes favourable to social transformation' and, as far as is possible, 'the organising of a consensus on the basis of such values'.[103] For this reason the party should equip itself with an ideological and programmatic synthesis based on these, as well as with organisational structures present in every vital centre of economic, social and political life which should mediate between the questions of its potential allies and its members and the requirements of its strategy. But neither one nor the other seems likely. On the contrary, the ideological synthesis is late in arriving if Lange was able to observe 'that *Rinascita* is full of analysis of the concept of hegemony' but one would 'search fruitlessly for systematic and authoritative treatments' on this point as on other prerequisites of a socialist society able to coexist with democracy.[104]

Furthermore, as far as the programmatic summary in the strict sense of the word is concerned, 'the major resources of analysis and research' available to the PCI in the socio-economic field have so far yielded only a *Proposal for a Medium Term Project* that Lange himself defines as 'disappointing'. In fact, he writes, the project 'does go, it is true, beyond previous documents in outlining the general principles and government objectives considered indispensable to improve the economy and Italian society. But the proposals are generic and rarely confront the difficult issue of priorities and the reasoning behind them. It expressly avoids, furthermore, supplying financial estimates for the proposed economic and social measures.' And while this could 'in part be explained by the party's intention to use the project to open up a wider discussion in the country', the fact is that 'there has been no discussion', either at the time of this comment (January 1978) or in the two succeeding years.[105]

Which is no motive for regret, however, if Lange's judgment is correct and if it is true that there is no need to be an economist to drive the criticism home. For this, in fact, 'it is enough to go and see for which and how many problems the project utilises the attribute "urgent" and its synonyms'. And then it will be discovered that 'according to the communist document the need for a new, far reaching and articulated industrial policy is "urgently pressing"; the "rapid" definition of an agro-industrial development programme is indispensable; the adoption of a national energy plan is required "without further delay", whilst the resumption of the accumulation process demands that a "rapid and constant" increase in productivity is achieved. Going on to the problems of employment, it is necessary "without delay" to develop a new employment policy by increasing job opportunities, the territorial redistribution of employment and the improvement and reunification of the employment market. As for educational issues, the "urgent" reform of upper-middle schools is called for, co-ordinated organically with a framework law for the upgrading of professional training; plus, the approval "in a short period of time" of university reform and numerous "urgent" interventions to do with decentralising university structures, the redefinition of professional development opportunities and the corresponding courses of study, and the strengthening and programming of scientific and other research. Regarding problems of the environment (housing, land and transport) a "priority commitment" to the construction of new homes by the state must be considered while "in the short-term" a general transport plan is required to put to best use, and to make investments which are mutually compatible and integrated, in the railways, the main and medium road networks, and maritime and air communications.

Further, it is essential to elaborate and "rapidly" put into action a plan for hydro-geological adjustment to prevent immense damage in even the immediate future, and to tackle the issue of soil degradation and the water crisis. This requires, as an "indispensable" condition, the creation of new skilled job opportunities in agricultural areas. And more, on the topic of public administration: there has to be "urgent" intervention to create conditions for the instruments of public intervention and the government of the economy to be adequately functional and effective, beginning with the reorganisation of the national statistics system, an "urgent" reform of the state budget, an "urgent" general reorganisation of the administrative apparatus and, finally, the redefinition "with particular urgency" of the relationship between parliament, government and the administrative agencies within the framework of an organic review of the current structure of the public sector economy. As for the administration of justice, the "rapid" creation of a plan suitable for equipping the judicial offices with the structures essential for their work is pressing while, turning to relations between Italy and the European Community, profound review is "absolutely urgent" of: the community agricultural policy, the definition of a common energy policy, the approval of common actions and programmes in the fields of scientific research, protection of the environment, the definition of the statute for European limited companies and control over the activities of multinational enterprises. Finally, it is "urgent" to proceed to a real reform of the international monetary system, as well as to new issues of special drawer rights whilst at the same time ensuring a true democratisation of the functioning of the supreme international monetary organism.'[106]

Please accept my apologies for the quotation, without doubt too long; but, anyway, useful for clarifying beyond any reasonable doubt that the medium-term project is only a greatly exasperated version of the 'shopping lists' for which the communists continually rebuked the governments of the centre-left. Certainly it does not bear any comparison with the more balanced documents of that period – from La Malfa's Additional Note to Project 80 – which in principle at least fixed priorities and indicated who should make sacrifices (that is: incomes policy), for what and to what extent.

It follows that, currently, 'the PCI is not only probably incapable of devising an economic programme able to obtain a wide consensus, but is afraid of putting forward proposals that could damage its relations with those social strata that are determined to defend their own corporate interests'.[107] For this reason it throws everything together, simultaneously, generically and indiscriminately: for lack of a genuine will to reform and maybe because of, yet again, the constraints of the situation and in particular the behaviour of the DC. In fact, it must not be forgotten that this party also pursues on its behalf a strategy of acquisition and/or consolidation of consensus through the distribution of particularistic material incentives to a vast network of supporters. And although this strategy will have suffered setbacks with the economic crisis, which may even have deprived it of huge resources,[108] nothing shows that it has collapsed due to the effects of the crisis.[109] On the contrary, the constant increase in current account public spending, the never-terminated policy of salvaging loss-making industries and the ever more luxuriant remuneration jungle are unequivocal signs that the old way of governing continues. And it probably remains solvent enough to offer an attractive alternative, comprising immediate rewards for all, to a policy of more far-sighted but painfully selective reforms. Thus, it is plausible that even a PCI better intentioned than it seems at present to be, must abandon such a policy or remain stuck with the approximate elaborations that we have seen. Otherwise, it would risk losing a move in the continuing game to those who promise, and give most, to as many petitioners as possible.

All the same, in acting thus, this party can aspire at most to becoming a representative and mediator of interests as is the DC already, and certainly not to becoming the dominant force of a hegemonic coalition. So, this idea continues to shimmer in the limbo of intentions wherein, come to that, the present state of communist organisation also holds it. It is to the communist party organisation that the diffusion in society of the ideological and programmatic directives of the party, and their consolidation, would be entrusted. But it is doubtful whether it is capable of this task, of manoeuvring the mobilisation and participation to acquire consensus on these directives. So much so that Lange was already formulating a generally negative opinion on this issue. And yet he could still find at least one point in favour of the PCI's capacity for initiative in the continual expansion of its members since he stopped, evidently, with the 1976 data.[110] But we know that in the following two years membership recruitment went badly in response to the party's political decisions. These decisions may, then, have brought the party closer to power; but they threatened to remove the resources necessary to put into practice the hegemonic aims that its leadership is now trying to articulate from the opposition from where it previously wanted to escape, recognising that hegemony was better constructed from governmental positions.

If this is so, then lulls or steps backward should follow future steps forward in the same sterile pendulum action that we have seen hinder the take-off of the consociational alternative. This oscillation would probably leave unresolved, or maybe aggravate, the deficiencies in the party's organisational machine which are not limited to the total pattern of membership recruitment. This can in fact be disaggregated to obtain a measure of the degree of territorial and social penetration of the organisation in its growth phase (1968–76), with the aim of checking to what extent the PCI was able to hegemonise the collective movements of those years, to use them for its own ends. And the result is, in brief, that the widespread improvement in its strength has found less or no confirmation in the areas (provincial capitals of the north-west) and in the groups (workers, youth, women) which were most violently affected by the mobilisation process and which took on its leadership.[111]

In particular, the rate of worker adhesion to the party 'grows from '68 to '76, but less than one would expect if one thinks of its overall growth and above all specifically that of the middle classes'. With the result that 'of the extraordinary process of mobilisation of the working class in 1968–72, the organisation of the PCI has gained little fruit'. And the communist leaders themselves spoke often in these years 'of the inability to identify a specific role for the party within the workplace in the new situation shaped by the emergence of large movements of autonomous masses, by the new role of the factory works council, by the very process of union autonomy and unity'. Justified fears, if it is true that 'as for the workers, one cannot speak of the transformation of the movement's energy into institutional participation', neither on the basis of the membership data nor on the basis of the dynamics of the 'renewal of the leadership groups'. These, in fact, were characterised by a net reduction of the worker cadres which, in truth, doesn't really constitute anything new because it was already noticeable 'after 1945–55'. But while at that time 'a period of retreats and defeats for the working class was beginning, what is surprising is that this process continued at an even more noticeable rate in the seventies, at the end of a new and exceptional cycle of struggle in which thousands of new worker cadres were formed'. And yet the data show 'dramatically' that 'the extraordinary renewal of the communist leadership cadres of the last years has not come about through the recruitment and promotion of these', but rather has to be put down to a large increase in the number of middle class officials.[112] And there are risks in this, authoritatively signalled by Giovanni Berlinguer, starting with an unwanted 'alteration in the class identity of the PCI' and the clear contrast that would result from this with the political line of a party that struggles for the participation of the working classes in government, for the re-evaluation of productive and manual labour and the affirmation of the values of the working class within the national culture. These are all objectives which a disproportionate weight of the middle class in the organisation threatens to obscure, since this brings about the emergence of the 'propagandistic, verbal, mediatory skills typical of intellectuals' to the detriment of the capacity for 'agitation, mass mobilisation, the organisation of struggle and an immediate rapport with the people'.[113]

Exactly the opposite, of course, of what was needed for a hegemonic project, for which the PCI, apart from anything else, does not seem to be prepared either with regard to its strongholds in central Italy (where its organisational abilities 'begin to present not a few obscure aspects') judging from the political crisis of its sections or, in fact, if one thinks of its peripherality compared to the most mobilised areas and groups – which has certainly worsened in the years of deterioration in membership that followed 1976.[114] So? Well, it is clear that this alternative is anything but close at hand. And, in truth, it would be futile to expect the contrary even if the conditions examined here were more favourable. Looking at it closely, in fact, hegemony is a long and slow affair, perhaps of centuries; it has less to do with political engineering, however intelligent and able, than with the historical process and maybe even anthropological revolution. So, when one is discussing hegemonic outcomes one should always be extremely prudent, and even more so when the few relevant factors available are all negative, as in the Italian case. But this case, on the other hand, is not one which is good ground for the cultivation of consociational democracy, as I have tried to show. And since there do not seem to be any other solutions – except perhaps on paper[115] – that are being pursued with the necessary firmness and conviction, all that I would risk saying, by way of conclusion, is that the situation could continue to stagnate for a long time without having to endure irreversible involutions, yet without even decisively evolving either, unless some imponderable event intervenes to push things in one or other direction.

Notes

1 'Typologies of Democratic Systems', in *Comparative Political Studies*, I (1968), p.21, and *Democracy in Plural Societies*, New Haven, Yale University Press, 1977, p.103.
2 'Segmented Pluralism: Ideological Cleavages and Political Cohesion in the Smaller European Democracies' in *Comparative Politics*, III (1971), p.144 n.
3 For a thorough demonstration of this affirmation see my 'Le condizioni della democrazia consociativa. Una critica logica e empirica', in *Rivista Italiana di Scienza Politica*, IX (1979), pp.367–445.
4 Ibid. pp.383–408, 425–434.
5 *Democracy*, op.cit. p.54.
6 For all these points Pappalardo, op.cit. pp.378–381, 398–403, 428–430.
7 *Democracy*, op.cit. pp.2–3.

8   'Cultural Diversity and Theories of Political Integration', in *Canadian Journal of Political Science*, IV (1971), p.10 [actually p.13].
9   As the already mentioned case of the Netherlands shows.
10   As Lijphart, after all, also recognises; *Democracy*, op.cit. p.54.
11   *Typologies*, op.cit. pp.22–24.
12   That the psychological and behavioural prerequisites of the elites are explained by appropriate structural and/or cultural conditions has already been discussed by E.A.Nordlinger, 'Conflict Regulation in Divided Societies', Harvard University, Centre for International Affairs, Occasional Paper n.29, pp.68–72, which I make extensive use of in the following paragraph. All the same, at many points my treatment of this issue diverges from (or amplifies) that of this author and, in particular, is completely different with regard to the second prerequisite.
13   *Typologies*, op.cit. p.22 (my emphasis).
14   Ibid.
15   Ibid. p.23.
16   Ibid.
17   On the possible reasons for this growth of discontent, see the later analysis of the fourth prerequisite.
18   *Typologies*, p.23.
19   Obviously, this is the reason why consociational theory grants only the elites the probability of democratic stability in profoundly divided societies. But the same conviction is at the root of other studies which argue that this stability depends on there being a greater degree of consensus between the elites than between non-elites. See I.Budge, *Democratic Argument and Democratic Stability*, Chicago, Markham,1970.
20   See, amongst others, L.Pellicani, 'Verso il superamento del pluralismo polarizzato?', in *Rivista Italiana di Scienza Politica*, IV, 1974, pp.645–673, now in L. Pellicani, *Il centauro comunista*, Firenze, Vallecchi, 1979, pp. 9–48; P.Farneti, 'Una democrazia consociativa in Italia?', in *Biblioteca della Libertà*, n. 51, July-August 1974, pp.43–47; G.Pasquino, 'Il sistema politico italiano fra neo-trasformismo e democrazia consociativa', in *Il Mulino*, XXII, 1973, pp.549–566; A.Lombardo, Le condizioni istituzionali del compromesso storico. Cooperazione e conflitto tra Dc, Pci e Psi: problemi e prospettive della politica consociativa, report to the annual session of AISPS, September 1978; P.Lange, 'Il Pci e i possibili esiti della crisi italiana', in L.Graziano & S.Tarrow (eds), *La crisi italiana*, Torino, Einaudi, 1979, pp.657–718. Note that Lange prefers talking about a 'modernising semicorporatist coalition' in place of consociational democracy. But the difference is more terminological than material.
21   Concessions that are all the more unjustified in that the Italian elites operate in a system of polarised pluralism less susceptible to being established with consociational methods than segmented societies such as Austria, Belgium and the Netherlands. The following, as is well known, have insisted on this point: G.Sartori, 'Il caso italiano: salvare il pluralismo e superare la polarizzazione', in *Rivista Italiana di Scienza Politica*, IV, 1974, pp.675–687, 'Lo scenario del compromesso storico' in J. La Palombara, G.Sani & G.Sartori, 'Il Pci dall'opposizione al governo. E dopo?', Torino, Quaderni di Biblioteca della Liberta, 1978, pp.79–108, *Parties and Party Systems: A Framework for Analysis*, New York, Cambridge University Press, 1976, pp.180–185; and G.Di Palma, *Sopravvivere senza governare. I partiti nel parlamento italiano*, Bologna, Il Mulino,1978, pp.295–338. However, I will not linger on the arguments of the two authors here, even though I need to stress that I agree with them; my analysis proposes a different perspective, although complementary to theirs, and is meant to reinforce the rejection of the consociational hypothesis at which they themselves arrive.
22   Thus, the most biased writing in favour of the consociational hypothesis is that of Pellicani who does not make any reference to conditions at all. More cautious and balanced, on the other hand, are Pasquino, Lombardo and Lange, in whom there is an analysis of the conditions and – in the case of Lange – he systematically and amply confronts some important points which in any case I had already myself pointed out in *Partiti e governi di coalizione in Europa*, Milano, Angeli, 1978, pp.90–114.
23   On the insurmountable pervasiveness of the spiritual families in the classic consociational

democracies, see the comparative analysis presented by Lorwin, op.cit. On Italy, the point has been made by G.Sani, 'Political Traditions as Contextual Variables: Partisanship in Italy', in *American Journal of Political Science*, XX (1976), pp.375–405.

24   On this point see G.Sani, 'Le elezioni degli anni settanta: terremoto o evoluzione?', in *Rivista Italiano di Scienza Politica*, VI (1976), now in G.Parisi & G.Pasquino (eds), *Continuità e mutamento elettorale in Italia*, Bologna, Il Mulino, 1977, pp.79–83. The author summarises what we know on the subject from various pieces of research, concluding that in the postwar period over 80% of voters have regularly repeated the choice made in previous elections in subsequent ones. A slightly lower estimate, speaking of oscillations 'between 70 and 80%', is in M.Barbagli et al., *Fluidità elettorale e classi sociali in Italia*, Bologna, Il Mulino, 1979, p.18. Oscillations 'decisively inferior' compared to 1972–76 were apparently also verified in 1979 according to A.Parisi, 'Mobilità non significa movimento' in *Il Mulino*, XXVIII (1979), esp. pp. 651–658. As one can see, these are results which, for all that they clearly indicate a decisively less *static* situation than some had, in the past, claimed, do not all the same contradict the rule of continuity on the whole.

25   Sani, 'Le elezioni', op.cit. p.80. On the size of these movements see the net flows calculated by G.Urbani ('Un anno di elezioni' in G.Urbani (ed.) *1978: elezioni con sorpresa*, Torino, Quaderni di Bdl, 1979, pp. 25–26), which give an indicative measurement, albeit very approximate, in that it tends 'to ignore those voters who transmigrating from one party to another "cross over each other", annulling the possibility of accounting for such reciprocal movements' (p.26). And so – it has rightly been observed – these flows are at the most a measurement of the *stability of the electoral support of the parties*, to which could correspond a far lesser *stability* (or a larger *fluidity*) of individual voter behaviour. Nonetheless, the authors who formulate this opportune distinction (and apply techniques able to distinguish the two dimensions in research carried out in Bologna) arrive at exactly the same conclusion that 'the percentage of votes that shift from one party (or political alignment) to the opposing one between elections is extraordinarily small' both absolutely and as a percentage of total fluctuations. See Barbagli et al., op.cit. p.121; for an analogous conclusion regarding the elections of 1979 see Parisi, op.cit. pp.653–658.

26   G.Sani, 'La composizione degli eletttorati comunista e democristiano', in A.Martinelli & G.Pasquino (eds), *La politica nell'Italia che cambia*, Milano, Feltrinelli, 1978, pp.117ff.; B.Bartolini, 'Insediamento subculturale e distribuzione dei suffragi in Italia', in *Rivista Italiana di Scienza Politica*, VI (1976), now in Parisi & Pasquino, op.cit. pp.103–144.

27   All the more so if one takes two facts into account: that in the future the new cohorts of young voters arriving at the ballot boxes will be smaller, while the exit of the larger cohorts of the ageing population is yet to come; and that amongst the young, the centre-right seems to have recovered some ground in 1979, although to a limited and nonhomogeneous extent. See M.Rossi, 'Veri sconfitti e finti vincitori: la Dc e il centro-destra', in *Il Mulino*, XXVIII (1979), pp.669–693.

28   Indeed, the first global and partial analyses of these last elections reveal a modest yet significant return flow of voters to the DC who, in 1975 and 1976, had left for the PCI. See R.Mannheimer, 'Un'analisi territoriale del calo comunista', pp.709–711 and P.Corbetta, 'Novita e incertezze nel voto del 3 giugno: analisi dei flussi elettorali', both in *Il Mulino*, XXVIII (1979), pp.727–732, 735–741.

29   I refer in particular to the process of expansion of the opinion vote at the expense of the vote of belonging [*appartenenza*] that for A.Parisi & G.Pasquino ('Relazioni partiti-elettori e tipi di voto', in Parisi & Pasquino, op.cit. pp.215–249) already manifested itself in 1974–76 and should become more and more relevant in the future, provoking growing electoral mobility. All the same, according to the same authors 'this does not mean that fundamental orientations can be put radically under discussion ... On the contrary, the growing opinion vote means that {these} shall be confirmed', whereas the 'specific party to which the various flows of mobility will be directed' {within the opposing alignments} should become less certain and more variable (pp.243–244). This is, in part, what happened on 3 June 1979, which confirmed a substantially reduced mobility between the alignments (but not an increased intra-area mobility which, even though it remained the larger, may actually have declined according to Parisi, op.cit. p.658). Anyway, it is clear that Urbani's (op.cit.) expectations and explanations were much disappointed, although, prudently, he had in fact hypothesised (or hadn't excluded) a possibly stronger affirmation of the different

tendencies revealed by the local elections of 1978. In fact, both these elections and other previous and successive consultations (the referendum, the European, the Sardinian regional elections, etc.) seem only to demonstrate (for now) that split voting, however important it may be, is not incompatible with the results that continue to be registered in elections.

30   See Di Palma, op.cit. pp.135–180, and 'Risposte parlamentari alla crisi del regime: un problema di istituzionalizzazione', in Graziano & Tarrow, op.cit. pp.370–379.

31   As has in fact been observed, 'the main themes of the "via italiana"... could not be understood if one were to forget the essentially defensive and pessimistic perspective from which they originated'. See S.Hellman, 'La strategia della alleanze del Pci e la questione dei ceti medi', in D.L.Blackmer & S.Tarrow (eds), *Il comunismo in Italia e Francia*, Milano, Etas Libri, 1976, p.253.

32   See amongst others Hellman, op.cit. pp.251–292; S.Tarrow, 'Il comunismo in Italia e in Francia. Adattamento e trasformazioni', D.Blackmer, 'Continuità e mutamento nel comunismo italiano del dopoguerra', P.Lange, 'L'applicazione della strategia del Pci a livello locale', all in Blackmer & Tarrow, op.cit. pp.357–398, 15–55, 159–196; D.Blackmer, *Unity in Diversity: Italian Communism and The Communist World*, Cambridge, MIT Press, 1968; S.Tarrow, *Partito comunista e contadini nel mezzogiorno*, Torino, Einaudi, 1972; H.Timmerman, *I comunisti italiani*, Bari, De Donato, 1974.

33   On this uncertainty see most recently S.Hellman, 'The Longest Campaign: Communist Party Strategy and the Elections of 1976', in H.R.Penniman (ed.), *Italy at the Polls*, Washington, American Enterprise Institute for Public Policy Research, 1977, p.166.

34   Ibid. pp.166–167.

35   Ibid. pp.160–161.

36   Ibid. p.167.

37   Ibid. p.168.

38   E. Berlinguer, 'Riflessioni sull'Italia dopo i fatti del Cile', now in *La questione comunista*, Roma, Editori Riuniti, 1975, p.633.

39   Relazione al C.C. of June 1974, now in *La questione comunista*, op.cit. pp.758–759.

40   E.Berlinguer, 'Lavorare per l'unità di tutte le forze popolari', now in *La questione comunista*, op.cit. p.653. For a recent affirmation of the same concept see 'Fare emergere tutta la forza innovatrice della nostra politica di austerità e di rigore', in *L'Unità*, 26 May 1978.

41   G.Vacca, 'Perche stupirsi per il voto DC?', in *Rinascita*, 16 July 1976; Hellman, 'The Longest Campaign', op.cit. pp.175–178; the PCI's consociational strategy in the course of the 7th legislature is analysed in detail by Lombardo, op.cit.

42   G.Di Palma, 'Christian Democracy: The End of Hegemony?', in Penniman, op.cit. pp.147–148.

43   The most authoritative Communist confirmation of these points is in E.Berlinguer, 'Relazione e Replica al C.C.', in *L'Unità*, 4 and 7 July 1979, and 'Il compromesso nella fase attuale', in *Rinascita*, 24 August 1979. As is known, the last article in particular stimulated the relaunching of the strategy of 'confrontation' by the Christian Democrat Secretariat.

44   G.Sani, 'La composizione', op.cit. p.123; A.Marradi, 'Immagini di massa della Dc e del Pci', in Martinelli & Pasquino, op.cit. pp.66–103; G.Sani, 'The Italian Electorate in the mid-1970s: Beyond Tradition?', in Penniman, op.cit. pp.98–109.

45   Sani, 'La composizione', op.cit. p.122.

46   See G.Sani, 'La strategia del Pci e l'elettorato italiano', in *Rivista Italiana di Scienza Politica*, III (1973), pp.576–577.

47   Sani, 'La composizione', op.cit. p.123. Note that the self-placement of the Italian voter on the left-right spectrum presents the greatest divergence if compared with the distribution of other countries. See G.Sani, G.Sartori, 'Frammentazione, polarizzazione e "cleavages": democrazie facili e difficili', in *Rivista Italiana di Scienza Politica*, III (1978), pp.339–361.

48   See 'Typologies', op.cit. and *The Politics of Accommodation: Pluralism and Democracy in the Netherlands*, Berkeley, University of California Press, 1975, pp.78, 103–104.

49   See the source quoted in n.4.

50   See G.Pasquino, 'Crisi della Dc e evoluzione del sistema politico', in *Rivista Italiana di Scienza Politica*, V (1975), p.460.

51   Such is the opinion of G.Pasquino, who is the only one up to now to have dealt systematically with these problems. See his 'Recenti trasformazioni nel sistema di potere della Democrazia cristiana',

in Graziano & Tarrow, op.cit. pp.609–656, and 'La Democrazia cristiana: trasformazioni partitiche e mediazione politica', in Martinelli & Pasquino, op.cit. pp.124–143.

52 As Pasquino has rightly observed, 'Recenti trasformazioni', op.cit. pp.644–645.

53 Thus M.De Carolis, 'La Democrazia cristiana oggi', in *Il Mulino*, XXVI (1977), p.439.

54 Ibid. p.438.

55 Of course, this is not exactly what the representatives of this political alignment say in so many words. They concern themselves, indeed, with emphasising the intention to democratise the life of the party by way of its organisational reinforcement. See G.Galloni, 'Una evidentissima tendenza al cambiamento investe il partito nelle più intime strutture', in *La Discussione*, 4 April 1977. But similar justifications are of course the customary cover for every attempt to regiment the rank-and-file before it takes place.

56 See G.Baget Bozzo, 'Requiem in memoria della sinistra Dc', in *La Repubblica*, 14 March 1978. The author points to the hardening of the moderate bloc, reflected in the Andreotti government of 12 March 1978.

57 See Lijphart, *Democracy*, op.cit. p.102.

58 On these points see A.Pizzorno, 'I sindacati nel sistema politico italiano', in *Rivista Trimestrale di Diritto Pubblico*', XXI (1971), pp.1510–1559, and G.P.Cella, 'L'azione sindacale nella crisi italiana', in Graziano & Tarrow (eds), op.cit. pp.271–301.

59 Cella, op.cit. p.287.

60 Ibid. pp.288–292. Some of Lama's moderate stands are summarised and critically analysed by D.Fisichella, *Quel Giano bifronte del Pci*, Milano, Editoriale Nuova, 1979, cap.VI.

61 See for example V.Foa, 'Sindacalismo responsabile e sindacalismo militante', in *Prospettiva sindacale*, VII (1976), pp.128–135, and B.Manghi, *Declinare crescendo. Note critiche dall'interno del sindacato*, Bologna, Il Mulino, 1977.

62 Cella, op.cit. p.288; V.Foa, 'Sindacati e classe operaia', in V.Castronovo (ed), *L'Italia contemporanea*, Torino, Einaudi, 1975, p.262.

63 See for example, the interventions of the Communist leader and the Flm secretary Pio Galli at the XV Party Congress, in *L'Unità*, 2 and 3 April 1979.

64 M.Barbagli, P.Corbetta, 'Partito e movimento: aspetti e rinnovamento del Pci', in *Inchiesta*, VIII (1978), p.11.

65 Ibid. Tab.2 for the 1977 date. The 1978 data have been calculated by myself based on the numbers given by *Supplemento all'almanacco Pci '79* edited by the PCI central section for the press and propaganda. At this moment (November 1979) complete and official information on the latest membership is not available, even if the daily newspapers have indicated a figure (1,775,000 members) that would suggest a year of stagnation.

66 Barbagli & Corbetta, op.cit. p.40 and fig.8.

67 Ibid. pp.20–21.

68 Ibid. p.21, fig.2 and tab.19; *Supplemento*, op.cit.

69 The most reliable estimates on the extent of this reorientation are those of G.Sani, of whom see most recently: 'Ricambio elettorale, mutamenti sociali e preferenze politiche', in Graziano & Tarrow (eds), op.cit. pp.303–328.

70 Barbagli & Corbetta, op.cit. pp.10–11.

71 Ibid. pp.40–41.

72 See M.Barbagli & P.Corbetta, 'Una tattica e due strategie. Inchiesta sulla base del Pci', in *Il Mulino*, XXVII (1978), pp.924–938.

73 That is, in the event of the PCI assuming responsibility for government in a coalition with the DC. As the data of Barbagli & Corbetta show (ibid. pp.947–950), this coalition is approved by a good part of the members. They have an instrumental conception; they consider it to be an instrument to accelerate the DC crisis to encourage a decisive change in the balance of forces between the parties thus shortening the path to the left alternative [government] (pp.951–957). This means that the 'conceptions of the historic compromise that the leadership and the base of the party hold are profoundly different' because 'for the leadership the historic compromise is not a tactic, but a strategy, a long-term position', whilst 'for the members, the truth is exactly the opposite' (p.951). And they would both be destined to enter into a full collision on this point.

74   Ibid. pp.943–944.
75   Ibid. p.947. That growth in the dissatisfaction of party members resumed from the late spring (that is from the formation of the programmatic majority) is a reasonable inference made by myself based on the negative outcome of the 1978 membership.
76   Barbagli & Corbetta, 'Partito e movimento', op.cit. p.41.
77   This in consideration of the fact that the mass of the voters are much less politicised and jealous of the ideological purity of the parties than are the members and especially the active members. See on the point P.Converse, 'The Nature of Belief Systems in Mass Publics', in D.Apter (ed.), *Ideology and Discontent*, New York, The Free Press, 1964, pp.206–261; D.MacRae Jr., *Parliament, Parties and Society in France 1946–1958*, New York, St. Martin's Press, 1967, pp.299–302.
78   See the surveys reported by G.Sani, 'La nuova immagine del Pci e l'elettorato italiano', in Blackmer & Tarrow, op.cit. p.348, and 'L'elettorato comunista: tendenze e prospettive', in La Palombara, Sani & Sartori, op.cit. p.62. It is to be noted, however, that the majorities in favour of the historic compromise are formed on questions of the type 'for or against', not, that is, on questions which offer alternative solutions such as the left alternative. When, on the other hand, this formula is mentioned, the PCI electorate decidedly prefers it, as is clear from the latest of the Doxa-L'Espresso surveys, in *L'Espresso*, 21 January 1979 and 20 May 1979.
79   See n. 73. That at least some communist voters consider the historic compromise a short-lived tactic (as do members) is clear from the interviews commented by Marradi, op.cit. pp.93–95.
80   See the surveys Doxa-L'Espresso quoted in n.78, the second of which shows that only 37 communists in a hundred were for the [government] formula 'left plus the DC' in April 1979 and 50 in a hundred for the formula 'left without the DC'.
81   Barbagli & Corbetta, 'Una tattica', op.cit. p.943
82   Which are votes lost by or not given to the PCI by first-time voters, dispersed in the great majority among the Radicals, the Pdup, the Nsu and to a party hostile to the historic compromise as is the PSI, as well as to abstention out of protest. See Mannheimer, op.cit., p.710; and Corbetta, op.cit., pp.727–735.
83   In other words, nothing seems to have changed since Lange conjectured that 'the nature of the PCI electorate is such as to make one think' that a policy of direct agreements with the DC 'would not attain the consensus of the communist voters'. See 'Il Pci', op.cit. pp.687–688. In fact the most recent events only strengthen this prediction, advising one to continue to abide by it.
84   See Bartolini, op.cit. p.126.
85   Sani, 'L'elettorato comunista', op.cit. pp.66–67.
86   Despite the absence of any rigorous research on this point I believe that in fact one can safely affirm that on 3 June the PCI paid for the deterioration of its organised strength which, if in itself small, becomes a lot more serious in the context of the increased demands placed on it by the successes of 1975 and 1976. Thus also G.Pasquino, 'Suggerimenti scettici agli ingegneri elettorali', in *Il Mulino*, XXVIII (1979), pp.752–753.
87   On this position of the PCI leadership see Fisichella, op.cit. pp.75–87.
88   Ibid. pp.21, 17–41, 49. L.Cavalli, *Italia promessa*, Bologna, Il Mulino, 1976; F.Diaz, 'La ricerca dei presupposti della "scelta democratica" del Pci', in AA.VV., *Egemonia e democrazia*, Roma, ed. by Mondoperaio, 1977; and Pellicani, op.cit. esp. pp.71–87 also insist on the contradictions and ideological ambiguities of the PCI.
89   See *La Repubblica*, 2 August 1978, and *L'Unità*, 18 September 1978.
90   As documented by Fisichella, op.cit. pp.50–56.
91   Ibid. p.59.
92   In which the communists have only re-obtained the presidency of the Chamber with a majority which is anything but consociational.
93   Sopravvivere, op.cit. p.180.
94   Ibid. p.139.
95   And the Italian elites are particularly inclined to second [public opinion], sharing on the whole a 'party-populist' conception of representation in which satisfying the wishes of one's own party members is more rewarding than an attitude of reciprocity and compromise. Ibid. pp.228–235. The

quote in the text is the comment of a local communist leader on the defeat suffered by the PCI in the local government elections in Castellamare di Stabia. See *Il Corriere della sera*, 20 April 1977.

96 On the dissatisfaction towards the communist administration's policies, accused of moving too timidly in order not to disturb the party's consociational strategy, there are many testimonies in the daily newspapers and periodicals and a few scientific studies. Among which, see the reports of R. Nanetti & R. Leonardi, Betting on Cities: The Urban Strategy of the Italian Communist Party (PCI), and R.Seidelman, The PCI and Municipal Decentralization: The Case of Florence, both presented at the permanent seminar on Italy, Centre for European Studies, Harvard University, November 1977; F.Ferraresi & A.Tosi, 'Crisi della città e politica urbana', in Graziano & Tarrow, op.cit. pp.559–605.

97 On all these points see my 'Le condizioni', op.cit. and *Partiti*, op.cit. pp.105 ff.

98 Il Pci, op.cit. p.677.

99 Ibid. p.678.

100 Such is the case of L.Graziano, 'Compromesso storico e democrazia consociativa: verso una "nuova democrazia"'?, in Graziano & Tarrow, op.cit. pp.719–767.

101 Relazione al C.C., of July 1971, Relazione al C.C. of November 1974, and Relazione al C.C. of December 1974, now all in *La questione comunista*, op.cit. pp.332–383, 919, 929–930.

102 Contra Berlinguer see Graziano, op.cit. for whom whether the PCI will succeed in moving the DC to the left is at most 'an unknown'; and, although he declared it 'central', it actually appears marginal to his essay as he dedicates only two-and-a-half lines to it (p.760) out of some fifty pages.

103 Lange, 'Il Pci', op.cit. p.678.

104 Ibid. p.698.

105 Ibid. p.700.

106 D. Fisichella, 'Le contraddizioni dei comunisti', in *Il Tempo*, 13 September 1977, now in op.cit. pp.121–123.

107 Lange, 'Il Pci', op.cit. pp.700–701 for a negative opinion on the current capacity for programmatic elaboration by the PCI (and the DC) compared to the 'fervour of activity and of studies, of projects and reflections' of the centre-left; see Pasquino, 'Recenti trasformazioni', op.cit., p.648.

108 As for example Pasquino, 'Recenti trasformazioni', op.cit. pp.638–639.

109 Or for the effect of the shift to the left of the administration of the big cities in 1975. From this it seems excessive to deduce 'the sudden fall of interest factionalism' in the DC, as does Di Palma, Christian Democracy, op.cit. p.133.

110 Lange, 'Il Pci', op.cit. pp.701–707.

111 Barbagli & Corbetta, 'Partito', op.cit. pp.14–30.

112 Ibid. pp.28, 30. See also Lange, 'Il Pci', op.cit. pp.702–704.

113 'Perche meno quadri operai e contadini?', in *Rinascita*, 10 June 1977, p.8. As confirmation of the importance of the problems raised by Berlinguer's article and of the concerned attention with which the party followed them, see the ample debate dedicated to them between leaders and members in subsequent editions of the same magazine.

114 On all these points see Barbagli & Corbetta, *Partito*, op.cit. p.30 ff.

115 I refer to, for example, the solution of Fisichella, op.cit. pp.141–146, who hopes for a new-found autonomy from the PCI of the centre and centre-left forces (even if one has few illusions in this respect). For others, the political stability of the country passes primarily along the road of electoral and/or institutional reforms, despite the fact that the disadvantage is their proven impracticability. See the contributions of P.Farneti, G.Urbani and others in 'Le ricette dei politologi', in *Biblioteca della libertà*, XVI (1979). Lastly, a different solution again is the one of Sartori, 'Il caso italiano', op.cit. that would be decisive but requires a long time.

[38]
Towards a History of Transformism (1883–1983)

Sandro Fontana

Translated by Mark Donovan

---

1. The Cavourian Alliance

As recently pointed out elsewhere,[1] 1983 marked the centenary anniversary of transformism: that is, the anniversary of the birth of the fifth Depretis government which marked the end of the distinction between the Historical Right and the Historical Left and the beginning of the political and parliamentary practice according to which, in the words of Crispi, a protagonist of the time – 'each group, instead of comprising an ordered set of ideas, consisted of an association of individuals each of whom, as circumstances warranted it, inevitably changed their opinion', so that 'disloyalty and apostasy were an advantage for promotion'.[2]

To be truthful, one can say, as Bollati himself notes,[3] that the practice of transformism was operative from the very first Italian parliamentary experiences, that is to say from the subalpine parliaments [i.e. from the Piedmontese parliament, before Italy's unification] and from the birth of Cavour's famous alliance [*connubio*]. In fact, it is not difficult to identify, via a close examination of the famous parliamentary operation which, towards the end of 1852 carried Cavour, with mounting success, to the leadership of the Piedmontese government, at least two aspects which, as we shall see, were to characterise transformist practice right up to the present. We can identify these characteristics as follows. (1) In the first place, the fact that the formula of the alliance represents the only solution able to guarantee, at one and the same time, both a constitutional regime and a reformist governmental practice. In fact, as Romeo has clearly demonstrated,[4] the real alternative to the 'centrist' choice of Cavour came not so much from the left of the alignment as from the Balbo-Revel right-wing which was supported by clerical groups and by the court, with the risk, therefore, that the fragile constitutional experience would come to an end. Certainly the wind of authoritarian restoration, coming in those years primarily from France, did not blow in a liberal direction. (2) In the second place, in the tendency to use parliament not so much as an arena for the dialectical representation of political and ideal positions but more as an instrument for the repeated formation and coagulation of the so-called *government party*, understood in the sense indicated by Cavour himself when he asserted that 'the cabinet ... in a parliamentary government ... must also represent a political party, that is, must be the leader of a party' (speech of 7 February 1852).[5]

Alongside these precursor elements, as we can call them, of the practice of transformism, we must nonetheless remember that during the so-called 'decade of preparation' the relationship between the state and civil society – that is between liberal institutions and the growth requirement of the Piedmontese bourgeoisie – developed in a very close way, and to their reciprocal benefit. In little Piedmont – Caracciolo observes – the establishment of a liberal political class and of new institutions took place in a fashion which was in harmony with the development of the social fabric.[6]

It follows that 'men who had a highly militant democratic past, from Lanza to Rattazzi and Cadorna, set about making their entrance into the governing class, thus opening the way for other old exponents of radical democracy who, in later years, would follow them from every part of Italy to form that which would be called the Historical Right, and which had, in the alliance, the first act of its birth'.[7]

In substance, Cavour's political operation not only moved in harmony with the general development of society and of the active forces of the Piedmontese bourgeoisie, but favoured the formation of a governing class which was, in terms of interests, culture and attitudes, amongst the most homogenous to guide the unitary state.[8] This harmony and homogeneity were to decline when the borders of the unitary state came gradually to be extended to include other regions 'where the capitalist formation of the economy and a more diffuse civic conscience were not mature'[9], provoking, in the end, the fall of the Right (1876). For these reasons, notwithstanding the presence of some important anticipatory elements, it is perhaps not historically correct to take the origins of the transformist practice all the way back to the political and parliamentary actions of Cavour.

It is not a coincidence, in fact, that even as late as 1873, during the government of the Historical Right, a major initiative by Minghetti (perhaps the most prepared and long-sighted figure of that political group) to co-opt Depretis into the government failed. It was Depretis who, ten years later, in collaboration with Minghetti, successfully inaugurated the true and great stage of Italian transformism.[10]

2.   The Characteristics of Transformism

It is, therefore, only in 1883 that the transformist practice comes officially, so to speak, out into the open; is made the object of political polemic and of cultural analysis, as well as being defined in its essential and enduring characteristics which would then manifest themselves throughout Italy's entire political experience, from the birth of the unitary state to the present day. In certain respects, to write a history of transformism means to recount the entire national political history and to offer key elements of analysis to phenomena such as Giolittism or fascism, the centre-left or the historic compromise, which otherwise would be difficult to understand.

In fact transformism has been identified with a certain style of Italian political struggle. It is, that is to say, one of its structural characteristics to the extent that, as can be seen from the articles by Bollati, many consider it to be an integral part not only of political custom but also of the character of all Italians. On the other hand, it is enough to observe contemporary Roman political news with a certain critical detachment, and to compare it with Depretis's time, to come across surprising similarities of behaviour and style, as if the personalities concerned today had to obey the same mechanisms, or play the same role, as then. All of which tells us that we are in the presence of a phenomenon which has to be confronted and studied with the greatest seriousness, that is to say it has to be historically understood in order to prevent it being considered as something doomed, at least at the cultural level, to repeat itself, for which there is no remedy.

3. Two Opposite Interpretations

We need first of all to start by outlining, albeit rather schematically, the main judgements which have been expressed over time about this phenomenon. Naturally these judgements conflict with each other and they are of course linked to the political struggles of the time.

They can be said to fall into two opposing categories: that of negative or moralistic judgements and that of positive or realistic judgements. The famous 1886 invective of Giosuè Carducci is prominent in the first category: one might say that it represents the prototype of an attitude of moral repulsion which has lasted right up to the present day. For the poet, transformism meant betrayal ('he betrayed his party and introduced the trojan horse into the old Left'), clientelism (his politics are 'a coat rack where each deputy believes he can hang his overcoat with at least one wallet inside'), corruption and inadequacy ('Italy, just as it lacks any steadiness internally, has no force abroad; just as it is corrupt inside, so it appears abject from outside').[11]

At the end of his analysis, Bollati summarised the principal elements which are to be found at the basis of these negative judgements thus: 'A gap between declared intentions and actual behaviour; the ability to make the themes and words of one's adversary one's own, to empty them of significance; the willingness to let oneself be won over; disagreement in public – and agreement behind closed doors. Transformism is appearance, spectacle, indifference to the merits of the question. Its aim is power for its own sake.'[12] It should be added that, in general, judgements of a negative and moralistic character flourish amidst people of a cultural and literary background, that is personalities who are rich in civil passion but distant from direct political participation.

Amongst the positive or realistic judgements, those expressed by the major protagonists of transformist practice are prominent, above all, of course; from Depretis right through to Andreotti. For Giolitti, for example, transformism represents nothing but the inevitable metamorphosis of he who passes from opposition into the government of public affairs and is constrained to use 'one of the principal gifts of the man of government: good sense' and to abandon certain positions which 'serve the opposition in attacking the government opposite: but not to govern'.[13] But it is above all to Benedetto Croce that we owe not only the defence, but indeed the ennobling, of the practice of transformism which, for the liberal historian, represents a given necessity for political action and for anyone who seeks to pass from ideas and from programmes to their implementation, taking into account the evolution of things and the existing relation of forces.

In Croce's work one discovers a sarcastically imbued criticism of the moralism of 'academics and other innocent souls upset by the revolving door of ministerial change, by the repeated disappointment of their melancholy hope for stable government and, in sum, by the ever-changing nature of things; because, in their heart of hearts, things should stay the same'.

Of particular interest in Croce's work is the criticism of recurrent dogmas which, disregarding the material reality of Italian history, are led to condemn everything which lies outside of the bi-party or bipolar scheme of things: that is, the existence of two normal parties confronting each other, one conservative, the other progressive. The great historian compares such abstractions to those used by certain art critics who, having identified certain literary and artistic genres and the rules that identify them, 'were at a loss when confronted by standard pieces of work which, yet, were not works of poetry; and by works of poetry which, yet, were not standard; and who could not understand why people rushed to see not where there was conformity, but where there was poetry, that is – life'.[14]

These two extreme positions – the one of rejection, the other of justification – have been recounted here not because they make evident the aspects of truth which are to be found in both, but above all in order to underline how they are both inadequate for a historical understanding of the phenomenon. It cannot be explained solely using a moralistic key even if political action does become 'immoral' precisely when it aims not simply to serve ideas but to exploit them for reasons of power or of personal interest. Nor can it be explained solely using the key of justification, because then it would indeed be necessary to argue, in Hegelian mode, that 'all that is real is rational', even if the criticisms made by Croce vis-à-vis certain academics and professional moralists, maintain an enduring vitality.

4.   Beyond Value Judgements

It is necessary, then, to go beyond value judgements to identify the *structural* reasons which have allowed transformist practice to have such long-term success. Two distinguished 'observers', Silvio Spaventa and Antonio Gramsci, can help us considerably in this regard. The first, taking up some of the intuitions of Stefano Jacini, seeks to uncover the causes of the failure to form, at the dawn of the new state, a conservative party or pole and the birth, in its stead, of an agglomerate of moderate and heterogeneous forces at the centre of the political spectrum which ruptures the conservative-progressive dialectic and which exalts the practice of transformism. Silvio Spaventa identifies the causes of this development in, above all, the so-called 'Catholic question': this issue not only prevented the entire Risorgimento bourgeois class gravitating towards the political management of the liberal state without obstacles of an ideological nature, but also functioned in a more profound and subtle manner: it deprived the new state of the 'cement' of religious belief; it denied its moral legitimation amongst the popular classes and, in consequence, it removed from the ruling classes the support of a party which would have had 'as its aim the conservation of the institutions of the state itself'. 'Thus it is,' concludes Spaventa, 'that the modern, free [*liberi*] governments of the Catholic countries have not been able, to this day, to base themselves on trusted and secure parties; indeed, they have had to do without these, contenting themselves with half-way parties, the name of which everywhere has been that of the moderate party. ... The new state is the product of this party which, however, entirely lacks the force necessary to maintain it. Insofar as the new state is the work of the moderate party, this is essentially, at one and the same time, a conservative and progressive party.'[15]

For Antonio Gramsci, transformism is the 'physiological' instrument with which a ruling group exercises hegemony over the socially similar forces which gradually aspired to have an active role in the government of the state. 'The moderates (that is the hegemonic class)', writes Gramsci, 'continued to lead the Action Party even after 1870 [the capture of Rome] and 1876 [the switch to government by the Historical Left]; so-called transformism was nothing more than the parliamentary expression of this intellectual, moral and political hegemony.'[6] In essence, for Gramsci – as one also gathers from the analysis of Cavourian politics outlined above – transformism represents a sort of 'spontaneous' osmosis which takes place within one and the same social class wherein, that is, not only the ideological reference points are common, but also the hegemonic and material interests.

But if the observations of Spaventa and Gramsci are precious for understanding the historical genesis of this phenomenon, they do not, however, explain why it endured beyond the historical period characterised by the hegemony of a single social class; why it continued to manifest itself, that is, even when the social bases of the state were radically changed, with the enlargement of the suffrage and, above all, with the advent of the large popular parties. Not by chance has the major scholar of Depretis, Carocci, written recently of the politics of the 'centre left' (1963–1968): 'Moro too, like his predecessors Depretis and Giolitti, who tried to increase the social base of the state, made great use of a transformist technique. But while the transformism of Depretis and Giolitti worked on single persons (deputies, notables and influential figures), Moro's transformism had to work on those rigid and massive bodies the political parties, with results which were much more wearying for, and paralysing of, government action.'[17]

5. The Structural Causes of Transformism

It is therefore necessary to look deeper still to understand other 'structural' causes at the origins of the phenomenon which allowed it to survive and prosper beyond the age of Depretis. In fact we can see clearly that already in this initial phase there are at least two other causes which nourished transformism in a decisive manner. The first concerns the incoherent and non-homogenous character of the development of the Italian economy: it concerns, that is, the existence of powerful imbalances between bourgeois, capitalist interests and parasitic interests, between economically advanced zones with a developed civil society, and zones which are backward from every viewpoint, and so on. The direct and indirect consequences of this situation made themselves felt above all in the objective difficulty of elaborating a programme of political economy which was valid for the entire country and capable of promoting the diverse interests of the bourgeoisie of the time. Worse, the very same 'national' choices, that is decisions concerning the entire national territory, such as, for example, the protectionist measures introduced by Depretis and made definitive by Crispi and Giolitti, had diverse and contrasting consequences on the various bourgeois realities: in the North they favoured the birth of the new industrial bourgeoisie, while in the South they wiped out any attempt at entrepreneurial growth or the intensive development of agriculture in favour of the most backward classes and absentee landlords.

It follows that, in the absence of a common project, political and parliamentary aggregation took place on the basis of particularistic and personal interests often contradictory to each other. It was not by chance that, already in Depretis's time, transformism spread in an endemic fashion, primarily in the South, where the fragmentation of bourgeois interests was most apparent; whereas it faced greater resistance in the North where the needs of the Italian bourgeoisie were more compact and homogenous. Thus, Carocci writes: 'This tendency, which in the North and in the Centre was as a pathology of the organism was, in the South, its physiology. In the South more than in the other region, the political struggle was no more than a facade which hid narrow personal interests which were so absolutely dominant and so taken for granted as to take the form, cynical and frank at the same time, of explicit blackmail.'[18]

It would not otherwise be possible to explain why, right from the beginning, the diffusion of the mentality and practice of transformism took place, as Gramsci did not fail to observe, spontaneously, even whilst being sought out from above. Carefully analysing the 1882 parliamentary elections, Carocci, again, writes that 'the transformist phenomenon, to whatever extent promoted by Depretis and by Minghetti, took place spontaneously, constituency by constituency, determined by the necessity which the individual candidates felt to come to agreements between themselves in order to guarantee their victory, rather than by any general programme which had its origins in the centre'.[19] It is not a coincidence that transformism developed organically and continuously following the enlargement of the suffrage: that is, when the number of voters increased from 400,000 to two-and-a-half million, and when that homogeneity of class and social orders represented by the Historic Right came to an end with the emergence of a larger and more heterogeneous area constituted by the petty bourgeoisie, the nascent industrial bourgeoisie and the urban classes comprising professionals and dependent workers. But the clearest evidence of the link between socio-economic imbalance and transformism is given by the activity of the Giolitti government which, with the support, which was nearly always unanimous, of the southern deputies, managed to divert the economic growth of the entire country and to concentrate it in the northern industrial triangle.[20]

6. The Consequences of Bureaucratic Centralisation

Another 'structural' cause of the transformist process is to be found in the so-called 'system of government' which was installed with the political and administrative unification of the country. Dual legislative and administrative centralisation had precise and enduring consequences for the type of political struggle which developed in Italy and for the behaviour of the political classes, the parties and state officials. Particularistic needs, unable to find a response in their natural location, that is at the local level, transferred themselves to the summit of the state and heavily influenced every attempt to provide more general political responses to the country's problems. From this stemmed also the necessity for each single deputy to 'immerse himself in real life', that is, to renounce his own ideas and his national role in order to obtain from the government majority the solution to those local problems on which his own re-election depended.

Stefano Jacini and Gaetano Salvemini provided textbook analyses of the phenomenon: these need to be re-read in order to understand how, within this government mechanism, the defence of corporatist and local interests became a necessity for the survival of the local ruling classes as much as the national ones.[21] But let us look at what Marco Minghetti – a protagonist with Depretis of the transformist operation of 1883 – writes regarding the favours and exemptions granted by the central government to the local communities in order to reward them for their electoral loyalty: 'Backed by the favour of the centre, the winning party occupies the town hall, the province, the executive committees of the religious charitable works, of the schools and sometimes even of the credit institutes, absolutely excluding their opponents from them; and thus pursues, with no restraint whatsoever, its own interests. Taxes are determined in the interests of the winning party. One reads of certain communities where the customs authorities let the merchandise of those belonging to the winning side enter unobstructed, making up the loss to the local authority budget by increasing the amount taken from their adversaries.'[22]

A sort of short circuit was thus established between local interests, parliamentary majorities and the state administration (one thinks simply of the role of the prefects) which finished by corrupting the local ruling classes – because it rendered them weak and subaltern vis-à-vis the central authority – just as much as the national ruling classes – because it rendered them incapable of placing the general interest of the country before the interests of their own clienteles.[23] And since transformism draws great strength from this short circuit, it is destined to endure as long as the causes underlying it endure. The same point applies, obviously, with regard to the enduring dualistic situation of our socio-economic development.

All this explains why transformism survived beyond the age of Depretis and strengthened itself during the course of Italy's history. But there is more. If one looks closely, the transformist technique has been, right from the time of Depretis, in a certain sense, the necessary path for reconciling the unequal development of the country and administrative centralisation with the progressive enlargement of the social bases of the state: it is, that is to say, a constituent component of reformist politics itself. This is proved not only by the fact that every phase of reformist development (from Depretis, to Giolitti, to Moro) is accompanied by the exaltation of transformist tendencies, but also by the fact that the real alternatives to each of these transformist operations were always located – right from the time of Cavour – on the right of the political spectrum. These alternatives are marked above all by the desire to liquidate every reformist and democratic drive and by the hegemonic ambition of bourgeois elites which feel most compact and homogenous, and indeed solidly represented, in the centralised administrative structures of the state.

It is no coincidence that up to the advent of fascism, each transformist phase ends with the birth of authoritarian government: after Depretis, Crispi; after Giolitti, first Salandra and then Mussolini. All this has to be remembered not only in order to underline the elitist and often reactionary character of a certain recurrent moralism hostile to transformism, but also to repeat how transformism gives rise, in effect, to further imbalances in economic and social development and further authoritarian centralisation of the state administration. In fact transformism, often quite without the intention of those who exercise it, ends by increasing the unhealthy interconnections between particularist interests (the true obstacle to every politics seeking social and economic harmonisation) and the state bureaucracy (which becomes ever more partisan and servile towards private interests, both open and hidden). Such a practice, that is, while on the one hand it represents, so to say, the necessary price for launching each reformist politics, on the other hand is destined in the long run to corrupt and to suffocate every democratic and innovative thrust. In short, transformism ends by worsening the causes which produced it and therefore finishes, sooner or later, by giving birth to more or less masked forms of reactionary authoritarianism.

7. The Absence of Autonomy

As one can see, it is enough to analyse the genesis and nature of transformism to discover both the ambiguous character of the Italian political system – a congenital ambiguity rooted in the simultaneous adoption of the parliamentary system (the liberal reformist face) and the Napoleonic administrative system (the authoritarian face), and to lay bare the democratic precariousness which characterises the entire history of united Italy. This latter appears to oscillate unremittingly between moments of reformist opening contaminated by transformism, and moments of authoritarian involution.[24] Yet we shall still not get to the heart of the phenomenon if, as the scholastics would put it, we do not get to the 'first cause' which condenses and includes all of the other causes, and which is at the base of every transformist attitude: and that is the lack of autonomy which we continually rediscover in each historical phase and at every level of Italian society. Lack of autonomy in relations between the central authority and local authorities, between civil society and political society, between social forces and political forces, between the factors of production and the public authorities, between politics and culture, and so on.[25]

It is this endemic, diffuse and generalised absence of autonomy which has made difficult, in various historical situations, the formation of independent subjects having their own integrity, and which has debased via pragmatic compromises the historical vocations and characteristics of the various social realities emerging over time: which has, in short, allowed transformism to become a habit and style of life and to provoke a sort of genetic mutation in the character of Italians to the point at which – not only in political life – men and groups capable of remaining faithful to themselves and to resist the temptation to run 'in aid of the victors', as the writer Ennio Flaiano liked to put it, are ever more rare.

However, in order not to give in to some moralistic regression on our own part, it is useful to direct historical research to the two essential characteristics and aspects of Italian transformism: that relating to cultural forces and that relating to industrial and productive forces.

It has often been asked why is it that our unitary history has known only two antithetical and mirror-image versions of participation by the man of culture: that of advisor to the prince and that of the rebel contestant.

And it is true to say that examples of intellectuals capable of exercising an autonomous and creative role distant from both the temptation of the court and the temptations of rebellion are rather scarce in the history of Italian culture. The reason for the existence of such a phenomenon, which has had such an influence and which has determined the collective behaviour of an entire country, is to be found once again in the inadequately autonomous character of a large part of the national cultural institutions: in the fact, that is, that the various economic and organisational structures which, since the eighteenth-century through to the present day, have shaped cultural activities (from music to the theatre, from universities to research institutions, from the cinema to mass communications) are configured as autarchic fortresses, lacking, one should say, lateral, non-subaltern linkages with civil society, fortresses to which one gains access, in general, only by co-optation from above.[26] One is dealing with oligarchic realities which act as a shield to the power of the intellectuals and which confront the 'excluded' with a dilemma: either surrender or brutal marginalisation which, sooner or later, leads to the 'idealistic revolt' against the entire system.[27]

It is within this objectively given environment that the disease of transformism has grown in the world of culture; also because, in general, servility on the one hand and rebellion on the other are no more than two faces of the same coin, or better, of one and the same script which foresees attitudes all the more revolutionary, the more unexpected and satisfying are the subsequent concessions. In fact, the biographies of Italian intellectuals who have switched, from the nineteenth-century onwards, from one attitude to the other, not apparently without critical torment, are innumerable.

Nor would it otherwise be possible to explain the most extended and significant transformist operation to have been witnessed by Italian culture when, towards the end of the Second World War, one saw the passage of numerous intellectuals from idealism to Leninism: the switch that, according to the testimony given by Franco Fortini in relation to the biography of Giaime Pintor, took place in a virtually painless fashion thanks to the elitist and anti-democratic character which the two conceptions have in common, and which allowed many intellectuals to maintain their traditional positions of prestige and power and simultaneously to save their *progressive* spirit in a new and triumphant ethico-political role.[28]

Similarly worthy of separate treatment would be the transformist attitude which characterised Italian industrial interests during the period of the first industrialisation from the end of the nineteenth century to the collapse of fascism: a period distinguished, as is known, by the high level of dependence of the nation's large-scale industry on political power thanks to exaggerated protectionist measures, the direct interventionism of the state and the expansion of the war economy.[29] But it is sufficient for the purposes of our research to dedicate attention specifically to that masterpiece of transformism which we see incarnated in the history of the largest private Italian industry: Giolittian under Giolitti, interventionist under Salandra, fascist under Mussolini, ready to join the opposite camp when the latter fell, centrist with De Gasperi, the first of the Italian industries to support the switch to the Centre-Left, pro the 'historic compromise'. Fiat always showed great tactical awareness and brilliant timing in drawing advantage from the various regimes which, one after the other, alternated in our country. This is a concrete history, which, more than any theoretical argument, allows us to see directly the processes of opportunistic adaptation and the social and political cost by which the first Italian industrialisation took place.[30]

8.   The Rise of the Mass Parties

With the emergence in the period immediately after the First World War of the large popular parties and with the introduction of the proportional electoral system – wanted above all by Luigi Sturzo – a decisive blow was struck against transformism. The failure of the last Giolitti government and the advent of fascism, in fact demonstrate how the changed situation placed insurmountable obstacles to parliamentary attempts to deconstruct and reconstruct the parties and ministerial majorities, forcing the traditional government system to abandon its liberal face and openly to show an authoritarian one.

It should not be forgotten, nonetheless, that fascism imposed itself as a totalitarian regime only after a period which saw a series of coalition governments and which finished with the destruction of the parties and unions and with the liquidation of the proportional electoral system: an able and subtle operation of attrition which once again made use of the resources of transformism as well as instruments of repression and blackmail which had already been available in the central and peripheral administrative system of the state for some time. What remains to explain, however, is why it is that, with the collapse of fascism, and notwithstanding the advent of the new republican constitution, transformist inertia managed once again to dominate.

In a 1926 article reviewing the work of Dorso, *The Southern Revolution*, Luigi Sturzo, taking to heart the tragic experience of fascism and keeping his eye fixed on the political and economic condition of the south, indicated four programmatic points the complete and simultaneous realisation of which would have *freed* the south and the entire country from the plague of transformism.

First came, obviously, a proportional electoral system. As Sturzo observed, 'the southern "right minded" people were hostile [to this]: because ... the dominant bourgeois classes always repulsed the peasant masses and the working classes from organised participation in public life, fearing the loss not only of their monopoly over local and provincial life, but also of their uncontrolled and unlimited economic domination'.

In second place, Sturzo put the problem of the latifondo [great estates] which 'did not regard the technical aspect ... but the political issue of rural emancipation'. The solution of this problem would have delivered 'another great blow for the development of political life in the south'.

'The third blow', still quoting Sturzo, 'would have been the construction of the regions and the giving of greater autonomy to local life in order to be able to create (even via harsh experience) a politico-administrative consciousness among large parts of the southern population.'

Last but not least, Sturzo put the problem of 'reducing the system of patronage and initiating and setting the country on the path of economic liberty'. With the solution to this problem, he concluded, 'the south would have passed from the rank of colony to that of province integral to the kingdom'.[31] It would seem that the Sturzian programme was largely implemented in the post-Second World War period, with the readoption of the proportional electoral system, the further extension of suffrage, the liberalisation of international trade and the consequent destruction of the 'agro-industrial bloc'.[32]

One is dealing, nonetheless, with the reversal of a trend which did not manage, in the short run, for reasons known to the experts, to relaunch a process of socio-economic development able to overcome the country's secular dualism,[33] nor to break the continuities in the state administrative apparatuses which remain both highly centralised and authoritarian. As a consequence, the two principal causes which we have seen to lie at the origins of the transformist phenomenon survived for a long time in the new historical situation, notwithstanding the substantial rupture brought about by the Resistance.

What was missing in the political forces and culture of the time was, above all, a perception of the importance of the administrative reform of the state. The large, people's parties were fully occupied by the attempt to aggregate and integrate into political and trade union life the millions and millions of citizens who had always been forced into abstention or political and social marginalisation. They paid little or no attention to this crucial theme, with the result that the exercise of local self-government, the one true educational training ground for democratic politics, appears still to be regulated by the fascist law of 1934.[34]

Two further circumstances have favoured the renewal of the transformist phenomenon. The first has to do with the gradual, but ever more extensive and massive identification of the parties with the state, caused by the permanence of those same political forces at the head of the republic's governments.[35] The second concerns the unshakeable survival of Leninist dogma in the principal opposition party: a dogma which has, on the one hand, rendered impracticable the physiological practice of alternation and, on the other, has favoured the diffusion of the transformist bacillus – the famous 'doppiezza' [double-dealing or ambiguity] which Bollati would say makes the history of the PCI, from the Salerno U-turn onwards, so *Italian* – even in a force excluded from central government.[36] Taken together, these various causes allowed transformist tendencies to put down deep roots even in the new terrain: unable to take shape at the parliamentary level, where the proportional system tends to maximise the identity and the formal unity of the political forces, these tendencies have spread inside the parties. It is thence, in fact, that real political power and the job of selecting the ruling class have been transferred. It is there that the corporatist and particular interests find their outlets and their rewards and, consequently, it is there that the majorities which matter form and break up.

The instruments of the new transformist alchemy are, therefore, the party factions and the numerous 'groups of friends' which form around the various notables, and which remind one so much of the cliques which, at the time of Depretis and Giolitti, held hostage the heterogeneous parliamentary majorities.

With the second industrial revolution, however, which within a few decades carried Italy to a position among the top ranks of the world hierarchy of advanced industrial democracies, Italian society experienced, in terms of the redistribution of wealth, the diffusion of welfare and of culture, and the mobility of classes and social groups; a social revolution which was without precedent in its entire history. Entire classes of people which the protectionist bloc had held fixed in a miserable subsistence economy and prisoners of a greedy bourgeoisie, which was able to see only in autarchy and war the instruments of the industrial expansion of the country, were liberated from their ancient moral and material subservience and undertook a vast and deeply-rooted process of economic and civil growth, often ignored by the dominant culture which had remained attached to its ancient idealistic and elitist outlooks.[37] The challenge of 'populism' launched by Sturzo had proved victorious. Sturzo was the only great leader in the history of united Italy who had known how to resist the enticements of transformism and had believed in the autonomous capacities of civil liberation and social emancipation of a people considered, on the right as on the left of the political spectrum, as permanently in need of guidance and guardianship from above.

Certainly the state continued its often incoherent role of intervention, sought not only for reasons of support to large scale industry but also by the sacrosanct necessity to alleviate and absorb the social consequences provoked by the vast process of industrialisation taking place. Equally the islands of social and geographic oppression and of economic and civil backwardness still appear numerous. Nevertheless, it is a fact that, as a consequence of these vast social and economic transformations, Italian society has come to know a degree both of homogeneity in its overall development, and of autonomy vis-à-vis political power, without comparison in united Italy's history.[38]

It would not otherwise be possible to explain the failure of the last great transformist operation undertaken towards the end of the 1970s which sought directly to involve the PCI in the government of the country.[39] The fact is that, with the gradual but irreversible ending of both the dualism of Italian society and its dependence on political power, some of the principal causes which had sustained transformism and rendered it victorious in the past had also disappeared. This also means that, perhaps for the first time in history, the objective conditions exist to undertake an authentic reformist policy without the need to adopt opportunist solutions; to finally root out the unhealthy practice of transformism without having to run the risk of a new authoritarianism.[40]

Notes

1   G.Bollati, *L'italiano*, Torino, 1983.
2   F.Crispi, *Scritti e discorsi politici*, Torino s.d., pp.567 ff.
3   G.Bollati, op.cit. p.x.
4   On the Cavourian alliance [*connubio*] see: Chapter 8, R.Romeo, *Cavour e suo tempo (1842–1854)*, vol.2, tome II, Bari, 1977, pp.527 ff. According to Romeo, 'The Centre majorities derived from the experience of the alliance at least guaranteed the gradual absorption of the old conflict into the new Italian reality and, with this, the gradual progression towards the higher levels of liberty and democracy which characterised the history of Italy from 1861–1915, and which no serious historiography can deny'. He adds, regarding the negative aspect of transformism: 'This does not mean that one must ... forget or underestimate the costs of this mediating function in terms either of the clarity, or the robustness, of parliamentary life, or of effective correspondence between the institutions and the will of the citizens. But one is talking of costs which cannot be eliminated from the reality which one is called upon to judge, and which cannot be detached from this without placing oneself, for this very reason, on a plane external to critical and historiographic reflection.'
5   R.Romeo, op.cit., p.572.
6   A.Carrociolo, *Stato e società civile*, Torino, 1960, p.14.
7   R.Romeo, op.cit. p.572.
8   The most complete and thorough analysis of the political and cultural formation of the Historic Right remains Chabod's *Storia della politica estera italiana dal 1870 al 1896*, I, *The Foundations*, Bari, 1951.
9   A.Carraciolo, op.cit., p.14.
10 On the politics of the Right, see A.Berselli, *La Destra storica dopo l'unità*, Bologna, 1965. By the same author see: 'Un tentativo di combinazione ministeriale tra Marco Minghetti e Agostino Depretis (24–29 June 1875)' in *Strenna storica bolognese*, Bologna, 1956, pp.7 ff.
11 Obviously all the vast anti-Giolittian writings, of Gobetti, Salvemini, Dorso, Sturzo et al, can be placed in this category, with the necessary references and quotations. The Carducci quotes are from G.Carducci, *Opere*, Zanichelli national editions, Series II, pp.33 ff.
12 Bollati, op.cit., pp.xiii–xiv. For a complete and systematic overview of the pro- and anti-transformism polemics during the Depretis period, see G.Spadolini, 'Lineamenti di storia del trasformismo' in *I radicali dell'Ottocento da Garibaldi a Cavallotti*, Firenze, 1982, 4th edn., pp.109–179. Spadolini's work also contains an ample bibliography of the period.
13 G.Giolitti, *Memorie della mia vita*, Milano, 1922, vol.I, pp.36 ff.
14 B.Croce, *Storia d'Italia dal 1871 al 1915*, 7th edn., Bari, 1943, pp.17 ff. Even if more elaborate and nuanced, the argument of R.Romeo cited above with regard to Cavour can be assimilated with that of the Neapolitan historian [i.e. Croce].
15 On the attitude of Silvio Spaventa, see the anthology edited by Nino Valeri, *La lotta politica in Italia (dall'Unità al 1925)*, 5th edn., Firenze, 1973, pp.116 ff. On the position of S.Jacini as intended to prevent the 'Catholic question' blocking the formation of a national, liberal-conservative party, see the perceptive introduction by S.Traniello to S.Jacini, *La riforma dello Stato e il problema regionale*, Brescia, 1968, pp.35 ff.
16 A.Gramsci, *Il Risorgimento*, Torino, 1948, pp.70 ff.
17 G.Carocci, *Storia d'Italia dall'Unità ad oggi*, Milano, 1975, p.355. Carocci's analysis of the

centre-left, unlike that of Depretis's politics (*Agostino Depretis e la politica interna dal 1876 al 1887*, Torino, 1956) appears to be marred by excessive moralising and contingent political prejudices.

18 G.Carocci, *A.Depretis*, op.cit., p.300.

19 Ibid. p.284.

20 On the Giolittian majorities and in particular on the ministerial 'vocation' of the southern deputies (the so-called *ascari*) it is always informative to re-read Salvemini (G.Salvemini, *Il ministro della malavita e altri scritti sull'Italia giolittiana*, Milano, 1962).

21 As far as the thought of Jacini and Salvemini is concerned, see the works already cited. See also G.Galli (*I partiti politici*, Torino, 1974, pp.1-52) who furthers the analysis of the relationship between state centralisation and transformism. Galli also shows, adopting some theses from M.Duverger (*I partiti politici*, Milano, 1961), that, immediately following unification, localistic preoccupations impeded the formation of a conservative party on national programmatic and organisational bases.

22 M.Minghetti, *I partiti politici e la pubblica amministrazione*, edited by B.Widmar, Bologna, 1969, p.41.

23 'The Chamber', wrote R.Bonfadini in the *Nuova Antologia*, 15 February, 1894, 'seemed to transform itself into a huge provincial council in which every deputy represented his constituency, and the government only pretended to represent the nation.' Also, G.Spadolini, op.cit., p.166.

24 On the ambiguous character of the Italian political system, see S.Fontana, 'Origine e sviluppo del sistema italiano: dalla polemica di Cattaneo alla situazione attuale,' in *L'opera e l'eredità di Carlo Cattaneo*, edited by C.Lacaita, Bologna, 1975, pp.119–143.

25 The author has sought to denounce this 'structural' lack of autonomy in every sense and every sector of activity (from local government to trade unions, from the parties to the cultural institutions) in: *Autonomia della cultura e cultura delle autonomie*, Bologna, 1980.

26 The research of various authors: *Intelletuali e potere* in *Storia d'Italia* (Annali 4) published by Einaudi, Torino, 1981, does finally, if not exhaustively, fill in a gap in Italian historiography regarding the role of intellectuals in the history of our country and their relations with political power. Bibliographical references can be found here too. With regard to this field of research, that is transformism, see in the same volume, above all, the worthy study by A.Asor Rosa, 'Il giornalista: appunti sulla fisiologia di un mestiere difficile', (pp.1277 ff.) dedicated to the analysis of the behaviour, simultaneously servile and blackmailing, of the press to political power from 1800 to the present. On the theme of intellectuals and power, see too the collection critically edited by G.Turi, 'Intelletuali senza potere' in *Italia contemporanea*, June 1982, pp.5 ff., to which we refer you for further bibliographical details.

27 It is interesting to note how 'rebellion' understood as a cultural and literary phenomenon always explodes in Italy coincidentally with the advent of reformist and transformist politics. For the Depretis period see on this the work cited by Spadolini. For the Giolittian era see R.D'Agata, 'Ancora sul ribellismo del primo novecento' in *La rivista trimestrale*, May 1972, and also R.Del Carria, *Proletari senza rivoluzione*, Milano, 1970, vol.I, pp.348–353. The same phenomenon occurs, albeit in a highly specific context which should be reconstructed with the utmost precision, during the period characterised by the long agony of the politics of the 'centre left' (1968–1974) and from the hypothesis of the insertion of the PCI into the central government (1976–1980): a period which not by chance saw the violent and endemic explosion of terrorism both of the right and of the left.

28 A vast literature exists on Italian culture between the end of fascism and the advent of the republican regime which is rich in direct testimony and historical analysis. For a critical overview of the studies dedicated to the argument, see A.D'Orsi, 'La cultura nell'Italia fascista. Un decennio di studi', in Quaderno 12, 1983 of the *Istituto per la storia della resistenza in provincia di Allesandria*, pp.7–65. For a statistical and biographical outline of the Italian intellectuals who participated in the Fascist cultural contests [littoriali] and who subsequently held positions of power and prestige in the popular anti-fascist parties, see U.Alfassio-Grimaldi and M.Addis Saba, *Cultura a passo romano*, Milano, 1983. For the testimony of F.Fortini re the diary of Giaime Pintor (*Doppio diario, 1936–43*, Torino, 1978) see S.Fontana, *Autonomia della cultura*, op.cit., pp.16–18.

29   An enormous literature on the first Italian industrialisation also exists. Nevertheless, to grasp the links between industrial development and state intervention, between political power and a protected economy, it is sufficient to consult the classic work by R.Romeo, *Breve storia della grande industria: 1861–1961*, Bologna, ed. 1972.

30   An effective synthesis of Fiat politics from its birth to the advent of the republican regime can be found in the more wide-ranging research by Valerio Castronovo, *Agnelli*, Torino, 1971 and, for the successive period, in the work of P.Barile, *Valletta*, Torino, 1983.

31   The article cited is in L.Sturzo, *Il partito popolare*, vol.III, Bologna, 1957, pp.366 ff.

32   On the gradual process of substitution of the class of large-scale landowners by that of farmers [*coltivatori diretti*] as a political pressure group, and on the role played by these in the country's economic development in the second post-war period, see S.Fontana, 'Industrializzazione e classi sociali negli anni cinquanta' in *Il dibattito*, Venezia, Jan-March, 1983, pp.56 ff.

33   On the enduring north-south divide in the second post-war era, despite the prodigious increase in national income and the massive intervention of the state (agrarian reform, Fund for the South, etc.), see P.Saraceno's contribution to the 'Keynes in Italy' conference held in Florence, 4–5 June, 1983 in *Banca toscana studi e informazioni*, VI, 3, 1983, pp.7–31.

34   On the subjective and objective causes which favoured the continuity of the pre-fascist and fascist state apparatuses in the second post-war period, the research of C.Pavone is fundamental: 'La continuità dello Stato: uomini e istituzioni', in *Italia 1945–48: le origini della Repubblica*, Torino, 1974. There are also stimulating contributions in E.Rotelli, 'La restaurazione post-fascista degli ordinamenti locali' in *Italia contemporanea*, Jan-March, 1979, pp.46–72 and by F.Traniello, 'Stato e partiti alle origini della repubblica nel dibattito storiografico', *Italia contemporanea*, April-June, 1979, pp.3–15.

35   F. Traniello (loc. cit., p.13) correctly observes that, following the rupture in anti-fascist unity (May 1947) and the advent of the *Cold War*, the stress shifted on the part of the DC to 'purely the control dimension, and a defensive posture based on the occupation of the state, whilst the PCI abandoned the notion of progressive democracy, replacing it with the primacy of the party as the compact nucleus, guaranteed by democratic centralism, of a society and a state alternative to those of the bourgeoisie'.

36   On the 'Salerno U-turn's' link to the centralised organisation of the PCI, and on the consequent 'doppiezza' of the PCI's relationships with the other parties and the democratic institutions, see in particular G.Quazza, *Resistenza e storia d'Italia*, Milano, 1976, pp.37–8 and 201. See also the evidence of G. Amendola where he writes that 'the party's centrist strategy was accepted, but with great reservations, with that *doppiezza* which has been so widely discussed and which was not an attitude simply of Togliatti or a few leaders, but a position widely found at the base of the party and in its functionaries. Yes, it was necessary to use the legal opportunities available to win the local authority and parliamentary seats – but in order to occupy positions which would be useful when H-hour finally arrived' ('De Gasperi e la lotta politica nel trentennio repubblicano', in *Rinascita*, 2 September 1977, p.9). For the discussions in the PCI at the time of the Salerno U-turn, see the anthological selections in A.Lepre, *Dal crollo del fascismo all'egemonia moderata: l'Italia dal 1943 al 1947*, Napoli, 1974, pp.81 ff. To fully understand the attitude of the PCI vis-à-vis transformism, the well-known 1950 work of Togliatti on Giolitti is emblematic (now to be found in *Momenti della storia d'Italia*, Roma, 1963) where the Communist leader not only re-evaluated Giolittian politics but liquidated as moralistic the principal criticisms always directed at the Piedmontese statist (clientelism, electoral fraud, transformism, etc.)

37   For a useful statistical outline of Italian economic and social growth from 1945 to the present, of the many publications, see in particular M.Deaglio and G.De Rita, *Il punto sull'Italia*, Milano, 1983.

38   On the 'popular' character of Italian industrial expansion and on its extension beyond the traditional borders of the 'industrial triangle' see in particular G.Fuà and C.Zacchia (eds), *Industrializzazione senza fratture*, Bologna, 1983. The 1971–81 census shows that there are 950,000 local industrial units in Italy (that is approximately one firm per 60 inhabitants), and that this phenomenon of *mass industrialisation* has grown in the decade in question by 33.8 percent (*Punto sull'Italia*, op.cit., pp.54–5).

39   For an initial and summary historical reconstruction of the period between the election of 1976 and
      the DC Congress of February 1980, which seemed to be characterised by the gradual *insertion* of
      the PCI into central government, it is necessary to consider the testimonies of E.Berlinguer, *La
      questione comunista*, Roma, 1975; F.Rodano, *Questione democristiana e compromesso storico*,
      Roma, 1977; G.Andreotti, *Diari 1976–1979*, Milano, 1981; F.Di Giulio and E.Rocco, *Un ministro
      ombra si confessa*, Milano, 1979. On the role played in those years by A.Moro, whose actions
      should not be confused with those of G.Andreotti, see S.Fontana, 'Moro e il sistema politico
      italiano' in P.Scaramozzino (ed), *Cultura e politica nell'esperienza di Aldo Moro*, Milano,
      published by *Il Politico*, 1982, pp.125 ff. and 'Partito e società nell'ultimo Moro' in Quaderno 11,
      of the *Istituto per la storia della resistenza in provincia di Alessandria*, IV, 1983, pp.135 ff.

40   See V.Murra, 'Il trasformismo: fenomeno specifico o costante storica del sistema politico
      italiano?', *Studi di filosofia, politica e diritto*, 1983, n.9.

[39]

Party System Change in Italy: 1987-1996 [1]

Luciano Bardi
Università di Bologna
Dipartimento di Politica Istituzioni Storia
Strada Maggiore 45, I-40125 Bologna, Italy
Fax: + 39 51 239 548
bardi@spbo.unibo.it

1. Introduction

For at least thirty years Giovanni Sartori's "polarized pluralism" (1966) has been the dominant analytical model of the Italian party system after it emerged as the clear winner in the debate with Giorgio Galli's (1966) interpretation. During this period only few attempts were made towards the formulation of alternative models. The most serious challenges to Sartori's model's primacy were made in the early 1980s. Paolo Farneti maintained that the Italian party system was evolving towards centripetal pluralism characterized by competition patterns oriented towards the formation of center coalitions (1983, 231); and Ivo Daalder's conclusions were rather similar: with seven relevant parties, the Italian party system was still pluralistic, but, as a consequence of a (near) disappearance of anti-system parties, it was becoming de-polarized.[2] Neither interpretation effectively challenged Sartori's interpretation's dominant position in the literature.

In the last two years, the ongoing process of party system transformation in Italy has revitalized the debate (Bartolini and D'Alimonte 1995; Melchionda 1995; Bardi 1996a, 1996b; Morlino 1996; Pappalardo 1996). In general such efforts analyze changes in the party system's structural elements such as number of relevant parties, ideological distance, direction of competition, size and distribution of opposition parties, referring more or less explicitly to Sartori's (1976) criteria. According to at least two of these contributions, the Italian party system has changed enough to warrant its re-classification. Pappalardo (1996, 140) argues that it is evolving towards "moderate pluralism", as "relevant actors, ideological distance, number of poles" have changed. Morlino, on the other hand, supports the view that there is continuity with the past and defines the present system as neo-polarized pluralism (1996, 25). The departure from traditional polarized pluralism is due to the absence of anti-system parties and of a strong central actor (1996, 23).

Some of the conditions at the basis of these analyses may have already been changed by a number of events, most importantly the 1996 elections. This report will try to outline the research questions that have to be addressed in order to assess the extent of change in the Italian party system. In particular, this project will try to focus on Sartori's properly structural variables: number of parties and ideological distance, concentrating on two major aspects: a) an assessment of the degree of party system stabilization; b) measurement of changes occurred in party system structure, especially in the number of parties and to a more limited extent in ideological distance and polarization. Party system stabilization will be studied by looking at electoral volatility (total and bloc). Party system structural changes will be

9

assessed through two sets of indices: 1) fractionalization and number of effective parties will be used for counting the number of parties; 2) voters left-right self-placements will be used to assess ideological distance. The analysis will also take into account the existence of a particular condition in the present Italian situation. Two different party systems seem to co-exist during this phase: an electoral party system, consisting of the parties and the coalitions that participate in the electoral competition, and a parliamentary party system, consisting of the parties and groups that are formed in parliament after an election. This distinction is justified by the different competition rules they have to follow respectively in the electoral and in the parliamentary arena.

2.   Party system structure and change

There is very little question that the Italian party system has experienced a dramatic change in recent years. Certainly there has been change in the identity and in the nature of the basic units of the system, that is the parties themselves. As important and dramatic as they may appear, such changes do not concern Sartori's model structural variables. According to Sartori polarized pluralism is characterized by high fragmentation and very high polarization. The number of parties in a system can very well be considered the most important structural variable. Sartori combines mathematical (quantitative) and nominal (qualitative) criteria to count the number of parties in a system and concludes that a system is to be considered fragmented if it consists of more than five relevant parties. Ideological distance or proximity determine the system's degree of polarization. A high degree of polarization discriminates between moderate or polarized pluralism in highly fragmented party systems. The operationalization of ideological distance has been more difficult than the operationalization of the number of parties. The most satisfactory indicator appears to be the difference between the two extreme parties' electors' average left-right self-placement scores. Only if these two variables undergo significant change (i.e. if the number of relevant parties drops below six or left-right self-placement differences drop to values close to four points[3] can we say that the party system has changed.

An assessment of the extent and nature of the current change in the Italian party system is rather complicated by the very fact that such change is still under way. Changes in the structure of electoral competition (the electoral law, the increasing importance of the media)[4], anti-party sentiment, the erosion of sub-cultures, and even the emergence of new cleavages or the rekindling of dormant ones have all been blamed or praised, depending on viewpoints, for being factors in the party system's transformation. Although they, and perhaps some other long term causes, all deserve consideration, only a few direct causes appear to be really relevant. In fact three major direct causes can be considered to be responsible for the current change: 1) change in political demand towards specific parties or even parties in general, resulting from greater potential voter mobility,[5] 2) change in the political supply provided by the parties a) as a result of the scandals and judicial actions that followed *Tangentopoli*; and b) as a consequence of the need by political parties to make new and different strategic choices in response to the new electoral law; 3) direct effects of the electoral law on individual parties parliamentary delegations.

Our research will therefore take into account the different impact that these three causes can have on party system structure and its stabilization. The first two have effects mostly on the stability of citizens' electoral behaviour, while the third one should have an impact on the number of the parties that make up the system.[6] We can surmise that the first cause, change in citizens' attitudes, is the one likely to produce the most important and lasting obstacles to the stabilization of the Italian party system. Some of the factors that made the Italian electorate relatively stable, such as the strength of sub-cultures and ideologies in determining partisan and electoral choices have been dramatically eroded; moreover, electors are showing a greater propensity to change their preferences as a consequence of the more pragmatic character of the centripetal competition typical of plurality systems and also of the greater marginal utility of alternating electoral choices in such systems. We can therefore conclude that the Italian party system will most likely continue to be characterized by a greater potential voter mobility than in the past.

As for the second cause, change in electoral supply, the effects of *Tangentopoli*, might have already exhausted its impact on the structuring of political and electoral supply. After the disruption caused on the party system between 1992 and 1994, *Tangentopoli*'s impact appears to be exhausted: even the possible discovery of the involvement of more, and so far "clean", politicians in new corruption cases would probably have no effect on their parties but only on their personal and political image.[7] If anything an *anti-Tangentopoli* investigations backlash is under-way. This could have some effect on the party system if attempts to re-found the PSI should prove to be successful. Still in terms of change in electoral supply, an assessment of the potential efficacy and persistence of party responses to the new electoral law is more complex. The two elections that have taken place after the reform could have already allowed Italian parties to revise their strategies according to the new electoral law. The creation of two electoral coalitions, the *Ulivo*, on the left, and the *Polo delle Libertà*, on the right, is a consequence of

this process. But the consolidation of electoral coalitions into permanent elements of a possible two-party system is far from certain: during the 1996 electoral campaign various groups candidly admitted that their strategies may be valid for only one election. This indicates that the electoral law is still producing effects on the party system. Undoubtedly the electoral competition's dual (proportional and plurality) nature exerts contrasting pressures on the parties and forces them to pursue less than consistent strategies. This delays the party system's stabilization. The PPI's 1995 split can be considered to a large extent a consequence of the plurality competition's pressures towards bi-polarization; but the maintenance of separate identities by the two catholic components (the PPI and the *Cristiani Democratici Uniti* - CDU) within the two electoral coalitions seems to respond to the proportional competition's logic. But both the *Ulivo*'s and the *Polo delle Libertà*'s inability to consolidate into more permanent party-like organizations must be imputed also to the already mentioned different nature of political competition in-between elections which permits the survival of parties and movements that are not even strong enough to obtain proportional seats in the Chamber of Deputies and/or in the Senate (Greens and Pannella's list).

Finally the last cause, the electoral law's direct effects on the strength of party parliamentary delegations must also be considered in its dual, proportional and majoritarian, aspects, even if both should exert pressures towards a reduction of the number of parties, albeit with different efficacy. In fact even in the proportional part of the competition the four percent threshold and the relatively small number of proportionally allocated seats (155) represent very serious hurdles to the entry of new parties into the system and even to the survival of some of the old ones. The efficacy of the plurality competition in limiting the number of parties could and should be even greater, even if in Italy voting is characterized by a strong territorial differentiation.

3.   Change and stabilization in the Italian party system

To be sure any assessment of party system change requires an in-depth analysis of a wide array of data and information on the country's socio-economic make-up, on citizens' values and attitudes, on the institutional context, on political information and communication, on political leaders' perception and strategies, besides a study of electoral results and their effects on parliament (party groups in particular). In this section we shall consider these last two types of data.

Table .1 lists scores on a number of indicators of the extent of changes in the party system concerning voter mobility and the number of parties between the 1987 election, whose scores well summarize the continuity experienced by the Italian party system since at least 1958, and the 1996 election.[8] The immediate impression one gets from at least some of the indices is that the Italian party system has indeed undergone a very important transformation. As has already been observed, an increase in electors' potential mobility could be one of the most important and persistent causes of party system change in Italy. Such potential mobility produces, in individual level electoral behaviour, votes for different parties in different elections, and causes, at the aggregate level, visible oscillations in political parties' overall results. Aggregate level

effects can be measured at the party system level with volatility indices. Table 1 lists total volatility (TV) and bloc volatility (BV) values. It is well known that volatility indices do not reveal completely variations in electoral behaviour; in fact they are calculated on the basis of political parties' electoral results' net differences between two consecutive elections. Consequently they do not take into account compensations that may occur as a consequence of identical numbers of electors' switching allegiances from one party to another and vice-versa.[9] But voters' mobility effects on the party system are determined by net differences, and changes in electors' behaviour that are not revealed by volatility indices can be considered as irrelevant. Consequently, examining total volatility indices' values can give us a first, albeit rough, impression of the system's stability.

As we have already mentioned, volatility is a synthetic measure of all direct causes' effects on the party system. An evaluation of each of the three causes' individual impacts should be made possible by the fact three elections have already taken place, under different institutional and, broadly speaking, environmental conditions, since the beginning of the change in 1992, 1994, and 1996 respectively. Certainly it can be surmised that in 1992 the change produced by those elections was the exclusive consequence of changes in electors' party choices; in 1994, the first elections held under the new electoral rules and after the beginning of the *Tangentopoli* investigations, all three sets of factors were most likely at work; in 1996, the impact of *Tangentopoli* on the shaping of electoral supply was probably exhausted.

TABLE 1
Italian party system 1987-1996
Volatility and number of parties indicators

	TV	BV	MP	F	EP	PwS	PG
1987	8.4	1.3	9	0.78	4.1	14	12 9
1992	14.2	7.5	10	0.85	5.7	16	13 10
1994	36.2	8.9	10	.87 .78	5.7 3.6	3.6	8 10
1996	18.2	8.9	9	.86 .67	6.2 2.7	8 14	9 11

Sources:

TV = total volatility; BV = Block volatility; MP = Number of major parties; F = Fractionalization; EP = Number of effective parties: my own calculations based on official electoral results.
PwS = Number of parties that obtained seats; PG = Number of parliamentary parties: Bartolini and D'Alimonte (1995) for 1987-1994; official electoral results and parliamentary records for 1996.

Notes:

All scores refer to the Chamber of Deputies' proportional election, unless otherwise indicated. The TV, BV, and MP indices were calculated according to criteria used by Bartolini and Mair (1990); the EP index is from Laakso and Taagepera (1979) and F is from Rae (1967).
TV, BV, PG, and F values are based on vote percentages. EP values are based on seat distributions.
F: the second figures in the 1994 and 1996 cells relate to the Chamber of Deputies' plurality election.
PG: the first figure in each cell relates to the Chamber of Deputies and the second one to the Senate.
EP: (1994 and 1996) the first figure in each cell relates to individual parties and the second one to electoral coalitions.
PwS: (1994 and 1996) the second figure in each cell relates to the elections' overall outcome.
EP: in 1994 is 3.1 for the plurality election and 6.0 for the proportional one
EP: in 1996 is 2.6 for the plurality election and 6.2 for the proportional one.

For all three post-1987 elections TV values are much higher than in the past. The 1992 value, the only one exclusively determined by many electors' autonomous decisions to modify their electoral behaviour, is particularly important. In fact, at 14.2 it was the highest registered up to that point between two parliamentary elections and almost double the average (7.2) of all previous elections.[10] The BV value (7.5) was even more impressive, considering the average (2.1) for the 1953-1987 period (Bardi 1996a).

The analysis of 1994 values is somewhat more complicated. While the 1994 BV value is only slightly higher than the 1992 one, that election's 36.2, perhaps the highest TV score ever observed in non-exceptional democratic elections (Bartolini and Mair 1990, 69), is two and half times higher and gives a dramatic impression of the change. But this time the change cannot be entirely imputed to increases in electors' mobility. Two very important developments had taken place between 1992 and 1994: the *Tangentopoli* investigations and electoral reform, whose effects were indeed first experienced in 1994. To be sure, both could have contributed to increasing voter mobility and political demand

13

induced party system change. But both factors had dramatic effects on the side of political supply. In fact volatility is a measure that is very much affected by changes that may occur in the composition of the field of parties contesting the election. At least a portion of the electorate, and probably a relevant one, although not necessarily more potentially mobile, were forced to alter their habitual electoral choices because of differences in the electoral supply. Some of these differences, such as those caused by the split and transformation that affected the DC, and the complete dissolution and only partial regrouping of the four center-left secular parties (PSI, PSDI, PRI, PLI) were clearly determined by the legitimacy crisis triggered by *Tangentopoli*. In the final analysis, the 1994 TV value describes accurately the change, but it cannot be considered as exclusively caused by changes in citizens' attitudes and electors' potential mobility. It is possible that without changes in electoral supply, the 1994 TV value would have been much closer to the 1992 one.

The 1996 TV score (18.2) is the second highest ever observed between two post-war parliamentary elections. It is closer again to the 1992 one and reveals a diminished, even if still present, importance of changes in electoral supply. Certainly, as we have mentioned, the effects of *Tangentopoli* have been absorbed. But at least one important change, the split of the PPI, has taken place between the last two elections and it can be interpreted as a response to the electoral competition's prevalently majoritarian logic.[11] Also this direct cause of party system change could be on the point of losing most of its importance. Only a new reform capable of changing again the logic of electoral competition, could perhaps resurrect electoral supply side causes of party system change. Summing up, the 1992-1996 period was

characterized by rather high levels of party system instability, but most of its direct causes appear to be exhausted. What remains is a relatively high level of potential voter mobility. It is probably lower than in 1992, when it was the only direct cause that started the change, but certainly higher than in the whole pre-1992 period.

The third direct cause of party system change, the new electoral system, determined the collapse of those parties that were situated in the center of the political spectrum and the formation of two alternative left and right coalitions. In 1994 two parties overtly decided to keep a centrist position against the two major blocks: PPI and the Segni Pact. Although the two parties represented the heritage of the former DC - still capable of attracting almost 30% of votes in 1992 - they obtained very disappointing results in 1994, largely as a consequence of the new electoral law. The PPI obtained a modest 11.1% and collected only 5.2% of the seats; similarly, the Segni Pact got 4.6% of the votes and 2.1% of the seats. All together the percentage of seats was less than half the percentage of votes. Out of 46 seats obtained by the two parties, only 4 were plurality seats while the rest came from the proportional part of the election. The voters/seats ratio (.46) gives an accurate idea of the two parties' under-representation. Beyond the decline in electoral appeal, the center was smashed by the logic of the electoral system. Finally the threshold of 4% in the proportional part of the competition had dramatic effects on the minor parties. In 1992, in what was then a fully proportional competition, 16 parties obtained seats. In 1994 and 1996 only 7 and 8 parties respectively passed the threshold. This forced most minor party to join electoral cartels in the plurality competition as the only means to obtain seats at all.

4.   The two party systems and their structure

The most visible, and normally most studied, party system structural element is number of parties. Indeed any consideration on party system structure and/or its change must take into account this crucial variable. Unfortunately such analysis is complicated by the need to chose criteria for the identification and counting of the relevant parties in the system (Sartori 1976). In the Italian case, this task is made even more difficult by contemporary existence of two superimposed party systems: the electoral party system and the parliamentary party system. These are different both in terms of the number of parties and character/direction of competition, which creates evident distortions in the observation of their characteristics and disturbances in the analysis of their dynamics. As we have anticipated, this phenomenon is probably due to the different competition logics that respectively regulate electoral and parliamentary politics in Italy.

Electoral competition now responds to what appear to be prevalently majoritarian pressures. The present Chamber of Deputies' electoral law, like the referendum that had modified the Senate's, introduced the single-member district plurality system for 75% of the seats. This was expected by many to produce structural effects on the party system, namely a visible reduction in the number of parties. Critics of this view asserted that the remaining 25% of the seats, still to be assigned through proportional representation, were a sufficiently large portion to help perpetuate the Italian party system's chronic fragmentation. Two elections are certainly not enough to produce the full effects of electoral reform, but at least some were expected. The new electoral law, indeed forced a multitude of parties to join electoral cartels. But post-election political dynamics (i.e. the

formation of parliamentary parties) showed that some parties and groups interpreted electoral alliances as means to obtain more seats in the election, and not as first steps towards the formation of more permanent common party structures. As we just said, this was indeed expected by critics of the new law (for one Giovanni Sartori) even before the 1994 elections. But this is not to be ascribed exclusively to inadequacies of the new electoral law. In fact, only electoral competition rules were changed, whereas parliamentary organization and procedures, government formation tactics and rules, coalition strategies and dynamics, all virtually remained the same.[12] In other words, even if new electoral competition rules can foster tendencies towards a reduction in the number of relevant parties in what we have called the electoral party system, such pressures lose much of their importance after the election, and other sets of rules condition inter-party relations in the parliamentary party system. Obviously this is an analytical more than a conceptual or even substantial distinction. The two labels actually represent two facets of party systems that in the present Italian one appear to be particularly distinct: the "electoral" one responds to the requirements of plurality competition and is structured accordingly around two major coalitions, the *Polo delle Libertà* (center-right) and the *Ulivo* (center-left); the "parliamentary" one is on the other hand regulated by other features of the Italian political system and is still characterized by very high fragmentation.[13] As we have said, the two "systems" coexist, with the electoral one surviving even between elections, but, so far, with a limited impact on inter-election dynamics.[14]

As we have mentioned, these two facets of the party system exist in all polities, but in the Italian case they diverge more than commonly observed elsewhere. We have also surmised that this may be due to a shortcoming of the institutional reform, limited as it was to electoral reform. For this reason, one could expect the electoral party system to have undergone more profound structural changes than the parliamentary one. Table 1 lists values for a series of indicators which can reveal the degree of divergence between the two systems. The first two indicators, MP (parties that obtained at least 2% of the vote) and F (Rae's fractionalization) are calculated on the basis of vote percentages obtained by parties in the various elections; EP (effective number of parties) is calculated on the basis of the number of seats obtained as a consequence of the elections; the meaning and calculation of PwS (number of parties that obtained seats) and PP (number of parliamentary parties) is self- explanatory.

MP values reflect very limited variations for the four elections considered. It would appear that the three direct causes of change have not made a big difference in the ability of political parties to pass at least a minimum (2%) electoral threshold. The highest MP value in Italian electoral history was reached in 1992 (see also Bartolini and Mair 1992) and confirmed in 1994. In 1996 the MP score reverted to the 1987 level, which had been the highest up to that point. The tendency that had started in 1979 towards a redistribution of electoral preferences in favour of relatively minor parties does not appear to have been modified by electoral reform. It is possible that Italian electors still perceive themselves to be in a relatively wide and/or crowded electoral space, contrary to the expectations of those who thought that such space should shrink and/or become less crowded as a result of plurality competition.

This impression is confirmed and even strengthened if one looks at F indices based on the proportional representation part of the elections. Also in this case 1992 is the year of change, whereas only slight variations from that value can be observed for 1994 and 1996.

And even plurality election based F indices do not portray a radically different picture. Actually in 1994 this index had a score of .78, the same as in 1987, when it was naturally calculated on the basis of a proportional election! Only in 1996 the index reverts to a value, .66, lower than all of those observed in prior, proportional and plurality, elections with the sole exception of 1948's (Bardi 1996a).

The last three indices in table 1, PwS, EP, and PP, allow for a more in-depth analysis of the overall extent of change in the Italian party system and at least some considerations on the two, electoral and parliamentary, systems' different configurations. The three indices' values confirm that change, in the form of greater fragmentation, becomes manifest in 1992. The overall situation is perhaps best summarized by looking at EP index scores. These are based on the number of seats obtained by political parties and not on their share of the vote. As such they can reveal better than F values direct and indirect effects of the new electoral law. The 1987 EP score, 4.1, is slightly above the average (3.7) for all the elections contested up to that point, whereas for the following three elections we can observe much higher and very similar scores. On the basis of these data alone, it would appear that the greater fragmentation, probably produced by increased voter mobility between 1987 and 1992 was not offset by the direct effects of the new electoral law and in general by developments that occurred between the last two elections and influenced electoral supply.

This impression is even strengthened if one looks at the other two indicators. The number of parties that obtained seats (PwS) in Chamber of Deputies' elections, which had been following a growing trend since 1976, reached in succession two peaks in 1983 (13) and 1987 (14). The index sky-rocketed in 1992 (16) and 1994 (20) to revert to a more modest but still very high 14 in 1996. It is true that the number of parliamentary groups (PG) decreased in 1994 and 1996 in the Chamber of Deputies, but this appears to be a consequence of a more rigid application of rules for the formation of parliamentary groups (Bartolini and D'Alimonte 1995, 432) and not, as we have just seen, to an actual reduction in the number of parties that obtained seats.[15] In the Senate, where the rules for the formation of parliamentary groups are more relaxed, PG actually rose from 9 to 11 between 1987 and 1996. Thus, in terms of number of parties, the Italian party system changed somewhat (becoming more fragmented!) between 1987 and 1992, but did not change much at all between 1992 and 1996.

The picture is different if one considers changes in the electoral party system. In 1994, the EP index, if calculated on the basis of electoral cartels rather than individual parties was 3.6, a score slightly below the general Italian average and much lower than the 1992 one. In 1996 it dropped to 2.6, the lowest ever. On the basis of this indicator, the only one that permits us to make direct comparisons between the two party systems, it would appear that the divergence between the electoral and the parliamentary party systems is clear and growing.

Sartori (1976, 315, *et passim*) considers mathematical indicators useful and perhaps even important, but certainly prefers what he calls "nominal routes" for counting relevant parties. In 1992, the combined effects of the proportional and plurality electoral competitions were different in the two chambers: in the Chamber of Deputies the right coalition's strong overall majority (366 seats out of 630) made, in Sartori's terms, every other group irrelevant, with the sole exception of the leftist opposition (213 strong); but in the Senate, the right's failure to obtain an absolute majority allowed also the centrist pact (31 seats) and even the three senator strong *Südtiroler Volkspartei* (SVP) to

meet Sartori's relevance criteria by giving them coalition potential.[16] In 1996, the victorious leftist coalition was weakened, especially in the Chamber of Deputies, by its scarce cohesion. As a result, besides the dominant PDS, at least two of its components, *Rifondazione Comunista* and Dini's *Rinnovamento Italiano*, have coalition potential and meet Sartori's relevance criteria. Overall, however, the number of relevant parties in the electoral party system appears to be significantly lower than in the pre-1994 system even if we use nominal criteria.

In the parliamentary system the situation is quite different. Shortly after the 1994 elections, when the Lega Nord withdrawal from the right wing coalition brought down the Berlusconi government, the Italian party system was returned to its pre-1994 fragmentation in both houses, with the additional complication represented by the absence of a strong center pivot such as the DC (Morlino 1996). Even what appears to be a deliberately conservative count made according to Sartori's nominal criteria identified six relevant parties, *Alleanza Nazionale* (AN), FI, PPI, *Lega Nord*, PDS, and RC. These could be reduced to five (Sartori's crucial threshold) only by admitting that the *Lega Nord* lies outside the left/right dimension (Pappalardo 1996, 123). RC's or *Rinnovamento Italiano*'s possible defection from the governmental coalition could produce an even more fragmented situation in the present legislature. One could in fact expect at least all eight electorally autonomous parties to be relevant in such a context.[17] Thus the divergence between the two party systems remains, at least potentially, even if we use non-numerical criteria.

Of course any conclusion, and perforce prognosis, requires an analysis of the other structural variable: ideological distance. The assessment of ideological distance, just like counting the relevant parties in the system, depends on the indicators one chooses, but also on the type of party system, electoral or parliamentary, one considers. Two contributions that have recently tackled the task of measuring or assessing ideological distance in the post-1994 party system (Morlino, 1996; Pappalardo, 1996), have come to rather diverging conclusions, possibly as a result of the different indicators they used. Moreover Pappalardo's own indicators can have different values depending on the level (type of system) chosen in the analysis.[18]

Morlino observes that after a period of party system de-radicalization, that lead to the 1994 elections, we are now observing a new radicalization resulting from post-election instability (high volatility, uncertainty about the rules of the game, low institutionalization and weak societal rooting of the new actors). This new radicalization, and the associated increase or maintenance of ideological distance at values typical of the old, polarized, system is illustrated with electoral data, which show a post-1994 increase in support for left and right and a drop for the center, and with the description of an "accentuated verbal violence in political discourse throughout 1994 and 1995", and of the associated intensity of the political conflict.

Pappalardo uses other indicators attributing most importance to one based on mass-surveyed left-right self-placements which he calls "left-right polarization". The index is calculated as the difference between the two extreme parties' identifiers' left-right self-placement averages, customarily measured on a one to ten scale. Pappalardo traces the evolution of the index with time-series data between 1975 and 1995. During this period, and as a consequence of the already described party system transformation (at least in terms of its basic units, as we are still looking at the structure), the two extreme parties have undergone some changes: on the left, the PCI has been replaced by one of its splinters, RC;

on the right, the MSI has evolved into AN, an organization that includes it, while at the same time trying to appeal also to broader, more moderate, sectors of the electorate. It is felt that both these parties no longer have their predecessors' anti-system characteristics (Morlino 1996), but this does not produce a dramatic change in ideological distance, which drops from 5.8 to 5.4 between 1975 and 1995 (Pappalardo 1996). The corresponding polarization index drops from .64 to .60, a value that maintains Italy in the highly polarized systems group.[19]

This finding would seem to confirm Morlino's differently based analysis according to which the Italian party system is presently at least as radicalized as it was in its polarized pluralism heyday. But according to Pappalardo extreme parties and lateral "poles" are no longer one and the same thing: the latter now coincide with the center-left and center-right "blocks", as a consequence of shifts in both the electoral and the inter-electoral competition's "centers of gravity". The system's relevant maximum ideological distance has to be measured as the difference between electoral-coalition averages. If this is done, the 1995 maximum-distance score drops to 4.2, a value considerably lower than those previously observed in Italy and corresponding to a .47 polarization index score. This value places Italy, along with Spain, in the in-between group, and closer to the majority of western democracies that are characterized by much lower polarization, like Germany and Great Britain (respectively .28 and .33 in 1993). Even if we are not yet in a position to accept Pappalardo's argument that both the electoral and the inter-electoral competition's "centers of gravity" have shifted, his analysis confirms the differences that exist between what we have defined as coexisting party systems. In fact his center-left and center-right blocks are nothing but the basic units of the electoral party system.

5. Conclusions

This report addressed two basic questions concerning the ongoing process of party system transformation in Italy: 1) what is the degree of party system stabilization; 2) what is the actual extent of the change. On the first question the answer is that the party system is close to becoming stabilized but most likely at levels of stability that are lower than in the pre-1992 past. Although at least two of the three direct causes of party system transformation, changes in electoral supply and direct effects of the electoral law on political parties, appear to have all but exhausted their impact on the Italian party system, this continues to be characterized by very high volatility. This is most likely due to a higher potential voter mobility than in the pre-1992 period. This is a feature that might not change in the near future and that might even be enhanced by increasing voter familiarity with the rules of plurality electoral competition.

The answer to the second question is necessarily more tentative. While it is clear that the system's basic units, the political parties, have individually undergone profound transformations, change in the system's structure is much more difficult to assess, also because of the co-existence of two separate party systems. The two party systems, electoral and parliamentary, created by the electoral reform, are not only formed by different basic units, but also present different structural characteristics. To be sure, the parliamentary party system's transformation concerns its basic units more than its structure: number of relevant parties and ideological distance seem to be practically unchanged. It still appears to be very close to Sartori's polarized pluralism type.[20] The electoral party system, on the other hand, in terms of number of relevant parties and ideological distance, tends towards a form of moderate pluralism. After the 1994 election it appeared that the electoral party system and its actors were playing a subordinate role. The 1996 election campaign and even some of the events that followed the election seem to indicate that the electoral system is exerting some pressure on the parliamentary one. This is certainly visible in the efforts made by the various components of the two major electoral coalitions to present united fronts on most major questions. In the long run this could foster a reduction in the number of relevant parties in the parliamentary party system. Effects on polarization are not as visible in this transitional phase, even if on specific policy questions, such as institutional reforms, a degree of convergence can be observed at least between selected components of the two major electoral parties.

Endnotes

1. This report outlines some of the research questions at the basis of a broader project on party system change in Italy I am currently developing. The end product should be published as a book (in Italian) in 1997 or early 1998. Some of these ideas have already been discussed in articles (Bardi 1996a, 1996b) and conference papers (Bardi 1996c; Bardi and Ignazi1996). I wish to thank: Stephen Helmann, Giacomo Sani, Giuseppe Di Palma and Renato Mannheimer for the comments and suggestions they offered during the discussion of the paper I presented with Piero Ignazi at the CONGRIPS panel in the context of the 1996 APSA Annual Meeting; Adriano Pappalardo for his detailed and insightful commentary on an earlier draft of this report; and Piero Ignazi for his much appreciated and stimulating criticism

2. According to Daalder's (1983, 232), the extreme-right *Movimento Sociale Italiano* (MSI) was "becoming increasingly smaller to the point that its systemic relevance [was] being questioned" and on the left the PCI's (*Partito Comunista Italiano*) increasing legitimacy made its anti-system character less than certain.

3. Based on Sartori (1982).

4. See the article by Valentina Padula in this issue of *Italian Politics and Society*.

5. This is perhaps the only one among several long term causes of change that is still producing direct effects on the party system.

6. The assessment of direct causes' individual effects is rather difficult as various factors and feed-back mechanisms create mutual conditioning effects among the various causes: parties' general and electoral strategies and electors' attitudes are influenced by the wide-spread conviction that the current electoral law will be reformed; the 1993 electoral law introduced a majoritarian principle of competition in an institutional and political system that follows a political competition model that could be characterized as bargain-oriented; elections at the municipal, provincial, regional, national, and European levels are regulated by as many different electoral laws.

7. As is well known, Italy's two largest parties PDS and FI are still being investigated by Italian magistrates. But even if this should lead to indictments of their top leaderships, traumatic effects on the two parties are unlikely. The PDS still has a strong organization and leadership and would probably be able to weather the disgrace of one of its leaders. Most likely this would also be true of FI, even if the movement's success is still very strongly identified with its leader's. FI's history has demonstrated that even in Italy there is room for a non-ephemeral, non-confessional, moderate or conservative party. This has suggested the development, currently in process, of a stronger organization and leadership structure.

8. Analyses of such continuity and pre-1987 values for most Table 1 indices can be found in Bardi (1996a) and Morlino (1996).

9. In multi-party systems compensations can also follow a circular pattern (from A to B to C to A) and not necessarily only a bi-directional one (from A to B and from B to A).

10. The next highest value (13.3) was registered in 1953. In 1948 TV was 22.8, but it was calculated on the basis of differences with the 1946 Constituent Assembly election.

11. The PPI's split has forced us to revise our BV calculation criteria and to include in the leftist bloc, besides all the secular groups included in the *Ulivo*, the *Popolari per Prodi* as well. This explains the persistence of high values for this index, which were caused in 1996 by an increase of the left, whereas they were caused by increases of the right in the previous two elections.

12. Not even the President of the Republic's decision to consult only the leaders of the two coalitions and not the leaders of the individual parties that make them up in the government formation process after the 1996 elections seems to have substantially reduced single parties' inter-election contractual power.

13. The two labels simply highlight the nature of the units making up the two systems' units (electoral cartels and parliamentary groups). The latter, however, in most polities, especially those where the identification of extra-parliamentary parties is easier than in the current Italian situation, would correspond to parties proper.

14. The two electoral cartels even have official leaders (Silvio Berlusconi for the center-right, Romano Prodi for the center-left), but it is clear that the political game is again the prerogative of individual party leaders, who often express positions that cut across electoral cartels as is the case of the debate on institutional reforms. According to Giovanni Sartori (1996), Italy has a two-layer political system whose units are "the cartels at the official level ... and the parties at the actual operational level" and whose dynamics are highly dysfunctional.

15. It is interesting to note that the high PwS scores in 1994 and 1996 result from the allocation of plurality seats to the various components of the electoral cartels, as the number of parties that obtained seats in the proportional part of the election was much lower (7 in 1994 and 8 in 1996).

16. Actually even individual senators were relevant in the election of the Senate's President which was decided, in favor of the right coalition's candidate, Carlo Scognamiglio, by only one vote.

17. In 1996 eight parties (AN, FI, CCD/CDU, LN, PPI, RI, PDS, and RC) obtained at least 4 percent of the vote in the proportional part of the Chamber of Deputies' election. According to Pappalardo (1996, 122) only such parties can be considered relevant, because only autonomous parties can afford to bring down a government. Indeed it was an autonomous party, LN, to bring down the Berlusconi government during the past legislature. This criterion, however, can be too reductive: once a government is brought down, the support of non autonomous parties can be crucial for the birth and survival of a new government, as was the case with *Alleanza Democratica*'s (AD) and the Greens' support of the Dini government.

18. As we shall see, in measuring ideological distance, Pappalardo examines two sets of values of his indicators, but his conclusions are based on only one set, relative to electoral cartels, which he considers more relevant than individual parties.

19. The polarization index is obtained by dividing the two extreme parties' ideological distance value by 9, its theoretical maximum (see: Sartori 1982, especially fig. 10.1).

20. The present system is characterized by the disappearance of anti-system parties. This means that even if the system is very fragmented and radicalized, it no longer responds to Sartori's polarized pluralism model. Hence, probably, Morlino's (1996) definition of the current system as "neo-polarized pluralism".

21

References

Bardi, L. 1996a. "Anti-Party Sentiment and Party System Change in Italy." In *The Politics of Anti-Party Sentiment*, ed. T. Pogunkte and S. Scarrow. Special Issue the *European Journal of Political Research* 29: 345-363.

Bardi, L. 1996b. "Change in the Italian Party System." *Res Publica* 38: 79-294.

Bardi, L. 1996c. "L'evoluzione del sistema partitico italiano." Presented at the Meeting of the Società Italiana di Scienza Politica, Urbino, 13-15 June.

Bardi, L., and P. Ignazi. 1996. "The Italian Party System: still the Case of Polarized Pluralism?" Presented at the Annual Meeting of the American Political Science Association, S. Francisco, August 29 - September 1.

Bartolini, S., and R. D'Alimonte. 1995. "Il sistema partitico: una transizione difficile." In *Maggioritario ma non troppo*, ed. S. Bartolini and R. D'Alimonte. Bologna: Il Mulino.

Bartolini, S., and P. Mair. 1990. *Identity, Competition and Electoral Availability. The Stabilization of European Electorates*. Cambridge: Cambridge University Press.

Daalder, I. 1983. "The Italian Party System in Transition: The End of Polarized Pluralism?" *West European Politics* 6: 216-236.

Farneti, P. 1983. *Il Sistema dei Partiti in Italia*. Bologna: Il Mulino.

Galli, G. 1966. *Il bipartitismo imperfetto*. Bologna: Il Mulino.

Katz, R., and P. Mair. 1995. "Changing models of Party Organization and Party Democracy: the Emergence of the Cartel Party." *Party Politics* 1: 5-28.

Laakso, M., and R. Taagepera. 1979. "Effective' Number of Parties: A Measure with Application to Western Europe." *Comparative Political Studies* 12: 3-27.

Lijphart, A. 1984. *Democracies*. New Haven and London: Yale University Press.

Melchionda, E. 1995. "Il bipartitismo irrealizzato. Modelli di competizione nei collegi uninominali." In *L'alternanza inattesa. Le elezioni del 27 marzo 1994 e le loro conseguenze*, ed. G. Pasquino. Rubbettino: Saveria Mannelli.

Morlino, L. 1996. "Crisis of Parties and Change of Party System in Italy." *Party Politics* 2: 5-30.

Pappalardo, A. 1996. "Dal pluralismo polarizzato al pluralismo moderato. I modelli di Sartori e la tradizione italiana." *Rivista Italiana di Scienza Politica* 26: 103-146.

Rae, D. 1967. *The Political Consequences of Electoral Laws*. New Haven and London: Yale University Press.

Sartori, G. 1976. *Parties and Party Systems*. Cambridge: Cambridge University Press.

Sartori, G. 1982. *Teoria dei partiti e caso italiano*. Milano: Sugarco.

[40]

Tangentopoli or the democratization of corruption: considerations on the end of Italy's First Republic

Donald Sassoon

Reader in History
Queen Mary and Westfield College, University of London

The aim of this article is to provide the basis for an analysis of the corruption scandals which rocked the Italian political system after 1992. As the affair is still far from concluded and as its repercussions will be felt for years to come it may be appropriate to set it in context.

As all commentators have pointed out for years, Italy has been, since 1947, a *democrazia bloccata*: the opposition, dominated by the Italian Communist Party (PCI), has never been in a position to constitute an alternative to the coalition governments which succeeded one another. The PCI was forced to seek an entente with some or all the members of the ruling coalition. This strategy, in all its variants, namely *compromesso storico* or *alternativa democratica*, was never able to break up the increasingly fractious entente between the Italian Socialist Party (PSI) and the Christian Democratic Party (DC). This situation had not altered even after the PCI, following the fall of the Berlin Wall in November 1989, had changed its name and renounced the Communist tradition – the climax of a process which had been under way for a number of years. Political *immobilismo* seemed to prevail in spite of the vociferously modernist rhetoric of the PSI led by Bettino Craxi, the widespread realization that Italy's public economy was diverging from that of its European partners, and the felt need for a major overhaul of the state bureaucracy and of the public sector. Outside Italy momentous changes were under way: the end of the Cold War and the collapse of Communism in eastern and central Europe, the system of apartheid breaking up in South Africa, a new economic course under way in China, and the decision of the European Community to proceed towards full monetary and political union. Italians, always worried about being out of step with the rest of Europe and the world and about missing, so to speak, the train of modernity, realized that something had to change, though it was not clear what or how. The *trasformismo* of its political elite, the principle 'everything must change so that everything can stay the same' – celebrated in the novel *The Leopard* – had degenerated into 'nothing must change otherwise everything will have to change'.

As it turned out, something did change and, afterwards, nothing was quite the same again. Three years after the beginning of the corruption

© 1995 Routledge   1354–571X
Journal of Modern Italian Studies 1(1) 1995: 124–143

scandals, Italy has a new, though unstable, party system and new electoral laws. The parties which dominated the government of the country for fifty years have disappeared. Like many momentous events, the initial trigger was unremarkable. The story began on 17 February 1992 when Mario Chiesa was arrested. The name meant nothing to the overwhelming majority of Italians. He was the Socialist-appointed president of the municipal old people's home of Milan, the Istituto per anziani Pio Albergo Trivulzio. Chiesa's racket was familiar to most entrepreneurs bidding for public sector contracts. If you wanted to win a bid you had to pay a kickback to be shared between the party and the party appointee. Chiesa's demands had become increasingly immoderate and he was denounced by one of the companies involved. He was caught *in flagrante* with a few million lire in ready cash. Chiesa named names and those names named more names until the Top Names came out, the names everyone knew: Craxi, Andreotti, Forlani.

The Milan magistrates, known as the Mani pulite (Clean Hands) team, uncovered a series of corrupt arrangements whereby private and public enterprises financed politicians and political parties in exchange for favours including the passage of special legislation and the awarding of public contracts. The sums collected were used to bribe more people to obtain further financial and political support or were used, quite simply, to sustain the lifestyles of the politicians and their cronies.[1] Though there is evidence that all parties, including the PCI, participated in these activities, the main protagonists of this system were the two largest government parties: the DC and the PSI.

More than one-third of those elected to Parliament in 1992 were investigated. Two thousand people were arrested including some of the country's most powerful politicians. Of the five parties that had dominated Italy since the war, four, the PSI, the Republicans, the Social Democrats and the Liberals, were virtually wiped out in the March 1994 election. The PSI, the linchpin of nearly all coalitions since 1962, obtained less than 2 per cent of the vote. The DC, the most successful government party in Europe since 1945, having been continuously in power as the majority party in all general elections and having appointed nearly all prime ministers, split, changed its name and barely survived to fight another day. In 1992 it obtained just under 30 per cent of the vote, its worst result but, in 1994 the DC, now the Partito popolare italiano (PPI), was reduced to 11.1 per cent and was out of power. Bettino Craxi, erstwhile leader of the PSI, and Prime Minister in the longest continuously serving government since Mussolini, took refuge in his splendid villa in Tunisia and has refused to attend his trial in Italy. He has since been convicted *absente reo*.

The most important consequence of *Tangentopoli* (*tangente* can be translated as kickback, hence 'Kickback City' referring to Milan where it all started) has thus been the end of the most stable political system in Europe apart from Switzerland's. Imagine a team of intergalactic historians visiting Europe in 1948 and returning in February 1991. Their second report, surveying the modifications of the intervening years, would note significant novelties. The authoritarian regimes of Spain and Portugal had been transformed into parliamentary systems. Greece had become a fully-fledged democracy. Even the Swedish Social Democrats – continuously in power since the 1930s – had been occasionally out of office since 1976. The French Left, effectively in opposition since the 1930s, had finally returned to power in 1981. Our travellers would have also noted the biggest change of all: the collapse of Communism throughout central and eastern Europe. Italy, however, would offer the intergalactic team a case study in continuity. The party which had triumphed in 1948, the Democrazia cristiana, was still around, not quite as strong electorally, but still the strongest, still in power, still the keystone of all coalition governments, with Giulio Andreotti and Amintore Fanfani still around. The Communists, albeit under a new name, were still in opposition, still hankering after power, still frustrated. The only change of any significance was that the Socialists, like the Social Democrats before them, had broken with the Communists in the late 1950s. Hardly worth reporting. Of local interest only. Yet had the team stayed around, it would have been offered the most interesting case – so far – of regime discontinuity within a democratic system.

The Italian press was prompt to baptize this change the unlamented death of the First Republic and to call the outcome 'la Seconda Repubblica'. This is not surprising. For many Italians the First Republic could only be understood in terms of the so-called *centralità* of the Christian Democratic Party. The DC was the central pivot of the system, the element of stability and continuity in what was otherwise a constantly evolving society. Many Italians have grown up not knowing a political system without Fanfani or Andreotti. Craxi, generally regarded as a 'new' politician, had actually been leader of the PSI for sixteen years when Mario Chiesa was arrested. No doubt there will be a long debate on the continuity and discontinuity between the First and the Second Republics. As in all historiographical controversies, some will argue that nothing has changed, others that there has been a revolution. Most historians, who, on the whole, are prudent creatures, will be more subtle. However, even at this early stage it is possible to state, unequivocally, that 1992–4 has presented observers with the most important discontinuity so far in the history of the political system of postwar Italy.

Of the democratic countries of western Europe, only the French transition from the Fourth to the Gaullist Fifth Republic in 1958 can aspire to rival the discontinuity exhibited by the Italian political system in 1992–4. But in France the background to this transition was the end of empire, an unwinnable colonial war, a threatened revolt by generals: the authentic stuff of major political crises. Moreover, the Fourth Republic in France was far weaker and more unstable than the Italian Republic. Instability in terms of coalition governments – in itself not very significant – was similar in the two countries but France lacked a hegemonic party of the centre to provide ballast. Italian coalitional instability disguised a phenomenal continuity. Governments were replaced by near-identical governments often with exactly the same personnel. So-called government crises, and there were dozens of them, were simply ways to resolve, temporarily, internal disagreements.

It is true that – in France – the transition between the Fourth and Fifth Republics had a constitutional dimension so far lacking in the Italian case. The French, after all, moved from a parliamentary system to a presidential one, and drafted a new constitution. Nothing like that has yet occurred in Italy. The 'Second Republic' – if it exists at all – is far from being well established. The main legal-political reform has been that of the electoral system on the basis of absurd expectations that the new system would lead to stable coalitions, strong government and the end of corruption.

This reform had been accelerated by *Tangentopoli*. For years a *riforma istituzionale* had been debated. A special parliamentary commission had been set up. This interested only a few specialists and politicians. In reality, without *Tangentopoli*, nothing would have been done about it. Electoral laws are seldom changed because those in power are usually the beneficiaries of the existing ones. As more politicians were being investigated, the popular desire for a change became focused on the electoral system. Politicians, consciously or unconsciously, encouraged this. The electoral system was an ideal target for public censure because it drew attention away from the political class. It provided an easy solution: change the electoral system and everything will be all right. This goes a long way towards explaining the speed at which the signatures were collected for the referendum held in 1993 which, by an overwhelming majority, abolished existing electoral laws and forced Parliament to draw up new ones. The French system of two electoral rounds was adopted for municipal elections. Where no candidate obtained an overall majority in the first round, a second ballot would be held among the top two candidates. Thanks to this system, the former Communists and their allies had done rather well in municipal elections in Rome, Naples and Turin at the end of 1993. A victory of the Left at the national election was a distinct possibility. However, the system adopted for general elections was quite different: 75 per cent of the seats were allocated to single-member constituencies where the candidate with the largest share of the poll would win. The remaining 25 per cent would be distributed in proportion to the votes gained nationally by the parties. Each elector would therefore have two ballots, one for the constituency vote and one for the party list.

Clearly this system required the setting up of pre-electoral pacts in order to maximize the results in the single constituencies. Parties could, of course, stand separately in the list section. The result of the March 1994 general election was a real electoral earthquake. The PDS (Partito democratico della sinistra) – the party created in 1991 out of the old PCI – survived. All the old parties were either wiped out or emerged much weakened – as was the case with the DC, now the PPI.

The most substantial changes occurred in the party system and in the composition of the new coalition. None of the victors of 1994 – Silvio Berlusconi's Forza Italia, Umberto Bossi's Lega Nord and Gianfranco Fini's Alleanza nazionale (AN) – have roots in the First Republic. Berlusconi's party was created a few months before the election. The Lega Nord did not exist before 1992. Its predecessors, the Lega Lombarda and the Lega Veneta, were seen as the eccentric recipients of ephemeral and inconsequential protest votes. The Alleanza nazionale is the recycled Movimento sociale italiano – Destra nazionale (MSI – DN) whose roots are in Italy's monarchist and Fascist past. Under the First Republic – itself the outcome of an anti-Fascist struggle and the product of a historic compromise between Communists, Socialists and Christian Democrats – the MSI was a pariah party, kept away from all levers of power at municipal, regional and national level. Even as late as 1993 few would have seriously envisaged a government with ministers representing the far Right.

The discontinuity between the First and the Second Republics is visible even at the level of the opposition. This remains monopolized by the PDS. There is obviously much continuity between the PDS and the PCI but one should not overemphasize it. In the first place Rifondazione comunista – the party created by those who objected to the dissolution of the PCI – has as much claim as the PDS to be the successor to the PCI. Second, the PDS, unlike the old PCI, is rife with organized factional infighting. By abandoning even a diluted form of democratic centralism, the PDS in fact relinquished one of the few traits which still distinguished the old PCI from mainstream west European social democratic parties such as the German SPD. The present PDS is thus now Italy's 'social democratic party', member of the Socialist International. One of the chief characteristics of the First Republic, the unelectability to office of its opposition, has now been removed.

Thus it is legitimate to claim that Italy's regime discontinuity was greater than that between the French Fourth and Fifth Republics.

A word of caution may be necessary here. The Second Republic is still far from consolidated. Will the electoral system be changed again? Will there be a new constitution? Will the existing party system survive? Will Forza Italia devour the Lega? Will it merge with Alleanza nazionale and become the conservative party Italy never had? Time will tell. Should the eventual outcome be a succession of coalition governments all led by Forza Italia or some such party in more or less perpetual coalition with junior partners, then all that would have happened would be yet another edition of the ancient game of *trasformismo* with Berlusconi/Forza Italia stepping into the shoes of Andreotti/Christian Democracy with Fini/Alleanza nazionale playing out the role of the junior partner which was that of Craxi/PSI. The old Marxian dictum, the first time a tragedy, the second a farce, might be fitting were it not for the possibility that 'both times a farce' might be more appropriate. Such speculations are amusing but ultimately unproductive. We simply do not possess sufficiently precise analytical tools to engage in worthwhile predictions of this magnitude.

Sudden political discontinuities in democratic societies – that is a transition from one democratic regime directly to another – are exceptional, not least because a democracy can seldom be called a regime. A regime can be said to have existed in Italy only because of two features: the lack of alternance in government and the systematic occupation by the governing parties of the state and civil society. In other words the present crisis is exceptional because the system was exceptional. Had something like *Tangentopoli* occurred in Britain, all that would probably happen would be the discrediting of the existing government, an election and a likely victory of the opposition. The former governing party would produce a new leadership and everything would return to normal. Thus Italy's main exceptional feature, the lack of alternance, was at the root of the crisis. It meant that the parties ensconced in power could proceed unchecked. Internal disputes within the establishment could be resolved by extending the spoil system. This systemic lack of alternance is what makes it difficult to study the case in comparative terms – even though corruption, kickbacks, nepotism, clientelism, the link between politics and organized crime, scandals, spoil systems, tax evasion, illegal funding of parties, etc. exist in other countries as any student of French or German or Spanish or Greek or American politics knows perfectly well. Only Japan and Mexico provide comparable instances, but the marked differences in historical traditions suggest that even a study focusing on these three instances may have limitations.

The surge of Lega Nord and *Tangentopoli* are the two principal causes of the destabilization of the First Republic. There is a symbiotic relationship between the two. Magistrates and *leghisti* had the same target: the political establishment (the PSI and the DC); both originated in the north and arose at the same time. The magistrates' action reinforced the Lega and the Lega's success reinforced the magistrates. Yet there was never any complicity or coordination. The Lega's support for the magistrates was unenthusiastic. Indeed it eventually turned out that the Lega itself had received 200 million lire (*c.* $128,000) from Raoul Gardini, the financier involved in the biggest kickback so far uncovered.

Perspectives and debates

The corruption scandal was gathering momentum just as the 1992 electoral campaign got under way. As a result the Lega, whose popularity had been growing for some months, emerged as the major force in much of the north. Though it obtained only 8.7 per cent of the national vote (a higher percentage than in 1994), it destroyed in one fell swoop the monopoly of power achieved by the Christian Democrats and the Socialist Party in Lombardy, Venetia and some areas of Piedmont where it obtained between 30 and 40 per cent of the vote. By the end of 1993 the Lega had won all local elections held in Italy's richest region, Lombardy, and captured its most coveted prize, the municipality of Milan.

The central campaign theme of the Lega was the same as the object of the magistrates' investigation: the misappropriation of public money by political parties. Though the Lega's overt political appeal was regionalist, at times even secessionist, it was never a classic 'nationalist' party like the Scottish National Party in Britain or the Corsican nationalists in France or the Basque in Spain. In spite of the efforts made to invent it, there is no nationalist Lombard or Venetian consciousness. Even to talk of a strong regional consciousness in Lombardy or Venetia would be an exaggeration. With the exception of Sicily and Sardinia there is little deep-seated regional awareness in Italy. There is, of course, a strong city-based consciousness: people may be proud to be Milanese or Turinese but being a Lombard or a Piedmontese is less significant. The Lega Nord appealed to a diffuse anti-southern sentiment with strong racist overtones. Accordingly, northerners are 'modern', 'European', honest, frugal, hard-working, efficient, enlightened, educated; southerners are 'backward', practically Africans or Arabs, thieving, lazy, inefficient, ignorant, beat their women, prostitute their wives and daughters, and are insanely jealous. The more sophisticated would claim that the south and the southern question (defined as a question of backwardness) have somehow perverted the Italian state, dragging it down into an unhealthy and parasitic *mafioso* capitalism sustained by public handouts and creating a culture of dependency.

The central characteristic of the Lega was that it gave political form to a taxpayers' revolt against an increasingly dysfunctional welfare state. The typical Lega Nord voters were not Lombard nationalists but angry and frustrated taxpayers for whom the Italian state had become a corrupt machine whose main purpose was to siphon off their hard-won resources and transfer them to southerners in exchange for votes.

Southerners thus became the Italian equivalent of those single mothers, welfare scroungers and undesirable immigrants who, elsewhere, have become the principal targets of conservative politicians.

According to the popular northern prejudice which the *leghisti* have embraced, if northern Italy were allowed to go its own way, it would rapidly become modern, efficient and clean. Everything would work. It would be just like Switzerland instead of being like North Africa. Its inhabitants would pay less tax and be more prosperous. There would be no corruption. The Lega is the Italian expression of the pro-market ideology which has been sweeping the western world since the end of the 1970s. The DC could not appropriate this ideology because it was the party of public spending, a role performed elsewhere by social democratic parties. Craxi tried to adopt it, under the cover of modernization, but unlike Felipe González in Spain, he was unable to achieve credibility for three reasons: first, because he was forced into coalition with the DC, second, because of the socialist tradition still surviving in his party, and, third, because the PSI was competing with the DC for a share of public spending to sustain its ever expanding clienteles. The Lega paved the way for an even more credible pro-market party: Forza Italia which had the added advantage of not threatening the unity of the country. It should be added that the pro-market ideology of Bossi or Berlusconi may have worked as good electoral propaganda. The promise to cut taxes by cutting down on public waste is always alluring. Things turn out to be difficult when those who make these promises are in power and have to cut not 'public waste' in general, but the generous pensions which are one of the main causes of Italy's budget deficit. Berlusconi's rhetoric was sorely tested in December 1994 when, faced with a massive wave of strikes and protest, he was forced to back down. Bossi withdrew his support and Berlusconi was out of office.

To say that *Tangentopoli* and the Lega Nord were the key elements in the destabilization of the Italian party system does not mean that they were the only ones. The entry of Berlusconi's Forza Italia into the political scenario destroyed the already slim chances that a refurbished and somewhat cleaned-up Christian Democratic Party might have had. Berlusconi entered the fold in order to stop what many feared would be an inevitable victory of the Progressive coalition set up by the PDS. Until then, this had been the only organization able to obtain electoral support throughout the national territory. The Lega, for obvious reasons, could not aspire to significant electoral support south of the Po Valley, while the Alleanza nazionale had little support north of Rome (except in the Trentino). Berlusconi's role was to provide a *trait d'union* between the Lega and AN forcing them into an alliance which would never have occurred without a mediator from the centre. Of course, indirectly, Berlusconi offered the moderate and conservative section of the Italian electorate, i.e. a majority, the prospect of a government which was untainted by corruption while not being of the Left. This is the main reason why, once Berlusconi appeared on the scene, a large proportion of potential Lega voters defected.[2] Berlusconi would give them what they wanted: tax reduction and less bureaucracy. He offered them a government which, it was felt, would do what its predecessors had always done – minus the

Perspectives and debates

massive corruption of the past. He thus offered a new face and, at the same time, continuity. This is precisely what the DC had achieved in the immediate postwar period: conservation with new faces and a new image, tradition and modernity.

The Left (I mean here the PCI/PDS and the hard-line Rifondazione comunista) contributed very little to the end of the First Republic. To some extent this is not surprising. It is true that it had always attacked the system of corruption and kickbacks, and that, with some important exceptions, it was relatively clean. But the PCI never made anti-corruption an important part of its propaganda. This was noted by Bettino Craxi who remarked that the Communists never denounced the accounts presented to Parliament by the ruling parties because 'all party accounts were fraudulent'.[3] Back in the 1970s, Berlinguer had launched a campaign around *la questione morale*, 'the moral question', but this had received little support even within his own party. Why such reticence? In the first place the PCI's insistence on its 'peculiarity' as the one clean party was always double-edged. Its opponents seized on it to stress that the PCI's specificity was precisely that it was not fit to rule in a modern western country, that somehow it did not belong to the western political system. Second, the PCI needed allies if it was ever to become a party of government. Allies were required not just because no party could possibly hope to obtain an absolute majority in Parliament under the old electoral system but also because a Communist party, however reformed, in power on its own in a western country would have caused a national and international crisis. But where would the PCI find allies except among parties already in power? Its constant dilemma was whether to opt for an alliance with the DC (the *compromesso storico*) or with the PSI (the *alternativa di sinistra*). It could carry out neither strategy while demanding the active criminal investigation of the leaders of the parties in question. The polemic of the PCI was, consequently, always a general one: against the 'system of power' of the DC and against the *lottizzazione* (the spoil system) which in practice it accepted and in which, I think inevitably, it occasionally took part.

One final word on the PCI. Public opinion played a major role in the development of *Tangentopoli*, in the collapse of the First Republic, in the rise of the Lega and in the popularity of the investigating magistrates. The massive support behind the referendum for the abolition of the old electoral system (1993) was, in substance, a vote against the First Republic. What really mattered, however, was that 'moderate' public opinion had shifted against the DC-led regime. Left-wing public opinion had always been intolerant of corruption and voted, accordingly, for the PCI. Until 1992, moderate opinion was prepared to tolerate the corruption of the DC and the PSI partly because few people realized that it had reached such formidable proportions and partly because the alternative to the DC and PSI was the Communists in power. Better the thieves you know than the reds you don't. Once alternatives emerged – first the Lega, then Berlusconi and then even the now more acceptable neo-Fascists led by clean-cut Gianfranco Fini – moderate and conservative public opinion discovered it had somewhere to go. Conservatives – who usually need to believe in the state – were also reassured because the attack on corruption had come not from untrustworthy Communists but from magistrates, 'honest' representatives of the state. It was difficult to believe in the state of Andreotti and Bettino Craxi but far easier, and understandably so, to believe in the state of Antonio Di Pietro, the leading investigating magistrate, and his colleagues. Conservatives had found in the magistrates local heroes who were neither corrupt nor Communist. Furthermore they had the exceptional advantage of not being politicians. They were people who were simply doing their duty, while so many politicians were so obviously not doing theirs.

Why were the magistrates not stopped? Why was the powerful DC–PSI coalition, for so long the master of Italy, unable to obstruct the investigation? The history of contemporary Italy has been punctuated by unresolved political scandals: the attempted plots to overthrow the state, the *affare* Borghese in 1970, that of Sogno in 1974, the existence of a parallel 'secret' secret service (the *Sid parallelo*), the Masonic Lodge P2 (which included also Berlusconi) whose full membership list has never surfaced.[4]

We still do not know who placed a bomb in Piazza Fontana in 1969, who was really behind the right-wing terrorism of the 1970s, who, if anyone, really helped the Brigate rosse. There have been numerous unresolved financial scandals, from that of the building of Fiumicino airport (1961), to that of the Federconsorzi (the Farmers Association, 1963), of the Azienda monopolio banane (1963) and of the Banco Ambrosiano. Did Roberto Calvi (the Ambrosiano boss) really commit suicide?[5] How did the financier Michele Sindona die? The Lockheed bribery scandal has never been satisfactorily resolved. How could the Mafia survive for so long? Who killed the journalist Pecorelli who was investigating Andreotti's alleged links with the Mafia and who worked for the secret services?

Seldom have corruption, scandal and the arrogance of power been less disguised than in Italy. It would be sufficient to read through old copies of weeklies like *L'Espresso* to realize how aware everyone was of the extent of this disease: 'Capitale corrotta e nazione infetta' ('Crooked capital of a corrupt nation'), lambasted *L'Espresso* as early as January 1958.[6] Five years previously, in 1953, Ernesto Rossi had published a book called *Settimo: Non rubare* ('Seventh: Thou Shalt Not Steal'), a book of nearly 500 pages denouncing the complicity between politicians, the public sector and private firms, the abuses of power, the corruption.[7]

There are several current hypotheses on why Di Pietro and his colleagues were able to turn the tide.

Perspectives and debates

The most popular appears to be the Cold War hypothesis. According to this, everything stems from the single Italian peculiarity, namely that the PCI monopolized the opposition, making the prospect of an alternance of the parties in power highly unpalatable. Had the Communist Party been elected to power there would be an international crisis of momentous proportion – or so it was widely believed. It was therefore perfectly justified to use all means, including covert action, to keep it out of power. It was necessary to strengthen the political resources of all governing parties while preparing for the worst: a Communist victory. All this cost money and the only way to fund the battle against Communism was to do it covertly. Hence the unofficial legitimation of the parallel state (P2, secret services, Gladio), and the development of uncontrolled and uncontrollable parallel funding. Once the habit of illegally funding a political battle is established it is difficult to check its expansion. This creates the possibility for further corruption, private gain and, more simply, intraparty competition for these resources. The strength of the hypothesis is that it explains how the system arose. Its weakness is that it does not explain why the system came to an end. The conclusion of the Cold War, after all, cannot automatically bring to an end the political practices generated by it. It is argued that the collapse of Communism enabled people not to vote for the DC and the PSI to stave off the Communist threat. This argument has limited validity. After all, a majority of people did not vote for the Left in 1994 and did not even vote for the PDS whose broad coalition obtained fewer votes than the PCI of Berlinguer had on its own in 1976. The largest share of the poll was obtained by the parties of the Right led by Berlusconi which energetically campaigned on an anti-Communist platform using a Cold War language which even Andreotti's DC had not used for years.

It is necessary to bring into play a second hypothesis, namely that the system was running out of money. For a long period it could be argued that clientelism was politically functional. It enabled the ruling coalition to fulfil tasks of redistribution which in other countries were assigned to the welfare state. Because much of this redistribution depended on an informal network and on access to political resources, the ruling parties derived a special advantage. A universalist welfare system distributes benefits to all citizens. A clientelist welfare state distributes benefits only to those who accept that a favour has been granted and must be returned. It is a contractual relationship based on exchange. In a clientelist welfare state even universal benefits may be withheld. For example, Italy provides a state pension to all citizens who have reached a certain age or worked for a specified number of years. If the state machine were efficient it would allocate a pension automatically to all those entitled to one. In reality getting a pension may take years. It may therefore often be necessary to bypass normal procedures and seek the help of influential people. In this instance state inefficiency becomes functional to state clientelism.[8] It is part of the system, not a peculiarity due to national characteristics stereotypically attributed to Italians (or Spaniards or Greeks). Those who receive a pension 'as a favour' when it is in fact due to them as a right have a contradictory position. On the one hand they have actually received the pension and paid back the favour by voting for someone in power who, it is assumed, may go on looking after them. They are part of the system. On the other hand, they have not received anything 'extra', particularly if they have paid their taxes and various contributions, so they would have an interest in ending the system. However, ending the system may bring forward unknown, perhaps unpleasant consequences. At best it may simply deliver a pension they would get anyway. Thus it would not be irrational to vote for the status quo particularly if you hold conservative or traditional values anyway and you have no faith in politicians in general.

Corruption and clientelism do not weaken the system. They reinforce it and each other. To denounce them as extensive and deplorable phenomena paradoxically strengthens them. It publicizes what everyone suspects: that it is widespread, vast, enormous, that 'everyone is doing it'. The action may be illegal, strictly speaking, but, if everyone participates, it is not immoral. Those who are discovered would not be considered by their community to be amoral or asocial individuals who should be treated as pariahs. The spread of petty corruption – its democratization – is its best protection. It was also the last, desperate defence of those accused of large-scale corruption. It is the justification most frequently involved. As Craxi put it: 'all major industrial and financial groups of the country have financed the political system. They are all liars.'[9] The more corruption and clientelism were exposed in novels, films, television serials and by investigative journalism the more they were reinforced as an omnipresent system. It creates a parallel system of social regulation which receives a double democratic legitimation: formal and informal. Informal because the majority participates in it and formal because the system is upheld electorally.[10]

A large proportion of those who used to vote for the five governing parties which constituted the political establishment had a high level of tolerance for corruption because they themselves participated in some form of clientelism, however marginally. This is not to say that all Communist and neo-Fascist voters were untouched by it. The distinction between clientelism and corruption, analytically valid, breaks down in practice. Corruption involved entrepreneurs funding political parties in exchange for state contracts and other business-related favours. Clienteles involved political parties 'funding' citizens (jobs, privileges, undeserved benefits) in exchange for votes. Thus political parties are at the centre of this flow of transactions. The precondition which makes everything else possible is the *de facto* continuous control and possession of the state by the ruling parties. Corruption and clientelism contribute to this continuous control. Thus the system is self-perpetuating.

Tangentopoli dealt with the most exposed part of this system because the least democratically legitimized: corruption. It could not deal with the clientele system. This is what, paradoxically, protected the magistrates from the risk of a popular backlash. To move against the rich and powerful, particularly when the sums involved defy the popular imagination, is one thing, to seek out the 'little people' is another.

Who is to be included in the system of clientele? Here are some random examples:

- all those employed in the informal economy who, by definition, do not pay taxes on their earnings (though they or their spouses pay their taxes for their main 'legal' occupation if they have any);
- all those who can obtain payment for their services in cash in order to be able to avoid taxes: these include doctors, plumbers, dentists, waiters, lawyers and virtually all piece-rate home workers;
- all those who build their own home illegally or who add an extension to it in defiance of Italy's complex regulations: it is normal for an 'architect' (in reality an overqualified surveyor) to add an extra sum which will be used to make sure that there will be no inspection;
- all those who engage in a legal activity for which a permit is needed but who either perform it without the permit or have obtained a permit through the personal intervention of a politician or a bureaucrat – for instance street vendors;
- all those who claim an invalidity pension while perfectly healthy because they have been able to obtain a certificate from a doctor and are protected by a local political boss; almost one in three of the twenty-one million pensions paid out annually goes to an invalid;
- all those with two jobs, one of which is a public sector sinecure which does not require regular attendance, obtained thanks to networking with influential people. Some of these jobs can even be subcontracted to others: an example familiar to all those who have had to spend many hours consulting books in Italian libraries is the *guardiani* who sit in every room making sure that no one defaces or damages the books being used.

I could go on. The crucial point is not that this is an exclusively Italian phenomenon but that, in Italy, it is part of an established and accepted system. For instance, so-called 'welfare scroungers' undoubtedly exist in Britain but they are the regular objects of attack by politicians, especially Conservative politicians, and are singled out as a group to be blamed. But in Italy no politician has ever launched a campaign against 'welfare scroungers'.

'Normal', that is legitimized, taxation could not be expected to fund this peculiar Italian-style welfare state; hence the ever-increasing public debt and the escalating costs incurred by firms, especially those operating in the public sector. The signing of the Maastricht Treaty and the requirement to meet its convergence criteria accelerated the need for an austerity programme which was increasingly incompatible with the old system. Fiscal crises, which elsewhere have destabilized the so-called social democratic model, in Italy destabilized the Christian Democratic state. A multiplicity of controls were imposed to decrease tax evasion. These singled out certain categories and forced them to establish complex accounting procedures. For instance restaurant owners and shopkeepers were forced to purchase specially sealed cash registers or adapt existing ones, to be subject to controls and either submit to them or find costly ways round them. Moreover, as anyone who has ever had an espresso coffee in an Italian bar knows only too well, each transaction requires the seller to provide the customer with a special 'tax receipt' or *ricevuta fiscale* which customers, in turn, must keep until they are at a certain distance from the place of purchase and must show to the police if requested to do so. Direct income tax is widely evaded by the self-employed but cannot be avoided by employees. The consequence is that the state has had to resort to massive increases in indirect taxes and to multiple controls. Thus Italians found themselves increasingly controlled by an alien state, in turn increasingly unable to perform its duties properly. As we know, people resent paying taxes even in 'normal' circumstances. To have to pay them knowing that a considerable proportion of the population avoids them is, understandably enough, extremely frustrating.

The Left opposition could never really channel this resentment, any more than any party of the Left anywhere in Europe could become the convincing leader of a taxpayers' revolt. The Left, inevitably, is always seen as the party of public spending and hence of taxation. But, in Italy, unlike other countries, the ruling parties of the centre could not be the taxpayers' parties for the reasons we have suggested. For structural reasons, as well as ideology, Christian Democrats could never be Thatcherites. As we have seen, only a new party such as the Lega, or Berlusconi, could pick up this issue, and only as pre-electoral propaganda.

Tangentopoli had a powerful effect on public opinion because of the extent of the sums involved and the power and arrogance exhibited by those being investigated and arrested. What was involved was not so much the principle as the amounts stolen, just as big business is often attacked by populists because it is big, rather than because it is business. *Tangentopoli* did not reveal the existence of corruption. No Italian could be unaware of it. What no one had realized was the actual size of the sums involved.

Imagine an average Signor Rossi, the owner of a small bar in Milan. He keeps three or four tables and chairs on the public pavement just outside the bar – an advantage because he can legally charge customers sitting at tables several times what he charges those standing at the bar. However, he does not have a permit for this. It would take too long to obtain one. He does not know the right people. He might not get it. So whenever the local policeman comes around he gives him a *mazzetta*, the traditional plain brown envelope with a bit of ready cash, say 50,000 or 100,000 lire ($30–$60). Sometimes the policeman warns him of an inspection and Signor Rossi removes the tables and chairs or bribes the inspector or pays the fine. Rossi is always worried but does not complain: after all playing by the informal rules is advantageous. He will go on voting for a ruling party because he might need help some day and, in any case, what would happen if the Communists came in? Either nothing would change, in which case he might as well keep things as they are. Or they would launch a crusade for clean government and he might not be able to keep his tables and chairs outside or he would have to pay more for his licence than he pays out in bribes. Rossi, like many Italians, does not like the government and dislikes most politicians but puts up with them just as he puts up with the rain. In these circumstances 'to lack a proper *senso dello stato*', which Italians are regularly accused of by civic culture theorists, seems to me quite rational.

One morning Signor Rossi reads in the newspapers that Raoul Gardini, the much-admired boss of Montedison, the 'king' of Italian chemical industries (who has since committed suicide), had spent 150 billion lire (*c.* $95 million) in kickbacks; that, of this amount, perhaps 60 billion (*c.* $38 million) ended up in his own secret accounts abroad; that the rest was distributed to Craxi, Forlani, various socialists and Christian Democrats. Or he reads that, according to a memorandum written and kept in a drawer by Vincenzo Balzamo, administrator of the PSI until 1992 (when he died of a heart attack), the party had received between 1987 and 1990 a total of 186 billion lire (*c.* $119 million) of which 136 billion (*c.* $87 million) came from private entrepreneurs, 30.2 billion (*c.* $19 million) from public sector firms, and 20.6 billion (*c.* $13 million) from various sources – on top of official state funding. [11]

Signor Rossi is, understandably, furious. These are the same people who humiliated him, forced him to resort to petty bribery, imposed on him the most absurd and bureaucratic financial controls in the whole of Europe. He is angry with the establishment. The point is that Rossi, like most Italians in his situation, does not think that he is himself involved in the corruption racket. Corruption, 'real' corruption, belongs to a minority of deviants. [12] He feels hard done by. He worked hard and only paid out what was in fact protection money. He cannot bring himself to vote for the Communists. He is, after all, the archetypal petty bourgeois and thinks he knows what his class interests are. But he will no longer support the DC or the PSI particularly because he can vote for someone else. Because our Signor Rossi is Milanese he will vote for the Lega. Had he been in the south he would have voted for the neo-Fascists. The magistrates are now his heroes. They are not politicians. They are clean. They will humiliate the rich and powerful. When wealthy industrialists are dragged out in the middle of the night, handcuffed, surrounded by journalists and photographers, stripped of their filofaxes and portable telephones, deprived of cronies and secretaries, with no access to their private planes and their chauffeur-driven cars, when they stand trembling before Di Pietro on prime-time television, Rossi is overjoyed. It is the great revenge of the petty bourgeois.

The establishment cannot stop the investigations. It has been deprived of popular complicity. This strengthens the magistrates who no longer conduct a lonely battle. They are strengthened and psychologically supported by the knowledge that politicians would find it impossible to stop them. It is thus not inappropriate to speak of the magistrates as acting like a surrogate political party with a specific programme and requiring political support.

The magistrates themselves, of course, have rejected this explanation which is also advanced by their opponents. They declared:

> Those who say that this investigation is proceeding because it is supported by the people are incorrect. It is proceeding because the mentality of the people has changed. Support makes a difference to the psychology of the magistrate, but a change in mentality has an effect on the behaviour and the psychology of those involved in the investigation. Honest magistrates do not react to popular opinion, they are answerable only to the law.[13]

This, of course, is the way it should be, not necessarily the way it is. What matters is to establish the conditions which permit magistrates to do their jobs effectively. Popular opinion, in this case, was a condition but not the only one. There were institutional constraints which empowered Di Pietro and company. The most important of these was the autonomy of the *magistratura*. This does not mean that individual magistrates – who are appointed for life – are not party supporters or that the Supreme Council of the *magistratura* is not made up of factions connected to political parties. It means that the *magistratura*, as a body, has remained independent of the executive though appointed by it – just like the US Supreme Court.

This independence had to be defended. In the early 1980s Bettino Craxi and his deputy Claudio Martelli (when Minister of Justice) tried to subject investigating magistrates to the executive. These attempts failed mainly because the professional corporation – like all professional corporations in Italy – was extremely strong. This independence meant that, even when politicians attempted, often successfully, to block investigation, they had to respect the formal autonomy of magistrates. They could move a magistrate or an investigation to another area. What they could not do was to 'colonize' the *magistratura* and transform it into the personal possession of some party or other, as they had done with the public sector media or the banking system. To have its way the executive branch had to negotiate informally with highly placed members of the *magistratura*. For instance in March 1981 the magistrates Gherardo Colombo (now in the Mani pulite team), Giuliano Turone (now in the national anti-Mafia squad) and Guido Viola had discovered the P2 conspiracy but were repeatedly advised by their senior colleagues to be less zealous about it. Eventually the investigation was moved from Milan to Rome where little was done. By 1983 the Swiss authorities had responded to an original request from Milan and had prepared a report on the Conto Protezione (Craxi's secret bank account), and were ready to send it to Rome. Rome never answered.[14] Similarly the investigations on the secret funds of the Istituto per la ricostruzione industriale (IRI), on Roberto Calvi, and many others were stopped by the simple mechanism of finding a good reason why the jurisdiction should fall elsewhere – where the magistrates were more pliable.[15]

Clearly honesty, diligence and formal political independence were necessary, but without wider political and popular support, without a shift in public opinion, there would have been no *Tangentopoli*. This shift and this support made the magistrates feel, to use a famous expression of Chairman Mao, 'like a fish in the water', unlike the *inquisiti* (as those being investigated are called) who felt, perhaps for the first time, isolated. Used to a life of power, they discovered what it was to be powerless. One or two weeks in jail was usually sufficient to break most of them.[16] They did not have the strength of character of Resistance fighters, who were often able to withstand far more unpleasant situations because they were fighting for a cause or because they didn't want to let down their comrades. Nor were the *inquisiti* like *mafiosi* who feared that, if they talked, they would be reached by the long hand of the Mafia. Without the accoutrements of power, they were weak and unprepared. When released on bail, they found themselves treated without respect, jeered at in the streets, while only shortly before they had basked in the inner satisfaction of being recognized as powerful and honourable people. No wonder they quickly cracked up and talked.

The fact that the vanguard role in this quasi-revolution has been played by magistrates and a 'social movement' turned into a party like the Lega appears to confirm various hypotheses on the triumph of the non-political. In a global economy the room for manoeuvre of national politicians in relatively small countries highly dependent on trade flows is so reduced that they all campaign on similar economic programmes.[17] They are consequently less and less distinguishable from each other. It follows that non-political characteristics become important: how they look, how they speak, whether they sleep around or not. The corruption

scandals have reinforced the tendency to perceive all professional politicians as crooked. Observers have noted the intense politicization of so
many aspects of Italian social life. This is not a reflection of the Italians'
interest in politics but of the extent political parties have invaded civil
society. Dislike of politics and politicization go hand in hand. This brings
about two tendencies. On the one hand there is the almost universal
longing for an anti-political politician – the classic 'man' of destiny (so far
no Italian woman has stepped into Mrs Thatcher's shoes). On the other,
political parties desperately seek non-politicians as their standard bearers,
partly to curry favour with the public, partly because they realize that
unpopular decisions have more chance of being acceptable if they are taken
by those who, allegedly, have no long-term political ambitions. This is the
advantage Berlusconi enjoyed at the beginning of his political itinerary –
though his business success could not have occurred in the way it had
without the help of political parties. This also played into the hands of
Bossi and his new party, facilitated by the non-political (and rather vulgar)
language he used throughout in contrast to the highly complex and in
some instances virtually unintelligible jargon traditional politicians use.
Since the victory of Forza Italia in 1994 anti-politician feelings have further
escalated. At every local election, political parties try to find some
candidates with little or no previous political experience in the belief that
some of their popularity will rub off onto the party. The fall of Berlusconi
himself, in December 1994, was immediately followed by a government
led by Lamberto Dini, a former senior official of the Bank of Italy and,
before that, of the IMF, made up entirely of *tecnici*, i.e. people who are in
power not because they are politicians or because they have been elected
but because they can use their technical (i.e. non-political) expertise to help
the nation. This, of course, rests entirely on the unfounded belief that there
is such a thing as a neutral and impartial way of resolving political
problems. The PDS, which in the past had promoted the candidacies of
independenti (mostly non-Communist left-wing intellectuals), has decided
to seek 'its' own *tecnico* to be its standard-bearer and appears to have found
him in the person of Romano Prodi, a former president of the stateholding
giant IRI and a Catholic. Their hope is that this will make an alliance with
the PPI less improbable and that it will reassure the middle classes who still
see the PDS as too left-wing.

In Italy the anti-political has old roots. In the immediate post-Fascist
period it arose, briefly, with a Poujadist party, the Uomo Qualunque,
which predated Poujade by nearly ten years. The mood of disillusion with
politics characteristic of those years has now, perhaps only temporarily,
resurfaced. It is not unique to Italy. It is the unmistakable sign of times of
rapid transition. Gramsci once wrote that during the passage from the old
to the new all sorts of morbid symptoms appear. *Tangentopoli* may have
contributed to opening up the transition, but it could not prevent its

Perspectives and debates

'morbid' consequences. What the result will be, whether Berlusconi and his allies will survive and become a permanent aspect of a new political system or whether they will be simply some of the morbid symptoms, is, at the time of writing, still an open question.

Notes

1 The mechanism is well analysed by Donatella Della Porta in 'La capitale immorale: le tangenti di Milano' in S. Hellman and G. Pasquino (eds), *Politica in Italia 1993* (Bologna: Il Mulino, 1993).

2 See comment by Ilvo Diamanti, 'La Lega', in Ilvo Diamanti and Renato Mannheimer (eds) *Milano a Roma. Guida all'Italia elettorale del 1994* (Rome: Donzelli editore, 1994), p. 55.

3 Cited in Andrea Pamparana, *Il processo Cusani. Politici e faccendieri della Prima Repubblica* (Milan: Mondadori, 1994), p. 146.

4 On the P2 see Marco Ramat, Giuseppe D'Alema, Stefano Rodotà and Luigi Berlinguer, *La resistibile ascesa della P2* (Bari: De Donato, 1983).

5 For a good journalist account see Rupert Cornwell, *God's Banker. The Life and Death of Roberto Calvi* (London: Unwin Paperbacks, 1984).

6 Arrigo Benedetti, 'Capitale corrotta e nazione infetta', in *L'Espresso*, No. 1, 1958, collected by the magazine in a paperback: *L'Espresso 1955–85. 30 anni di scandali*, edited by Giampaolo Pansa (Rome: Espresso spa, 1985).

7 Ernesto Rossi, *Settimo: Non rubare* (Bari: Laterza, 1953).

8 See the lucid comments on this by Giulio Sapelli in his *Cleptocrazia* (Milan: Feltrinelli, 1994), pp. 86–7.

9 Cited in Pamparana, *Il processo Cusani*, pp. 147–8.

10 Similar conclusions have been reached by Donatella Della Porta, *Lo scambio occulto. Casi di corruzione politica in Italia* (Bologna: Il Mulino, 1992); Franco Cazzola, *Della corruzione. Fisiologia e patologia di un sistema politico* (Bologna: Il Mulino, 1988) and *L'Italia del pizzo. Fenomenologia della tangente quotidiana* (Turin: Einaudi, 1992); and C. Sennet, *La coscienza dell'occhio* (Milan: Feltrinelli, 1991). Of a contrary opinion is Marco Marturano, *Mafia e corruzione. Un libro scritto da 150.000 italiani* (Milan: FrancoAngeli, 1994), p. 194. Though the survey data Maturano used simply show that ordinary people respond to pollsters by expressing their dismay at corruption, the opposite would be surprising.

11 Of the many instant books describing these intrigues see Marcella Andreoli, *Processo all'Italia. Il Belpaese alla sbarra: Storie di delitti ordinari e di castighi eccellenti* (Milan: Sperling & Kupfer Editori, 1994), and Pamparana, *Il processo Cusani*.

12 Surveys conducted in 1992 and 1993 show that 76.6 per cent of citizens think that the majority of Italians are honest. See Marturano, *Mafia e corruzione*, p. 183.

13 Gherardo Colombo, Piercamillo Davigo and Antonio Di Pietro, 'Noi obbediamo alla legge non alla piazza', *Micromega* 5(1993): 13.

14 This was revealed by the three magistrates to the Assize Court of Rome at the end of 1993; see the extracts in Maurizio De Luca, 'Mani pulite prima di mani pulite' *Micromega* 1(1994): 165–71; see also Edmondo Bruti Liberati, 'Magistrati e politici: una difficile convivenza', *Micromega* 5(1993): 31–45.

15 See Maurizio De Luca and Franco Giustolisi, 'Gli anni ottanta fra giudici e insabbiatori', *Micromega* 2(1993): 101–17.

16 The exceptions were few and significant; one was Sergio Cusani, the

protagonist of the main trial so far, the other was Primo Greganti, a Communist who said that he had stolen the money for himself not for the party. In Cusani's case, the reason for his silence may have been due to the assumption that he will never serve his full eight years and will be able to spend the rest of his life enjoying the vast sums distributed in bank accounts. As for Greganti, if he lied it was to protect his party, in which case his cause gave him strength.

17 In Italy the ex-Communists campaigned on a programme which could have been written, and some say was written, by the Bank of Italy.

[41]

The partitocracy of health

Towards a new welfare politics in Italy?

by Maurizio Ferrera

Maurizio Ferrera is Professor of Public Administration at the University of Pavia.

I. Healthcare, political logic and party government

Healthcare is undoubtedly one of the most delicate areas of state intervention: what governments do or do not do directly, and almost literally, affects the chances of life of their citizens. The very complex nature of the production and distribution of health services tends to give a primary role to players with a professional and technical background (doctors, researchers, administrators), in this area of policy: here, much more so than in other areas, knowledge (specific and general, medical and managerial) greatly influences the processes by which decisions are reached and their contents. The great visibility and high impact of these decisions, as well as a strong government involvement in regulating the most important aspects of healthcare (access, funding, organisation of services, etc.) nevertheless means that the specific preferences of political players - above all political parties - retain their own importance.

Despite the recent growth of a fruitful field of comparative research on healthcare policy, the relationship between the former and political parties still remains largely unexplored. [1] True, the literature has highlighted the links between ideological and programmatic positions of the various political families and the features of the healthcare systems which they have helped to build over time. But the direct link between political competition (especially party competition) and healthcare decisions has not been analysed systematically. Yet the hypothesis that this competition has had some impact, i.e. that there has been some "political exploitation" of healthcare by parties, with tangible effects on the content and results of public policy, appears to be highly plausible and, at least for political scientists, is certainly worth serious consideration.

Italy offers more than its fair share of material for the purposes of such research. The healthcare scandals of the early 1990s (the *malasanita* - or evil health care - as these scandal are known in Italy) have revealed practices of political manipulation of incredible levels of sophistication (and cynicism). Furthermore, these practices were just the climax of decades of use of the healthcare resource by Italian political parties for the purposes of obtaining consensus. Reconstructing this history would, therefore, appear to provide interesting material to enrich the comparative theory on the determinants of healthcare policy.

---

1 For a critical survey of these studies, see Immergut, 1992, chap. 1.

Besides, such a reconstruction could probably also lead to equally interesting indications for the current debate regarding the crisis of the so-called 'partito-crazia' (partitocracy). The healthcare scandals not only testify to the existence of massive exploitation of this sector by the parties but also - and perhaps above all - its spectacular failure both in terms of results and as a way of gathering consensus. The metaphor of a "giant with a clay foot" has been recently proposed as promising interpretative tool for understanding the ascent and - especially - the demise of Italy's partitocratic government (Cotta and Isernia, 1996). This metaphor appears to be highly suited to interpreting the relationship between the political parties and the healthcare system in Italy from the post-war period to the present, and to assess to what extent the dynamics of the national healthcare system contributed to the fall of the partitocratic giant. In the paragraphs that follow I, therefore, propose a re-reading of the events within healthcare policy over the last forty years, emphasising the rise and decline of Italian-style party government in this sphere, and showing how the rise was intimately linked with the decline.

II. From insurance funds to a National Health Service

The political exploitation of healthcare began in the 1950s by the DC, was perfected by the governments of the centre-left during the 1960s and reached its climax in the 1970s and into the 1980s, with the involvement of the PCI and the extension of the spoils system from national level to sub-national level (regions and local health units). The healthcare system generated political resources for the parties mainly through four channels.

The first (in chronological terms, as well) was the selective extension of healthcare rights to the various social groups. At the end of the Second World War, only employees (manual workers and white collar workers) were entitled compulsory healthcare insurance. In the 1950s and 1960s the right to free treatment was gradually extended to new sections of the working population, sometimes even including quite small groups: journalists (1951), domestic workers (1952), managers, (1953), retired state employees (1953), owner-occupier farmers, sharecroppers and tenant farmers (only those in work 1954), general compulsory pensioners (i.e. former private employees 1955) working artisans (1956), home workers (1958), fishermen (1958) working shopkeepers (1960), retired artisans (1963), traders, retired owner-occupier farmers, sharecroppers and tenant farmers as well as the unemployed (1966) and social pensioners (1972). Very often, this led to new insurance funds, with their own regulations (both in terms of contributions and provisions) and their own administrative structure. In some cases (such as the extensions to various categories of pensioners, or to the unemployed), they were true financial gifts: services for the newly insured could be paid for through greater contributions from the working and employed categories. And needless to say each of these little inclusions into the citadel of the welfare system was intelligently exploited by government parties (particularly the DC and the PSI) to retain or attract into their own electoral orbit the beneficiary groups. The political and distributive use of healthcare eligibility nevertheless had a natural limit in the universalisation of cover, which was achieved de facto at the beginning of the 1970s and formally established in 1974 (for hospital care), and in a more complete form in 1978 with the establishment of the Servizio Sanitario Nazionale (SSN - National Health Service).

The second channel that generated political resources was the distribution of economic and legal privileges to the providers of services. The most courted category was undoubtedly the doctors, especially the *medici della mutua* (health insurance doctors), whose caricature in films (a mixture of incompetence and greed) is still seen today as a sort of cultural landmark of Italian society in the 1950s and 1960s. The centre and centre-left governments bought political and administrative support from these doctors by giving them large emoluments and various social guarantees (including paid leave for marriage) (Paderni, 1981). It should be noted that especially in Southern Italy, insurance doctors also acted as electoral advisors to patients (and in some cases as mediators in clientelistic voting). These clientelistic ties between parties and doctors ensured consensus, but also helped greatly to push professional standards down.

The third channel was the intense sub-governmental exploitation of the health-care institutions. The proliferation and solidification of the insurance funds created new public (para-statal) sector jobs that the parties were able to distribute among their supporters and, most of all, to their peripheral lieutenants (with little attention to the requisites of technical expertise and, as a result, considerable negative effects on the operating efficiency of the funds) (Bonaccorsi, 1979). In the 1950s and the 1960s, the *Istituto Nazionale per l'Assicurazione contro le Malattie* (National Institute for Health Insurance or INAM) became a major stronghold of Christian Democrat sub-government (*sottogoverno*). The use of health-care institutions as political spoils continued even after the dissolution of the funds and, indeed, intensified (as we shall see) after the 1978 reform.

Finally the construction of the *selva mutualistica* (a true forest of separate health insurance funds) created new opportunities to obtain secret funds. Culminating in 1993 with the indictment of Poggiolini (the head of the Health Ministry's pharmaceutical services, arrested on charges of corruption), the story surely began at the time of the insurance funds system - although, unfortunately, this will be difficult to document.

The clientelistic practices targeted to the various occupational categories and the shareout of posts produced a long "distributive cycle" in Italian healthcare politics, based on the proliferation of measures characterized by "concentrated benefits and diffuse costs". [2] As I mentioned above, these measures could easily be financed in a relatively painless way, due to the existence of quite generous "contributory dividends"; i.e. operating surpluses within the funds' budgets thanks to the expansion of working contributors, especially in the private employment sector. This syndrome was not exclusive to the state healthcare system. As a matter of fact it took on an even more acute form in the sector of transfer payments: entire generations of pensioners (e.g. within the self-employed) were blanketed in the new old age insurance schemes created in the 1950s and 1960s without paying any contribution at all. What, if anything, was unusual about the health insurance system, was the fact that financial difficulties came to a head much earlier than in other sectors: debt was already rising around the mid-1960s, especially in the case of hospitals. Various factors were responsible for the early onset of a financial crisis: changes in demographic and employment trends and the consequent imbalances in the actuarial equilibria of the insurance funds, rising levels of healthcare consumption by the insured population, ever rising costs of medical technology and its relative cost, particularly inefficient Italian healthcare bodies, the irrationality of some funding methods (Ferrera, 1993). There is obviously no link between some of these factors and the parties. Nevertheless, what

---

2 The concept of "distributive cycle" is dealt with in more detail in Ferrera, 1996a.

is certain is that the dynamics of political exploitation of the insurance system, described above, did worsen the general situation, by generating waste and inefficiency and placing distributive interests before the requisites of good management. Typical of this was the hospital reform of 1968, which was approved shortly before the general election of that year; a vast shareout agreement between government parties, trade unions and the PCI introduced the funding of hospitals on the basis of *per diem* payments [3]: "The one minor drawback of this reform, noted Salvati (1978, p. 10) - was that hospital costs tripled in five years".

In short between the 1960s and the 1970s the healthcare sector witnessed an 'ante litteram' version of the "partitocratic giant with clay feet" syndrome. The distributive obsessions of politicians, on the one hand, and their planning and management incapabilities on the other, provoked a policy crisis of considerable proportions, especially with regard to funding. At the time of their dissolution (in 1977) the insurance funds had accumulated total debts of 6,151 billion lira (ca. 3.2% of that year's GDP): a shortfall which has rightly been considered as the main component of Italy's "original" public debt (Mapelli, 1984 and Panella, 1984). Italian-style party government was able, however, to come out of this crisis unscathed through a double operation: the extraordinary write-off of the insurance debt (which was transformed into public debt) and the approval of the health reform of 1978.

Although the first strategy ridded the party-system of the "small nuisance" of previous financial difficulties, the reform of 1978 in many ways crowned and gave new life to a long cycle of political exploitation of the healthcare system. It would be unfair to look at the establishment of the SSN as just another of the usual large shareout deals. Many players who helped to see the reform through (even from the parties) were really inspired by concerns of efficiency, justice and (to a lesser extent) of effectiveness. These goals were, however, unable to take precedence in the decision-making process and ended up being practically suffocated by the stranglehold of ideological pressures, on the one hand, and self-interest, on the other. At a political level, the reform was the result of a double compromise. A compromise of high politics, above all, preceded by an intense ideological competition, centred on general principles and normative references: State vs. Market, Public vs. Private, Democratic vs. Professional Control, Planning, Universalism, etc. (the political and cultural climate of the second half of the 1970s should be borne in mind). The emphasis on principles prevented serious debate on the methods and ways - in law no. 833/1978 - of rationally organising the infrastructure. The second compromise was purely based on a shareout deal. The parties (including the PCI) agreed to broaden the health care *party governmentness*, by creating additional important instruments of distributive government in the newly formed *Servizio Sanitario Nazionale* (National Health Service or SSN). [4] The main way was through the Management Committees, the controlling organs of the *Unita' sanitarie locali* (local health units or USL), which were politically appointed and in which the reform had concentrated all powers. It is a well-known fact that such organs were allotted immediately: and their *lottizzazione* was of-

---

3 The daily bill for a hospital stay invoiced by hospitals was calculated by dividing the annual operational costs by the number of stay days - a mechanism which provides no incentive to curb costs.

4 For a political and comparative analysis of the Italian healthcare reform see Freddi, 1984 and the articles by Freddi and Ferrera in Freddi, 1989.

ten based on regional legislation which specified the percentages of members government and opposition could appoint in each single Management Committee. Research carried out on the composition of these committees gives a rather desolate picture regarding the technical expertise of the staff recruited during the first legislature (1980-1985); the majority did not even possess a higher education degree (Ferrera, 1986). It should be noted that the parties themselves had difficulties in filling all the positions allocated to them. These totalled about 11,000 posts ranging from Presidents, Vice-Presidents and ordinary members. In many cases not only did the committees contain members without any technical competence, but also persons who had poor political credentials such as candidates who had lost in administrative elections (Berlinguer, 1994). Also the trade unions supplied their own "manpower" to fill the new posts: it is important in this regard to note that throughout the 1980s the trade unions have been prominent participants of the distributive games played within the health care arena.

There has been a barrage of word written about the damage done by the spoils system for the USLs in terms of results in the last fifteen years. That experienced at the beginning of the 1980s was the last "feast" of the healthcare partitocracy - at least in terms of visible politics at national level. A few years after the write-off of the insurance debt, the issue of debts was, once again, on the agenda with growing urgency and the clay began to crumble more quickly under the heavy weight of the spoils system.

III. The 1980s and the new financial government of the healthcare sector

In the 1980s endogenous and exogenous problems surrounding the healthcare service led to a renewed worsening of the problem of (rising) costs and (falling) yields. Healthcare gradually changed from an easy spending resource into a "hot potato" for the parties, especially those in the centre. As it became impossible to pass an effective reform of the reform (which had actually been first mooted in the middle of the decade), the sector came under the "axe of the three Cs" (copayments, ceilings and cuts) (Vicarelli, 1995), wielded by the Treasury with the parties forced to go along. The reform of the reform was only passed in the autumn of 1992 by the Amato government, in the wake of an alarming currency crisis. Making costs explicit through the "three Cs" and through the new reform of 1992, nevertheless, slowly eroded the old consensus based on distributive deals and induced a polarisation of interests (social and political) which manifested itself for the first time clearly during the elections of 1994.

Let us consider the various stages of the sequence sketched out, starting with the financial problems. After the reform, Italian style party government found itself having to run a sector of vast and complex proportions, and one which was growing in economic terms, but whose ramifications as well as technical and management implications were still widely unknown. The law enacting the SSN had a system of administration based on a multi-step programming, (national economic programme, national health plan, regional plans etc.) based on "need" considerations rather than available resources. This system never got off the ground (Granaglia, 1990). The first five-party governments shifted the emphasis from needs to resources and appointed a liberal politician with a business background as head of the Health Ministry (Mr. Altissimo), in the illusion that it would be easy to curb expansionist tendencies in the sector - at least in macro-financial terms. Let us remember that at the same time inflation, debt and the deficit were spiralling up, while the external constriction of Italy's membership to the European Monetary System began to have an effect. In the first two years of the SSN (which entered in full operation in 1980) there were nevertheless some worrying turbulence. In 1980 on top of a planned expenditure of 15,594 billion lira (4.6% of GDP) the government was forced to allocate another 2,000 billion in October and another 400 at year end (public health expenditure thus amounting in 1980 to 5.3% of GDP). In 1981, the gap between budgeted and actual was once again nearly 2,500 billion. The heated discussions on the *lottizzazione* of the USLs and on the confused organisation generated by the reform at the peripheral level in turn created pressures to return the management of the SSN under some form of control from the centre. The government (especially the Treasury Ministry) took cover and launched a new phase of financial administration of the sector, aimed, on the one hand, at curbing the demand for services by making users pay in part for services and secondly by making the regions and USLs accountable through the imposition of a number of aggregated ceilings of expenditure.

Copayments have been without doubt the most visible (and most unpopular) instrument of government action in the healthcare sector in the last fifteen years. Significantly, the year of change was 1983. Alarmed at the worrying excessive growth in healthcare costs (especially for medicines) in the previous two years, that year the government decided to change the copayment from a (modest) fixed fee to a percentage, making consumers pay 15% of the cost of drugs. This percentage was then raised on several occasions in later years (1986, 1988, 1989 and 1992) reaching 50% in 1995 (limited to the so-called class B set of drugs) - one of the highest copayment rates in Europe (Ferrera, 1995). The policy of copayments was not, however, limited just to the introduction of tougher measures, but also accompanied by action on three other fronts.

The first was the modulation of the taxable pharmaceutical basis, through ever more restrictive revisions of the Therapeutical Catalogue aimed at reducing the number of drugs that could be prescribed at the expense of the state. This process culminated in the reclassification of drugs into three groups: a verly limited class A of "life-saving" drugs (available with just a fixed prescription copayment); a class B of drugs obtainable with a percentage charge and a residual class C (payment of full price by the consumer).

The second line of action was the extension of the use of the copayment system first to diagnostic tests (1982) and later to specialist consultations (1986). Finally, the third line of action was the introduction of more detailed legislation on exemptions, based on therapeutic criteria (exemptions due to illness), income, family situation, and age. The copayment policy was heavily criticised for a long time as an ineffective way of bringing down prescription consumption, as having unfair distribution effects, etc. (Censis, 1988). From the point of view of governments which have pursued this policy, however, it generally achieved its aims, which were mostly financial. Pharmaceutical spending has, in fact, stabilised, copayments now represent 30% of this expenditure (compared to 10% in 1980) and the use of prescribed drugs has actually fallen (Ferrera, 1995).

The second major line of government action regarding the SSN, as mentioned before, was the introduction of ceilings on expenditure. Once the intended multi-step planning fell through, from 1983 onward the five-party governments (once again) tried to keep expansionist pressures in the sector under control by placing budgetary limits. The budget bill becomes the instrument par excellence to run the healthcare system from the centre: it is this bill that sets the global allocation for the National Health Fund (NHF) on the basis of available public funds, to be shared out among the regions; and it is again the budget bill that determines both the copayments and the cuts (the third C: reduction of facilities, staff, investments etc.) deemed necessary to remain in line with the ceilings. Generally under the sway of the Treasury Ministry at the centre, the policy of ceilings (and cuts) was mainly implemented by the regions. As these had little say in the fixing of ceilings, and were not bound by any fiscal accountability, they had little interest in keeping spending down, and objectively did not possess powers of control over the USLs or, above all, over the main "demand-inducers", i.e general practitioners. The regions in turn engaged in a tug of war with central government (Pistelli, 1995 and Veronesi, 1994). Throughout the decade 1984-1993 the typical sequence of events in each financial year with regard to the health service was the following: fixing of expenditure ceilings, of copayments and cuts in the autumn/winter budget; spring adjustment of the previous year's deficit; alarm in the summer due to the insufficiency of the funds allocated to the regions, consequent delays in USL payments to suppliers (such as pharmacies) and threats of insolvency, lockins etc.; agreement in September between central government and regions on further allocations; new ceilings and more severe copayments and cuts in the next budget. There has been a gradual escalation over time in this sequence of events. On the one hand, the government, under increasing pressure of budgetary restrictions (internal and external), has begun to set ceilings that are quite unrealistic; on the other hand, local health units have made very little effort to curb spending. To give but just one example, very few regions (and USLs) have introduced the systems of effective monitoring of medical prescriptions recommended by the government and clearly set out in the national agreements with doctors. This escalation of the financial stakes between centre and periphery is borne out by the growing gap between the funds budgeted ex ante for the regions and actual ex post expenditure. In percentage terms, this gap rose from 4.5% of ex ante expenditure in 1983 to 20.3% in 1990 (Veronesi, 1994).

In the second half of the 1980s, the issue of fiscal unaccountability of the regions and of the USLs became a *leitmotiv* of the debate on the reform of the reform (Balassone and Franco, 1995). The budget for 1992 attempted to modify this situation for the first time, by officially mooting the transfer of direct responsibility for the financing of health services to the regions. The actual transfer from the centre to the regions of the responsibility for balanced budgets in the SSN was decided by the Amato government only in the autumn of 1992 (even though, as we shall see, it is still to be actually implemented).

Although less visible to the eyes of the general public, the policy of ceilings (and cuts) has also come in for a good deal of criticism for both technical and political reasons: it is said to have had generally negative effects on the technical efficiency of the sector as well as the non-clinical quality of services (France, 1995). Once again, from the point of view of the successive governments applying the policy, however, it has resulted in some quite remarkable changes. It is true that budget allocations to the SSN have constantly risen (social contributions now cover just 50% of the expenditure), and that the gap between budgeted and actual costs has grown. Nevertheless, in percentage terms of GDP, public expenditure on healthcare did not rise much between 1980 and 1992 (from 5.3 to 6.5%) and remains at values that are fully in line with (if not lower than) those of other European countries (OECD 1994).

It should, however, be noted that there is a big mortgage to be paid for this apparent success: the huge hidden accumulated debt of the USLs towards their creditors over time, as a result of operations "off the books" (Veronesi, 1994). Tolerated (and sometimes even directly encouraged) by the regions and already partly written off by lenient governments, this debt has been the hidden cost of the policy of ceilings and cuts. Estimated at twenty billion lire in 1995 (ca. 1.2% of GDP), this debt is a real Sword of Damocles hanging over the still precarious conditions of Italy's public finance system - a new "hot potato" which the First Republic is sadly about to bequeath to the Second Republic.

IV. The reactions of parties at national, sub-national, visible and invisible levels

The institutional re-organisation brought about by the reform and cost containment pressures at the macro level re-structured party interests in the health-care sector during the 1980s. This re-structuration has been somewhat complex. To fully understand its various forms it is useful to distinguish between national and sub-national levels, on the one hand, and between visible and invisible politics, on the other.

At the national level, the opportunities to exploit the SSN directly became increasingly scarce. The only measures that made sense were the "3 Cs", i.e. those which placed sacrifices on users, producers/suppliers, on regional and local politicians and local administrators. The initiative to work out and introduce such measures was willingly left to "technical" Ministers and to the Cabinet which acted in union with senior levels of the civil service (Court of Accounts, Bank of Italy, Central Service for Health Planning etc.). The parties have kept their distance from cabinet actions: events in the health care system confirm that the functional needs of policy management (in a restrictive sense), which came to the fore in the 1980s, contributed to the institutionalisation of the executive and its independence from the party system. This withdrawal of the parties from the executive sphere has nevertheless been accompanied by the their mobilisation - at national level - in two directions. Firstly, in blame avoidance so as to prevent erosion of support from the categories that were hit by government measures. Secondly, in cross-vetoing all proposals aimed at structural change.

Avoiding blame (and consequently punishment from the electorate) is a primary objective of all political players in general. However, it becomes the primary objective when politics turns into a negative sum game, where only losses are being distributed. The comparative literature has identified many possible strategies of blame avoidance (Weaver, 1986; Pierson and Weaver, 1993). Italian parties in the 1980s adopted, above all, two strategies: "passing the buck" and "finding a scapegoat". As noted above, the introduction of unpopular measures was left to the cabinet, while the parties played off the political responsibility for them against each other, often assigning the "blame" to the regions or the European Community and its pressures for austerity. In some cases, this gave rise to a sort of "jumping on the bandwagon", but in reverse - with parties outbidding each other in proposing attenuations of the "3 Cs".

The strategy of avoidance was particularly cautious when it came to co-payments, the most visible and unpopular measure in the eyes of the mass electorate. Here the syndrome of blame avoidance worked more or less as follows. The government proposed the introduction, extension, and/or higher levels of co-payment (and perhaps passed a decree to this effect). The opposition parties and trade unions protested strongly and, in some cases, took their protests to the streets. The five parties of the majority thus began a sort of 'reverse auction', proposing concessions, new exemptions etc. in parliament. In 1986, for example, charges on medicines were raised from 15% to 25% and then brought back down to 15%. In some cases, the 'reverse auction' (sparked off also by Communist intransigence and social protest) even led to the abrogation of the measure. Once again, in 1986, the attempt to increase the copayment on diagnostic tests to 25% raised such protests that in the end the five-party government decided to eliminate it completely. The same thing happened to the attempt to introduce a copayment of ten thousand lire a day (ca. five ECUs) on hospital stays, proposed by the government in 1989 (and practised in many other countries). The left-wing opposition organised a general strike, the government parties initially proposed a series of ceilings and exemptions and then gave up the idea. In the case of the "doctor tax" introduced in 1992 (eighty-five thousand lire a year - ca. 42 ECUs - to retain free access to general practicioner consultations), the parties agreed to the introduction of the measure, but later withdrew support from government and from administrative attempts to verify payment, following an almost mass evasion.

The second direction that mobilisation took was the issue of the reform of the reform. Discredited by the furore at the unfettered division of the USLs spoils at the beginning of the 1980s, the parties realised that they had to loosen their control over health (at least at the visible level): as noted previously, the debate on the de-politicisation of the USLs and the professionalizaton of medical staff and managerial competence had already begun in the mid-1980s. In actual fact, however, the parties vetoed the reform of the reform (especially on the revised USLs) and it appeared that approval would be postponed sine die. It was only the financial crisis of 1992 (and the beginning of 'Tangentopoli') which finally opened a window of political opportunity so that the Amato government was able to finally get the bills through parliament (law no. 421, and later, delegated decree no. 502).

In short, the political exploitation of the healthcare system was scaled down considerably in the 1980s at national and visible level. For government parties, at least, the balance in terms of support and resources was negative; the only electoral strategy possible was the transfer of blame onto other parties; within the spoils system, competition was only defensive, taking the form of a veto on those proposals that directly threatened single shares of power.

At the national, invisible level, however, the party system continued to make full use of the health sector as a source of illegal and secret funding. A fourth C (corruption), through a very refined clientelistic network, was piloted by the Ministry of Health with large bribes flowing through the *Commissione Unica del Farmaco* (CUF or Single Drug Committie, approving new drugs and their classification within the Therapeutical Catalogue) and the *Comitato Interministeriale Prezzi* (CIP or Inter-ministerial Committee on prices): the *malasanità*. The Court of Accounts has estimated that the kickbacks alone which were paid to politicians by pharmaceutical companies between 1983 and 1993 amounted to a total of 15,000 milliard lira (0.9% of the 1995 GDP) and added, on average, 3,000 milliard a year (ca. 0.3 percentage points) to the public finance bill (due to artificially higher prices) (Il Sole-24 Ore, 19/7/1994).

The sub-national level allowed even more opportunities for political exploitation of healthcare than from the centre, even at a visible level, throughout the 1980s. The political administrators of the region and the USLs are, as I mentioned before, not institutionally bound to financial accountability. At this level, therefore, there are no political incentives to distinguish between administrative government and party interests. The local, political and administrative decision makers (especially in the USLs) are, in addition, imbued with a 'debt culture', that has developed with many years of practice and learning, perhaps in the administration of public hospitals or insurance funds. [5] To a large extent, the local partitocracy can continue its own distributive games unhindered, claiming credit for the appropriation of resources from the centre and in sharing them out locally or for its own accounting creativity. Being by far the most important sector of decentralised government, healthcare has allowed and promoted the development of a peripheral party government, distinct from (and perhaps in some ways rivalling) the national one, undoubtedly with its own dynamics which are still widely unknown. This local partitocracy suffered a serious blow with the appointment of external administrators to run the USLs (1990) firstly, and with the managerialistion later, introduced by the reform of the reform. The "giant" seems, nevertheless, to be more resistant at this level, at least with regard to the regions. And in the sphere of invisible behaviour its appetite appears to be just as voracious as at ministerial level. As research is beginning to show (Della Porta and Vannucci, 1994), individual USLs were the scene of large-scale corruption, especially with regard to external contracts and commissions.

V. A new political demand in healthcare: prospects for the future

From 1993 onwards the healthcare partitocracy was caught up in the whirlwind of 'Tangentopoli' (Bribesville). The wrongdoings of various health Ministers, bureaucratic chiefs of Ministry, members of the CUF and the drugs CIP have perhaps dealt the final blow against Italian-style party government. Speculation "on people's lives" has, in fact, had a particularly marked impact on public opinion. The reform of the reform - finally passed in 1992, as already mentioned - has erected institutional barriers to the presence of parties in the management of the sector and in the continuation of the distributive games at the sub-national level. Following the disbanding of the management committees, the USLs are now run by General Managers who, at least on paper, must possess verifiable technical expertise. The USLs (and large hospitals) are, in addition, becoming public companies, with increased powers of independent management and a duty to balance budgets. The regions, for their part, must make good any financial debts through their own resources. The new institutional model is slowly taking off while old habits die hard: in the spring of 1995 the Italian press reported on continuing attempts by regional councils (i.e. parties) to shareout posts. The regions, for their part, have engaged in a battle against central government through legal appeals, in order to reduce their fiscal accountability: they argue (and they are not totally unjustified) that they do not have effective powers to monitor local spending. The institutional system of healthcare is nevertheless restructuring and its level of party governmentness is gradually diminishing, albeit with great difficulty.

---

5 It has been noted that one of the main causes of regional irresponsibility was "the operational culture of the USLs, heirs of other institutional bodies (hospitals and funds) that were generally run with a shortage of resources to meet objectives (necessary or unnecessary). As a result, incurring debts without the means to pay them off became an accepted state of affairs, and skill was used to obtain more credit from suppliers of goods and services" (Veronesi, 1994, p. 180). These observations provide the basis for developing an interesting theory as to how the healthcare debt grew (and perhaps the public debt, in general), based on a cognitive - cultural and policy learning perspective (Gualmini, 1995).

THE PARTITOCRACY OF HEALTH   457

The account I have just given suggests that this restructuring is to a large extent the result of the failure of party governmentness: its shareout excesses, its corrupt practices, and its ineffectiveness at the planning and management levels. The "financial" government of the SSN by technical Ministers has prevented the declining standards from developing into a complete breakdown of the system. But it has not been able to protect the old parties from the long term political consequences of their behaviour and the progressive erosion of those resources that have traditionally been obtained through these behaviours. Indeed, the financial government of the healthcare system has, in itself, ended up accelerating the break-up of the partitocratic system, generating an ever greater political demand for change. This is a very important point and requires greater development.

During the 1980s, not only did the parties run the SSN at the macro level badly, halting the dynamics of organisational and institutional innovation at the meso and micro levels: they also failed to make choices of a purely political nature regarding the distribution of costs of healthcare services among social groups. It has been said that the reform of 1978 was, on the one hand, a compromise of high politics on principles and, on the other, a compromise on the sharing out of power. Besides ignoring the "middle ground" of managerial and organizational considerations, the reform also failed to be accompanied by clear redistributive decisions (who receives what and, above all, who pays what) - the very healthcare choices which in other developed countries are normally made by the parties themselves (at least in the sense of parties-in-government). These choices, in fact, constitute the "wherefore" of party action in the various policy domains (the *partyness of government*, if you wish). The "financial government" of the SSN could not do much on this aspect: it has imposed sacrifices where it has been able to do so (technically as well as socially), while the parties have tried to manipulate the social distribution of these sacrifices so as to protect their own share of the electorate from copayments and cuts. To illustrate this point, we could mention the failure to shift from conributory to tax financing of the SSN, the retention of contribution differences between categories, the selective concession of exemptions (for example various types of disabled) as well as the tolerance of widespread fraud in this sector, and inaction against large pockets of evasion (contributions from self-employed workers, health tax and, finally, the above mentioned doctor tax). Applied against such a background, the copayment policy has only generated further inequalities (honest tax payers versus evaders). The policy of ceilings has for its part indirectly contributed, as has been said, to a fall in standards, at least at a non-clinical level.

In the long term, all theses dynamics have generated widespread ill-feeling among the consumers of the SSN and have created a constellation of potentially favourable interests for change. This constellation, it should be noted, is tendentially anti-universalist and anti-state, exasperated by the excessive taxes (although ready to avoid them where possible), by operational inefficiencies, by the wrongdoings of politicians, etc. The comparative literature has shown that it is difficult to create and mobilise anti-universalist coalitions in the health sector due to the typical model of service utilization in this sector: everyone needs health services sooner or later and, therefore, everyone is interested in retaining the right of access (Moran, 1991). The case of Italy shows that - under certain conditions - such a coalition can be formed even in a mature welfare state, lending itself to be mobilised at a political level.

As a result of the inability of the old parties (given the well-known macro-political and institutional constraints of the First Republic) to break of the distributive cycle and make bold redistributive choices, the process just described has contributed - and I wish to emphasise this - to the break up of the partitocratic system as a whole. The anti-universalist and anti-state interests in some major social groups have, in fact, been mobilised by the new parties: initially the Lega Nord and later Forza Italia. It is worth remembering that the Lega supported a referendum (rejected by the Constitutional Court) on the abrogation of compulsory membership of the SSN. Forza Italia's electoral manifesto in the elections of 1994 included plans for the dismantlement of the public service and its replacement with a system of vouchers reserved for the most needy (the most radical proposal ever officially put forward by any European party). In other words (and to conclude): the healthcare system shows how the inadequacy of the partitocratic system to produce a policy of redistribution has created fertile ground for the emergence of a new political demand and new political entrepreneurs. The elections of 1994 signalled a re-orientation of the political system in this direction: at least in their manifestos the parties formulated quite detailed proposals. In the coming years, the pendulum of healthcare reforms might well swing (for the first time in Italy) towards greater partyness in the running of healthcare, together with the dismantling of the spoils system. The margins of choice will not be great. Comparative experience shows that the "extremist" options (all public or all private, all state or all market) are technically and politically very dangerous in this sector. The adoption of a mixture of various instruments appears to be the most promising strategy to achieve good results in terms of efficiency, effectiveness and fairness (France, 1994). A serious debate between left and right on the kind of state healthcare towards which to aim (a debate which is pragmatic but also based on value options), open to "non-partisan" voices, but promoted by parties, and subjected to the electoral test, would nevertheless be an important sign that the *malasanità* is truly a thing of the past.

VI. Towards a new model of welfare

A development in a similar direction would be extremely positive not only for the health care sector, but also for other social policies as well. As mentioned in passing throughout this article, the whole welfare state has been the object in Italy of a systematic and pervasive exploitation by the First Republic's partitocracy. In certain sectors (e.g. invalidity pensions or unemployment subsidies) parties (and trade unions) have been able to set up extremely elaborated patronage machines for the individualized delivery of benefits to their voters. The Italian academic debate of the 1980s has coined the label of a "paricularistic-clientelistic welfare model" to characterize the Italian case vis-à-vis the other Continental welfare states belonging to the same "Bismarckian" family. [6] Whether the emerging Second Republic will be able to effectively reform this model and break with the legacy of partisan patronage, without however dispensing with the idea of a national welfare state is a crucial, but still uncertain question.

The debates and proposals made during the 1996 electoral competition have sent some promising signs - but they have also switched on an alarm bell. The positive signs are the programs of welfare reform presented by the two opposing

---

6 See for instance Ascoli, 1984 and Ferrera, 1984. For an update on the particularistic-clientelistic model (with references also to the other Southern European countries) see Ferrera, 1996b.

THE PARTITOCRACY OF HEALTH 459

coalitions. These programs are clearly differentiated on the basis of typical left-right principles: but the relevant thing is that they are both serious, pragmatic and realistic documents, devoid of the ideological clichés and simplifications of the past. The PDS has for instance abandoned its traditional, intransigent "etatisme", while Forza Italia no longer questions in its turn the maintenance of a public and compulsory social insurance. The alarm bell is represented by the Lega Nord. This party advocates a dismemberment of the national welfare state and its radical regionalization: regional health services and even regional pension systems, with only a moderate amount of inter-regional redistribution. It will not be easy either to accomodate the demands of the Lega: but it could be very risky to ignore them. Amongst the many challenges confronting the new "Olive tree" government (and, more broadly, the new Parliament), welfare reform is certainly a very compelling one - and possibly even the most important of all.

Abstract

This article illustrates the relationships between political parties and the health-care sector in Italy since the 1950s. The several ways though which parties have "exploited" health policies are explored, ranging from the selective extension of care entitlements to the various occupational categories to the clientelistic ties with doctors, from the placement of party personnell in the various administrative posts to illegal financing. The author argues that the partitocratic exploitation of the health care sector has greatly contributed to the failure of the 1978 reform establishing a National Health Service. This failure has in its turn backlashed against the partitocratic government, accellerating its demise in the early 1990s. The article concludes with some considerations on the future of Italy's health policy and, more generally, welfare state policy.

[42]

The Reform of Finance and Administration in Italy: Contrasting Achievements

GIACINTO DELLA CANANEA

This assessment reviews the changes which have affected Italian financing and the administration in recent years. In particular, it considers why public administration is in a worse state than finance, and why this issue has been relatively neglected. An assessment of the extent to which the questions of finance and administration are linked is made first. The evolution and current state of both issues is then analysed, before explaining why moves have been made towards greater financial rigour when, by contrast, the public administration remains largely unreformed.

The poor state of Italian finances and the inefficiency and ineffectiveness of the Italian administration have been well-known since the 1970s, as have the difficulties in achieving an improvement in either. In recent years, however, there has been a marked divergence in the paths followed by financial and administrative reform. This discussion analyses the changes which have affected both areas. In particular, it considers why public administration is in a worse state that finance, and why the former issue has not been adequately addressed. The evolution and current state of both areas is analysed before an attempt is made to explain why the 1990s have witnessed moves towards greater financial rigour, while the administration remains largely unreformed.[1] Before doing so, however, it is necessary to examine the extent to which the two areas of finance and the administration are linked.

THE LINK BETWEEN FINANCE AND THE ADMINISTRATION

There are three reasons for treating the questions of finance and administration together.[2] The first is that both have grown considerably in importance with respect to the Constitution and the political system. Financing and administration, as basic components of public power, received little attention from the Constituent Assembly which was responsible for drafting the Italian constitution of 1948, and this state of affairs continued until the early 1970s, when there was a move to expand the competencies and scope of both. Public finance, according to recent estimates,

FINANCIAL AND ADMINISTRATIVE REFORM   195

now absorbs more than half of Gross Domestic Product (GDP), with the deficit amounting to about 10 per cent. Moreover, decisions affecting financing – such as major funding legislation – have risen to the top of the political agenda. The administration, meanwhile, has witnessed an increase in both its normative powers and personnel. Today, it is Italy's largest employer. Furthermore, its reputation depends much more than in the past on satisfying citizens' interests. In the course of this century, fundamental interests have developed which cannot be satisfied without state intervention to provide such things as a good educational system and an efficient health service.

The second reason is that both finance and administration have been subject to clientelistic party interference, which has had undesirable effects. The fact that from 1950–90 political parties assumed a greater role in state and society than was in the general interest has been well-documented. It is important, however, to note the effects of this expanded role on finance and the administration. Public spending sustains political power through the distribution of group benefits, and is regulated by the constitutional rule governing finance limits (Art.81, last sub-section) and other constitutional principles of impartiality and administrative efficiency (Art.97, §2). Yet, the huge intake of public employees who have not passed the requisite competition – as required by the Constitution (Art.97, §3) – and the lack of selection by merit has caused a crisis in public finance and reduced efficiency in the administration. In effect, the administration has come to perform the social function of guaranteeing employment, rather than providing services. Moreover, as protection of its personnel has become more important, so responsibility for performance has declined. As a result, there have been hostile confrontations between politicians and bureaucrats over efficiency controls. The bureaucracy has accepted an undermining of its independence and role through party interference, and has willingly subjected itself to stringent controls, which are often based upon fulfilling the requirements of individual laws. This has produced numerous levels of co-decision making between politicians and the bureaucracy, which, while in accordance with the law, tend nevertheless to overlook the main objectives behind the collection and distribution of public resources, for which the administration is responsible.[3]

The third reason for considering finance and the administration together is that the reform of one has an effect on the other. The extent to which the reform of public finances is contingent on overhauling the administration became increasingly clear during the 11th legislature (1992–94). In order to begin the reorganisation of public finances, the governments of Giuliano Amato (1992–93) and Carlo Azeglio Ciampi (1993–94) initiated a comprehensive reform of the administrative system. The Amato

196   CRISIS AND TRANSITION IN ITALIAN POLITICS

government effected a major reform of the main public spending sectors –
(health, social security, employment and local financing) and, after years
of debate, began to privatise public enterprises. The Ciampi government,
for its part, paved the way for the modernisation of public administration,
in all of its dimensions – organisation, procedure, personnel and controls.[4]
But then the reform of finance and administration began to diverge.

THE REFORM OF PUBLIC FINANCE

From the mid-1970s onwards, there were increasing demands from various
institutions and public opinion for a restructuring of the public accounts.
A succession of reforms gradually changed the profile of financial institutions. Two sets of changes were particularly noteworthy: (1) clearer links
were established between the various sectors of public finance (the state,
the regions, and local and other public bodies); and (2) the instruments for
intervention at the disposal of public institutions were modified.[5]

To understand the importance of the first set of changes, it should be
noted that the state, while being almost exclusively responsible for
collecting resources, redistributes them via the budget which passes them
on to other bodies. These are either sub-national authorities (at the regional
or local level) or auxiliary institutions (such as social security or local health
agencies). The separation of the collection and distribution of finances has
tended to make the different spending bodies or agencies largely irrespon-
sible, resulting in dysfunction and waste. To remedy this, laws were introduced to control public financing *in toto* during the yearly cycle of financial
decisions: the economic and financial planning act (law of 14/8/1988,
no.362) and the finance law (law of 5/8/78, no.468, amended under law
no.362/1988). Moreover, fixed spending levels were established for all
bodies in the enlarged public sector (a figure for public administration costs
was provided by the protocol on excessive deficits linked to the Maastricht
Treaty). These aimed to conform to regulations on keeping individual
accounts, to provide information for the Ministry of the Treasury and to
keep treasury capital near to the state Treasury in order to reduce the costs
of obtaining funding on the financial markets.[6] Finally, controls were
introduced which applied to public financing in general. These were
entrusted to the Court of Accounts which, as the body controlling state
accounts, became the Court of Public Accounts (the National Audit Office).

The second set of changes concerned the instruments of intervention at
the disposal of public institutions:

- Whilst the Constitution (under Art.81, §4) requires single items of
  spending to be covered by revenue (which has often had to be ignored

FINANCIAL AND ADMINISTRATIVE REFORM   197

by legislators), ordinary law requires that projected medium-term spending (over three years) is also covered by revenue. Law no.384/91 extends constitutional law and demands that medium-term spending should also be adequately covered.

- Whereas previously the budget could restrain areas of spending, but could not modify the norms established, this capacity has now been included in the annual Finance Bill. At the level of quantitative regulation, the finance law now assesses the total cost of financing, and determines what the maximum level of market funding should be (thus establishing a ceiling for spending). It also determines the commitments to longer-term spending and modification to the rates of taxation. The laws linked to the Finance Bill, which contain many norms, have also modified previously existing arrangements, and were used during the eleventh legislature to reform the organisation of public administration.
- The system of procedures affecting public finance have been modified. These are now divided between two consecutive sessions (spring and autumn) and concern almost exclusively economic and financial measures (excluding decree laws) in order to guarantee a fixed calendar for parliamentary debate. Furthermore, limitations were placed on the modifications which the Chamber of Deputies (the Lower House) can make to proposals submitted by the government. Amendments can no longer be considered if they alter the total cost of the proposed Finance Bill. Finally, the order of voting is such that it now gives priority to the vote on the revenue side of the Bill which subsequently sets the limits on spending.
- Finally, five measures were introduced to allow the identification and measurement of the negative effects arising from fixed and proposed spending. On the one hand, because a law can increase spending or reduce income, an appropriate technical report must now be made which measures the law's effects. This report is submitted to the State Accounts Department (*Ragioneria generale dello Stato*) for scrutiny. On the other hand, the Ministry of the Treasury must inform Parliament of the actual costs as compared with the initial forecasts; it should also propose solutions to overcome the discrepancies between the two. Furthermore, the Court of Accounts carries out checks on the limits on spending and where these fail, before referring them to Parliament.

The reform of the financing system, summarised above,[7] has certainly not resolved all of the problems of public finance inherited from previous legislatures. Among the unresolved problems there is the sheer scale of the public debt, which has deterred more productive investment and has left Italian finances vulnerable to fluctuations in the financial markets.

198 CRISIS AND TRANSITION IN ITALIAN POLITICS

Furthermore, it has not solved the (still legal) legislative and administrative evasion of fixed levels of spending and public debt. Legislative evasion stems from the reluctance of the government and Parliament to respect the rules; it also derives from the weakness of the existing limits, which, being established under ordinary, rather than constitutional, law, can be altered by another ordinary law.[8] Administrative evasion is the result of the accounting regulations by which the Treasury ensures the formal respect of limits, artificially determining the distribution of certain resources (for example, those destined for the regions or tax returns demanded by citizens). Moreover, some activities which increase spending have not been changed, such as the mechanisms which are incorporated into the laws governing social welfare, which are still divided into approximately 6,000 sections, and which prevent the setting of clear financial limits.[9]

There are also problems created by the reforms themselves. Although state expenditure has been reined in, this does not mean that spending is disbursed according to need (rather than the pressure of interests) or that it is managed in an efficient and economic manner. Furthermore, financial centralisation has reduced the autonomy of the regions and of local bodies. At the same time, the reform of public finance has brought the conflicts between different groups and interests over state funding into the very heart of the process by which financial decisions are made and adopted.

That said, placing financing at the centre of the institutional and political agenda has also had many positive effects. The growth of spending has been stemmed and fiscal pressure alleviated.[10] The deficit – the substantial reduction of which is fundamental to Italy's future role in the European Union (EU) – has been brought down to within more manageable limits. Italy's primary surplus has risen faster than that of any other member of the G7. In other words, tax receipts are now higher than public spending. Mention should be made, however, of the presence of high interest rates demanded for servicing the debt. These are the result of errors made in the past, which pushed the state into debt, and of financing from current expenditure (family benefits and funding public companies).

These changes have also had an effect at the institutional level. Since 1988, the Finance Bill has been approved within the time schedule set by budgetary policy, whereas in the previous decade, there were instances when provisional budgets were used (twice in 1985 for example). The new law, if correctly employed (i.e. on the basis of realistic estimates) allows for an effective control of spending. During the first few years of using the new rules, the number and quality of technical reports has grown. Parliament has been able to produce more considered decisions, thanks to the new budgetary reports which it has received. The government, for its part, has managed to avoid changes to established budgetary targets, although there

FINANCIAL AND ADMINISTRATIVE REFORM 199

TABLE 1

PUBLIC SECTOR DEBT: 1970–95 (AS PERCENTAGE OF GDP)

Year	%	Year	%
1970	34.2	1983	68.4
1971	38.4	1984	73.3
1972	42.7	1985	81.1
1973	44.0	1986	85.3
1974	44.1	1987	89.9
1975	49.9	1988	92.7
1976	48.7	1989	96.0
1977	51.2	1990	98.7
1978	57.0	1991	101.9
1979	56.6	1992	108.6
1980	54.8	1993	115.9
1981	57.7	1994	124.3
1982	62.7	1995	123.8

Source: Bank of Italy

has still been the problem of compensatory parliamentary amendments which do not alter the level of spending but which nevertheless can significantly affect the government programme.

Finally, there has been a strengthening of independent financial powers. Since 1981 the Bank of Italy has been relieved of its obligation to buy public paper not purchased during sales of ordinary Treasury bonds. This has allowed it to improve its capacity to function autonomously in the monetary sphere, as required by the agreements instituting the European Monetary System (EMS). More recently, the law of 26 November 1993, no.483, implementing the Treaty on European Union, has severed the remaining links between the Bank of Italy and the Treasury. Monetary policy has thus been separated from budgetary policy, with the stabilisation of prices as its primary objective.[11]

THE MIXED FORTUNES OF ADMINISTRATIVE REFORM

Thus, despite its inconsistencies, the reform of public finance has followed a relatively coherent and progressive course. In contrast, administrative reform went through three phases which were so disjointed that they hardly amount to a single, coherent programme of reform.

In a first phase (until the end of the 1970s) there was a move away from the idea that administrative reform should be 'global' in nature towards *ad hoc* reform. In the 1980s, whilst the conviction that major institutional reform was necessary spread, the administration at the lower levels became – wrongly, as it turned out – the object of *ad hoc*, organisational changes

200   CRISIS AND TRANSITION IN ITALIAN POLITICS

with no clear, overall plan (for example, the introduction of a general law for administrative procedures, under law no.241/1990, and of new regula- ions for local autonomy, in law no.142/1990). Consequently, while there was an obvious path to be followed in financial reform, there was no clear vision of comprehensive administrative reform. For example, the govern- ment of Giovanni Goria (1987–88) instigated measures in disparate areas with no common thread: the Prime Minister's office, public works, local autonomy, civil protection, simplification of administrative procedures, and administrative justice. Moreover, even where some of these reforms were achieved by successive governments at the legislative level, they had little concrete effects. For example, in 1988, the Parliament approved, under law no.400, the reform of the Prime Minister's office and the normative powers of the government. Yet, the directive in the law on the removal from the legal sphere of areas only partially governed by law was not implemented; as a result, many areas became subject to legal intervention, despite being matters originating in other spheres (public investment, for example). Nor did the government instigate the reorganisation of interministerial committees, something which happened only some years later under the Ciampi government.

The contradictions became even clearer in the period after 1989, when a general move towards improving the exercise of public power emerged. The demand for the separation of centre and periphery led to the statutory empowerment of autonomous bodies, such as universities (law no.186/1989) and local bodies (law no.142/1990), but these remained linked to the financial decisions of the central agencies. The demand for the separation of administration and politics produced new institutions, divided according to function and organisation, in the areas of radio and publishing (law no.223/1990), competition (law no.287/1990) and strikes in essential public services (law no.146/1990). The demand for the simplification of administrative procedures pushed the legislators to provide relevant instru- ments, such as the services conference and programme agreements (law no.241/1990); but in other cases they preferred simply to suppress controls or defer their implementation (e.g. in matters of public works).

Between 1992 and 1994, however, there was a noticeable change of tack, due to several factors. First, the state of public finances made more rigorous measures inevitable. Second, the political and institutional crisis resulting from the investigation of political and administrative corruption reduced the scope of action of political parties. And third, the completion of the Single Market tightened the margins between the public resources which could be targeted at unproductive investment and the level of goods and services (resourced by the administration) which could be restricted to national firms. These were to be at the centre of the abrogative referenda

FINANCIAL AND ADMINISTRATIVE REFORM   201

of April 1993. Seven out of the eight referendums held that month
concerned the administration (further referendums being avoided only
through legislative reforms); so this might be described as a form of public
reappropriation of the administration. These developments lay at the heart
of a series of structural interventions without parallel in recent Italy history,
and which can be grouped into six areas or themes, dealt with during the
Amato and Ciampi governments:[12]

- *Separating the political and administrative spheres.* This included measures
  to separate the executive (the domain of the political organs) from the
  administration (entrusted to the 'managers'), as set out in the legislative
  directive no.29/1993, and prohibiting politicians and trade unionists from
  sitting on jury panels for public office appointments (directive of the
  Prime Minister, 17 December 1993, instigated by judgement no.416/
  1993 of the Constitutional Court). New, semi-independent, bodies were
  also created, such as the *Agenzia per l'ambiente* (Environmental Agency)
  and the *Autorità per l'informatica* (Information Technology Agency)
  (legislative directive no.39/1993).
- *The reduction of the scope of the public sector.* The number of ministries
  was reduced, some by referendum, some under law no.537/1993. Further
  reductions, envisaged by this law, were prevented by conflicts inside the
  executive and the hostility of Parliament towards any kind of 'Jacobean'
  reform. Many public bodies and local organisations were also eliminated.
  The legal status of other groups was altered, to make way for
  privatisation. The first step towards privatisation was taken through law
  no.356/1990 for state-sector banks. This was followed by law no.359/1992,
  relating to the large state-holding groups, such as IRI, ENI and ENEL.
  Some privatisation was achieved, but it did not have the desired effect,
  namely the creation of a wider shareholding base. Instead, it produced
  a rapid consolidation of control by a limited number of private groups.
- *A change in status of personnel* who, except for certain categories
  (magistrates, directors, university professors), became employed mainly
  on a contractual basis, and subject to private-sector type efficiency
  norms. This did not, however, solve the problems in the upper echelons.
- *The reorganisation of administrative procedures*, initiated by law
  no.241/1990, but still on the drawing board. Only a few modifications
  have, thus far, been adopted into law. Nevertheless, more than 50
  regulations for the simplification of procedures originated with this law,
  including some dealing with the regulation of financing and supplies.
  Other regulations were focused on liberalising economic activity
  previously under state control (d.p.r. Nos.407 and 411/1994).
- *Modifying the system of controls.* In the same way that law no.142/1990

limited the number of controls on the decisions of local bodies, this also occurred at the regional level (legislative directive no.40 and 476/1993) and at the level of the state (law no.20/1994). Furthermore, controls on public administration management were widened, and entrusted to the Court of Accounts. Finally, controlling bodies were introduced into all administrative agencies, under the secondary supervision of the Court.

* *Altering the links between the administration and citizens*. Norms governing access to administrative documents were introduced, the first being rather restrictive (d.p.r. no.352/1992), but its successor being far more open (d.p.r. no.130/1994). With the Public Services Charter, laws protecting the rights of users of public services were promised both in specific sectors, such as health (legislative directive no.502/1992), and more generally (directive of the Prime Minister, 21 February 1994).

This phase of reform was interrupted in 1994 by an event of the utmost constitutional and political importance. A primarily majoritarian electoral system was introduced for the Chamber of Deputies under laws no.276/1993 and no.277/1993, following a similar change enacted for the Senate via a referendum held in April of that year (the rules on electoral campaigning were also changed under law no.515/1993). However, the form of government was not amended in any way. This partly explains why, in the first attempt at a 'majoritarian' government, Prime Minister Silvio Berlusconi was forced to bargain and compromise as much as previous governing coalitions. Furthermore, this government witnessed a retreat from the ideal of separating clearly the executive from the administration, not only in the sectors traditionally most affected by political influence (such as the RAI broadcasting agency), but also for autonomous or nominally independent groups, such as the Bank of Italy.

At the same time, the priority given to administrative reform by previous governments was downgraded. There was no mention of administrative reform in the government's 'one hundred day programme', save one ambivalent reference: the revision of the new norms governing contracts, whose aim was to reduce 'contractual obstacles', produced instead a reduction in the administration's power and an increase in conflict through judicial action. Moreover, the commitment to economic liberalisation was contradicted by the introduction of controls and permits by the government control agency, *l'Osservatorio*. The goal of reducing the public sector had some success. Certain bodies were reorganised, although the restructuring of ministries under law no.537/1993 was abandoned. The main preoccupation of the governing coalition was, instead, with the acquisition and occupation of existing institutional positions, rather than their rationalisation and reduction.

FINANCIAL AND ADMINISTRATIVE REFORM   203

The subsequent government, led by Lamberto Dini, set itself a few objectives: further financial reorganisation (if possible), reform of the regional electoral system; the reorganisation of the pension system; and the guarantee of equal access to the media during electoral campaigns. Administrative reform, therefore, was not at the centre of its programme. Nevertheless, some measures were taken of relevance to the administration. For example, certain steps were taken regarding the regulation of public services (law no. 483/1995) as already required by law no.537/1993. Furthermore, under decree no.163/1995 (converted into law no.273/1995), the introduction of charters of public service was made obligatory in certain sectors of public service (schools, health, electrical energy for example).

In short, there was no systematic reform of the public apparatus – in particular the administrative sector – either before or after the 11th legislature . Instead, there was a series of initiatives (such as law no.241/1990 on administrative procedure) put together with varying degrees of effectiveness. However, these were still isolated cases, in so far as they were not co-ordinated with other structural reforms, and were not followed up by a period of committed implementation, either at the regulatory or administrative level. Thus, even if the Italian system has experienced the introduction of a large number of innovative norms, aimed at improving the functioning and transparency of administrative activity, the effects have not been as positive as expected.[13] In particular, a lack of incisive action in the political sphere has reduced the savings envisaged under law no.537/1993 (which accompanied the 1994 finance law), resulting in an increasing call for investment by subscribers in government bonds as of the summer of 1994.[14]

WHY IS PUBLIC ADMINISTRATION IN A WORSE STATE THAN FINANCE?

At this point, it is worth returning to our initial question: why, if public administration is in a worse state than finance, has this not been remedied, particularly when it is precisely in this area that one of the fundamental forces for financial restructuring is to be found? There are various possible answers to this question, some more convincing than others.

To begin with, it is not convincing to argue that, while the costs arising from problems in public accounts are quite evident, it is difficult to calculate the costs caused by the absence of administrative reform. Leaving aside the parameters set by the EU, this argument is doubtful for two reasons. First, there are two types of administrative cost analysis available today: direct economic costs (which derive from taxes) and indirect costs, such as non-paid taxes, time-wastage, failure of services – in short, any dysfunction which forces citizens, if they have the means, to resort to private alternatives to the public sector (which continues to incur costs regardless). Second, the belief that the Italian administration is less efficient than those in other EU states has been frequently demonstrated through institutional comparison. This view has become increasingly prevalent amongst Italians, as shown by the abrogative referendums of 1993, where a clear majority called for the abolition of parts of the administrative apparatus. Furthermore, initial attempts to measure the attitudes of public service users have all unearthed considerable dissatisfaction.

Explanations which highlight the exceptional nature of the governments of the eleventh legislature are more convincing. Indeed, in contrast with previous governments, there was only minimal intervention from political parties in the distribution of ministerial posts. That this was an aspect common to both governments was confirmed by their respective prime ministers who both reaffirmed 'the decisional autonomy of governing bodies in relation to the role that parties exercised earlier in surpassing all reasonable bounds that might be deemed to be within the sphere of the public interest'. Another communication, of 26 May 1993, from Ciampi to his ministers, underlined his desire for a united government, in the face of 'a delicate and difficult context ... [for] this government, and one which is different from the coalitions which preceded it'.

Yet, this argument is of too general a nature to explain satisfactorily why particular attention has been paid to administrative reform only under certain governments, and why the consequent solutions have been such that the same fate awaits them as the temples of Central America: of gradually becoming covered in the very vegetation that they had briefly replaced. To explain this phenomenon, two factors need to be considered: the first derives from the difference in costs and benefits in the reforms of finance and the administration; the second relates to the interests of those responsible for protecting the general interest.

As for the first, it is arguable that the administration is difficult to reorganise, and the effects of reorganisation are hard to see, because it is a structure with many centres, inevitably leading to fragmentation, whereas finance is a unitary phenomenon, with centralisation of its instruments of function and control. The source of revenue is singular (national wealth), as is responsibility for the financial balance and the deficit (which the EU assigns to central governments). Moreover, it is possible – as was demonstrated by the Ciampi government – to reduce and rationalise public spending 'without implementing cuts, at least in terms of eliminating waste in public services', in other words 'by making each lira spent on public services more efficient' (Declaration of Programme, 6 May 1993).

As for the second factor, any attempt at administrative reorganisation confronts two major obstacles. First, changing the criteria for the

FINANCIAL AND ADMINISTRATIVE REFORM   205

organisation and functioning of these bodies will inevitably conflict with vested interests, especially those – widespread in Italy – which view public posts as sinecures. This can be seen in the case of the recruitment of people to jobs without open competition (running counter to Art.97 of the Constitution, which requires a meritocratic and egalitarian system). In general, the opposition of a large number of public employees – or at least the better organised of them – to changes in their employment status has deflected the process of reform and changed the terms of reference (something to which the mass media has also contributed): instead of *administrative* reform, people now speak of *bureaucratic* reform.

Second, while the inefficiency of public services has adverse consequences for most people, it nevertheless has advantages for those responsible for providing those services, and whose utility would be reduced were the administration able to function efficiently. The best example (although others could be cited, such as commercial licensing) was the press campaign promoted by the National Union of Driving Instructors (*Unione nazionale delle autoscuole*) against the simplification of the driving test, on the basis of the (claimed) negative effects that would be caused by the proposed measures. This is a case of intransigent hostility to reform caused by vested interests, which have made decision-making procedures more complex and arduous.

It remains to be explained, however, why a reform so likely to damage individual interests, such as financial reform, met with so little opposition. The majority of recent governments, rather than reforming finance for the purpose of governing, have given the impression of governing for the purpose of reforming finance, in order to resolve the crisis in the state accounts inherited from previous governments. This focus depended a great deal, to borrow a phrase from Giuliano Amato, on a climate of 'obvious financial crisis ... as a consequence of a lack of control', but also on two other factors: the emphasis placed on the renewal of public institutions, and the symbolism attached to such reform in the context of pressures from the EU.

The Changing Role of Public Institutions

In Italy, interest in the functioning and impartiality of public offices has never been strong. The Ministry of Public Administration has, in fact, been more responsive to the needs of its employees than to those of the administration and public service administration. Examples abound of it behaving more as an advocate for spending than as an agent of the Treasury, with requests for increases in salaries irrespective of the efficiency of the personnel and the quality of services provided to citizens and other users.

This situation changed under the Ciampi government, when the Minister

206   CRISIS AND TRANSITION IN ITALIAN POLITICS

for Public Administration, Sabino Cassese, targeted the interests of the 'clients' rather than those of the employees, something which was noticed immediately by the trade unions. Moreover, he reorganised the department so that its prime concerns were with its internal organisation, procedures and controls, rather than simply its staff. This altered role also emerged through an internal requirement of the Cabinet (directive of 30 November 1993) that the presentation of government amendments for discussion in Parliament should be preceded by a meeting of the Ministers of Public Administration and of the Budget if the amendments refer to the organisation and functioning of the administration (Art.17, §1). The Prime Minister, however, can defer analysis of measures which impinge on the government's general policy (Art.18, §1).

There has, therefore, been a change in role of the Ministry of Public Administration. which, 'for the first time has aligned its own objectives with the reduction of administrative costs'.[15] Nevertheless, as a ministerial task without portfolio, administrative reform has depended a great deal on the importance given to it by the Prime Minister, whatever the intentions of public administration ministers may have been. This probably explains the differing performances of the ministers who succeeded Cassese (Giuliano Urbani and Franco Frattini) because there was a decline in interest in administrative reform during the 12th legislature.[16]

The monitoring of public finance is rather different, resting, as it does, with the Ministry of the Treasury. The Treasury must check the coherence of government decisions and their effects across different sectors. To this end, every measure that incurs costs must receive its assent (Articles 17 and 18 of internal regulations). At the political level, the extent of the Treasury's importance is reflected in the number of times a Minister of the Treasury has been called upon to lead a government.[17]

Nevertheless, the Treasury has, in the past, often yielded to pressure from particular interests. For example, it has often allowed non–accountable spending to occur, or has used resources acquired through debt as an instrument to finance direct aid (rather than investments). The detrimental effects of this laxity, however, have been offset by the role played by a stricter guardian of public finances, the Bank of Italy. The Bank of Italy has never failed to convey to political institutions and the public the seriousness of the state of the public accounts. A glance at the *Considerazione finali* of the Governor of the Bank of Italy during the 1980s reveals demands for the relocation of financial procedures under the auspices of Art.81 (1981), and references to the chronic imbalance between income and spending and the need to balance the various items of current spending in the budget (1983). The financial rigour of the Bank has been greatly valued. The draft law presented by Giuliano Amato (Prime Minister 1992–93) which proposed

FINANCIAL AND ADMINISTRATIVE REFORM 207

the delegation of emergency economic and financial powers to the government, gave a prominent role to the Governor of the Bank of Italy. Following this, in 1993, the Governor of the Bank, Carlo Azeglio Ciampi, was asked to form a government, as was, in 1995, Lamberto Dini (who had been Director-General of the Bank before becoming Minister of the Treasury under Berlusconi in 1994).

A significant contribution to maintaining more rigour in public finance has also come from the Court of Accounts. In spite of widespread hostility to this new regime of control (based on the primacy of public accountability and management efficiency), the external controlling bodies gradually modified their perception of their own role. Proof of this can be seen through the consolidated orientation on the basis of which it sought the intervention of the Constitutional Court, in order to confirm the constitutional legitimacy of the spending laws approved by Parliament, but which the Court of Accounts considered to be lacking the necessary financial cover.

External Influence on Public Finance

The reorganisation of public finances cannot be explained purely by the widespread belief amongst institutions and broad sections of public opinion of its urgency, or by the high profile of the institutions responsible. External factors also played a role, especially pressure from the EU.

The launch of the EMS in 1979 – in which the Bank of Italy played a supporting role[18] – reimposed an external constraint on national monetary policy which had been in decline since the crisis of Bretton Woods in 1971. This clearly had far-reaching political implications. The discipline imposed on excessive deficits placed considerable pressure on member-states if they wished to enter the third phase of European Monetary Union (EMU). In the process, the power of central banks and bankers was increased. Convergence with the Maastricht criteria has also had considerable symbolic value. If one considers that adhesion to European integration has been one of the few constants in Italian foreign policy in the post-war period, and that the Maastricht Treaty offers the possibility of measuring governmental financial activity according to fixed parameters, the importance of European influence on Italian public finance becomes clear. The political and economic costs of exclusion from the single currency would be devastating for Italy, not only symbolically but possibly also for future financial rigour.[19] The financial markets make daily judgements on the policies of government which are no longer able to protect themselves from such external pressures by regulating the flow of capital. As Guido Carli has confirmed, the policy constraint imposed by the EU fulfils 'a positive function with respect to the revitalisation of public finance'.[20]

None of this, however, is applicable to the administration, even it is

208 CRISIS AND TRANSITION IN ITALIAN POLITICS

crucial that its problems are resolved if Italy is to enjoy the benefits of European integration, without coming into conflict with other countries which are better organised and have a more developed capacity to support the interests of their citizens in the European arena. It follows that, if support from the public administration is absent, it is improbable that financial reorganisation will be sufficient to ensure a satisfactory government of the *res publica*. For this reason, a session on the functioning of public administration might be usefully included in the EU's intergovernmental conference.

NOTES

Giacinto della Cananea would like to thank Professor Sabino Cassese for his helpful comments on a draft version of this article, but as the author, G. della Cananea, takes full responsibility for any errors and omissions.

1. For a fuller analysis of these issues, see G. della Cananea, *Indirizzo e controllo della finanza pubblica* (Bologna: Il Mulino 1996).
2. The link between finance and administration is explored in M. T. Salvemini, 'Riforma dell'amministrazione e riduzione del disavanzo nella politica di bilancio del governo Ciampi', *Politica economica* 11/1 (1995) p.4.
3. See S. Cassese, 'L'inefficienza della pubblica amministrazione e i suoi costi', *Rivista trimestrale di scienza dell'amministrazione*, 1989, p.71ff. On the role of political parties see P. Scoppola, *La Repubblica dei partiti. Profilo storico della democrazia in Italia* (Bologna: Il Mulino 1992). Also of use are D. Della Porta, *Lo scambio occulto. Casi di corruzione politica in Italia* (ibid. 1993) and M. D'Alberti and R. Finocchi (eds.) *Corruzione e sistema istituzionale* (ibid. 1994).
4. See Carlo Azeglio Ciampi, *Un metodo per governare* (Bologna: Il Mulino 1996) pp.105ff.
5. The legal instruments adopted to keep spending and the deficit under control are examined in S. Cassese, *La nuova costituzione economica* (Bari: Laterza 1995) pp.142ff. On controls, the most recent and accurate study is U. Allegretti (ed.) *I controlli amministrativi* (Bologna: Il Mulino 1995).
6. The law creating a single budget line for the public administration (law of 29 Oct. 1984, no.702) was also spared being subject to the abrogative referendum. Art.75 of the Constitution grants immunity from this only for financial acts, fiscal laws and the budget. However, the Constitutional Court extended this privilege to financing laws and 'related' laws (judgement no.2/1994 in *Giurisprudenza costituzionale*, 1994, pp.9ff., with a comment by G. Gemma), and subsequently to law no.702/1984, because – in the Court's view – these laws also affected the use of available resources (judgement no.12/1995, ibid. 1995, pp.54ff.).
7. For further details, see D. Franco, *L'espansione della spesa pubblica in Italia* (Bologna, Il Mulino 1992), G. Morcaldo, *La finanza pubblica in Italia* (ibid. 1993), L. Bernardi (ed.) *La finanza pubblica italiana. Rapporto 1995* (ibid. 1995) and A. Monorchio (ed.) *La finanza pubblica italiana dopo la svolta del 1992* (ibid. 1996) (which includes the U-turn of the Amato government).
8. An example of the overlapping competences of the government and the Treasury is provided by the U-turn effected by the law of 30 June 1994, no.423 (A.S. no.526, 12th legislature) in which financing was traced using a global figure, without taking into account the limit set by the finance law on the rate of redemption of loans, and the limits to such engagements.
9. Giuliano Amato, *Due anni al Tesoro* (Bologna: Il Mulino 1990) provides a good account of the work of the Treasury minister.

FINANCIAL AND ADMINISTRATIVE REFORM   209

10. Public spending reached 56.6 per cent of GDP in 1993, then fell to 52.5 per cent in 1994; at the same time, fiscal pressure (taxation as a proportion of GDP) dropped from 44.3 per cent to 43.9 per cent. On the progress of the deficit, see Table 1. In the programme for Italy's presidency of the EU (Jan.–June 1996) the Prime Minister, Lamberto Dini, drew on the forecasts of the Dpef (the government's rolling medium-term financial strategy) from 1995 to 1997, which predicted a reduction of the national deficit from 5.8 per cent to 4.4 per cent of GDP in 1997, and to 3 per cent in 1998, a figure which would prevent Italy from joining the third phase of EMU.

11. The autonomy of the Bank of Italy with respect to the Treasury is described in M.T. Salvemini, *Le politiche del debito pubblico* (Bari: Laterza 1994) pp.178ff.

12. The administrative reforms undertaken during the eleventh legislature are described in N. Lupo, 'Le deleghe del governo Amato in Parlamento', *Rivista trimestrale di diritto pubblico*, 1994, pp.85ff.; and in C. Lacava and G. Vecchi, 'L'amministrazione nella XI legislatura', *Riformare la pubblica amministrazione* (Turin: Fondazione Agnelli 1995), pp.157ff. For a critical account, see S. Cassese, 'La riforma amministrativa all'inizio della quinta Costituzione dell'Italia unità', *Il Foro italiano*, 1994, V, p.9 and G. della Cananea, 'Reforming the State: The Policy of Administrative Reform in Italy under the Ciampi Government', *West European Politics* 19/2 (April 1996) p.321ff.

13. For further analyses of administrative reform, see S. Cassese, 'Hypotheses on the Italian Administrative System', *West European Politics* 16/2 (April 1993) pp.316ff, G. Capano, *L'improbabile riforma* (Bologna: Mulino 1993) and S. Cassese and C. Franchini (eds.) *L'amministrazione pubblica italiana. Un profilo* (ibid. 1994). On the independent authorities see, S. Cassese and C. Franchini (eds.) *I garanti delle regole* (ibid. 1996).

14. On the 12th legislature, the analyses provided by the 'Osservatorio sull'attività normativa del Governo' are quite useful, coordinated by G. Vesperini, and published every two months in *Giornale di diritto amministrativo* from 1995. The report on the six months of the Berlusconi government is in *Vita italiana. Documenti e informazioni*, 1994, nos.8–12 (on p.15, the programmatic proposals are outlined, and p.60 contains a section on actions relevant to personnel).

15. E. D'Albergo, 'Rendimento istituzionale e logiche di azione organizzativa nella politica di bilancio', in F. Bassanini and S. Merlini (eds.) *Crisi fiscale e indirizzo politico* (Bologna: Il Mulino 1995) p.744.

16. See S. Cassese, 'Il difficile mestiere di Ministro della funzione pubbliche', in *Riformare la pubblica amministrazione* (note 12) p.135ff; and P. Marconi, 'Gli interventi di riforma delle amministrazioni pubbliche nella politica di bilancio per il 1994–96', *Politica economica* 11/1 (1995) p.99ff.

17. These have, in the past, included Giovanni Goria, Bettino Craxi and Amintore Fanfani. More recently, Giuliano Amato, Minister of the Treasury under Goria, was Prime Minister 1993–93; and Lamberto Dini, Minister of the Treasury under Berlusconi, was Prime Minister 1995–96, while remaining at the Treasury.

18. The commitment of the Bank of Italy to the formation of the EMS was shown by its then governor Paolo Baffi, 'Il sistema monetario europeo e la partecipazione dell'Italia', in P. Ciocca (ed.) *La monetà e l'economia. Il ruolo delle banche centrali* (Bologna: Il Mulino 1983) pp.261ff.

19. On the importance of the European constraint, see A. Manzella, 'Il 'vincolo europeo' sul governo dell'economia', in *Studi in memoria di Franco Piga*, Vol.2 (Milano: Giuffrè) p.1491ff.

20. This phrase is taken from the memoirs of Guido Carli, according to whom external influence plays a greater role in Italy than in other nations. This is because 'the market economy, open to the outside, is always in a precarious position, fragile, exposed to the continual effects of an autarchic mentality. External influence has maintained Italy's position amongst the free nations. Our choosing this influence is a constant that has lasted throughout the post-war period.' This choice was 'born out of pessimism based on the conviction that the basic instincts of Italian society, left to develop naturally, would have carried our country elsewhere'. See Guido Carli, *Cinquant'anni di vita italiana* (in collaboration with P. Peluffo) (Bari: Laterza 1993).

[43]

**Hollowing and Hardening the State: European
Integration and the Italian State**

Vincent Della Sala
Carleton University
Department of Political Science
Ottawa, Ontario
Canada K1S 5B6
vdsala@ccs.carleton.ca

Paper presented to the Annual Meeting of the American Political Science
Association, San Francisco 29 August - 1 September 1996

It is somewhat ironic that shortly after scholars were calling for the state to be "brought back in" as a central focus of inquiry, a number of volumes have emerged that have contemplated its demise and possible disappearance. What is at the heart of works with titles such as, "What Future for the State?", "After the Nation State", and "The Crisis of the State" is the question of whether national states continue to have the capacity to organise collective responses to social and political demands.[1] There have emerged two broad, and not exclusive, themes in the discussion of the state in advanced industrialised societies. The first concentrates on the "hollowing out" of state authority and capacity. While not denying that the state will remain an important political and discursive arena, these arguments emphasise the displacement of national state authority away from national states towards other levels of governance and to parts of civil society. A second set of arguments highlight the attempts to strengthen certain decision-making institutions within state structures, especially the executive and its agencies. In this instance, it is not the future of the national state that is in question but the balance of powers between state institutions so that Robert Dahl's democratic dilemma between system effectiveness and representation is decided in favour of those institutions that are more appropriate for the former.[2] As a consequence, it is much more difficult for societal interests to find access points and to penetrate decision-making structures.

The aim of this paper is to bring together these two sets of concerns to argue that the "hollowing out" of the state and the "hardening of its shell" are complementary processes; that is, the displacement of national state authority requires state structures that are less permeable to penetration from interests and demands emanating from civil society. In turn, a "hollow" national state becomes the basis for claims for less inclusive representation in decision-making and for a reduced space for policy-making discourse. The paper will look at the case of what has been called a "weak" and permeable" state to explore whether it is indeed the case that national states are becoming hollow entities coated by a hard shell. It will focus on budgetary politics in Italy in light of the convergence criteria for entry into the single currency established by the Treaty on European Union (TEU).

If Harold Lasswell's claim that the essence of politics is about who gets what, when and how, then budgeting is the quintessential political activity. By definition, it is about making choices that represent the values, priorities and structures that are prized in a particular society. How these choices are made and the relative authority of the structures that make them may tell us something about state capacity for economic management. Increasingly, these choices are made by national states whose economies are highly integrated into international financial markets, and therefore, sensitive to the capital movements.[3] The world of international finance is often described using terms that leave no doubt about its velocity and ability to transform economic, social and political structures. It conjures images of a Darwinian struggle where only the

---

[1] P. Evans, D. Rueschmeyer and T. Skocpol, eds., *Bringing the State Back In* (Cambridge: Cambridge University Press); Special Issue of Daedulus on, "What Future for the Nation State?", *Daedulus*, 124:2 (Summer 1995); Special Issue of Political Studies on, "Contemporary Crisis of the Nation State", *Political Studies*, 42 (1994); P. McCarthy and E. Jones, eds. *Disintegration or Transformation? The Crisis of the State in Indistrialised Societies* (New York: St. Matin's Press, 1995).

[2] Robert Dahl, "A Democratic Dilemma: System Effectiveness and Citizen Participation", *Political Science Quarterly*, 109:1 (Spring 1994), 23-34.

[3] Richard O'Brien, *The End of Geography* (London: Routledge, 1992); J. Camilieri and J. Falk, *The End of Sovereignty?* (Aldershot: Edward Elgar, 1992).

quickest, smartest, most cunning and the strongest will survive. National governments are divided into the virtuous and the condemned, the credible and the waverers. They must operate on two fronts in making public policy decisions: first, they must create the conditions to maximise access to this financial world; second, they must provide rapid, coherent decisive policy responses once they have opened themselves up to this environment. Even the quickest, most decisive and "strongest" national states will see their capacity for economic management constrained in the "borderless" world. Moreover, the more intrusive and interventionist state action, the more likely that the national state will not be a welcome member of the world of international finance.

This raises the question of how a national state that is not known for its rapid and coherent decision-making makes budgetary choices in a world of the quick and the dead. Italy provides an opportunity to examine how "weak" states survive in the interdependent global economy. As we will see shortly, it is often described as a "weak" state, lacking the capacity to aggregate demands into coherent policy programmes. Moreover, it is highly integrated into the global economy; and more specifically, it now operates within a regional economy whose borders have been almost entirely removed for capital mobility. In the case of budgeting, it has one of the highest debt-to-GDP ratios amongst OECD countries; and it faces great challenges to meet the convergence criteria set out in the TEU. The aim of our discussion is to examine how Italian policy-makers have responded to these challenges, and to what extent pressures to weaken state capacity for economic management have affected states that are known to already be "weak" in this respect.

Italian budgetary politics is a useful case study in that it allows for the exploration of the displacement of state authority through regional polities; and the convergence criteria create pressures to reduce the role of the state in many areas of social and economic life. As Wildavsky points out, budgetary politics reflect the distribution of power, and the authority of the government is expressed by its ability to make and approve its budgetary choices.[4] The Italian budgetary process will reveal the weakness of the Italian executive and the ability of societal interests to capture parts of the decision-making structures. European integration raises the qyestion of whether a permeable state will give way to less inclusive decision-making structures.

The discussion will be divided into two main sections. The first will explore some of the arguments about the future of the national state and make the case for hollow, hard states. It will illustrate that Italy has been characterised as a "weak", "permeable" state, captured by sectional interests. The second section will provide some background to the Italian case, and will focus on budgetary politics in light of the criteria for entry in a European single currency set in the Treaty on European Union (TEU). It will demonstrate that budgetary politics in Italy reveal both a "hollowing out", as further authority is assumed by EU commitments or by market forces and principles; and a "hardening" of the state as pressures to create more timely, coherent policy-making have made it more difficult for societal interests to penetrate state structures.

HOLLOW STATES WITH HARD SHELLS

It is interesting to note that discussion about the state in advanced industrialised societies has shifted from a concern in the 1980s with understanding and identifying different types of states - such the distinction between "weak" and "strong" states, or

---

[4] Aaron Wildavsky, *Budgeting: a comparative theory of budgetary processes* (Boston: Little, Brown and Co., 1975), xii-xiii.

between pluralist and corporatist states - and with exploring the limits of state autonomy, to the more recent questions of whether there is a future at all for national states. Most of the change in focus may be understood by the emergence of a number of challenges that have led to a displacement of national state authority in decision-making: economic interdependence, financial deregulation, technological change, greater capital mobility, and greater consolidation of regional economic and trading blocs.

It is not surprising that increased economic interdependence and globalization has contributed to the generation of an intense argument about the future of the national state. On the one hand, arguments about the continued importance of the role of national states in the global economy persist, and not simply amongst realist and neo-realist scholars of international relations. States continue to be the only vehicle that can make authoritative decisions at the transnational level. Moreover, their role is enhanced by capital mobility as they are the only form of regulation of economic and social life that may deal effectively with the demands generated by an interdependent global economy. The emphasis on "national competitiveness" enhances states rather than diminishes their authority.[5] In addition, while the state may be losing its capacity to act in some area such as control of capital movements, it is trying to enhance its powers in others such as the control of the movement of people, immigration and law and order.[6]

A number of works have begun to address this issue by suggesting that we are witnessing the "hollowing out of the state".[7] None would argue that national states have become obsolete or will disappear in the near future, as is the case with enthusiasts of alternative structures such as Kenichae Ohmae.[8] But there is widespread agreement that state authority to affect outcomes in civil society has been curtailed in many areas of economic and social life.[9] As Susan Strange argues, "State authority has leaked away, upwards, sideways and downwards. In some matters, it seems to have gone nowhere, just evaporated."[10] The sources of this displacement are traced back to processes that have encouraged or created greater capital mobility and economic interdependence. This has led, in part, to the shifting of political authority upwards to supranational organisations; downwards to regional and local governments seen as better situated to provide responses in areas such as training and education[11]; sideways to new polities such as the European Union whose emerging federal processes have assumed many of the responsibilities assigned to national states. In addition, state authority has disappeared as elements of civil society have assumed (or re-assumed) the capacity to

---

[5] Vincent Gable, "The Diminished State: A Study in the Loss of Economic Power", *Daedulus*, 124:2 (Spring 1995), 24; Philip Cerny, "The limits of deregulation", *European Journal of Political Research*, 19 (1991), 181-184.

[6] It is useful to understand the displacement of state authority by emphasising "state capacity" which Michael Mann refers to. "The capacity of state to actually penetrate civil society, and to implement logistically political decisions throughout the realm. See: Michael Mann, "The Autonomous Power of the State: Its Origins, Mechanisms and Results," *Archives Europeenes de Sociologie*, 25 (1984), 189.

[7] Susan Strange, "The Defective State," *Daedulus*, 124:2 (Spring 1995), 55-75; Bob Jessop, "Towards a Schumpeterian Workfare State?" *Studies in Political* Economy, 40 (Spring 1993), 7-39; R.A.W. Rhodes, "The Hollowing Out of the British State." *Political Quarterly*, 65:2 (April 1994), 138-151.

[8] Kenichi Ohmae, "The Rise of the Region State," *Foreign Affairs*, 72 (1993), 78-87.

[9] Manfred Bienefeld, "Financial Deregulation: Disarming the Nation State," *Studies in Political Economy*, 37 (Spring 1992), 31-58.

[10] Strange, *op.cit.*, 56.

[11] There also is a heightening of regional and local identities as a response to the erosion of national state authority.

make decisions in a number of areas. The most obvious instance in this respect has been the emphasis on markets as a means of economic and social regulation; but it also includes attempts to have the "third sector" or non-governmental structures replace both markets and states in the delivery of many services.[12] The result is that national states have become "defective"; or, "Like old trees, hollow in the middle, showing signs of weakness and vulnerability to storm, drought, or disease, yet continuing to grow leaves, new shoots, and branches."[13]

The "hollowing out" analogy provides a number of useful insights. First, it suggests that changing state capacity is a process that takes place at a number of different levels; and can lead to a focus on what state capacities remain within the core, and what has been transferred or eroded. It highlights that there is a close relationship between pressures to change the balance of powers between national states and sub-national governments, and those to change boundaries between states and other forms of social regulation such as markets. Second, Strange's description highlights that even as states are being "hollowed out", they may assume new responsibilities and may try to respond to emerging political demands. National states will continue to search for a basis for authority as their capacity to regulate social and economic life is eroded; but this is part of processes that will continue to develop.

One area that the literature has not developed is that which focuses on the political and institutional features of the "hollowed out" state. Although some mention is made about the continuing importance of executive authority, the link between displacement of state authority and the type of state structures that will emerge has not been addressed. On the other hand, part of the literature that has looked at what kind of state governs in industrialised societies has focused on elements of executive authority, leading partly to notions "weak" and "strong" states. Weak states may be described as those that lack the capacity to "achieve the kinds of changes in society that their leaders sought to achieve through state planning, policies and actions."[14] The capacity of executives to make and implement policy decisions is seen as the key variable that places states at particular points on the weak-strong state spectrum.[15] Moreover, "strong" states were seen to be those that had clear distinctions between state and civil society, while those closer to the weak end of the spectrum tended to have a blurring of the lines between the two.[16] States that are subject to penetration by societal interests, it is argued, are less likely to have the capacity to implement the objectives set out by executives.

However, the link between the boundaries of executive authority and the "hollowing out" of the state has not been addressed entirely. As Vivien Schmidt points out, one response of the national state to international pressures has been, "[A] strengthening of executive authority vis-a-vis societal interests".[17] This is the case not simply because many of the consequences of economic interdependence and

---

[12] For instance, see: Paul Hirst, *Associative Democracy: new forms of economic and social governance* (Amherst, MA: University of Massachusetts Press, 1994).

[13] Strange, *op.cit.*, 57.

[14] J. Migdal, *Strong Societies and Weak States* (Princeton: Princeton University Press, 1988), pp. 4-5.

[15] John Zysman, *Governments, Markets and Growth* (Ithaca: Cornell University Press, 1983), 295-6.

[16] Peter Katzenstein, "Conclusion: Domestic Structures and Strategies of Foreign Economic Policy," in Peter Katzenstein, ed. *Between Power and Plenty* (Madison: University of Wisconsin Press, 1978), 322.

[17] Vivien Schmidt, "The New World Order, Incorporated: The Rise of Business and the Decline of the Nation State," *Daedulus*, 124:2 (Spring 1995), 86.

globalization fall within areas that are normally under the executive's jurisdiction.[18] It is also the case that inclusive, representative decision-making requires a broader consensus amongst a wide range of societal interests than that left simply to the executive and its agencies. Pressures for a "hollowing out" of the state would directly affect many of those interests; and any attempt to displace state authority would find obstacles in those institutions and structures that had been permeated by societal interests. Therefore, the paradoxical situation arises in that "weak" states would face greater problems in being "hollowed out"; while in "strong" states, where clear boundaries have been established between state and civil society, it is much easier to displace state authority and harder to mobilise resistance to "hollowing" out.

A number of works have argued that the displacement of state authority towards markets is not inevitable but the result of state actions, implying that not all states may be able to make and implement decisions that give greater space to markets in regulation social and economic life.[19] Andrew Gamble argues that a "free economy" requires a strong state to, amongst other things, limit the power of trade unions and quell resistance to changes to the welfare state.[20] Gamble's argument is a useful one but perhaps describing the state as "strong" may be a bit misleading. It suggests that state capacity to affect outcomes in civil society is enhanced. This may be the case in some instances but the overall effect of displacing state authority is that state capacity will be limited. It may seem that the state is "stronger" in that its impermeability to penetration from some societal groups has been enhanced. On the other hand, a "hollowed out" state has less capacity to penetrate civil society and regulate social and economic life.

It is more useful to speak of a state that is being "hollowed out" while its shell is being hardened. This implies that it becomes more difficult for societal interests to penetrate the state and affect decision-making. In fact, states must harden this shell before being hollowed out if they want to overcome resistance. For instance, seeking consensus from a broad range of groups that includes trade unions, students, and social movements on fiscal restraint and austerity will be difficult if decision-making structures are permeable and provide access and veto points. In turn, displacing state authority will help establish clear lines between the state and society, making it harder for societal interests to break through to permeate the hollowed out state.

The "hardening" of the shell takes on a number of forms that go beyond the strengthening of the executive with respect to more inclusive institutions. It also refers to the discourse of "post" politics which suggests that certain realms of decision-making are purely technical exercises with no feasible political alternatives. This may be the case in many member states of the EU, where discussion about market liberalisation, fiscal restraint and meeting the convergence criteria are presented as the only feasible choices for economic policy. Policy making becomes a "technical", not a political, exercise that is to be rendered immune from civil society, or at least certain interests. This is clearly the case with the use of the Bundesbank as the model central bank and instrument for

---

[18] For instance, a great deal of the literature on the "democratic deficit" in the European Union has focused on the fact that it is the executives of the member states that are involved in decision-making. See: Brigitte Boyce, "The Democratic Deficit of the European Community," *Parliamentary Affairs*, 46:4 (October 1993), 149-170..

[19] For instance, see: L. Pauly, *Opening Financial Markets* (Ithaca: Cornell University Press, 1988); T. Porter, *States, Markets and Regimes in Global Finance* (Basingstoke: Macmillan, 1993).

[20] Andrew Gamble, *The Free Economy and the Strong State* (London: Macmillan, 1988).

monetary policy: independent of political control, emphasis on fiscal restraint and pursuit of "sound money" policies.

Italy provides a good example to explore the complementary processes of the "hollowing out" and "hardening" of the shell of the state. As in other advanced industrialised states in the post-war period, the Italian state played an active and extensive part in the regulation of economic and social life. Moreover, beginning in the late 1960s and early 1970s, pressure from trade unions and other social movements led to a wide range of social and labour market policies that ensured a state protection of social and economic benefits.[21] This reflected another important change: the increasing penetration of decision-making structures by a wide range of social and economic interests. Italy was seen as the classic "weak" state in which the political authority of the executive was limited so that it could not achieve its policy objectives.[22] The result was a state that has been described as a "nonstate" state; that is, state structures that had been "captured" by such a broad range of societal interests that its authority was seriously curtailed.[23] This is especially the case in economic policy-making since the early 1970s as it is characterised as incremental, serving micro-sectional interests, and without any clarity or coherence. It is not that major policy decisions are not taken in as much as these decisions are not the product of processes and structures that can set clear objectives, establish procedures and instruments to achieve them and then use the instruments of government to implement them. Rather, they are incremental, reactive policies that do little to enhance the government's ability to anticipate and deal with socio-economic demands.[24]

Decision-making became more open and accessible to a wide range of social and political forces, including the opposition parties, in the period since the late 1960s.[25] Pressures for greater political participation and the continuing anomaly of Italian democracy - that is, the lack of an alternation in power - led to the full implementation of the Constitution, the dispersion of power and strict limits on the use of executive power. Both informal rules and the 1948 Constitution provided the basis for a very diffuse, inclusive pluralist policy-making structure. The problem was no longer that important policy decisions were avoided; rather, it was that the state did not have the capacity to

---

[21] Giancarlo Morcaldo, *La finanza pubblica in Italia* (Bologna: Il Mulino, 1993), 65-73.

[22] Alan Posner, "Italy: Dependence and Political Fragmentation," in Peter Katzenstein, ed. *Between Power and Plenty* (Madison: University of Wisconsin Press, 1978); Pippo Ranci, "Italy: the weak state," in F. Duchene and G. Shepherd, eds., *Managing Industrial Change in Westren Europe* (London: Frances Pinter, 1987).

[23] Gianfranco Pasquino argues that these interests have "permeated" the state. See: Gianfranco Pasquino, "Rappresentanza degli interessi, attivita dei lobby e processi decisonali: il case italiano di istituzioni permeabili," *Stato e Mercato*, 21 (December 1987), 403-29; Sergio Fabbrini makes the case that the state is a large arena for the negotiation of the distribution of public resources between private interests. See: Sergio Fabbrini, "Lo stato 'nonstato': L'Italia tra disaggregazione e federalismo," Paper presented to the Convegno Annuale della Societa Italiana Politica, Urbino, 13-15 June 1996.

[24] John Ikenberry argues that these are the essential components by which to assess the state strength or state capacity. See: John Ikenberry, "The irony of state strength: comparative responses to the oil shocks in the 1970s", *International Organization*, 40:1 (Winter 1986), p.136.

[25] Bruno Dente, "Le politiche pubbliche in Italia," in Bruno Dente, ed. *Le politiche pubbliche in Italia* (Bologna: Il Mulino, 1990).

set out clear objectives and pursue policies in a decisive, timely manner.[26] The open, consensual decision-making process allowed for a broad range of interests and micro-sectional demands to affect policy choices. In many cases, parts of the state were parcelled out to these interests and the political parties that represented them. The dispersion of power meant that it was difficult to locate the centre of political and policy decision-making. The result is that policy-making in Italy demonstrates many of the characteristics of what may be described as "weak states"; that is, those states that, "lack the ability to provide strong direction in steering the nation-state through troubled economic waters".[27]

The Italian Road to Europe

The European Dimension
        A state with weak economic management capacity, such as that in Italy, should be quite susceptible to the transforming forces of markets and supranational authority such as the European Union. This leads the discussion to a brief examination of the impact of European integration. The aim of this section is not to debate whether European integration is an economic or political project, or whether a federal European structure will eventually replace national state authority. Rather, it will simply provide a short description of some of the key developments in the last decade that have placed policy-making pressures on state authorities in Italy, as elsewhere in the European Union.
        It is generally accepted that the recession of the early 1980s created a consensus amongst member states and business elites in the European Community.[28] It centred on two key points that reflected a profound transformation in thinking about the role of national states in economic management. First, no single government could hope to pursue autonomous industrial and economic policies without raising serious doubts in financial markets; especially, if those states were part of arrangements such as the European Monetary System (EMS).[29] Second, there emerged a consensus on limited government intervention in the economy, as the primary objective should be promoting productivity and competitiveness through the control of inflation.[30] The emphasis was on a policy of "sound money", with the German Bundesbank as the model for removing politics from the making of monetary policy. This was a clear signal that the Keynesian commitment to demand management and full employment by national states was confined to the mythology of the post-war economic recovery of the 1950s and 1960s. The event that symbolised the new consensus was the *virage* of economic policy by the

---

[26] Sergio Ristuccia, "Quadro generale: potere dell'esecutivo, rapporti con gli altri levelli di governo, rapporto con le forze sociali," CNEL, ed., *Continuita e Rinnovamento della Politica Economica* (Roma: CNEL, 1992), 18-21.

[27] William Chandler and Herman Bakvis, "Federalism and the Strong-state/Weak-state Conundrum, " *Publius, 19 (Winter 1989)*, 60.

[28] David Cameron, "The 1992 Initiative: Causes and Consequences, " in A. Sbragia, ed. *Europolitics* (Washington: Brookings, 1992); Wayne Sandholtz and John Zysman, "Recasting the European Bargain, " *World Politics,* 42:1 (October-July 1990), 95-128; Anrew Moravcsik, "Negotiating the Single European Act," in R. Keohane and S. Hoffamn, eds. *The New European Community* (Boulder: Westview Press, 1991).

[29] Bernard Connelly and Jurgen Kroger. "Economic Convergence in the Integrating Community Economy and the Role of Economic Policies," *Recherches Economiques de Louvain,* 59:1-2 (1993), 37-40.

[30] Tommaso Padoa-Schioppa, *L'Europa verso l'unione monetaria* (Torino: Einaudi, 1992), xiv-xv.

Socialist government in France in 1983. The Mitterrand experience with an expansionary policy in the face of recession was rejected by the markets and the Socialists were faced with the choice of abandoning their policy or the EMS. The Socialists opted for the former and embarked on a path that would see France become one of the strongest proponent of economic and monetary union.

The recession of the early 1980s, the policy shift in France, conservative governments in Germany and Britain, and mobilisation by European business elites helped generate support for the completion of the internal market in the mid-1980s. The completion of the internal market galvanised efforts to liberalise the movement of goods, capital, and to a lesser extent, people, not only across EC borders but also within the member states. Many member states had to take policy measures to prepare their own internal markets for the greater competition that the SEA would bring, and to conform to European directives. The liberalisation of economic activity within and across European borders helped generate momentum to go further and aim for full economic and monetary convergence. There is an economic debate as to whether the completion of the internal market required or resulted in monetary union. It certainly created the political conditions that made it easier for political leaders in the late 1980s to consider economic and monetary union by the end of the century.

The negotiations that led to the commitment to achieve economic and monetary union enshrined in the Maastricht Treaty were long and intense, but they were based on a few widely shared assumptions. First, that the room for manoeuvre for national governments in monetary policy was limited and that their commitment to policies of "sound money" - that is, low inflation, low government debt, control of public finances, and to market efficiencies - was tested almost daily by international financial markets. In practice, this meant that countries that were suspected of wavering in their policy of sound money were sources of frequent speculation as to whether they could maintain their position within the EMS. Solutions were sought in binding national states to stronger commitments to maintaining "sound money" policies. Second, the negotiations leading to economic and monetary union in the Maastricht Treaty assumed that there would be structures to monitor that convergence of economic policies was taking place in the transition to a single currency, and long after.

Both these assumptions led to two fundamental features of economic and monetary union that will accelerate the transformation of economic management in national states: the so-called "convergence criteria" and multilateral surveillance.[31] The convergence criteria reflect the consensus on "sound money" policies. Any member state that wishes to e part of the single currency must have public deficits at 3 percent of GDP (or making significant progress in that direction); public debt at 60 percent of GDP; and inflation at no higher than 1.5 percent of the three best performing countries. In preparation for monetary unions, the central banks in member states will have be made independent of direct government control, with the German Bundesbank serving as the model. The Commission and the Council will be charged with implementing a series of procedures that will monitor closely the policies and their outcomes in the member states so that these may be moving closer to convergence. All member states have had to submit multi-year convergence programmes that details budgetary and policy expectations and objectives. These are scrutinised by the Commission along with other member states through the Council. The convergence programmes are supplemented

---

[31] Alexander Italianer, "Convergence in Europe: State of Affairs," in A. Wildavsky & E. Zapico-Goni. eds., *National Budgeting for Economic and Monetary Union* (Dordecht: Martinus Nijhoff, 1993).

by annual reports by each country. Member states that are not performing well in terms of economic convergence are issued recommendations by the Council, the Commission and after 1994, the European Monetary Institute. In addition to this, in preparation for monetary union, there is an annual publication of a list of countries that are deemed to have "excessive deficits". These close surveillance mechanisms of government economic management will be even more acute if and when monetary union is achieved. One might argue that the issuing if reports and recommendations carries little threat of sanction by the European authorities. However, they are signals that international markets respond to, and the threat of sanction here is in the form of capital flight.

Although the Maastricht Treaty did provide for a social chapter, the essence of economic and monetary union is to enshrine the consensus that was formed in the mid-1980s around limited government intervention in the economy and limited policy autonomy for member states. It may be described as an economic constitution for Europe that closely binds its members to pursuing a clearly defined course of economic management. There is nothing in the Treaty that forces governments to adhere to its economic and monetary criteria. However, given the close interdependence of European economies and their integration in world financial markets, few governments could risk the sanctions that might accrue for being "unconstitutional" in their economic policies.[32]

Italian Budgetary Politics

Italy has struggled to bring its public finances under control for about twenty years but it has met little success as its level of public debt has grown at a significant rate as annual deficits accumulated throughout the 1980s.[33] The figures in Table 1 reveal that there was a significant jump in public deficit levels between 1970 and 1975; and that it is not until 1992 that there is a noticeable trend to drop below the 10 per cent figure. The jump in the early 1970s may be traced to two developments. The first was economic slowdown in the wake of the first oil shock after nearly a quarter century of significant economic growth. The second, and related source, was that the economic slowdown highlighted a number of the social policies that were won by the labour movement in the unrest of the late 1960s and early 1970s. Student and labour movements secured a number of concessions that included the protection of incomes, a generous pension scheme for wage earners, health services and access to university.[34] The result was that there would be in place a number of structural demands on public expenditures, many of which, such as income maintenance programmes, would be particularly sensitive to economic slowdowns. The figures in Tables 2 and 3 indicate that this is indeed the case when looking at social policy expenditures during the recessions of the early 1980s and again in the early 1990s.

---

[32] Stephen Gill, "The Emerging World Order and European Change: The Political Economy of European Union," in Ralph Miliband and Leo Panitch, eds. *Socialist Register 1992* (London: Merlin Press, 1992).
[33] Camera dei Deputati. Servizio Studi. "Debito pubblico e fabbisogno: Evoluzione e politiche di rientro (1983-1994)", *Documentazione e ricerche*, XII Legislatura, n.35 (September 1994), p. 3-6.
[34] Daniele Franco. *L'espansione della spesa pubblica in Italia (1960-1990)*, (Bologna: Il Mulino, 1993), 35-50.

Table 1 - Public Debt and Deficit (Percentage of GDP)

	Public Deficit	Public Debt	Primary Balance**
1970	3.7	38.0	2.1
1975	11.6	57.6	8.1
1980	8.5	57.7	3.2
1981	11.4	59.9	5.2
1982	11.3	64.9	4.2
1983	10.6	70.0	3.1
1984	11.6	75.2	3.6
1985	12.6	82.3	4.6
1986	11.6	86.3	3.1
1987	11.0	90.5	3.1
1988	10.7	92.6	2.6
1989	9.9	95.6	1.0
1990	10.9	97.8	1.3
1991	10.2	101.4	0.0
1992	9.5	108.0	-1.9
1993	9.6	117.3	-2.6
1994	9.0	121.4	-1.7
1995	7.5	122.9	-3.5
1996*	5.9	122.7	-4.3
1997*	4.4	121.1	-5.4
1998*	2.6	117.9	-6.4

* Bank of Italy estimates
** Primary balance removes interest payments from calculation of expenditures and revenues.
Source: Data collected from annual report to parliament by the Treasury and Budget ministries;
        and from data presented by the Governor of the Bank of Italy, Antonia Fazio to the
        Interministerial Committee on Economic Planning in: Banca d'Italia, *Bollettino
        Economico*, n.25 (October 1995), 152-155.

It is not surprising, given the consistently high levels of public deficits, that Italy would eventually have high levels of public debt. The first column in Table 1 reveals that by the time Italy agreed to the convergence criteria in the TEU, its public debt to GDP ratio was at about 100 per cent, with little sign of significant decrease in the horizon. In fact, even after the level of public deficit begins to show a consistent decline after 1992, debt levels continue to rise (albeit at a slower rate). This reflects the fact that the size of the deficit is greater than the rate of economic growth, making it difficult to begin to pay down the debt.

12

Table 2 - Allocation of public expenditures (% of total)

	1979	1981	1983	1985	1987	1989	1991	1993
Total spending (billion lire)	103947	178744	259890	353456	439762	488213	579966	634690
General Administration	3.5	3.0	3.3	2.7	3.0	3.1	3.4	3.3
Defence	4.6	3.8	4.0	4.1	3.9	4.0	3.6	3.2
Justice	0.9	1.0	1.0	1.0	0.9	0.8	1.0	1.0
Internal Security and Civil Protection	2.4	2.1	2.0	2.0	2.1	2.4	2.4	2.8
International Affairs	2.3	2.2	2.1	2.5	2.7	3.1	3.0	3.4
Education and Culture	12.2	10.6	10.2	9.1	9.4	10.1	10.3	9.9
Housing	1.0	1.4	1.4	1.0	1.4	0.8	0.9	0.5
Social Policy	22.1	22.6	21.7	22.8	27.6	24.1	24.3	17.8
Transport and Communication	7.8	7.7	8.0	8.6	7.5	6.5	5.8	5.2
Agriculture	0.9	1.4	1.3	1.0	1.4	1.5	1.1	0.7
Industry, trade and state intervention	9.2	11.3	10.5	8.8	6.3	5.7	3.1	4.2
Regional and local government transfers	20.7	16.8	13.4	13.6	12.9	12.7	12.6	12.3
Interest charges on public debt	7.9	11.2	15.6	16.4	15.9	19.2	23.1	28.1
Other Financial commitments	4.4	4.9	5.4	6.3	5.1	6.0	5.4	7.7

Source: Data collected from annual report on the state of the economy presented to Parliament by the Minister for the Budget and the Minister for the Treasury.

Table 3 - Increases in government spending (%)

	1981	1983	1985	1987	1989	1991	1993
Total spending	71.9	45.4	36.0	24.1	11.0	18.8	8.6
General Administration	43.9	62.0	12.6	35.3	15.0	29.9	6.7
Defence	43.8	52.8	39.3	17.4	13.9	6.1	-1.3
Justice	49.4	45.7	27.5	17.5	-8.1	52.3	15.2
National Security	49.7	42.3	36.7	28.9	24.3	22.6	24.2
International Affairs	57.5	43.4	58.1	33.9	31.0	14.9	22.2
Education and Culture	48.7	40.8	21.3	27.8	20.0	20.5	5.1
Housing	142.5	44.6	-5.8	74.1	-33.3	23.7	-32.9
Social Policy	75.8	39.8	42.8	50.5	-3.1	20.0	-19.9
Transport and Communication	70.5	49.9	45.9	8.4	-3.4	6.0	-2.6
Agriculture	167.3	34.2	9.3	72.0	17.0	-17.4	-29.2
Industry, trade and state intervention	111.5	35.1	14.6	-11.1	-.1	-34.0	46.9
Regional and local government transfers	39.7	15.7	37.8	18.5	9.2	17.4	7.1
Interest charges on public debt	143.0	101.4	43.3	17.0	34.3	43.2	32.8
Other Financial commitments	91.6	61.6	59.4	.13	31.1	7.4	54.3

Source: See Table 2.

Tables 2 and 3 provide an indication of where spending priorities have been placed, and some indication of what have been the spending sources of deficits and debt. Interest payments have taken over as the largest spending envelope; and there is a significant decrease in the percentage allocated to social policy (broadly defined to include health, pensions and income maintenance), transfers to regional and local governments, and direct state intervention in industry (including regional assistance to southern Italy). The increases in the percentage assumed by social policy in the mid-1980s may be traced to the transfer of funds to bail out the state pensions scheme as contributions by employers and workers could not shore the shortfall. There also has been a noticeable cut in the percentage assumed by spending on education. The extent to which spending on programmes have been cut to make up for the larger role assumed by interest payments on the debt is demonstrated by the final column in Table 1. By 1991, revenues covered all current spending; and beginning the following year, governments continued to cut away at current spending so that there would have been surpluses in the absence of interest payments.

The figures in the tables presented above indicate that 1992 was a major turning point in the evolution of Italian public finances and budgetary processes. Processes that were already underway, such as changing budgetary priorities, were accelerated; and major reversals in terms of deficit levels were signalled for the first time and have continued since then. There are a number of factors that help to understand the changes that took place in 1992. First, the convergence criteria in the TEU established clear reference points and a timetable for budgetary targets. Governments could choose to ignore the criteria, and risk being accused of jeopardising Italy's chances of being part of the single currency. Conversely, governments could now use the criteria as the reason for bringing about changes to public expenditure, affecting the role of the state in economic and social life. The introduction of clear reference points was particularly important in a budgetary process where debt and deficit targets had been met only in and 1986 in the period between 1983 and 1992.

Second, the pressures from international currency markets that forced the Italian government to pull out of the exchange rate mechanism (ERM) in September 1992 immobilised opposition to spending cuts, and, to a lesser extent, tax increases. The newly formed government, composed largely of non-political technocrats in key economic ministries and led by Giuliano Amato, not only introduced a mini-budget that combined tax increases and spending cuts for 38 800 billion lira (approx. $25 billion U.S) but also announced major privatisation programmes. Moreover, the currency crisis paved the way for the approval of a government bill that delegated to the government the authority to change four areas considered to be structural sources of deficits: health, pensions, public sector employment and local government finance. The legislation was an important development not simply because it introduced structural changes that brought immediate savings of about 13 000 billion lire ($8.6 billion), and long-term savings. For instance, changes introduced to pensions gave the government flexibility in limiting early retirement packages; and in health services, it introduced income brackets for families which would determine prescription and doctors' fees.[35] Moreover, the delegated legislation provided the executive a virtual free hand to introduce changes in the four areas with little possibility for Parliament to obstruct or amend the reforms. Given the relatively weak position of government legislation in the parliamentary process, delegating to the government the powers to reform four areas of major public expenditures was seen by political and economic observers as an "historic" turning point.[36]

---

[35] *D.L. 382, 1992.*
[36] Marco Rinforzi. "Con la fiducia del Senato la legge delega va in porto ", *Il Sole 24 Ore* 23 October 1992.

The Amato government put through a series of measures in its first six months, beginning in July 1992. In addition to the mini budget and the delegated legislation, it introduced further savings of 41 700 billion lire ($27.8) in the 1993 budget approved in December 1992, including 7 000 billion lire to be raised through privatisation. In total, the Amato government's action led to cutting the size of the budget deficit by about $60 billion in a single year. It was followed by subsequent budgets brought forward by governments led by Carlo Ciampi (1994) and Lamberto Dini (1996), and to a lesser extent Silvio Berlusconi (1995), that continued the trend to cut the size of the deficit. What makes the reversal since mid-1992 even more impressive in Italian terms is that it took place during a period of recession and later sluggish economic growth.

While Italy will not, in all likelihood, meet the convergence criteria for deficit levels in 1997, the Prodi government projects to be within the 3% range by 1998.[37] More importantly, political discourse on economic policy has been taken over by the objectives the Italian government set for itself in signing the TEU.[38] Amato, in a speech before the Senate vote to confer confidence in his government, said there was no alternative to the European commitments. The choice was not whether Italy would leave the EU, but whether it would be relegated to its second division and become its "Disneyland", or whether it would choose to concentrate its efforts on meeting the convergence criteria.[39] Budgetary politics, which include privatisation plans, now have a focal point that mobilises a broad range of political and social forces: employers' organisations, the Bank of Italy, all the parties on the centre-left with the exception of the die-hard Communist Refoundation, most of the parties on the centre-right, with the ex-fascist National Alliance ambivalent on major cuts to spending, and the reluctant support of trade unions.

What is striking about this broad consensus is that the reversal in budgetary politics has been carried out largely through cuts in spending, at a ratio of two to one with respect to tax increases. This may reflect the fact that increases in expenditures in the 1970s and 1980s were not matched by increases in revenues raised through taxation; leading some economists to argue that if Italy had increased taxes at rates similarly to OECD averages for the period, debt and deficit levels would have been at more manageable levels.[40] The most significant measures on the revenue side in the 1990s include the privatisation of state-held firms which, although not always carried out with the speed that some had hoped for, brought close to 30 000 billion ($20 billion) to the state coffers between 1992 and 1995.[41] Another revenue measure has been to be more aggressive in reducing levels of tax evasion; this includes simplifying the tax code and enhancing the powers of tax inspectors. Alesina and Mare argue that tax evasion in 1991

---

[37] There is no chance of meeting the public debt figure of 60% of GDP in the near future. Italy, like Belgium, is hoping that it can convince its partners to invoke the TEU clause which allows member states into the single currency f they can rove to be making significant progress in meeting the criteria figure.

[38] An interesting example of this was an editorial that appeared in the newspaper *La Repubblica*. The author, trying to recall attention to the perennial problem of many parts of Sicily and southern Italy lacking running water, gas and electricity. called for the delivery of these basic services as criteria for entry into the single currency. The assumption is that by only policy objectives that are seen as gateways tot he single currency will gain attention from policy makers. Antonio Ramenghi, "Acqua. luce e gas per Maastricht," *La Repubblica*, 17 July 1996.

[39] Senato della Repubblica, XI Legislatura, *Resoconto Stenografico*, 30 June 1992, 12.

[40] Vito Tanzi, "Il Sistema Tributario Italiano: Una Prospettiva Internazionale ", in Andrea Monorchio. ed. *La finanza pubblica italiana dopo la svolta del 1992* (Bologna: Il Mulino, 1996), 23.

[41] These include major banks, insurance companies and almost the entire state holdings in steel. See: Alfredo Macchiato, *Privatizzazioni: tra economia e politica* (Roma: Donzelli. 1996), 43.

amounted to 15% of GDP, higher the deficit level. They argue that if tax evasion in Italy since the 1970s would have been at levels in the United States, the debt to GDP ratio in the 1990s would be at about 80%; if tax evasion would have been at UK levels, the debt ratio would be 60%. However, tax evasion was part of a political compromise that would have been difficult to abandon without causing major problems for fragile governing coalitions.[42] Concessions made to industrial workers in the form of pensions and incomes policies, to students in the form of low university tuition fees, and regional aid to southern Italy were countered by a relaxed approach to collecting taxes, especially from shopkeepers, professionals, and small and medium enterprises.

Interestingly, it has been the ex-Communist Democratic Party of the Left (PDS) that has provided the most consistent public and parliamentary support for reversing the trend in public finances through privatisation and major changes to key areas of social policy and public expenditure. This reflects a change in the terms of political discourse. In effect, whether or not Italy will be part of a single currency at its inauguration, it has begun to implement the objectives of "sound money" policies that were at the heart of the Maastricht criteria; and by the time the process is over, the boundaries of state intervention will be changed drastically in key areas such as health, pensions, state ownership of firms and key industries.

It may be argued that the evolution of budgetary politics in Italy reveals both the "hollowing out" of the Italian state and the "hardening of its shell." The state's authority is being displaced in at least two directions. First, although ultimate responsibility for budgetary decisions continues to rest with the national state, Italian governments throughout the 1990s have pointed to Europe as the source of fiscal restraint and rigour. In political discourse, not only Europe but international financial markets are presented as an external force dictating budgetary policy. For instance, the assessment of budgetary plans by the Bundesbank, the Commission, and bond rating agencies are given precedence over that of trade unions or even political parties.[43] In accepting the convergence criteria, Italian governments accepted not only further limits on monetary policy but also on levels of spending and taxation.

These and other European commitments also have contributed to a second source of "hollowing out"; the retreat of the state from many areas of social and economic life, and the primacy of market principles and forces. Italy embarked on major plans for privatisation and restructuring of the welfare state relatively later than other industrialised states. It is only in the 1990s, and with the blunt instrument of the convergence criteria to marginalise resistance, did governments put through major reforms that introduced greater market forces to many parts of the economy; and put into private hands major state holdings. For instance, Italian governments tried at least on two occasions in the 1980s, with little success, to introduce or increase user fees for medical and health services. In the 1980s, not only did governments not deal with the large financial problems of the pension system, they made many pensions even more

---

[42]Alberto Alesina and Mauro Mare, "Evasione e Debito", in Andrea Monorchio, ed. *La finanza pubblica italiana dopo la svolta del 1992* (Bologna: Il Mulino, 1996), 70.

[43] A good example was the controversy raised by the Italian Commissioner Mario Monti who criticised in July 1996 the Prodi government's economic statement that continued deficit and debt projections for the three year period from 1997-1999. Monti's comments received front page coverage, along with the government's reaction which was to point out that Commission President Santer and international financial markets approved of the government's budgetary plans. Elena Polidori, "Brava Italia, manovra ok: L'Europa e l'FMI promuovono Prodi," *La Repubblica, 29 June 1996.*

generous. In the period since 1992, changes that have increased user fees in health and university education have been implemented relatively easily; and not only was the pension system reformed in 1995, the government has also started to crack down on fraudulent claims.[44] An indication of the extent to which there has been an acceptance of the new boundaries of state intervention in economic and social life is the recent refusal by almost all social and political forces to accept the call by Communist Refoundation leader, Fauso Bertinotti, to resist government plans to privatise the state telecommunications conglomerate.[45]

There may be political contingencies that help to explain the recent reversals in Italian economic policy. First, the collapse of all the traditional parties has radically changed the entire political landscape. None of the parties that ran for office in the 1994 elections were present under the same banner just seven years earlier. More importantly, judicial investigations, leading to one-third of the members of the Chamber of Deputies being under investigation or facing corruption charges in 1994, unmasked an extensive patronage network that, directly or indirectly, drained public resources. Second, the emergence of new political forces, such as the Northern League, put directly on to the political agenda fiscal responsibility and tax reduction. The Northern League's base of support is in the provincial cities of northern Italy, especially in Lombardy and the north-east. These are the areas characterised by small and medium-sized industries that are largely export-oriented. The new political forces were able to combine anti-tax sentiments with reaction to the corruption crisis of the 1990s, creating an environment that led many political and business leaders to fear a major tax revolt.

The political conditions, while helping to create a political opportunity structure for change, do not provide a complete account. First, the commitments made at Maastricht were agreed to by Prime Minister Giulio Andreotti (facing charges for collusion with the mafia) and Foreign Minister Gianni De Michelis (convicted of accepting illegal political contributions), well before the corruption crisis broke. Amato's changes in 1992 were introduced well before major political figures such as Andreotti and Socialist leader Bettino Craxi were charged. Moreover, Amato's parliamentary majority included of the old Socialist Party and the Christian Democrats. In addition, the primary balance was already balanced in 1991, indicating that a reversal in budgetary politics was already underway. Third, the extent of change in the parliamentary class should not be over-estimated; over 100 ex-Christian Democrats were re-elected in 1996 along with a number of ex-Socialists and ex-Liberals. Finally, there is no reason to assume that simply changing party labels or even the members of the parliamentary class will lead to a change in approach to budgetary politics and economic policy-making. The question remains of why so little resistance was offered by most political and social forces.

It may be argued that the "hollowing out" that has taken place could not be carried out without the complementary process of making the state less permeable to societal interests. Paradoxically, the objectives set in the Treaty that weakened national state capacity were accepted by the Italian government precisely because they would strengthen the decision-making capacities within the state. In order for the state to give way to market forces and supranational authorities, the boundaries within its own borders between the state and society must be redrawn. As we saw earlier, the

---

[44] Maurizio Ferrara, "The Rise and Fall of Democratic Universalism: Health Care Reform in Italy, 1978-1994", *Journal of Health Politics, Policy and Law*, 20:2 (Summer 1995). 275-302; Giuliano Cazzola. *Le nuove pensioni degli italiani* (Bologna: Il Mulino, 1996).

[45] Francesco Verderami, "Il Pds da l'altola a Rifondazione ", *Corriere della Sera*, 20 August 1996.

17

conventional view is that the Italian state was "captured" or "expropriated". Decision-making required extensive cumbersome negotiations to produce a consensus across a broad range of social and political forces. Quite often, that consensus was forged by using finances to trade benefits between different groups or perhaps providing state protection for parts of the economy. It was easier to appease different social interests through public expenditures than it was to mobilise social and political forces to cut government spending, liberalise the economy or cut the size of the public sector.

The Maastricht Treaty ensured that the boundaries of state-society relations in the economy could no longer ignore outside pressures. It introduced a new set of binding rules that forced upon all social and political interests serious questions not unlike those posed by the French Socialists in 1983. If Italy wants to be part of the economic and monetary union, it needs to change the terms of state intervention in the economy; and in order to do that, national state structures must have the capacity to set policy objectives and pursue them autonomous from social and political constraints. Moreover, the convergence criteria has helped to remove partisan, ideological and political considerations from the discussion of drastic measures. A consensus has emerged across political boundaries that goes from centre-left to centre-right that claims that there are no alternative policies available if Italy wants to be at the centre of economic and monetary union. Politics, then, becomes simply a technical exercise of how to best achieve the objectives set out in the convergence criteria.

It is not surprising, then, that between 1992 and 1996 Italy's Prime Ministers were: Giuliano Amato, who made his mark as Minister of the Treasury in the late 1980s; Carlo Azeglio Ciampi, a former Governor of the Bank of Italy, who also led a government of "technocrats"; Silvio Berlusconi, whose claim to fame prior to entering politics four months before leading his coalition to victory in the 1994 elections was as one of Italy's leading entrepreneurs; Lamberto Dini, a former director general of the Bank of Italy, also led a government of technocrats that assumed power when the Berlusconi government fell in late 1994; and Romano Prodi, an economics professor who formed a centre-left government after the 1996 elections that included Dini as Foreign Minister and Ciampi as the new minister of both the Budgetary and Treasury portfolios. Italians were not happy just to have an independent central bank, they wanted to have the bank officials leading the country. Dini, speaking to the Chamber of Deputies in support of his government's mini budget in March 1995 said, made virtue of the fact that the cuts to spending and tax increases being considered were not the product of a government expressing the will of a majority but of "technocrats" with a specific mission.[46]

In addition to the "removal" of politics from the budgetary process, thereby making it less accessible for contestation by societal interests, there has been a growing consensus that the permeability of the process itself needs to be addressed. A series of measures have Been taken to strengthen the executive, and within that, the role of key economic ministries such as the Treasury.[47] Changes to the electoral law in 1993 moved to a mixed system, with three-quarters of the seat based on first-past-the-post and one-quarter assigned according to proportional representation. It has helped to mobilise political groups into two coalitions, and focused attention on candidates to lead the government. This is in marked contrast to previous practice where any number of factions and groups could influence the choice of the head of the executive. More importantly, changes to parliamentary rules and procedures have given the government

---

[46] Camera dei Deputati, XII Legislatura, *Atti Parlamentari - Discussioni*, 13 March 1995.
[47] D. Hine and R. Finocchi, "The Italian Prime Minister," *West European Politics, 14:2 (1991), 79-86.*

greater control of the budgetary process in the legislature. There is now a clear time-table for the budget, and the executive can set budgetary targets early on in the process.[48] While governments still have few guarantees that the budget that emerges from Parliament will look exactly how it was presented, it does have greater assurance that at least the broad objectives, such as deficit and spending levels, will not be breached. Within Parliament, the Budget Committee of the Chamber of Deputies (to a lesser extent in the Senate)has emerged as a champion of fiscal restraint, and has become a gateway for all spending decisions in Parliament. Interests seeking budgetary concessions no longer have the broad array of access points to achieve their objectives. Moreover, many commentators claim that restricting this access is necessary if the budget targets of the TEU are to be met.[49] The Dini government introduced a bill to "rationalise" public finances that would see the executive strengthened in its capacity to determine spending levels.[50]

Conclusion

The "hollowing" out of states is a process with little prospect of being reversed in the near future; and it will have consequences for state structures. The Italian case demonstrates that even "permeable" states will face the pressure to displace state authority, and as a consequence, will begin to address questions about the penetration of societal interests within state structures. The political arena becomes a shrinking one in which the space for societal interest to represent claims continues to be narrowed. In turn, as the space for the articulation of claims diminishes, it becomes easier to make decisions to continue to displace authority.

Italy embarked on the road to reverse the direction of its public finances before bringing about institutional changes. The introduction of a new electoral law and the gradual process of strengthening the executive have made it easier to mobilise support for fiscal restraint. Conversely, the convergence criteria have made it easier for the executive to claim greater authority in the decision-making process. The result is a process of "hollowing out" of the Italian state as the capacity to penetrate its structures is being decreased. The question remains, however, of whether a hollow state with a hard shell can mobilise support and maintain social cohesion in a period of economic and political transition. The Italian state was "penetrated" partly as a means of consolidating democracy and maintaining social peace. The gamble is that a hollow, hard state can do the same.

---

[48] Camera dei Deputati, XI Legislatura, *Ciclo annuale di bilancio* (Rome, 1993)
[49] Andrea Manzella, "Interventi istituzionali: la logica di coordinamento tra politica ed istituzioni," inCNEL, ed., *Continuita e Rinnovamento della Politica Economica* (Roma: CNEL. 1992).
[50] *D.L., n.3438, 1995.*

[44]

Judith Adler Hellman   1

ITALIAN WOMEN'S STRUGGLE AGAINST VIOLENCE: 1976-1996

Judith Adler Hellman, Professor of Political Science, York University, Toronto[1]
* * * *

Italian women's struggle for legislative protection from violence has spanned twenty years. From the establishment in 1976 of a Center against Violence in Rome to document cases of rape and violence against women, the struggle for a law criminalizing rape and redefining violence was carried forward -- sometimes vigorously, sometimes haltingly -- through a variety of means until the approval of a law in the spring of 1996.

As a general principle, feminist movements are best understood in the context of the local, regional, and national political cultures in which they arise[2]. Italian feminists' mobilizational effort around the issue of violence against women is a case in point. To be sure, the basic problem of women's vulnerability as victims of assault -- both sexual and non-sexual -- is properly understood as a phenomenon that transcends class, racial, religious, ethnic and, of course, national boundaries. In this paper, however, I will show how the form that feminist mobilization against violence takes and the outcomes of that organizational effort are strongly conditioned by specific political cultures and social conditions

Three particularities of the Italian context that need to be borne in mind if we are to understand how and why Italian feminists mobilized against violence in the ways they did. The first is the legislation -- inherited from fascism -- that was on the books in 1976 when feminists first set to work to conceptualize the kind of law that was needed to protect women from violence. The second is the political and party system through which feminists -- even those who militantly eschewed all contact with what they regarded as the sexist political institutions of their society -- were ultimately forced to work. The third is the nature of the battles to legalize abortion and divorce that led up to the mobilization against violence.

I. Fascist Concepts of Women and Family Law

The law on sexual violence that was contested by Italian feminists from the mid 1970s to the present, like all of Italian family law -- and much else in the Penal Code put in place in the 1948 Constitution -- was inherited from the years of fascist rule. Under fascism (1922-1943), Italian women had suffered a loss of legal status from which they would not recover until the modern women's movement began to systematically challenge women's inferior status. To contextualize the fascist legislation on rape, it is important to recall that fascist legislation pushed women out of the work place and out of the schools and explicitly excluded them from a variety of civic and political activities. In 1927 women's salaries were reduced to half those of men. From 1928 they could no longer serve as administrators in secondary schools or universities. From 1933 they were excluded from civil service examinations. By the mid-1930s, girls were obliged to pay higher school fees than boys. In 1936 fascist law made abortion a "crime against the race," for which only women were culpable. Under fascist law Italian women were not permitted to apply for passports or leave the country without permission of their husband or father. Family law inherited from the fascist period placed all family decisions, including the question of children's schooling in the hands of the father.[3]

Thus the struggle for new legislation on rape and violence against women must be viewed within the context of the legal condition of women under fascism. It must also been seen in reference to the persistence of retrograde attitudes bolstered by an Italian Catholic Church that, under John XXIII, had moved in a reformist direction in some areas, but in matters of family law and women's control of their bodies remained staunchly reactionary even as other changes swept the Church and the country.

The fascist legislation that the women's campaign sought to overturn and replace, Title IX of the Penal Code, defined rape as a crime "against public morality and right living (buon costume)," which is to say, as an attack on society and its moral strictures rather than as an assault on the physical or psychological person of the victim.[4] The code further distinguishes between penetration and other violent sexual acts.[5] Under this 1930 law, an offense to society occurs when a man has "carnal knowledge" of a girl under the age of 14, when a person in a position of authority has carnal knowledge of a girl under age 16, or anyone who is mentally incompetent, or when a man has violent carnal knowledge of a woman to whom he is not married.[6]

The fascist code differentiated among rape for the purpose of forcing a woman into a "reparatory marriage," with her abductor (1-3 years); seduction of woman through the promise of marriage by a person already married (3 months to 2 years); rape of a prisoner or detainee by a public official (1-5 years); and a variety of other forms of "carnal violence."[7] In the case of abduction of a woman by a would-be suitor, when the rapist "makes restitution to the victim's family and to the victim by marrying her, 'all execution [of the law] and its penal effects cease."[8]

Karen Beckwith notes that the most pernicious effects of the law were that the crime of rape went unpunished if the victim chose not to prosecute; that the rape victims themselves had to produce evidence of violence employed in the crime; that rape within marriage was not recognized and that rape could be transformed from a "crime against society" to acceptable behavior in cases where "the victim restores the honor of the state by marrying her assailant" (i.e. by accepting a "reparatory marriage").[9]

II. The political and party system

It would fall beyond the scope of this chapter to analyze in detail all of the features of the Italian political system that bear on the form that the anti-violence campaign was to take. This is particularly the case insofar as the party system that was in place when the women's movement developed in the late 1970s was radically transformed by the 1990s; the three political parties that had been the most important protagonists in the parliamentary battles around women's legal

3

status in Italy [the Italian Communist Party, (PCI), the Italian Socialist Party (PSI), and the Christian Democratic Party (DC)] had, by the early 1990s been swept from the political scene or reincarnated as different political forces in the radical transformations that marked the passage in Italy from the so-called First to the Second Republics.[10]

If it is impossible to explore all the dimensions of the political system that conditioned women's mobilization around violence, it is nonetheless important to underscore the fact that the women's movement, like other Italian new social movements, emerged in the 1970s in a situation in which the organizational network of the traditional political forces covered every corner of society, and tended to compel even the most anti-institutional, anti-hierarchical movements to take on a more organized form. It is not surprising, then, that a constant theme of the politics of protest in Italy was a tension between social movements -- the student movement, the women's movement, the peace movement, the neighborhood councils, the environmentalists -- and the organized mass parties, above all the Communist Party. The potential for conflict between groups pushing for change from below, and the political forces that wished to control or "mediate" change from above was always present in Italian life. But this tension became acute in the 1960s and 1970s and was expressed in terms of a strong, often bitter resentment on the part of movement activists toward a party that was interested in incorporating the new subjects as part of its own mass base, but at the price of deradicalizing the demands of the social movement.

Thus the Italian Communist Party claimed to have a vision of a future society and a grand strategy for realizing that vision. But the party's program generally required that the movement subsume its goals to this broader strategy. Movement activists were, in essence, asked to join the political party, incorporating their adherents and contributing their collective energy to the general efforts of the party in return for the support of an organizational structure and parliamentary presence that only a mass party can provide. Given their reluctance to give up their independent identity and capacity for autonomous political activity, central to the ideology of many, if not most of the new social movements that emerged in Italy in the 1960s and 1970s was a rejection of the PCI's and other traditional parties' efforts to mediate on their behalf.

And yet the nature of the parliamentary system and the way in which policy is formulated and translated into legislation in Italy reinforced the dependency of movements like the women's movement on the mediation of parties. In the Italian bicameral, multiparty system based on alliances and coalitions, the formulation, debate, and passage of new legislation was inevitably very slow. Seats in both chambers were divided among representatives of anywhere between nine and twelve parties (depending on how we count and what definitions we use), and only two parties regularly gained more than 15% of the vote. With a Left divided between Communists and Socialists, (but thoroughly dominated by the Communists), a Center (really a Center-Right) about the same size as the Left, occupied by the Christian Democrats and three small non-religious parties, and a small but persistent extreme Right of neo-fascists, the arithmetic of the situation required the formation of governing coalitions that left little room for maneuver. As a consequence, through 1990, all of the legislative victories of Italian women -- including the abortion law, the divorce law, labor legislation, and changes to the family law -- were won, slowly and painfully, through the process of negotiation and trade-offs that this system demanded.

The period from the fall of the Berlin Wall to the passage of the antiviolence legislation that concerns us here was marked in Italy by radical changes in political life that include: the transformation of the Italian Communist Party into a "post-communist" Democratic Party of the Left (PDS), the break-up and disappearance of the Socialists and the Christian Democrats in the aftermath of the political corruption scandals, the development of the regionalist, often separatist, sometimes racist Northern League, the emergence of a newly "respectable" National Alliance Party comprised of the former neofascists, and the reconfiguration of the party system to incorporate both new parties and new party alliances. Moreover the period was also characterized by persistent efforts at constitutional reform to create a new, less cumbersome political system that would, among other things, streamline the process of legislation. Yet for all that these changes were radically transformative, with regard to an initiative like that of the women's movement for a law to protect women from violent assault, the system continued to creak on in very much the old manner: that is, as a system of trade-offs and compromises among partisan forces. As we will see, the law on violence that would eventually pass reflects the continuity of the system of alliance formation and compromise even in the face of dramatic change in other aspects of the party system.

III. The History of Feminists' Parliamentary Struggles

Karen Beckwith has argued that the approach used by feminists around the sexual violence issue was, in itself, an outcome of the frustrations feminists had experienced in their efforts to work through the existing party system in their struggle for abortion rights. As Beckwith notes, organized women's groups had not directly initiated the abortion debate in parliament, choosing instead to work through political parties to which they had "preestablished ties and obligations."[11] As a consequence, women were constrained in their ability to bring pressure on the parties to push for more complete abortion rights and when, in 1977, the Senate rejected the abortion bill that had already passed in the Chamber, the sponsoring parties moved to modify the bill, watering it down in the hope of making it acceptable to more conservative legislators.

Thus one of the striking things about feminists' mobilization to push forward a law was that they chose to use the device of the proposta popolare or popular proposal rather than working to persuade one of the more progressive political parties to carry an initiative forward through the normal legislative channels. Under the Italian constitution of 1948, a popular initiative may be carried forward by ordinary citizens who obtain at least 50,000 signatures on their petition. In fact the women's movement succeeded in amassing more than 300,000 signatures on the violence law petition.

Thus what made the campaign different from any previous effort by organized women to bend the institutions of the state to feminist purposes was that the decision to move ahead without bringing progressive legislators on board first. This meant that feminist jurists were able to put before parliament model legislation that was not the outcome of the kind of preemptive compromise that normally accompanies the efforts of legislators to hammer out a law acceptable to a sufficient number of deputies and senators to assure passage. It was, instead, the law that feminists wanted to see in place.

Moreover, the feminists' campaign for this law reflected a clear recognition that if genuine change was to come about it would need to be promoted on two fronts: among the legislators themselves and among their constituents.[12] Bringing forward a popular proposal supported by signatures on a petition required a mass mobilization of public opinion and process of public education on the issue. This form of public education was meant to create an atmosphere favorable to more radical changes in the concepts underpinning the Penal Code on rape.

It is important to underscore that what has -- over the decades -- been presented in the media as "the women's movement's initiative" was the brainchild of a relatively limited group of feminists who belonged to the Radical Party affiliated Movimento della Liberazione della Donna, the Union of Italian Women, (UDI), the Roman feminist collective of Via Pompeo Magno, and the women's coordinating committee of the FLM, the very progressive Metalmechanical Workers' Union. From the very start many Italian women who considered themselves to be a central part of what could be called "the women's movement" disagreed with this approach. Either they objected on the grounds that it was inappropriate to use the institutions of the state to advance women's cause, or they questioned the use of the Penal Code, or they had problems with all legislation that singles out women for special protection. However, notwithstanding the lack of enthusiasm of many militant feminists for the "parliamentary road," the women's movement proposal on sexual violence set the terms of discussion on the issue over the next two decades.

IV. The New Proposal

The popular proposal redefined sexual violence as assault; as a crime of violence "against the person," a crime against an individual rather than against public morality. While it retained the parts of the old Title IX on minors and mentally incompetent people, all other distinctions, that is, different penalties for rape within marriage, the rape of a prostitute, or gang rape were erased. It abolished the distinction between forced penetration and other violent sexual acts, and introduced the concept of "sexual molestation," a crime for which less severe penalties were assigned. Reparatory marriage would be abolished and trials would be public. The bill also proposed the removal from the penal code of references to "seduction" and "infanticide to protect one's honor," as offensive to women's dignity as equal citizens.[13] The state, rather than the victim, would bring the case against her attacker, and testimony regarding the victim's personal conduct or past history would be inadmissable in court. Significantly, the bill provided the opportunity for feminists organized in women's "associations" or "movements" to participate in trials as formal plaintiffs on behalf of the victim or of women in general.

The popular proposal strategy succeeded insofar as the major progressive parties of the time immediately responded to the popular initiative with legislative proposals of their own. Several different proposals were introduced in the course of the debates, with the parties trying, in all cases, to redefine the problem within the framework of their own discourse. The PCI quickly drew up its own legislative proposal which was similar to the feminists' in many respects, but differed in that it removed sexual violence from the context of an analysis of society as patriarchal and placed rape in the broader context of societal violence. Not surprisingly it also rejected the notion that the feminist movement as a whole could be a formal legal party to any such trial.[14]

The Socialists, for their part, also attempted to reconfigure the issue. They moved away from the notion that women were assaulted as women and framed the debate in terms more general to Italian society: as crimes "repugnant to democracy."[15] In a peculiar manner that made it difficult for feminists to determine whether the Socialists represented potential allies in the struggle, the PSI also proposed to alter the discourse on rape by making it a "crime against sexual freedom." Moreover, the PSI advocated "a legal role for women's associations which represent collective interests... but did not specify which associations or that those associations be feminist."[16]

In looking at the sexual violence campaign as a whole, Tamar Pitch views the mobilization an attempt to promote the political visibility of the women's movement through a new kind of political presence. She argues that rape was chosen as an organizing tool in the late 1970s not because it spontaneously emerged as a primary issue in the process of discussion and consciousness raising in the feminist collectives operating at the time. "Rather," she writes, "rape was chosen as an issue ...for expressly political motivations: as an issue likely to bring women back into the streets. Such political motivations are evident in the forms of struggle chosen and in the contents of the bill written."[17] Pitch also argues that with the collection of signatures for the popular proposal, the notion of politics had implicitly changed, reacquiring "the traditional meaning of a specific, sectorialized activity to gain specific, sectorial objectives," and with this, feminists accepted the language of state institutions, enhancing their legitimacy.[18]

As Pitch reminds us, the sexual violence campaign represents a different way in which the law could be used by women. The law for which women were mobilized was a penal law rather than a piece of legislation designed to enable women to transform their social situation or expand their sphere of activities.

> It is very significant that the rape campaign dealt with penal law. The penal code is the symbolic organizer of the hierarchy of 'goods' which a community deems worth defending and therefore affirming. The use of such an instrument by the women's movement signaled a shift of political emphasis from questions related to social transformation to questions of principle. Law was here used as a symbolic means to affirm one's status as an equal citizen, one's official recognition as a political actor.[19]

In this way, Pitch argues, "the solemn declaration of one's 'worth' was delegated to law." The bill was written, "not in order to decrease the number of rapes nor even solely to offer better legal protection to the victim." Instead, the law was given the task of "subverting the hierarchy of 'goods,' by declaring that an offense to women's bodies is a very serious crime, that women are 'persons,' that women are 'equal citizens,' that women are autonomous political actors." The proposal was framed in order to alter the "dominant wisdom" about the nature and status of women.[20]

V. The current situation

The story of the new law on sexual violence that was finally approved by the Chamber of Deputies on 7 February 1996 and by the Senate on 14 February 1996 is in fact a story of the creation of a new consensus and the alteration of the "dominant wisdom" of which Tamar Pitch speaks. In the earliest phase of its movement through parliament, what was debated was the women's movement model law, in modified form. The text initiated by popular proposal was debated in the Chamber in 1984 and in the Senate in 1985 along with the versions of the law put forward by the PCI, PSI, and DC.

To give some sense of the levels of conflict around an issue about which we might expect to find some broader consensus, it is worth noting that the Christian Democrats' bill was also designed to protect women from sexual violence and to punish rapists, but the DC proposal sought to provide completely different processes for rape of a wife by a husband or common law partner as distinguished from rape by a stranger. In the formulation of the legislation that passed from the Chamber to the Senate, a distinction between sexuality regulated within the family and outside of the family began to creep into the new versions of the law, inserted by the Christian Democrats and by those who hoped to please the DC. At this point in the process, the notion of women constituting themselves as collective plaintiffs on behalf of the victim also definitively disappeared from the versions of the legislation that the parties were willing to consider seriously.

By 1987 a new proposal came forward, promoted by female senators of all the non-religious parties who pushed for a proposal closely resembling that of the initial proposta popolare. Then, in a backward step, in 1988, the Senate proposed a text that reopened the question of who was required to bring suit against a rapist. Thus, by 1989, when the debate returned to the Chamber, it continued to bog down around the issues of objections to the regulation of sex within marriage, the question of whether the state, the victim or an association of women should bring the case against the rapist, and the issue of a double standard applied to husbands "with sexual rights" as distinguished from "real rapists."

From 1989 to 1995, altogether 17 different bills on sexual violence were presented in the two chambers.[21] On International Women's Day, 8 March 1995, 500,000 new citizens' signatures were presented to the President (i.e. the Speaker) of the Chamber of Deputies, Irene

Pivetti, and by 23 March a group of 67 female deputies from all the parliamentary groups ranging from the former fascists to the former Communists, held in a press conference to present the text of a new proposal which was substantially that which finally won approval in February 1996.

In the ten months in which it was debated, discussion turned on the old points of contention (the breakdown in definitions of various forms of rape and sexual assault, and the question of who may bring a case of sexual violence.) However important new issues also arose that clearly reflect dramatic changes from the realities of Italian society in the late 1970s to the realities of 1996. These focused on the spread of AIDS, increased awareness of incest and sexual abuse within the family, and the recognition of sexual activity of minors and the potential for mutual consent between sexually active adolescents.

VI. The Passage of the Law

A good deal of work in the area of Women and Politics focusses on the increase of women's presence in parliamentary bodies as a predictor of success in struggles for feminist legislation. Yet, the passage of the Italian sexual violence law in 1996 cannot, in fact, be attributed to the increased numerical influence of female parliamentarians. Through the 1980s, in a reflection of the broad acceptance of the demands of the women's movement, all Italian parties demonstrated some awareness of the need to assure women's election to the Chamber and the Senate by placing women at or near the top of the party lists. As a consequence, the proportion of female parliamentarians rose steadily through the 1980s. However, the 1994-96 legislature that finally passed the sexual violence law, was, in fact, characterized by a significant decline in the number of female deputies and senators from a high of 15 percent in 1992 to less than 8 percent in 1994.

Rather than seeing the long delayed passage of the sexual violence law as a direct consequence of women's numerical influence in parliament, it is more persuasive to pose it as a reflection of the spread of feminist ideas through the broader society. This general change in attitudes found expression in the Italian Senate and Chamber in the expanded feminist consciousness of female legislators from a wide range of partisan experiences who put women's needs ahead of partisan quarrelling to co-sponsor and work vigorously together for the passage of the law. Moreover, the bill passed amid the widespread feeling among both male and female parliamentarians that, after literally decades of delay, some kind of law, however imperfect, would be preferable to further delay.[22]

In the end the bill is a bundle of compromises, which provide the following:

1> Definition of the crime: rape is redefined as a crime against a person, not against public morality. Likewise, in a further effort to remove the sexual dimension from the event, a "crime for libidinous purposes" is abolished; anyone who carries off another person for sexual purposes is simply charged with kidnapping (sequestro di persona.)

2> Recognition of adolescent sexuality: sexual relations are permissible between minors aged 13 to 16 with no penal consequences if the two partners are no more than three years apart in age. If the age spread is greater than three years, or if one of the partners is younger than 13, the law on statutory rape is applied.

3> Responsibility for bringing charges: Only when the victim reports the crime may the law proceed against the rapist, although the victim has 6 months in which to make this report. To protect the victim from pressure, the law states that once reported, the charge cannot be withdrawn. The state only becomes involved bringing charges against the rapist in the case of a victim under the age of 14, or when the accused rapist is a parent of the victim.

The notion that other people in society (in general, feminists) could press charges, a principle that was so central to the early versions of the legislative proposal, was lost in the many changes the proposal suffered. This reflects a profound rejection by the organized political forces of groups in civil society like autonomous feminist collectives. But it also reflects the diminished mobilizational capability of the women's movement to constitute itself on a regular basis as a "civil party" to bring a case against a rapist.

4> Victim's rights: significantly, the law is very explicit on the victim's rights and the need to protect the victim's privacy, public image, and that of the victim's family. Adult victims may choose a hearing behind closed doors: a closed hearing is obligatory in the case of minors. It rules out all questions regarding the victim's personal life or sexual behavior except where necessary to reconstruct the exact circumstances of the crime. Neither the name nor photo of the victim may be used in the media on pain of three to six months imprisonment to those who violate this rule and reveal the identity of the victim.

5> Sanctions: Minimum punishment for rape is raised from 3 to 5 years, although the maximum penalty remains ten years. In the case of violence against a minor under 14, the law calls for imprisonment of 6 to 12 years, and 7 to 14 years for sexual violence against a child under 10. In the case of mitigating circumstances, all of these penalties, however, may be reduced by two-thirds according to the discretion of the judge.

6> Gang rape: A penalty of 6 to 12 years is assigned to gang rape, but the law recognizes the possibility of a gang member who, "although participating the violence did not actually rape the victim, but also did nothing to stop the act." In such cases the judge may apply a more lenient penalty.

7> AIDS: The accused must submit to tests for AIDS and other sexually transmitted diseases.[23]

VI. Conclusions:

To what, then, may we attribute the successful passage of a legislative initiative that, for nearly twenty years, had been blocked by parliamentary wrangling? In the end, the new law won approval because of the persistence of its sponsors and the persistence of the problem the legislation sought to address. Above all, the proposal finally became a law because the social context of Italy has changed. What was once a country shaped by conservative Catholic values has undergone radical transformations. Among the many indicators that could be cited it should suffice simply to note that the majority of women have left home to join the paid workforce and Italy now has the lowest birthrate in the world.

One of the ironies of the debates around the law on sexual violence is that, in the late 1970s early 1980s, the changes to the fascist law proposed by feminists were seen as too radical with respect to the values of the broader society. Its movers faced strong resistance to the notion that women's bodies belong to them; they were dealing with general public opinion and with parliamentarians of all parties who believed fundamentally in the control of husbands over wives and the "sanctity of the domestic sphere.' Moreover, feminists were confronted with the inflexibility of lawmakers who subscribed to the underlying principles that sustained the practice of "reparatory marriage": that is, the concept of virginity as sacred; idea of a rape victim as used or spoiled goods; and the idea that the only man who would marry an unchaste women would be the man who had "used" her, who had "taken" her virginity.

The other irony is that opposition to the bill in its final form came in a context of radically changed popular values in which teenagers were now understood to be sexually active. Under the circumstances, all of the language of the proposal that concerned statutory rape of the "under-aged" -- originally conceived as protecting girls from predatory men -- now risked being applied either to teenage girls or boys who were engaging in sexual relations with underage partners.

Thus the final bill reflected not only a transformation of social values, attitudes toward women, toward the family, the Church, and patriarchy, but also changing conditions and new realities: the terrifying problem of AIDS, an increased awareness of the occurrence of incest and sexual abuse within the family, the recognition that teenagers are often sexually active and that consensual sex may take place among minors.

A decade ago, evaluating the responsiveness of governments to the legislative demands of the Italian feminist movement, Karen Beckwith argued that "the extent to which the feminist movement can force increased responsiveness to the model law will be determined by the outcome of the movement's second plan: its effort to mobilize support outside parliament, in public opinion."[24] Indeed, the struggle fought outside the parliamentary arena has, in the case of this law, been the key to its passage. In the twenty years since the ideas contained in the original popular proposal were first mooted, the party system collapsed and was recomposed. The great adversaries of Italian politics — the Christian Democrats and the Communists — disappeared from Italian politics to reemerge in new forms, scandal followed scandal and touched almost the entire political class, the so-called First Republic gave way to the Second, and lawmakers seriously searched for a whole new constitutional model. Through all of this radical transformation in the broader political context, the fight went on for progressive legislation to protect women, and finally public opinion changed to the point that the proposers were at last successful in gaining passage of a bill, however imperfect.

1. I wish to acknowledge the support of the Social Science and Humanities Research Council of Canada and the Faculty of Arts, York University in funding the research on which this chapter is based.

2. Judith Adler Hellman, Journeys Among Women: Feminism in Five Italian Cities, (New York: Oxford University Press, 1987); and Judith Adler Hellman, "Toward a Comparative Model of Women's Movements," APSA, New York, September 1994.

3. On women under fascism see Antonella Marrazzi and Enrica Tedeschi, Donna: Riforma o rivoluzione? (Roma: Edizioni Controcorrente, 1977), p. 67; Piero Meldini, Sposa e madre esemplare, (Firenze: Guaraldi, 1975); Maria Antonietta Macciocchi, La donna nera, (Milan: Feltrinelli, 1976), p. 44; and Aida Tiso, I comunisti e la questione femminile, (Roma: Editori Riuniti, 1976), pp. 57-9.

4. Karen Beckwith, "Response to Feminism in the Italian Parliament: Divorce, Abortion, and Sexual Violence Legislation," in Mary Fainsod Katzenstein and Carol Mueller, eds. The Women's Movements of Western Europe and the United States: Changing Theoretical Perspectives. Philadelphia: Temple University Press, 1987), p. 162.

5. Tamar Pitch, "The Political Uses of Laws: The Italian women's Movement and the Rape Campaign," American Legal Studies Association Forum, 7: 22-3 (1983), p. 141.

6. Beckwith, op.cit.

7. Mirella Alloisio, "50 mila firme contro la violenza sessuale," Noi Donne, anno XXXIV, n. 35, 7 September 1979, pp. 17-34; Elena Medi, Giordana Masotto, Silvia Motta and Simonetta Jucker, Contro la violenza sessuale: le donne...La legge, Atti del convegno tenuto a Milano, Umanitaria, 27-28 October 1979.

8. "On crimes against Public Morality," 1930, art. 519-144, quoted in Beckwith op.cit., p. 162.

9. Beckwith, op.cit., p. 163.

10. For a summary of this period of radical transition see Stephen Hellman, "Italy," in Mark Kessleman and Joel Krieger, European Politics in Transition, 3rd edit., (Boston: Houghton Mifflin, forthcoming 1996), chapter 16.

11. Beckwith, op. cit., p. 162.

12. As Beckwith notes, however, there was a fair bit of disagreement regarding who was more likely to lag behind the elected politicians or the general public. see MLD, Documento del movimento della liberazione della donna sulla porposta di legge sull liberta sessuale, 1981, typescript, cited in Beckwith, op. cit., p. 163.

13. Pitch, op.cit., p. 142.

14. Beckwith, op. cit., p. 164.

15. Ibid.

16. Ibid.

17. Pitch, op. cit., p. 147.

18. Ibid.

19. Ibid., pp. 147-8.

20. ibid. p. 148.

21. Il Manifesto,,15 February 1996, art 28. (on line version)

22. Giovanna Grignaffini, "La Legge Contro La Violenza Sessuale," (Intervento nel dibattito parlamentare alla Camera dei Diputati del 7/2/1996), Femminismi: Bollettino delle muove accessioni in biblioteca, Centro di Documentazione Delle Donne, Bologna, #1, 1996, pp. 22-24.

23. Raffaello Masci, "E' nata la legge anti-stupro," La Stampa, 15 Feb. 1996.

24. Beckwith, op. cit., p. 165.

[45]

Mafia: The Sicilian Cosa Nostra

PINO ARLACCHI

Revelations in recent years by high profile Mafia members allow for a better understanding than was previously possible of the organization, rules, norms of behaviour and activities of the Sicilian Cosa Nostra as well as other Italian organized crime groups. This article uses these, in combination with other information, to examine the internal functioning of Cosa Nostra (its ideology, admission criteria, structure, relations and modes of conflict regulation) and to consider the nature of its contemporary transformation in terms both of economic activities and its changing relationship with Italy's political class and secret societies.

INTRODUCTION: THE TWO PARADIGMS

Until 1984, analyses of the Mafia phenomenon were based almost exclusively on indirect sources or sources outside the criminal world such as parliamentary acts, judicial documents, travel summaries, political and criminological essays, doctoral theses and so on. Because of the difficulty of reconstructing the rules, hierarchies and values of a social sub-system of uncertain scale – whose actors, moreover, are diffident or hostile to the researcher – our knowledge was extremely restricted. In the past, 'Mafia' crimes and 'Mafioso' activities, as well as the network of relations and powers defined as 'Mafioso', were understood to be part of a larger system of values and norms held to be valid for all natives of Sicily, Calabria or other regions: depending on the point of view, the Mafioso was seen simply as a strong or weak ideal-typical version of a Sicilian or southern Italian (Hess 1973: 96–106).

Similarly, the Mafia was defined as a form of behaviour and power that responded to the general needs of social order and integration, or to the demands of class domination and socio-political control (Arlacchi 1983: 41–63). According to some researchers, Mafia groups multiplied more in certain areas of Sicily and the continental part of the Mezzogiorno because of specific socio-economic structures, as well as the peculiar relations between these structures, the market and the State

Translated by Claire M. O'Neill

South European Society & Politics, Vol.1, No.1 (Summer 1996) pp.74–94
PUBLISHED BY FRANK CASS, LONDON

MAFIA: SICILIAN COSA NOSTRA   75

(Arlacchi 1980, Sylos Labini 1966: vii–ix). Most scholars attributed the Mafia phenomenon to the presence of local power groups in relations of co-operation or, at times, violent conflict, that sought control of territory and resources. These groups or 'clans' enjoyed the active consensus of the population and were 'politically' protected from police and judicial repression. Few believed the Mafia to be more than an informal institution within a wider, and analogous, socio-cultural milieu; there was precious little evidence that it was a secret society with its own initiation rites, statutes, dynamics and hierarchy. The conception of the Mafia as simply a 'delinquent association' is present in all of the political and legal literature on the phenomenon up until the mid-1950s (Montalbano 1953, Reid 1956).

Although some authors maintained that the Mafia had its own 'legal order' – a 'State within the State' (Romano 1918: 122–5) – based on unwritten laws, and profoundly rooted in the traditions and customs of Sicily (Lo Schiavo 1962: 24–43), this was a minority view and, owing to lack of proof, one that was virtually abandoned (in academic and informed journalistic circles) between the 1950s and the early 1980s. At the time of Henner Hess's study-trip to Sicily (in the late 1960s) it was feasible even to assert that the Mafia did not 'exist' as a secret criminal organization (Hess 1973). The police never confiscated codes, rules, account books or membership lists. No defendant ever admitted belonging to a sect called 'Mafia', 'honorary society' or any other name before a Court. Nor did any defendant ever provide evidence which could lead to the identification of a secret association among so-called 'men of honour'.

Even when judicial authorities or the police were confronted with detailed disclosures about the existence of a formal, secret association, such disclosures were considered neither credible nor worthy of investigation. Magistrates, intellectuals and politicians held rigidly to the quasi-dogma originally laid down by the Palermo folklorist Giuseppe Pitré in the late nineteenth century and widely believed until the mid-1980s: that the Mafia is neither sect nor association and has neither regulations nor statutes (Pitré 1889: 289). Moreover, the Supreme Court has often stated that the actions and crimes attributed to the 'Mafia' were to be considered the work of local criminal groups, entirely unrelated to any central organization. If ministers or examining judges requested the amalgamation of various 'Mafia' trials against the wishes of defence lawyers or other judges, the Supreme Court sided with the latter.

The most recent significant controversy in this regard took place in the second half of the 1980s between Judge Giovanni Falcone and the head of the prosecution office of Palermo's central court. Falcone claimed that the confessions of the Mafia *pentito* (super-grass) Antonio Calderone suggested the need for a single trial of the Mafia members identified. But since the Palermo prosecutor did not believe Calderone's deposition, or those of the other 'super-grasses' regarding Cosa Nostra, he decided that the proceedings should be handled separately by different courts in the various local areas of Mafia activity. The scepticism of the Supreme Court regarding the existence of a 'Mafia' organization was shared by most scholars in the 1970s and 1980s. It persisted until 1992 and the high profile trial of Cosa Nostra, which itself resulted from the confessions of the former Mafia 'boss' from Palermo, Tommaso Buscetta.

The confessions of Tommaso Buscetta to Judge Falcone, between July and October 1984, represent a watershed between two eras of insight into, and conflict with, the Mafia. As a result of these disclosures, an investigation was begun which enabled the magistrates of Palermo's anti-Mafia 'pool', led by Falcone, to put the entire senior level of the Sicilian Cosa Nostra on trial in 1986. The material provided by Buscetta was verified by hundreds of depositions from Mafia members who subsequently became informers, as well as by thousands of inquiries undertaken independently by the investigators. Since the mid-1980s, 'super-grasses' have also enriched our knowledge of organized crime groups such as the Calabrian 'ndrangheta and the Campanian Camorra. Unfortunately, until recently use of this knowledge has been limited to court rooms.

I was authorized to conduct a series of interviews in 1991 and 1993 with two informers – Antonino Calderone, a member of Catania's Cosa Nostra, and Tommaso Buscetta. The following analysis is based on these interviews as well as research carried out since the late 1970s.

MAFIA AND COSA NOSTRA: TRADITION AND MODERNIZATION

The distinction between 'Mafia' and 'Cosa Nostra' within the Sicilian criminal world has been clarified by the super-grasses. 'Mafia' is a more generic term, but 'Cosa Nostra' is restricted specifically to the groups of individuals that operate – in Sicily and elsewhere – within certain key 'families' or *cosche* ('clans') belonging to a secret sect born in Sicily about two centuries ago. Initially called the 'Carbonari', then the 'Beati Paoli', only during this century has it been referred to as 'Cosa Nostra'.

Origins and Present Structure

'Cosa Nostra' ('Our Thing') is a confederation of Mafia groups originating from the provinces of Palermo and Trapani, and whose more

Italy II

important branches are to be found in Agrigento, Caltanissetta and Catania. In the last few decades, Cosa Nostra settlements have spread into the remaining Sicilian provinces and southern Calabria. According to Tommaso Buscetta, Cosa Nostra does not have a real organizational centre, but rather a centre of gravity located between Palermo and Trapani. All of the major families in the rest of Sicily are either transplants from, or have been recognized by, the families of these two cities (Arlacchi 1994: 107–8).

According to Antonino Calderone, the first Catania 'family' was created in 1925 by a group of 10 to 15 so-called 'men of honour' *(uomini d'onore)* who were 'authorized' by the Palermo families (Arlacchi 1992: 3). The gradual expansion of Cosa Nostra in Sicily and Calabria seems to have occurred after the national and international expansion of the sect. Nuclei of Cosa Nostra (families or sub-parts of a single family called the 'tens') were already present in the rest of Italy, the south of France, Tunisia and in the United States in the first decades of the 1900s – an expansion driven not so much by the need to broaden its illegal interests as by massive migration and sporadic anti-Mafia campaigns by the Italian authorities.

Various authors have noted how Sicily in the second half of the last century was full of secret 'associations of bad elements', 'brotherhoods', parties and cabals. These were present virtually everywhere on the island and active – using methods of intimidation, blackmail and violence – in political struggles, family feuds, and business competition (Montalbano 1953). All of them had initiation rites, passwords and internal links similar to those described by the older super-grasses of Cosa Nostra, who were able to cast their memories back to mid-century. Their interviews with the author suggest that, alongside an expansion from the Palermo 'centre of gravity', there were processes of 'recognition' as well as absorptions of local groups, of various origins, into the central unit of Cosa Nostra.

According to the 'map' of Mafioso groups, which is periodically updated by the Ministry of the Interior, there are today around 56 families operating in the province of Palermo, with a little more than 1,300 members known to the police. In the province of Trapani there are 11 clans with a total membership of 550, composed of 'men of honour' and affiliates; in the province of Agrigento, 16 families with a total of 242 members; and in the province of Catania (where Cosa Nostra has never dominated criminal society) there are only three federated clans, composed of 64 'men of honour' and 271 affiliates. However, there are no reliable estimates of the number of families associated with Cosa Nostra in other Sicilian provinces, since these are not classified separately from other Mafia groups and gangsters in the same area.

For not all of the Sicilian criminal world is controlled by Cosa Nostra. In at least seven of the island's provinces, excluding Palermo and Trapani, there are Mafioso groups that do not adhere to Cosa Nostra. But even these groups tend to aggregate, as is evident from the loose formation of 'cartels' of various types. But the fragility of their structures – caused by less stringent recruitment criteria, the temporary nature of their alliances and weak defences – renders them incapable of either further development or a durable presence. 'Galaxies' of criminals can emerge and exist for a short time, and even include thousands of members, but they are unable to withstand clashes or prolonged competition with the federated families of Cosa Nostra or, for that matter, with the forces of law and order. Knowing that they represent a closed, elite circle of *malavita* (criminality) is very important for the 'men of honour' and is one of the reasons for their deadly reputation.

The term Mafia is often used in a rather extensive way and has even become a synonym for organized crime. But in reality, only the major criminal coalitions operating in the continental part of the Mezzogiorno can be compared to the Sicilian Mafia – namely the Campania groups belonging to the Camorra (Sales 1988) and the 85 families of the 'ndrangheta (Ciconte 1992). Whilst these groups are different from Cosa Nostra families in terms of internal rules and levels of centralization, they present important common traits: a significant continuity over time, an elaborate internal division of labour, formalized procedures for association, a substantial capacity for manipulating official institutions and extensive international networks. Legislators have therefore ensured that the cases punished by the new crime of Mafia-type 'delinquent association' (Article 416a of the criminal code) included not only Sicilian groups but also these other serious manifestations of organized crime.

Ideology and Admission Criteria

The families of Cosa Nostra and their members have a dual cultural identity. Notwithstanding their integration into international business networks, and cosmopolitan modes of behaviour and customs, they remain traditionalists, heavily anchored in the world of their cultural origin – the world of the family, relatives, village and neighbourhood. The traces of this 'localism' live on in Cosa Nostra's creed and practice.

Cosa Nostra's original creed consists of an ideology, in opposition to the law and official institutions, the essence of which was the defence of the weak and the oppressed from real or presumed abuses of power. According to Tommaso Buscetta, in the past the 'men of honour' and those around them considered the law of Cosa Nostra superior to that

MAFIA: SICILIAN COSA NOSTRA   79

of the state and a means of defending Sicily at a time when the island seemed to have been abandoned by its rulers (Arlacchi 1994: 15–16). The 'men of honour' and their friends/allies always carefully promoted these aspects of Mafia ideology, and it will always be hard to ascertain how close it corresponds to reality. But a number of socio-economic and political integration functions were attributed to the traditional 'men of honour' by both local society and the State. Preserving order, mediating conflicts and forming patron-client relationships were all central to Mafia activities in the years preceding the expansion of illegal markets. Buscetta has pointed out that, while by the 1980s the power of the 'men of honour' was based on force, in the past it had been based on their capacity for serving people and on a reputation for resolving difficult situations, including those involving the State (Arlacchi 1994: 113–14).

Traditional ideology and tasks of social integration have been considerably weakened in recent decades and have given way to a straightforward quest for power and wealth. But they have not disappeared completely. Traces of the old tendencies were evident, for example, in the plan for the separation of Sicily from the rest of Italy which, according to one informer, was conceived at the beginning of the 1990s by Cosa Nostra together with certain Masons, members of the security services and local businessmen in response to the State's large-scale, anti-Mafia offensive. More significantly, although the traditional ideology of Cosa Nostra may have declined, the long-standing internal relations, family roles, selection criteria and rules of behaviour for the families and their members remain much as they were at the turn of the century.

Even before Leonardo Vitale, a Mafioso from the Altarello di Baida family in Palermo, who first revealed his clan's secrets to the investigators in 1973 – and was literally considered to be a madman – there had been at least one other significant breach in the Mafia's wall of silence. A document of exceptional interest has been available to investigators since 1937. It is a deposition made by a doctor from Castelvetrano, Melchiorre Allegra, who declared to a police official that, since 1916, he had belonged to a powerful criminal association, including so-called 'men of honour' from all sections of society. Known locally in Sicily as 'mafia', and composed of 'families' led by a *capo* ('boss'), based on groups of 'ten', it was powerful enough to deliver votes to whichever politicians were best able to offer its members political protection (Allegra 1937). He also listed most of the 'men of honour' he knew personally in Palermo and western Sicily. His statements were even published in one of Palermo's daily newspapers, *L'Ora*, in January 1962. However, the deposition led to neither an investigation nor a court testimony. The precious key of knowledge provided by Allegra was dropped and forgotten.

In the light of more recent revelations, Allegra's statement reveals the historical continuity of Cosa Nostra. The doctor described his entry into this secret society in essentially the same terms as those used by today's informers. Admission criteria do not seem to have changed fundamentally since the entry of the young Buscetta into Cosa Nostra in 1946. As we shall see later, they have in fact been strengthened in recent years. The rigidity of recruitment procedures is still apparent in the strict personal and family control of candidates in order to establish their criminal trustworthiness (Arlacchi 1992: 7). This entails not having parents or close family members in the forces of order or judiciary; and the exclusion of women, non-native Sicilians, and militants and sympathizers of left-wing parties, as well as those with dubious reputations according to the more conventional canons of family and sexual morality (illegitimate children, homosexuals, separated or divorced men, bigamists etc.). The relatives of Cosa Nostra victims are also excluded for two reasons: if the killing of their relatives by Cosa Nostra were justified, they would not merit admission; and if it were an error or an unjust elimination, once they were accepted, they could identify the killers and seek revenge, threatening the internal equilibrium of the organization.

Entry into Cosa Nostra involves a fundamental 'test' – murder. There is an exception for adults who come from non-Mafia backgrounds, who are valuable because of their professional know-how or their position of power (lawyers, doctors, businessmen, politicians, etc.). The selection of future 'men of honour' entails a long period of observation. From early childhood, sons and grandsons of Cosa Nostra members are closely scrutinized in order to identify those with the requisite personal qualities. Such rigorous and well-established recruitment procedures have ensured that most of today's Sicilian 'men of honour' come from Mafia backgrounds or long Cosa Nostra blood lines. If we add to these strong family links the fact that each member is obliged to belong to a Mafia family of his commune or neighbourhood of birth, we begin to understand the strong stability of this criminal association: in Palermo, Mafia affairs have been run by the same fifty or so 'families' for more than a century. In areas of heavy Cosa Nostra concentration, such as Palermo, Trapani or Agrigento, these take the form of quasi-social groups, microcosms of the economic, social and political dynamics of the wider, surrounding society. But despite the fact that many 'men of honour' come from long-standing Mafia families, groups operating within Cosa Nostra try to avoid too close an identification between the

MAFIA: SICILIAN COSA NOSTRA   81

personnel or interests of a biological family and those of the clan. According to Tommaso Buscetta, one of the first acts of Palermo's Provincial Commission, when it was established in 1957, was to confirm the pre-existing ban on more than two close relatives belonging to the same Cosa Nostra 'family' (Arlacchi 1994: 79–80).

Such limitations clearly distinguish Sicilian families from their Calabrian counterparts. Superimposing the blood family on the *'ndrina* (the Calabrian Mafia family) is a generalized practice that has, in more recent years, created a strong disincentive to informers. The tough selection criteria in personnel recruitment used by the Sicilian Cosa Nostra have been strengthened recently precisely because of the risk posed by such informers and the decline of popular support for the Mafia. The exceptional procedures that were in the past reserved for influential members of legitimate society (businessmen, politicians, professionals), whose know-how and powers were necessary for the promotion of Mafia interests, have now been extended to ordinary members of Cosa Nostra.

Organization: Secrecy, the 'Commissions' and Internal Relations

Secrecy has always been a fundamental resource and rule of Cosa Nostra, and is one of the traits that distinguishes it from other Italian criminal gangs. The cult of secrecy entails an absolute ban on conserving written documents concerning the internal order, composition and location of Cosa Nostra families. As a consequence, information is fragmented and compartmentalized; and usually no 'man of honour', not even a family 'boss' (*capofamiglia*), fully knows the details of a crime that he himself has not committed.

The internal hierarchy of each Cosa Nostra unit seems almost identical to that described by Melchiorre Allegra almost 50 years ago. 'Men of honour' who do not hold responsibility are the 'soldiers' or *picciotti* (Sicilian for 'boy') and are co-ordinated, usually in groups of five or ten, but sometimes more, by a 'boss of ten'. At the head of each family there is a 'representative' or a 'family boss' who is helped by a 'vice', who substitutes for him in case of absence, and by one or more advisors who are responsible for assisting and backing him up. In all Cosa Nostra families, the representative and advisors are elected, while the vice-representatives and 'bosses of ten' are normally nominated by the family boss. At most, elections take place every five years and all clan members participate (Stajano 1992: 41, Arlacchi 1992: 21–4). In smaller families, an assembly of all those who have the right to vote is called and new bosses are elected by raised hands, whereas in the larger clans the procedure is more formalized.

82   SOUTH EUROPEAN SOCIETY & POLITICS

This selection strategy ensures that a Mafia clan belonging to Cosa Nostra can be divided into three main circles of members: the nucleus, the crown and the periphery. The nucleus of the clan is the most cohesive and restricted level and is composed of two groups: the 'men of honour' and the affiliates. The 'men of honour' are admitted through a formal initiation rite and have potential access to all information, as well as the possibility of a career inside the family. The affiliates do not have any formal initiation rite, but they collaborate full-time in the illegal and legal activities of the clan. They constitute an integral part of the clan but have incomplete access to information. However, there is a very close relationship between 'men of honour' and affiliates since it is from the ranks of the latter that the clan's new soldiers are recruited.

As a result of the recent restriction on admission criteria, the majority of Cosa Nostra groups have a rather contained nucleus. For example, the nucleus of Salvatore Riina's family was composed of only 38 members, including refugees from justice and prisoners. These were bands of older 'men of honour', with an average age of 62. The nucleus of another powerful clan, that of Minore from Trapani has been reduced to 7 'men of honour' and 17 affiliates. In contrast to this trend for consolidation, other clans have begun to increase the quota of new followers linked by a close family relationship to existing 'men of honour' in order to protect themselves from the possibility of future 'betrayals'. The Cinisi family's inner circle is currently composed of 49 'men of honour' and affiliates, half of whom come from only 3 blood families (Badalamenti, Di Trapani and Palazzolo).

However, the families also have to mobilize enough personnel to carry out illegal activities and provide a military force able to control and earn respect from neighbouring families. Such demands have prevented the major Catania Mafia family – Santapaola – from following the direction of the other Palermo families. The 221 members of the Santapaola clan make up the largest federated criminal coalition in Cosa Nostra. Until the capture of its boss in 1993, this clan succeeded in expanding its legal and illegal activities while other powerful Palermo groups were scaling them back. And it managed to do this while simultaneously waging war with local groups of gangsters. The Santapaola family's solution was to increase slightly the number of 'men of honour' (from 35 in the early 1980s to 44 in 1993), whilst expanding considerably the number of affiliates (up to 177 of a relatively young age by Mafia standards – under 43 on average, against 48 for 'men of honour') and increasing even more the scale of the crown and the periphery of the clan.

The *corona*, or crown, of a Mafia family consists of persons connected by biological or artificial bonds (through the practice of *comparaggio* – creating bonds of obligation) to members of the nucleus. They come from the most disparate classes of society, from the liberal professions to the most valuable and sensitive positions of public administration, and enjoy the trust of the families – which they provide with information, advice, hide-outs and loans – even if their relationship with them is not especially visible. Finally, the periphery of a Cosa Nostra clan includes those who do not have formal or blood ties with family members, but are linked to it for various reasons. They may be motivated by mere convenience and self-interest without having any wider involvement. They are generally members of the criminal world such as kidnappers, thieves, money-lenders, swindlers, etc., as well as economic and financial criminals, politicians and 'friendly' officials. Both the crown and periphery of a Mafia family frequently experience rapid contractions and expansions. In the absence of official repression and anti-Mafia public mobilization, the entourage of an important Mafia coalition can number a couple of thousand, only to be scaled back to a few hundred in times of conflict or serious difficulties.

Two institutions of 'government' that are superior to individual families – the Provincial Commission of Palermo and Cosa Nostra's Regional Commission – arose from the most important organizational reforms ever to occur in Cosa Nostra. According to informers, the Provincial Commission was founded in 1957 on the initiative of Joe Bonanno, then boss of one of the five New York families, and modelled on the American Cosa Nostra Commission. In order to improve decision making, the families in the province were grouped together into constituencies of three families, called *mandamenti* (districts). The new collegial body was thus composed of 14 to 15 members (rather than 50 or more), who elected a secretary. In order to avoid an excessive concentration of power, the *mandamento* boss would not have any function within his own family. However, because of the opposition of some family bosses which threatened to undermine the entire project, some exceptions were allowed from the outset (Arlacchi 1994: 60–71; Stajano 1992: 42). In any case, an overlapping of roles seems to have become common practice, at least in the last twenty years.

The Provincial Commission was dissolved in 1963 following the vigorous reaction of the State to the Ciaculli massacre: this caused considerable difficulties for Cosa Nostra and forced the Mafia bosses to emigrate in order to avoid arrest. It was reconstructed in the mid-1970s after an interim period during which the leadership of Cosa Nostra was taken over by three of its most representative exponents (the so-called 'triumvirate') (Tribunale di Palermo 1984). An institution similar to the

84 SOUTH EUROPEAN SOCIETY & POLITICS

Provincial Commission of Palermo seems to have been created in other provinces too. Where the presence of Cosa Nostra is less widespread, however, internal affairs are still regulated by a single figure, the 'Provincial Representative', chosen periodically from the most important family bosses of the province (Tribunale di Palermo 1989).

The regional Commission was established in the mid-1970s by Giuseppe Calderone, then boss of the Catania family, as the locus for conflict resolution among the provinces and for elaborating strategies for the entire association. It was a committee made up of six 'men of honour', each of whom represented one of the traditional Mafia provinces (excluding the provinces of Messina, Siracusa and Ragusa) (Arlacchi 1992: 122–33, CPM 1992: 279–80).

The declarations of informers and the results of numerous recent inquiries have provided a much more detailed and a deeper understanding of Cosa Nostra's internal relations. Despite the fact that it has much in common with other secret societies using initiation rituals, selection techniques, and rules of management and operations – organizations with which historians and sociologists are familiar – Cosa Nostra does not appear to be a static sect of conspirators. Its internal order is based on a combination of two fundamental types of relationship: relationships of 'purpose' (Weber 1968: 23–9) regarding its members' economic interests, characterized by a high level of market freedom and personal autonomy; and a 'status' relationship (ibid.), involving loyalty and absolute submission to the family and its representative bodies. The latter may require a 'man of honour' to place his own life and that of others in danger when executing high-risk tasks to defend the common interest of the clan (assassination attempts, murders, punishments, etc.). The status of 'man of honour' is acquired through a contract for life, expressed symbolically in a blood oath.

The distinction and balance between the two relationships are fundamental. They enable Mafia groups to establish an equilibrium between the coercive dimension of Cosa Nostra 'militancy', and the economic, pragmatic aspects of daily life. Without such a double dimension, Cosa Nostra would not possess the flexibility and the economic strength that it has. Thus the system of business relationships among the members of a Cosa Nostra family ensures a rigorous respect for private property and the free enterprise of each member. Every 'man of honour' manages his own quota of legal and illegal activity (bars, restaurants, hotels, farms, construction, craft and transport firms, petrol stations, networks of money-lending, clandestine gambling houses, fraud, robbery) in full autonomy. Partnership with other members of the family is frequent but in no way obligatory. The family can 'regulate', tax and, in certain extreme cases, even prohibit specific illegal activities for the sake of the common interest or territoriality. However, the concept of economic freedom for each 'man of honour' and for each family, in relation to others, is never questioned.

But this does not mean that Cosa Nostra's Commission is the executive board of a large criminal firm. The Mafia, as such, is not a 'crime multinational'. The worldwide expansion of illegal trafficking is the result of single investment decisions taken by individual criminals and families that from time to time, for certain business purposes, have become partners. For example, joint-ventures or investor pools are frequently created among members of different families in the international narcotics trade, and oligopolistic cartels are common in securing public contracts. Even though in such cases the Commission can distribute responsibilities and arbitrate disputes, these functions are not central to the Commission's work. Large amounts of Mafia profits are invested in such co-ordinated ways, and the use of the same banks and financiers, in certain areas of Italy and Europe, can give the impression of a plan or unified strategy. However, this is more the result of choices made by illegal businessmen who influence one another's behaviour, for example in the case of the advice-order to divert clan investments to Germany after the entry into force in 1982 of the Rognoni-La Torre law on the confiscation of illegal property.

Mafia families are businesses and present-day Mafiosi are businessmen in the full sense of the word. But the families of Cosa Nostra are not mere businesses and its Commission is not simply an illegal business cartel. The Provincial Commission of Palermo and the Regional Commission are both essentially political organisms. They are a sort of Mafia 'government', a crude attempt to introduce order and co-ordination between traditionally sovereign and independent entities. This 'government' is not highly bureaucratized and its management expenses are minimal, since many crucial services are internalized by the individual families. Legal assistance for example, which represents one of the higher costs for the United States Commission and families, has not been a huge problem for the Sicilians or for the Palermo Commission. Even repression and specialized services of violence are provided by the families and the *mandamenti* when the Provincial Commission needs them. Each *mandamento* has a *gruppo di fuoco* (task force) of 'men of honour' with proven reputations for reliability and efficiency as killers, used for murdering other 'men of honour' or persons of importance under Commission instruction. They also carry out minor killings on their own account but must keep the Commission informed (Procura della Repubblica di Palermo 1993a: 78).

Conflict Regulation and Primitive Law

Notwithstanding the fact that the Commissions have made economic transactions between Cosa Nostra members more secure, their principal function consists of limiting violent internal conflict. In recent years, the number of murders has remained at slightly lower levels in areas where there is a large concentration of Cosa Nostra clans compared with areas where there are independent or non-Cosa Nostra gangs. For nine years, Sicily has had the highest absolute levels of murder in Italy – over 400 in 1989 – which began to fall only in 1992. Nevertheless, the two provinces of the island with the highest concentration of Cosa Nostra families (Palermo and Trapani) – where a third of the island's population lives – made a fairly small contribution to the region's statistics (a maximum of 39.8 per cent in 1988 and a minimum of 9.4 per cent in 1993). The majority of organized crimes take place outside the areas that are strictly controlled by Cosa Nostra families. In Messina, which was traditionally a province without a Mafia tradition, the absolute number of murders is actually higher for recent years than in Palermo which has almost double the population. The rapid growth in murders in eastern Sicily, which has no historical Cosa Nostra settlements, can be attributed to the formation during the 1980s of vast groupings of Mafia-gangsters and numerous bands of young delinquents which make a symbolic-demonstrative use of lethal violence. Such criminal groups lack any regulatory and co-ordinating organs capable of preventing clashes and defining territories and sectors of influence. The latter are established ex-post as a result of armed confrontations in the streets, piazzas and local hangouts.

But the firm control of inter-Mafia conflicts by the Commissions should not be confused with the Mafia's exaggerated capacity for guaranteeing law and order. Today's Cosa Nostra is not particularly inclined to repress or contain small-time criminals or common delinquency. Current Cosa Nostra families tend to 'overlook' a significant amount of illegal activity. Indeed, provinces with the highest number of 'men of honour' also have a rate of 'normal' crime (burglaries, robberies, extortion) among the highest in the country. This can be explained in part by the need to maintain a large reserve army of criminal labour for the purpose of mobilization by the clans.

Even though it has numerous legal-political-administrative traits such as territorial organs of government, and formal norms and sanctions, it would be wrong to overestimate the level of development of Cosa Nostra's legal order. It cannot be understood as an 'illegal State' *tout court* since its 'constitution' is embryonic and far cruder than the basic laws and constitutions of modern states. Its precepts are ignored, manipulated, suspended and contradicted so frequently that they become a form of 'primitive law', to be interpreted using the tools of legal anthropology rather than of criminal law. They are closer to the institutions and codes, used for resolving controversies and punishing non-conformist behaviour, found in pre-industrial society than to the rational structures of a modern state (Pospisil 1971, Motta 1994). Characteristic elements of states include the prohibition of the use of force among citizens, with the exception of legitimate defence, and the delegation of three principal functions – the production, assessment and implementation of law – to parliament, the courts and the police (Cassese 1984: 20). Such institutions are only embryonic in Cosa Nostra and a process of functional differentiation has only partially come about: the Provincial Commission and the Regional Commission simultaneously carry out 'legislative', 'executive' and 'legal' functions. Their decisions are not based on a corpus of consolidated and recognized norms but express the largely arbitrary will of the Mafia group or coalition in power.

This has become especially evident in recent years. Between 1957 and 1963, when Cosa Nostra had a 'horizontal' order that was based on a plurality of families, each sovereign in its own territory, the Commission performed a function of mediation between the positions and interests of the various *mandamenti* bosses. The decision to murder a 'man of honour' who had committed a serious violation had to have the approval of all the *mandamenti* bosses and often less drastic measures were preferred, such as the suspension of the offender or his expulsion. But with the ascent to power of the Riina-led coalition, murder was no longer used simply to punish behaviour which contravened Cosa Nostra rules; it became the main instrument for guaranteeing the stability and supremacy of the leadership group against attempts by individual 'men of honour' to increase their own autonomy and power (Procura della Repubblica di Palermo 1993b: 212).

MODERN-DAY MAFIA: ECONOMIC AND POLITICAL TRANSFORMATION

Economic Activities

The business transformation of the Mafia happened fairly recently. Until the end of the 1960s, the main illegal activity was contraband tobacco, providing a basic source of income for a minority of affiliates, since the majority of 'men of honour' kept their legal occupations. Even extortion was not practised in the systematic way that it is now in most parts of Sicily. In exchange for a monthly contribution and occasional favours, the Mafiosi performed a surveillance service, were so-called 'caretakers' of estates belonging to well-to-do locals, and, more rarely, they 'protected' certain big businessmen (Arlacchi 1992: 42–4).

Before the 1970s, no single Mafia boss or Mafia family ever succeeded in acquiring massive wealth and power. For example, the financial resources of one of the five New York families studied by the anthropologist Francis Ianni amounted to no more than $15 million at the beginning of the 1970s (Ianni 1972). Even Sicilian Mafia bosses had rather limited economic strength until the end of the 1960s. Only in the course of the 1970s did they become more closely involved in illicit big business. In the case of Cosa Nostra clans, the major transformation came about when they achieved dominance in two particularly lucrative markets – the wholesale drug trade and public contracts. The Sicilian families took control from French criminal groups of heroin imports from south-east Asia and heroin exports to the US, and Sicily became an important centre for heroin refining and distribution. From 1975–76, to the discovery of the first laboratory in 1980, Sicily produced 4–5 tons of pure heroin per annum – sufficient to satisfy 30 per cent of the American market, with a value of around 700–800 billion lire per annum (Arlacchi 1983: 232).

During the 1980s, however, the quota of the US market for heroin held by Sicilian clans fell steadily. The alliance that emerged victorious from the Mafia wars of 1981–83 failed to maintain its dominant position in the international drug trade. This was caused in part by the intense anti-Mafia offensive launched in 1984 with the legal co-operation agreement between Italy and the US (Fondazione Falcone 1994: 331). By the end of the 1980s, the US market was supplied with heroin mainly from south-east Asia by Chinese criminal groups (NNICC 1990). The marginalization of the Cosa Nostra in the drugs business was also linked to a gradual concentration of refining activity in the countries of cultivation (Lewis 1985: 15). Yet it would be wrong to assume that Cosa Nostra clans are no longer involved in large-scale narcotics trade. They still have an important role in importing and in the wholesale distribution of drugs in the main piazzas of the Italian Centre North and other European countries. Since the end of the 1980s, Sicilian groups have joined forces with Colombian trafficking operations in Europe and, thanks also to their network in Latin America, Cosa Nostra imported substantial quantities of cocaine into the major West European markets.

From the mid-1980s, the Corleone families made more profits from public contracts than from the drugs trade. Cosa Nostra was helped to achieve this by formally 'clean' businessmen who manipulated the distribution of major orders. These businessmen were in charge of

MAFIA: SICILIAN COSA NOSTRA   89

managing competition and designating winning businesses according to
agreed criteria of ordered rotation. This generally occurred without
particular pressures or explicit threats. Recourse to violence occurred
only when it appeared indispensable to ensure compliance with the
established 'rules' or that Mafia interests in certain areas of competition
were respected (DIA 1993). That Cosa Nostra managed to control the
assignment of 20 public works contracts awarded in Sicily, each
amounting to 50 billion lire in 1992, gives some idea of the scale of the
Mafia profits in this area.

The scope for organized crime activities and their capacity for
penetrating the legal economy have been extended considerably by
recycling and reinvesting illegal profits. Moreover, illegal profits are
exported to foreign countries where there are incomplete and archaic
regulations on recycling and organized crime, or to 'tax paradises' where
regulations favour 'hot' and 'dirty' money (Naylor 1986). In the last few
years, Mafia groups have also extended their investments to ex-socialist
bloc countries. Finally, it should be noted that old-fashioned extortion
continues to provide a major source of illegal income. During the last 20
years, Cosa Nostra families and other criminals have imposed a
widespread regime of extortion on their territories to finance legal bills
and provide for the families of detained 'men of honour' and affiliates.
It is even possible that the intensification of this activity has resulted
from the increased vigour of the anti-Mafia opposition. The arrests of
their leaders, as well as the difficulty of carrying out lucrative trafficking,
have obliged the families to return to their more traditional activity.

Political Relations

The development of its business interests has enabled the Mafia to
redefine its relationship with politics. Vast wealth allowed organized
crime to develop unprecedented economic, political and military power
and put an end to its traditional role of political and cultural mediator
between central state and periphery. Without such vast economic
resources, the Sicilian bosses would not have been able to carry out the
assassination attempts on high-ranking legal and political figures that
have bloodied Sicily for the last 15 years. Nor would they have been
capable of the campaign of Mafia terrorism that hit Italy in 1992 and
1993.

There had been no major confrontation between Cosa Nostra and the
State for a long time. Mafiosi and representatives of public power,
theoretically antagonists in the sense that they compete for the
monopoly of violence, have in reality collaborated in achieving a
common objective – the preservation of the social and political order.

For decades, many Mafia leaders enjoyed a de facto delegation from the Italian State for the exercise of public order functions in large areas of most southern regions. They did so in the conviction that they were acting legally: as mayors in many Sicilian communes during the Anglo-American occupation, as an auxiliary police force during the repression of bandits and peasant protests just after the war, and as conciliators in civil and criminal matters whose role was recognized and praised publicly by State officials (Hess 1973, Pantaleone 1962, Renda 1987, Violante 1994: 8–57). The Mafia was assigned some of the most delicate public functions in the context of an intense exchange relationship between Mafia groups and politicians. The Mafia leader was almost always an important figure of political influence whose support was necessary for candidates in national and local elections. From the 1880s until a little over a decade ago, the majority of Sicilian members of government owed a large part of their electoral success to their links with, or membership of, Cosa Nostra.

In exchange for their electoral support – provided through 'legal' methods of political clientelism as well as by threats and the corruption of voters, Mafiosi received favours and protection for themselves and for their friends for more than a century (Tranfaglia 1992). But over the last 30 years, the relationship between Mafia and politics has changed considerably, mainly because the State has withdrawn from the Mafia the task of mediating and repressing political and social conflict. After the first Anti-Mafia Commission was set up in 1962, and especially in the 1980s after the assassination of General Dalla Chiesa, the Mafia power was no longer legitimated by the State: an ethical-political protest movement against the Mafia and corruption emerged with its own leaders and electoral lists. The relationship between government members and Mafia leaders was no longer flaunted but surreptitious, and, in some recent cases, has damaged reputations and careers.

Encouraged by the development of an anti-Mafia civil movement, the magistrature began an enquiry into the relations between the Mafia and State institutions in the 1980s: this led to the incrimination and arrest of hundreds of politicians. Between 1991 and 1995, more than half of the deputies in Sicily's regional parliament, as well as 17 national parliamentarians, were accused of corruption or collusion with the Mafia. Cosa Nostra reacted by abandoning its usual tactics of collusion and adopting a frontal terrorist attack on State institutions, as manifest in the assassination attempts and the massacres of the spring-summer of 1992 and 1993, when Judges Falcone and Borsellino, among others, lost their lives.

It was in fact the increase in the clans' economic power in the 1970s that was to destroy the long-standing and stable relationship between

Cosa Nostra and Sicilian politics. The subordination of the latter to criminal power, and the emergence of an evenly matched confrontation between leaders of Cosa Nostra and national political figures, became more and more evident. Informers have described some of the meetings between Giulio Andreotti and Bontade, Riina and other Mafia leaders that took place between 1979 and 1987 during which the latter showed little deference to the seven times prime minister of Italy, now accused of 'association with the Mafia' by the judges in Palermo. On the contrary, the representatives of the two orders of power faced each other, conscious of their respective prerogatives, and even jealous (in the case of the Mafiosi) of the territorial extent of their power. In one of these meetings, Bontade threatened to withdraw votes from Andreotti's Christian Democrat party in Sicily, Reggio Calabria and elsewhere in southern Italy and threatened 'serious consequences' if Andreotti's government adopted special anti-Mafia powers (Procura della Repubblica di Palermo 1995).

The story of the relationship between Cosa Nostra and State institutions and politicians over the last 40 years can be found in the life history of Salvo Lima, Andreotti's Sicilian 'lieutenant'. In conjunction with other members of the Fanfani faction in Palermo – who subsequently became *Andreottiani* (supporters of Andreotti) – Lima began in the mid-1950s to take hold of almost all of the fundamental levers of regional power, assuming the leadership of a powerful political machine that left the Mafiosi with little room for independent manoeuvre. The 'men of honour' were obliged to operate within the clientelistic networks controlled by a group of political bosses who were very similar to the Mafiosi in terms of birth and socialization (Lima himself was the son of a Mafioso). At the beginning of the 1960s, Salvo Lima had the same power and prestige as Mafia boss Tommaso Buscetta. However, in the 1980s, with the ascendance of the Corleone family, Lima's power diminished and he was murdered for failing to honour his task of 'fixing' the anti-Mafia maxi-trial in the Supreme Court.

Although it would be inaccurate to say that Cosa Nostra has exercised untrammelled rule over Sicilian public institutions over the last few decades, its influence on electoral lists and campaigns should not be underestimated. Our knowledge of the hidden ties between parliamentary candidates and the clans is today much greater thanks to disclosures by super-grasses. Taking only those referred to by Tommaso Buscetta in interviews with the author, as well as those named by the Palermo super-grasses Gaspare Mutolo and Marino Mannoia, it is possible to assess this influence on national elections in western Sicily between 1958 and 1979.

If we compare the names of parliamentarians known to the informers as 'men of honour', or elements close to Cosa Nostra, with the number of elected Christian Democrats (DC) and other parties' members, we obtain the following results (Table 1).

The data demonstrate how from half to three quarters of DC deputies, and about 40 per cent of all deputies, elected to the lower house of Parliament in western Sicily from the end of the 1950s to the end of the 1970s were actively supported – when they were not themselves 'men of honour' – by Cosa Nostra families.

TABLE 1
MAFIA SUPPORT FOR ELECTED POLITICIANS IN WESTERN SICILY, 1958–1979

Elections to the lower house of Parliament	Deputies supported by Cosa Nostra elected on DC list (a)	Deputies elected on DC lists (b)	% a/b	Deputies supported by Cosa Nostra elected on other lists	Total deputies supported by Cosa Nostra(c)	Total deputies elected in west Sicily(d)	% c/d
1958	8	13	61.5	2	10	25	40.0
1963	9	12	75.0	2	11	26	42.3
1968	7	12	58.3	3	10	26	38.5
1972	7	13	53.8	2	9	26	34.6
1976	7	13	53.8	3	10	23	43.5
1979	6	13	46.1	3	9	22	40.1

Relations with Covert Masonic Lodges

Cosa Nostra reacted to the State's withdrawal of delegated power, as well as the ethical-political maturing of Sicilian civil society, by increasing the clandestine nature of its activities and even by becoming more closely involved with other, covert criminal networks. Relations with 'covert' Masonic lodges have been particularly intense. The Masonic sects provided Mafia groups with the specialized knowledge and the power to manipulate the State's central institutions which they did not possess themselves. In turn, Cosa Nostra provided the lodges with two resources they actively sought: professional violence and money. Such an exchange was facilitated by the particular characteristics of Masonic association. The secrecy surrounding Freemasonry and the relationships among Masonic 'brothers' makes interpersonal relationships between the Mafia and Masonry more difficult to investigate. At the same time, the bond of solidarity and mutual help that binds the 'brothers' has made the production of favours for Cosa Nostra much easier thanks to the

MAFIA: SICILIAN COSA NOSTRA   93

widespread participation of State officials and liberal professionals in the lodges.

Since the beginning of the 1970s, the reciprocal involvement of Cosa Nostra and Sicilian Masonic lodges has grown in such a way as to create a situation of 'dual membership' for dozens of the more influential Mafia bosses. But this has not meant their subordination to the interests and the aims of the Free Masons. On the contrary, an equal partnership for the illegal exploitation and plundering of public resources was established (CPM 1993). The infiltration of Mafia bosses into networks of illegal lobbying and the collusion of Masonic affiliates with members of organized crime emerges clearly from the numerous inquiries and trials of the last 15 years. The preliminary investigation and hearing into the assassination of the lawyer Giorgio Ambrosoli, the liquidator of the Banca Privata Italiana, proved, for instance, that the false kidnapping in 1979 of the bankrupt Sicilian Michele Sindona was managed by Cosa Nostra in Sicily and the US in collaboration with covert Freemasons.

The relationship with this 'deviant' form of Masonry allowed Cosa Nostra to overcome the impasse created by the expansion of the scale of its trafficking, which otherwise would have opened its ranks uncontrollably as well as threatening its standards of secrecy. These links also helped Cosa Nostra deal with the damage inflicted by the super-grasses and the State's anti-Mafia offensive. Its level of secrecy has increased and its rules and codes have changed. Furthermore, its close alliance with covert Masonry enabled Cosa Nostra to avoid internal demands for modernization and change. Its future, therefore, will continue to have an old heart.

REFERENCES

Allegra, M. (1937): 'Come io, medico, diventai mafioso', *L'Ora*, 22–25/1/1962.
Arlacchi, P. (1980): 'Mafia e tipi di società', *La Rassegna Italiana di Sociologia*, 1.
—— (1983): *La mafia impreditrice: L'etica mafiosa e lo spirito del capitalismo*, Bologna: Il Mulino.
—— (1992): *Gli uomini del disonore. La Mafia siciliana nella vita del grande pentito Antonino Calderone*, Milano: Mondadori.
—— (1994): *Addio Cosa Nostra: La vita di Tommaso Buscetta*, Milano: Rizzoli.
Cassese, S. (1984): *Il diritto internazionale nel mondo contemporaneo*, Bologna: Il Mulino.
Ciconte, E. (1992): *La 'ndrangheta dall'Unità a oggi*, Bari: Laterza.
Commissione Parlamentare d'inchiesta sul fenomeno della mafia e delle altre associazioni similari (CPM)(1992): *Audizione del collaboratire di giustizia Antonino Calderone*, 11 Nov.
—— (1993): *Relazione sui rapporti mafia e politica*, April.
Direzione Investigativa Antimafia (DIA)(1993): *Rapporto semestrale sulle criminilità organizzata*, Rome: Ministero dell'Interno.
Fondazione Falcone (1994): *Giovanne Falcone: Interventi e proposte (1982–1992)*, Firenze: Sansoni.
Hess, H. (1973): *Mafia*, Bari: Laterza.

94   SOUTH EUROPEAN SOCIETY & POLITICS

Ianni, F. (1972): *Affari di famiglia*, Milano: Bompiani.
Lewis, R. (1985): 'Serious Business: the Global Heroin Economy', in A. Henman, R. Lewis
    and T. Maylon, *Big Deal: the Politics of the Illicit Drug Business*, London: Pinter Press,
    pp.5–49.
Lo Schiavo, G.G. (1962): *100 anni di mafia*, Roma: Bianco.
Montalbano, G. (1953): 'La mafia e il banditismo', *Rinascata* No.10, Oct.
Motta, R. (1994): *L'addomesticamento degli etnodiritti: Percorsi dell'antropologia giuridica
    teorica e applicata*, Milano: Unicopli.
Naylor, T. (1986): *Denaro che scotta*, Milano: Comunità.
NNICC (1990): National Narcotics Intelligence Consumers Committe, *The Supply of
    Illicit Drugs to the United States.*
Pantaleone, M. (1962): *Mafia e politica (1943–62): Le radici sociali della mafia ed i suoi
    sviluppi più recenti*, Torino: Einaudi.
Pitrè, G. (1889): *Usi, costume, credenze e pregiudizi del popolo siciliano*, Vol 2, Palermo.
Pospisil, L.J. (1971): *Anthropology of Law: A Comparative Theory*, New York: Harper and
    Row.
Procura della Repubblica di Palermo (1993a): *Richiesta di applicazione di misure cautelari
    contro Agate Mariano + 57*, 20 Feb.
—— (1993b): *Richiesta di applicazione di misure cautelari contro Abbate Luigi + 87*, 23
    Dec.
—— (1995): *Memoria depositata dal Pubblico Ministero nel Procedimento Penale, No.
    3538/94 nei confronti di Andreotti Giulio.*
Reid, E. (1956): *La mafia: Dalle origini ai giorni nostri*, Firenze: Parenti.
Renda, F. (1987): *Storia della Sicilia, Vol. 3*, Palermo: Sellerio.
Romano, S. (1918) [repr. 1977]: *L'ordinamento giuridico*, Firenze: Sansoni.
Sales, I. (1988): *La camorra, le camorre*, Roma: Editore Riuniti.
Stajano, C. (1992): *Mafia: L'atto di accusa dei giudici di Palermo*, Roma: Editore Riuniti.
Sylos Labini, P. (ed.) (1966): *Problemi dell'economia siciliana*, Milano: Feltrinelli.
Tranfaglia, N. (1992): *Mafia: Politica e affari, 1943–1991*, Bari: Laterza.
Tribunale di Palermo (1984): *Interrogatori resi da Tommaso Buscetta.*
—— (1989): *Interrogatori resi dal collaboratore di giustizia Francesco Marino Mannoia*, 7
    Nov.
Violante, L. (1994): *Non è la piovra: Dodici tesi sulle mafie italiane*, Torino: Einaudi.
Weber, M. (1968): *Economia e società*, Milano: Comunit.

[46]

The Judiciary in the Italian Political Crisis

CARLO GUARNIERI

In post-war Italy the judiciary has played an increasingly significant role in the political system. The roots of this development have to be traced to the Constitution of 1948 and to the way in which it was implemented. The institutional setting of the Italian judiciary has been radically altered, in an attempt to make it as independent as possible from the political branches of government. However, for many years judicial power was somewhat constrained, with political parties exploiting the internal divisions of the judiciary. After 1992, the collapse of traditional governmental parties, partly brought about by judicial actions, has made Italy a example par excellence of judicialised politics.

THE TRADITIONAL SETTING AND ITS TRANSFORMATION

For a long time the Italian judiciary was structurally very similar to those elsewhere in the European continent. Especially during the period of Unification (1859–70), the influence of Napoleonic models of government organisation was very strong. Even later, notwithstanding some minor adjustments, the basic structure did not change very much, at least until the period following the Second World War. For this reason, the Italian judiciary displayed the well-known characteristics of civil law judicial bureaucracies:

- Applicants for the judiciary were selected on the basis of their general institutional knowledge of the law, as tested by written and oral exams and guaranteed by a university degree.
- Professional training and experience was to be acquired inside the judicial organisation, starting from the bottom of the pyramid-like hierarchy, since candidates for the judiciary were encouraged to enter the competition soon after graduation.
- Promotions to higher positions were granted, according to the traditional criteria of seniority and merit, by hierarchical superiors enjoying considerable discretion, with the government playing an important role in appointments to higher positions.
- The approach to work performance and role assignment was of a 'generalistic' type, whereby members of the judiciary were supposed to

158   CRISIS AND TRANSITION IN ITALIAN POLITICS

be able to perform equally all organisational roles formally associated with their rank: for example, adjudicate a criminal case, a bankruptcy case, a family case or to perform as a public prosecutor.[1]

The role played by the judiciary in the political arena more or less conformed to the classical stereotype of the civil law tradition, according to which judges are – and have to be – the *bouche de la loi*, merely giving voice to the will of the legislator. However, notwithstanding the fact that judicial independence was guaranteed, a vast array of hierarchical controls and continuous oversights by Justice Ministers ensured that this role had to be performed in such a way that it did not conflict with government policies.

Immediately after the Second World War, in 1946, as a first reaction to past abuses – occurring, although with different intensity, during both the Liberal and the Fascist regimes – the guarantees of judges and public prosecutors *vis-à-vis* the executive were somewhat reinforced, even though the hierarchical character of the judiciary was left untouched. But much more important reforms were contained in the Constitution enacted in 1948.[2] Indeed, the Constitution triggered a long process which has led to a deep transformation of the political role of the Italian judiciary. In the Constituent Assembly the memory of the past contributed to a general attitude of distrust towards executive power, often seen as a potential threat to democracy. Therefore, the Constitution envisaged the institution of a self-governing body of the judiciary, the Higher Council of the Judiciary (*Consiglio Superiore della Magistratura*), two-thirds of which was composed of magistrates elected by their colleagues and one third of lawyers or law professors elected by Parliament, to which all decisions concerning the status of magistrates had to be referred.

However, after the sweeping victory of the Christian Democrats (DC) at the 1948 legislative elections, the constitutional design in the realm of the administration of justice was, at first, not implemented. At least until the end of the 1950s, the Italian judiciary was governed mainly by the higher-ranking magistrates, acting very often in full agreement with the Minister of Justice. Thus, direct pressures by the executive in judicial affairs were rare, since the hierarchical setting allowed more discrete interventions through senior magistrates. Apart from some minor cases, there were no serious tensions in this period between the higher judiciary and Christian Democratic governments.

Only after 1959 did things begin to change, leading to a great increase in both the internal and external independence of Italian judges. In that year, the constitutionally-mandated Higher Council of the Judiciary was instituted, progressively taking away the powers of the executive in the

THE JUDICIARY'S POLITICAL ROLE   159

administration of judicial personnel, namely, of judges and public prosecutors. Since 1975, this body has had 33 members:[3] in addition to the President of the Republic, and the President and Prosecutor General of the Court of Cassation, ten are elected by Parliament (the electoral quorum – 60 per cent – is such that representation has been guaranteed for parties of the left, i.e. Socialists and Communists) and 20 are elected via proportional representation by all magistrates. Its main institutional function is to make all decisions concerning judicial personnel: recruitment, promotions, transfers from one judicial office to another, disciplinary sanctions, and so on. Even this summary of the functions and composition of the Higher Council suggests how it broke with the traditional bureaucratic structure of the judiciary, in so far as lower- and middle-ranking magistrates participated for the first time in decision-making processes regarding the distribution of organisational awards and sanctions, not only with respect to their peers, but higher-level magistrates as well.

The reforms of the post-war period also affected the position of public prosecutors. From Unification until 1946, the public prosecutor was considered to be the representative of the executive inside the judiciary. The prosecuting officers were members of the judiciary, following the same career path as judges, but could be transferred into the ranks of the latter group – at least formally – only under special circumstances. The prosecution offices were structured according to hierarchical principles. The prosecutor-general attached to each court of appeal had powers of direction and supervision over all subordinate offices of its district. At the top of the pyramid was the Minister of Justice. In 1946 the traditional dependence of the public prosecutor on executive instructions was abolished. The Constitution of 1948 recognised the principle of compulsory prosecution of criminal offences by the public prosecutor, reaffirmed that prosecutors had to be members of the judiciary, and proclaimed their equality of status with judges, guaranteeing their autonomy from every other branch of government, a goal that was fully achieved after the institution of the Higher Council in 1959.

The institution of the Higher Council, therefore, brought about a remarkable increase in the independence of the Italian judiciary *vis-à-vis* the executive, the traditional point of reference of its so-called 'external' independence. However, another major modification in the organisational set-up of the judiciary concerned the system of promotion. The traditional system was sharply criticised by the majority of lower-ranking magistrates, strongly organised inside their professional association – the *Associazione Nazionale dei Magistrati* (ANM) – which claimed that promotions contradicted the principle of judicial independence (or at least its 'internal' aspects) as sanctioned by the Constitution. In the face of this pressure, Parliament

160   CRISIS AND TRANSITION IN ITALIAN POLITICS

passed a series of laws, between 1963 and 1973, which dismantled step by
step the traditional system of promotions and with it the traditional power
of the higher ranks. The consequence is that, today, those candidates with
the seniority required to compete for promotion at the different levels of
the judicial hierarchy are no longer evaluated – as they were until the 1960s
– either by written and oral exams, or on the basis of their written judicial
works, but rather by a 'global' assessment of their judicial performance.
Once promoted, even in excess of existing vacancies, they enjoy all the
material advantages of the new rank, even though they may continue to
exercise the lower judicial functions of their previous rank. In fact, all candidates who fulfil the seniority requirements are promoted to the highest
ranks. It is a phenomenon that can be explained to a great extent by the
way in which the composition of the Higher Council is determined, its
judicial members being elected by the very colleagues they have to evaluate.[4]

By the end of this process, in the mid-1970s, the Italian judiciary had
assumed considerable political significance. Its guarantees of independence,
both external and internal, are considerable. Moreover, it is the only case,
among democratic polities, in which the same corps of career magistrates
performs both judicial and prosecuting functions in conditions of full
independence.

THE GROWTH OF JUDICIAL POWER IN THE 'FIRST REPUBLIC'

As we have seen, deep changes have been brought about inside the judiciary
by reforms of the status and the career of magistrates. An important
phenomenon related to this development has been the emergence of
organised factions (*correnti*). Due to the internal conflict over career structure, since the late 1950s, the professional associations of Italian magistrates
have been officially divided into ideological factions, each with a stable,
although limited, organisational structure. After a long history of divisions
and reunifications, the most important today are, from left to right:
*Magistratura Democratica, Movimento per la Giustizia, Unità per la
Costituzione*, and *Magistratura Indipendente*.

The *correnti* have played a remarkable role in furthering the interests of
the magistrates. After realising that not much could be obtained from the
government – which, at least until the end of the 1960s, supported the
highest ranks – they turned their attention first to public opinion, trying to
enlist its support for their cause, and later to political parties. In fact, the
laws dismantling the traditional career structure were passed thanks to the
support of the parties of the left, and especially of the Socialist Party (PSI),
during the years when it became part of the new centre-left governing
majority. The Socialists were obviously interested in developing contacts

THE JUDICIARY'S POLITICAL ROLE 161

with a strategic body like the judiciary and in strengthening its guarantees of independence from an executive branch they could not hope fully to control. In this situation, the traditional party of government, the DC, found itself confronted by new and powerful competitors. Its internal fragmentation, with growing competition among various factions, gave the judiciary ample opportunities for finding allies within its ranks. In the process, new and stronger relationships developed between association leaders, political parties and public opinion, as represented by the media. At the same time, the traditional pro-active definition of the judicial role came under fire. The more 'progressive' groups – like *Magistratura Democratica* – began to stress the need for a 'less positivistic' approach to the interpretation of the law by judges and the duty to take into account the principles – above all, that of equality – set out in the Constitution. The result was the development of more activist conceptions of the judicial role which, although shared only by a minority, nevertheless began to exert a slow but steady influence on judicial decisions.

As already mentioned, the demands put forward by the judicial groups were well received, above all, in the PSI. The other important party of the left – the Communist Party (PCI) – supported the reforms, but at the time had a much more cautious attitude towards them. Inside the party, there was still considerable mistrust of the judiciary, since it was perceived, according to traditional Marxist ideology, as a 'bourgeois', repressive institution. Things began to change after 1968. In that year, the eruption of mass movements nearly everywhere in Italian society triggered a new, and deeper conflict inside the judiciary as well. Some left-wing magistrates – grouped around *Magistratura Democratica* – further developed the activist conceptions of the judicial role (which were by now widespread within the profession) and began sharply to criticise traditional judicial policies. This critique was much more than doctrinal: it produced concrete judicial decisions, frequently defying the traditional jurisprudence of the Court of Cassation, and often involved the direct participation of 'progressive' magistrates in mass meetings and demonstrations. One of the consequences of these new developments inside the judiciary was a slow shift in the attitude of the Communist Party. The judiciary came to be considered a profession in which 'democratic' magistrates were also at work and whose decisions could be supportive of the workers movement.[5] This changing position of the PCI was accelerated by its electoral successes of 1975 and 1976 and by its growing involvement in the policy process.[6] Indeed, the law which introduced the principle of proportional representation with competing lists of candidates for the election of judicial representatives in the Higher Council, and which erased the last prerogatives of the judicial hierarchy, was enacted, with Communist support, at the end of 1975.

162   CRISIS AND TRANSITION IN ITALIAN POLITICS

The changes in the institutional setting of the judiciary have also strengthened the role of the Higher Council. The very growth of judicial associations – a phenomenon that can also be found elsewhere, for example, in France, Portugal and Spain – has acquired a greater relevance in Italy because of the unparalleled role played by the *correnti* in the Higher Council of the Judiciary – an important decision-making body. The changes in that institution's electoral rules, especially the reform of 1975, have made the *correnti* stronger: since 1976, all magistrates elected to the Higher Council have belonged to one or another corrente (see Table 1). In fact, with this last reform the possibility of being represented in the Council has been offered to all the main groups.[7] Yet, the significance of the *correnti* cannot be understood without taking into account the fact that, by *de facto* associating rank exclusively with length of service, the dismantling of the hierarchical structure has deprived the Council of the criteria with which to evaluate magistrates when making appointments to higher positions or deciding on transfers or when many applicants compete for the same position. In these cases, since the Council finds itself in a position to choose among candidates of the same rank, – all of which, at least formally, are equally qualified – the links between a candidate to a faction or a party could become highly relevant. In other words, the transfer or 'promotion' to a given position occurs, when not on the basis of the simple seniority, very likely as the result of a deal among the factions and parties, which often support one another in a process reciprocal exchange. On the other hand, the relevance of the Higher Council is also supported by the fact that, thanks to the decline of the powers of the Ministry of Justice, it has become the most effective institutional link between the judiciary and the political sphere.[8]

In this new context, there was a slow but steady growth of judicial interventions in politically relevant matters, which were greeted with varying degrees of enthusiasm by the political class. In fact, part of it was not enthusiastic at all. Some examples are particularly interesting. The part played by the judiciary in the fight against political terrorism was, without doubt, very important. Government and Parliament granted extensive powers to the judiciary, allowing public prosecutors and investigating judges to direct criminal investigations. This trend was especially strong in the years of 'National Solidarity' (1976–79) when the PCI lent its support to the governing majority. This could be seen in the PCI's expanded participation in the criminal policy process, since many of the magistrates in charge of these affairs were well-known PCI sympathisers or, at least, sympathetic to the left. On the other hand, the PCI strongly supported the fight against political terrorism, both left and right, at the institutional level – for example, in Parliament – and at the mass level, mobilising its organisation in support of the judiciary and the police forces.

THE JUDICIARY'S POLITICAL ROLE 163

TABLE 1

ELECTIONS TO HIGHER COUNCIL BY CORRENTE (1976–1994):
VOTES, PERCENTAGES AND SEATS

Left		<===>		Right		
Year	Magistratura Democratica (MD)	Movimento per la Giustizia[9] (MG)	Unità per la Costituzione (UC)	Magistratura Indipendente (MI)	Others[10]	Voters
1976	755		2526	2156	506	5943
	13%		42%	36%	9%	
	2		9	8	1	
1981	803		2557	2263	297	5990
	14%		43%	38%	5%	
	3		9	8		
1986	1107		2517	2078	402	6159
	19%		41%	34%	6%	
	3		9	7	1	
1990	1337	714	2236	1828		6115
	22%	12%	36%	30%		
	4	3	8	5		
1994	1620	1133	2854	1230		6837
	24%	16%	42%	18%		
	5	4	8	3		

Note: Superscript figures 9 and 10 refer to the endnotes on p.173.

One of the most important consequences of this period was the build-up of investigative capabilities inside the judiciary, well exemplified by the growing influence of public prosecutors and investigating judges over the police forces. In the 1980s, these capabilities began to be employed in another important field, the fight against organised crime. We cannot deal here with the well-known historical strength of organised crime in some Italian region, such as Sicily, Calabria or Campania.[11] It is sufficient to note that, for different reasons, the beginning of the 1980s saw a resurgence of organised crime in these regions and their spread to the more industrialised regions of the North. Some parts of the judiciary – often, but not only, those which had already played an important part in the fight against terrorism – began to conduct important investigations in this field as well. This time, the attitude of the political class was less straightforward. While it cannot be said that it fought against judicial initiatives, its attitude was much more passive than in the case of terrorism. This statement however, applies mostly to government parties since, broadly speaking, the PCI also supported this new judicial trend, which in any case led to defining the maintenance of public order as the responsibility of the judiciary, rather than, as was traditionally the case, the executive.

The first part of the 1980s witnessed a definite growth in judicial power. Another, striking example is the case of judicial salaries. Between the end of the 1970s and the middle of the 1980s, judicial salaries were increased substantially, thanks to favourable legislation and to the even more favourable interpretations of it by higher courts, like the Court of Cassation, the Council of State and the Court of Accounts. What must be emphasised is, first, that judicial salaries have become the highest in the state sector, outpacing their traditional point of reference, the higher civil service. Second, all parties more or less willingly supported judicial demands – including the Communists who broke with their traditional stance of not supporting salary increases for higher-ranking state officials.[12]

However, as we have already noted, not all the political class welcomed this expansion of judicial power. Indeed, some groups were strongly opposed to it. The most important was the PSI, under the leadership of Bettino Craxi, even though opposition towards judicial interventionism was not confined to this party but could also be found in minor centrist parties as well as among the Christian Democrats. The tensions between the PSI and the judiciary, or at least that part of it more prone to intervene in politically relevant matters, erupted in the early 1980s in the course of the Ambrosiano scandal.[13] The aim of checking the expansion of judicial power led the PSI and its allies to back proposals for a system of civil liability for magistrates, who had hitherto been more or less exempt from it. Capitalising on widespread dissatisfaction with the performance of the judicial system and on some miscarriages of justice like the Tortora affair,[14] the proponents of the referendum were able to attract wide popular support. The move was an astute one, since those parties usually much more sympathetic to judicial interests, like the Communists, had to give in and advise their electors to vote yes in the popular referendum as well. But the Socialists were also helped in achieving their aim by the stubbornness of the leadership of the ANM, which refused any kind of compromise on the matter and asked the electorate to vote no. Therefore, the results, with more than 80 per cent of votes in favour of introducing some form of civil liability for the judiciary, was seen as a defeat of the judiciary as a whole, as it was unable to enlist the support of the majority of the voters.

The weakening of the judiciary, and especially of its associational leadership, opened the way to a more important reform: that of criminal procedure. Since 1930, Italian criminal procedure has been governed by the code enacted by the then justice minister, Rocco, which more or less followed the traditional Napoleonic inquisitory model of an instructing judge in charge of the investigation, at least for serious cases. Even though its more authoritarian aspects were removed in the 1950s and 1960s by legislative reforms and by the Constitutional Court, criminal procedure was thought to contradict the values of the new democratic regime. However, attempts at reform came up against the careful, but always strong, obstruction of the judiciary, which was afraid of losing some of its powers. Only after the referendum of 1987 was the situation ripe for the reform to be introduced, under the aegis of the justice minister, the Socialist jurist, Vassalli. A new, more accusatory code was introduced with the intent of reducing the powers of the judiciary and abolishing the role of the instructing judge. But, as we will see below, the results have not been those anticipated by the reformers.[15]

Thus, the end of the 1980s was characterised by an attempt, especially by Socialists, to resist the expansion of judicial power. The Socialist leadership found an ally in the President of the Republic, the Christian Democrat, Francesco Cossiga (1985–92), and the tension thereby created spread inside the Higher Council. But this attempt also met with the opposition of the Communists, who remained the most faithful, long-term, ally of the judiciary, and of a large part of the DC.[16]

Summing up, from the 1970s onwards, Italy has witnessed an intense process of political judicialisation.[17] The growth of judicial power was confronted by the political class in different ways. Some parties, like the PCI and, in part, the DC, have supported the trend while others, like the Socialists, have tried different means to undermine it. However, the growing political significance of Italian magistrates has given a strong incentive to the political class to cultivate the judiciary. Personal ties are difficult to document in full but they have often been reported and are based, above all, on the flourishing of extra-judicial duties, assigned with remarkable frequency to many magistrates by the political – and social – environment.[18]Furthermore, another sign of the development of such connections and of their ramifications in other institutions is, without doubt, the growing number of magistrates elected to Parliament and not-so-rare cases of rapidly advancing political careers. Personal ties often supported more complex relationships among groups, or factions, of magistrates and parties. In the latter case, there are naturally some connections of an ideological nature – the most visible, but not the only one, being that between *Magistratura Democratica* and the parties of the left.[19] But there are also different ties which might be called 'opportunistic'. In any case, such connections – that have not been without the occasional tensions and conflicts – have allowed an exchange of reciprocal favours between magistrates and parties, with the Higher Council providing a useful institutional setting for these exchanges. As a result, the growth of judicial power has in some ways been balanced by this set of informal checks.

166   CRISIS AND TRANSITION IN ITALIAN POLITICS

THE POLITICAL CRISIS AND THE ROLE OF THE JUDICIARY

This 'equilibrium' has been radically altered by the political crisis brought about by the set of *'Mani Pulite'* ('Clean Hands') or *Tangentopoli* ('Bribe City') corruption investigations. The investigations leading to *Tangentopoli* began in Milan in February 1992,[20] but they acquired momentum only in May, after the April parliamentary elections. The result of the elections – a setback for the Socialists and Christian Democrats and a victory for the Northern League, scoring very good results in Milan and in all of Lombardy – triggered a major crisis among the traditional governing parties, further aggravated by the resignation of President Cossiga. In a context marked by tragic events, such as the assassination of Giovanni Falcone by the Mafia, and with executive power weaker than ever (the Presidency of the Republic was vacant and there was no government with full powers) the Milan prosecutors profited from the weakness of the traditional political class and began progressively to expand their investigations, reaching by the end of that year the national leader of the PSI, Bettino Craxi.

As is well known, as a result of judicial investigations, the traditional party system was completely overhauled in less than two years. The parties which had most participated to government – the so-called, *pentapartito* – were those hit most: some of them disappeared altogether (the Social Democrats); others were drastically weakened and lost any importance (Liberals and Republicans); others, after heavy electoral losses and several schisms, finally decided to change their names (Socialists and Christian Democrats). The most important consequence has been the sudden and radical dissolving of the most important political forces of post-war Italy, producing a crisis of the traditional networks of party power. Since the parties were no longer able to exert influence on the policy processes, the old complicities – for example, in the assignment of public works – declined in importance, facilitating the investigative efforts of the judiciary. At the end of the process, the only parties surviving were, besides the extreme right, the heirs of the Communists, that is, the *Partito Democratico della Sinistra* (PDS) and *Rifondazione Comunista* (RC) – in other words, those traditionally more responsive toward judicial demands. As a consequence of this change in the political environment, the informal mechanisms of checking judicial powers lost their effectiveness. A sign of this has been the much smoother functioning of the Higher Council since the resignation of President Cossiga – with President Scalfaro taking a more conciliatory line – and of the Socialist justice minister Claudio Martelli, in February 1993, because of his involvement in the Ambrosiano scandal. Moreover, judicial investigations into political and administrative corruption were greeted with much enthusiasm by public opinion. The popularity of the judiciary

THE JUDICIARY'S POLITICAL ROLE 167

increased, with the media supporting judicial actions as well as amplifying their consequences.[21]

The context was ripe for the expansion of judicial power. It has already been emphasised how the institutional independence of the judiciary has been steadily strengthened since the end of the 1950s. We have also seen that this evolution has been followed by the development of more activist conceptions of the judicial role. However, it is the structure of the criminal process that has been the crucial factor in enabling the judiciary to so effectively prosecute political and administrative corruption. As already noted, public prosecutors are part of the judiciary and have enjoyed, at least since the end of the 1950s, the same status as judges. The growth of the prosecutors' independence has been made easier by the fact that, unlike the case in all other democratic countries – with the possible, partial exception of Germany – in Italy criminal initiative is mandatory. In other words, the Italian criminal process is governed by the principle of compulsory prosecution, as required under the Constitution itself: 'the public prosecutor has the duty to institute criminal proceedings' (Art.112). The concrete meaning of the principle of compulsory prosecution is far from clear. It 'is currently interpreted in Italy as denying to the public prosecutor any discretion in deciding whether or not to start a criminal prosecution. It is maintained, at least by the great majority of Italian jurists, that in every case where a suspicion arises that a crime has been committed the public prosecutor must request a decision from the judge, even if he is convinced of the innocence of the accused'.[22] The Italian legal system – with more than 100,000 laws on its books and frequently vaguely-defined criminal offences[23] – entrusts the prosecutor with wide margins of discretionary powers. Therefore, by requiring prosecutors to start a prosecution and to ask for a judicial decision every time there is *some* evidence that a crime has been committed, it assigns to the prosecuting authorities a task which is impossible to perform. However, the principle seems to have been very often interpreted in a formalistic way: that is, when the prosecutor finds some evidence of a crime she or he must open a file. Nothing more is required and often criminal initiatives lag behind until the statute of limitations has to be applied.

Thus, the lack of substantial controls on prosecutorial activity, which arises from the way the principle of compulsory prosecution has been interpreted, has made the prosecution virtually unaccountable for the choices it has inevitably to make. Moreover, the general structure of the prosecution is characterised by a high level of decentralisation, since the old hierarchical relationships no longer work and every prosecutorial office is autonomous from the others.[24] On the other hand, the weak accountability of public prosecutors has to be coupled with the powers they actually enjoy.

168   CRISIS AND TRANSITION IN ITALIAN POLITICS

As we have seen, especially since the 1970s, the fight against terrorism and organised crime has steadily increased the role of magistrates – (prosecutors and investigating judges) – in the criminal process. The trend has not been reversed by the 1989 reform of the Code of Criminal Procedure which, introducing, at least on paper, an adversarial-style process, has given investigative powers to public prosecutors. Subsequent legislation, issued after the assassination by the Mafia of the public prosecutors, Falcone and Borsellino, and rulings by the Constitutional Court further reinforced this trend, entrusting the prosecutor to a large extent, with the power of instructing the process. Currently, the wide powers enjoyed by the prosecution and the organisational connection between prosecutor and judge, both belonging to the same corps, tend to strike an uneven balance between the two conflicting parties, openly disadvantaging the defendant, whose rights do not seem to be well guaranteed. In this context, even apparently minor elements can become significant. For example, according to Italian procedural law, a person under investigation must be notified by the prosecution. The prosecutor has some discretion over when to send the notification: at the beginning of the investigation or just before the first court appearance. This discretion, which in ordinary cases can have only a limited impact, can have a tremendous effect in politically significant cases, especially in connection with media intervention. Notwithstanding the fact that notification should not be made public, the media are invariably able to find out about it. Given the strong inquisitorial tendencies of Italian political culture,[25] a notification – which *per se* does not signal any criminal responsibility – is often interpreted as a guilty verdict and in any case cannot but damage the public image of politicians.

Thus, after 1992, free from previous restraints, the judiciary, or at least those parts willing to act, began to put to use the formidable weapons accumulated hitherto. The main field chosen was political and administrative corruption, with extremely effective results. For example, the Amato government (July 1992–April 1993) came under heavy fire: seven of its ministers resigned after having been notified of being under judicial investigation. But also much more serious charges were raised. As is well-known, one of the most important politicians of the 'First Republic' – Giulio Andreotti – is presently standing trial because of his alleged connections with organised crime.

The victory of the right-wing coalition at the 1994 election did not bring to power a group particularly welcomed by the judiciary. Just before the elections, the Milan prosecutors had started to investigate Silvio Berlusconi's financial company, and arrested his brother Paolo for corruption. In fact, the judiciary seemed to have campaigned for other groups, as can be seen from the fact that as many as 18 magistrates were elected in the leftist alliance and only four on the right.[26] Moreover, many inside the winning coalition were openly in favour of curbing judicial power. Senator Previti, for example – thought likely to be appointed minister of justice in the Berlusconi government, who ended up in charge of Berlusconi's defence – openly advocated a reform of the Higher Council in order to 'depoliticise' it and make it more in tune with governmental majorities. However, Berlusconi initially tried to appease the judiciary. He offered the interior ministry – a key portfolio since it is in charge of the police – to Antonio Di Pietro, perhaps the most popular of the Milan magistrates. Moreover, Berlusconi was the first – and, so far, the last – head of government in post-war Italy to formally meet the judicial association in order to explain his programme. In the course of the meeting Berlusconi promised that judicial independence – and, above all, the independence of public prosecution – should not be endangered by the policies of his government.

But the honeymoon was short-lived. In July the government issued a decree-law[27] granting, among other things, a form of conditional amnesty to people involved in corruption investigations and making preventive detention more difficult. This was perceived as a kind of political solution to *Tangentopoli*, as a way of stopping judicial investigations into the matter. The Milan prosecutors vociferously opposed the decree, using television to promote their cause, and mass demonstrations followed in their support. The governing coalition began to vacillate. The 'post-Fascists' in the *Alleanza nazionale* and the Northern League expressed their, at least partial, disagreement. Eventually, the government was forced to withdraw the decree, although this did not end the conflict. The investigations led by the Milanese magistrates into the financial activities of Berlusconi continued, with Berlusconi being publicly notified of his judicial investigation when attending the UN Conference on the fight against crime in Naples, in November 1994. Even though the Milan investigations cannot be said to have brought about the fall of the Berlusconi government the following month, it did much to tarnish his image. Investigations by the Milan prosecutor's office into Berlusconi's affairs continued throughout 1995 and the first trial in the case opened in January 1996.

PERSPECTIVES: TOWARD JUDICIAL DEMOCRACY?

The political significance of the Italian judiciary seems likely to endure. As already emphasised, institutional arrangements give Italian magistrates significant scope for intervention in the policy-making processes. Moreover, this expanded participation is still finding a welcoming response in academic doctrine, whose legitimising role in civil law countries should not be discounted. Despite some disagreement, the overwhelming majority of

Italian lawyers tends to support judicial intervention: only the 'excesses' are sometimes reprimanded, and they are attributed to individual faults rather than to the institutional setting.

Judicial interventions will also be encouraged by the relative support enjoyed by the judiciary in public opinion, especially when compared to that of the political class. However, the support for the judiciary is a relatively new phenomenon and its strength should not be overestimated, as the results of the 1987 referendum showed. But the Italian judiciary does have some other weak points. The most important is a consequence of the virtual abolition of the career structure in the 1960s and 1970s. Since the recruitment process has remained unchanged, after entering the corps in their late twenties, young magistrates today, after a short and casual apprenticeship of more or less one year, are entrusted with judicial – or prosecuting – functions and their professional competence is not subject to further assessment, while salaries increase automatically with seniority until reaching the highest level. Therefore, the selection process is still providing the corps with inexperienced young people, while the abolition of the traditional career – with its deep, even if debatable, socialising effects – has not been replaced by other equally effective methods. In other words, institutional identification among Italian magistrates seems to be rather low, since there are no organisational mechanisms at work to ensure it[28]. Therefore, capture by outside interests is always possible, if not probable, because of the political salience of many judicial – and especially prosecu-torial – decisions. Having little to gain – or fear – from the organisation, it is likely that at least some magistrates will be ready to listen to those interests, especially those able to provide them with some reward. On the other hand, the dismantlement of the career structure has further accentu-ated the already lax working habits of the majority of magistrates, harming the performance of the judicial system.[29] Since the poor performance of the system affects directly or indirectly large groups of citizens, they may sooner or later blame the judiciary, even though, so far, the judiciary has been able to transfer this dissatisfaction on to the political class.

Potentially most damaging for the power of the judiciary is its internal divisions. We have already pointed to the decentralised structure of the corps, where traditional forms of control are no longer in use and institu-tional socialisation is extremely weak: every unit – and, to some extent, also every magistrate – is autonomous from the other. This structural fragmenta-tion is compounded by ideological and political divisions. As we have seen (see Table 1), the corps is presently divided into four organised groups, each with a small organisational structure enjoying a share of the Higher Council's seats, and, therefore, participation in the government of the corps. Even though the factions tend to coalesce strongly when common interests

THE JUDICIARY'S POLITICAL ROLE 171

come into play, their divisions are rather deep and offer to external political groups opportunities to influence the corps, pitching one *corrente* against the other, for example, when appointments to key positions appear on the Higher Council's agenda. However, rectifying this situation requires the emergence of a strong external actor, which is unlikely under current political circumstances.

On the other hand, the judiciary seems to have stronger relationships with groups on the centre-left, even if it seems to be the dominant partner. The participation of many magistrates as candidates in the leftist lists at the elections of March 1994 has already been noted. The election of the vice-president of the Higher Council in July 1994 pointed in the same direction: the magistrates in the Council split their vote between the candidate of the left and that of the centre (who was elected), while no magistrate voted for the candidate put forward by the right.[30] Also, the recent case of former Justice minister, Mancuso, seems to indicate at least a tactical convergence between the judiciary and the political left. Mancuso, a retired magistrate appointed minister in the Dini government, was dismissed in October 1995 after a no-confidence vote in Parliament, which censured his policy of sending inspectors into magistrates' offices which, as in the case of Milan, were engaged in anti-corruption or anti-organised crime investigations. The votes censuring Mancuso, who was also criticised by the ANM, came from the parliamentary groups of the centre and left. However, the decentralised structure of the judicial corps, as well as its ideological divisions, prevents the development of a homogeneous judicial policy. Judicial decisions can therefore still have negative consequences for individuals or interests normally identified with the left.[31]

As has been noted elsewhere,[32] there is a trend towards judicialisation in contemporary democratic regimes. However, the extent and nature of this expansion of judicial power seems to differ from case to case and depends much on their political context. In the Italian case we should remember the importance of the authoritarian legacy. The experience of Fascism led the founding fathers of the Constitution to reinforce constitutional guarantees and, above all, the checks on executive powers. Consequently, the independence and the role of the judiciary was strengthened. Thus, the Constitution of the 1948 had *in nuce* represented an important step in the development of the relationships between justice and politics. As the Constitution was gradually implemented in the 1950s and the 1960s, the traditional Napoleonic model of judicial organisation underwent a radical transformation leading to its substantial demise. While in other civil law countries, the political branches tend to exercise influence on a judiciary organised along bureaucratic, hierarchical lines through their powers over higher-ranking judges, in Italy, even though the selection of

172   CRISIS AND TRANSITION IN ITALIAN POLITICS

judicial personnel is still made through public examinations at a youthful age, the internal hierarchy has been dismantled. The power of higher-ranking magistrates, as well as of the government, has been dramatically reduced, even though the political system has been able to exercise some influence through its representatives in the Higher Council.

The Italian model has also exerted a strong influence – via academic doctrine and judicial associations[33] – in other Latin democracies such as Spain, Portugal and, to some extent, France.[34] But it has been implemented fully only in Italy, thanks to the consensual or proportionalist trend in Italian politics since the end of the 1950s.[35] The decisions which step by step dismantled the traditional institutional arrangements cannot be understood outside a context in which judicial demands receive a receptive political response. As we have seen, the new relationship between the judiciary and politics, together with the growth of Socialist and, above all, Communist influence on parliamentary decision-making, resulted in the approval of those reforms that fully satisfied magistrates' demands. However, if political trends helped to reinforce the role of the judiciary, the Constitution had already provided an institutional setting conducive to a higher degree of judicialisation.

If the process of judicialisation cannot be divorced from deeper trends in the political system, what are the likely consequences of the new majoritarian trend which has emerged in Italy, at least since the electoral referendum of 1993? We have to point out that the current state of judicialisation of Italian politics is an obstacle *per se* to such a development. However, it is likely that the emergence of a stronger executive could exploit the weak points of the judiciary outlined above and lead to a containment, and even reduction, of judicial power. But, so far, the influence of the majoritarian trend, if it exists at all, has still to be felt, at least in the field of the administration of justice.

NOTES

1. The general traits of the judiciary in civil law countries are presented in John H. Merryman, *The Civil Law Tradition* (Stanford UP 1985) pp.35–9. For a fuller account of the characteristics of Italian judicial personnel see Giuseppe Di Federico and Carlo Guarnieri, 'The Courts in Italy', in Jerold L. Waltman and Kenneth M. Holland (eds.) *The Political Role of Law Courts in Modern Democracies* (London: Macmillan, 1988), pp.161–70.
      In Italy, as in France, the term – *magistratura* – refers to personnel who are able to perform both prosecuting and judicial roles. It goes without saying that Italian magistrates must not be confused with English magistrates, i.e. lay judges.
2. For a fuller account of these developments see Carlo Guarnieri, *Magistratura e politica in Italia* (Bologna: Il Mulino 1993) pp.87–108. For an analysis of the political and

THE JUDICIARY'S POLITICAL ROLE 173

institutional developments of post-war Italy see David Hine, *Governing Italy* (Oxford: Clarendon Press 1993).

3. Between 1959 and 1975 the body was composed of 24 members: besides the three *ex-officio*, there were 14 magistrates and seven members elected by Parliament. The judicial component was elected with a majoritarian electoral law which tended to overrepresent the higher ranks.

4. For these developments, see G. Di Federico, 'The Italian Judicial Profession and its Bureaucratic Setting', *The Juridical Review* 1 (1976) pp.40–57; Giorgio Freddi, *Tensioni e conflitto nella magistratura* (Bari: Laterza 1978); Di Federico and Guarnieri (note 1).

5. Judicial decisions applying the Workers' Statute, a law issued in 1970, were highly influential in this change of perception. *Magistratura Democratica* has played a very important role in ensuring the full implementation of the rights established in the Statute. See Tiziano Treu (ed.) *Lo Statuto dei lavoratori: prassi sindacali e motivazioni dei giudici* (Bologna: Il Mulino 1976).

6. In the same years the party organised throughout Italy a series of meetings – attended by many lawyers, politicians and, above all, magistrates – on the reform of judicial organisation. See *La riforma dell'ordinamento giudiziario* (Roma: Editori Riuniti, 1977).

7. The electoral law was slightly modified in 1990, but with no important implications for this analysis.

8. We have to remember that the Higher Council is presently composed, outside of the 20 magistrates elected by the corps, of 10 lawyers or law professors chosen by Parliament, usually along strict party lines. See G. Di Federico, 'Le qualificazioni professionali del corpo giudiziario: carenze attuali, possibili riforme e difficoltà di attuarle', *Rivista trimestrale di scienza dell'amministrazione* 32/4 (1985) pp.21–60; Giorgio Rebuff, *La funzione giudiziaria* (Torino: Giappichelli 1993) pp.91–8.

9. MG was formed by splinter groups of MI and UC.

10. Includes some short-lived moderate and conservative factions.

11. See Salvatore Lupo, *Storia della mafia* (Roma: Donzelli 1993); Romano Canosa, *Storia della criminalità in Italia dal 1946 a oggi* (Milano: Feltrinelli 1995). On organised crime in Sicily, see, e.g. Pino Arlacchi, 'Mafia: The Sicilian Cosa Nostra', *South European Society and Politics* 1/1 (Summer 1996) pp.74–94.

12. See Francesca Zannotti, *La magistratura. Un gruppo di pressione istituzionale* (Padova: Cedam 1989); and 'The Judicialization of Judicial Salary Policy in Italy and the United States', in C. Neal Tate and Torbjörn Vallinder (eds.) *The Global Expansion of Judicial Power* (NY UP 1995) pp.181–203.
   It is interesting to note that the ANM was able to get the support of the trade unions movement for its demands for higher salaries. See Guarnieri (note 2) p.144.

13. In 1981 Roberto Calvi, the chief executive of the Ambrosiano bank – one of the major private banks in Italy – was arrested for violating the currency control law. The Socialists sharply criticised the magistrates of Milan in charge of the case and advocated a reform of the status of public prosecutors. The following year Calvi was found dead in London and the Ambrosiano ended up bankrupt. See Vladimiro Zagrebelski, 'La polemica sul pubblico ministero e il nuovo Consiglio superiore della magistratura', *Quaderni costituzionali* 1 (1981) pp.391–9; Canosa (note 11) pp.195–203. We can speculate that Craxi saw a judicial investigation which was undermining one of his financial supporters as an interference with his attempts at reinforcing Socialists' assets in their competition with the other two big parties: the PCI and the DC.

14. Enzo Tortora, a well-known television entertainer, was arrested in 1983 and accused of drug trafficking and association with Neapolitan organised crime. He was later condemned by the court of Naples but, in 1986, the court of appeal cleared him of all charges, the court declaring that none of the original accusations had any basis in fact, but were based only on hearsay collected mainly from career criminals. See G. Di Federico, 'The Crisis of the Justice System and the Referendum on the Judiciary', in Robert Leonardi and Piergiorgio Corbetta (eds.) *Italian Politics: A Review*, Vol.3 (London: Pinter 1989) pp.25–49.

15. For an enthusiastic account of the reform see Ennio Amodio and Eugenio Selvaggi, 'An

174   CRISIS AND TRANSITION IN ITALIAN POLITICS

Accusatorial System in a Civil Law Country: The 1988 Italian Code of Criminal Procedure', *Temple Law Review* 62 (1989) pp.1211–24.

16. It is difficult to define in one sense or another the DC's policies since, as it is well-known, the party was divided into different and conflicting factions. However, broadly speaking, leftist factions, being also in favour of a closer collaboration with the Communists, were more supportive of judicial positions. For example, Galloni, vice-president of the Higher Council and a prominent member of the left of the party, was always in disagreement with President Cossiga.

17. By which, following Vallinder, 'When the Courts Go Marching In' (note 12), we mean 'the expansion of the province of the courts or the judges at the expenses of the politicians and/or the administrators' (p.13).

18. The range of extra-judicial duties of Italian magistrates is extremely wide. Among them is an important role as well-paid arbitrators, possibly in disputes between state-owned companies, or by appointment as consultants for various governmental departments. For more details see F. Zannotti, *Le attività extragiudiziarie dei magistrati ordinari* (Padova: Cedam 1981) and the introduction by Di Federico.

19. See Zannotti, *La magistratura* (note 12) pp.70–155; and Sergio Pappalardo, *Gli iconoclasti. Magistratura Democratica nel quadro dell'Associazione Nazionale Magistrati* (Milano: Franco Angeli 1987).
    The number of magistrates in Parliament began to rise in the second half of the 1970s: in 1992 there were 13 and, by 1994, 22. There have also been some cases of magistrates becoming ministers or deputy ministers.

20. The investigations started even before 1992, but in Feb. the first arrest was made of a lower-level Socialist politician. In the 1980s the Milanese magistrates had already tried to investigate cases of corruption, but with insignificant results. On the growing intensity of judicial investigations into the political class, see Franco Cazzola and Massimo Morisi, 'Magistratura e classe politica. Due punti di osservazione specifici per una ricerca empirica', *Sociologia del diritto* 22/1 (1995) pp.91–143.

21. See Andrea Lavazza, 'La toga e la verità', *Il Mulino* 44/362 (1995) pp.1045–58. However, in the 1980s, the degree of trust in the judiciary did not seem very high. See Roberto Cartocci, *Tra Lega e Chiesa* (Bologna: Il Mulino 1994) p.23.

22. See Di Federico and Guarnieri (note 1) p.172; and also Di Federico, 'Crisis' (note 14) esp. pp.28–35. For the general problems involved in the implementation of this principle see C. Guarnieri, *Pubblico ministero e sistema politico* (Padova: Cedam 1984) pp.125–52.

23. There are no precise data on the number of statutes presently in force. However, according to conservative estimates there are no less than 100,000 (*Il Sole-24 Ore*, 6 July 1994). An example of a crime, whose definition is rather vague, is the 'abuse of power' (art.323 of the criminal code), according to which a public official who 'in order to provide for himself or others an unjust benefit, or to damage another unjustly, is guilty of an abuse of her or his office' and still be punished. The crime has been used to prosecute many public officials.

24. Only in the field of organised crime has disappointment with the lack of co-ordination in the fight against the Mafia has led to the establishment, in 1992, of a special structure – the Anti-Mafia District Offices, at the regional level, with the National Anti-Mafia Office at the top. The latter's senior personnel is appointed by the Higher Council and is in charge of all the investigations against the Mafia and organised crime. However, the power of the National Office should not be overrated.

25. For example, since they are members of the same corps, very often prosecutors are referred to by the media as 'judges', generating a dangerous confusion between two functionally very different roles.

26. See Giuseppe Di Federico, *Il Tempo*, 3 July 1995.

27. Namely, a decree with temporary value of law, but which must be approved before 60 days by Parliament. See Hine (note 2) p.149.

28. As Edward Gross and Amitai Etzioni, *Organizations in Society* (Englewood Cliffs, NJ: Prentice-Hall 1985), have pointed out, '... the degree to which an organisation selects ... its participants affects its control needs ... [since] the same level of control can be

THE JUDICIARY'S POLITICAL ROLE   175

maintained by high selectivity and a low level of organisational socialisation as by low selectivity and high level of organisational socialisation' (pp.125–7). The Italian judiciary has a low level both of selectivity and organisational socialisation.

29. See Di Federico and Guarnieri (note 1) pp.168–70. The unsatisfactory performance of the Italian judiciary was stressed once again by the Prosecutor General at the Court of Cassation in his annual report for 1995 (*Il Sole-24 Ore*, 19 Jan. 1996).

30. The Constitution prescribes that the vice-president must be chosen from among the lay members of the Council. However, on the right, *Alleanza Nazionale* seems to be the group on the best terms with the judiciary.

31. An example is provided by the investigations in Venice into the use of public funds by many co-operatives traditionally affiliated to the PCI and the left. A new phase of investigations from the autumn of 1996 has implicated a number of left-wing figures and provoked the ire of influential left-wing politicians.

32. See Kenneth M. Holland (ed.) *Judicial Activism in Comparative Perspective* (London: Macmillan 1991); Lawrence M. Friedman, 'Is There a Modern Legal Culture?', *Ratio Juris* 7/2 (1994) pp.117–31 and Tate and Vallinder (note 12).

33. Especially strong are relations between progressive groups of European magistrates. They have recently founded an international association – Magistrats Européens pour la Démocratie et la Liberté (MEDEL) – which advocates the adoption of the Italian model of judicial organisation.

34. See Carlo Guarnieri and Patrizia Pederzoli, *Pouvoir judiciaire et démocratie* (Paris: Michalon, forthcoming).

35. See Maurizio Cotta 'Il Parlamento nel sistema politico italiano. Mutamenti istituzionali e cicli politici', *Quaderni costituzionali* 11 (1991) pp.201–23.

Name Index